The Law and Policy of Environmental Federalism

The Law and Policy of Environmental Federalism

A Comparative Analysis

Edited by

Kalyani Robbins

Associate Professor of Law, Florida International University College of Law, USA

Cheltenham, UK • Northampton, MA, USA

© The Editor and Contributors Severally 2015

All rights reserved. No part of this publication may be reproduced, stored in a retrieval system or transmitted in any form or by any means, electronic, mechanical or photocopying, recording, or otherwise without the prior permission of the publisher.

Published by
Edward Elgar Publishing Limited
The Lypiatts
15 Lansdown Road
Cheltenham
Glos GL50 2JA
UK

Edward Elgar Publishing, Inc.
William Pratt House
9 Dewey Court
Northampton
Massachusetts 01060
USA

A catalogue record for this book
is available from the British Library

Library of Congress Control Number: 2015945456

This book is available electronically in the **Elgar**online
Law subject collection
DOI 10.4337/9781783473625

ISBN 978 1 78347 361 8 (cased)
ISBN 978 1 78347 362 5 (eBook)

Typeset by Columns Design XML Ltd, Reading
Printed and bound in Great Britain by
TJ International Ltd, Padstow, Cornwall

Contents

List of contributors vii

Introduction ix
Kalyani Robbins

PART I   MAJOR UNITED STATES ENVIRONMENTAL STATUTES

1   Debunking revisionist understandings of environmental cooperative federalism: collective action responses to air pollution   3
    Robert L. Glicksman and Jessica A. Wentz
2   Dynamic federalism and the Clean Water Act: completing the task   28
    William L. Andreen
3   CERCLA, federalism, and common law claims   49
    Alexandra B. Klass and Emma Fazio

PART II   REGULATION OF NATURAL RESOURCES

4   Fragmented forest federalism   71
    Blake Hudson
5   Coordinating the overlapping regulation of biodiversity and ecosystem management   94
    Kalyani Robbins
6   Evolving energy federalism: current allocations of authority and the need for inclusive governance   114
    Hannah J. Wiseman

PART III   CLIMATE CHANGE AND FEDERALISM

7   Climate federalism, regulatory failure and reversal risks, and entrenching innovation incentives   145
    William W. Buzbee
8   The enigma of state climate change policy innovation   169
    Kirsten H. Engel

9 Cooperative federalism and adaptation 188
    Alice Kaswan

PART IV   THEORIES OF DIFFUSE REGULATORY POWER

10 Reverse preemption in federal water law 213
    Ann E. Carlson
11 The cost of federalism: ecology, community, and the pragmatism
    of land use 243
    Keith H. Hirokawa and Jonathan Rosenbloom

PART V   COMPARING INTERNATIONAL REGIMES

12 The Australian experience with environmental federalism:
    constitutional and political perspectives 271
    Robert Fowler
13 German environmental federalism in the multilevel system of the
    European Union 304
    Nathalie Behnke and Annegret Eppler
14 The paradox of environmental federalism in India 327
    Sairam Bhat

PART VI   CONCLUDING THOUGHTS

15 Environmental federalism's tug of war within 355
    Erin Ryan

Index 419

Contributors

William L. Andreen, Edgar L. Clarkson Professor of Law and Director of the UA-ANU Exchange Program, University of Alabama School of Law, USA

Nathalie Behnke, Full Professor of Administrative Science, Department of Politics and Administration, Konstanz University, Germany

Sairam Bhat, Associate Professor and Coordinator for Centre for Environmental Law Education, Research and Advocacy and the Environmental Law Clinic, National Law School of India University, India

William W. Buzbee, Professor of Law, Georgetown University Law Center, USA

Ann E. Carlson, Shirley Shapiro Professor of Environmental Law, Faculty Co-Director, Emmett Institute on Climate Change and the Environment, UCLA School of Law, USA

Kirsten H. Engel, Charles E. Ares Professor of Law, University of Arizona James E. Rogers College of Law, USA

Annegret Eppler, Assistant Professor, Innsbruck Center for European Research, Department of Political Science, University of Innsbruck, Austria

Emma Fazio, Associate, Stoel Rives LLP, USA

Robert Fowler, Adjunct Professor of Law, Law School, University of South Australia, Australia

Robert L. Glicksman, J.B. and Maurice C. Shapiro Professor of Environmental Law, The George Washington University Law School, USA

Keith H. Hirokawa, Associate Professor of Law, Albany Law School, USA

Blake Hudson, Burlington Resources Professor in Environmental Law and Edward J. Womac, Jr. Professor in Energy Law, *Joint Appointment*, LSU Law Center and LSU School of the Coast and Environment, USA

Alice Kaswan, Professor and Dean's Circle Scholar, University of San Francisco School of Law, USA

Alexandra B. Klass, Distinguished McKnight University Professor, University of Minnesota Law School, USA

Kalyani Robbins, Associate Professor of Law, Florida International University College of Law, USA

Jonathan Rosenbloom, Professor of Law, Drake University Law School, USA

Erin Ryan, Professor of Law, Florida State University College of Law, USA

Jessica A. Wentz, Associate Director and Postdoctoral Research Fellow, Sabin Center for Climate Change Law, Columbia Law School, USA

Hannah J. Wiseman, Attorneys' Title Professor, Florida State University College of Law, USA

Introduction

Kalyani Robbins

Federalism considerations remain every bit as critical at each successive stage of growth within a federalist regime as they are at initial formation. Many policy issues attract interest at multiple levels of government, each of which is likely to have a different set of priorities at stake. Environmental and natural resources law provides both an excellent example of this phenomenon, and also its own microcosm of federalism generally, given the wide array of approaches utilized throughout the field. If we want a testing ground for the various tenets of federalism theory, we find no better battlefield than that of environmental and natural resources policy, which represents the front line of federalism controversy. Powerful federal interests in environmental quality and human health face stark opposition by entrenched local expectations regarding land-use control and property rights. As Erin Ryan notes in the concluding chapter of this book, environmental law is "the canary in federalism's coal mine."

The goal of this book is to bring together the variety of approaches to environmental federalism and consider what is working and what is not working, what might be translated into another environmental field to improve it, and what works best in just the field in which it presently exists. Each contributor has focused on a different environmental statute or regime, both directly analyzing the relevant statutes or other sources of law and contemplating the possibilities with an eye towards evolution via implementation. We have, collectively, taken a comparative approach, and summed up with a concluding chapter comparing the various methods and considering what one area might draw from another.

This theme – examining existing regimes and determining both how successful they are in practice as well as how context-dependent that evaluation is – stems from the hope of bringing value from experiences in one environmental area into our policy choices in another. With such a variety of approaches in use, there is quite a bit of experiential data to work with. Further, because the authors are seasoned environmental federalism scholars, they bring their own ideas and theories to the table. This collective effort to offer a broad overview of the field (including helpful descriptive portions for improved accessibility to students) and then draw potential policy exchanges from that work, is unprecedented and sure to contribute great value to our understanding of environmental federalism as well as to our policy-making future.

The contributors represent legal academia in five different countries and their law schools number around a score. Many are already leaders in this field; others are well on their way. They have one thing in common: an interest in the manner in which regulatory power is divided among the federal government, states and local governments, and a desire to improve on how that division is structured wherever possible.

Part I of this Introduction will briefly introduce the concept and history of federalism generally. This will be followed by the environmental federalism basics in Part II. In both parts I shall refrain from delving too deeply into the complexities or relevant theories, as this is the task of the substantive chapters of this volume, and has been expertly accomplished within them. After laying this basic foundation for the book, Part III will preview the chapters to follow.

I WHAT IS FEDERALISM?

In the United States, as indicated by the country's name, we have separately governed states that are united into one country. This is a federalist structure, and was designed with the goals of avoiding a tyrannical national government, promoting more accessible government and public participation, and encouraging policy innovation at the state level. In his Federalist Paper #10, James Madison noted the importance of each level of government serving as a check on the other.

Federalism is a system wherein the same territory is governed by more than one government, each at a different scale. The US Constitution grants certain powers to the federal government, typically in ways that have been interpreted as broad categories, such as regulating matters that impact interstate commerce. Powers that do not fit into any of these categories are reserved to the states in the Tenth Amendment. States can create local governments, which in turn have the power to tax and legislate, so these functions take place at all levels. Because there are so many governing bodies in one country, representing different scales, different geographic locations and, consequently, different constituent interests, we must determine who will govern what. In light of the myriad policy issues in need of regulation this is no easy question, and is the focus of most federalism scholarship.

II FEDERALISM IN THE CONTEXT OF ENVIRONMENTAL AND NATURAL RESOURCES LAW

There is traditionally an effort in federalism to match the scale of governance to the scale at which the interest lies, such as establishing currency at the national level and regulating land use at the local level. This logic is weakened, however, in the environmental context, where there are such intense interests at every level, interests that may be at odds with each other. Although there are a handful of older environmental statutes, most of which did very little to actually advance environmental improvement, environmental law in the US was largely born in the early 1970s with a burst of legislation covering enormous ground in just a few years. This is where the key innovation took place to address the problem of multilevel interests: carefully structured cooperative federalism. In two of the numerous new environmental statutes from this time – the Clean Air Act and the Clean Water Act – Congress gave states the power to create their own implementation programs while giving the EPA the responsibility of defining expectations and overseeing the state implementation. There were also some aspects, those that were more nationally uniform or that addressed interstate impacts, left to federal implementation directly. This careful division of power into a cooperative system has been very successful for this area of law, and is evolving into even more complex multiscalar approaches.

III THE ORGANIZATION OF THIS BOOK

The book is divided into six parts. In the first part, we look at the carefully designed cooperative federalism schemes created in three major federal environmental statutes. Two of these statutes were pioneers of federalism innovation, but time has highlighted their weaknesses. We then turn to federalism issues relating to US regulation of natural resources in the second part of the book. In the third part we consider the need to address the threat of climate change, both in terms of mitigation of greenhouse gas emissions and the policy choices that will become necessary in the context of adapting to the changing climate. The fourth part provides us with some intriguing theoretical insights, which consider more complex divisions of power than traditional dualism theory has. Part V adds several non-US regimes to the discussion, drawing insights from India and Australia, as well as the European Union from Germany's point of view. In the final part Professor Erin Ryan considers all that preceded and draws some overarching concluding thoughts on environmental federalism.

A. Major United States Environmental Statutes

A great deal of federalism pioneering has taken place in the context of US federal environmental statutes, through which Congress carefully laid out its plan for shared federal and state involvement in pollution control implementation and policy-making. Chapter 1 takes us right to the beginning of this story, as Robert Glicksman and Jessica Wentz explore the foundations of the cooperative federalism approach to environmental law, first developed in the Clean Air Act. They find ample evidence of Congressional intent to address collective action problems via this new approach. They also find that this effort led to some successful experiences in practice, in spite of the many failures that accompany them, and consider whether these experiences suggest realistic potential for addressing climate change via the Clean Air Act.

The next major US statute implementing a cooperative federalism model was the Clean Water Act, which closely followed on the heels of the Clean Air Act, but with a somewhat different model. In Chapter 2, William Andreen provides the structure of the Act and its dynamic federalism methodology, which he finds to be rather successful in achieving marked reductions in water pollution. Unfortunately, notes Andreen, the approach in the Clean Water Act is inadequately comprehensive, failing to address either run-off pollution (that which is not released into the waters via a point source) or in-stream flows. Run-off pollution has thus become the greatest remaining source of pollutants in US waters, and those concerned with protecting the water levels that aquatic ecosystems require have been forced to resort to other inadequate sources of protection, with water levels ultimately not well preserved. The dual federalism model, which had long failed when applied to water quality overall, was left in place in these two areas, even while proactively replacing it in the context of point source pollution. The clean water chain is thus broken at its weakest link and cannot achieve its goals without sealing this gap. Andreen proposes increased federal authority over these areas in order to ameliorate this problem.

Finally, the materials on federal environmental statutes conclude in Chapter 3 with a move into the realm of post-hoc liability for environmental harms, specifically those resulting from land disposal of hazardous waste. Alexandra Klass and Emma Fazio review the reach of the liability scheme in the Comprehensive Environmental Response,

Compensation, and Liability Act (CERCLA), which provides remedies for hazardous waste clean-up expenses but falls short of compensating for other related damages resulting from the contamination. The latter is traditionally included in state common law claims, and the authors opine that these should remain intact, at least to the extent they do not conflict with CERCLA. They similarly address several other areas of potential preemption, reaching the same conclusion, and suggesting that in ambiguous cases weight should be given to CERCLA's remedial purpose.

B. Regulation of Natural Resources

Although the US regulates the protection and exploitation of natural resources somewhat pervasively as well, this area lacks the structure and clarity of environmental regulation (pollution control). Indeed, natural resources law and policy approaches are extremely varied and rarely comprehensive even within a given area. In Chapter 4, Blake Hudson discusses an area of natural resource regulation that serves as a perfect example of this disjointedness: forests. He notes that only 35 percent of forest land is federally owned and regulated, while the other 65 percent is subject to widely varying and unpredictable state regulation (or no regulation at all). Unlike regimes addressing resources such as air, water, biodiversity, fisheries, wetlands and hazardous waste – regardless of whether they happen to be on federally owned land – the federal government has little to no involvement in managing this other 65 percent of critically needed and rapidly dwindling forests. This leads to wide variation in policies at a time when we are on a path toward even more widespread deforestation. Hudson advocates for a more holistic approach to forest management, while acknowledging the challenges to increasing federal control.

Although federal regulation of endangered species protection, via the Endangered Species Act, is far more comprehensive, it may go too far in the other direction. Rather than leaving too much to the states, it takes on so much at the federal level that we have never, in over four decades, managed to implement it. Kalyani Robbins takes on this problem in Chapter 5, noting that federal oversight is key to avoiding the collective action problems of state governance, but arguing that we could achieve greater implementation success by tapping into state and local expertise and implementation potential that is presently going to waste. The ESA leans so heavily on its implementing federal agencies that state action, even conservation efforts, can sometimes be hamstrung. This will become increasingly true as climate change brings the need for increasingly proactive species management and renders static preserves less helpful.

Robbins finds that endangered species law could benefit from a more cooperative federalism approach, and suggests informal ways of achieving this, in light of the improbability of Congress designing an entirely new ESA.

The "Regulation of Natural Resources" part concludes in Chapter 6, in which Hannah Wiseman explains the importance of shared authority over energy development and suggests approaches for ensuring that all governments and stakeholders have a role in energy governance. Wiseman observes that there are key interests at stake at all levels – federal, state and local – and describes how the concentration of power at the state level tends to shut out some of these interests in a detrimental manner. To address this problem she recommends inclusive and coordinated governance for energy development.

C. Climate Change and Federalism

The US has yet to enact legislation to address comprehensively the need to mitigate the emission of greenhouse gases that lead to global climate disruption, but such legislation is expected. In its absence, some states have been regulating in the area, resulting in the need to determine the extent to which eventual federal legislation should preempt state efforts. Some scholars have argued that it should preempt the field and replace all state governance of climate mitigation, but in Chapter 7 William Buzbee provides good reason to reconsider this position. While acknowledging that a single administrator is ideal for a comprehensive market-based (credit trading) system, Buzbee notes that leaving state laws in place would provide a better safety net in the event that federal policy choices change or there is implementation failure. It also enables us to keep the value of innovation at the state level that may result in positive policy change at the federal level. Finally, overlapping jurisdiction can provide valuable gap-filling and result in even greater mitigation benefits than we otherwise might observe.

Kirsten Engel, in Chapter 8, takes us through the logical next step, considering how much state innovation is really happening. States have for decades been filling the gap left by the federal government's failure to enact climate change legislation, which is generally viewed as policy innovation. This has surprised some, as it contradicted their expectations that states would free-ride off other states' innovations, thus minimizing innovation overall. However, Engel suggests that what we have observed is not (usually) so much policy innovation as it is "scale innovation," as most of these state policies were already in use at the national level elsewhere. This is still valuable, she explains. Given the overarching necessity of cutting back on greenhouse gas emissions, policy adoption on multiple scales is arguably of greater social value than developing new and original policy tools. This is also in line with Buzbee's proposal in Chapter 7.

No section on climate change would be complete without turning to adaptation. The IPCC has made very clear in its recent reports that it is too late for mitigation alone, we will need to both mitigate greenhouse gases to slow the progression of climate change and also adapt to the climate change that has already been irreversibly set in motion. Given that this could mean mass migrations and changes in land use and infrastructure needs, it naturally raises substantial questions about federalism. In Chapter 9 Alice Kaswan reviews the array of regulatory areas raised by the various climate adaptation requirements and suggests the need for more cooperative multiscale governance in many of these areas, including those traditionally kept local, such as land use and water policy.

D. Theories of Diffuse Regulatory Power

Preemption of one regulatory program by another, more supreme, program is an important federalism topic. Typically, the question is like that discussed in Chapter 3 – the extent to which a federal law preempts state law. Does it preempt the entire field and wipe out state law entirely, or does it allow states to govern the same behavior more strictly with statutes that go further than the federal statute? The latter is more common, in which state regulation remains in effect with the sole exception of conflicts with the federal law. Ann Carlson has noticed a somewhat unusual circumstance, however, which she calls "reverse preemption," as she explains in Chapter 10. Using the context of water law, she points out two scenarios in which states can actually veto federal regulatory implementation. For example, the Coastal Zone Management Act enables a state with a federally approved Coastal Zone Management Plan to veto federal actions it deems inconsistent with its plan, such as offshore oil drilling leases. Carlson also identifies a similar provision in the Clean Water Act. Her analysis of these provisions leads to the conclusion that they allow Congress to utilize states (especially those with strong environmental values) to keep the federal administration in check, thus furthering separation of powers values.

In Chapter 11, Keith Hirokawa and Jonathan Rosenbloom take a stance against excessive preemption. They explore whether imposed homogeneity or sameness at the federal level defeats the benefits of self-identifying communities through land use controls at the local level. They argue that federal environmental regulation and widespread state preemption of local environmental governance detaches a community from its local ecosystem. As such, preemption can in some instances drown the potential for greater levels of regulation in those communities that would do so.

E. Comparing International Regimes

The international chapters are especially diverse, and best contribute to the comparative law flavor of the book. First, in Chapter 12, Robert Fowler takes us through the recent turmoil in Australia, which has significantly impacted its federalism structure. Although Australian constitutional law gave the Commonwealth (federal government) broad power to regulate environmental issues, the Commonwealth has in practice followed a system of substantial cooperation with the states. It avoided preempting or duplicating what was being accomplished on the state level, but maintained its power, governed in the area, and retained oversight. The recently elected Abbott Coalition government is pushing this tradition further in the direction of state sovereignty and threatens to take environmental governance out of national control. While the ultimate resolution of these issues remains to be seen at the time of writing, Fowler provides a solid foundation for understanding the issues as they evolve.

From Australia we travel to the European Union, where countries must work within an extra level of government. In Chapter 13, Nathalie Behnke and Annegret Eppler provide the German approach to existing within that larger regime, which has been relatively successful. The authors analyze the complex policy-making network of actors, institutions and processes in a system with more levels to coordinate than is typical. They find that the Europeanization of environmental policy led to relevant changes and adaptations in the institutional structure within Germany. As a result, and in spite of numerous potential veto points and opportunities for deadlock due to the need for interaction among all levels of government, environmental decision-making in the German system is actually functioning quite well.

Our final destination in this non-US section is India, where Sairam Bhat takes us in Chapter 14. Bhat describes the significant tension between state and local autonomy on the one hand and federal control on the other. In spite of substantial pressures toward decentralization, the uniformity gained from federal control over environmental matters is holding strong, especially since the Bhopal industrial tragedy triggered greater support for federal environmental protections. In the end, this tension has developed into a cooperative federalism approach to environmental regulation in India.

F. Concluding Thoughts

In the final chapter of the book, Erin Ryan takes on the enormous task of pulling together all the chapters that precede hers, reviewing the issues relating to environmental federalism holistically, and providing her analysis and conclusions. Drawing from her own extensive body of work in federalism generally, including her book on the subject, she observes that there are certain differences with environmental law and related constituent interests that merit it a special case in the federalism discussion. Because the interests are so strong at all levels, the need to determine the right balance of power is as high as it gets. It is also an area that in practice has served as a testing ground for federalism innovation. For these and other reasons, Ryan gives environmental federalism the title of federalism's "canary in the coal mine." Ultimately, she views the approaches to environmental federalism as valuable federalism innovation to be considered for other fields. Environmental federalism brings us further in the direction of multiscalar and cooperative methods of governance, and this is a good thing.

PART I

MAJOR UNITED STATES
ENVIRONMENTAL STATUTES

1. Debunking revisionist understandings of environmental cooperative federalism: collective action responses to air pollution

Robert L. Glicksman and Jessica A. Wentz

From its inception in 1970, modern environmental law has been a joint venture between the federal government and the states. When Congress enacted the Clean Air Act (CAA) of 1970[1] it crafted the model for much of the pollution control legislation enacted in the ensuing decade. Commonly referred to as cooperative federalism, the model entailed delegating authority to a federal agency, the Environmental Protection Agency (EPA), to enact standards and take other action to achieve clean air protection and enhancement goals[2] and inviting states to participate in implementation, permitting, and enforcement.[3] With some variations, Congress built subsequent statutory efforts to protect water quality and prevent land pollution along similar lines, 'shar[ing] governmental responsibilities for regulating private activity' with the potential to create environmental harm between the federal government and the states.[4] In the environmental context, cooperative federalism involves federal

---

[1] Pub. L. No. 91-604, 84 Stat. 1676 (1970) (codified as amended at 42 USC §§ 7401–7671q).

[2] 42 USC § 7401(b)(1) (declaring purpose to 'protect and enhance the quality of the Nation's air resources').

[3] For a description of the basic cooperative federalism model reflected in the federal pollution control statutes, see Glicksman, Robert L., 'From Cooperative to Inoperative Federalism: The Perverse Mutation of Environmental Law and Policy' (2006) 41 Wake Forest L. Rev. **719**, 719–21, 737–43.

[4] Coggins, George Cameron and Robert L. Glicksman, *Public Natural Resources Law*, vol. 1, 2nd edn (Thomson/West, Eagan, Minn. 2007) § 5:3.

inducement, but not coercion of state participation in a coordinated federal program.[5]

Despite decades of experience with the CAA's version of cooperative federalism, fundamental disagreements persist not only about the merits of that model, but also about what Congress intended when it delineated EPA and state roles in the 1970 Act and subsequent amendments. One view is that the pollution laws that Congress adopted in the 1970s, beginning with the CAA, fundamentally changed the structure of environmental law by carving out 'a significant role [for states] to play under this "cooperative" approach to federalism,' while 'clearly [making] EPA the senior partner in the relationship. The states had lost their predominant position.'[6] The Court of Appeals for the Tenth Circuit expressed a similar understanding, summarizing the CAA model as one in which states are responsible for adopting plans to implement EPA's national ambient air quality standards (NAAQS), but 'with federal oversight.'[7]

Some judicial decisions provide a significantly different depiction of the roles of federal and state regulators under the CAA. The most prominent such decision is Justice Kennedy's dissenting opinion in *Alaska Department of Environmental Conservation v EPA*,[8] in which the Supreme Court held that the CAA authorizes substantive review by EPA of state permitting decisions for stationary sources in prevention of significant deterioration (PSD) areas. Justice Kennedy responded to EPA's contention that such review helps prevent a 'race to the bottom' in which states lower environmental standards to attract industry by finding 'EPA's distrust of state agencies' to be 'inconsistent with the Act's clear mandate that States bear the primary role in controlling pollution.'[9] According to Kennedy, 'Congress made the overriding judgment that States are more responsive to local conditions and can strike the right balance between preserving environmental quality and advancing competing objectives.'[10] He protested EPA's lack of trust in the states and charged that vesting in EPA veto power over state PSD permits violated

---

[5] Fischman, Robert, 'Cooperative Federalism and Natural Resources Law' (2006) 14 NYU Envtl LJ **179**, 184.

[6] Andreen, William L., 'Of Fables and Federalism: A Re-Examination of the Historical Rationale for Federal Environmental Regulation' (2012) 42 Envtl L. **627**, 629.

[7] *Oklahoma v EPA* 723 F.3d 1201, 1204 (10th Cir. 2013).

[8] 540 US 461 (2004).

[9] Ibid. at 506–07.

[10] Ibid. at 507.

'the established presumption that States act in good faith.'[11] Justice Kennedy was also dismayed by the 'broader implications' of the Court's decision:

> The CAA is not the only statute that relies on *a close and equal partnership between federal and state authorities* to accomplish congressional objectives. Under the majority's reasoning, these other statutes, too, could be said to confer on federal agencies ultimate decision-making authority, relegating States to the role of mere provinces or political corporations, instead of coequal sovereigns entitled to the same dignity and respect. If cooperative federalism is to achieve Congress' goal of allowing state governments to be accountable to the democratic process in implementing environmental policies, federal agencies cannot consign States to the ministerial tasks of information gathering and making initial recommendations, while reserving to themselves the authority to make final judgments under the guise of surveillance and oversight.[12]

Echoing Justice Kennedy's dissent, the Court of Appeals for the Fifth Circuit recently interpreted the CAA as 'confin[ing] the EPA to the ministerial function of reviewing [state implementation plans] for consistency with the Act's requirements,' reasoning that this narrow reading of EPA's authority 'reflects the balance of state and federal rights and responsibilities characteristic of our federal system of government.'[13] Similarly, a minority report issued by the Senate Committee on Environmental and Public Works in 2013 expressed concern that 'EPA, instead of cooperating with the States as equal and valued partners, is coopting and coercing the States by treating them as mere regional offices of a massive federal environmental bureaucracy.'[14]

Thus, despite decades of experience with the CAA, courts and commentators offer dramatically different descriptions of its cooperative

---

[11] Ibid. He also asserted that even EPA agreed that 'States, by and large, take their statutory responsibility seriously,' and that EPA itself had admitted that its 'fears about a race to the bottom bear little relation to the real-world experience under the statute.' Ibid.

[12] Ibid. at 518 (emphasis added) (citations omitted).

[13] *Luminant Generation Co., LLC v EPA*, 675 F.3d 917, 921 (5th Cir. 2012). See also *Luminant Generation Co., LLC v EPA*, 714 F.3d 841, 846 (5th Cir. 2013).

[14] US Senate, Comm. on Environment and Public Works, Minority Report, Cooperative Federalism, Neglecting a Cornerstone Principle of the Clean Air Act: President Obama's EPA Leaves States Behind 13 (31 October 2013) (hereinafter Cooperative Federalism). The report also postulated that 'mere inadequacy of a [state implementation plan] in the eyes of EPA is not a sufficient basis for disapproving' the plan. Ibid. at 17.

federalism enterprise. Either the statute makes EPA the dominant partner, and the opportunity afforded to the states to participate in fashioning air pollution control policy, albeit significant, 'is the power of the servant, not the sovereign,'[15] or Congress intended to make EPA and the states equal partners.[16]

This chapter demonstrates that the vision of CAA cooperative federalism as an equal partnership bears no resemblance to the allocation of power Congress established in adopting the CAA. Congress made EPA the dominant partner because experience convinced it that the states lacked the will or the capacity to achieve its air quality protection goals. While it recognized that states' familiarity with local conditions made a significant state role in deciding how to implement some federal standards desirable, it also acted on the premise that a series of collective action problems could be effectively addressed only by vesting predominant policymaking authority in a federal agency. Experience in implementing the 1970 CAA reinforced these sentiments, inducing Congress to tilt the balance of power even more heavily toward EPA in the 1977 and 1990 amendments. Congress allowed the states to avoid federal supervision or constraints only when they adopt emission controls more stringent than the floors established by EPA (except in limited areas such as emission controls for new motor vehicles). This approach does not disrespect state sovereignty. As the Supreme Court recognized in a 1981 decision upholding a statute regulating surface mining, this cooperative federalism approach is less intrusive than the complete preemption of state authority to regulate activities creating environmental harms with interstate effects to which Congress could have resorted.[17]

This chapter emphasizes the predominant role of EPA vis-à-vis the states in various CAA programs. It refutes recent characterizations of its cooperative federalism design as intended to create an 'equal partnership' between EPA and the states. Instead, the legislative history reveals that Congress crafted key statutory programs to address collective action problems that it regarded the states as incapable of solving. Finally, the chapter briefly examines the desirability of this cooperative federalism model both in controlling conventional air pollution and in seeking to

---

[15] Gerken, Heather K., 'The Federalis(m) Society' (2013) 36 Harv JL & Pub Pol'y **1**, 3.

[16] In limited contexts under other pollution control statutes, Congress has given the states the power to override federal actions. See Carlson, Ann E., 'Reverse Preemption' (2013) 40 Ecology LQ 583.

[17] *Hodel v Va. Surface Mining & Reclamation Ass'n, Inc.*, 452 US 264, 289–91 (1981).

address greenhouse gases (GHGs) that contribute to climate disruption. The authors find that the CAA's delegation to EPA of the dominant role in controlling conventional air pollution, subject to state power to exceed federal minimums, has largely succeeded in addressing conventional air pollution problems. Moreover, this version of cooperative federalism promises to be an effective approach for regulating GHG emissions. Unfortunately, judicial decisions circumscribing EPA's authority under the CAA have undermined federal efforts to address lingering collective action problems such as interstate air pollution. An accurate application of the cooperative federalism model actually established under the CAA is imperative for the successful implementation and enforcement of the statute's programs and goals.

THE CAA MAKES EPA THE DOMINANT COOPERATIVE FEDERALISM PARTNER

That Congress sought to protect and enhance air quality through a cooperative federalism venture is not in dispute. The CAA finds that 'Federal financial assistance and leadership is essential for the development of cooperative Federal, State, regional, and local programs to prevent and control air pollution.'[18] Congress committed the federal government to providing technical and financial assistance to state and local governments to help them develop and implement air pollution control programs.[19] EPA must encourage cooperative activities by state and local governments and improved laws to control air pollution, in pursuit of uniformity to the extent it is practicable 'in the light of varying conditions and needs.'[20] EPA may make grants to support regional, state, and local programs.[21] None of these provisions, however, establishes the states as equal partners with EPA.

The Act declares air pollution control at its source to be 'the primary responsibility of States and local governments.'[22] Moreover, as indicated below, it authorizes EPA to step in if the states do not fulfill that responsibility. Notably, the statute refers to state responsibilities, not rights. Responsibilities imply duties, whose breach carries consequences. The reference to responsibilities contrasts with the Clean Water Act's

---

[18] 42 USC § 7401(a)(4).
[19] Ibid. at § 7401(b)(3).
[20] Ibid. at § 7402(a).
[21] Ibid. at § 7405.
[22] *Id.* at § 7401(a)(3).

enunciation of a federal policy of recognizing, preserving, and protecting 'the primary responsibilities *and rights* of States to prevent, reduce, and eliminate pollution,'[23] and with the same law's renunciation of any intent to supersede, abrogate, or impair state authority to allocate quantities of water within a state's jurisdiction.[24] When the CAA refers to states' 'rights,' it preserves their right, with exceptions for mobile source controls, to enact standards more stringent than applicable federal rules.[25] States are therefore free to craft air pollution control policy without EPA supervision only when they choose to exceed federal minimum standards.

The CAA's allocation of authority between EPA and the states is usually clear-cut. EPA is responsible for adopting the NAAQS that form the Act's central pollution control mechanism, although it may seek technical input from state and local governments, among others.[26] Each state has 'the primary responsibility for assuring air quality' within its borders by adopting a state implementation plan (SIP) for each NAAQS.[27] States must submit each SIP to EPA to determine whether it meets mandatory requirements.[28] EPA must approve an SIP that meets these requirements;[29] the Supreme Court in an early CAA case concluded that EPA has

> no authority to question the wisdom of a State's choices of emissions limitations if they are part of a plan which satisfies [the Act's minimum requirements]. Thus, so long as the ultimate effects of a State's choices of emissions limitations is compliance with the [NAAQS], the state is at liberty to adopt whatever mix of emission limitations it deems best suited to its particular situation.[30]

---

[23] 33 USC § 1251(b) (emphasis added).
[24] Ibid. at § 1251(g).
[25] 42 USC § 7416.
[26] Ibid. at § 7408(a)–(b).
[27] Ibid. at § 7407(a).
[28] Ibid. at § 7410(a)(1)–(2). Each SIP must include, among other things, enforceable emissions limitations and other control measures, schedules and timetables for compliance, monitoring requirements, enforcement provisions, and measures to prevent interstate pollution. Ibid. at § 7410(a)(2).
[29] Ibid. at § 7410(k)(3).
[30] *Train v Natural Res. Def. Council, Inc.*, 421 US 60, 79 (1975). See also ibid. at 86–87 (stating that Congress 'left to the state considerable latitude in determining specifically how the [NAAQS] would be met. This discretion includes the continuing authority to revise choices about the mix of emissions limitations.').

Nevertheless, Congress specified the mandatory components of each state plan, delegated to EPA the power to assess whether a plan meets those requirements, and authorized EPA to adopt a federal implementation plan if a state fails to abide by its responsibilities.[31] Likewise, the statute gives the states the first opportunity to enforce SIP provisions or permits, but allows EPA to enforce if the states do not.[32]

Other CAA programs provide less authority to the states, or none at all. Whereas the states are responsible in the first instance for developing and imposing controls on sources that emit pollutants covered by the NAAQS, Congress gave EPA the power to issue technology-based emission standards for new stationary sources[33] and newly manufactured mobile sources,[34] and to issue technology-based and, if necessary, health-based standards for hazardous air pollutants.[35] States may adopt and submit for EPA approval a program to implement and enforce emission standards for hazardous air pollutants to displace the federal program, but state standards may not be less stringent than EPA's standards.[36] EPA is responsible for enforcing all of these federal emission standards.[37]

States may adopt controls more stringent than EPA's standards for new sources or sources of hazardous air pollutants, but the statute completely preempts state power to adopt tailpipe emission standards for new motor vehicles.[38] EPA may waive this prohibition by allowing California to adopt more stringent standards,[39] and, if it does so, any other state may adopt California's standards in lieu of EPA's.[40]

---

[31] 42 USC § 7410(c).
[32] Ibid. at § 7413(a).
[33] Ibid. at § 7411. EPA may require states to submit plans establishing standards of performance for existing sources in industrial categories covered by the new source standards of performance issued under § 111. EPA retains backup regulatory authority, with the discretion to issue a plan for a state failing to submit a satisfactory one. Ibid. at § 7411(d).
[34] Ibid. at §§ 7521, 7547, 7571.
[35] Ibid. at § 7412.
[36] Ibid. at § 7412(*l*).
[37] Ibid. at §§ 7413(a)(3), (b)–(c), 7523–24.
[38] Ibid. at § 7543(a).
[39] Ibid. at § 7543(b).
[40] Ibid. at § 7507. Congress included this waiver procedure in the 1970 CAA because it recognized that California regulators might need to impose more stringent tailpipe emissions standards to address the state's uniquely severe pollution problems and to enable California to meet the NAAQS. See 116 Cong. Rec. 19,231–37 (1970). Air quality in Los Angeles, for example, was five times

EPA is also largely responsible for implementing the programs added in the 1990 amendments to control acid deposition[41] and emissions of substances that deplete the stratospheric ozone layer.[42] The 1990 amendments also authorized states to seek EPA approval of permit programs that encompass all aspects of the CAA's emission controls for stationary sources, but the statute prescribes the mandatory minimum contents of state programs and authorizes EPA to determine whether a state program is adequate. State-issued permits must incorporate all controls applicable to the source covered by the permit, including those issued solely by EPA.[43] EPA may reject a state's proposed permit and if the state does not make changes identified by EPA, EPA may deny or issue the permit itself.[44] EPA also may revoke a state permit program if it determines that the state is not adequately administering and enforcing the program.[45] Thus, with the exception of state power to adopt controls more stringent than federal standards for stationary sources, EPA either unilaterally adopts pollution control standards or determines whether state provisions meet state responsibilities. It is difficult to conceptualize the states as equal partners with EPA under virtually any aspect of the statutory program (other than the power to adopt controls more stringent than EPA's), no less under the statute as a whole.

COLLECTIVE ACTION RATIONALES FOR FEDERAL ENVIRONMENTAL REGULATION

A significant federal role in environmental lawmaking requires justification, given the traditional state role in protecting health and safety through exercise of the police power, and the preference for policymaking by state and local officials in light of their superior political accountability and familiarity with local conditions. Collective action theory justifies environmental laws such as the CAA that carve out a predominant role for the federal government. That theory examines the

---

worse than in any other city in the country. Ibid. at 19,237 (remarks of Rep. Springer).
 [41]   42 USC §§ 7651–51*o*.
 [42]   Ibid. at §§ 7671–7671q.
 [43]   Ibid. at §§ 7661a, 7661c(a).
 [44]   Ibid. at § 7661d(b)–(c).
 [45]   Ibid. at § 7661a(i).

dynamics of individual behavior in cooperative group settings.[46] Much of environmental regulation generally can be explained as an effort to avert the tragedy of the commons, which is a collective action problem that causes shared resources to be overused.[47] Five more specific collective action problems justify significant federal authority to adopt and implement environmental law instead of leaving such matters within state control: transboundary externalities, the benefits of resource pooling, avoidance of a race to the bottom, the need for uniformity, and avoidance of the 'not in my backyard' syndrome.[48] With the exception of the last one, Congress relied on all of these collective action problems in authorizing EPA to adopt and implement air pollution controls itself or to supervise state implementation and displace the authority of underperforming states.

Transboundary Externalities

One of the clearest justifications for federal intervention is the fact that air pollution can create negative externalities in states downwind from the pollution source.[49] The core concern is that a state enjoying the economic benefits of the activity producing interstate air pollution without having to address adverse environmental impacts will abstain from regulation. Federal intervention is justified because the source state has no incentive to regulate in-state sources that pollute downwind states and downwind states have no authority to regulate those sources.

Resource Pooling

The federal government can pool resources from across the country to develop and implement regulatory programs, giving it more resources than any individual state has to collect technical information, conduct scientific studies, and develop and enforce standards. In some instances,

---

[46] Glicksman, Robert L. and Richard E. Levy, 'A Collective Action Perspective on Ceiling Preemption by Federal Environmental Regulation: The Case of Global Climate Change' (2008) 102 Nw U.L. Rev. **579**, 579 n.1. See generally Olson, Mancur, *The Logic of Collective Action: Public Goods and the Theory of Group* (Cambridge, Mass.: Harvard University Press 1965).
[47] Glicksman and Levy, *supra* n.46, p. 593.
[48] *See* ibid., pp. 593–602.
[49] *See* Merrill, Thomas W., 'Golden Rules for Transboundary Pollution' (1997) 46 Duke L.J. 931; Revesz, Richard L., 'Federalism and Interstate Environmental Externalities' (1996) 144 U. Pa. L. Rev. 2341.

the federal government can carry out these activities more efficiently than could multiple states acting independently.

Race to the Bottom

Concerns about a 'race to the bottom' among states may justify federal regulation. If states have different environmental standards, regulated industries may migrate from jurisdictions with more stringent standards to those with less stringent standards. This dynamic creates a perverse incentive for each state to relax its environmental standards to gain the economic benefits and tax revenues that polluting businesses provide. Interstate competition for industry can lead all states to settle on a lowest common denominator of environmental degradation. States imposing stringent standards are penalized.[50] Federal regulation can halt the race by establishing a floor below which the states may not go.

Uniform Standards

Exclusive federal regulation provides uniform standards. The key advantage of uniform regulation is that it reduces production and transaction costs for regulated entities supplying goods and services in interstate commerce, such as manufacturers of new vehicles.[51] Uniform standards avoid the need for industries whose products have a national market to comply with multiple, divergent state standards. Although states are free to harmonize their standards, it is typically easier to achieve uniformity through the imposition of exclusive federal standards.

The 'Not In My Backyard' (NIMBY) Syndrome

Local opposition to the siting of undesirable (but sometimes necessary) land uses can prompt strict state or local laws that seek to drive those activities elsewhere. If all jurisdictions adopt such laws, socially important activities that necessarily generate adverse environmental effects may

---

[50] See Engel, Kirsten, 'State Environmental Standard-Setting: Is There a "Race" and Is It "to the Bottom"?' (1997) 48 Hastings LJ 271; Esty, Daniel C., 'Revitalizing Environmental Federalism' (1996) 95 Mich. L. Rev. 570; Swire, Peter P., 'The Race to Laxity and the Race to Undesirability: Explaining Failures in Competition Among Jurisdictions in Environmental Law' (1996) 14 Yale L. & Pol'y Rev. 67.

[51] See Engel, *supra* n.50, at 369.

be permitted nowhere. NIMBYism is the inverse of the negative externality problem in that the host state bears all or most of the associated environmental burdens, while the economic benefits are more broadly distributed among the states. Although this phenomenon may present a compelling rationale for federal regulation in contexts such as waste disposal,[52] it is not the basis for federal air pollution control.

CONGRESS RELIED ON COLLECTIVE ACTION RATIONALES TO MAKE EPA THE DOMINANT CAA PARTNER

Until the mid-twentieth century, air pollution control was the domain of state and local governments. Worsening pollution, growing awareness of its public health consequences, and the perceived failure of states and localities to adequately address pollution combined to generate public demand and congressional support for a dramatic shift in the direction of greater federal power. When Congress passed the 1970 CAA, it chose to vest in the newly created EPA the dominant role in pursuing statutory goals. In doing so, it subscribed to the belief that collective action problems made federal dominance essential for effective air pollution control. Amendments adopted in 1977 and 1990 reinforced the states' subsidiary role, either because states had not responded adequately to past responsibilities under the Act or because collective action problems made it unlikely that they would be able to manage newly discovered problems.

The 1970 Act

When Congress adopted legislation during the 1960s to protect the public health from air pollution, it carved out a relatively limited role for the federal government. Aside from taking the lead in controlling interstate air pollution and regulating new motor vehicle emissions, federal agencies would primarily set goals and provide financial and technical assistance to state regulators. According to Senator Edmund Muskie, a principal author of the 1970 Act, Congress established a strong regulatory role for the states because it wanted 'to preserve the federal system' and 'recognized that the task of implementing and enforcing the clean air

---

[52] See Glicksman and Levy, *supra* n.46, at 600–01 (discussing the Low-Level Radioactive Waste Policy Act of 1980).

program was so enormous that it would be helpful to have effective agencies at the state and local level to get the job done more quickly and thoroughly.'[53] By 1970, however, a House committee report characterized progress under the pre-1970 legislation as inadequate and emphasized the urgency of more expeditious control of sources and more effective enforcement.[54] The states would continue to participate significantly in pollution control efforts primarily for practical reasons; the federal government lacked the resources to implement the statute by itself and the states and localities were best situated to implement land use and transportation control policies thought to be critical to effective pollution control.[55]

Congress passed the 1970 Act with near unanimity, and yet '[f]ew members of Congress ... expressed any sentiments for the abstract values of state autonomy.' Indeed, 'federal legislators viewed state autonomy with suspicion because the states had failed to impose adequate air pollution controls' when they had the opportunity to do so under the pre-1970 legislation.[56] Sentiments in favor of state autonomy related principally to state authority to adopt more stringent motor vehicle emission standards than EPA's. Some legislators referred to the states' 'right to have higher standards.'[57] Congress eventually decided to allow California alone to adopt more stringent tailpipe emission standards, but permitted other states to adopt California's standards.[58]

Some policymakers were concerned about protecting rights, but they focused on individual rights to a healthy environment and the need to protect states that took their environmental protection responsibilities seriously. A 1970 Senate report justified vesting in EPA authority to adopt NAAQS by asserting that 'the air is a public resource, and ... those who use that resource must protect it from abuse, to assure the protection of the health of every American.'[59] Similarly, President Nixon supported the NAAQS program because it would 'provide a minimum standard for

---

[53] Muskie, Edmund S., 'Role of the Federal Government in Air Pollution Control' (1968–1969) 10 Ariz. L. Rev. **17**, 17.
[54] H.R. Rep. No. 91-1146, pp. 1, 5 (1970). See also *Alaska Dep't of Envtl. Conservation v EPA*, 540 US 461, 469 (2004) (describing the 1970 Act as the outgrowth of 'dissatisfaction with the progress of existing air pollution programs').
[55] See e.g. S. Rep. No. 1196, p. 2 (1970).
[56] Dwyer, John P., 'The Practice of Federalism under the Clean Air Act' (1995) 54 Md L. Rev. **1183**, 1192–93.
[57] See e.g. 116 Cong. Rec. 19, 231 (1970) (remarks of Rep. Saylor).
[58] 42 USC §§ 7507, 7543.
[59] S. Rep. No. 91-1996, at 4 (1970).

air quality for all areas of the nation, while permitting States to set more stringent standards.'[60] Legislators also feared a race to the bottom, notwithstanding Justice Kennedy's contrary protestations. As one House member put it, 'if we do not have [NAAQS], we find what has happened is that States begin to bid against each other to attract polluting industries ... So I say it is not fair to those States who are trying to do something about pollution to allow such lowering of standards to attract polluting industries into other States.'[61] Similarly, Nixon noted that the NAAQS would protect the interests of industries subject to stringent state controls, which 'would otherwise be disadvantaged with respect to competitors' subject to less rigorous controls.[62] Uniform NAAQS would level the playing field.

The 1970 Act vested responsibility to implement the NAAQS in the states, which could craft pollution control strategies suitable to their social and economic needs. But, as one legislator put it, '[i]f a State hangs back and fails to move out, the Federal government will take over and make rules and regulations amounting to a State plan.'[63] Thus, although Congress afforded the states the opportunity to choose their own paths for meeting the NAAQS, it hardly made the states equal partners with EPA. Rather, as the Supreme Court put it, Congress reacted to disaffection with pre-1970 state progress by 'taking a stick to the States in the form of the [1970 Act],' which 'sharply increased federal authority and responsibility in the continuing effort to combat air pollution.'[64] For the first time, the states had to attain air quality of specified standards on a federally specified timetable. Notwithstanding Justice Kennedy's later characterization, congressional distrust of state performance also provided the rationale for jointly authorizing EPA and the states to enforce SIP provisions, and for providing a safety net in the form of citizen suit enforcement.[65]

---

[60] President Richard M. Nixon, Special Message to the Congress on Environmental Quality (10 February 1970) (transcript accessed 28 June 2015 at www.presidency.ucsb.edu/ws/?pid=2757).

[61] 116 Cong. Rec. 19,213 (remarks of Rep. Preyer).

[62] Nixon, *supra* n.60.

[63] 116 Cong. Rec. 19,206 (1970) (remarks of Rep. Springer).

[64] *Train v Natural Res. Def. Council, Inc.*, 421 US 60, 64–65 (1970). Cf. *Union Elec. Co. v EPA*, 427 US 246, 249, 256–57 (1976) (repeating the stick metaphor and noting that although the CAA gave states the primary responsibility to formulate control strategies, it subjected them to 'strict minimum compliance requirements' of a technology-forcing character).

[65] See S. Rep. No. 91-1196, at 21 (1970).

Congress cited several collective action rationales for increasing the federal role in air pollution control. First, it relied on race-to-the-bottom concerns to justify delegating to EPA the power to adopt nationally uniform emissions standards for new sources and hazardous air pollutants. According to a House report, both sets of standards would 'preclude efforts on the part of states to compete with each other in trying to attract new plants and facilities without assuring adequate control of extra-hazardous or large-scale emissions therefrom.'[66] Second, legislators cited superior federal expertise and resources (the resource pooling rationale for federal action) to support uniform federal standards.[67] Third, Congress decided to delegate to EPA exclusive power to adopt tailpipe emissions standards (with an exception for California) to address the need for uniformity. A Senate report accompanying earlier air pollution legislation stated that 'it would be more desirable to have national standards rather than for each State to have a variation in standards and requirements which could result in chaos insofar as manufacturers, dealers, and users are concerned.'[68] Senator Muskie later explained that restricting state authority in this manner was appropriate because it was 'obviously in the public interest to reduce the variation in automotive emissions standards to an absolute minimum.'[69] Congress accommodated state interests primarily by authorizing the states to adopt controls (except for new motor vehicles) more stringent than EPA's.[70]

The 1977 Amendments

The 1977 amendments extended the deadlines for compliance with the NAAQS due to many states' failure to meet the original statutory timetable. They also added new programs, including permitting requirements for major stationary sources in both air quality control regions that had not yet met the NAAQS (nonattainment areas) and regions with air quality better than required by the NAAQS (PSD areas). Although some

---

[66] H.R. Rep. No. 91-1146, at 2 (1970). *See also* S. Rep. No. 91-1196, at 49 (1970) (seeking to prevent states with adequate controls from being placed at a competitive disadvantage).
[67] See e.g. 116 Cong. Rec. 19,206 (1970) (remarks of Rep. Springer).
[68] S. Rep. No. 89-192, at 6 (1965).
[69] Muskie, *supra* n.53, at 20. As indicated above, Congress allowed California to seek permission to enact more stringent standards because of its early efforts to control auto pollution and the severity of the state's pollution problems.
[70] See S. Rep. No. 91-1196, at 15 (1970) (explaining the purpose of § 116 of the 1970 Act).

lawmakers expressed concerns about rising regulatory costs and increasing federal intrusion on state prerogatives, the dominant theme expounded throughout the legislative debate was the need for an even stronger federal role vis-à-vis the states. Legislators again invoked the specter of a race to the bottom, identifying as a key purpose of the amendments the prevention of industry's ability to foster competition for new business through the adoption of ever weaker state controls.[71] A House report referred to this practice as 'environmental blackmail.'[72] The nonattainment provisions subjected states failing to meet NAAQS deadlines to new penalties and required them to submit SIP revisions.[73] The amendments reduced state discretion to determine the appropriate mix of emissions controls needed to achieve the NAAQS by, among other things, requiring states with nonattainment areas to ensure that existing stationary sources in those areas implement reasonably available control measures for the nonattainment pollutants[74] and to ensure that new or modified major stationary sources install emissions controls reflecting the lowest achievable emissions rate for those pollutants.[75]

Opponents of the new PSD provisions complained about unfair discrimination against the economic interests of states with clean air resources and protested the unwarranted federal intrusion on local governments' ability 'to protect clean air from people.'[76] The House committee report, however, actually lists the 'protection of States' rights' as a key justification for the PSD program.[77] The Act delegated to the states 'primary responsibility' for administering the program, but required that they abide by minimum standards (measured as percentages of the NAAQS) regarded as 'essential to guarantee the individual States the right to decide to maintain air quality superior to minimum federal

---

[71] H.R. Rep. No. 95-294, at 11, 133–35 (1977). *See also* Dwyer, *supra* n.56, at 1195 ('Because of their willingness to relax environmental standards to attract or keep economic development, states could not be trusted to adopt adequate standards.').
[72] H.R. Rep. No. 95-294, at 195.
[73] The amended sanction provisions are at 42 USC § 7509.
[74] 42 USC § 7502(c)(1).
[75] Ibid. at §§ 7502(c)(5), 7503(a)(2), 7501(3).
[76] See e.g. 123 Cong. Rec. 18,135 (1977) (remarks of Sen. Garn). Some even charged that the PSD program amounted to a federal land use control system. See e.g. ibid. at 16,964 (remarks of Rep. Rousselot).
[77] H.R. Rep. No. 95-294, at 105 (1977). Specifically, the PSD program was intended to protect states' rights to be free of interstate air pollution and to avoid the practice of 'environmental blackmail' described above.

standards.'[78] Indeed, a House report asserted that without the PSD provisions, the pre-existing guarantee that states would retain the power to adopt standards more stringent than EPA's would be meaningless.[79] The same report also noted that the PSD program would help avoid the race to the bottom by precluding sources from 'shopping around' for locations with clean air and weak controls.[80]

Congress had authorized federal regulation of interstate pollution even before 1970 as a necessary response to transboundary externalities.[81] The 1977 amendments sought to facilitate EPA efforts to enforce statutory restrictions on interstate pollution and authorized states to petition EPA for a finding that an upwind state was violating the statute by inadequately restricting emissions that prevented attainment or maintenance of the NAAQS in the petitioning state.[82] The goal was to protect downwind states' interests by 'making a source at least as responsible for polluting another State as it would be for polluting its own State,' even if the source state's SIP did not prevent it from doing so.[83]

The 1990 Amendments

The 1977 amendments tilted the balance of federal–state authority significantly toward greater EPA control, protecting state autonomy mainly by reinforcing states' freedom to adopt controls more stringent than EPA's and by constraining the power of one state to prevent another from effectively controlling air pollution. The 1990 amendments took another step away from a regime even remotely resembling an 'equal partnership' between the two levels of government. The amendments were spurred by the persistent failure of some states to comply with the NAAQS and by the need to address newly discovered or inadequately addressed problems such as acid deposition and stratospheric ozone

---

[78] Ibid. at 136. The Supreme Court described EPA's authority to issue orders halting construction of major facilities permitted by states notwithstanding regulatory deficiencies as 'notably capacious.' *Alaska Dep't of Envtl. Conservation v EPA*, 540 US 461, 473–74 (2004). Another court later rejected the contention that EPA's implementation of the CAA's related visibility protection provisions 'trample[d] on discretion that Congress afforded states,' noting that the exercise of state responsibility is subject to federal oversight. *Oklahoma v EPA*, 723 F.3d 1201, 1204 (10th Cir. 2013).
[79] H.R. Rep. No. 95-294, at 136–37 (1977).
[80] Ibid., at 133.
[81] See Glicksman and Levy, *supra* n.46, at 594–95.
[82] 42 USC § 7426.
[83] S. Rep. No. 95-127, at 40 (1977).

depletion. The amendments set new deadlines for NAAQS compliance in nonattainment areas, defined in much greater detail the steps necessary to move states with nonattainment areas toward compliance (and refined the sanctions available if states did not do so[84]), established a cap-and-trade program for coal-fired power plants that emitted acid rain precursors, stiffened interstate controls still further,[85] phased out the manufacture and use of ozone-depleting chemicals to comply with US treaty commitments under the Montreal Protocol, and established a new permit program to help consolidate in one document all regulatory requirements applicable to a source.

Individual legislators predicted economic disruption. Senator Minority Leader Bob Dole called the bill 'the toughest environmental medicine America has ever had to take,' but supported it anyway.[86] Other legislators protested the burdens the legislation would impose on some regions, such as those producing or whose sources burned large amounts of high-sulfur coal.[87] Congress adopted the amendments in the face of this opposition. Senator Bentsen's response to those who opposed the acid rain provisions was that 'fairness' considerations had to be supplemented by state responsibility for the downwind harms caused by their sources, consistent with the 'polluter pays' principle.[88] A House report noted that the amendments signaled that Congress was 'very serious' about air pollution control and 'will require all States to comply fully' with their CAA duties. States not making good faith efforts to comply would be severely sanctioned.[89] The 'stick' Congress wielded in 1970 got larger in 1977 and larger still in 1990, notwithstanding preservation of the CAA's basic cooperative federalism architecture.

---

[84] 42 USC § 7410(m).
[85] See e.g. *GenOn REMA, LLC v EPA*, 722 F.3d 513, 523 (3d Cir. 2013) ('Congress viewed the Federal government as continuing to play an essential role in the fight against interstate pollution despite the fact that the states are the primary actors for implementing NAAQS and formulating SIPs.').
[86] 136 Cong. Rec. 36, 130 (1990).
[87] See e.g. ibid., at 35,007 (remarks of Rep. Luken); ibid., at 35,016 (remarks of Rep. Applegate).
[88] Ibid., at 36,129.
[89] H.R. Rep. No. 101-490 (1990).

THE PERFORMANCE OF COOPERATIVE FEDERALISM UNDER THE CAA

Congress's initial venture into environmental cooperative federalism is largely a success story. A 2013 minority report of the Senate Committee on Environment and Public Works, while highly critical of the Obama administration's implementation of the CAA, concluded that '[a]ir quality has significantly improved in the United States over the past 40 years, and the [CAA's] cooperative federalism arrangement deserves credit.'[90] Both emissions and ambient concentrations of the criteria pollutants covered by the NAAQS – the centerpiece of the statute and the primary focus of public health concern – have fallen significantly on a national basis, notwithstanding economic growth and population increases.[91] Some programs administered by EPA without significant state assistance also have fared well. The acid deposition control's cap-and-trade program, for example, has reduced emissions of acid rain precursors generated by fossil fuel combustion at lower costs than anticipated.[92] The statutory phaseout of ozone-depleting chemicals has helped shrink the hole in the ozone layer that increases risks for skin cancer and cataracts, although the hole is not expected to fully close before 2070.[93] Retained state authority to adopt more stringent state controls has borne fruit in the form of ambitious state programs which have gone further than federal

---

[90] Cooperative Federalism, *supra* n.14, at 11. The criticism was directed at EPA's alleged treatment of states not as 'equal and valued partners,' but as objects of cooptation and coercion, and as 'mere regional offices of a massive federal environmental bureaucracy'. Ibid., at 13.

[91] See Glicksman, Robert L. et al., *Environmental Protection: Law and Policy*, 7th edn (Wolters Kluwer, Austin, Boston, Chicago, New York, the Netherlands (2015), pp. 428–30. David Adelman, however, attributes most of the reduction in criteria pollutants to direct federal regulation, not the NAAQS program. See Adelman, David, 'Environmental Federalism: When Numbers Matter More than Size' (2014) 32 UCLA J. Envt'l L. & Pol'y **238**, 301–304.

[92] See e.g. Glicksman et al., *supra* n.91, pp. 586–88; Goffman, Joseph, 'Title IV of the Clean Air Act: Lessons for Success of the Acid Rain Emissions Trading Program' (2006) 14 Penn. St. Envtl L. Rev. **177**, 179–80.

[93] See Culaba, Anne (January 2014) 'Good News: Ozone Hole Closing. Bad News: It Won't Recover Until 2070', *RYOT News*, accessed 30 June 2015 at www.ryot.org/full-recovery-ozone-layer-wont-happen-2070/499477. See also Driesen, David M. and Amy Sinden, 'The Missing Instrument: Dirty Input Limits' (2009) 33 Harv. Envtl L. Rev. **65**, 85 ('Scholars recognize the phaseout of ozone-depleting chemicals as the major (some say the only) example of successful international environmental protection.').

controls (such as California's control of motor vehicle emissions) or preceded such controls (such as California's restrictions on GHG emissions). In some instances, one state's programs have spurred efforts by other states or EPA.[94] Indeed, adoption of stringent state standards by a jurisdiction (like California) with a large market share for a regulated product such as new cars may induce manufacturers to conform their products globally to the standard to increase economies of scale, even in the absence of copycat regulation by other jurisdictions.[95]

The CAA is not an unalloyed cooperative federalism success story, however. Nonattainment persists, especially in major urban areas. Decades after Congress first mandated compliance with the NAAQS, more than 40 percent of US residents (more than 131 million people) live in counties with unhealthy levels of either ozone or particulate matter.[96] Persistent nonattainment problems are due principally to emissions from mobile and small stationary sources (such as gas stations, paint emissions, and agricultural field burning), not from large industrial sources (with the exception of fossil fuel-fired electric power plants).[97] Because the states are primarily responsible for regulating emissions from smaller sources under their SIPs (for example, through land-use plans and stationary source regulations), one might argue that nonattainment problems reflect inadequate federal oversight of NAAQS compliance

---

[94] See e.g. Pawa, Matthew F., 'The Very Definition of Folly: Saving the Earth from Environmentalists' (2011) 38 BC Envtl Aff. L. Rev. **77**, 80–81 (describing adoption by a dozen states of California's vehicle emission standards); Buzbee, William W., 'Preemption Hard Look Review, Regulatory Interaction, and the Quest for Stewardship and Intergenerational Equity' (2009) 77 Geo. Wash. L. Rev. **1521**, 1551–52 (describing other states' desire to adopt California emissions standards for GHGs). See also *Rocky Mountain Farmers Union v Corey*, 740 F.3d 507, 511 (9th Cir. 2014) (Gould J, concurring in denial of rehearing en banc) (arguing that 'once states appreciate the benefits of [California's Low Carbon Fuel Standard], there may be a cascade of similar laws throughout the country – and perhaps federal action – aimed at stemming the tide of global warming').

[95] See Stewart, Richard B., Michael Oppenheimer and Bryce Rudyk, 'Building a More Effective Global Climate Regime through a Bottom-Up Approach' (2013) 14 Theoretical Inquiries L. **273**, 297–98.

[96] American Lung Ass'n, Report on State of the Air 2013, at 8, accessed 30 June 2015 at www.lung.org/assets/documents/publications/state-of-the-air/state-of-the-air-report-2013.pdf; Adelman, *supra* n.91, at 301. For a complete list of nonattainment areas for all criteria pollutants, see 'Currently Designated Nonattainment Areas for All Criteria Pollutants', EPA, accessed 30 June 2015 at www.epa.gov/oaqps001/greenbk/ancl.html.

[97] See Adelman, *supra* n.91, at § IV A–B.

efforts.[98] On the other hand, some characterize the new source review (NSR) program that requires permits for major stationary sources in nonattainment and PSD areas as unduly burdensome and needlessly intrusive on state prerogatives.[99]

Perhaps the most dysfunctional CAA provisions, however, are those restricting interstate air pollution. Before 1990, these restrictions accomplished little, as EPA and the courts consistently held that downwind states failed to prove that upwind sources significantly contributed to downwind state nonattainment.[100] The 1990 amendments lessened the burden of proof for states soliciting EPA assistance in controlling upwind state sources contributing to downwind state nonattainment and allowed EPA to require upwind state regulation based on the aggregate contributions of groups of sources instead of having to trace problems to a single source.[101] Judicial interpretation of the amended statute left EPA's efforts to mitigate interstate pollution in a shambles, however. The DC Circuit

---

[98] EPA and the states actually share regulatory authority over motor vehicles: EPA establishes federal tailpipe emission standards, but states can also significantly reduce such emissions through transportation planning efforts and other regulatory mechanisms.

[99] See e.g. *Alaska Dep't of Envtl. Conservation v EPA*, 540 US 461, 502–18 (2004) (Kennedy J dissenting); Gaines, Sanford E., 'Reflexive Law as a Legal Paradigm for Sustainable Development' (2003) 10 Buff Envtl LJ **1**, 9 (raising possibility that NSR is impeding, not promoting emissions reductions); Murkowski, Senator Frank H., 'The Kyoto Protocol Is Not the Answer to Climate Change' (2000) 37 Harv. J. on Legis. **345**, 361–62 (describing NSR as intrusive). Others have criticized NSR's grandfathering of existing sources, which arguably creates perverse incentives not to modernize old plants or competitive advantages for such plants. See e.g. Nash, Jonathan Remy and Richard L. Revesz, 'Grandfathering and Environmental Regulation: The Law and Economics of New Source Review' (2007) 101 Nw U.L. Rev. **1677**, 1709–11; Revesz, Richard L. and Allison L. Westfahl Kong, 'Regulatory Change and Optimal Transition Relief (2011) 105 Nw U.L. Rev. **1581**, 1628–32. Professor Adelman recommends scrapping NSR, thereby removing constraints on state regulatory choices in nonattainment and PSD areas. At the same time, he suggests giving EPA increased power to work with states and localities to address transportation control and small source emissions, which collectively are more responsible for nonattainment than large industrial sources. See Adelman, *supra* n.91, at § IV A–B.

[100] See Glicksman, Robert L., 'Watching the River Flow: The Prospects for Improved Interstate Water Pollution Control' (1993) 43 J Urb & Contemp L **119**, 166–68; Crider, Kay M. 'Interstate Air Pollution: Over a Decade of Ineffective Regulation' (1988) 64 Chi-Kent L. Rev. 619.

[101] See Glicksman, *supra* n.100, at 566–67.

invalidated major regulatory initiatives by the Bush and Obama administrations.[102] The Supreme Court reversed the DC Circuit's latest invalidation, upholding EPA's Cross-State Air Pollution Rule.[103] The Court's decision did not resolve all issues concerning the Rule, however, and EPA's efforts to implement it are likely to face significant delays, including the possibility of additional litigation.[104] The irony is that Congress authorized federal control of interstate air pollution in 1963, before authorizing any other federal air quality-related regulation. Fifty years later, the collective action problems arising from these transboundary externalities remain seemingly intractable.

A COLLECTIVE ACTION-BASED RESPONSE TO CLIMATE CHANGE MITIGATION

Climate change is the most significant problem facing environmental policymakers in the US and elsewhere. In the absence of a federal statute directed to controlling GHGs that contribute to climate change, EPA has addressed the problem under the CAA.[105] Some contend that the CAA is ill suited to addressing climate change mitigation, a global problem with characteristics different from the localized air pollution problems targeted by the NAAQS program.[106] Nevertheless, the CAA already addresses both regional (acid deposition) and global (stratospheric ozone depletion) transboundary problems, apparently quite effectively. The question is

---

[102] *EME Homer City Generation, L.P. v EPA*, 696 F.3d 7 (DC Cir. 2012), *rev'd & remanded*, 134 S Ct 1584 (2014); *North Carolina v EPA*, 531 F.3d 896 (DC Cir.), *modified on reh'g*, 550 F.3d 1176 (DC Cir. 2008).

[103] *EPA v EME Homer City Generation, L.P.*, 134 S Ct 1584 (2014).

[104] See e.g. *EME Homer City Generation, L.P. v. EPA*, ___ F.3d ___, 795 F.3d 118 (DC Cir. 2015); Ambrosio, Patrick, 'Attorney Says "Live Issues" Remain Following Supreme Court Decision on Cross-State Rule' (8 May 2014) 45 Env't Rep. (BNA) 1467; Childers, Andrew, 'Challenges Remain Despite Supreme Court Decision Reinstating EPA Cross-State Rule' (29 April 2014) BNA Env't Rep., accessed 30 June 2015 at www.bna.com/challenges-remain-despite-n17179890025/.

[105] See *Massachusetts v EPA*, 549 US 497 (2007) (holding that emissions of GHGs such as carbon dioxide are pollutants for CAA purposes, authorizing EPA to regulate them from mobile sources under § 202 of the Act); Endangerment and Cause or Contribute Findings for Greenhouse Gases Under Section 202(a) of the Clean Air Act; CAA rulemakings, 74 Fed. Reg. 66,496 (15 December 2009).

[106] Cf. *Massachusetts v. EPA*, 549 US at 559 (Scalia J. dissenting) (insisting that regulation of GHGs 'is not akin to regulating the concentration of some substance that is *polluting* the *air*').

whether the CAA's version of cooperative federalism, in which the federal government solicits state assistance but ultimately retains control, is a good fit for climate change mitigation.

Some environmental law experts, including Holly Doremus, have endorsed a cooperative federalism-based approach to climate change mitigation.[107] Such an effort could entail direct federal technology-based regulation of mobile and new stationary source emissions, supplemented by state and local planning and implementation roles. As noted below, this is the approach that EPA has undertaken thus far, by establishing technology-based performance standards for motor vehicles and fossil fuel-fired power plants. Although there is not much state discretion in the implementation of the standards for motor vehicles and new power plants, EPA has issued a rule for existing power plants that allow states to experiment with a variety of implementation approaches – however, EPA retains final authority to review the adequacy of state implementation plans and issue a federal implementation plan if necessary.

A cooperative federalism approach to GHG regulation can be justified by collective action concerns.[108] The presence of transboundary externalities, for example, justifies nationally (and internationally) led efforts to control GHGs. These externalities do not support preemption of more stringent state regulation, however, because such regulation will benefit all jurisdictions, not just the adopting state. As a result, California should retain its authority to adopt more stringent tailpipe emission standards and low carbon fuel standards.[109]

Retained state authority risks non-uniform regulation in the form of multiple state standards, but no more so than does the CAA's current

---

[107] Doremus, Holly and W. Michael Haneman, 'Of Babies and Bathwater: Why the Clean Air Act's Cooperative Federalism Framework Is Useful for Addressing Global Warming' (2008) 50 Ariz. L. Rev. 799. Cf. Schapiro, Robert A., 'Not Old or Borrowed: The Truly New Blue Federalism' (2009) 3 Harv L & Pol'y Rev. **34**, 42 ('It is clear that the national government must be part of any solution. ... No one believes that global warming is best addressed by the states rather than the national government.').

[108] See generally Glicksman and Levy, *supra* n.46, at 610–47.

[109] For some examples of recent state policies to address GHG emissions, see Klass, Alexandra B. and Elizabeth Henley, 'Energy Policy, Extraterritoriality, and the Dormant Commerce Clause' (2013–2014) 5 San Diego J of Climate & Energy L. 127. Such efforts may be vulnerable to challenges alleging unconstitutional extraterritorial application, however. See e.g. *North Dakota v Heydinger*, 15 F. Supp. 3d 891 (D Minn. 2014) (invalidating Minnesota's Next Generation Energy Act, which established energy and environmental standards relating to carbon dioxide emissions).

preemption waiver. California has already demonstrated its leadership in controlling GHG emissions from mobile sources.[110] Moreover, the uniformity rationale for exclusive federal regulation of new motor vehicle emissions does not apply to stationary source regulation, and does not justify preemption of more stringent state controls. Race-to-the-bottom concerns justify a federal floor on stationary source emissions to preclude states from competing for business by adopting weak GHG emission controls, but they do not justify preemption of more stringent state controls.

Superior resources suggest a significant federal role in developing climate change scientific information and at least a backup role in enforcement of mandatory state requirements. A closer question might be whether state regulation would undermine the international bargaining position of the US in extracting commitments from reluctant foreign nations, but at least two federal courts have rejected that rationale as a reason to preempt state GHG emission controls.[111] Finally, the design of a climate change regime need not dwell on the NIMBY phenomenon because GHG emissions in one state generally have the same effects on climate change as emissions in any other place. Efforts to exclude a GHG-emitting source will therefore not benefit a state if its stringent regulations prompt a source to operate elsewhere. Indeed, the more salient problem may be the reverse in that a state that regards itself as at low risk from climate change (such as a landlocked state that need not fear sea level rise or coastal flooding) may be more inclined than a more vulnerable state to allow high levels of GHG emissions.

EPA has sought to achieve a balance between federal leadership and state autonomy in its regulation of GHGs under the CAA. In addition to developing federal performance standards for CO_2 emissions from motor vehicles and some stationary sources,[112] EPA issued technology-based emission

---

[110] See *Green Mountain Chrysler Plymouth Dodge Jeep v Crombie*, 508 F Supp 2d 295, 394 (D Vt 2007).

[111] Ibid.; *Cent. Valley Chrysler-Jeep, Inc. v Goldstene*, 529 F Supp 2d 1151 (ED Cal. 2007), *reconsideration denied*, 563 F Supp 2d 1158 (ED Cal. 2008).

[112] Greenhouse Gas Emissions Standards and Fuel Efficiency Standards for Medium- and Heavy-Duty Engines and Vehicles 76 Fed. Reg. 57,106 (15 September 2011) (codified at 40 C.F.R. pts. 523, 534, 535, and 49 C.F.R. pts. 523, 534, 535); 2017 and Later Model Year Light-Duty Vehicle Greenhouse Gas Emissions and Corporate Average Fuel Economy Standards; Final Rule, 77 Fed. Reg. 62,624 (15 October 2012) (codified at 40 C.F.R. pts. 85, 86, 600, and 49 C.F.R. pts. 523, 531, 533, 536, 537); Standards of Performance for Greenhouse Gas Emissions from New, Modified, and Reconstructed Stationary Sources: Electric Utility Generating Units 80 Fed. Reg. 64,510 (23 October 2015) (to be codified at 40 C.F.R. pts. 60, 70, 71, 98), www2.epa.gov/sites/

guidelines in 2015 under § 111(d) for state regulation of CO_2 emissions from existing electric generating units.[113] The guidelines aim to reduce CO_2 emissions from the power sector by approximately 32 percent from 2005 levels by 2030. To achieve this goal, EPA has created a 'partnership between the EPA and the states' under which EPA will establish state-specific emission rate-based CO_2 goals for the power sector and states will 'take the lead' on meeting those goals by creating plans that are consistent with EPA guidelines.[114] According to EPA, the guidelines are 'based on, and reinforce, the actions already being taken by states and utilities' to upgrade existing electricity infrastructure.[115] The regulatory approach also

> provides flexibility for states to build upon their progress, and the progress of cities and towns, in addressing GHGs, and minimizes additional requirements for existing programs where possible. It also allows states to pursue policies to reduce carbon pollution that: (1) Continue to rely on a diverse set of energy resources; (2) ensure electric system reliability; (3) provide affordable electricity; (4) recognize investments that states and power companies are already making; and (5) tailor plans to meet their respective energy, environmental and economic needs and goals, and those of their local communities.[116]

Like the state implementation plan process that governs achievement of the NAAQS,[117] EPA's § 111(d) rule relies heavily on a cooperative federalism partnership: EPA establishes quantitative pollution reduction targets, states are afforded flexibility in deciding how they wish to achieve the federally specified targets, and states remain accountable

---

production/files/2015-08/documents/cpp-final-rule.pdf; Oil and Natural Gas Sector: Emission Standards for New and Modified Sources 80 Fed. Reg. 56,593 (18 September 2015) (to be codified at 40 C.F.R. pt. 60).

[113] Carbon Pollution Emission Guidelines for Existing Stationary Sources: Electric Utility Generating Units 80 Fed. Reg. 64,662 (23 October 2015) (to be codified at 40 C.F.R. pt. 60, subpart UUUU), www.epa.gov/airquality/cpp/cps-final-rule.pdf).

[114] Ibid. at 64,665. Although EPA will be responsible for setting the CO_2 reduction goals, EPA has crafted these goals based on the unique position of each state, taking into account pre-existing state programs and policies such as state-wide regional cap-and-trade programs and renewable portfolio standards. See Section V ('The Best System of Emission Reduction and Associated Building Blocks') of the Final Rule for a detailed description of how EPA intends to establish state-specific CO_2 emission reduction goals for the power sector. Ibid. at 64,663-811.

[115] Ibid. at 64,678.

[116] Ibid. at 64,678-79.

[117] Nevertheless, EPA has identified distinctions between the SIP and § 111(d) processes. Carbon Pollution Emission Guidelines for Existing Stationary Sources: Electric Generating Units; Proposed Rule, 79 Fed. Reg. 34,830, 34,834 (18 June 2014).

through EPA review of state plans and their implementation. The § 111(d) rule is noteworthy not only as an ambitious effort to use the CAA to reduce GHG emissions that contribute to climate change, but also as a program that recognizes and accommodates the need for states to craft policies and programs suited to their own needs and the capacities of affected stakeholders. Notwithstanding this accommodation, and consistent with the cooperative federalism model threaded throughout the CAA, the federal government retains the final say over pollution reduction goals and the capacity to step in if states fail to abide by their responsibilities.[118]

CONCLUSION

The CAA initiated cooperative federalism in US environmental law. Its design should be well understood, along with the strengths and weaknesses of its federalism model in combatting air pollution. Fundamental misconceptions nevertheless persist about why Congress relied on both federal and state governments to control air pollution. Despite judicial characterizations that the CAA created an equal partnership between EPA and the states, it was never intended to do so. EPA has always been in charge, notwithstanding delegation of discretion to the states to determine how best to fashion an emission control strategy capable of achieving the NAAQS set by EPA to meet federally determined air quality goals. Even in that realm, EPA's authority increased and state prerogatives narrowed as states failed to satisfy NAAQS deadlines. The statute was not principally an effort to protect states' rights, notwithstanding traditional state police power authority to address public health risks. Congress repeatedly chose to protect state authority to regulate more rigorously than the federal government, not the authority to reach divergent judgments about the appropriate balance between promoting economic activity and protecting human health.

An accurate understanding of the nature of cooperative federalism under the CAA is critical. It is difficult for policymakers to fix problems and for judges to review implementation of the statute if they do not appreciate how the statute was meant to work. Similarly, efforts to adapt the CAA to meet climate change challenges by increasing or decreasing the federal or state role for particular tasks are more likely to succeed if they are based on a proper understanding of the existing statutory foundation.

---

[118] See Federal Plan Requirements for Greenhouse Gas Emissions from Electric Utility Generating Units Constructed on or Before January 8, 2014; Model Trading Rules; Amendments to Framework Regulations; Proposed Rule, 80 Fed. Reg. 64,966 (23 October 2015).

2. Dynamic federalism and the Clean Water Act: completing the task

William L. Andreen

I. INTRODUCTION

The Clean Water Act (CWA)[1] is a lengthy and complicated statute that gave rise to a vast array of implementing regulations and agency guidance.[2] The sheer breadth of the program reflects the complexity of its subject matter and the ambitious nature of its objective,[3] namely, the restoration and maintenance of the "chemical, physical, and biological integrity of the Nation's waters."[4] Amazingly, despite all of the obstacles that inevitably confront such a major reform effort, the CWA has proved remarkably successful.[5] Both municipal and industrial point source discharges have fallen sharply, broadly enhancing water quality throughout the United States.[6] This improvement has been so dramatic that some

---

[1] Act of October 18, 1972, Pub. L. No. 92-500, 86 Stat. 816 (codified as amended at 33 U.S.C. §§ 1251–1387 (2006)).

[2] See Adler, Robert W., "The Decline and (Possible) Renewal of Aspiration in the Clean Water Act" (2013) 88 Wash. L. Rev. **759**, 760–61.

[3] Ibid., at 761.

[4] Federal Water Pollution Control Act (Clean Water Act) § 101(a), 33 U.S.C. § 1251(a) (2014).

[5] See Andreen, William L., "Water Quality Today – Has the Clean Water Act Been a Success?" (2004) 55 Ala. L. Rev. 537. According to two respected academics, the "big question" is not "why major political and policy reforms so often fail to achieve what is promised," but "why (beyond sheer luck), given the process that seems to dominate, some major reforms succeed." Aberbach, Joel D. and Tom Christensen (2013) "Why Reforms So Often Disappoint" 44 Am. Rev. Pub. Admin. **3**, 14.

[6] Andreen, William L., "Success and Backlash: The Remarkable (Continuing) Story of the Clean Water Act" (2013) 4 Geo. Wash. J. Energy & Envtl L. **25**, 28–30 (hereinafter Andreen, "Success and Backlash").

have deemed it the eleventh greatest government achievement of the second half of the twentieth century.[7]

The success that the CWA has enjoyed was due in large measure to the experience and foresight of its drafters. Many of them had been intimately involved for over a decade in both the oversight of an earlier statutory program and in a series of amendments to that program.[8] Not surprisingly, however, given the limits of individual and political capacity, the design of the CWA was not perfect. Perhaps the greatest single imperfection lies in the lack of more uniformity in the CWA's approach to federalism.

The CWA produced substantial progress in precisely the areas where Congress expanded the federal government's role in 1972. In the view of Congress, many states had failed to adopt, implement and adequately enforce acceptable standards despite years of substantial federal assistance, both financial and technical.[9] As a result, the CWA empowered the newly created US Environmental Protection Agency (EPA) to take a more direct hand in regulating water pollution from industrial and municipal point sources such as discharge pipes and other discernible conveyances. Although the EPA became the senior partner in this new regulatory enterprise, the states retained a significant role in its implementation, subject to EPA oversight.[10] It is this new, more dynamic form of federalism that has proven effective.

---

[7] Light, Paul C., 'Government's Greatest Achievements of the Past Half Century' (2000) 2 *Reform Watch* **1**, 4. The significance of this achievement was likely understated in Light's study since water quality improvement undoubtedly played a role in reducing disease, an achievement that placed fourth, and in ensuring safe food and water, which placed sixth. See ibid., Hoornbeek, John A., "Water Pollution Policies and the American States: Runaway Bureaucracies or Congressional Control?" (2011) at 229.

[8] See Andreen, "The Evolution of Water Pollution Control in the United States – State, Local, and Federal Efforts, 1789–1972: Part II" (2003) 22 Stan. Envtl L.J. **215**, 242–60.

[9] See Hoornbeek, *supra*, n. 7, at 57; William L. Andreen, "Delegated Federalism Versus Devolution: Some Insights from the History of Water Pollution Control" in Buzbee, William W. (ed.) *Preemption Choice: The Theory, Law, and Reality of Federalism's Core Question* (Cambridge University Press, New York, 2009) **257**, 258 (hereinafter Andreen, "Delegated Federalism"). As Oliver Houck succinctly put it: "We have a federal CWA for one reason: programs run by the states with federal assistance had failed utterly for 25 years." Houck, Oliver A., "Cooperative Federalism, Nutrients, and the Clean Water Act: Three Cases Revisited" (2014) 44 Envtl L. Rep. **10426**, 10426.

[10] See *infra*, nn 31–32, 37–45 and accompanying text.

Congress unfortunately failed to apply the new model to two significant sources of water pollution: non-point source pollution – diffuse runoff from, for example, fields and logging operations – and hydrologic modifications, such as water withdrawals, impoundments and diversions for offstream uses.[11] In both cases Congress bowed to the old concept of dual federalism, the notion that the states and the federal government operate in separate and independent spheres.[12] But the separation was not complete. A planning scheme and eventually financial support were provided to states to assist them in dealing with non-point source pollution,[13] and the CWA does recognize a federal role with regard to hydrologic modifications.[14] Nevertheless, both areas lie primarily within state prerogative, and most states have failed to regulate non-point source pollution[15] and have avoided restricting water use to protect water quality.[16]

In contrast to the progress that has been achieved under the point source program, the less directive approach towards non-point sources has proved ineffective.[17] Non-point source pollution is now considered to

---

[11] I refer to water quality problems produced by hydrologic modifications as pollution because the Act defines "pollution" broadly as "the man-made or man-induced alteration of the chemical, physical, biological, and radiological integrity of water." Federal Water Pollution Control Act (Clean Water Act) § 502(19), 33 U.S.C. § 1362(19) (2014).

[12] See Lieber, Harvey, *Federalism and Clean Waters: The 1972 Water Pollution Control Act 1* (Lexington Books, Lexington, Mass. 1975).

[13] See *infra*, nn 50–58 and accompanying text.

[14] See *infra*, nn 75–82 and accompanying text.

[15] See *infra*, nn 91–92 and accompanying text.

[16] See Benson, Reed D., "Pollution Without Solution: Flow Impairment Problems Under Clean Water Act Section 303" (2005) 24 Stan. Envtl L.J. **199**, 204–05.

[17] Two other CWA programs are primarily federal in orientation. First, the Act prohibits unpermitted discharges of dredged or fill material into waters of the United States. Federal Water Pollution Control Act (Clean Water Act) §§ 301(a), 404, 33 U.S.C. §§ 1311(a), 1344 (2014). This program is administered by the US Army Corps of Engineers although its permits are crafted pursuant to EPA guidance and are subject to EPA review and veto. Ibid. § 404(b), (c), 33 U.S.C. § 1311(b), (c). Only two states have obtained authority to issue these permits for their non-navigable waters and adjacent wetlands. See "State Delegations – Clean Water Act, Envtl. Council of the States," accessed 14 July 2015 at www.ecos.org/section/states/enviro_actlist/states_enviro_actlist_cwa. Despite a number of programmatic and jurisdictional problems, this program, together with conservation provisions found in a number of farm bills, has reduced annual wetlands losses by over 90 percent. See Andreen, "Success and Backlash," *supra*,

be responsible for over 75 percent of the rivers and lakes that fail to meet water quality standards.[18] One particular kind of non-point source, runoff from agriculture, tops the charts as the principle source of impairment in US waters,[19] while hydromodifications constitute the second-leading cause of impairment on our flowing waters.[20] Natural stream flow regimes, moreover, have been altered on 86 percent of the rivers and streams in the contiguous United States, and such anthropogenic changes have wreaked extensive ecological damage.[21] Our current approach to these polluting activities is simply not working.

The rigid approach of dual federalism has failed in both instances. While some states have taken strong action to combat non-point source pollution, most have not, federal support notwithstanding.[22] The same is true of efforts to ensure stream flows that reasonably reflect the natural hydrograph in terms of flow, timing, duration, and rate of change.[23] A more dynamic approach is necessary, one that utilizes the strengths and policy advantages that exist at both levels of government and recognizes

---

n. 6, at 30. The second program deals with oil spills. Both section 311 and the Oil Pollution Act of 1990 are federally administered. Since section 311 was enacted in late 1972, both the number of spills and the amount of oil that is released annually into US waters have been on a downward trend with the exception of several notable events like the Deepwater Horizon spill. Office of Investigations & Compliance Analysis, U.S. Coast Guard (2012) "Polluting Incidents in and around U.S. Waters: A Spill/Release Compendium: 1969–2011" at 3.

[18] See Glicksman, Robert L. and Matthew R. Bezel, "Science, Politics, Law, and the Arc of the Clean Water Act: The Role of Assumptions in the Adoption of a Pollution Control Landmark" (2010) 32 Wash. U. J. L. & Pol'y **99**, 132.

[19] See Adler, Robert W., "Agriculture and Water Quality: A Climate-Integrated Perspective" (2013) 37 Vt L. Rev. **847**, 854 (hereinafter Adler, "Agriculture and Water Quality").

[20] Office of Water, U.S. Envtl Prot. Agency (2009) National Water Quality Inventory: Report to Congress 16, fig. 3.

[21] Carlisle, Daren M. et al., "Alteration of Streamflow Magnitudes and Potential Ecological Consequences: A Multiregional Assessment" (2011) 9 *Frontiers in Ecology & the Env't* **264**, 264 (assessing streamflow alteration at 2,888 monitoring stations).

[22] Only seven states regulate non-point source pollution to some extent. U.S. Gen. Accountability Office (2013), Clean Water Act: Changes Needed if Key EPA Program Is to Help Fulfill the Nation's Water Quality Goals 26 (listing California, Florida, Hawaii, Oregon, Pennsylvania, Washington, and Wisconsin) (hereinafter GAO, Clean Water Act).

[23] See Benson, *supra*, n. 16, at 214 (stating that it is "extremely uncommon" among the states to regulate water quantity in pursuit of water quality).

the limitations, legal and otherwise, that constrict the ability of either level of government, acting alone, to complete the task of restoring the integrity of the nation's waters.

After setting forth the CWA's current bifurcated approach to cooperative federalism, containing both dynamic as well as more dual approaches, the chapter examines at greater length the question whether the states have been creative and capable leaders within the realms left to their authority or whether they have demonstrated the lack of capacity or willingness to meet the challenge. That story demonstrates the limits of relying primarily upon state action and underscores a principal reason why we have not more successfully tackled the problems of non-point source pollution and flow impairment. The chapter concludes by discussing a number of ways in which a more dynamic form of federalism could help to fill the voids that lie at the heart of the CWA.

II. THE CLEAN WATER ACT'S BIFURCATED APPROACH TO FEDERALISM

Early in the decade of the 1970s, Congress grew impatient with rivers that resembled "sewers" flowing to the sea.[24] Convinced that water pollution was a national problem meriting a national response and armed with the experience of over a decade of legislating in the area, Congress set forth in bold fashion. It cast aside an earlier program that had called upon states to adopt and implement water quality standards since many states had failed to adopt acceptable standards or implementation plans.[25] In its stead, Congress adopted a wholly new approach for dealing with the most obvious and, at that time, the largest sources of water pollution – industrial and municipal point sources.[26]

---

[24] The primary author of the Act, Senator Edmund Muskie, alluded to "sewers" when describing the appalling condition of many of the nation's rivers and streams on the floor of the Senate. 2 (1973) "A Legislative History of the Water Pollution Control Act Amendments of 1972," 1253 (hereinafter "Leg. Hist. 1972").

[25] Just over half of the states had fully approved water quality standards by the end of 1970. Hort Holmes, Beatrice, *History of Federal Water Resources Programs and Policies 1961–70* (Dept of Agriculture, Economics, Statistics, and Cooperatives Service, Washington, 1979), p. 190.

[26] Congress also understood, however, that non-point source pollution was a "major source of pollution." S. Rep. No. 92-414, at 39, reprinted in 2 Leg. Hist. 1972, *supra*, n. 24 at 1457.

A. The Point Source Program

The new point source program vastly increased the federal role in fighting water pollution. EPA was directed to promulgate uniform, technology-based effluent limitations[27] that would be implemented through a new permit program,[28] which would apply to all point source discharges.[29] Rather than wholly discarding state water quality standards, Congress kept the program, incorporating it into the permit system in order to supplement technology-based limits in cases where a uniform approach would fail to ensure compliance with water quality objectives.[30] The states, however, retained important roles. They could, for example, obtain authority to administer the permit system, and the vast majority of states have done so.[31] In addition, they can establish regulatory standards and limits that are more stringent than those required by federal law.[32] So while Congress nationalized the business of water pollution control to a significant degree, the CWA created a complex set of overlapping and shared functions.

EPA, nevertheless, is the senior partner in this system. EPA has the sole authority to set uniform effluent limitations, unless of course a state has the capacity and desire to establish more protective limits. Furthermore, EPA has oversight authority over many aspects of the program.

---

[27] Federal Water Pollution Control Act (Clean Water Act) §§ 301(b)(1)(A), (b)(1)(B), (b)(2), 306(b)(1)(B), 33 U.S.C. §§ 1311(b)(1)(A), (b)(1)(B), (b)(2), 1316(b)(1)(B) (2014).

[28] Ibid. § 402, 33 U.S.C. § 1342.

[29] See ibid. § 301(a), 33 U.S.C. § 1311(a).

[30] Ibid. § 303, 33 U.S.C. § 1313.

[31] Ibid. § 402(b), 33 U.S.C. § 1342(b). Forty-six states and the Virgin Islands currently possess authority to issue CWA permits. U.S. Envtl Prot. Agency, Nat'l Pollutant Discharge Elimination System (NPDES), Specific State Program Status, accessed 14 July 2015 at cfpub.epa.gov/npdes/statestats.cfm?program_id=45&view=specific. In some of these states, however, the authority does not extend to every kind of discharge. See ibid. In those instances, EPA remains the permitting authority.

[32] Federal Water Pollution Control Act (Clean Water Act) § 510, 33 U.S.C. § 1370 (2014). EPA estimated in 1986 that 40 percent of major municipal permits and perhaps an equal fraction of major industrial permits were based in some manner upon water quality standards. Office of Tech. Assessment, U.S. Cong., Wastes in Marine Environments 205 (1987). The fraction of minor sources, both municipal and otherwise, with water quality related permit parameters is likely much lower.

EPA may veto state-issued permits;[33] in extreme cases, EPA may withdraw state permitting authority;[34] EPA is directed to review state water quality standards and has the authority to disapprove a standard if it is not consistent with the requirements of the CWA;[35] and EPA has the power to help shape state programs through the provision of federal financial assistance and the promulgation of program regulations.[36] Despite EPA's expansive role, the states remain significant actors in the point source program.

In addition to permitting activities, the states set their own water quality standards – consisting of designated uses and the criteria designed to meet those uses[37] – and are responsible for implementing those standards directly through their permits[38] or more indirectly through the establishment of waste load allocations and the application of those allocations to permits.[39] They are also responsible, in significant measure, for enforcing the permit program,[40] although this authority is shared with both EPA and private citizens in a thoroughly redundant enforcement scheme.[41] Furthermore, states and local governments play a vital role in the implementation and enforcement of the pretreatment program, which regulates toxic industrial discharges to municipally owned wastewater treatment plants.[42]

States also have the freedom to take steps that directly or through incentives provide additional protection to their waters since the CWA utilizes floor preemption rather than ceiling preemption.[43] This approach is given added force through a certification provision that effectively endows states with authority to veto or impose conditions upon federal licensing or permitting activities that may adversely affect the quality of

---

[33] Federal Water Pollution Control Act (Clean Water Act) § 402(d), 33 U.S.C. § 1342(d) (2014).
[34] Ibid. § 402(c), 33 U.S.C. § 1342(c).
[35] Ibid. § 303(c), 33 U.S.C. § 1313(c).
[36] Ibid. § 106, 33 U.S.C. § 1256; 40 C.F.R. Pts. 123–24, 130, 131 (2013).
[37] Ibid. § 303(c), 33 U.S.C. § 1313(c).
[38] Ibid. §§ 402(a), 301(b)(1)(C), 33 U.S.C. §§ 1342(a), 1311(b)(1)(C).
[39] See ibid. § 303(d), 33 U.S.C. § 1313(d).
[40] See Andreen, William L., "Motivating Enforcement: Institutional Culture and the Clean Water Act" (2007) 24 Pace Envtl L. Rev. **67**, 74–75 (hereinafter Andreen, 'Motivating Enforcement').
[41] Federal Water Pollution Control Act (Clean Water Act) §§ 309, 505, 33 U.S.C. §§ 1319, 1365 (2014).
[42] Ibid. § 307(b), (c), 33 U.S.C. § 1317(b), (c).
[43] Ibid. § 510, 33 U.S.C. § 1370.

state waters.[44] Another considerable font of state power is found in the savings clause contained in the Act's citizen suit provision. Despite the creation of a federal statutory right to sue polluters who violate the Act, this provision expressly preserves the right of persons to utilize state tort law to sue dischargers for the injuries they cause.[45]

While many problems and challenges remain,[46] the point source program has produced a tremendous amount of progress. In 1977, 91 percent of the United States' water basins were experiencing water quality problems resulting from point source discharges, while 87 percent were suffering from non-point source problems.[47] Today, on the other hand, non-point source pollution, rather than point source pollution, is the primary culprit.[48]

B. The Non-Point Source Program

Rather than directly regulate non-point pollution, Congress chose to leave the problem – as politically and administratively difficult as it is to address[49] – to the states. Thus, the CWA in 1972 relied upon a state planning process that was supposed to produce management plans to address non-point source impaired waters.[50] This program proved

---

[44] Ibid. § 401, 33 U.S.C. § 1341.

[45] See ibid. § 505(e), 33 U.S.C. § 1365(e).

[46] See e.g. Andreen, William L. and Shana Jones, "The Clean Water Act: A Blueprint for Reform" (2008), accessed 14 July 2015 at www.progressive reform.org/articles/CW_Blueprint_802.pdf.

[47] Office of Water Planning & Standards, U.S. Envtl Prot. Agency, Nat'l Water Quality Inventory: 1977 Report to Congress 9 (1978).

[48] See Nat'l Summary of State Information, U.S. Envtl Prot. Agency, accessed 14 July 2015 at iaspub.epa.gov/waters10/attains_nation_cy.control. As the Congressional Research Office has noted, "Over time, as [point source discharges] have abated pollution, uncontrolled non-point sources have become a larger relative portion of remaining water quality problems." Copeland, Claudia, Cong. Research Serv., R42752, Clean Water Act and Pollutant Total Maximum Daily Loads 5 (2012).

[49] Garovoy, Jocelyn B., "A Breathtaking Assertion of Power? Not Quite" (2003) 30 Ecology L.Q. 543 (noting the difficulties presented by the diffuse and varied nature of non-point source pollution and the political opposition to controls posed by agricultural, timber, and development interests).

[50] Federal Water Pollution Control Act (Clean Water Act) § 208, 33 U.S.C. § 1288 (2014). The only action EPA could take if a state program was deemed inadequate was to withdraw state approval and grant funds. Ibid. § 208(b)(4)(D), (f)(3), 33 U.S.C. § 1288(b)(4)(D), (f)(3).

ineffective, so Congress added a new provision in 1987.[51] Unfortunately it was "not significantly different in its overall approach."[52] The new section 319 called upon the states to identify those waters impaired by non-point source pollution and to then develop "best management practices" (BMPs) to remedy the problem "to the maximum extent possible."[53] Although these plans are subject to EPA review, Congress permitted states to use non-regulatory approaches such as technical assistance, education, training, and demonstration projects as alternatives to regulation.[54] The only sanction EPA has at its disposal, in the event that a state program is found wanting, is to withhold funding for the state non-point source program – rather than establish an adequate program in its stead.[55] Since withholding funds would deprive a state of much of its ability to make at least some progress in controlling non-point source pollution, EPA has been unwilling to take that step.[56] As a result of the reluctance of most states to establish regulatory programs,[57] limited federal leverage over state programs and inadequate funding, the section 319 program has failed to make great progress in combating non-point source pollution.[58]

Another tool exists under the CWA to deal with non-point source discharges. Under section 303(d), states are directed to identify those waters that are not meeting water quality standards.[59] The states are then required to establish a pollution budget, known as a "total maximum daily load" (TMDL) for those pollutants responsible for the water's impaired condition. The TMDL is essentially a numeric target that is required to restore the water to compliance with water quality standards with a margin of safety while also taking into account seasonal variations

---

[51] Percival, Robert V. et al., *Environmental Regulation: Law, Science, and Policy*, 7th edn (Wolters Kluwer, Austin, Boston, Chicago, New York, the Netherlands 2013), p. 794.

[52] Adler, 'Agriculture and Water Quality', *supra*, n. 19, at 861.

[53] Federal Water Pollution Control Act (Clean Water Act) § 319(a), (b), 33 U.S.C. § 1229(a), (b) (2014).

[54] Ibid. § 319(b), 33 U.S.C. § 1229(b).

[55] Ibid. § 319(d)(2), (h)(8), 33 U.S.C. § 1229(d)(2), (h)(8).

[56] Dubrowski, Fran, "Crossing the Finish Line" (July–Aug. 1997) Envtl F. **28**, 32–33.

[57] See *supra*, n. 22. Most states use an incentive-based or voluntary program instead of regulations to address non-point source pollution. Copeland, *supra*, n. 48, at 17.

[58] Percival, *supra*, n. 51, at 795.

[59] Federal Water Pollution Control Act (Clean Water Act) § 303(d)(1)(A), 33 U.S.C. § 1313(d)(1)(A) (2014).

in flow.[60] This budget or loading capacity must in turn be allocated, as appropriate, to point sources (wasteload allocation) and non-point sources (load allocation).[61]

TMDLs are subject to EPA review. In the event that a state TMDL is found inadequate, EPA is not only empowered but ordered to adopt one.[62] EPA, however, has no particular authority to implement TMDLs. That presents no particular problem for point source discharges since wasteload allocations are defined as a form of water quality-based effluent limitation.[63] Thus, they should be included in point source permits as long as a state is properly implementing the program or where EPA is the permitting agency. On the other hand, there is no statutory or regulatory provision requiring the implementation of load allocations for non-point sources. That task is left entirely to state initiative or the lack thereof.[64]

States took little action to set TMDLs until a host of citizen suits established the proposition that EPA had a duty to establish TMDLs for states that had failed to do so.[65] Since the early 1990s, nearly 50,000 TMDLs have been developed, many of which were the result of consent decrees in mandatory duty cases filed against EPA.[66] State TMDL coordinators report that 83 percent of wasteload allocations for point sources have been met in long-established TMDLs. In contrast to that relatively high level of compliance, only 20 percent of load allocations for non-point sources have been met.[67] The difference may well be ascribed to the fact that non-regulatory mechanisms are overwhelmingly relied upon to implement TMDLs for the non-point source community and that inadequate funding has been available for encouraging compliance with the BMPs that TMDLs either call for or implicate.[68]

---

[60] Ibid. § 303(d)(1)(C), 33 U.S.C. § 1313(d)(1)(C).
[61] 40 C.F.R. §§ 130.2(g), (h); 130.7.
[62] Federal Water Pollution Control Act (Clean Water Act) § 303(d)(2), 33 U.S.C. § 1313(d)(2) (2014).
[63] 40 C.F.R. § 130.2(h).
[64] Adler, "Agriculture and Water Quality," *supra*, n. 19, at 868. The states, however, are directed to incorporate TMDLs (including load allocations) into their continuing planning processes. Federal Water Pollution Control Act (Clean Water Act) § 303(d)(2), 33 U.S.C. § 1313(d)(2) (2014).
[65] See Percival, *supra*, n. 51, at 768.
[66] GAO, Clean Water Act, *supra*, n. 22, at 3.
[67] Ibid. at 35.
[68] See ibid. at 62 (reporting that, according to state TMDL coordinators, 86 percent of long-standing TMDLs have not had adequate funding for implementation of non-point source controls).

C. Flow Impairment

Water quality is intimately related to water quantity. Healthy aquatic systems simply cannot exist on rivers and streams with little or no flow.[69] All too often, however, water has been treated as a commodity for exclusive human use and consumption. In the West, water withdrawals, impoundments and diversions "routinely dry up rivers – including some of the major ones in the region – or reduce them to a relative trickle."[70] In the East, water diversions have spawned regional conflict,[71] while the operation schedule of hydroelectric dams produce excessively high and low flows in rapid succession producing wide-ranging adverse effects upon the aquatic environment.[72] Anthropogenic flow alterations can also increase water quality problems by increasing the concentration of pollutants in a stream.[73] Simply providing a minimum flow in order to maintain certain species is not an adequate response. In order to sustain aquatic diversity and protect the ecological services provided by flowing

---

[69] *PUD No. 1 of Jefferson Cnty. v Wash. Dep't of Ecology* (1994) 511 U.S. **700**, 719 (declaring that "a sufficient lowering of the water quantity in a body of water could destroy all of its designated uses, be it for drinking water, recreation, navigation or ... as a fishery").

[70] Benson, *supra*, n. 16, at 202. Hydraulic fracturing will produce even greater stress in our more arid areas since the production of shale gas using this process typically requires the use of 2–4 million gallons of water per well. Office of Res. & Dev., U.S. Envtl Prot. Agency, Draft Plan to Study the Potential Impacts of Hydraulic Fracturing on Drinking Water 19 (2011) (hereinafter EPA, Potential Impacts of Hydraulic Fracturing).

[71] See Andreen, William L., "Alabama," in Kelley, Amy K. (ed.) *Waters and Water Rights*, 3rd edn (LexisNexis (Michie), 2015), pp **AL-1**, AL-16 to AL-27 (discussing the dispute between Georgia, Florida, and Alabama over the Apalachicola–Chattahoochee–Flint River system and the dispute between Alabama and Georgia over the Alabama–Coosa–Tallapoosa system).

[72] Arthington, Angela H., *Environmental Flows: Saving Rivers in the Third Millennium* (University of California Press, California 2012), pp. 116–17 (2012) (stating that "hydroelectric dams cause extreme daily variations in water level that have no natural analogue in freshwater systems and represent an extremely harsh environment of frequent, unpredictable flow disturbance"). Even in the East, the use of hydraulic fracturing to produce shale gas may impact flows in the headwaters of many watersheds. See EPA, Potential Impacts of Hydraulic Fracturing, *supra*, n. 70, at 21.

[73] See Benson, *supra*, n. 16, at 203. Rapidly fluctuating water levels can also produce increased sedimentation and siltation due to erosion.

waters one must seek to establish and maintain "natural flow variability, or some semblance of it."[74]

The CWA recognizes that the alteration of stream flows can constitute water pollution. "Pollution," in the Act, is broadly defined as "the man-made or man-induced alteration of the chemical, physical, biological, and radiological integrity of water,"[75] and the biological integrity of streams is certainly impacted by low flows and other flow impairments.[76] Moreover, the Act explicitly states that "pollution" can result from "changes in the movement, flow, or circulation" of our rivers and streams.[77] Despite this recognition, Congress also provided in the Act's preemption provision that nothing in the CWA may "be construed as impairing or in any manner affecting any right or jurisdiction of the States with respect to the waters ... of such State."[78] During the 1977 amendments to the Act, Congress added more precise language pertaining to water quantity issues to the provision dealing with the goals and policy of the Act. This amendment declares that "[i]t is the policy of Congress that the authority of each State to allocate quantities of water within its jurisdiction shall not be superseded, abrogated or otherwise impaired by this chapter."[79]

According to the Supreme Court, these latter two provisions do not exclude the regulation of water quantity from the purview of the Act. Rather, they preserve traditional state authority "to allocate water quantity as between users; they do not limit the scope of water pollution controls that may be imposed on users who have obtained, pursuant to state law, a water allocation."[80] Recognizing the intertwined interests of both federal and state governments in water quality and water quantity issues,[81] the CWA also directs federal agencies to "co-operate with State

---

[74] Arthington, *supra*, n. 72, at 10.
[75] Federal Water Pollution Control Act (Clean Water Act) § 502(19), 33 U.S.C. §1362(19) (2014).
[76] See *PUD No. 1 of Jefferson Cnty. v Wash. Dep't of Ecology*, 511 U.S. **700**, 719 (1994).
[77] Federal Water Pollution Control Act (Clean Water Act) § 304(f), 33 U.S.C. § 1314(f) (2014).
[78] Ibid. § 510, 33 U.S.C. § 1370.
[79] Ibid. § 101(g), 33 U.S.C. § 1251(g).
[80] *PUD No. 1 of Jefferson Cnty*, 511 U.S. at 720. In *California v FERC*, 495 U.S. **490**, 498 (1990), the Court interpreted somewhat similar language in the Federal Power Act and said that "minimum stream flow requirements neither reflect nor establish 'proprietary rights'" to water.
[81] While state law has traditionally governed water rights, the federal government has played a pivotal role in the management of the nation's water

and local agencies to develop comprehensive solutions to prevent, reduce and eliminate pollution in concert with programs for managing water resources."[82]

Despite the call for a more integrated approach to water management, the regulation of water quantity and water quality have remained highly compartmentalized. It is an approach that defies logic, science and the apparent will of Congress. Most states have been reluctant to regulate water quantity in order to protect water quality.[83] EPA, however, has recently encouraged states to consider the explicit expression of flow as part of their water quality standards either through a numeric standard (for example, no more than a specific percentage change from the natural flow regime) or through a narrative standard (for instance, flow adequate to support the aquatic criteria).[84] Unfortunately, these efforts have prompted some states to object to "the ever increasing encroachment of federal entities" into issues of "water quantity [that] have been [traditionally] managed by the State."[85]

III. THE STATES: LABORATORIES OF DEMOCRACY OR LAGGARDS?

Most states have not been zealous guardians of their water resources. Although the CWA gives states the authority to set more stringent water pollution standards, they seldom do so.[86] In fact, 28 states have enacted statutes or rules that either forbid or restrict the authority of state

---

resources. This role runs the gamut from huge water and irrigation projects to hundreds of flood control dams; from water subsidies to navigational improvements and the licensing of water power projects; and from the protection of endangered species and wetlands to a proprietary interest in water flowing through federal land. See e.g. Water Res. Council, Water Resource Policy Study, 42 Fed. Reg. 36788 (1977).

[82] Federal Water Pollution Control Act (Clean Water Act) § 101(g), 33 U.S.C. § 1251(g) (2014).

[83] Benson, *supra*, n. 16, at 214.

[84] See e.g. Letter from Joanne Benante, Chief, Water Quality Planning Branch, U.S. Envtl Prot. Agency, Region 4, to James McIndoe, Chief, Water Div., Ala. Dep't of Envtl Mgmt (20 August 2010).

[85] See e.g. Letter from Jess Nix, Deputy Attorney Gen., State of Ala., to J. Brian Atkins, Div. Dir., Ala. Office of Water Res. (1 November 2012).

[86] Selmi, Daniel P. and Kenneth A. Manaster, *State Environmental Law* (looseleaf) (ThomsonReuter 2013) §§ 11:3, 11:10.

agencies to exceed federal water pollution standards.[87] Even after the duty to prepare TMDLs became clear in the early 1990s, many states dragged their feet in preparing TMDLs, citing numerous difficulties with the process, despite the fact that they have historically expressed a preference for using water quality standards rather than uniform effluent limitations to control water pollution.[88] Even when TMDLs have been set, most states lack any effective way in which to compel non-point sources to comply with identified BMPs.[89] As a result, "few TMDLs have been implemented for non-point source pollution" and, even when they have been implemented, "progress has generally been incremental."[90]

Only a handful of state agencies possess the authority to regulate non-point source pollution.[91] And even that authority may be limited in scope; in some cases, moreover, it may not even be used. Pennsylvania, for example, requires farms to have a plan to control sediment runoff over a certain threshold amount. Nonetheless, state officials report that this provision has never been enforced despite the fact that it has been in effect for over 40 years.[92]

This lack of zealousness extends to many other areas as well. Not only have most states been reluctant to regulate water quantity to protect water quality, but a few have actually forbidden restrictions on water use based on water quality considerations.[93] Furthermore, state water pollution enforcement has been on a downward trajectory since the mid-1990s,[94] and many state enforcement programs continue to underperform.[95] In addition, instances where states have vetoed or conditioned federal permits on the basis of water quality concerns have been relatively rare.[96]

---

[87] Envtl Law Inst., State Constraints: State-Imposed Limitations on the Authority of Agencies to Regulate Waters Beyond the Scope of the Federal Clean Water Act 1 (2013).

[88] Houck, Oliver A., *The Clean Water Act TMDL Program: Law, Policy, and Implementation*, 2nd edn (Environmental Law Institute, Washington, DC 2002), p. 63.

[89] GAO, Clean Water Act, *supra*, n. 22, at 61.

[90] Ibid. at 62.

[91] Ibid. at 26 (including California, Florida, Hawaii, Oregon, Pennsylvania, Washington and Wisconsin).

[92] Ibid. at 61.

[93] Benson, *supra*, n. 16, at 214.

[94] Andreen, "Motivating Enforcement," *supra*, n. 40, at 75.

[95] See Office of Inspector Gen., U.S. Envtl Prot. Agency, EPA Must Improve Oversight of State Enforcement (2011).

[96] Andreen, "Delegated Federalism," *supra*, n. 9, at 260–61.

Some states, however, have been leaders rather than laggards. This was true even before the 1970s. During the 1920s, two states created rudimentary stream classification systems that were forerunners of what became state water quality standards.[97] In the late 1940s, Pennsylvania began to utilize a simple form of effluent limitations,[98] and by the late 1960s Oregon had devised a permitting system for point source discharges requiring compliance with secondary treatment limitations or the equivalent and even more stringent limitations when necessary to meet water quality standards.[99] Many of the provisions in the CWA were based on these early state efforts. A number of states, moreover, have continued to act as laboratories of democracy.

Perhaps the most obvious instances of where some states have pushed beyond minimum federal standards are found in two water quality certification cases. In *PUD No. 1 of Jefferson County v Washington Department of Ecology*, the Supreme Court upheld the state agency's use of its section 401 authority to impose minimum flow conditions on a hydroelectric project.[100] The Supreme Court also upheld a Maine certification that stipulated not only a minimum stream flow but also fish passage requirements in the federal re-licensing of five hydroelectric dams.[101] Some states, such as California, also enforce various non-point source requirements,[102] while a number, such as Oregon, California and Florida, have well-articulated schemes for protecting instream flows.[103]

---

[97] Andreen, "The Evolution of Water Pollution Control in the United States – State, Local, and Federal Efforts, 1789–1972: Part I" (2003) 22 Stan. Envt. L.J. **145**, 182.

[98] Ibid. at 192–93.

[99] Or. Dep't of Envtl Quality, Water Quality Control in Oregon 2, 10 (1970). Oregon was commonly lauded as a model state program in the early 1970s. See Robbins, William G., *Landscape of Conflict: The Oregon Story, 1940–2000* (University of Washington Press, Washington, DC 2004), p. 270 (citing the EPA Regional Administrator in Seattle as saying in the fall of 1971 that he "didn't know of a water quality program in the nation that is better" than Oregon's).

[100] 511 U.S. **700**, 709–10 (1994).

[101] *S.D. Warren Co. v Me. Bd. of Envtl. Prot.*, 547 U.S. 370, 375 (2006).

[102] See *Pronsolino v Nastri*, 291 F.3d 1123, 1129–30 (9th Cir. 2002).

[103] See Gillilan, David M. and Thomas C. Brown, *Instream Flow Protection: Seeking a Balance in Western Water Use* (Island Press, Washington, DC 1997), pp. 139–43; Adler, Robert W. et al., *Modern Water Law: Private Property, Public Rights, and Environmental Protections* (Foundation Press 2013), pp. 244–46 (2013).

For the most part, however, the states appear to have neither the capacity nor the will to go further than federal law or funding requires them or incentivizes them to go.[104] In fact, many may not even be willing or able to go that far if the 58 petitions that have been filed to withdraw state program authorizations shed any light on the quality of many state programs.[105]

IV. MOVING TOWARD A MORE UNIFIED, DYNAMIC FORM OF FEDERALISM

History has demonstrated that a dynamic form of federalism, with overlapping and intertwined federal and state responsibilities, has worked well with respect to point source regulation. Where Congress relied more heavily upon a dual approach to federalism, the CWA has come up short. Technical and financial assistance, jawboning and cajoling have proven inadequate for controlling non-point source. And the near total ceding of environmental flows to state discretion has resulted in serious aquatic impairment.

When Congress enacted section 319 in 1987, members of Congress indicated that it was just "a first step in tackling the problem – a trial run, to see if allowing the States the option to develop a control program will indeed abate non-point source pollution across the Nation."[106] Eventually, a decision would have to be made as to whether a voluntary program could work or whether "Congress should consider a regulatory and

---

[104] See *Res. Renewal Inst., The State of the States v* (2001) (concluding that most states lag well behind in preparing themselves for increasingly complex environmental problems); Rabe, Barry G., "Permitting, Prevention, and Integration: Lessons from the States," in Kettle, Donald F. (ed.) *Environmental Governance: A Report on the Next Generation of Environmental Policy* (Brookings Institution Press: Harrisonburg, Va. 2002) pp. 14, 51 (stating that "many states ... appear unprepared to step up to the formidable challenges of integration and prevention"); Houck, *supra*, n. 88, at 147 (asserting that the majority of states have been reluctant to do "hard things" which would alienate "powerful constituencies" such as "the forest, farm, and construction industries").

[105] See Hammond, Emily and David L. Markell, "Administrative Proxies for Judicial Review: Building Legitimacy from the Inside-Out," (2013) 37 Harv. Envtl L. Rev. **313**, 343. The petitions raised numerous concerns including inadequacies as to public participation, permitting, inspections, enforcement, state resources, and state authority. Ibid. 345.

[106] 132 Cong. Rec. 32,382 (1986) (statement of Sen. Robert Stafford during the Senate debate on the conference report).

enforceable approach in the next phase of the program."[107] Twenty-seven years later, it is clear that the first step has not worked. The time is ripe for considering a regulatory approach to take the place of the initial voluntary scheme.

A possible starting point for such an approach may be found in the 1990 Coastal Zone Act Reauthorization Amendments (CZARA).[108] CZARA requires each state with an approved management plan under the Coastal Zone Management Act (CZMA)[109] to develop a Coastal Non-Point Pollution Control Program and submit it to EPA and the National Oceanic and Atmospheric Administration (NOAA) for approval.[110] These coastal non-point source control programs must provide for the implementation, at a minimum, of management measures that conform to guidance developed by EPA and NOAA.[111] That guidance sets forth a number of technology-based options for controlling non-point source pollution and gives state officials a good deal of flexibility in choosing among them.[112] If a state fails to submit an approvable program, it is subject to the loss of a portion of its CZMA grant.[113]

The CZMA requires that state CZARA programs contain "enforceable policies and mechanisms" to implement non-point source management measures.[114] While "enforceable policy" is statutorily defined to mean "legally binding" laws and regulations,[115] EPA and NOAA, as a matter of policy, will approve programs containing voluntary or incentive-based elements in order to give the states more flexibility.[116] So far, all of the

---

[107] 130 Cong. Rec. 18,811 (1984) (statement of Rep. James Oberstar during House debate on the initial House bill).
[108] Pub. L. No. 101-508, 104 Stat. 1388 (codified at 16 U.S.C. § 1455b (2006)).
[109] Pub. L. No. 92-583, 86 Stat. 1280 (codified as amended at 16 U.S.C. §§ 1451–1466 (2006)).
[110] 16 U.S.C. § 1455b(a)(1) (2006). The CZARA program was not intended to replace the existing state non-point source program but rather to update and expand upon it. Ibid. § 1455b(a)(2).
[111] Ibid. § 1455(b).
[112] See Office of Water, U.S. Envtl Prot. Agency, Guidance Specifying Management Measures for Sources of Nonpoint Pollution in Coastal Waters (1993).
[113] 16 U.S.C. § 1455b(c) (2006).
[114] Ibid. § 1455(d)(16).
[115] Ibid. § 1453(6a).
[116] U.S. Envtl Prot. Agency & Nat'l Oceanic & Atmospheric Admin. Final Administrative Changes for the Coastal Nonpoint Program Guidance 4 (1998).

states participating in the CZMA program have submitted non-point source programs, and all have received either full or conditional approval.[117] The federal agencies have had little choice. A cut in funding would hurt water quality, and, in any case, federal funding of the program has been dwindling.[118]

A better approach under a revised section 319 of the CWA would require states to establish truly enforceable best management practices – BMPs that could be drawn from a menu of technology-based options set forth by EPA to give the states some flexibility in selecting the practices that are most appropriate for their state. And instead of being all "carrot" and no "stick," EPA should have the authority, in cases where a state submits an inadequate management plan and fails to remedy the problem, to disapprove the plan and promulgate a federal plan in its stead. Increased and stable federal funding is also necessary to provide small-scale farmers and other appropriate grant recipients with the wherewithal to comply with these new requirements. Of course, the new requirements would have to be implemented over a period of years in order to give the newly regulated entities the time and, where appropriate, access to the funding necessary to come into compliance. This new approach should be coupled with revisions to the TMDL provisions in the CWA to make it clear that load allocations developed for specific non-point sources through the TMDL process would have to be implemented and enforced. Thus, in cases where the technology-based approach found in section 319 proves inadequate to remedy water quality impairment in particular waters, the more finely crafted section 303(d) process could produce the additional steps necessary to ensure compliance with water quality objectives.

Although EPA has at times encouraged states to bridge the divide between water quality and water quantity, the agency has done little more than exhort states to act.[119] The agency's lack of commitment to this task may be due, at least in part, to the passage of the Wallop Amendment in 1977. The amendment added section 101(g) to the Act stating that it was congressional policy that nothing in the Act should be construed to

---

The agencies added, however, that voluntary or incentive-based programs must be "backed by existing state enforcement authorities" that could be used to prevent non-point source pollution, if necessary. Ibid.

[117] Upton, Harold E., Cong. Research Ser., RL34339, Coastal Zone Management: Background and Reauthorization Issues 9 (2010).
[118] Ibid. at 9–10.
[119] Benson, *supra*, n. 16, at 204.

impair traditional state authority over the allocation of water.[120] Its authors, Senators Malcolm Wallop and Gary Hart, were troubled by certain options that had been floated as part of the Water Resource Policy Study[121] being conducted at the request of President Carter.[122] Senator Wallop, for instance, expressed concern that several of the options under consideration might involve using the CWA for purposes not strictly related to water quality, such as federal land use planning, in a way that could interfere with state water rights systems.[123] He recognized and accepted, however, that "legitimate and necessary water quality considerations" could have an impact at times upon individual water rights.[124] Thus, Justice O'Connor made it explicitly clear in the *PUD No. 1* case that while the Wallop Amendment protects state authority to allocate water quantity, the provision does "not limit the scope of water pollution controls [including minimum stream flows] that may be imposed on users who have obtained" a water allocation under state law.[125]

An obvious place to begin would be for EPA to require state agencies to set water quality criteria for environmental flows since appropriate flows in terms of timing and quantity are necessary to sustain the vast majority of designated uses including the protection and propagation of fish and wildlife. EPA's regulations actually direct states to include in their water quality standards "criteria sufficient to protect the designated use."[126] A resource-starved and politically harassed agency like EPA,[127] however, is unlikely to take such a bold step, especially since these criteria cannot be enforced under the current TMDL program, limited as it is by statutory language that restricts TMDLs to "pollutants" introduced into waters[128] rather than the broader term "pollution" that would include flow conditions.[129]

---

[120] Federal Water Pollution Control Act (Clean Water Act) § 101(g), 33 U.S.C. § 1251(g) (2014).
[121] Water Res. Council, Water Resource Policy Study: Issue and Option Papers, 42 Fed. Reg. 36,789 (1977).
[122] 123 Cong. Rec. 39,211 (1977) (Senate debate on the conference report).
[123] Ibid. at 39,211–12.
[124] Ibid. at 39,212.
[125] *PUD No. 1 of Jefferson Cnty. v Wash. Dep't of Ecology* (1994) 511 U.S. **700**, 720.
[126] 40 C.F.R. § 131.6 (2013).
[127] See Andreen, "Success and Backlash," *supra*, n. 6, at 31–34.
[128] Federal Water Pollution Control Act (Clean Water Act) § 303(d)(1)(C), 33 U.S.C. § 1313(d)(1)(C) (2014).
[129] See *supra*, nn 75–77 and accompanying text.

While EPA could take a number of steps to begin to address the problem,[130] Congress will ultimately have to act, just as it will have to act in order to invigorate the non-point source program – assuming, of course, that the nation will one day emerge from the dysfunctional gridlock that has gripped Congress for much of the past quarter-century. Congress could explicitly find that environmental flows are a necessary ingredient of water quality criteria; require states to place flow-impaired waters on their TMDL lists – at least to shine a spotlight on these problem waters; extend TMDLs to include "pollution" rather than just "pollutants" or at least encourage states to consider flow restoration in developing TMDLs for their pollutant-impaired streams; make flow impairment a priority under the non-point source program; and appropriate adequate funds to both EPA and the states to enable them to undertake the research that will be necessary to set instream flows reflecting the natural variations in stream levels and the subsequent monitoring that will be necessary to help fine-tune the flows in an adaptive manner. Congress could also require all federally owned or operated hydromodifications, including dams and water diversions as well as federally permitted dams, to comply with state instream flow criteria. The states, however, must cooperate in this effort.

As the Wallop Amendment recognized, the allocation of water in this country is, for the most part, a matter of state law.[131] Nevertheless, a long-neglected provision contained in the Wallop Amendment should be dusted off and put into action. That provision directed federal agencies "to co-operate with State and local agencies to develop comprehensive solutions to prevent, reduce and eliminate pollution in concert with programs for managing water resources."[132] The states and EPA, in short, must work together to address the problem of adequate stream flow, and Congress should reemphasize this obligation and provide some incentives for state participation. Congress could, for example, provide funding to western states to enable them to purchase water rights for flow restoration and a similar form of funding could be provided to the eastern states that utilize a form of regulated riparianism.[133] In addition, grants could be made available, where necessary, to assist agriculture, which is

---

[130] See Benson, *supra*, n. 16, at 257–62.

[131] See Tarlock, A. Dan, et al., *Water Resource Management*, 7th edn (Foundation Press, St Paul, Minn. 2014), p. 527.

[132] Federal Water Pollution Control Act (Clean Water Act) § 101(g), 33 U.S.C. § 1251(g) (2014).

[133] Over half of the eastern states have adopted permitting programs that are commonly referred to as regulated riparianism. Adler, *supra*, n. 103, at 232.

responsible for approximately 80 percent of the nation's consumptive water use,[134] to utilize more efficient forms of irrigation[135] or switch to less water-intensive crops. The list of policy options could go on and on. The most important thing, however, is that the nation must move toward the integration of water quality and water quantity law and policy.

V. CONCLUSION

Progress towards achieving the CWA's goals of restoring and maintaining "the chemical, physical, and biological integrity of the nation's waters" has stalled largely because we have failed to control non-point source pollution and because we have failed to ensure that our waters receive the environmental flows that are necessary to sustain their aquatic ecosystems. Much of the blame for these failures can be attributed to an outmoded approach to the allocation of governmental authority. While a number of states have demonstrated the capacity and the will to meet the challenge of dealing with one or both of these problems, the majority have not, and that leaves a gaping hole in our ability to complete the task that was begun in 1972. If the point source program is a reliable guide, its success should point to the use of a more dynamic form of federalism to help fill those gaps and thereby fulfill the promise of clean waters that was heralded by Congress in 1972.

---

[134] Econ. Res. Serv., Irrigation & Water Use, U.S. Dep't of Agric., accessed 14 July 2015 at www.ers.usda.gov/topics/farm-practices-management/irrigation-water-use.aspx.

[135] Although the number of irrigated acres using sprinkler and micro-irrigation systems has grown, 44 percent of irrigated acreage still relies upon surface (flood) systems. See Kenny, Joan F. et al., U.S. Dep't of Interior & U.S. Geological Survey, Estimated Use of Water in the United States in 2005 (2009), 1.

3. CERCLA, federalism, and common law claims

Alexandra B. Klass and Emma Fazio

INTRODUCTION

This chapter considers federalism concerns raised by the Comprehensive Environmental Response, Compensation, and Liability Act (CERCLA) in the context of common law claims for relief caused by hazardous substance contamination. Congress enacted CERCLA in 1980 to provide a vehicle for the federal government, state and local governments, tribes and private parties to recover costs associated with contamination from releases of hazardous substances that occurred in the past, often decades ago, during a time when there were few requirements for the disposal of hazardous substances. In this way, CERCLA is as much about looking backwards to past harm as it is about looking forward to set regulatory standards for future harm – the hallmark of the other federal environmental statutes covered in this book such as the Clean Air Act, the Clean Water Act and the Endangered Species Act. Through its draconian liability provisions Congress also intended to deter parties generating, transporting and disposing of hazardous substances from engaging in the types of activities in the future that had caused such serious contamination in the past. Although EPA and the states often work closely together to set cleanup standards and remediate contaminated sites, the heart of CERCLA is made up of its provisions that allow for recovery of cleanup costs associated with past harm. Thus, a central federalism question for CERCLA is how the provisions of CERCLA should impact, if at all, state statutory and common law claims to recover damages associated with the past releases of hazardous substances.

Like most federalism issues involving the impact of federal statutes on state law, the answer is a matter of determining the extent to which Congress intended CERCLA to preempt (that is, displace) state law. The answer to this question depends on express statutory language, evidence of Congressional intent and the overall purpose of the federal statute.

This chapter concludes that to the extent state law provides remedies for harm caused by releases of hazardous substances that go beyond the remedies provided in CERCLA, CERCLA should not bar such remedies except to the extent that there is a direct conflict between state and federal law. Moreover, where CERCLA is ambiguous courts should look to the remedial purposes of CERCLA in resolving those ambiguities. This chapter explains these conclusions by exploring (1) preemption of state statutory and common law claims for relief that provide remedies in addition to CERCLA and (2) preemption of state statutes of limitations and statutes of repose that may apply to state law claims for relief associated with hazardous substance contamination.

I. CERCLA OVERVIEW[1]

CERCLA, also known as "Superfund,"[2] was enacted in 1980 to create a federal framework to address the problems associated with the existence of hazardous substances in the environment. Although CERCLA's legislative history is not a model of clarity, most courts and commentators agree that the purposes of the statute were to facilitate the remediation of hazardous waste sites, to make the polluter pay the costs of cleanup, and to deter new site contamination.[3]

---

[1] Much of the background on CERCLA in this chapter is taken from Klass, Alexandra B., "CERCLA, State Law and Federalism in the 21st Century" (2012) 41 Sw. L. Rev. 679.

[2] The term "Superfund" is from the five-year, U.S.$1.6 billion Hazardous Substances Response Trust Fund created to finance cleanups at CERCLA's inception. See 28 U.S.C. § 9507 (2014) (establishing fund). Superfund was initially funded by special taxes on oil and chemical companies and other businesses and supplemented by general revenues, as well as cleanup costs recovered from responsible parties. See Cooke, Susan M. and Christopher P. Davis, *The Law of Hazardous Waste: Management, Cleanup, Liability and Litigation* (looseleaf) (LexisNexis Matthew Bender 2004), § 12.03[3] (hereinafter "Cooke"). The special taxes on oil and chemical companies expired in 1995, and have not been renewed.

[3] See *Mehrig v KFC W., Inc.*, 516 U.S. 479, 483 (1996) (stating that the two main purposes of CERCLA were "prompt cleanup of hazardous waste sites and imposition of all cleanup costs on the responsible party" (quoting *Gen. Elec. Co. v Litton Indus. Automation Sys. Inc.*, 920 F.2d 1415, 1422 (8th Cir. 1990))); Aronovsky, Ronald, "A Preemption Paradox: Preserving the Role of State Law in Private Cleanup Cost Disputes" (2008) 16 N.Y.U. Envtl L.J. **225**, 280–81 (discussing purposes of CERCLA and citing cases); see also Klass, Alexandra B., "From Reservoirs to Remediation: The Impact of CERCLA on Common Law

A. Cost Recovery and Contribution Claims

Specifically, CERCLA provides that any private or government entity may sue under section 107(a) to recover for any "release"[4] of a "hazardous substance,"[5] from a "facility,"[6] resulting in "response costs,"[7] so long as those costs are incurred in a manner consistent with the National Contingency Plan (NCP).[8] The NCP is a set of federal regulations that provides the procedures EPA and private parties must follow in selecting and conducting response actions if the party conducting the cleanup wishes to recover those costs from responsible parties under CERCLA.[9] In addition to the section 107(a) cost recovery provisions[10] the federal government (and only the federal government) may seek judicial relief under CERCLA section 106 to require a responsible party to abate an imminent and substantial endangerment to the public health or welfare or to the environment as a result of a release or threatened release of a hazardous substance.[11]

CERCLA also creates a right to contribution under section 113(f) "during or following" a section 106 or 107(a) civil action asserted against a plaintiff seeking contribution from other responsible parties.[12] CERCLA's contribution provisions provide that (1) section 113(f) settlements "shall be governed by federal law;" (2) "[i]n resolving contribution

---

Strict Liability Environmental Claims" (2004) 39 Wake Forest L. Rev. **903**, 926–29 (discussing CERCLA's legislative history); Buzbee, William W., "Remembering Repose: Voluntary Contamination Cleanup Approvals, Incentives, and the Costs of Interminable Liability" (1995) 80 Minn. L. Rev. 35 (discussing the deterrence of new site contamination as an important purpose of CERCLA).

[4] 42 U.S.C. § 9601(22) (2014) (defining "release").
[5] Ibid. § 9601(14) (defining "hazardous substance").
[6] Ibid. § 9601(9) (defining "facility").
[7] Ibid. § 9601(25) defining "response").
[8] See ibid. § 9607(a) (setting forth prima facie case for CERCLA recovery); Klass, *supra*, n. 3, at 920–23 (discussing CERCLA's liability provisions). Which party bears the burden of proof on NCP consistency depends on whether the suit is brought by EPA, a state, or an Indian tribe under § 9607(a)(4)(A), or whether the suit is brought by "any other party" under § 9607(a)(4)(B). For suits brought by EPA, a state or an Indian tribe, the defendant bears the burden of proving costs are "inconsistent" with the NCP, whereas for suits brought by any other party, such as a private party or a local government, the plaintiff bears the burden of proving the costs are "consistent" with the NCP and "necessary."
[9] See 42 U.S.C. § 9607(a)(4) (2014).
[10] Ibid. § 9607(a).
[11] Ibid. § 9606.
[12] Ibid. § 9613(f).

claims the court may allocate response costs among liable parties using ... equitable factors;" (3) nothing in section 113(f) diminishes contribution rights in the absence of a section 106 or 107 action; (4) a responsible party who resolves its CERCLA liability with the government in a settlement may seek contribution from a non-settling responsible party; and (5) a settling responsible party "shall not be liable for claims for contribution regarding matters addressed in the settlement."[13]

B. CERCLA's Limitations

Despite its broad liability provisions,[14] CERCLA has significant limitations. Private parties are limited to recovering "response costs" or monies paid toward a cleanup under section 107(a). CERCLA does not provide a vehicle for private parties to recover damages associated with personal injury, diminution in property value (often called "stigma damages"), lost profits, lost rents or other damages that are typically associated with contaminated property.[15] Moreover, Congress defined the term "hazardous substance" to exclude petroleum and natural gas, which means the widespread contamination resulting from activities such as gas station spills and natural gas pipeline leaks is not covered at all by CERCLA.[16] Thus, while CERCLA has been monumental in governmental and private party efforts to remediate contaminated property and recover those costs from responsible parties, there remain significant types of contamination

---

[13] Ibid.
[14] See Klass, *supra*, n. 1, at 684–85 (reviewing CERCLA's liability provisions).
[15] See 42 U.S.C. § 9607(a)(4) (2014) (limiting recovery to "response costs"); Cooke, *supra*, n. 2, at § 16.01[8] (collecting cases holding that lost business profits and diminution in value to property are not within the definition of response costs); Falcone III, Joseph L. and Daniel Utain, Comment, "You Can Teach an Old Dog New Tricks: The Application of Common Law in Present-Day Environmental Disputes" (2000) 11 Vill. Envtl L.J. **59**, 60–61 ("CERCLA does not offer a private plaintiff the opportunity to collect damages other than those which are necessary to cover the cleanup costs of the subject site.").
[16] See 42 U.S.C. § 9601(14) (2014):

The term [hazardous substance] does not include petroleum, including crude oil or any fraction thereof which is not otherwise specifically listed or designated as a hazardous substance under paragraphs (A) through (F) of this paragraph, and the term does not include natural gas, synthetic gas, natural gas liquids, liquefied fuel (or mixtures of natural gas such as synthetic gas).

See also Klass, *supra*, n. 3, at 937 and n. 139 (discussing CERCLA's petroleum exclusion).

and damages that CERCLA does not cover, and thus state statutory law and common law, as discussed below, continue to play an important role.[17]

II. CERCLA AND PREEMPTION OF STATE LAW

A. CERCLA Purposes, Savings Clauses, and the Role of State Law

In cases where the plaintiff brings both a CERCLA claim to recover remediation costs and state law claims to provide an additional basis for recovering such costs or to obtain other relief not available under CERCLA, such as damages or for injunctive relief, the question is whether CERCLA preempts those state law claims. Federal preemption occurs when (1) Congress preempts state law by saying so in express terms (express preemption); (2) Congress and federal agencies create a sufficiently comprehensive federal regulatory structure in an area where the federal interest is so dominant that it requires the inference that Congress left no room for state law (implied field preemption); or (3) Congress does not completely displace state regulation but the state law actually conflicts with federal law or "stands as an obstacle" to achieving the full purposes and objectives of Congress (implied conflict preemption).[18] Courts also apply a "presumption against preemption" of state law in recognition of the fact that states are "independent sovereigns in our federal system," and thus courts assume that Congress did not intend to displace the states' historic police powers unless it expresses a "clear and manifest" purpose to do so.[19]

---

[17] Congress provided an explicit savings provision to ensure that those costs not recoverable under CERCLA could still be recovered under other statutes and the common law. See 42 U.S.C. § 9652(d) (2014); *PMC, Inc. v Sherwin-Williams Co.*, 151 F.3d 610, 617 (7th Cir. 1998) (purpose of 42 U.S.C. § 9652 "is to preserve to victims of toxic wastes the other remedies they may have under federal or state law"), *cert. denied*, 525 U.S. 1104 (1999). See also *infra*, nn 25–28 and accompanying text (discussing CERCLA savings provisions).

[18] See *Hillsborough Cnty. v Automated Med. Labs., Inc.*, 471 U.S. 707, 713 (1985) (citing *Hines v Davidowitz*, 312 U.S. 52, 67 (1941)); Nelson, Caleb "Preemption" 86 Va. L. Rev. **225**, 226 28 (2000) (describing the three types of preemption). The doctrine of federal preemption is based on the Supremacy Clause in the U.S. Constitution, which provides that the Constitution and U.S. laws "shall be the supreme law of the Land" notwithstanding any state law to the contrary. U.S. Const. Art. VI, cl. 2.

[19] See e.g. *CTS Corp. v Waldburger*, 134 S. Ct. 2175 (2014).

While Congress did not include express purpose language in CERCLA, courts often set forth one or more purposes of CERCLA in reaching various decisions under the statute. In a 2009 CERCLA decision, the Supreme Court quoted a Second Circuit opinion which stated that "[t]he act was designed to promote the 'timely cleanup of hazardous waste sites' and to ensure that the costs of such cleanup efforts were borne by those responsible for contamination."[20] This statement reflects the most common purposes courts have attributed to CERCLA, both when courts are addressing CERCLA preemption issues and otherwise.[21] Moreover, the Second Circuit has also stated that "it was not part of the legislative purpose that CERCLA be a comprehensive regulatory scheme occupying the entire field of hazardous wastes, nor does CERCLA prevent the states from enacting laws to supplement federal measures relating to the cleanup of such wastes."[22] In another case, the same court noted that states "play a crucial role in effectuating the purposes of CERCLA."[23]

Thus, the inquiry begins with a determination of whether Congress intended that CERCLA preempt state law completely, partially or not at

---

[20] *Burlington N. and Santa Fe Ry. Co. v United States et al.*, 129 S. Ct. 1870 (2009) (quoting *Consol. Edison Co. of N.Y. v UGI Util. Inc.*, 423 F.3d 90, 94 (2d Cir. 2005); see also *Mehrig v KFC W., Inc.*, 516 U.S. 479, 483 (1996) (distinguishing RCRA from CERCLA by indicating that RCRA was not designed to serve the purposes of CERCLA "to effectuate the cleanup of toxic waste sites or to compensate those who have attended to the remediation of environmental hazards"). But see *Cooper Indus., Inc. v Aviall Servs., Inc.*, 543 U.S. 157, 167 (2004) (refusing to take a position on the purpose of CERCLA and stating that

> [e]ach side insists that the purpose of CERCLA bolsters its reading of § 113(f)(1). Given the clear meaning of the text, there is no need to resolve this dispute or to consult the purpose of CERCLA at all. As we have said: "[I]t is ultimately the provisions of our laws rather than the principal concerns of our legislators by which we are governed" (internal citations omitted).

[21] *City of Los Angeles v San Pedro Boat Works*, 635 F.3d 440, 447 (9th Cir. 2011) (stating that CERCLA has two primary goals: "(1) to ensure the prompt and effective cleanup of waste disposal sites, and (2) to assure that parties responsible for hazardous substances [bear] the cost of remedying the conditions they created" (quoting *Carson Harbor Village, Ltd. v Unocal Corp.*, 270 F.3d 863, 880 (9th Cir. 2001))).

[22] *Bedford Affiliates v Sills*, 156 F.3d 416, 426–27 (2d Cir. 1998) (emphasis added), *overruled on other grounds*, *Cooper Indus., Inc. v Aviall Servs., Inc.*, 543 U.S. 157 (2004).

[23] *Niagara Mohawk Power Corp. v Chevron U.S.A., Inc.*, 596 F.3d 112 (2d Cir. 2010).

all. On that basic level, courts are in agreement that Congress did not intend to preempt the field of hazardous substance remediation and did intend to leave considerable room for state law.[24] The question is, how much? In addition to invoking the generally accepted purposes of CERCLA outlined above, courts can look to the statute's several savings clauses that provide a partial answer to this question. First, section 114 states that "[n]othing in this chapter shall be construed or interpreted as preempting any State from imposing any additional liability or requirements with respect to the release of hazardous substances within such State."[25] CERCLA section 114 also states, however, that any person who receives compensation for removal costs or damages or claims under CERCLA shall be precluded from recovering compensation for the same removal costs or claims or damages under any other state or federal law, and vice versa.[26] Second, section 302(d) states that "[n]othing in this chapter shall affect or modify in any way the obligations or liabilities of any person under other Federal or State law, including common law, with respect to releases of hazardous substances or other pollutants or contaminants."[27] Third, section 301(h) states that CERCLA "does not affect or otherwise impair the rights of any person under Federal, State, or common law...."[28] Thus, it is fairly clear that CERCLA did not intend to occupy the field of hazardous substance remediation and intended to preserve a significant role for state law.

B. State Law Claims for Damages and Injunctive Relief

Several states have their own superfund-type statutes that allow plaintiffs to recover response costs in a manner similar to that provided under CERCLA. In contrast with CERCLA, however, some state superfund statutes, such as those in Minnesota and Washington, allow recovery for personal injury, lost profits, diminution in value to property or other losses stemming from the contamination of property or harm to human health and the environment.[29]

---

[24] See Aronovsky, *supra*, n. 3.
[25] See 42 U.S.C. § 6914(a) (2014).
[26] See ibid. § 9614(b).
[27] See ibid. 9652(d).
[28] See ibid. § 9659(h).
[29] See e.g. Minn. Stat. §§ 115B.05, 115B.14 (2014) (allowing recovery for personal injury, lost profits, diminution in value to property, and other damages associated with the release of hazardous substances as well as reasonable costs and attorneys' fees); Wash. Rev. Code § 70.105D.080 (2014) (allowing recovery

For instance, Minnesota's superfund statute, the Minnesota Environmental Rights and Liability Act (MERLA), allows for recovery of costs and damages not available under CERCLA. CERCLA's primary liability provision allows only for recovery of "response costs" (that is, costs incurred on the actual remediation of contaminated property). MERLA, by contrast, provides for recovery of those costs but also has a separate provision that allows for recovery of: (1) damages for economic loss, including injury to or destruction of real or personal property, loss of use of real or personal property and loss of past or future income or profits resulting from injury to, destruction of or loss of real or personal property; and (2) all damages for death, personal injury or disease, including medical expenses, rehabilitation costs, burial expenses, loss of past or future income, loss of earning capacity and damages for pain, suffering and impairment.[30]

Although often overshadowed by CERCLA, plaintiffs in many environmental contamination cases continue to rely heavily on common law claims of trespass, nuisance, negligence and strict liability to obtain damages, injunctive relief and punitive damages in addition to or instead of CERCLA and state superfund claims. Sometimes this is because the contamination results from the release of petroleum, natural gas or another substance that is excluded from CERCLA and state superfund law coverage, so common law claims are the only legal means of recovering damages and other costs.[31] Sometimes this is because a party other than the plaintiff, such as the defendant, a third party or the government, is assuming responsibility for the actual cleanup of hazardous substances, but the plaintiff still has incurred damages such as lost profits, lost rents, stigma damages or personal injuries. Moreover, depending on the egregiousness of the conduct, a plaintiff may be in a position to seek punitive damages, which may dwarf any cleanup costs or other damages, and such relief is not available under CERCLA or state

---

of expenses and reasonable attorneys' fees in connection with cost recovery actions).

[30] See Minn. Stat. §§ 115B.04, 115B.05, 115B.14 (2014).

[31] See e.g. *Volunteers of Am. v Heinrich*, 90 F. Supp. 2d 252, 258 (W.D.N.Y. 2000) (finding that plaintiff's state law claims based on costs associated with the discharge of petroleum were not available under CERCLA and were therefore not preempted). But see *Members of Beede Site Grp. v Fed. Home Loan Mortg. Corp.*, 968 F. Supp. 2d 455 (D.N.H. 2013) (dismissing plaintiff's state law contribution claim as preempted by CERCLA because even though state law does not contain a petroleum exemption like CERCLA, allowing the claim would conflict with Congress's "political determination to exclude transporters of petroleum from liability").

superfund statutes but may be available under common law.[32] Notably, if the plaintiff's suit does contain a CERCLA claim, the CERCLA claim and any state law claims may be brought in federal court. If, however, the plaintiff's suit is only to seek relief for harm under state law, those claims will generally be brought in state court unless diversity jurisdiction is present or there is recovery under a separate federal claim.

C. CERCLA and Preemption of State Law Claims

Courts have struggled with the extent of CERCLA preemption of independent state statutory or common law claims to recover for response costs or damages in three main areas: (1) whether plaintiffs who incur response costs without complying with the NCP should be able to recover those costs under state superfund statutes or state common law claims such as nuisance, negligence or strict liability; (2) whether plaintiffs should be able to bring state law claims for contribution, restitution, unjust enrichment and the like despite CERCLA's contribution provision under section 113(f); and (3) whether specific language in CERCLA preempts both state statutes of limitation and state statutes of repose that do not apply a "discovery rule" or only state statutes of limitation.

1. Claims for cost recovery, damages and injunctions

With regard to whether plaintiffs who incur response costs without complying with the NCP should be able to recover those costs under state superfund statutes, most courts have found that such state law claims are viable because by not complying with the NCP the plaintiff is not attempting to recover CERCLA response costs.[33] Courts have also

---

[32] See Klass, Alexandra B., "Common Law and Federalism in the Age of the Regulatory State" (2007) 92 Iowa L. Rev. **545**, 583; Klass, "From Reservoirs to Remediation," *supra*, n. 3, at 905.

[33] See e.g. *MPM Silicones, L.L.C. v Union Carbide Corp.*, 931 F. Supp. 2d 387, 398 (N.D.N.Y. 2013) (explaining that a state law contribution claim for costs incurred outside CERCLA is not preempted); *City of Waukegan. v Nat'l Gypsum Co.*, 587 F. Supp. 2d 997, 1011 (N.D. Ill. 2008) (finding claims available under the Illinois Water Pollution Discharge Act that would not otherwise be available under CERCLA, including recovery for cleanup costs not in compliance with the NCP); *One Wheeler Rd. Assocs. v Foxboro Co.*, No. Civ. A. 90-12873-RGS, 1995 WL 791937 (D. Mass. Dec. 13, 1995) (allowing for recovery of attorney's fees under state environmental statute in a case where other damages were awarded under CERCLA); *Village of DePue, Ill. v Exxon Mobile Corp.*, 537 F.3d 775, 787 (7th Cir. 2008) (finding that a local claim was

generally found that state common law claims for nuisance, negligence, strict liability, trespass and other substantive tort theories are not subject to preemption under CERCLA despite failure to comply with the NCP, and that damages and other relief not available under CERCLA can be recovered under such state law claims.[34] For instance, two Eighth Circuit cases allowed common law negligence, strict liability and nuisance claims to proceed alongside CERCLA cost recovery claims.[35] Moreover, in at least one case where a plaintiff brought claims for negligence, nuisance and trespass, the court found that CERCLA did not preempt recovery of future damages under state law even though such relief is not available under CERCLA.[36]

---

preempted by a state claim, but that CERCLA does not apply to a consent order handled only at the state level); *N.J. Dep't of Envtl. Prot. v Minn. Mining and Mf'g Co.*, 2007 WL 2027916, at *6 (D.N.J. July 5, 2007) (finding no preemption of state law claims in a removal action and reasoning that preemption "would disturb the congressionally approved balance of federal and state judicial responsibilities"). For a broader discussion of CERCLA preemption of state law claims see Aronovsky, *supra* n. 3, at 284–92.

[34] See e.g. *Board of County Com'rs v Brown Group Retail*, 598 F. Supp. 2d 1185, 1192 (D. Colo. 2009) (finding that claims including negligence, negligence per se, and strict liability for abnormally dangerous activity were not preempted because they provided for recovery not otherwise allowed under CERCLA); *Quapaw Tribe of Oklahoma v Blue Tee Corp.*, 2009 WL 455260 (N.D. Okla. 2009) (finding that plaintiffs could recover under state common law claims for nuisance, trespass, strict liability, and natural resources damages because any interference with CERCLA compliance was too remote). But see *Ashtabula River Corp. Group II v Conrail, Inc.*, 549 F. Supp. 2d 981, 985–86 (N.D. Ohio 2008) (finding that common law nuisance claim seeking recovery for the same costs as those claimed under CERCLA was preempted when CERCLA claims were barred because of CERCLA s. 114 prohibiting duplicative recoveries). See also Aronovsky, *supra*, n. 3, at 314–17 (discussing "Generic Preemption of State Common Law Claims").

[35] See *Kennedy Bldg. Associates v Viacom, Inc.*, 375 F.3d 731, 735 (8th Cir. 2004) (reversing the plaintiffs' common law strict liability claim not because it was preempted by CERCLA, but because it was not viable under state law); *Union Pac. R. Co. v Reilly Indus., Inc.*, 215 F.3d 830, 842 n. 11 (8th Cir. 2000) (following the district court in declining to decide whether the plaintiff's common law indemnity and contribution claims were preempted by CERCLA, since the district court had found that the claims were not viable under state law).

[36] See *Walnut Creek Manor, LLC v Mayhew Center, LLC*, 2010 WL 653661, at *5 (N.D. Cal. 2010). The court clarified that double recovery was not a concern because CERCLA expressly limits double recovery, and, therefore, if the party were to bring later claims for damages under CERCLA, those would be precluded by the recovery for future damages. Ibid. For a discussion of

2. Contribution claims

As to whether plaintiffs should be able to bring state law contribution, restitution, unjust enrichment and other similar claims, most courts have found that such state law claims would disrupt CERCLA's contribution scheme and interfere with the settlement protection the federal statute provides.[37] The Second Circuit in *Bedford Affiliates v Sills* characterized this as conflict preemption, noting that allowing common law restitution and indemnification claims to proceed in state court would circumvent the "carefully crafted system" of CERCLA section 113 and thereby frustrate Congress's goals, thus finding an actual conflict between state and federal law.[38] The court was concerned that "PRPs would choose not to settle their claims with the government out of fear that other defendants could thwart section 113's contribution protection by bringing identical contribution claims under the state common law."[39] Another Second Circuit decision, *Niagara Mohawk Power Corp. v Chevron U.S.A., Inc.*, asserted that "§ 113 was intended to provide the only contribution avenue for parties with response costs incurred under CERCLA," and thus claims under state law that attempt to recover CERCLA response costs are preempted.[40]

---

preemption of future cleanup costs see Aronovsky, *supra*, n. 3, at 301–03 (discussing case law in which CERCLA preempted future recovery).

[37] See e.g. *Niagara Mohawk Power Corp. v Chevron U.S.A., Inc.*, 596 F.3d 112, 139 (2d Cir. 2010) (finding that state indemnification and unjust enrichment claims were preempted by CERCLA); *Chitayat v Vanderbilt Assocs.*, 702 F. Supp. 2d 69, 83 (E.D.N.Y. 2010) (state law contribution and unjust enrichment claims are preempted by CERCLA); *Ford Motor Co. v Mich. Consol. Gas Co.*, No. 08-CV-13503-DT, 2009 WL 3190418 (E.D. Mich. Sept. 29, 2009) (ruling that the plaintiffs could assert common law indemnification claims as a fallback if the CERCLA claims fail). For further discussion of CERCLA preemption of state law contribution claims, see Aronovsky, *supra*, n. 3, at 308–14, 312 n. 399.

[38] 156 F.3d. 416, 427 (2d Cir. 1998).

[39] *New York v Hickey's Carting, Inc.*, 380 F. Supp. 2d 108, 114 (E.D.N.Y. 2005) (summarizing *Bedford*).

[40] 596 F.3d 112, 138 (2d Cir. 2010) (explaining that § 113 was intended to "standardize the statutory right of contribution and, in doing so, avoid the possibility of fifty different state statutory schemes that regulate the duties and obligations of non-settling PRPs who might be viewed as tortfeasors under the law of any particular state."); see also *Fireman's Fund Ins. Co. v City of Lodi*, 302 F.3d 928, 946 & n. 15 (9th Cir. 2002) (citing *PMC, Inc. v Sherwin-Williams Co.*, 151 F.3d 610, 617–18 (7th Cir. 1998)); *Bedford Affiliates*, 156 F.3d at 426–27; *In re Reading Co.*, 115 F.3d 1111, 1117 (3d Cir.1997) (finding CERCLA preempted a municipal hazardous waste ordinance to the extent that it

Circumstances exist, however, in which courts have found CERCLA does not preempt these state claims.[41] In *New York v West Side Corp.*[42] the U.S. District Court for Eastern District of New York distinguished one of the most frequently cited contribution preemption cases, *Bedford Affiliates v Sills*,[43] in situations where the plaintiff asserting the state claims is not a potentially responsible party (PRP) under CERCLA.[44] The district court ruled both that conflict preemption could not apply where there was no claim under CERCLA section 113, and that the potential for double recovery was not enough to trigger preemption.[45] The court in *West Side Corp.* relied on its earlier decision in *Hickey's Carting*, which reasoned that when a state brings a state law claim along with a section 107(a) claim, there is no reason to worry that the state would be attempting to circumvent the comprehensive settlement system in section 113.[46] The U.S. District Court for the Northern District of New York in *MPM Silicones, LLC v Union Carbide Corp.*[47] even extended this ruling to private PRPs bringing state law contribution claims alongside their section 107 claim, because the presence of the state law claims do not affect the PRPs' incentive to settle with the United States, and because the court overseeing the case would "undoubtedly prohibit the suing PRP from recovering the same costs under its state-law

---

legislatively insulates [the municipality] from contribution liability under state and federal law, and noting that this "holding is not inconsistent with the reasoning of other circuits that have held that litigants may not invoke state statutes in order to escape the application of CERCLA's provisions in the midst of hazardous waste litigation.").

[41] See e.g. *Queens W. Dev. Corp. v Honeywell Int'l, Inc.*, No. 10-4876-PGS, 2013 WL 163306 (D.N.J. Jan. 15, 2013) ("[O]ther district courts in the Second Circuit have declined to dismiss restitution claims as being preempted by CERCLA because some damages recoverable under a restitution theory may not be recoverable under CERCLA.").

[42] 790 F. Supp. 2d 13 (E.D.N.Y. 2011).

[43] 156 F.3d 416 (2d Cir. 1998).

[44] Specifically, in *New York v West Side Corp.*, the court described *Bedford*'s reach as "diminished or outright neutralized," in a CERCLA § 107 action because the state is bringing the cost recovery action, not private PRPs. 790 F. Supp. 2d 13, 22 (E.D.N.Y. 2011). See Aronovsky, *supra*, n. 3, at 309–10 (describing *Bedford* as a "frequently cited case" addressing the issue of CERCLA preemption of state law contribution claims).

[45] *West Side Corp.*, 790 F. Supp. 2d at 29.

[46] *New York v Hickey's Carting, Inc.*, 380 F. Supp. 2d 108, 117 (E.D.N.Y. 2005).

[47] 931 F. Supp. 2d 387 (N.D.N.Y. 2013).

claims."[48] The court concluded that "ultimately ... whether state-law claims are preempted by CERCLA boils down to whether double recovery of CERCLA response costs will occur."[49] In addition, in *Board of County Com'rs v Brown Group Retail*[50] the U.S. District Court for the District of Colorado held that because the plaintiff's unjust enrichment and other similar state law claims sought relief that was not identical to that pursued under the CERCLA claims, the state claims were not preempted.[51]

These last cases aside, however, courts generally have found state law contribution, indemnity and similar claims preempted. The Seventh Circuit found that CERCLA preempts state law contribution claims even when the plaintiff does not comply with the NCP, and is therefore not seeking recovery of CERCLA response costs.[52] When a plaintiff who did not follow the NCP attempted to seek contribution under the Illinois contribution statute, the court explained that CERCLA denies contribution claims to non-NCP compliant plaintiffs as a "sanction," and therefore seeking contribution under a state statute "is an attempt to nullify the sanction that Congress imposed for [this] kind of CERCLA violation."[53] A district court illuminated another aspect of the issue: while a plaintiff is permitted to bring a state law claim for unjust enrichment, for example

---

[48] Ibid. at 402–03. The court noted further that

permitting private PRPs and states alike to bring state-law claims alongside their § 107(a) claims accomplishes CERCLA's remedial purpose of "encouraging prompt and effective cleanup of hazardous waste sites" by "assuring that those responsible for any damage, environmental harm, or injury from chemical poisons bear the costs of their actions."

Ibid. at 405–06 (quoting *Niagara Mohawk Power Corp. v Chevron, Inc.*, 596 F.3d 112, 120 (2d Cir. 2010)).

[49] Ibid. at 406; see also *Ashtabula River Corp. Grp. II v Conrail, Inc.*, 549 F. Supp. 2d 981, 986 (N.D. Ohio 2008) ("Where, however, a plaintiff's CERCLA and state law claims seek recovery of the same response costs, courts have found that CERCLA preempts the plaintiff's right to recover under the state law.").

[50] 598 F. Supp. 2d 1185 (D. Colo. 2009).

[51] Ibid. at 1192 (stating specifically, "Plaintiff seeks monetary damages that are unavailable to private parties under CERCLA."). It should also be noted that the decision was on a motion to dismiss, and the court indicated that regardless of any preemption question, the claims could stand because the plaintiff could argue alternative legal theories even if only one of those theories could "bear fruit at trial." Ibid.

[52] *PMC, Inc. v Sherwin-Williams Co.*, 151 F.3d 610, 618 (7th Cir. 1998).

[53] Ibid.

alongside a section 107 cost recovery claim,[54] a state law contribution claim conflicts directly with the comprehensive contribution scheme in section 113 and is therefore preempted.[55]

Certainly, the courts are far from uniform on the extent of CERCLA preemption of state law contribution claims. But the weight of authority holds that contribution claims are somewhat unique among state law claims for relief because of their potential to interfere with CERCLA's remedial goals and settlement scheme. As a result, courts are far more likely to find state law contribution claims preempted but at the same time allow recovery for other state law claims for relief.

3. CERCLA and preemption of state law statutes of limitations and repose

In addition to CERCLA's several statutes of limitations for actions to recover response costs,[56] CERCLA contains a provision, 42 U.S.C. § 9658 (CERCLA section 309), entitled "Actions under State Law for Damages from Exposure to Hazardous Substances." This section provides that in any action brought under state law for personal injury or property damage which is caused or contributed to by exposure to hazardous substances, pollutants or contaminants, the state limitations period may not begin to run until the "federally required commencement date" – the date the plaintiff knew or reasonably should have known that the personal injury or property damages were caused or contributed to by the hazardous substance or pollutant or contaminant concerned.[57] Thus,

---

[54] See Pharmacia L.L.C. v Union Elec. Co., No. 4:12CV2275 CDP, 2013 WL 1965122, at *3 (E.D. Mo. May 10, 2013); Bd. of Cnty. Comm'rs v Brown Grp. Retail, Inc., 598 F. Supp. 2d 1185, 1192–93 (D. Colo. 2009) (allowing a state law unjust enrichment claim to proceed alongside a § 107 claim, so long is there is no double recovery for the same response costs, because plaintiffs are permitted to "pursue alternative and legally inconsistent theories up until the point where one of the inconsistent theories prevails to the exclusion of the others").

[55] Pharmacia LLC, 2013 WL 1965122, at *2 ("Section 113(f) was intended to 'standardize the statutory right of contribution' and 'provide the only contribution avenue for parties with response costs under CERCLA.'") (quoting Niagara Mohawk Power Corp. v Chevron U.S.A., Inc., 596 F.3d 112, 138 (2d Cir. 2010)).

[56] See 42 U.S.C. § 9613(g)(2)(A) (2014) (three-year statute of limitation after completion of a removal action to recover response costs); ibid. § 9613(g)(2)(B) (six-year statute of limitation after construction of remedial action to recover response costs).

[57] See ibid. § 9658.

while CERCLA does not alter any state's limitations period for bringing an action to recover for personal injury or damages associated with hazardous substances, it does impose a "discovery rule" on the accrual of such claims for those states that do not already have a discovery rule under their own state statutory or common law.[58]

As noted above, CERCLA itself does not provide recovery for claims of personal injury or for damages associated with hazardous substances; it allows for recovery only of remediation costs. Thus, the purpose of section 9658 is to assure that plaintiffs are not time barred from bringing personal injury or property damage claims under state law prior to the time they knew or should have known of the connection between their damages and the hazardous substances at issue.[59] Typically, when interpreting 42 U.S.C. § 9658, courts have found that CERCLA's authority preempts state statute of limitations accrual dates that would otherwise bar state law claims, reasoning that where the deadline provided by CERCLA is more generous, preemption is appropriate.[60] As

---

[58] See e.g. *A.S.I., Inc. v Sanders*, 835 F. Supp. 1349, 1358 (D. Kan. 1993) ("Under [CERCLA], state law creating limitations periods which begin to run earlier than under federal law are preempted.").

[59] See *Waldburger v CTS Corp.*, 723 F.3d 434, 442 (4th Cir. 2013) (noting "Congress's unmistakable goal of removing barriers to relief from toxic wreckage"), rev'd, *CTS Corp. v Waldburger*, 134 S. Ct. 2175 (2014); *Burlington N. & Santa Fe Ry. Co. v Poole Chem. Co.*, 419 F.3d 355, 363 (5th Cir. 2005) (reviewing the legislative history of § 9658 and concluding that "Congress added § 9658 as part of the 1986 CERCLA amendments to respond to a report by a congressional study group that determined that many state systems were inadequate to deal with the delayed discovery of the effect of a release of a toxic substance.").

[60] CERCLA states specifically:

In the case of any action brought under State law for personal injury, or property damages, which are caused or contributed to by exposure to any hazardous substance, or pollutant or contaminant, released into the environment from a facility, if the applicable limitations period for such action (as specified in the State statute of limitations or under common law) provides a commencement date which is earlier than the federally required commencement date, such period shall commence at the federally required commencement date in lieu of the date specified in such State statute. 42 U.S.C. § 9658 (2014).

Barton v NL Industries, Inc., No. 08–12558, 2010 WL 4038738, at *3 (E.D. Mich. Sept. 30, 2010) (applying *O'Connor v Boeing N. Am., Inc.*, 311 F.3d 1139 (9th Cir. 2002)); see also *Union Pac. R. Co. v Reilly Indus., Inc.*, 215 F.3d 830, 840 (8th Cir. 2000) ("[U]nder § 9658, the federally required commencement date arguably yields to state law if the commencement date under the applicable state

one court reasoned, "CERCLA is a remedial statute whose terms should be construed liberally to carry out its purposes."[61]

One issue that had divided courts regarding section 9658 was whether it preempts both conflicting state statutes of limitation and state statutes of repose or only conflicting state statutes of limitation. In June 2014 the U.S. Supreme Court resolved the issue in favor of a narrow reading of section 9658 in *CTS Corporation v Waldburger*,[62] applying the federally required commencement date only to state statutes of limitations and not state statutes of repose.

Statutes of limitation and statutes of repose serve different purposes. Statutes of limitation are often referred to as "procedural," a way of promoting "fairness to defendants" by "encourag[ing] prompt resolution of disputes" and "extinguishing stale claims."[63] By contrast, a statute of repose "creates a substantive right to be free from liability after a legislatively determined period. In other words, a statute of repose establishes a 'right not to be sued, rather than a right to sue.'"[64] According to the Fifth Circuit:

> A statute of limitations extinguishes the right to prosecute an accrued cause of action after a period of time. It cuts off the remedy ... A statute of repose limits the time during which a cause of action can arise and usually runs from an act of a defendant. It abolishes the cause of action after the passage of time even though the cause of action may not have yet accrued.[65]

As a result of section 9658, state statutes of limitations for hazardous substance contamination claims do not begin to run until the plaintiff has discovered the injury. If section 9658 does not also preempt state statutes

---

statute of limitations is later than that federally required commencement date."). But see *Angle v Koppers, Inc.*, 42 So.3d 1 (Miss. 2010) (finding that because the appellant failed to make CERCLA preemption claims in its initial pleadings, time barred state claims must be dismissed).

[61] *Abrams v Ciba Specialty Chems. Corp.*, 659 F. Supp. 2d 1225 (S.D. Ala. 2009); *McDonald v Sun Oil Co.*, 548 F.3d 774, 783 (9th Cir. 2008) (stating that "Congress's primary concern in enacting [§ 9658] was to adopt the discovery rule in situations where a plaintiff may lose a cause of action before becoming aware of it.").

[62] 134 S. Ct. 2175 (2014).

[63] *First United Methodist Church of Hyattsville v U.S. Gypsum Co.*, 882 F.2d 862, 866 (4th Cir. 1989).

[64] *Burlington N. & Santa Fe Ry. Co. v Poole Chem. Co.*, 419 F.3d 355, 362 (5th Cir. 2005).

[65] Ibid. (citation omitted).

of repose, a plaintiff's claim could be abolished before he or she even discovers the injury.

Before the Supreme Court's 2014 decision in *Waldburger*, lower federal courts had split on the scope of section 9658. For instance, the Ninth Circuit in *McDonald v Sun Oil Co.* noted that when section 9658 was enacted in 1986 it was not clear whether the term "statute of limitations" included statutes of repose or not.[66] The court went on to examine the legislative history behind the provision, finding that "Congress's primary concern in enacting [section 9658] was to adopt the discovery rule in situations where a plaintiff may lose a cause of action before becoming aware of it."[67] Because that situation is more likely to occur with a statute of repose than with a statute of limitation, and given the ambiguity in the term "statute of limitation," the court reasoned that Congress intended for section 9658 to preempt both statutes of limitation and repose.[68] The Fourth Circuit majority in *Waldburger v CTS Corp.* agreed that section 9658 preempts statutes of repose, finding the provision to be ambiguous on that issue and consequently looked to Congress's purpose for guidance.[69] The court noted that Congress had a remedial purpose in enacting CERCLA as compared to other environmental statutes, and therefore "CERCLA, as all remedial statutes, must be given a broad interpretation to effect [*sic*] its ameliorative goals."[70] The court argued that interpreting the provision to exclude statutes of repose would not be "an honest attempt to effectuate Congress's intent."[71] By contrast, the Fifth Circuit had ruled that section 9658 preempts only state statutes of limitation, not statutes of repose.[72]

In reversing the Fourth Circuit decision in *Waldburger*, the U.S. Supreme Court found first that the heading of section 9658 refers to

---

[66] 548 F.3d 774, 781 (9th Cir. 2008) ("At that time, although some cases recognized the differences between statutes of limitation and repose, a number of cases confused the terms or used them interchangeably."). See also *Abrams*, 659 F. Supp. 2d at 1234 & n. 13 (detailing numerous cases where courts have considered statutes of repose to be encompassed in the definition of "limitations period," which is the term used in § 9658(a)(1)).

[67] *McDonald*, 548 F.3d at 783.

[68] Ibid.

[69] 723 F.3d 434, 442 (4th Cir. 2013), *rev'd*, *CTS Corp. v Waldburger*, 134 S. Ct. 2175 (2014).

[70] Ibid. (quoting *First United Methodist Church of Hyattsville v U.S. Gypsum Co.*, 882 F.2d 862, 867 (4th Cir. 1989)).

[71] Ibid. at 444 (internal quotation marks omitted).

[72] *Burlington N. & Santa Fe Ry. Co. v Poole Chem. Co.*, 419 F.3d 335 (5th Cir. 2005).

"statutes of limitations" and that Congress could have included the term "statutes of repose" in the scope of the provision if it wished to include those statutes as well.[73] The Court also relied on the "presumption against preemption" of state law in finding that Congress needs to be clear when it is displacing state law and thus ambiguity will result in upholding the application of state law.[74] Finally, the Court also found that although the terms statute of limitations and statute of repose were sometimes used interchangeably when section 9658 was added to CERCLA, the distinction between the two was still recognized at the time, and it was reasonable to believe, based on the statutory language, that Congress chose to preempt statutes of limitations but not statutes of repose.[75]

The decision was subject to a dissent by Justices Ginsburg and Breyer. In authoring the dissent, Justice Ginsburg relied on the remedial purposes of CERCLA, the problem with potential plaintiffs not knowing the fact or extent of their harm until decades after the contamination took place, and the language in section 9658 referring to the "federally required commencement date" which could apply equally to statutes of limitations and statutes of repose.[76]

In reaching its decision in *Waldburger*, the Supreme Court appeared to follow the approach of lower courts in CERCLA cases generally of preempting state law only where the statutory language is clear or there is a direct conflict. The Court departed from prior CERCLA cases, however, in allowing the presumption against preemption of state law to override the more general remedial purposes of CERCLA, which courts have relied on for decades in addressing federal–state conflicts in the area of hazardous substance contamination.

CONCLUSION

The goal of this chapter has been to highlight recent federalism debates in CERCLA. Notably, the *Waldburger* case was the first time the U.S. Supreme Court weighed in on section 9658 of CERCLA and also the first time the Supreme Court had the opportunity to expressly consider the extent to which Congress intended CERCLA to impact state statutory and common law claims for relief relating to hazardous substance

---

[73] *Waldburger*, 134 S. Ct. 2175.
[74] Ibid.
[75] Ibid.
[76] Ibid. (Ginsburg J. dissenting).

contamination. While the Supreme Court was not able to consider its own precedent in CERCLA cases on this point, there is a long history of focus in the lower courts on the remedial purposes of CERCLA in determining the extent to which state law that differs from CERCLA is in actual conflict with its terms and is preempted. These cases have generally concluded that to the extent state law promotes the voluntary remediation of hazardous substances and the recovery of costs from responsible parties, such state law claims do not conflict with CERCLA. But to the extent such claims interfere with CERCLA's remedial purposes, like some state law claims for contribution, those claims are preempted. Applying these principles to CERCLA section 9658 would have supported the conclusion that if the language is determined to be ambiguous, principles of federalism and CERCLA itself should weigh in favor of finding that section 9658 preempts both state statutes of repose and state statutes of limitation. That was the rationale of the dissent in *Waldburger*. But in focusing more on the general presumption against preemption of state law, the *Waldburger* majority interpreted the ambiguous language of CERCLA in favor of state autonomy and against CERCLA's remedial purposes, thus elevating its general rule in preemption cases over CERCLA-specific principles. Whether the Supreme Court applies these principles more broadly in future CERCLA cases remains to be seen.

PART II

REGULATION OF NATURAL RESOURCES

4. Fragmented forest federalism
Blake Hudson

I. INTRODUCTION

United States forest policy is fragmented, both horizontally across state and local jurisdictions and vertically across federal, state, and local levels of government. In fact, it is a bit of a misnomer to use the phrase "US forest policy," since the US has no coordinated policy for holistically managing the nation's forests. Vertically, though the federal government has gained a substantial foothold over most resource management in the US, such as in the areas of air,[1] water,[2] biodiversity,[3] fisheries,[4] wetlands,[5] and toxic and other waste,[6] its role in US forest policy is limited almost exclusively to federal forests. The federal government uses only a scattered handful of voluntary, financial incentive programs to influence forest activities on other lands.[7] While useful, these programs as currently

---

[1] Clean Air Act, 42 U.S.C. §§ 7401–7671g (2014).
[2] Federal Water Pollution Control (Clean Water) Act, 33 U.S.C. §§ 1251–1387.
[3] Endangered Species Act, 16 U.S.C. §§ 1531–1544 (2014).
[4] Magnuson Stevens Fishery Conservation and Management Act, 16 U.S.C. §§ 1801–1884 (2014).
[5] Federal Water Pollution Control (Clean Water) Act, 33 U.S.C. §§ 1251–1387 (2014).
[6] Comprehensive Environmental Response, Compensation, and Liability Act, 42 U.S.C. §§ 9601–9675 (2006); Resource Conservation and Recovery Act, 42 U.S.C. §§ 6901–6992k (2006).
[7] See "Conservation Reserve Program," USDA Natural Res. Conservation Serv., accessed 14 July 2015 at www.nrcs.usda.gov/wps/portal/nrcs/detail/national/technical/nra/ceap/?cid=stelprdb1041269; "Forest Legacy Program: Protecting Private Forest Lands from Conversion to Non-Forest Uses," U.S. Forest Serv., accessed 14 July 2015 at www.fs.fed.us/spf/coop/programs/loa/about flp.shtml; "Healthy Forests Reserve Program," USDA Natural Res. Conservation Serv., accessed 14 July 2015 at www.nrcs.usda.gov/wps/portal/nrcs/main/national/programs/easements/forests; "Conservation Stewardship Program,"

utilized are unlikely to be substantial enough to forestall threats facing the nation's important forest resources in the coming decades. Federally owned forests make up only approximately 35 percent of US forestlands, while 60 percent of forests are privately owned and 5 percent are state owned. Though certain federal statutes, such as the Endangered Species Act and Clean Water Act, have tangential, case-by-case effects on private forest management, the federal government maintains no inputs into direct forest management activities on private forests. State and local governments, rather, are the primary managers of the 65 percent of forests in subnational ownership, and the regulation of subnational forests has long been considered a land use regulatory function in the same category as zoning or land use planning more generally.

A lack of direct federal inputs into subnational forest policy may not be a problem – and by some accounts may be preferable[8] – as long as state and local governments do an adequate job of protecting forest resources across the nation. Yet, horizontally, state and local governments vary widely with regard to both the types of forest policies they maintain – if they maintain any at all – and those policies' level of stringency. Most jurisdictions containing important forest resources simply do not maintain adequate forest management, conservation or preservation standards.

This vertical and horizontal fragmentation of US forest policy is likely to have significant ramifications for the future of US forests, which face a number of pressures potentially placing regions of the US on a path of deforestation not seen since the turn of the twentieth century. For example, a recent US Forest Service's Southern Forests Futures Project Summary Report ("Futures Report"),[9] highlights that as much as 23 million acres (13 percent) of forests in the US South may be lost by 2060 due to the combined effects of urban sprawl, population growth, invasive species, climate change and a shift in timber markets from the US to overseas. In short, a vast acreage of forested lands has changed hands – forests previously owned by large industrial timber operators are now owned by real estate investment trusts and similar entities. At the same time, population pressures in the South, combined with the desire to

---

USDA Natural Res. Conservation Serv., accessed 14 July 2015 at www.nrcs.usda.gov/wps/portal/nrcs/main/national/programs/financial/csp.

[8] See Adler, Jonathan, "Let Fifty Flowers Bloom: Environmental Federalism for the 21st Century" (unpublished manuscript) (on file with author).

[9] Wear, David N. and John G. Greis, U.S. Forest Serv., The Southern Forest Futures Project: Summary Report 26–31, 35 (2011), accessed 14 July 2015 at www.srs.fs.usda.gov/futures/reports/draft/summary_report.pdf.

stimulate economic growth through lax land use regulation, will see urban sprawl continue to replace important forest resources. While other areas of the country may be reforested, as agricultural and other lands revert to forests, the overall trend is likely to be deforestation on a level not seen since the turn of the twentieth century. Even if other areas of the country are reforested, the most biodiverse and forest rich region of the US, the South, will be irreparably damaged if forests continue to be paved over at current rates.

Importantly, vertical and horizontal fragmentation of US forest policy has both political and legal components. Politically, while the federal government has not sought inputs into subnational forest policy, it has not done so at least in part due to perceived constitutional constraints. Similarly, state and local governments politically are all over the board with regard to the types of forest policies they have implemented, if any at all. Yet, at least at the local level, legal concerns over state preemption may chill the development of stringent forest policies that seek to curb commercial, residential or industrial development of forested lands.

The use of the term "fragmented" in this chapter not only describes the huge number and myriad types of forest policy spanning vertical and horizontal levels of government, but is also meant to convey with normative force a view that US forest policy should be more holistic. There are clear reasons for maintaining a degree of policy tailoring and flexibility across regions of the US forest landscape. Each of the many different types of forest in the US is unique ecologically and the pressures each faces are somewhat distinct in different regions of the country. Even so, all forests, regardless of ecological makeup, are important resources – especially in the context of climate change. The strain these forests will increasingly face in the coming decades supports arguments for a more holistic national policy aimed at protecting them.

This chapter is by no means groundbreaking, but aims simply to highlight regulatory fragmentation in US forest policy and the related challenges it poses as well as to offer analysis of a number of drivers of fragmentation. The further study of these drivers can allow policy-makers to understand where to direct efforts to overcome fragmented forest federalism and to facilitate better management of this crucial domestic resource. These drivers include both institutional and political elements. Part II will first provide context by briefly discussing the two primary policy tools for managing forests. Part III will next detail both institutional and political drivers for forest policy fragmentation. Institutional drivers include constitutional federalism and the distribution of forests in the US between public and private actors, while political drivers include the political culture of certain regions of the US with weak forest policy and the historical inertia that perpetuates that culture and political predisposition. Part IV briefly concludes.

II. WAYS OF MANAGING FOREST RESOURCES

There are two primary approaches to managing forests. The first is managing the means by which forests are harvested and cultivated as a source of economic and environmental goods and services, primarily in the form of timber. Timber operations management standards are important to regulate timbering impacts on water, carbon, habitat and other environmental resources. This type of management involves crafting standards related to riparian buffer zones, stand density, afforestation/ reforestation, clear-cutting, annual allowable cut, forest road building, controlled burning, fertilizer usage, among other standards.[10] Riparian buffer zones protect water bodies from erosion, eutrophication and negative impacts on fisheries from increased water temperatures. Stand density, afforestation/reforestation, clear-cutting and forest road building standards protect against erosion, regulate carbon and protect water resources. Controlled burns protect against the buildup of forest fuel that could later spawn devastating forest fires, while fertilizer regulation protects watersheds from the harmful effects of nutrient pollution. Many forest operators, of course, implement these standards as best practices, but many do not in the absence of regulatory standards set by government.

Currently, these standards are left entirely within the regulatory purview of state and local governments, presenting a vertical fragmentation of US forest policy between federal and subnational governments. Politically the federal government has never claimed authority over such activities, and legally the question will remain unsettled until the federal government does so (though there are good arguments under the Commerce Clause that the federal government could regulate the means by which extractive forest products are cultivated and managed).[11] Subnational government forest policy is also highly fragmented horizontally, as some states establish substantial policies aimed at managing the extraction and cultivation of forest resources, while a great many more

---

[10] McDermott, Constance L. et al., *Global Environmental Forest Policies: An International Comparison* (Earthscan, London, Washington 2010).

[11] See generally Hudson, "Commerce in the Commons: A Unified Theory of Natural Capital Regulation Under the Commerce Clause" (2011) 35 Harv. Envtl L. Rev. 375.

states maintain some of the least stringent timber extraction policy standards in the world (maintaining only voluntary best management practices).[12]

The second primary means of managing forests is implementing policies that simply keep forests forested. In other words, these policies aim to prevent forested lands – whether utilized for timber or for other environmental services – from being replaced by industrial, commercial, agricultural or other developed uses. While such policies may tip the scales toward primarily protecting the environmental goods and services provided by forests rather than the extractive value of the resource – a more pure form of forest preservation – extractive timber operations may also occur on these lands. Such extraction may be intensive or may be selective in order to maximize other values such as carbon, biodiversity or water quality protection. The foremost way to achieve these management goals is through direct land use controls, such as the establishment of development density requirements, the use of urban growth boundaries or development limits lines, or other outright restrictions or qualifications on the removal of forest acreage or even on the removal of individual trees.[13]

From a vertical, legal perspective these standards are even more clearly within the realm of traditional state and local regulation than are the development of forest extraction standards, since they implicate local land use planning related to keeping open spaces free of development. As with extractive forest management standards, constitutional arguments remain available to the federal government in the private forest preservation context (and may be quite sound under Commerce Clause analysis[14]). Even so, the federal government may be even more hard pressed to claim regulatory authority to craft policies that prevent private land development and that mandate that those lands remain forested to some degree, given traditional understandings of constitutional federalism. This plays a role in stymying political action to test the federal government's legal standing to do so. In addition to this vertical fragmentation, this type of forest policy is also highly fragmented horizontally, as a scattered handful of state and local governments maintain development restrictive policies aimed at forest and other natural capital preservation, but the vast majority of state and local jurisdictions do not.

---

[12] See McDermott et al., *supra*, n. 10.
[13] See Leon County, Fla., Environmental Management Act, Ch. 10, § 10-1.101 (2014).
[14] See Hudson, *supra*, n. 11.

A number of drivers have culminated in the fragmented nature of US forest policy. These include both institutional and political factors, as described in the next section.

III. DRIVERS OF FRAGMENTED FOREST FEDERALISM

A. Institutional Drivers: Constitutional Federalism and the Public/Private Forest Ownership Divide

1. Constitutional federalism

Constitutional considerations contribute to fragmented forest federalism in at least two ways. First, perceptions of legal constraints on the federal government's ability to regulate land use planning plays a role in driving political inaction at the federal level, even if federal intervention is ultimately needed to address failure on the part of state and local governments to protect forest resources. In this context, I construe "political action" broadly, meaning that perceived legal constraints make it more difficult even to begin a political discussion on potential federal minimum standards for private forests. So in the event that private timbering or land development interests do not responsibly manage forest resources, and state and local governments do not design adequate forest management policies, constitutional federalism acts as a vertical constraint on the federal government's ability to intercede.

As with most environmental subject matter, the US Constitution provides no explicit authority to the federal government to regulate forests (except for those that it owns, pursuant to its power under the Property Clause, of course). Though the federal government could claim such authority under its Commerce Clause power and test the reach of its control, it has yet to do so. The result is that subnational forest management regulatory authority has long been considered the sole purview of state and local governments under their police power to regulate land use.[15]

---

[15] See Rose, Gerald A. et al., "Forest Resources Decision-Making in the U.S,", in Colfer, Carol J. Pierce and Doris Capistrano (eds), *The Politics of Decentralization: Forests, People and Power* (Earthscan, London 2005) pp. 238, 239; and Laitos, Jan G. et al., *Natural Resources Law* (Thomson West, St Paul MN 2006); see also *Mugler v Kansas*, 123 U.S. 623, 646–47 (1887); May, James R., "Constitutional Law and the Future of Natural Resource Protection" in Lawrence J. MacDonnell and Sarah F. Bates (eds) *The Evolution of Natural*

Private forest management is not the only resource category where there is a notable absence of federal inputs due to perceived constitutional constraints on federal control over land use. In the area of water pollution, the CWA does not regulate non-point sources of pollution in part because Congress viewed (and continues to view) those sources as state and local government land use regulatory responsibilities.[16] And this is despite the fact that non-point source water pollution remains perhaps the most significant water pollution problem in the US. The CWA also exempts a number of point sources, such as those arising from agricultural and private timber operations, due again in part to their association with land use planning. One of the most recent disputes over point source exemptions under the CWA came in the context of private forest management. The recent Supreme Court case of *Decker v Northwest Environmental Defense Center*[17] involved a dispute over whether private foresters were required to receive a national Pollutant Discharge Elimination System (NPDES) permit under Clean Water Act section 402 for stormwater channeled through ditches along logging roads. The case was ultimately rendered moot because the Environmental Protection Agency, while the case was pending, decided to exempt logging roads from NPDES permitting requirements. Nonetheless, the reaction of state and local government groups to the mere potential of federal regulation of private forest management activities was remarkable, and demonstrated the predisposition of subnational governments to maintain the fragmented

---

Resources Law and Policy (American Bar Assoc., Section of Environment, Energy and Resources, 2010), 124, 132; Nolon, John R. et al., *Cases and Materials on Land Use and Community Development*, 7th edn (Thompson West, St Paul MN 2008), p. 17.; Hamilton, Marci A., "Federalism and the Public Good: The True Story Behind the Religious Land Use and Institutionalized Persons Act" (2003) 78 Ind. L.J. **311**, 335; *Vill. of Euclid v Ambler Realty Co.*, 272 U.S. 365 (1926); Goldstein, Paul and Barton H. Thompson, Jr., *Property Law: Ownership, Use and Conservation* (Foundation Press, St Paul MN 2006), p. 967; *Rapanos v United States*, 547 U.S. 715, 738 (2006).

[16] Professor Craig has argued that "[c]omprehensive federal regulation of nonpoint source pollution would thus arguably engage the federal government in land use regulation – a type of regulation historically viewed as belonging almost exclusively to more local levels of government" and that "because of federalism restrictions, Congress cannot and has not forced states to assume any regulatory burden with respect to nonpoint sources of water pollution. Therefore, regulation of nonpoint source polluters is left largely to states' individual regulatory discretion." Craig, Robin Kundis, "Local or National? The Increasing Federalization of Nonpoint Source Pollution Regulation" (2000) 15 J. Envtl L. & Litig. **179**, 182, 186.

[17] 133 S.Ct. 1326 (2013).

status of US forest policy. The National Governors Association, National Association of Counties, National Conference of State Legislatures, International City/County Management Association and Council of State Governments filed an amicus brief[18] arguing that federal regulation of private forestry under the CWA was unlawful in part because the forest management activities in question were "traditionally regulated by state and local governments under their own laws"[19] and that "[the US Supreme] Court has held that the Constitution's Commerce Clause ... limits Congress' power to enact laws that 'effectually obliterate the distinction between what is national and what is local ... .'"[20] Consider that at issue in *Decker* was a regulatory target *indirectly* related to traditional forest management objectives (water quality) under a federal statute that primarily regulated resources *other* than forests (the Clean Water Act). *Decker* provides a glimpse into how subnational governments and private property owners would likely respond to any claimed federal authority over more direct timber extraction or subnational forest preservation standards.

Perhaps the strongest constitutional doubt cast on federal power over land use regulation is in the area of wetlands. While not basing a ruling on the precise constitutional question to date, the US Supreme Court has explicitly called into doubt whether federal regulation of isolated wetlands – those without a requisite surface connection to navigable waters – would be constitutional under Commerce Clause analysis.[21] The Court relied on precedent finding that "regulation of land use [is] a function

---

[18] Brief for the Nat'l Governor's Ass'n et al. as Amicus Curiae Supporting Petitioners, *Decker v Nw. Envtl. Def. Ctr.*, 133 S.Ct. 1326 (2013), accessed 14 July 2015 at www.americanbar.org/content/dam/aba/publications/supreme_court_preview/briefs/11-338_petitioneramcungaetal.authcheckdam.pdf.

[19] Ibid. at 15. The amici's primary argument was actually that the statute did not authorize intrusion by EPA into traditional state and local government regulatory spheres unless clearly articulated by Congress in the statute. The amici argued

> If an agency interprets a statute as authorizing federal intrusion into areas traditionally regulated by state and local governments, such as water use and land use, countervailing principles of federalism come into play that limit deference to the agency's interpretation. Under these principles of federalism, Congress presumptively does not authorize federal intrusion into areas traditionally regulated by state and local governments unless it speaks clearly and unequivocally. Ibid. at 16–17.

[20] Ibid. at 17.
[21] See *Rapanos v United States*, 547 U.S. 715, 738 (2006).

traditionally performed by local governments,"[22] and that "regulation of land use is perhaps the quintessential state activity."[23] Though forests, like isolated wetlands, have hydrological connections to interstate waters, proponents of local control over forests would argue that forests' connection is even more tenuous than isolated wetlands, and that forests are more clearly anchored to intrastate lands than are wetlands since wetlands by their very nature store and channel water that may ultimately cross state lines. As a result, any federal prohibition on the removal of forest acreage and replacement with other developed uses without a government permit, for example, would likely be resisted far more stringently than is the limited Clean Water Act prohibition on filling in wetlands, at least from a constitutional perspective.

The second way constitutional considerations contribute to fragmented forest federalism does not involve a vertical constraint "up the chain," so to speak, on federal power. Rather, there may be a constraint "down the chain," as state government displacement of local government policies looms as a potential threat to local efforts to more stringently protect forest resources. This may occur due to state preemption of local policies or failure to empower local governments with regulatory authority (through home rule laws, for example).[24] It is true that local governments face a number of countervailing incentives that undermine natural capital protection.[25] Yet even if local governments did choose to enact strict forest management standards en masse – in the absence of state or federal policies – states may very well prevent them from doing so by attempting to take back or preempt powers initially allocated to local governments under the state's constitution. Local governments are not recognized by – and therefore do not maintain any authority under – the US Constitution, and therefore must derive authority from the state. Recently, states have more aggressively taken back land use planning authority when local government efforts to protect lands from environmental harms run counter to state economic goals, such as in the context

---

[22] *Solid Waste Agency of N. Cook Cnty. v Army Corps of Eng'rs*, 531 U.S. 159, 174 (2001) (citing *Hess v Port Auth. Trans-Hudson Corp.*, 513 U.S. 30, 44 (1994)).

[23] *FERC v Mississippi*, 456 U.S. 742, 768 n. 30 (1982)

[24] See Hudson, Blake and Jonathan Rosenbloom, "Uncommon Approaches to Commons Problems: Nested Governance Commons and Climate Change" (2013) 64 Hastings L.J. **1273**, 1306–12.

[25] See Hudson, Blake, *Constitutions and the Commons: The Impact of Federal Governance on Local, National, and Global Resource Management* (Routledge RFF, New York and Abingdon 2014).

of fracking. The Pennsylvania legislature, for example, recently attempted to carve out exceptions from local zoning laws for various oil- and gas-related activities and to preempt local governments from restricting such activities through regulation.[26] Local governments in Pennsylvania challenged this preemption of their authority as unconstitutional under the state constitution. In *Robinson Township v Commonwealth of Pennsylvania*[27] the Pennsylvania Supreme Court held that preempting local governments' abilities to plan for environmental concerns related to oil and gas operations violated the Environmental Rights Amendment of the state Constitution.[28] Despite the fact that Pennsylvania citizens succeeded in preventing their state from taking away local authority to protect landed natural capital in the face of industrial and economic development, as of 2012 over 100 municipalities nationwide had banned fracking activities within their borders,[29] and other states have successfully preempted these policies. Courts in Ohio and Louisiana, for example, have upheld state preemption of local regulation of fracking activities.[30] It is easy to envision states doing the same if local governments engaged in forest preservation efforts that the state perceives will stifle economic growth and development, especially during a time when so much economic growth seems to be associated with increased urban sprawl that replaces forest resources.[31]

Ultimately, the potential legal constraints entrenched by our constitutional institutions demonstrate disregard for the complex, interconnected nature of forest resources. Private forests have historically been placed in the local government/land use planning category because they are anchored to the soil of discernable plots of land. But the role of forests in regulating climate and protecting biodiversity, water and air quality call into question our institutional division of legal authority in this area. Further, these legal constraints ignore the interstate impacts private forest management has both economically and environmentally and restricts the

---

[26] 58 Pa. Cons. Stat. §§ 2301–3504 (2012) (seeking to preempt local zoning ordinances that regulate oil and gas operations).

[27] 83 A.3d 901 (2013).

[28] See Pa. Const. Art. I, § 27 (the "Environmental Rights Amendment").

[29] Goho, Shaun A., "Municipalities and Hydraulic Fracturing: Trends in State Preemption" (2012) 64 Planning & Envtl. L. 3, accessed 14 July 2015 at blogs.law.harvard.edu/environmentallawprogram/files/2013/03/Municipalities-and-Hydraulic-Fracturing-Trends-in-State-Preemption.pdf.

[30] See *State ex rel. Morrison v Beck Energy Corp.*, 989 N.E.2d 85 (Ohio Ct. App. 2013); *Energy Mgmt. Corp. v City of Shreveport*, 467 F.3d 471 (5th Cir. 2006).

[31] See Hudson, *supra*, n. 25.

development of policies at multiple levels of government where they may be needed. As long as current understandings of constitutional federalism remain in place, forest federalism is likely to remain fragmented.

2. Public/private forest ownership divide

The second institutional driver of fragmented forest federalism is the private property/public property divide in ownership over US forest resources. States vary greatly regarding the balance of public and privately owned forests within their borders. Eighty-six percent of forests in the southeastern United States, for example, are privately owned,[32] whereas in the primary forested western states only 33 percent of forests are in private ownership.[33]

In North America in particular, forest policy scholars have found that whether forests are publicly or privately owned is a strong predictor of policy prescriptiveness, primarily because "private property rights, including the requirement to compensate forest owners once a regulation has been deemed by the courts to infringe upon such rights, make it much more difficult for governments to regulate private rather than public forests."[34] Governments, on the other hand, are more likely to make swift policy changes and respond to slighter pressures from civil society regarding the regulation of their own resources. Indeed, scholars have noted that "[g]overnments in developed countries respond to pressure from environmental activists and the community for high forest management standards by developing high levels of policy prescriptiveness, and high performance thresholds, for public forestlands."[35] These governments "can set the terms for access to [public] forest resources, impose more onerous restrictions on harvesting activities, and use more intrusive policy instruments for regulation than would be tolerated if private forest lands were involved."[36]

This has led forest policy scholars to highlight what has been termed a public forest management "spillover effect," whereby states with a greater percentage of more stringently managed public forest lands also manage private forests more stringently through a "ratcheting up" of

---

[32] Wear and Greis, *supra*, n. 9, at 58.
[33] McDermott et al., *supra*, n. 10, p. 80 tbl.3.3.
[34] Ibid. at 346.
[35] Ibid.
[36] Howlett, Michael and Jeremy Rayner, "The Business and Government Nexus: Principal Elements and Dynamics of the Canadian Forest Policy Regime" in Howlett, Michael (ed.) *Canadian Forest Policy* (University of Toronto Press, Toronto 2001), pp. 23, 33.

forest management standards. These scholars have found that "[w]here there are substantial public and private lands within a given jurisdiction, greater regulation of public lands may, over time, result in increased pressures from civil society and environmental groups for greater regulation on private lands."[37]

This dynamic could very well be at play in the US. An average 67 percent of forests in the western states of California, Washington, Oregon, Idaho and Alaska are publically owned.[38] These states also maintain stringent forest policy standards for both public and private forests on a scale of 1 to 10 developed by forest policy scholars (a "6.7" average). In addition, the US Forest Service, which owns a significant portion of public forests in these states, ranks a "9" on the scale. Meanwhile, states in the southeastern United States, where 86 percent of forests are privately owned and the federal government owns less than 5 percent of the land,[39] average a "1.2."[40] There are simply far more public forests in the West than in the East, public forest management standards are quite robust[41] and these robust public standards have seemingly spilled over onto private forests in the West. So though a spillover effect can improve forest policy standards on private lands in states with large public forest holdings, the southeastern United States simply does not maintain the critical mass of publicly owned forests that would help facilitate such an effect. Of course, as described below in parts B.1 and 2, overall governance culture, limited administrative capacity of southeastern governments, historical political inertia, and other factors also contribute to the region's lax standards. Yet it seems that the lack of the requisite amount of public lands to create a spillover effect may be an institutional driver that contributes to the status quo. And indeed, perhaps the lack of public lands in the area fosters a culture that values private interests over public interests and perpetuates the historical inertia described below.

Southeastern forests, where forest policies are weakest, are not only almost entirely privately owned, but are also highly fragmented in ownership. Eighty-six percent of southern forests are privately owned. Though 60 percent of privately owned forests in the South are 100 acres or more, 59 percent of all private forest owners own less than 9 acres of

---

[37] McDermott et al., *supra*, n. 10, p. 347.
[38] See ibid. p. 80 tbl.3.3.
[39] Wear & Greis, *supra*, n. 9, at 71.
[40] Ibid. p. 58.
[41] McDermott et al., *supra*, n. 10, p. 346.

forestland.[42] Family forest holdings in the South average only 29 acres in size.[43] This high degree of private property fragmentation makes it incredibly difficult to craft stringent forest policies, for a number of reasons. First, the government is not regulating its own resources, but rather a vast array of private interests, which gives rise to stiff resistance. In addition, the interests possibly regulated are so disparate that crafting a uniform policy in these states would be all the more difficult. If most of the forestland were owned by, for example, the top 20 industrial forest companies in the region, then the government would be working with a more uniform set of regulated entities with similar interests, goals and management approaches.[44] Under this scenario, and assuming that the government has the political will to pass policies in the first instance (a large assumption), setting management standards for forests would at least be an easier task than doing so for the highly fragmented private forests in the South.

Perhaps more importantly, in recent years southeastern extractive timber operators have rapidly divested their holdings, creating smaller private properties "subject to new dynamic forces that encourage parcelization and fragmentation."[45] This parcelization has been described as "the most substantial transition in forest ownership of the last century," and industrial forest owners actually divested nearly three-quarters of their forest holdings.[46] Waiting to purchase many of these divested forest properties were real estate investment trusts (REITs), which represent a voting block whose interests may very likely be diametrically opposed to high forest management/preservation standards, especially if development of lands and conversion from forest uses is their primary goal. REIT ownership may also exacerbate concerns regarding urbanization and loss of forest cover over the next 50 years.[47]

Ultimately, the division of public versus private ownership of forests in the United States is potentially a significant institutional driver of forest policy fragmentation. This can be labeled an "institutional" problem because while some private lands may be purchased or donated to the

---

[42] Wear and Greis, *supra*, n. 9, at 62.
[43] Ibid.
[44] This is very much the situation in Canada, which has more stringent provincial regulations. See Hudson, Blake, "Fail-Safe Federalism and Climate Change: The Case of U.S. and Canadian Forest Policy" (2012) 44 Conn. L. Rev. **925**, 959–62.
[45] Wear and Greis, *supra*, n. 9, at 62.
[46] Ibid. at 60, 62.
[47] Ibid. at 60.

public, and some public lands may give way to private rights, the allocation of public and private forests within states is a virtually immutable characteristic. This immutability further demonstrates the difficulty of overcoming horizontal fragmented forest policy in the United States via subnational government volition alone. In this way, the public/private forest ownership divide also provides a normative grounding for claims that vertical forest policy fragmentation should be overcome.[48]

B. Political Drivers

Political drivers of fragmented forest federalism include the political culture of areas of the country that maintain lax forest and land use standards as well as historical inertia entrenching that culture in those areas. I should pause here to note that it is very difficult to talk about institutional and political drivers in a vacuum, because they overlap in complex ways. In this way, the institutional drivers highlighted above may be characterized as "mostly institutional" drivers, whereas the ones below are "mostly political." There are obviously elements of politics affecting institutions and elements of institutions affecting political outcomes.

1. Political culture

The first political driver affecting the fragmented nature of US forest policy is that in areas with lax standards, particularly the Southeast, the political culture is much more opposed to prescriptive regulation. This is no doubt due in part to the high percentage of privately owned lands in certain regions of the US, as discussed in part A.2 above. Though somewhat circular, the simplest evidence of political disdain for prescriptive forest regulations can be found in the fact that most all southeastern states have no prescriptive forest management standards, even though other regions of the country do. The Alabama Forestry Commission sums up the position of most southern entities that might otherwise be tasked with implementing forest regulations when it describes itself as the "lead agency for forestry in Alabama" but "not an environmental regulatory or enforcement agency," and that it "[avoids] environmental problems through voluntary application of preventative techniques."[49] Yet the presence of a high percentage of private forests alone does not explain

---

[48] McDermott et al., *supra*, n. 10, pp. 346–47.
[49] McDermott et al., *supra*, n. 10, p. 82.

the political culture of resisting prescriptive regulation. The state of Maine, for example, contains 94 percent of forests in private ownership,[50] yet maintains a number of prescriptive requirements that are lacking in southeastern states.[51] Southern states tend to be more politically conservative and political conservatives tend to resist regulation of private property more stringently.

Political culture plays out not only in the timber extraction context, but also in the context of utilizing land use planning to preserve forests and other natural capital. Granted, the use of urban growth boundaries is sparse across the entire United States – the most notable policy of the kind is perhaps Portland's growth boundary, or those of other Oregon municipalities, like Eugene. Yet, southern state and local governments have been particularly resistant to their use. The state of Tennessee is the only southern state that requires municipalities to enact growth boundaries, and while this mandate purportedly contemplates the reduction of urban sprawl, the policy is aimed primarily at ensuring that growth occurs in the most economically efficient manner possible.[52] A handful of southern cities have growth boundaries as well,[53] with Lexington Kentucky's being perhaps the most effective from an environmental perspective. Yet other southern cities, such as Miami, are arguably preoccupied with controlling how land is inevitably developed rather than whether it should be developed or not.[54]

Ultimately, the combination of private property and red state/blue state politics plays a role in the culture of southeastern states being more

---

[50] "Who Owns Maine's Forests?," Maine Tree Foundation, accessed 14 July 2015 at www.mainetreefoundation.org/forestfacts/Who%20Owns%20Maine's%20Forest.htm.

[51] "Maine Forest Service Laws and Ordinances," Me. Dep't of Agric., Conservation, and Forestry, accessed 14 July 2015 at www.maine.gov/dacf/mfs/policy_management/woodswise/laws_ordinances.html.

[52] "Tennessee Growth Policy," Tenn. Advisory Comm'n on Intergovernmental Relations, accessed 14 July 2015 at www.state.tn.us/tacir/growth.html.

[53] "A Coastal Community Enhancement Initiative: An Approach for Addressing Growth, Land Use & Environmental Impacts in Southern Delaware," University of Delaware, accessed 14 July 2015 at www.scc.udel.edu/sites/default/files/urbangrowthboundary.pdf.

[54] Mazzei, Patricia, "Miami-Dade Commissioners Expand Urban Development Boundary," *Miami Herald* (last updated 2 October 2013, 5:10 pm), accessed 14 July 2015 at www.miamiherald.com/2013/10/02/3666008/miami-dade-commissioners-expand.html.

resistant to prescriptive forest management standards or land use planning policies aimed at protecting forests. These same cultural nuances play out in other regions of the US, whether the Pacific Northwest, the Midwest, or the Northeast. In this way culture plays a role in the fragmentation of US forest policy, as it does with the regulation and management of any resources implicated by individual activities on private property.

2. Historical inertia
The second political driver of fragmented forest federalism is the historical inertia of lax state regulation of forest management in some regions of the US and the history of the US federal government deliberately avoiding regulatory inputs into private forest management. Again, this driver plays out most significantly in the South, which stands as the perpetual example of the degree of fragmentation in forest policy across regions of the US. As described in depth below, in the first half of the 1900s the southern forest resource was so degraded that the Franklin D. Roosevelt administration pushed to prescriptively regulate southern forests. This got the attention of the forest industry, which moved in and aggressively reforested the South and turned it into a forest product economic powerhouse. With forests restored across the Southeast and the forest economy booming, the federal government backed down from intervening in subnational forest policy in a more robust way. The resulting historical status quo – whereby industry self-regulates and the federal and state governments stay out of the way – is a driver for fragmented forest federalism today. Especially given that the economic and environmental stability long afforded US forests has changed and the threats that forests face have evolved, we should be reminded of the history of forest policy in the US South and should reassess what can be learned from that history to aid in crafting a more holistic US forest policy going forward.

Whereas urbanization and climate change are the primary threats facing southern forests today, in the early twentieth century the threat was fire. Professor William Boyd has undertaken an important and telling review of the history of southern forestry since the early 1900s.[55] At that time, southern forests were exploited almost out of existence during "probably the most rapid and reckless destruction of forests known to

---

[55] Boyd, William, "The Forest is the Future? Industrial Forestry and the Southern Pulp and Paper Complex," in Scranton, Philip (ed.), *The Second Wave: Southern Industrialization, 1940–1970s* (University of Georgia Press, Athens GA 2001).

history" – a period that William Faulkner referred to as a time of "the slain wood."[56] As a result, the federal government took an acute interest in private forest management in the South, a scenario hard to imagine today. In fact, federal prescriptions for private forests were proposed as part of the solution, and the mere specter of federal regulation played an important role in forging incentive-based policies that helped states and industry make the necessary changes to restore southern forests – even if those policies were focused primarily on the extractive timber value of forests. A key tipping point in the history of southern forests was the Roosevelt administration's push to expand the federal government's role in private forest management.

Not surprisingly, given the Roosevelt administration's view of federal power on most issues, President Roosevelt and members of Congress actually contemplated that constitutional federalism, as discussed in Part A.1, would not be a constraint on the federal government's ability to curb forest destruction in the South. This is evidenced by Article X of the Lumber Code of the National Industrial Recovery Act of 1933 (NIRA),[57] which aimed to "commit ... the lumber industry to principles of conservation and sustained yield."[58] The NIRA was ultimately found unconstitutional by the Supreme Court on a number of grounds.[59] One of those grounds was the view that "where the effect of intrastate transactions upon interstate commerce is merely indirect, such transactions remain within the domain of state power."[60] This ruling was, however, during a period of narrow Commerce Clause interpretation, and immediately preceded the 1937–1995 period when the Supreme Court failed to strike down one statute as beyond Congress's Commerce Clause authority.[61] Nonetheless, President Roosevelt did not give up on his push for a prescriptive federal role in southern private forest policy, arguing that "most of the States, communities, and private companies have, on the whole, accomplished little to retard or check the continuing process of using up our forest resources without replacement ... it seems obviously necessary to fall back on the last defensive line – Federal leadership and

---

[56] Ibid. at nn 25, 26.
[57] See National Industrial Recovery Act of 1933, 15 U.S.C. § 703 (1933), accessed 14 July 2015 at www.ourdocuments.gov/doc.php?doc=66.
[58] Boyd, *supra*, n. 55, at 187.
[59] *Schechter Poultry Corp. v United States*, 295 U.S. 495 (1935).
[60] Ibid. at 546.
[61] See e.g. Barnett, Randy E., "The Original Meaning of the Commerce Clause" (2001) 68 U. Chi. L. Rev. **101**, 101.

Federal Action."[62] As William Boyd recounts, President Roosevelt further stated that the "forest problem" was "a matter of vital national concern, and some way must be found to make forest lands and forest resources contribute their full share to the social and economic structures of this country, and to the security and stability of all our people." Evoking images of "denuded" watersheds and "crippled" forest communities "still being left desolate and forlorn," Roosevelt urged the Congress to study the problem and propose legislation that would include "such public regulatory controls as will adequately protect private as well as the broad public interests in *all* forest lands."[63]

Alabama Senator John Bankhead actually organized a committee whose investigation into southern forestry "concluded that the management of commercial forest land under private ownership represented the crux of the so-called forest problem."[64] This is yet another historical statement hard to imagine today since today's southern congressional representatives are not likely to criticize private management of resources, and in fact seem predisposed to support sprawling development even if it does pose a significant threat to southern forests and their services.[65]

The Roosevelt administration's push to prescriptively regulate private forests was actually the culmination of a series of federal studies and inquiries aimed at resolving deforestation of the South and the poor management of southern forests. Gifford Pinchot's[66] 1919 report predicted a timber shortage in the nation, which led to another US Forest Service Report, the "Capper Report," assessing the potential role of the federal government in regulating private forest management. The Capper Report concluded that the South would need to *import* timber in order to sustain timber supply if the destruction of southern forests was not remedied.[67] A number of laws were passed providing funding to state

---

[62] Ibid. at 189.
[63] Boyd, *supra*, n. 55, p. 188 (emphasis added).
[64] Ibid. at 189.
[65] See Hudson, *supra*, n. 25.
[66] Known as the "father" of the US Forest Service. Paulu, Tom, "Gifford Pinchot Was Father of U.S. Forest Service," *Daily News Online* (27 June 2008, 12:00 am), accessed 14 July 2015 at tdn.com/lifestyles/gifford-pinchot-was-father-of-u-s-forest-service/article_bba03335-149a-5611-bbe4-392d0ac62eec.html.
[67] Boyd, *supra*, n. 55, at 174–75.

agencies to curb forest destruction due to fire,[68] seeking to remedy the problems caused by state and local forest taxation practices that were encouraging premature cutting of what little timber was not destroyed by fire,[69] establishing the first nationwide forest survey in order to facilitate investment in southern forests,[70] and to establish federal–state cooperative programs to resolve pest and disease problems.[71] Southern states eventually adopted special tax provisions aimed at promoting industrial forestry.[72]

These actions, of course, were all voluntary, incentive-based, or merely fact-finding efforts, and by the time Roosevelt became interested in US forests, policy-makers were engaged in a debate "centered on whether the federal government should regulate private forestry directly or assist state governments and industry through cooperative institutions and programs" – a debate which "stemmed from the growing concern among professional foresters and political leaders over the extent of forest destruction in the US during the 1910s and 1920s."[73] Potential federal regulation of private forests came about because the voluntary assistance programs provided by federal and state governments were initially unsuccessful at forging appropriate private forest management standards.[74] In yet another move that is almost unimaginable in modern times, and in an effort to "ensur[e] that the nation's timberlands would be properly managed,"[75] one federal government report even recommended a massive federal acquisition of 224 million acres of private southern forests. This is an amount 10 million acres greater than the entire acreage of southeastern forests today.[76]

The federal government never sought to overcome vertical fragmented federalism in the forest sector through prescriptive regulation, however, because layers of federal and state assistance ultimately succeeded. As professor Boyd describes, southern forests transitioned from a virtual wasteland after the Civil War to the most productive commodity forests

---

[68] The Weeks Law of 1911 and the Clarke-McNary Act of 1924 were two such laws. Ibid. at 183–84.
[69] Ibid.
[70] This was the 1928 McSweeny-McNary Forest Research Act. Ibid. at 176.
[71] This was the Forest Pest Control Act of 1947. Ibid. at 181.
[72] Ibid. at 185.
[73] Ibid. at 187.
[74] Ibid.
[75] Ibid. at 187.
[76] Alvarez, Mia, Soc'y of Am. Foresters, "The State of America's Forests" (2007), accessed 14 July 2015 at www.safnet.org/publications/americanforests/StateOfAmericasForests.pdf.

in the world. It did so through three phases of transition, which Boyd describes as rationalization, regeneration and intensification.[77]

Rationalization involved solving the fire problem so that investors would feel confident investing in southern forests. As Pinchot said at the time, "[u]nless fires are checked, forestry in the Southern pineries will never appeal to men of good business sense."[78] The statistics on the fire problem in the South are quite telling. For example, a 1930s survey found that fires occurred on more than three-quarters of the state of Georgia's *total* forest acreage. Though the South contained only one-third of the nation's forests, it led the nation in both the frequency of forest fires and in the amount of acreage burned, accounting for 85 percent of all forest fires in the country in the 1920s and 1930s.[79] A large contributor to these fires was actually the "deep-seated cultural practice of annual woods-burning" that was "part of the very fabric of rural life in the South."[80] Woods-burning effectively involved going outside and setting the woods on fire for entertainment, a unique cultural pastime to be certain.

After stable markets for investment were created by rationalization, regeneration took place, whereby degraded forests and agricultural lands were reforested or afforested. Reforestation efforts were undertaken primarily by large industrial timber operators, bolstered by federal programs that "ushered in an era of cooperation between the federal government, state governments, and private actors on matters of forest policy and management."[81] Between 1948 and the late 1980s nearly 13 million acres of southern lands were converted to timberland by public and industrial private and non-industrial private landowners.[82]

Finally, after rationalization and regeneration, intensification took the newly rejuvenated southern forests and made them even more productive through the use of scientific advances. Cultivation of pest-resistant and fast growing genetically "superior" trees was at the forefront of these advances, and the forest industry increasingly looked to tree genetics to drive forest operations.[83]

---

[77] Boyd, *supra*, n. 55, pp. 171–72.
[78] Pinchot, Gifford, "Southern Forest Products, and Forest Destruction and Conservation Since 1865" in *The South in the Building of the Nation*, vol. VI, accessed at www.confederatelinks.com.
[79] Boyd, *supra*, n. 55, p. 178.
[80] Ibid. p. 178.
[81] Ibid. pp. 186–87.
[82] Ibid. pp. 192–93.
[83] Ibid. p. 194

After rationalization, regeneration and intensification, southeastern forests became the "wood basket of the world"[84] during the "grand march"[85] of the forest products industry southward. In a 20-year span, southern forests grew from a 15 percent share of the total US woodpulp capacity to a 55 percent share, and by 1990 this share had grown to 71 percent.[86]

A lesson learned from this history for resolving fragmented forest federalism is that the mere threat of federal regulation can play a key role in turning around the fortunes of an important national resource such as forests. This threat motivated pulp and paper companies to move toward a system of conservation, regeneration and minimum standards for forest protection. Non-industrial private landowners followed suit.[87] The 1937 "Statement of Conservation Policy of the Southern Pine Pulpwood Industry" committed industry to promote selective cutting, forest restoration and fire protection,[88] while the Southern Pulpwood Conservation Association forged a motto of "[c]ut wisely, prevent fires, and grow more trees for a better South," which "symbolized the extent to which forest protection and forest regeneration were being framed in the language of *moral duty*."[89]

While Roosevelt, members of Congress and industry representatives, at least through a skeptical lens, may not have been as concerned with environmental degradation of southern forests as with the devastating economic impacts that a degraded southern forest would have on the nation, it remains an important point of historical reference that the federal government backed away from any prescriptive role in private forest policy.[90]

With this historical context we can characterize climate change and urbanization of the South as the new fire problem, and we need a renewed push to overcome fragmented forest federalism as a result. Professor Boyd's analysis of southern forest history and fire rings just as true in modern times, as urban development, climate change, invasive

---

[84] Ibid. p. 172.
[85] Clark, Thomas D., *The Greening of the South: The Recovery of Land and Forest* (University Press of Kentucky, Lexington 1984), 114.
[86] Boyd, *supra*, n. 55, p. 170.
[87] Ibid. p. 190.
[88] Ibid.
[89] Ibid. (emphasis added).
[90] Alabama Senator Bankhead's committee report "effectively marked the end of the push for federal regulation." Ibid. at 213, n. 99.

species and other threats to forests "d[o] not respect political or administrative boundaries" and these threats "represent ... a collective action problem that demand[s] new forms of coordination."[91]

Not to be overlooked, however, is that the success of voluntary assistance and incentive programs in regenerating southern forests in the twentieth century corresponded with strong economic drivers – namely, to capitalize on the role of southern forests as a crucial component of the national economy. In the twenty-first century, however, economic drivers are running in the opposite direction. With the shift in forestland ownership from the forest industry toward REITs and other land development investment groups, combined with the rapid economic growth and land development exemplified by urban sprawl, the nation is poised to lose the focus that it has had over the last century on keeping forests forested. Increased fragmentation at the private forest owner level leaves smaller players with incentives to convert forests to other uses or to sell to others who will do the same. In other words, "[t]he gains made in reforestation during the first push for federal regulation of private forests are now set to be undone, not only in the carbon storage context, but also with regard to biodiversity, water quality, and many other areas where forests provide critical services."[92]

IV. CONCLUSION

Recall the two primary means of managing forests: as an extractive timber resource and as a more pure form of preservation in the form of keeping forests forested. The current threats to US forest resources attack on both of these fronts. Many state and local governments are failing to adequately manage timber extraction in a way that preserves other forest values, which has implications for the spread of invasive species, biodiversity and habitat protection, and water quality. Other state and local governments are doing better. Many state and local governments are also failing to engage in adequate land use planning to protect forests from pressure caused by urban development, climate change and related threats. A handful of state and local governments are doing better. Overcoming fragmentation in forest policy to keep forests forested is crucial for their carbon sink potential alone, not to mention preserving

---

[91] Ibid. at 178.
[92] Hudson, Blake, "Dynamic Forest Federalism" (2014) 71 Wash. & Lee L. Rev. 1643.

the biodiversity, water quality and other beneficial environmental protections forests provide. The federal government, in turn, is not involved in either of these approaches. This is the essence of vertical and horizontal fragmentation of US forest policy.

This chapter details a few drivers for this fragmentation. Identifying each of these (and perhaps more) institutional and political drivers for fragmented US forest federalism will be critical to determining where policy-makers should focus their energy in reducing fragmentation and crafting more holistic forest policy for forests of the twenty-first century. Otherwise, this critical resource in the US is in danger of being mismanaged in a way not seen since the turn of the twentieth century and with dire consequences not only for forests, but also for other important environmental resources.

5. Coordinating the overlapping regulation of biodiversity and ecosystem management

Kalyani Robbins

What is the ideal division of power among states and the federal government when it comes to protecting biodiversity and managing wildlife and ecosystems? There may not be a single right answer to this question, but it is worth giving some thought, as the current system developed somewhat disjointedly and by chance. This chapter will review that dual development in Part I. It will then take a present-day snapshot in Part II, which discusses the various cooperative aspects of our existing approach. In Part III, we consider the potential for a more precise model of cooperative federalism than the somewhat haphazard model that organically developed and exists today. Finally, Part IV will look toward the changing climate of the future in order to spot the aspects of our present system that are incompatible with that future.

I. A REVIEW OF OUR HISTORICAL RELATIONSHIP WITH WILDLIFE AND THE DEVELOPMENT OF POWERS TO REGULATE IT

Regulation of wildlife has evolved along two completely separate tracks at the state and national levels, nearly to the point where each system operates in a vacuum. It is no surprise, then, that we see substantial regulatory overlap and little cooperation. As I will discuss further in Part III, this overlap can be beneficial to vulnerable species and ecosystems, but creates regulatory inefficiencies as well. This Part sets the stage for the remainder of the chapter by reviewing the history of this dual lineage of wildlife law's development.

A. The States

For most of US history wildlife has been regulated by the states. Our relationship with wildlife, and attitude toward it, evolved substantially over that time. Early common law, especially through the nineteenth century, held that wildlife was state property. While this philosophy still exists somewhat, it has eroded over time, beginning with the Supreme Court's 1896 holding in *Geer v Connecticut*.[1] Although the *Geer* court upheld the states' special right to wildlife, it noted that wildlife in a state of nature cannot truly be owned at all and that, to the limited extent that the state was capable of owning it, it was for the benefit of all the people in common. State ownership of wildlife formally expired in 1979 when the Supreme Court overruled *Geer* in *Hughes v Oklahoma*,[2] holding that states do not have an ownership interest in wildlife that would trump Commerce Clause authority, but rather the same regulatory interest in wildlife as they do in other natural resources.

After the initial property-based power, the next phase of state wildlife regulation turned the focus to more traditional police powers. While *Geer* conceded limited state ownership of wildlife, it refocused the source of regulatory power as flowing from the general police powers within the state. *Geer* then limited this power for the first time, stating that it was subject to federal preemption, even though there were no federal wildlife statutes at the time. This tentative and prospective limitation was necessitated by the shift from a proprietary role to a police power focus. The Court's discussion of preservation for the common good was a precursor to the concept of trust duty in relation to wildlife. That said, it appears that the primary purpose of this shift into police power was to set up the future potential for federal preemption, and as such *Geer* arguably represents the dawn of wildlife federalism.

Around the same time as this shift was pushed forward by *Geer*, the public trust doctrine was taking shape in other contexts, and would ultimately play a role in wildlife regulation. In 1892, just four years before *Geer*, the US Supreme Court had established in *Illinois Central Railroad v Illinois*[3] that the public trust doctrine applies to the states, though in that case the focus was on land and waterways. This doctrine holds that certain natural resources belong to the public to enjoy or use, and that the state government has an affirmative duty to preserve these inalienable resources for the public, effectively serving in the role of a

---

[1] 161 US 519 (1896).
[2] 441 US 322 (1979).
[3] 146 US 387 (1892).

trustee. *Geer* began the process of extending this doctrine to wildlife, though somewhat vaguely, indirectly, and via dicta. By the late-twentieth century, court opinions routinely hinged on application of the doctrine to wildlife values. In *National Audubon Society v Superior Court*,[4] the famous 1983 Mono Lake case, the California Supreme Court ruled Mono Lake a public trust resource, holding that the doctrine extends to the value of the land or water *to wildlife*. A 1980 Washington case, *Washington Department of Fisheries v Gillette*,[5] held that the state's trust duty over the fish in the state *obligated* it to seek damages against a private party damaging that resource.

Biodiversity values developed slowly. Initially state fish and game management was entirely focused on commercial value: increasing supply and controlling demand via game restrictions. Part of the problem was that state fish and game commissions tend to be dominated by hunters, farmers and commercial fishers. Court challenges by organizations with non-consumptive interest in wildlife failed to change this council structure.[6] Thankfully in recent decades we have seen an explosion of state endangered species acts, so the legislatures have stepped in to fill the void often observed at the local level. All but a few states now have such statutes and list their own endangered species for protection, which demonstrates an evolution of state priorities, and perhaps a response to the development of public trust doctrine in relation to wildlife.[7] It is worth noting, in relation to some of the points to come, that the federal Endangered Species Act (ESA)[8] was designed in a world without state ESAs.

B. The Federal Government

1. The Lacey Act of 1900[9]

The nineteenth century saw serious wildlife depletion, due largely to our consumptive focus and state under-enforcement of game restrictions.

---

[4] 33 Cal.3d 419 (1983).
[5] 621 P.2d 764 (1980).
[6] See e.g. *Humane Soc. of U.S., New Jersey Branch, Inc. v New Jersey State Fish and Game Council* 70 N.J. 565 (1976) (reversing a lower court's holding that limiting the council to sportsmen, farmers, and commercial fishers was unconstitutional).
[7] In other words, if the states have a duty, as trustees, to protect wildlife, this might lead to greater formal protections such as endangered species laws.
[8] 16 U.S.C. §§ 1531–1544, ELR Stat. ESA §§ 2–18.
[9] 16 U.S.C. §§ 3371–3378.

Responding to this problem, the Lacey Act made violations of state game laws a federal crime if the illegal game was to be transported across state lines. This allows the federal government to prosecute state offenses in some cases, which represents the beginning of our current system of overlapping federalism. The Lacey Act also seeks to prevent the introduction of non-native species into new ecosystems, making it a first small step in science-based federal regulation of wildlife, which would eventually become the norm. It may not seem like much, but it was the first federal law protecting wildlife, which is in itself a big move.

2. The Migratory Bird Treaty Act of 1918[10]

Well into the twentieth century, states continued to cling to the view that their control over wildlife was more proprietary than regulatory.[11] The Migratory Bird Treaty Act, which implemented several international treaties to protect migratory birds, was immediately challenged in *Missouri v Holland*[12] under the Tenth Amendment. Missouri argued that birds were under exclusive state control. The Supreme Court rejected this notion and upheld the Act under the federal treaty power, securing its place as the next major federal statute protecting wildlife. Because states had bird-hunting restrictions already, this was another step in the development of overlapping authority over wildlife. In spite of *Geer*'s dicta, Congress had still not exercised its prerogative of preempting state law.

3. The Federal Aid in Wildlife Restoration Act of 1937[13]

The next method Congress used to address wildlife protection came in the form of federal aid. Commonly known as the Pittman-Robertson Act, this was the first federal effort to get states to do more to conserve wildlife and habitat. The federal government had thus far asserted so little authority to regulate wildlife that it had to pay the states to conserve and restore habitat. Before this, state agencies were entirely funded by taxes and fees on hunters and fishers, who consequently had great influence. The Act introduced the first conservation-driven funding of state wildlife agency administration, which in turn led to a greater balancing of interests in state and local wildlife management. This is why conservation-based funding is essential.

---

[10] 16 U.S.C. §§ 703–712.
[11] The latter is, of course, easier to preempt, as the *Geer* Court pointed out.
[12] 252 U.S. 416 (1920).
[13] 16 U.S.C. §§ 669–669i.

4. The Wild Free-Roaming Horses and Burros Act of 1971[14]

After using the Commerce Clause, the treaty power and then the funding approach, Congress next made use of the Property Clause. Slowly inching forward in terms of overall protective coverage, the next step was to protect wild horses and burros on federal land. What makes this step especially interesting for the purpose of this chapter is the impact it had on wholly *intrastate* wildlife and state actors. In *Kleppe v New Mexico*[15] the Supreme Court upheld the statute's application to prohibit the New Mexico Livestock Board from taking wild burros, under the federal property power. This is a significant step, given the early tradition of state ownership of all wildlife within the state, which did not formally come to an end until three years later in *Hughes v Oklahoma*.[16] The federal government was able to prohibit state actors from accessing wildlife within the state.

5. The Marine Mammal Protection Act of 1972[17]

The first meaningful precursor to the ESA,[18] albeit still extremely limited in scope (compared with what would follow), was the Marine Mammal Protection Act (MMPA). Not only was it a clear and unprecedentedly broad assertion of federal power in the realm of wildlife conservation, making use of the Commerce Clause power, but it also ushered in several key statutory innovations for the field. First, it had a scientific focus, expecting the use of science in its implementation as well as taking into

---

[14] 16 U.S.C. §§ 1331–1340.

[15] 426 U.S. 529 (1976).

[16] 441 U.S. 322 (1979) (rejecting the notion of state ownership over wildlife that might enable it to keep minnows in the state, and holding that wildlife is no different from other resources when it comes to regulations that discriminate against interstate commerce).

[17] 16 U.S.C. §§ 1361–1421h, ELR Stat. MMPA §§ 2–410.

[18] There were two federal statutes for wildlife protection that closely preceded the MMPA, which were the embryonic stages of ESA development, but neither had any teeth at all. They were at best warnings of the movement toward the meaningful protections provided in the ESA. First was the Endangered Species Preservation Act of 1966, which was the first species-listing statute, but had no enforcement potential. Next was the Endangered Species Conservation Act of 1969, which increased protections for invertebrate species and restrictions on interstate commerce in listed species, but still did not provide for external enforcement. For further discussion of these pre-ESA developments, see Robbins, Kalyani, "Strength in Numbers: Setting Quantitative Criteria for Listing Species under the Endangered Species Act" (2009) 27 UCLA J. Envtl L. & Pol. 1, 5–7.

account populations and ecosystems. Second, it preempted all state laws, as had been previously avoided, resulting in a strong assertion of federal power. Finally, the MMPA represented an effort to address competing political interests: on the one hand it shifted the focus to populations and away from yield, but on the other hand it still maintained a management focus rather than one of complete protection.

6. The Endangered Species Act of 1973

Finally, the ESA was passed and biodiversity was serious federal business. The ESA was enacted in 1973 as the first comprehensive US effort to preserve biodiversity. *Tennessee Valley Authority v Hill*,[19] the most famous ESA case, told us that the Act was intended "to halt and reverse the trend toward species extinction, whatever the cost."[20] The ESA requires the listing of threatened and endangered species for protection, as well as the designation of their critical habitat, also to be protected. It prohibits "take" of individual members of a listed species by any person, and requires all federal agencies to ensure that their actions (including permitting or funding private actions) neither jeopardize the continued existence of a listed species nor destroy or adversely modify its designated critical habitat. It was the biggest and boldest step Congress ever took to federalize conservation, and had amazing potential. Unfortunately, due largely to lack of funding and partly to political pressures, the ESA is not even close to being fully implemented. In spite of an inability to administer the statute federally, there has been little effort to involve the states, other than some assistance with recovery plan management.

II. EXPLORING THE EXISTING RELATIONSHIP BETWEEN STATES AND THE FEDERAL GOVERNMENT IN REGULATING WILDLIFE

Although the ESA did not create a true cooperative federalism scheme such as we see in the Clean Air Act (CAA)[21] and the Clean Water Act

---

[19] See *Tennessee Valley Auth. v Hill*, 437 US 153, 180 (1978) (the ESA was "the most comprehensive legislation for the preservation of endangered species ever enacted by any nation").
[20] Ibid.
[21] 42 U.S.C. §§ 7401–7671q, ELR Stat. CAA §§ 101–618.

(CWA),[22] the states have not been left completely out of its implementation. Several aspects either take state action into account or even directly involve the states. This is true in the text of the ESA itself, as well as in practice that can sometimes go beyond that mandated by the ESA.

A. Formal Cooperation Requirements

First, the ESA involves states in its critical habitat designation process. It requires the wildlife agencies to designate critical habitat for the species they list as endangered or threatened, and provides protection for that habitat. In determining which habitat to designate, the Act requires the agencies to consult "as appropriate with affected states."[23] Such consultation may focus on the economic impact of habitat designation (that is, other intended uses for the land areas in question), in addition to making use of local expertise regarding the habitat needs of the listed species. Given the value of such local expertise, this is an aspect of ESA implementation that could be expanded.

Second, state conservation programs are to be considered in determining whether a species needs to be listed. Among the factors the ESA provides for the wildlife agencies to consider in determining the listing status of a proposed species is "the inadequacy of existing regulatory mechanisms."[24] This factor is a nod to state regulation of wildlife, and appears to be somewhat of an effort to avoid excessively overlapping jurisdiction. If an intrastate species is being adequately protected by state legislation, it may not be necessary to list it federally. If, however, there are regulatory gaps in a species' protection, the ESA serves to cover them. This lends to greater overall efficiency, assuming it is actually followed, and assuming that a subsequent state failure to protect would lead to prompt federal attention.

Third, the ESA requires the federal wildlife agencies to create recovery plans for listed species, designed to get them to the point of delisting. The agencies are expressly permitted to procure the services of state agencies in developing and implementing recovery plans,[25] and must cooperate with the states in developing a monitoring system to determine the species' progress toward delisting.[26] This demonstrates the legislature's intent to make use of the substantial wildlife management expertise

---

[22] 33 U.S.C. §§ 1251–1387, ELR Stat. FWPCA §§ 101–607.
[23] 16 U.S.C. § 1536(a)(2).
[24] 16 U.S.C. § 1533(a)(1)(D).
[25] 16 U.S.C. § 1533(f)(2).
[26] 16 U.S.C. § 1533(g)(1).

to be found in state wildlife agency staff. As noted in the next subsection, this is the area in which such cooperation has most occurred, whereas other areas tend to fall short of what the ESA provides.

Finally, an entire section of the ESA section 6 is titled "Cooperation with the States."[27] It requires that the agencies, in implementing the Act, "cooperate to the maximum extent practicable with the States."[28] It also permits the agencies to "enter into agreements with any State for the administration and management of any area established for the conservation of endangered species or threatened species."[29] These provisions are not about allowing the states to administer primary ESA duties, simply about cooperating as the federal agencies do so. However, following this language, the section then sets up the one provision in the ESA that appears most similar to the cooperative federalism design of other environmental statutes:

> COOPERATIVE AGREEMENTS. – In furtherance of the purposes of this Act, the Secretary is authorized to enter into a cooperative agreement in accordance with this section with any State which establishes and maintains an adequate and active program for the conservation of endangered species and threatened species. Within one hundred and twenty days after the Secretary receives a certified copy of such a proposed State program, he shall make a determination whether such program is in accordance with this Act. Unless he determines, pursuant to this paragraph, that the State program is not in accordance with this Act, he shall enter into a cooperative agreement with the State for the purpose of assisting in implementation of the State program.[30]

In other words, much like the national pollutant discharge elimination system (NPDES) program under the CWA or the state implementation plan (SIP) program under the CAA, states may design their own programs for the protection and management of federally listed endangered and threatened species. In addition, likewise following the NPDES lead, if such programs would be successful, the wildlife agencies *must* accept them. This provision had immense potential to bring the efficiency and added regulatory value of cooperative federalism to the ESA, but unfortunately little has come of it. This is largely because it fails to grant states sufficient regulatory authority to entice them to do the work; courts have struck down the state plans due to the lack of ESA authority for

---

[27] 16 U.S.C.A. § 1535.
[28] 16 U.S.C.A. § 1535(a).
[29] 16 U.S.C.A. § 1535(b).
[30] 16 U.S.C.A. § 1535(c)(1).

states to allow incidental take.[31] It would be virtually impossible to run a state ESA management program without control over incidental take.

B. Cooperation among State and Federal Agencies in Practice

As mentioned in the previous subsection, section 6 of the ESA provides for both informal cooperation with the states in the federal implementation process and formal operation of complete state-run programs to protect federally listed species. Unlike the latter, the former has led to substantial state assistance with recovery planning and general management of listed species and their habitat. The US Fish and Wildlife Service (FWS) and the National Oceanic and Atmospheric Administration (NOAA) have a formal interagency policy requiring maximum possible utilization of state-level expertise and assistance in making key ESA decisions as well as in implementing recovery plans for listed species.[32] State wildlife managers generally value this opportunity, and in a recent Article authored by two of them, listed what they see as the three main reasons that "such cooperation is essential":

> (1) States have a deep understanding of local values and attitudes toward wildlife conservation, (2) states have principal management authority for resident fish and wildlife, so they are in the best position to assess and meet the conservation needs of at-risk species, and (3) states own and/or manage public lands and provide technical assistance to managers of private lands that contribute to conservation of federally listed species. In Florida, for example, where more than 25% of land is publicly owned, the Florida Fish and Wildlife Conservation Commission has helped manage more than 5.8 million acres of conservation lands that contribute to the recovery of numerous listed species, including the red-cockaded woodpecker.[33]

---

[31] See e.g. *Swan View Coalition, Inc. v Turner*, 824 F.Supp. 923, 938 (D. Mont. 1992) (holding that, in spite of cooperative agreement provision's appearance of allowing state program to govern, the ESA's strong preemption provision prevents state programs that are less restrictive than federal program from governing, in that case applying this result to a state regulation that did not treat habitat modification as a take).

[32] Interagency Policy Regarding the Role of State Agencies in ESA Activities, 59 Fed. Reg. 34275 (1994).

[33] Haubold, Elsa M. and Nick Wiley, "State Perspectives on the ESA: A Journey of Conflict and Cooperation," *The Wildife Society News*, 28 March 2013, accessed 14 July 2015 at news.wildlife.org/featured/state-perspectives-on-the-esa/.

Unfortunately, state wildlife managers Haubold and Wiley note that the ESA retains numerous impediments to properly maximizing their involvement: implementation by two agencies with differing policies to follow; the need to obtain incidental take permits for everything state wildlife managers do that may harm an individual listed animal, even when the project is designed to improve the overall status of the species; citizen-suit litigation against the federal agencies that can sometimes get in the way of their efforts to work with the states; the bad PR that can come from state actors implementing a federal program instead of their own; and what the managers call "federalization" of species that were already state-listed and under a management plan for their recovery.[34] It is not difficult to see that these concerns could be addressed by a system that allowed a state program to implement the ESA directly (at least as to post-listing management), rather than mere state cooperation with federal implementation. It is also important to see the dangers inherent in such a transfer of power and thus the need to retain federal oversight and automatically triggered take-over.

In 2010, the federal wildlife agencies and the states created the Joint Federal/State Task Force on Endangered Species Act Policy (ESA JTF). The ESA JTF is composed of eight state fish and wildlife agency directors and eight federal agency representatives, four from each of the wildlife agencies. Among its priorities are:

(1) to define the role of states in listing-petition reviews and status reviews of species so states can ensure that their species data and staff expertise are available to the Services when they evaluate species for listing; (2) to clarify the authority conveyed by the Section 6 Cooperative Agreements that each state enters into with one or both Services; and (3) to increase state involvement in federal recovery planning, critical habitat designations, and implementation of the ESA's mandate for "Interagency Cooperation" (Section 7).[35]

The ESA JTF collected reports from 49 states and territories, with an overwhelming trend of needing greater federal understanding of states' needs in implementing the ESA. As one example, state managers, who work most closely and regularly with landowners, expressed a need for better incentives for the regulated community to conserve. Given that the federal wildlife agencies have been woefully unable to actually enforce the ESA against violators, indeed missing the vast majority of violations and thus encouraging the "shoot, shovel and shut up" attitude, it is worth

[34] Ibid.
[35] Ibid.

considering the value of some compromise and other incentives. Due to inadequate enforcement resources, ESA policy has always been about walking that fine line between overly compromising the protective requirements and being just flexible enough to avoid the level of strictness that results in nobody following the law.[36] State managers may understand these needs better than Washington administrators do.

III. AREAS FOR POTENTIAL EVOLUTION OF THE FEDERALISM MODEL IN THE WILDLIFE CONTEXT

Do we need a more formal cooperative federalism scheme for the ESA? Consideration of the pros and cons to both state and federal control suggests that concentrating power at either level can be problematic. On the one hand, there are advantages to federal authority: federal regulation can reduce the complication of multiple rules for regulated entities to follow; states have conflicting interests and may not always prioritize the national interest in biodiversity, indeed may even engage in game-theoretic behavior with one another (the "race to the bottom"); and states are not adequately equipped to cope with transboundary issues. If states had been adequately protecting environmental interests, the 1970s boom in federal environmental statutes would never have taken place. On the other hand, there are advantages to state authority: federal implementation can have greater transaction costs at state and local levels; private parties tend to be less trusting and compliant with federal government than with states (and, on the flip side of the same coin, government accountability can be stronger at lower levels); state level expertise can go to waste; centralized implementation can lead to unreliable enforcement, given the frequent change in administrations; and states can serve as "laboratories of invention," a valuable service to the national interest.

Given the flaws with either level of concentration, it is worth considering the potential for a cooperative federalism approach. This will, of course, work well in some fields of regulation and be less appropriate for others. Environmental law has proved itself a strong area for statutes using cooperative federalism. In his discussion of the value of taking a

---

[36] Clinton's "no surprises" policy, in which he provided long-term certainty of ESA compliance to private parties entering into habitat conservation plans for incidental take permits (regardless of changing needs or newly listed species), is a good example of this. There was substantial disagreement regarding which side of that line it was on.

cooperative federalism approach in the context of environmental regulation, Professor Jonathan Adler provides

> three reasons for adopting the cooperative federalism model in the context of environmental protection. First, the federal government does not have the resources or personnel to implement detailed regulatory proscriptions in all fifty states. The federal government may set environmental priorities through legislation and regulation, but much of the actual implementation is dependent upon state agencies and personnel. Second, the geographic and economic diversity of the nation requires local knowledge and expertise that is often unavailable at the federal level. Environmental problems, and their solutions, will vary from place to place, limiting the federal government's ability to adopt nationwide solutions to environmental concerns that are equally applicable to multiple parts of the country. Third, enlisting state and local cooperation in the imposition of potentially costly or intrusive environmental controls can blunt local opposition to federal mandates. This facilitates the adoption of federal environmental standards while simultaneously blurring the lines of political accountability.[37]

While Professor Adler[38] and his Law and Economics colleagues generally advocate for the "matching" principle of federalism, in which power over an issue is placed at the jurisdictional level that best matches the scope of the issue,[39] the environmental context is a good example of where that will not work, due to the national interest in local harms, as well as other complications.[40] Thankfully, as discussed in the prior

---

[37] Adler, Jonathan H., "Judicial Federalism and the Future of Federal Environmental Regulation" (2005) 90 Iowa L. Rev. **377**, 385–86; but see Stewart, Richard B., "Pyramids of Sacrifice? Problems of Federalism in Mandating State Implementation of National Environmental Policy" (1977) 86 Yale L.J. **1196**, 1210.

[38] In Adler, Jonathan H., "Jurisdictional Mismatch in Environmental Federalism" (2005) 14 N.Y.U. Envtl L.J. **130**, 157.

[39] Butler, Henry N. and Jonathan R. Macey, "Externalities and the Matching Principle: The Case for Reallocating Environmental Regulatory Authority" (1996) 14 Yale L. & Pol'y Rev. **23**, 25 ("The Matching Principle suggests that, in general, the size of the geographic area affected by a specific pollution source should determine the appropriate governmental level for responding to the pollution. There is no need for the regulating jurisdiction to be larger than the regulated activity."); Esty, Daniel C., "Revitalizing Environmental Federalism" (1996) 95 Mich. L. Rev. **570**, 587 ("Whenever the scope of an environmental harm does not match the regulator's jurisdiction, the cost–benefit calculus will be skewed and either too little or too much environmental protection will be provided.").

[40] See Zerbe, Richard O., "Optimal Environmental Jurisdictions" (1974) 4 Ecology L.Q. **193**, 245 ("[W]hile the arguments show the case for local

section, there already exists some state involvement in the implementation of the ESA. Unfortunately, this involvement is haphazard and inadequate to attaining the full benefits of a cooperative federalism system. This Part considers what sort of system might work in the context of protecting biodiversity.

A. The Standard Cooperative Federalism Approach

By "standard," I only mean to refer back a few decades to the 1970s, when our entire scheme for environmental regulation was developed nearly overnight. I am referring especially to the CAA and the CWA. These statutes provided a structure in which the federal government sets the standards for the states to implement via their own programs under the federal statutes. If these programs meet the statutory requirements, the states enjoy great autonomy in determining the details, but if the programs fail to serve the federal purposes, the EPA is immediately to step in. This is the basic structure of environmental cooperative federalism, although of course different systems can vary in the details. Robert Percival and John Dwyer explained it well in a 1995 symposium on the topic:

> The cooperative federalism model seeks to exploit economies of scale by establishing national environmental standards while leaving their attainment to state authorities subject to federal oversight. As John Dwyer notes in this Symposium, this approach is a practical necessity because "the federal government cannot implement its air pollution program without the substantial resources, expertise, information, and political support of state and local officials." ... By encouraging the states to develop their own bureaucracies to administer environmental programs, Dwyer notes that cooperative federalism "paradoxically gives states greater opportunity and incentives to undertake policy experimentation." Considerable state autonomy is preserved because most federal environmental standards established under this model are minimum standards with states expressly authorized to establish more stringent controls if they so desire.[41]

---

jurisdiction [over environmental regulation] to be strong, important exceptions remain... where there is undue political influence at local levels, where there is sufficient interjurisdictional pollution, and where technological considerations give substantially greater efficiency to larger jurisdictions.").

[41] Percival, Robert V., "Environmental Federalism: Historical Roots and Contemporary Models" (1995) 54 Md. L. Rev. **1141**, 1174–75 (quoting John P. Dwyer, "The Practice of Federalism Under the Clean Air Act" (1995) 54 Md. L. Rev. 1183, 1224).

Wildlife regulation has many of the qualities that can benefit from such a regime: a national interest in sustaining biodiversity regardless of geographic proximity to a given ecosystem;[42] a scientifically complex field, conservation biology, in which expertise can often be quite narrow, applicable to a particular species or ecosystem type; numerous state and local conflicts of interest due to the competition between habitat and other land uses; the need for different and individualized treatment of different species and landscapes, which is a tall order for a single federal agency; and a regulated community with widely varying political sensitivities that might be best addressed by their own local regulators.

B. Enhanced ESA Cooperative Federalism

To some extent, informal practices provide further unofficial cooperative federalism beyond what is designed in the statute. Because of the potential for species to be listed, delisted and listed again, coupled with the consideration of state-program adequacy as a factor in both determinations, we can effectively see a situation similar to state-program cooperative federalism such as is found in the CWA and CAA. When the state program is failing, the feds step in, only rather than in the context of a statute creating federal oversight over the state program, the federal agencies must move completely in and out of their authoritative role over the species. While this can theoretically operate to the same effect, the danger of inertia and the added transaction costs of this ESA context render it inferior to the direct federal oversight model, as there is no automatic trigger for the return of federal authority.

An excellent example of this scenario, which is discussed at greater length in a case study by Lara Guercio and Timothy Duane,[43] is the Montana gray wolf population. The wolf had been listed as endangered since the inception of the ESA, but met its recovery criteria in late 2002. In 2005, Montana entered into a cooperative agreement with the FWS to engage in the limited level of management that program permits. It was not until 2011 that the wolf was delisted and Montana was able to take

---

[42] See *Alabama Tombigbee Rivers Coalition v Kempthorne*, 477 F.3d 1250 (11th Cir. 2007).

[43] Guercio, Lara D. and Timothy P. Duane, "Grizzly Bears, Gray Wolves, and Federalism, Oh My! The Role of the Endangered Species Act in De Facto Ecosystem-Based Management in the Greater Glacier Region of Northwest Montana" (2009) 24 J. Envtl L. & Litig. 285.

complete control over wolf management.[44] As the state program's website states, its "focus will be on ensuring that Montana's conservation and management program keeps the wolf off the federal endangered species list while pursuing a wolf population level below current numbers to manage impacts on game populations and livestock."[45] The ever-present threat of federal relisting serves as a substitute for the oversight provided for in other environmental statutes. Without that threat, without the potential for renewed federal authority, there would be little hope that the state would include conservation values in the balance – *even their own explanation of the inclusion of such values expressly bases it on the goal of keeping the feds off their backs.*

In many ways, the current system of ESA federalism is in tune with the modern trend in federalism theory, in which scholars advocate for such a shared system of power in schemes they describe as

> "empowerment federalism," "polyphonic federalism," "interactive federalism," "dynamic federalism," and even "vertical regulatory competition." This movement began as a response to a dualist model of federalism premised on preserving state sovereignty by delimiting spheres of state authority immune from federal interference. Finding the task as difficult as it is fruitless, early scholars have advocated strong, overlapping state and federal jurisdiction. Some scholars have gone so far as to argue that all regulatory matters should be presumptively within the authority of both the federal and state governments.[46]

There is certainly a bit of magic to the dance between state and federal actors with overlapping jurisdiction over a problem, as well as a logic to the notion that more entities in control might result in a field that is, well, more under control. However, this informal overlap, which in the context of biodiversity just developed by chance and not by plan, creates a great deal of uncertainty as to who is really in charge, as well as a danger that nobody will be. Just as studies have shown that the more spectators there are to observe a criminal act, the lower the chances anyone will render aid (with all assuming that someone else will do so), there is at least

---

[44] Actually, it was first delisted in 2009, but the delisting was struck down by a federal judge in 2010, so the ultimate delisting took place in 2011, as a result of congressional action via a rider to a federal budget bill. The general political mess of those few years is beyond the scope of this chapter.

[45] See "Montana Fish, Wildlife, and Parks, Wolf Program," accessed 15 July 2015 at fwp.mt.gov/fishAndWildlife/management/wolf/.

[46] Adelman, David E. and Kirsten H. Engel, "Adaptive Federalism: The Case Against Reallocating Environmental Regulatory Authority" (2008) 92 Minn. L. Rev. **1796**, 1807–08.

some risk that overlapping regulatory authority, combined with inadequate regulatory resources at all levels, will lead to a failure to assert power where it is needed. Professor William Buzbee refers to this circumstance as the "regulatory commons."[47] Buzbee later points out the advantages of such a system, however, such as allowing regulators to fill implementation gaps at the other level with power.[48] Naturally, such advantages can still exist within a more formal cooperative federalism scheme.

How to design such a scheme remains a tricky question, of course, given the risk of going too far in either direction, as in too formally structured versus too loose (as it tends to be now, when not just in full federal power mode, such as with Montana's wolves). Professors Adelman and Engel advocate for what they call "adaptive federalism," which

> would allow multiple jurisdictions to address a problem independently without circumscribing their roles or strategies. This would by no means preclude interjurisdictional coordination. To the contrary, an adaptive model contemplates innovative experimentation with regional initiatives and other midlevel regimes. The point is to allow this to occur more organically based on the specific attributes of the problem, as well as surrounding political currents and socioeconomic factors. The current system of cooperative federalism relies on forced coordination mediated through the federal government over the structural innovation-oriented approach of an adaptive model.[49]

The irony is that the ESA at present arguably comes closest to being such an adaptive model, given the organic way in which completely separate and overlapping authority developed,[50] but what we hear from the states is that the federal control is too suffocating – not in the sense that they want the freedom to be less stringent, and thus not as a matter of excessive baseline oversight, but rather in terms of federal implementation authority, which tends to be exerted haphazardly at best. If the federal agencies had the resources to consistently implement and enforce

---

[47] See Buzbee, William W., "Recognizing the Regulatory Commons: A Theory of Regulatory Gaps" (2003) 89 Iowa L. Rev. **1**, 30–33.

[48] See Buzbee, William W., "Contextual Environmental Federalism" (2005) 14 N.Y.U. Envtl. L.J. **108**, 114, 115–16 ("[W]hen federal environmental action appears to be 'underkill' of what written laws and regulations have historically allowed or required, it creates opportunities for environmentally oriented citizen and state actors (such as state attorneys general) to supplement federal enforcement or challenge the legal adequacy of the newly relaxed regulatory environment.").

[49] Adelman and Engel, *supra*, n. 47, at 1830–31.

[50] See Part I, *supra*.

the ESA, it might make more sense to maintain the power structure as it is (which would be more in tune with what Adelman and Engel suggest), but given how desperately the federal government needs the states' help, and given that the maintenance of full federal implementation authority is hamstringing that help, something needs to give.

The biodiversity context may well require its own brand of cooperative federalism, which we might call divided implementation authority. Rather than a completely state-run or federally implemented endangered species program, implementation authority for each aspect of the overall program could be placed at the level best suited to it. This approximates what is done in the clean air and water contexts, but adjusted for the unique needs of biodiversity and ecosystems. The primary difference between such a system and what is already in place would be true state authority over the aspects it implements, most notably the ability to approve incidental take when actions are taken as part of a program to recover the species and will not jeopardize it. The federal agencies would still have oversight authority, but this would be administratively more efficient than requiring their approval of every state conservation action ahead of time. This would also provide substantial workload relief at the federal level, which could improve the rate of progress on the federally retained implementation areas, such as listing and critical habitat designation. And because there is so much overlap already with state conservation goals, states could more efficiently absorb this work by eliminating duplicative enforcement of state/federal redundancies. Given the retained federal oversight, along with the citizen suit provision, the states would have incentive to exercise caution in implementing their programs.

IV. CLIMATE CHANGE AND ITS IMPACT ON THE FEDERALISM CHOICES REGARDING DIVISION OF POWER OVER WILDLIFE

In addition to the traditional concerns discussed above, species face unprecedented challenges in the coming decades, a circumstance that will require unparalleled cooperation among all scales of government. Climate change is impacting biodiversity across the board. Indeed, biodiversity may well be the catastrophe's greatest victim. We have already seen relatively dramatic changes in habitat and species behavior, and it is very clear that what has taken place so far is only the tip of the iceberg. As species living within the confines of our disconnected collection of conservation lands struggle to adapt,[51] failure will be inevitable absent a more comprehensive species and ecosystem management system. We will need people whose job it is to be constantly paying attention.

One notable characteristic of the impacts climate change will have on species and ecosystems is that they are largely unpredictable. Frontloaded policymaking requires predictability and is thus a mismatch for managing ecosystems in this time of rapid change (or ever, for that matter, as even under more typical circumstances nature can be unpredictable). Nor is it ideal to operate entirely reactively, both because this ignores prevention and because policy choices may excessively fall prey to special interest influences. Instead, as many of the broader policy principles as possible should be determined on the front end – goals should be set, with initial plans to achieve those goals and various adjustments to be made in response to the range of possible feedbacks – and the implementation details managed as we go. This is the adaptive management approach, which is the gold standard for modern ecosystem management. Consider it like writing a "choose your own adventure book" for nature to play: many possible storylines and outcomes depending upon which page the ecosystem turns.

Moreover, we have begun to see shifts in the geographic ranges of many species, and expect to see such movement increase substantially if not impeded. Species are seeking out their historic climates, the conditions in which they evolved. With a warming atmosphere, one must keep moving in order to stay the same, whether northward or upward in altitude. While this can sound like a self-managed problem, it is rare that such migrations are successful. If they need to move northward, they run quickly into the upper boundaries of their conservation island, unable to cross large areas of human development (or even something as narrow as a road, for some species), even if there is any suitable habitat to the north

---

[51] See Eastering, William E. III, Brian H. Hurd and Joel B. Smith, "Coping with Global Climate Change: The Role of Adaptation in the United States, Pew Center on Global Climate Change" (2004), accessed 15 July 2015 at www.c2es.org/docUploads/Adaptation.pdf:

> Although biological systems have an inherent capacity to adapt to changes in environmental conditions, given the rapid rate of projected climate change, adaptive capacity is likely to be exceeded for many species. Furthermore, the ability of ecosystems to adapt to climate change is severely limited by the effects of urbanization, barriers to migration paths, and fragmentation of ecosystems, all of which have already critically stressed ecosystems independent of climate change itself.

of it (which there may not be in any case). If they are moving up in altitude, some may find short-term success, due to there being less human development on mountains than elsewhere, but there is a rather obvious endpoint: the mountaintop itself. Even if there is suitable habitat on a higher mountain nearby, there is no way to survive the trip through the valley in between, so the population is stranded.[52] Finally, even where migration is not impeded, a population may be faced with leaving behind certain habitat needs or encountering a new predator. Ecosystems are complex interdependent webs, no more designed to be broken apart than the organs in your body. Studies show species populations at the southern end of the species range going extinct in spite of the availability of suitable habitat to the north.[53]

Adaptively managing ecosystems, along with sometimes relocating climate-impacted populations, not to mention handling the ecosystem impacts of doing so, will require multi-jurisdictional collaboration. While much of what needs to be done will absolutely require federal standards and oversight, it simply will not be possible for this type of work to happen at the federal level.[54] State and local land managers will take on greater national importance than ever before in the face of climate adaptation. Carefully targeted exceptions will need to be made for certain provisions of both the ESA and state species protection laws, in order to facilitate the far more proactive work that must be done. If land managers working within the existing static world of ecosystem management are complaining that they face too many obstacles due to federal bureaucracy, imagine how much worse it would be to attempt climate adaptation for struggling species. In order for meaningfully responsive adaptive management to occur, and especially species relocation and coping with its aftermath, we will need all players at the table. This will require, more

---

[52] This is happening now to the pika. See J.B. Ruhl, "Climate Change and the Endangered Species Act: Building Bridges to the No-Analog Future" (2008) 88 B.U. L. Rev. **1**, 2–4.

[53] See Karl, Thomas R., Jerry M. Melillo and Thomas C. Peters (eds), *Global Climate Change Impacts in the United States* (Cambridge University Press, New York, 2009) (report to Congress by US Global Change Research Program), 80, accessed 15 July 2015 at downloads.globalchange.gov/usimpacts/pdfs/climate-impacts-report.pdf.

[54] See Colburn, Jamison E., "The Indignity of Federal Wildlife Habitat Law" (2005) 57 Ala. L. Rev. **417**, 446 ("The fact that FWS actions must take the national stage and come only in the form of fully rational, finalized 'findings,' 'rulemakings,' and the like transforms FWS's ESA work into a series of proceedings the dignity of which impedes real improvisation and learning-by-doing.").

than ever before, greater authority over conservation implementation at lower government levels, which does not preclude federal oversight to prevent harmful choices. It does require a bit less micromanagement, however.

V. CONCLUSION

The greatest problems with the ESA's structure of authority relate to inefficiencies. The current system is theoretically sound, placing authority at a level that takes into account the value of biodiversity to all, regardless of geographic proximity, but does not work in practice. As a practical matter, the states are better able than the federal government to implement wildlife management programs, and largely just need oversight to protect our national interest in preventing species extinctions. By keeping the authority for species listing, critical habitat designation, multistate regional permitting and other non-state-specific matters at the federal implementation level, but granting states the authority to fully implement intrastate programs with federal oversight, we may be able to capture more of the wasted efficiency without sacrificing the big-picture goal.

ACKNOWLEDGEMENT

A substantial portion of the content of this chapter has been adapted from my article, "Cooperating with Wildlife: The Past, Present, and Future of Wildlife Federalism" (2013) 43 *Environmental Law Reporter* 10501.

6. Evolving energy federalism: current allocations of authority and the need for inclusive governance

Hannah J. Wiseman

INTRODUCTION

Accounts of federalism historically focused on the state–federal relationship and on relatively static divisions of authority, asking how and why authority is and should be allocated between federal and state governments.[1] However, in the energy context, recent changes in the production

---

[1] More recent federalism accounts challenge these traditional notions in a variety of ways, noting shifting governmental authority rather than static authority allocations and in some cases considering levels of government beyond the federal-state realm. See e.g. Buzbee, William W., 'Contextual Environmental Federalism' (2005) 14 N.Y.U. Envtl L.J. **108**, 112 (rejecting static 'snapshots' of authority allocations and emphasizing the 'myriad' forms of interaction among regulatory actors); Carlson, Ann E., 'Iterative Federalism and Climate Change' (2009) 103 Nw U.L. Rev. **1097**, 1106–08 (explaining that iterative federalism rejects notions of static allocations of authority and of states as a 'single analytic unit'); Engel, Kirsten H., 'Harnessing the Benefits of Dynamic Federalism in Environmental Law' (2006) 56 Emory L.J. **159**, 161 (rejecting traditional notions of clearly defined and rigid allocations of authority between federal and state governments); Gerken, Heather K., 'Foreword: Federalism All the Way Down' (2010) 124 Harv. L. Rev. **4**, 28–30 (focusing on the participation of all levels of government in a federalist system, including sublocal entities without traditional sovereign authority); Osofsky, Hari M., 'Is Climate Change "International"? Litigation's Diagonal Regulatory Role' (2009) 49 Va. J. Int'l L. **585**, 592–600 (arguing for multiscalar approaches to climate problems that incorporate the competencies of many levels of government, including local governments); Rodriguez, Daniel B., 'Turning Federalism Inside Out: Intrastate Aspects of Interstate Regulatory Competition' (1997) 14 Yale L. & Pol'y Rev. 149 (arguing for 'greater attention to the relationship between the national government (which is, itself, made up of many different parts) and the range of other units of government'); Ryan, Erin, 'Negotiating Federalism' (2011) 52 B.C. L. Rev. **1**,

and transportation of energy resources in the United States have turned the spotlight toward the state and local level. These changes demand an application of modern, more nuanced federalism accounts to the energy field.[2]

A growing number of issues, from gun control[3] to school funding,[4] have drawn new attention to state–local relationships and 'intrastate' preemption. But energy development in particular demands a heightened state–local focus and a better understanding of the fluid, overlapping authority wielded by a range of government actors in this area. Energy infrastructure is one of the classic sources of 'not-in-my-backyard' (NIMBYist) sentiment at the local level,[5] and for good reason. Transmission lines are unsightly and, some believe, dangerous to human health.[6]

13–14 (describing internal dynamics of federalism in the form of negotiations across federal and state lines); Schapiro, Robert A., 'Toward a Theory of Interactive Federalism' (2005) 91 Iowa L. Rev. **243**, 285 (through 'polyphonic federalism', rejecting views of governance as being allocated in clear, hierarchical layers, and arguing that '[t]he federal and state governments function as alternative centers of power').

[2] This effort has already commenced in the literature. See e.g. Burger, Michael, 'Fracking and Federalism Choice' (2013) 161 U. Pa. L. Rev. Online 150; Nolon, John R. and Steven E. Gavin, 'Hydrofracking: State Preemption, Local Power, and Cooperative Governance' (2013) 63 Case W. Res. L. Rev. 995; Osofsky, Hari M. and Hannah J. Wiseman, 'Hybrid Energy Governance' (2014) U. Ill. L. Rev. 1; Osofsky, Hari M. and Hannah J. Wiseman, 'Dynamic Energy Federalism' (2013) 72 Md. L. Rev. 773; Outka, Uma, 'Intrastate Preemption in a Shifting Energy Sector' (2015) 86 U. Colo. L. Rev. 927; Spence, David B., 'The Political Economy of Local Vetoes' (2014) 93 Texas L. Rev. 351; Spence, David B., 'Federalism, Regulatory Lags, and the Political Economy of Energy Production' (2012) 161 U. Pa. L. Rev. 431.

[3] See Blocher, Joseph, 'Firearm Localism' (2013) 123 Yale L.J. **82**, 121 (noting a Morton Grove, Illinois gun control ban that 'survived a Second Amendment challenge, but inspired a political backlash that helped lead to the passage of preemption laws in dozens of states').

[4] See e.g. *Claremont v Governor*, 144 N.H. 210 (1999) (striking down a portion of a New Hampshire statute that contained a tax phase-in, which temporarily taxed certain property owners more than others with a goal of eventually raising all property taxes to provide equal school funding).

[5] But see Outka, *supra*, n. 2 (noting the importance of local regulation – not all of which involves bans of energy development – in informing national energy policy).

[6] Vaheesan, Sandeep, 'Preempting Parochialism and Protectionism in Power' (2012) 49 Harv. J. on Legis. **87**, 113 ('In recent decades, transmission lines have generated controversy and fear in the public's mind because of the alleged effects of electromagnetic fields ('EMF') on human health.').

Oil and gas wells, although temporary, require concentrated, noisy industrial activity, which can cause pollution and large amounts of truck traffic.[7] On the other hand, many property-owners benefit from leasing their minerals or land, and state governments tend to welcome energy development for the money and jobs the development generates.[8] Due to this intense variation in preferences, and the fact that energy is an essential resource, state–local conflicts have long simmered in the energy area, and these conflicts are fast intensifying as the United States produces more of its own energy resources. Domestic energy growth has primarily occurred in the form of large-scale renewable energy development[9] and unconventional oil and gas production[10] – both of which require infrastructure that consumes large amounts of land[11] and is distributed throughout hundreds of communities.

---

[7] See (2008) National Park Service, 'Potential Development of the Natural Gas Resources in the Marcellus Shale', 9, accessed 15 July 2015 at www.nps.gov/frhi/parkmgmt/upload/GRD-M-Shale_12-11-2008_high_res.pdf (explaining that fracturing can require up to 1000 truckloads of fracturing materials per well).

[8] See e.g. University of Arkansas Sam M. Walton College of Business, 'Revisiting the Economic Impact of the Natural Gas Activity in the Fayetteville Shale: 2008–2012,' ii–iii (2012), accessed 15 July 2015 at www.aogc2.state.ar.us/OnlineData/reports/Revisiting_the_Economic_Impact_of_the_Fayetteville_Shale.pdf (noting that '[t]he oil and gas extraction industry had the highest growth rate in payroll employment among all other industries in Arkansas' between 2001 and 2010 – raising the number of payroll employees by 116.8 percent, as compared to overall state employment increases of only 0.6 percent – and that 'taxable sales in Fayetteville Shale counties increased by 20.0 percent from 2006 to 2011', as compared to statewide growth of 5.7 percent).

[9] 'Wind Industry Installs Almost 5,300 MW of Capacity in December', U.S. Energy Info. Admin., accessed 15 July 2015 at www.eia.gov/todayinenergy/detail.cfm?id=9931 ('Wind generators provided the largest share of additions to total U.S. electric generation capacity in 2012, just as it [sic] did in 2008 and 2009.').

[10] 'Annual Energy Outlook 2014, Market Trends: Natural Gas', U.S. Energy Info. Admin., accessed 15 July 2015 at www.eia.gov/forecasts/aeo/MT_naturalgas.cfm (projecting that the United States will become 'a net exporter of natural gas before 2020' due largely to unconventional natural gas from shale formations).

[11] Denholm, Paul et al., 'Land-Use Requirements of Modern Wind Power Plants in the United States' (2009, Natl. Renewable Energy Laboratory), accessed 15 July 2015 at www.nrel.gov/docs/fy09osti/45834.pdf; N.Y. State Dep't of Envtl. Conservation, Revised Draft Supplemental Generic Environmental Impact Statement on the Oil, Gas and Solution Mining Regulatory Program 5-51 (2011), accessed 15 July 2015 at www.dec.ny.gov/data/dmn/

In the past few years, US oil and natural gas production has boomed.[12] This 'revolution,' as it is often called,[13] is driven by unconventional oil and gas resources – low-density resources that are trapped within millions of acres of shale and tight sandstone formations underground. To access these resources, energy companies must drill and hydraulically fracture wells to expose more surface area of the formation and allow oil and gas to be released from the tiny pores within the formation. The fact that unconventional formations must be physically 'cracked' to expose the oil and gas trapped tightly within their pores means that numerous wells are required – at least 11,000 new wells are fractured each year.[14] These wells must be drilled and fractured wherever shale formations happen to be found, including in population centers like Fort Worth, Texas.[15]

Wind energy, too, is booming within US borders,[16] and wind, like oil and gas, is distributed at low densities over broad areas. Thousands of wind turbines must be installed to capture the most powerful and abundant onshore wind resources found in the regions like the Midwest. In 2012, more new wind energy capacity was built in the United States than any other type of generation capacity,[17] requiring land for wind towers and turbines and new transmission lines that carry electricity to load centers – the areas that use electricity. While most of this growth was in the form of large wind farms, smaller wind turbines are also increasingly common, with a high of 10,400 new small turbines installed

---

rdsgeisfull0911.pdf (explaining that well pad sizes range from 2.2 to 5.5 acres in the Marcellus Shale region).

[12] 'U.S. Crude Oil and Natural Gas Proved Reserves' (2014) U.S. Energy Info. Admin., accessed 15 July 2015 at www.eia.gov/naturalgas/crudeoilreserves/ ('U.S. oil and natural gas production both increased in 2012, reflecting the growing role of domestically produced hydrocarbons in meeting current and projected U.S. energy demand.').

[13] See e.g. Merrill, Thomas W. and David M. Schizer, 'The Shale Oil and Gas Revolution, Hydraulic Fracturing, and Water Contamination: A Regulatory Strategy' (2013) 98 Minn. L. Rev. 145; Pugliaresi, Lucian, 'The Lessons of the Shale Gas Revolution,' Wall St. J., Sept. 29, 2011, online.wsj.com/news/articles/ SB10001424052970204831304576596770729824868.

[14] 'Overview of Final Amendments to Air Regulations for the Oil and Natural Gas Industry, Fact Sheet' (2012) Envtl. Protection Agency, 1, accessed 15 July 2015 at www.epa.gov/airquality/oilandgas/pdfs/20120417fs.pdf.

[15] See 'Gas Well Drilling,' Fort Worth, accessed 15 July 2015 at fortworthtexas.gov/gaswells/ (showing 1991 producing gas wells in the city).

[16] See *supra*, n. 9.

[17] See *supra*, n. 9.

in 2008, dropping to 7,300 additional turbines installed in 2011 and 3,700 in 2012.[18] Solar energy is also growing, leading to more demand for land for generation infrastructure and transmission lines.[19]

This growth in domestic energy development, which is likely to continue due to political preferences for energy security and a cheap energy supply, calls for a new focus on federalism in the context of energy, and a closer examination of the shifting, overlapping relationships among multiple government actors in this area – relationships that recent federalism scholarship has analyzed in other contexts.[20] This chapter builds from a nascent energy federalism literature[21] to enhance this focus. It describes emerging state and local conflicts over energy issues and explores where the impacts of energy development tend to fall. It then places state–local energy federalism within the existing federalism framework, describing how state and local governments regulate energy development through full preemption, ceilings and floors, shared authority and other authority allocations already identified in the federalism literature. Finally, this chapter explores how we will need to implement creative governance approaches to more effectively regulate energy development. It notes that most existing analyses of energy governance seem to point toward the importance of a shared allocation of authority, and the chapter thus argues that effective energy governance will require an inclusive governance 'sphere' in which private actors and state and local governments – as well as, for certain issues, regional and federal government actors – all have a meaningful voice.[22] This, in turn, will

---

[18] U.S. Dept. of Energy, '2012 Wind Technologies Market Report' (2013), 4, accessed 15 July 2015 at www1.eere.energy.gov/wind/pdfs/2012_wind_technologies_market_report.pdf.

[19] *2012 Renewable Energy Data Book* (National Renewable Energy Laboratory, 2013), accessed 15 July 2015 at www.nrel.gov/docs/fy14osti/60197.pdf (noting that in 2012, 'cumulative installed solar photovoltaic capacity grew more than 83% from the previous year').

[20] See *supra*, n. 1.

[21] See *supra*, n. 2.

[22] This is somewhat similar to Blake Hudson's approach to other governance issues. See Hudson, Blake, 'Reconstituting Land-Use Federalism to Address Transitory and Perpetual Disasters: The Bimodal Federalism Framework' (2011) B.Y.U. L. Rev. **1991**, 2037 (arguing that 'federal, state, and local governments should share regulatory responsibilities, and none should be arbitrarily precluded or preempted from addressing any regulatory target,' although noting that sometimes bimodal (clear federal–state) allocations of authority will be necessary).

require a major reallocation of government authority in some states, particularly in states where governments currently leave nearly exclusive authority over energy to a state or local entity.

THE IMPACTS OF ENERGY DEVELOPMENT

All forms of industry – indeed, most human activities – have environmental, social, and cultural impacts, although these impacts vary substantially depending on the type, duration, intensity and location of the activity. This Part discusses the positive and negative impacts of energy development and the allocation of these impacts geographically, building from existing literature on this topic.[23]

A. Costs

Energy development is in some respects unique in terms of the types of the impacts it generates and the scope of its impacts. Unlike the manufacturing of widgets or the operation of a software company, energy development must be located wherever natural resources are found. Wind turbines or solar panels must be located where there is an abundant, relatively steady flow of wind or sunlight, whereas oil and gas wells must be drilled into formations that contain oil and gas in profitable, accessible quantities. Energy development also must be located near specialized transportation infrastructure that moves energy products to population centers – in the case of electricity, transmission lines and, in the case of natural gas, pipelines. In part due to these locational constraints, energy development is often unusually intense, in that it is concentrated geographically: thousands of wind turbines or oil or gas wells are sometimes located within a town or county that has particularly abundant natural resources and is near available transportation infrastructure.[24]

The costs of energy development imposed on communities and states – costs that can be very concentrated due to the location of energy resources – vary depending on the type of development. The drilling and

---

[23] For detailed examinations of the distribution of costs and benefits, see Spence, 'Regulatory Lags,' *supra*, n. 2; Spence, 'Local Vetoes,' *supra*, n. 2.
[24] See *supra*, n. 15.

hydraulic fracturing of oil and gas wells emit water and air pollutants, generate large amounts of truck traffic to and from well sites, and are noisy, dusty and, in many neighbors' opinion, aesthetically unsightly.[25] Tall drilling rigs, although temporary, also interrupt landscapes, as do wind and solar farms when they are built on 'green fields' (previously undeveloped land). Tall wind farms have blinking lights at the top of each turbine or at least on the turbines at the perimeter of the wind farm, which are required to warn aircraft of their presence.[26] These lights can be unsightly and annoying to neighboring residents. Wind turbines also cast moving shadows over neighboring property, and in cold areas they can throw large icicles from their blades, creating a safety hazard.[27]

The duration of energy development, and thus its impact, also varies. Oil and gas wells generate the most surface impacts when they are being drilled and fractured – for a period of approximately one month to one or more years.[28] Following the well drilling and fracturing process, the operator leaves a smaller amount of equipment on site, including a wellhead to control the flow of oil and gas out of the well, processing units to separate water from oil and gas on site (if needed), and gathering lines.

Renewable energy installations produce the most impacts during the site development phase when the site is leveled and graded, large trucks carry turbine blades, solar panels, transformers and wires to sites, and the equipment is installed.[29] The aesthetic impacts of renewable energy are

---

[25] For a summary of some of the impacts, see Wiseman, Hannah, 'Risk and Response in Fracturing Policy' (2013) 84 U. Colo. L. Rev. 729. See also Wells, Dale, 'Condensate Tank Emissions,' (undated) Colo. Dept. of Public Health and Env't. **2**, 10, accessed 15 July 2015 at, www.epa.gov/ttnchie1/conference/ei20/session6/dwells.pdf (describing air pollution emissions from tanks at oil and gas sites).

[26] Patterson, James W. Jr., 'Development of Obstruction Lighting Standards for Wind Turbine Farms' (U.S. Dept. of Transportation, Federal Aviation Admin., 2005), accessed 15 July 2015 at www.airporttech.tc.faa.gov/safety/downloads/TN05-50.pdf.

[27] Wiseman, Hannah J., 'Urban Energy' (2013) 40 Fordham Urb. L. J. **1793**, 1818 n. 136.

[28] See Dana, David A. and Hannah J. Wiseman, 'A Market Approach to Regulating the Energy Revolution: Assurance Bonds, Insurance, and the Certain and Uncertain Risks of Hydraulic Fracturing' (2014) 99 Iowa L. Rev. **1523**, 1534–41 (discussing the typical time spans of well development).

[29] See e.g. Bureau of Land Mgmt., 'Final Programmatic Environmental Impact Statement on Wind Energy Development on BLM-Administered Lands in

somewhat longer lasting than those of oil and gas development, however, as solar and wind farms sometimes operate for a period of 30 years or longer.[30] While oil and gas wells have some equipment on site during what can be a decades-long production process,[31] much of this equipment is less intrusive from an aesthetic perspective than, say, a tall wind tower and turbine.

The transportation infrastructure required for both fossil fuels and renewable energy also has long-lasting impacts. Natural gas requires 'compressor stations' to compress the gas and transport it long distances through pipelines, and these stations are noisy and emit air pollution.[32] Utility-scale renewable energy, unlike small-scale distributed renewable energy on rooftops and in parking lots and back yards, requires unsightly electric transmission lines and transformers to step up and step down voltages. Both buried pipelines for oil and gas and aboveground transmission lines for electricity fragment valuable habitat,[33] produce safety hazards,[34] and kill wildlife[35] or interrupt wildlife migration and breeding patterns.[36]

---

the Western United States, Executive Summary at ES-5–ES-8,' (2005) accessed 15 July 2015 at www.windeis.anl.gov/documents/fpeis/maintext/Vol1/Vol1Exec Sum.pdf (summarizing the likely environmental impacts).

[30] 'Element Power,' accessed 15 July 2015 at www.elpower.com/wind (estimating that '[a] typical wind farm's useful life is 30 years').

[31] After a well has been drilled and completed and enters the production phase, a several-foot-tall 'Christmas tree' remains on site to control the flow of oil and/or gas out of the well. Additionally, several tanks may remain on site to hold water that is produced from the well over time with oil and gas, and on-site processing equipment separates water from oil and gas.

[32] See Alamo Area Council of Governments, 'Oil and Gas Emission Inventory Improvement Plan, Eagle Ford, Technical Proposal' (2012), 7-1, accessed 15 July 2015 at www.aacog.com/DocumentCenter/View/8286.

[33] See e.g. Jankowitz, Rachel, New Mexico Dept. of Game and Fish, 'Oil and Gas Development Guidelines: Conserving New Mexico's Wildlife Habitat and Wildlife' (2007) 8 (noting habitat fragmentation from oilfield development); New Mexico Dept. of Game and Fish, 'Conservation Habitat Handbook, Recommendations to Minimize Adverse Impacts of Wind Energy Development on Wildlife' (2012), accessed 15 July 2015 at www.wildlife.state.nm.us/ conservation/habitat_handbook/documents/WindEnergyGuidelines.htm (noting habitat fragmentation from wind farms).

[34] 'Oil and Gas Extraction,' Occupational Safety and Health Admin., accessed 15 July 2015 at www.osha.gov/SLTC/oilgaswelldrilling/ (listing safety and health hazards); 'Green Job Hazards: Wind Energy,' Occupational Safety and Health Admin., accessed 15 July 2015 at www.osha.gov/dep/greenjobs/wind energy.html.

These many costs of energy development vary in their geographic scope and thus affect different groups of people and levels of government in different ways. The costs are most burdensome to the people who live closest to the energy infrastructure, and they therefore most powerfully impact communities – homeowners and renters, neighborhoods and local governments such as towns, boroughs, townships and cities.[37] Individuals who live near energy infrastructure see it, hear it, and sometimes smell it (in the case of oil and gas development) every day, at times experiencing direct pollution impacts from spills and other events. Local governments shoulder direct costs in the form of road damage from heavy trucks carrying renewable energy infrastructure or drilling and fracturing materials to and from sites.[38] During the most intense phases of energy development, they also experience heightened demands for emergency and fire services, housing, food and other supplies, and court services, among other public services.[39] Investment in infrastructure and services for energy workers can then be left stranded when workers leave, contributing to detrimental boom and bust cycles at the local level.

---

[35] See Ramirez, Pedro Jr., U.S. Fish & Wildlife Service, 'Reserve Pit Management: Risks to Migratory Birds' (2009), accessed 15 July 2015 at www.fws.gov/mountain-prairie/contaminants/documents/reservepits.pdf; Robbins, Kalyani, 'Awakening the Slumbering Giant' (2013) 63 Case W. Res. L. Rev. 1143 (describing the wildlife impacts of oil and gas development).

[36] See U.S. Fish & Wildlife Service, Briefing Paper: 'Prairie Grouse Leks and Wind Turbines: U.S. Fish and Wildlife Service Justification for a 5-Mile Buffer from Leks; Additional Grassland Songbird Recommendation' (2004), accessed 15 July 2015 at www.fws.gov/southwest/es/oklahoma/documents/te_species/wind%20power/prairie%20grouse%20lek%205%20mile%20public.pdf.

[37] See Spence, 'Regulatory Lags,' *supra*, n. 2, at 492 (concluding that 'most of the externalities of fracking are experienced locally' after examining a range of impacts).

[38] Local Road Research Bd., 'Estimating the Traffic Impact on County Roads from Wind Turbine Construction' (2013) Minn. Dept. of Transportation, accessed 15 July 2015 at www.dot.state.mn.us/research/TS/2012/2012 RIC11TS.pdf; Abramzon, Shmuel et al., 'Estimating the Consumptive Use Costs of Shale Natural Gas Extraction on Pennsylvania Roadways, J. Infrastructure Systems' 10.1061/(ASCE)IS.1943-555X.0000203, 06014001 (2014).

[39] See e.g. Williston Economic Development, Williston Impact Statement 2014, accessed 15 July 2015 at www.willistondevelopment.com/usrimages/Williston_Impact_Statement.pdf (describing heightened demands for infrastructure and services largely due to development of the Bakken Shale).

States, to some degree, also shoulder similar burdens of energy development. To the extent that services and infrastructure used by energy workers are funded by states, these costs rise as workers move in. Some environmental impacts can also be statewide in scope or even move beyond state borders, creating regional and federal concerns. For example, large spills of diesel from construction equipment can enter ground or surface water depending on where the spills occur,[40] certain types of air pollution can travel within states or interstate,[41] and blowouts (explosions) of wells during fracturing have sent fracturing chemicals into rivers that flow interstate.[42] For the most part, though, it appears that states may experience more benefits of energy development than costs,[43] leaving communities to shoulder many of the negative effects of development.

B. Benefits

Energy development, although generating substantial nuisances and costs locally, statewide, and sometimes regionally and federally, also has large positive effects at all of these levels. Locally, fossil fuel and renewable-based development produce income in the form of property taxes[44] (unless land with energy improvements receives property tax exemptions, as it sometimes does), sales taxes paid by workers who move into the area,[45] and, in some cases, direct payments or donations from industry to the town in the form of money, wastewater treatment, parks or other

---

[40] See Dana and Wiseman, *supra*, n. 28, at 1542–43, 1545 (providing examples of spills); Wiseman, *supra*, n. 25, at 794–96, 799–800.

[41] See e.g. Wells, *supra*, n. 25, at 10 (explaining that in the Denver area ozone nonattainment area, which includes nine counties and approximately 11,000 square miles of land, emissions of pollutants from condensate tanks at oil and gas sites were the largest contributor to ozone problems in the area in 2008).

[42] 'AG Gansler Secures Funding to Safeguard Susquehanna Water Quality,' Maryland Att'y General, 14 June 2012, accessed 15 July 2015 at www.oag.state.md.us/Press/2012/061412.html (describing a well blowout during fracturing, which sent chemicals into the tributary of an interstate river).

[43] For a detailed discussion of the allocation of costs and benefits, see Spence, 'Local Vetoes,' *supra*, n. 2; Spence, 'Regulatory Lags,' *supra*, n. 2.

[44] See e.g. Shale Public Finance, 'Eagle Ford Boosts Government Revenue Across Southern Texas,' Duke University, accessed 15 July 2015 at sites.duke.edu/shalepublicfinance/2014/01/17/eagle-ford-boosts-government-revenue-across-southern-texas/ (noting that 'revenues from property taxes have increased dramatically in DeWitt County,' which hosts oil production).

[45] See e.g. Shale Public Finance, 'Wyoming Counties See Large Revenue Growth, Cities Less So As Production Grows,' Duke University, accessed 15 July

public infrastructure.[46] Individual landowners also benefit from leasing their property to energy developers and receiving up-front bonuses and longer-term royalty income.[47] States, too, benefit from certain taxes generated from workers buying goods and landowners receiving lease income, as well as jobs created by the development (although many jobs are out-of-state). Some states also encourage in-state production of the infrastructure required for energy development by streamlining the permitting process for wind turbine manufacturing plants, for example, or providing tax breaks for such businesses.[48] These initiatives can create lasting jobs and income if leveraged effectively. Regionally and nationally, the United States benefits from increased income and job growth and 'energy security,' although, in a global energy market, it is difficult for any one nation to be truly energy independent.

II. FITTING ENERGY GOVERNANCE WITHIN EXISTING FEDERALISM FRAMEWORKS

With an understanding of the impacts of energy development, one can begin to assess whether existing governance schemes meet various governance goals, such as avoiding races to the bottom, maximizing utility, or equitably distributing costs. This Part explores existing allocations of authority over energy development within various federalism frameworks, setting the stage for a normative analysis in Part III.

2015 at sites.duke.edu/shalepublicfinance/2013/12/03/wyoming-counties-cities-largely-pleased-by-shales-fiscal-effect/ (describing revenues from a sales and use tax in Sweetwater County, which hosts natural gas production).

[46] See e.g. Christine Peterson, 'New water treatment facility would be first in Wyoming,' Casper Star Tribune, Dec. 18, 2013, accessed 2 September 2015 at http://trib.com/business/energy/new-water-treatment-facility-would-be-first-in-wyoming/article_93381566-fde7-5892-91f8-50d15444b10e.html (describing an energy company's contribution to a water treatment plant in an area in Wyoming that has hosted oil and gas production).

[47] See 'A Landowner's Guide to Leasing Land in Pennsylvania,' Penn State Extension (2013), 3, accessed 15 July 2015 at pubs.cas.psu.edu/FreePubs/pdfs/ua448.pdf ('Many landowners are realizing significant income by leasing their property to gas companies for exploration and drilling').

[48] See e.g. 'Economic Development Guide for Wind Energy in Oklahoma,' Oklahoma Dept. of Commerce, accessed 2 September 2015 at digitalprairie.ok.gov/cdm/ref/collection/stgovpub/id/16394 (describing tax breaks for manufacturers and the 'Fast Forward' program that makes the permitting process for manufacturing facilities easier).

A. The Division of Governmental Authority

This Part focuses on state–local relationships in energy because this is where most energy governance occurs,[49] but it is important to note that federal and certain regional actors are also involved in energy governance. For example, the Endangered Species Act prohibits all private actors from 'taking' an endangered species, and this impacts all types of private development.[50] Both oil and gas operators and renewable energy developers also must obtain a permit under the Clean Water Act before grading and disturbing sites of a certain size, although oil and gas operators enjoy some exemptions from this requirement.[51] The permit requires certain measures to reduce erosion and sedimentation from sites. Further, in some parts of the country, regional entities also play a role in energy regulation. The Susquehanna River Basin Commission, a group of states in the Appalachian region, governs all water withdrawals for hydraulic fracturing within its watershed, requiring operators to obtain a permit prior to withdrawing water and to maintain a minimum flow of water in streams during withdrawals in order to avoid harming aquatic species.[52]

At the state and local level, authority over energy development is rarely divided neatly between governments. This is in part because the governed activity is so broad in nature, spanning from the siting of wells, generation infrastructure, pipelines and transmission lines, and oil or gas processing plants to the regulation of environmental risks. Certain state–local arrangements for energy development, however, resemble

---

[49] See e.g. Nolon & Gavin, *supra*, n. 2, at 1000–13 (describing federal exemptions and explaining that most regulation occurs at the state and local level); Wiseman, Hannah J., 'Regulatory Adaptation in Fractured Appalachia' (2010) 21 Vill. Envtl L.J. **229**, 243–47 (discussing some of the exemptions).

[50] See Robbins, *supra*, n. 35 (describing the application of the Endangered Species Act to oil and gas development).

[51] 33 U.S.C. § 402(l) (Westlaw 2011); Envtl. Protection Agency, Regulation of Oil and Gas Construction Activities (9 March 2009) accessed 15 July 2015 at cfpub.epa.gov/npdes/stormwater/oilgas.cfm.

[52] See Susquehanna River Basin Comm'n Info. Sheet, 'Natural Gas Well Development in the Susquehanna River Basin' (2013), accessed 15 July 2015 at www.srbc.net/programs/docs/NaturalGasInfoSheetJan2013.PDF (describing water withdrawal permitting requirements). These regional approaches represent aspects of horizontal federalism. See Erbsen, Allan, 'Horizontal Federalism' (2008) 93 Minn. L. Rev. 493; Hall, Noah D., 'Toward a New Horizontal Federalism: Interstate Water Management in the Great Lakes Region' (2006) 77 U. Colo. L. Rev. 405.

models that have been identified in the federal–state context, such as William Buzbee's 'four preemption forms' that include 'no federal regulation,'[53] 'complete displacement of state regulation'[54] and floor and ceiling preemption, through which states may implement more protective or stringent regulations above a federal floor or may only implement less stringent standards below a federal ceiling.[55]

1. No state regulation, varied local standards

For certain aspects of energy development, some states leave nearly all government authority at the local level, providing no guiding top-down standard. This is often the case for the siting of energy generation infrastructure, such as wind farms or oil and gas wells. States like Texas, Oklahoma and Kansas, for example, allow local governments to determine where renewable energy infrastructure will be built, if at all.[56] Indeed, the Kansas Supreme Court has allowed full municipal bans on large wind turbines,[57] and the New York courts have done the same for oil and gas development when local governments ban this development using their land use authority.[58]

Other states also leave certain regulation of the operations of energy infrastructure to local governments to regulate. Local governments might limit the times during which drilling and fracturing may occur, for example,[59] the maximum permitted decibel level near wind farms or oil

---

[53] Buzbee, William, 'Asymmetrical Regulation: Risk, Preemption, and the Floor/Ceiling Distinction' (2007) 82 N.Y.U. L. Rev. **1547**, 1561.
[54] Ibid. at 1561.
[55] Ibid. at 1564–76.
[56] See Wiseman, Hannah et al., 'Formulating a Law of Sustainable Energy: The Renewables Component' (2011) 28 Pace Envtl. L. Rev. 827 (describing how these states have left decision-making to local governments for wind and solar); Bd. of Cty. Commissioners of Santa Fe County, Ord. No. 2008-19, accessed 16 July 2015 at www.santafecountynm.gov/userfiles/SFCOrdinance2008_19.pdf (showing a detailed local ordinance for oil and gas wells in New Mexico); Fort Worth, Texas, Ord. No. 18449-02-2009, accessed 16 July 2015 at fortworth texas.gov/uploadedFiles/Gas_Wells/090120_gas_drilling_final.pdf (showing this type of ordinance in Texas).
[57] *Zimmerman v Bd. of County Commissioners*, 289 Kan. 926 (2009).
[58] *Wallach v Town of Dryden*, 23 N.Y.3d 728 (N.Y. Ct App. 2014).
[59] See e.g. Fort Worth, Texas, Ord. No. 18449-02-2009, *supra*, n. 56, at § 15-42(B)(2) (prohibiting fracturing at night, with the exception of allowing the fracturing flowback process, in which the injected substances flow back out of the well, to occur at night); ibid. at § 15-42(B)(6) (limiting well workover operations to daytime hours). Note, however, that Texas has preempted most new local regulation of oil and gas development. See Tex. H.B. No. 40 at 1-3,

and gas wells[60] and the types of equipment that must be used during energy development operations.[61]

2. Uniform state standards with limited local regulation

On the opposite side of the authority allocation spectrum, some state governments fully or almost fully preempt local authority over certain aspects of energy development. In the siting context, some states provide a centralized siting process for large energy infrastructure such as large wind and solar farms.[62] Although local governments may often participate in the siting decision, and existing land use requirements may

---

enrolled version (2015), accessed September 2, 2015 at www.capitol.state.tx.us/tlodocs/84R/billtext/pdf/HB00040F.pdf.

[60] See e.g. Fort Worth, Texas, Ord. No. 18449-02-2009, *supra*, n. 56, at § 15-42(B)(2) (prohibiting drilling or equipment operations that cause noise at nearby properties to exceed ambient noise levels by more than five decibels during the day and three decibels at night, and prohibiting the noise from fracturing from exceeding ambient noise levels by more than ten decibels during the day); Howard County, Nebraska Planning and Zoning Regulation at § 4(c), accessed 16 July 2015 at www.howardcounty.ne.gov/pdfs/planning_zoning/zoning_regulations.pdf ('Small wind energy systems shall not exceed 60 dBA, as measured at the closest neighboring inhabited dwelling unit.'); ibid. at § 7(8)(a) (limiting noise to 50 dBA for large, commercial wind turbines).

[61] See Fort Worth, Texas, Ord. No. 18449-02-2009, *supra*, n. 56, at § 15-42(A)(25); Arlington, Texas, Ord. No. 11-068, at § 7.01 (A)(21), accessed 16 July 2015 at www.arlingtontx.gov/planning/pdf/Gas_Wells/Gas_Drilling_and_Production_Ordinance.pdf (both requiring exhaust mufflers); Howard County, Nebraska, *supra*, n. 60, at § 7(1)(c) (requiring commercial wind energy systems to be 'installed with a tubular, monopole type tower').

[62] See e.g. Minn. Stats. Annotated § 216F.07 (Westlaw 2014) ('The site permit [for large wind energy conversion systems] supersedes and preempts all zoning, building, or land use rules, regulations, or ordinances adopted by regional, county, local, and special purpose governments.'); Rev. Code Wash. § 80.50.040(1) (Westlaw 2014) (giving the state Energy Facility Site Evaluation Council the power to 'receive applications for energy facility locations'); Rev. Code Wash. § 80.50.110(2) (Westlaw 2014) ('The state hereby preempts the regulation and certification of the location, construction, and operational conditions of certification' of certain energy facilities.); Wyo. Stat. 35-12-106 (Westlaw 2014) (requiring a state-issued industrial siting permit for the construction of an industrial facility, including power plant projects of a certain size); Wyo. Stat. 35-12-115 (Westlaw 2014) (prohibiting other state agencies and local governments from imposing any additional requirements for facility 'construction, operation, or maintenance' after the state permit issues).

impact the state decision,[63] the siting certificate issued by the state – aside from certain building permits and engineering approvals – is the sole document needed to construct generation infrastructure. Some states provide similar preemption for the siting of electric transmission lines, oil pipelines and intrastate natural gas pipelines.[64] For oil and gas wells, Pennsylvania attempted similar, full preemption of local authority over the location of wells, requiring municipalities in the state to allow natural gas wells in all land use zones, including residential zones, while providing certain minimum setback requirements and other environmental regulations.[65] The Pennsylvania Supreme Court struck down this decision under the environmental rights and public trust provision of the Pennsylvania constitution, however, finding that the law failed to adequately protect natural resources held in trust by the Commonwealth for its citizens.[66]

Finally, many states also preempt local regulation of certain operational and technological aspects of energy development. For example,

---

[63] Cf. Wyoming Dept. of Envtl. Quality, Rules and Regulations of the Industrial Siting Council, Ch. 1, § 9(i)(i), accessed 16 July 2015 at deq.state.wy.us/isd/downloads/Chapter%201.pdf (requiring that applicants for an Industrial Siting Certificate submit information on 'whether or not the use of the land by the industrial facilities is consistent with state, intrastate, regional, county and local land use plans, if any'); Wash. Admin. Code § 463-28-070 (allowing Washington's Energy Facility Site Evaluation Council to preempt local regulations that are inconsistent with a project but requiring that the Council include 'conditions in the draft certification agreement which consider state or local governmental or community interests').

[64] See Klass, Alexandra B., 'Takings and Transmission' (2013) 91 N.C. L. Rev. **1079**, 1101, n. 134 (explaining that in some states, like Ohio, 'the PUC has exclusive authority over transmission lines above a specified kV capacity and length'); Ohio Rev. Code § 4906.01 (Westlaw 2014) (defining gas pipelines greater than 500 feet in length and greater than nine inches in outside diameter as a '[m]ajor utility facility'); Ohio Rev. Code § 4906.13 (Westlaw 2014) (providing that '[n]o public agency or political subdivision of this state may require any approval, consent, permit, certificate, or other condition for the construction or initial operation of a major utility facility'; only the Ohio Power Siting Board has this authority); 220 Ill. Compiled Stats. Annotated 5/15-401 (Westlaw 2014) (providing for licensing of pipelines by a state commission, although requiring that the commission consider impacts on affected 'local governmental units').

[65] 58 Pa.C.S.A. § 3304 (b)(5) (Westlaw 2014) (effective 2012, held unconstitutional 2013).

[66] *Robinson Twp. v Commonwealth*, 83 A.3d 901, 979-82 (Pa. 2013).

some states prohibit local governments from regulating the construction and operation of oil and gas wells.[67]

3. Shared state–local authority through floors and ceilings

For the operation of energy infrastructure, many states alternatively provide minimum regulatory standards and allow local governments to regulate more stringently above this statewide floor. Texas, for example, requires certain types of casing for wells and construction standards for pits,[68] but many local governments add more stringent requirements – mandating the use of tanks rather than pits for wastes, for example.[69] In 2015 Texas preempted most new local government regulation of oil and gas development, although it allowed local governments that had regulated this development for at least five years without prohibiting oil and gas development to continue regulating.[70] Minnesota, although superseding local siting authority over large wind systems above a certain capacity,[71] allows counties to implement more stringent standards than state standards contained in permits or rules.[72] Wisconsin, in contrast, has regulatory ceilings for wind energy development, providing a standard of maximum stringency for allowed decibel levels near wind farms, for

---

[67] See e.g. N.Y. Envtl. Conservation L. § 23-0303 (Westlaw 2014) (providing that '[t]he provisions of this article shall supersede all local laws or ordinances relating to the regulation of the oil, gas and solution mining industries'); *Wallach v Town of Dryden*, 23 N.Y.3d 728, 750 (N.Y. Ct App. 2014) (defining regulation of oil and gas to apply to the 'technical and operational aspects of oil and gas activities across the state' and not the zoning of these industries); Ohio Rev. Code § 1509.02 (Westlaw 2014) (providing 'uniform statewide regulation ... with respect to all aspects of the locating, drilling, well stimulation, completing, and operating of oil and gas wells within this state, including site construction and restoration, permitting related to those activities, and the disposal of wastes from those wells'); *State ex rel. Morrison v Beck Energy Corp.*, 2015 WL 687475 at *9 (Oh. Feb. 17, 2015) (interpreting this language to preempt local bonding and permitting requirements, not just the technical aspects of oil and gas development).

[68] 16 Tex. Admin. Code § 3.8 (d)(2), (d)(4) (Westlaw 2014).

[69] See e.g. Dallas Ordinance 29228 § 51A-12.204 (d)(5)(A) (2013), accessed 16 July 2015 at envirocenter.yale.edu/uploads/13 2139%20Dallas%20Gas%20Drilling%20Ordinance%20%282013%29.pdf ('Only closed-loop [pitless] drilling fluid systems are permitted.').

[70] Tex. H.B. No. 40, *supra* note 59.

[71] Minn. Stat. Ann. § 216F.07 (Westlaw 2014).

[72] Minn. Stat. Ann. § 216F.081 (Westlaw 2014).

example, but allowing municipalities to implement less stringent standards.[73] More stringent standards are permitted only in limited circumstances.[74] New Hampshire has a similar ceiling for small wind energy systems, prohibiting local governments from requiring that the systems be set back from property lines by more than 150 times the height of the system, '[s]etting a noise level limit lower than 55 decibels' and '[s]etting electrical or structural design criteria that exceed applicable state, federal, or international building or electrical codes or laws.'[75]

4. Hybrid and shifting allocations of authority

Many allocations of authority over energy development fall between the somewhat clear categories of full local authority, full state authority, or ceilings or floors. This is particularly true for the siting of energy infrastructure. These allocations of authority often involve collaborative frameworks in which states and local governments share regulatory space and work toward a joint governance solution.[76] Oregon provides a state-centric siting process for large renewable energy installations but requires a certification during this process that the siting complies with local zoning, and local officials participate in siting decisions led by the state.[77] Florida has a similar process for all thermal power plants of a certain size. Developers of the plant must obtain a state siting certificate as well as a land use consistency determination from the local government certifying that the plant complies with existing zoning and other local land use standards.[78] Similarly, some states issue the permit to drill an oil or gas well – a permit that typically specifies the location of the

---

[73] Wisconsin Stat. § 66.041 (Westlaw 2014).
[74] See Wisconsin Stat. § 66.041 (Westlaw 2014) (allowing more stringent local standards for wind turbines only when, *inter alia*, they are needed to protect public health and safety).
[75] N.H. Rev. Stat. § 674:63 (Westlaw 2014).
[76] Erin Ryan constructed the theoretical framework for this type of federalism. *See* Ryan, *supra*, n. 2.
[77] Oregon. Rev. Stat. § 469.401 (Westlaw 2014) (providing that after the issuance of a state site certificate for a power plant, the 'only issue to be decided' by any government or agency is whether the facility complies with the certificate terms, but allowing local governments to address issues not in the permit, including building code compliance); Oregon Rev. Stat. § 469.378 (Westlaw 2014) (providing for a determination of facility compliance with local land use requirements).
[78] Fla. Stats. Annotated § 403.50665 (Westlaw 2014).

well – but allow municipalities to exert certain zoning authority that influences the permitted location.[79]

B. Other Actors in the Energy Governance Process

A number of additional actors play important roles within the state and local governance processes described above, and these actors influence the governance process and sometimes fill in gaps. Some governments, for example, leave certain operational aspects of energy development to private standards. Some local governments require wind tower and turbine construction to meet international, industry-developed consensus standards in addition to state standards.[80] And some states require the cement that secures casing within an oil or gas well to meet a minimum American Petroleum Institute specification.[81]

In other cases, industry is beginning to voluntarily fill certain gaps in governance. The Center for Sustainable Shale Development, a collaboration between industry actors and environmental groups in the Northeast,[82] provides 15 performance standards for drilling and hydraulic

---

[79] See e.g. Tex. Admin. Code § 3.5(c) (Westlaw 2014) (allowing the commencement of drilling only after a permit to drill, deepen, plug back, or reenter a well has been granted by the Railroad Commission of Texas); Dallas Ordinance 29228, *supra*, n. 69, at § 1(B) (allowing oil and gas wells in all zoning districts only if the wells have received a special use permit (SUP) from the city); *supra*, n. 67 (describing the New York system, in which the state regulates oil and gas operations but municipalities can exercise zoning authority over wells). But see Tex. H.B. 40, *supra* note 59 (preempting most new local regulation of oil and gas development).

[80] See e.g. Kittitas County Code (Washington) § 17.61B.050 (7)(b), accessed 16 July 2015 at www.co.kittitas.wa.us/boc/countycode/title17.aspx#Chapter_17.61B ('All SWES [small wind energy systems] shall comply with all applicable sections of the Washington State Building Code and adopted International Building Codes.').

[81] See e.g. 25 Pa. Code § 78.85 (2011) (Westlaw 2014) (requiring well surface casing 'cement that meets or exceeds the ASTM International C 150, Type I, II or III Standard or API Specification 10' and adding other cementing standards); W. Va. Admin. Code § 35-4-11 (Westlaw 2014) (for well casing cement requiring 'American Petroleum Institute Class A Ordinary Portland cement with no greater than three percent (3%) calcium chloride').

[82] 'About the Center for Sustainable Shale Development,' Ctr. for Sustainable Shale Development, accessed 16 July 2015 at www.sustainableshale.org/about/.

fracturing of Marcellus Shale wells.[83] A growing number of hydraulic fracturing companies, in collaboration with state agency actors, also voluntarily disclose the chemicals they use at wells, even where state standards do not require disclosure.[84] While these voluntary efforts do not come close to filling certain governance gaps left by incomplete local or state authority – or by inadequate incentives to enforce regulation even where authority exists[85] – they are important components of the broader energy governance framework.

Allocations of authority over energy development are also rapidly shifting in some areas,[86] and courts play an increasingly important role as authority allocations are tested. Although New York has for some time preempted local control over oil and gas operations, for example,[87] the lower and middle state courts determined that municipalities may still ban natural gas drilling and hydraulic fracturing if they do so under their zoning authority,[88] and the highest court agreed.[89] The state has since implemented a ban on certain types of hydraulic fracturing.[90] Oil and gas operators in several other states have also demanded court intervention, arguing that local regulation of energy development is preempted by state regulation.[91]

---

[83] 'Performance Standards,' Ctr. for Sustainable Shale Development (2013), accessed 16 July 2015 at www.sustainableshale.org/wp-content/uploads/2014/01/Performance-Standards-v.-1.1.pdf.

[84] See FracFocus Chemical Disclosure Registry, FracFocus 2.0, accessed 16 July 2015 at www.fracfocus.org (showing 72,725 well sites registered). Note that many of the sites for which operators disclosed chemical use were in states that require disclosure through FracFocus.

[85] See e.g. Wiseman, Risk and Response, *supra*, n. 25 (documenting certain gaps).

[86] See *supra*, nn 65–66 and accompanying text.

[87] See N.Y. Envtl. Conservation L. § 23-0303 (Westlaw 2014) (enacted 1972, amended 1981).

[88] *Norse Energy Corp. v Dryden*, 108 A.D.3d 25, N.Y.A.D. 3 Dept., 2 May 2013.

[89] *Wallach v Town of Dryden*, 23 N.Y.3d 728 (N.Y. Ct App. 2014).

[90] Thomas Kaplan, 'Citing Health Risks, Cuomo Bans Fracking in New York State,' N.Y. Times, Dec. 17, 2014, accessed 2 September 2015 at www.google.com/search?q=cuomo+and+fracturing+and+ban&ie=utf-8&oe=utf-8.

[91] See e.g. *Colorado Oil and Gas Conservation Comm'n. v City of Longmont*, case no. 2013CV63 (District Ct., Boulder County, 2014) (holding that Longmont's ban was preempted); *State ex rel. Morrison v Beck Energy Corp.*, 2015 WL 687475 at *9 (Oh. Feb. 17, 2015) (holding that Munroe Falls's regulation of oil and gas development was preempted).

C. Governance Challenges

The extent to which these governance allocations 'work' is of course in the eye of the beholder and depends on the metric used, such as a utilitarian balancing of costs and benefits or an egalitarian standard in which costs and benefits of energy development are distributed as evenly as possible. From a variety of metrics, however, it appears that certain allocations of authority might be inadequate in that they exclude key government actors that could efficiently address a range of impacts – potentially in a way that would not impose large costs on industry.

In Texas, for example, where local governments control many aspects of renewable energy development, courts have asserted very little authority over certain energy issues. When citizens used common law nuisance claims to express concerns about the aesthetic and safety-based impacts of wind turbines, at least one state court suggested that aesthetic harms alone, combined with what the court viewed as unsubstantiated safety claims, are not recognized by Texas nuisance law.[92] This erases the role of courts in much of the energy governance process, which may be problematic. Courts can moderate the impacts of energy development 'on the edges,' where development complies with regulations but still has negative effects, and these effects could in some cases be easily avoided through small changes in the location or operation of energy infrastructure.

Problems may also arise where local governments have nearly exclusive authority over energy development, thus allowing too little energy development.[93] Where towns can fully ban wind and oil and gas development, for example, these towns import all of their energy and may benefit from relatively cheap and abundant energy while bearing fewer costs of energy development.

Alternatively, where states have attempted to fully preempt local control, this prevents local governments from locating energy development where it is compatible with other uses, thus causing unnecessary and inefficient harm. In Ohio, the state supreme court determined that a

---

[92] See *Rankin v FPL Energy*, LLC, 266 S.W.3d 506, 509, 512–13 (Tex. App. 2008).

[93] See e.g. De Avila, Joseph, '"Fracking" Goes Local,' Wall St. J., 29 Aug. 2012, accessed 16 July 2015 at www.wsj.com/articles/SB10000872396390444432720457761779355250847O (mapping numerous bans on fracturing and moratoria). But see Outka, *supra*, n. 2, at 43 (examining the state–local dynamics of wind energy and oil and gas governance and observing that overemphasis of the 'NIMBYist' aspects of local government hides the beneficial role that local governance plays in informing energy policy by highlighting local impacts).

town could not require operators to receive a permit from local officials before drilling,[94] and in Louisiana, Shreveport was prohibited from placing a buffer zone around a lake – a zone within which oil and gas drilling would not occur.[95] The city also could not regulate other 'aspects of drilling activities within 5,000 feet of the lake.'[96] Full exclusion of local governments from the energy governance process, particularly with respect to the location of energy infrastructure, seems unwise. Although full bans on energy development could be problematic if enacted in too many areas, local zoning efforts could encourage energy development in zones where it least interfered with other uses and could avoid unnecessary impacts on people and the environment.

III. IMPROVING ENERGY GOVERNANCE

A growing energy federalism literature uses a variety of metrics to determine whether allocations of authority in energy governance – allocations that are increasingly fluid – are effective. David Spence and Michael Burger have explored some of the more traditional metrics, such as potential races to the bottom; the 'matching principle,' in which the scope of governance should match the extent of the externalities; whether a 'national interest' in certain aspects of energy justifies federal pre-emption; maximization of utility; and the benefits and drawbacks of decentralized regulation.[97] Michael Burger has further noted the role of federal environmental statutes and regulations in oil and gas governance, suggesting that extensive exemptions of oil and gas from these public laws may be unwise.[98]

At the state and local level, David Spence has focused on the allocation of costs and benefits and how we might best initially place entitlements so as to allow effective Coasean bargaining and reach a positive utilitarian outcome. He concludes that choices of governance allocation depend on our 'decision criterion,' with states regulating if we want to aggregate the preferences of those who share benefits and costs,

---

[94] *State ex rel. Morrison v Beck Energy Corp.*, 2015 WL 687475 at *9 (Oh. Feb. 17, 2015).

[95] *Energy Management Corp. v City of Shreveport*, 467 F.3d 471, 475–76, 483–84 (5th Cir. 2006).

[96] *Energy Mgmt. Corp.*, 467 F.3d at 475.

[97] Burger, *supra*, n. 2; Spence, 'Regulatory Lags,' *supra*, n. 2; Spence, 'Local Vetoes,' *supra*, n. 2.

[98] Burger, *supra*, n. 2, at 157.

and local governments regulating if we want to 'maximize collective utility' and account for strong preferences at the local level.[99]

John Nolon and Steven Gavin emphasize the importance of shared authority, arguing that rather than focusing on who should govern, we must ask how state–local authority is best coordinated.[100] Further, Uma Outka notes that the large number of local regulations emerging in both renewable energy and oil and gas play an important role in informing national energy policy by calling attention to the local impacts of this development.[101] Indeed, communities that are close to the development are likely to be most familiar with these impacts.

Although the literature approaches the normative issue of energy governance allocation from many angles, there seems to be a growing consensus that locating all authority within one level of government is not the best approach. In a sense, energy governance is simply too large an issue to produce an easy federalism answer: it involves a range of social and environmental impacts and numerous steps, from the grading of sites to the drilling of wells to the construction of renewable infrastructure and eventual decommissioning. Further, a range of federal, regional, state and local regulations already apply to energy development. Although this chapter has focused on state–local relationships, it has provided a brief sampling of other laws that apply in both the renewable and oil and gas contexts.

The path forward seems to call for further exploration of some version of Erin Ryan's 'negotiated federalism,'[102] in which we do not rely on zero-sum allocations of authority but rather better enable bargaining for shared authority and shifting authority allocations among different levels of government, and further explore how this authority will and should change over time. Effective governance of energy development requires broadening of the 'energy governance sphere' – in other words, an allocation of authority that gives all actors, including federal, regional, state and local governments, and the stakeholders affected by governance, a meaningful role within the processes that determine where and how energy development occurs. While this proposal seems (and is) modest,

---

[99] Spence suggests that giving local governments the initial entitlement, including the power to ban oil and gas development, might incentivize more bargaining, as individuals would bargain over benefits (the possibility of lifting a local ban and thus profiting) rather than losses. Spence, 'Local Vetoes,' *supra*, n. 2.
[100] Nolon and Gavin, *supra*, n. 2, at 1036–39.
[101] Outka, *supra*, n. 2.
[102] Ryan, *supra*, n. 1.

and perhaps appears obvious, current governance structures often do not provide this inclusive sphere, as briefly discussed in Part II.

This Part discusses some of the mechanisms that could help to provide all actors with more access to decisions about the location of energy generation and oil and gas wells, as well as the operations and technology involved.

A. Avoiding Full Preemption and Preserving the Role of Courts

As introduced above, one important means of ensuring that all governments and individuals impacted by energy development have a role in energy governance is to avoid full preemption of any one government's control over this development, and instead to rely on overlapping or shared authority, which may shift over time. Furthermore, the permitting of an energy facility should not, in many cases, foreclose common law doctrines applied by the courts, such as nuisance. Permitting authorities might not fully anticipate the impacts of particular energy infrastructure, and common law doctrines are needed to address these unanticipated impacts.

B. Expanding Participatory Processes and Generating More Information About Impacts

In addition to including a range of government actors in the energy development process, including courts, this process must be open and allow for adequate participation by impacted governments and individuals. The environmental justice literature has long emphasized the importance of process in ensuring that affected communities have a voice in decisions about the location of infrastructure.[103] While process alone cannot fix massive disparities in industrial impacts – including impacts caused by energy development – it is exceedingly important. Local governments need a seat at the table when states issue a siting permit for a wind or solar farm, for example, or a permit that allows a company to drill an oil or gas well.[104] States often provide only limited notice

---

[103] See Wiseman, Hannah J., 'Remedying Regulatory Diseconomies of Scale' (2014) 94 B.U. L. Rev. **235**, 260, n. 127 (providing a brief summary of the environmental justice literature and some energy-specific environmental justice scholarship).

[104] See e.g. Nolon, Sean F., 'Negotiating the Wind: A Framework to Engage Citizens in Siting Wind Turbines' (2011) 12 Cardozo J. Conflict Resol. 327

requirements before a permit to drill issues,[105] and they often do not offer meaningful hearings beforehand.

Colorado and Maryland provide models for more open and inclusive well permitting processes, although even these processes might not allow for adequate community engagement. Colorado allows well operators proposing to drill to participate in a voluntary Comprehensive Drilling Plan process.[106] Through this process, the Colorado Oil and Gas Conservation Commission and the company that has proposed the well work with other state agencies, such as the wildlife agency, to identify and mitigate a range of likely impacts before drilling occurs.[107] Maryland has similarly proposed to require a Comprehensive Gas Development Plan that would consider a range of impacts and incorporate mitigation strategies into a well approval.[108] The same process could be applied to renewable energy generation, which can impact wildlife, landscapes and local human populations.

Where state processes allow numerous agencies and groups to influence a decision to site or operate energy infrastructure, these processes will be productive only if participants have the resources needed to effectively participate. This will require extensive citizen education about the impacts of development. It will also require more uniform collection and reporting of information. Regulatory officials, nonprofit groups, or industry actors should collect data about social and environmental baselines – the conditions that exist in an area prior to energy development – and monitor conditions throughout development. Post-development testing, monitoring and reporting are equally important.

(describing the importance of local participation in siting decisions and suggesting improvements for participatory processes).

[105] See e.g. W. Va. Code § 22-6A-10(b) (Westlaw 2014) (requiring notice to a limited number of landowners at and near the proposed well site); Colo. Oil & Gas Conservation Commission, Comparison of State Oil and Gas Permitting Requirements, accessed 2 September 2015 at http://cogccuat.state.co.us/RuleMaking/WorkGroups/Process/ComparisonofStateOil&GasPermittingRequire..pdf (showing some states that require certification of notice to landowners and/or nearby landowners).

[106] 2 Colo. Admin. Code § 404-1:216 (Westlaw 2014).

[107] Ibid.

[108] Md. Dept. of the Envt., Marcellus Shale Safe Drilling Initiative Study Part II, Best Practices (Draft for Public Comment), accessed 16 July 2015 at www.mde.state.md.us/programs/Land/mining/marcellus/Pages/MSReportPartII_Draft_for_Public_Comment.aspx.

This type of information gathering and reporting occurs, but only to a limited degree and in a non-uniform manner.[109] Wind energy developers under federal Fish and Wildlife Service guidelines conduct extensive pre-development investigations of wildlife populations, develop monitoring plans and measure impacts on birds, bats and other wildlife during operations – counting wildlife carcasses, for example.[110] For oil and gas, some states require or strongly incentivize pre- and post-development testing of groundwater.[111] States like Michigan also require monitoring of groundwater quality during the well development process.[112] But monitoring and reporting requirements vary widely among states, with some states requiring no information production. Regional collaboration or federal involvement will be needed to ensure that energy companies more consistently monitor for impacts and report this information uniformly, thus enabling more effective participation of agencies, nonprofit groups and citizens in regulatory processes for energy development.

C. Implementing Cooperative Federalism in the State–Local Context

In addition to opening up and improving decision-making processes that address the siting and operation of energy infrastructure, as well as generating information that supports effective participation in those processes, better enforcement of laws is needed. Even where centralized state standards are the best approach – technical standards that determine which types of cables safely secure wind energy equipment or which types of well lining prevent oil and gas wells from leaking, for example

---

[109] See, e.g., Richardson, Nathan et al., 'The State of State Shale Gas Regulation: Maps of State Regulations, Resources for the Future' (2013) at 5, accessed 16 July 2015 at www.rff.org/rff/documents/RFF-Rpt-StateofStateRegs_StateMaps.pdf (showing pre-drill testing requirements); Wiseman, Hannah J., 'Hydraulic Fracturing and Information Forcing' (2013) 74 Ohio St. L.J. Furthermore 86 (comparing testing requirements).

[110] 'U.S. Fish and Wildlife Service Land-Based Wind Energy Guidelines,' U.S. Fish & Wildlife Service (2012), accessed 16 July 2015 at www.fws.gov/windenergy/docs/weg_final.pdf.

[111] Wiseman, *supra*, n. 107 (describing Pennsylvania and West Virginia incentives).

[112] Mich. Admin. Code r. 324.1002(3)(a) (Westlaw 2014) (requiring '[a] minimum of 1 groundwater monitoring well downgradient which is in close proximity to all hydrocarbon or brine storage secondary containment areas' or, as an alternative, a tertiary containment system).

– local governments and citizens could be key players in helping to enforce these statewide standards. State officials cannot be everywhere at once and may not be aware of local conditions that require creative solutions for compliance. Thus, states should involve local governments, industry actors and other stakeholders in monitoring – requiring industry to electronically monitor and report certain emissions of pollutants and other impacts, for example, or enlisting citizen brigades to periodically investigate sites and report back certain information.

D. Limiting Harms and Providing Compensation

A final means of improving the governance of energy development and ensuring that more governments are included in the governance process is to limit local impacts or, alternatively, to provide compensation to the people and governments harmed by energy development. David Spence has identified this latter approach as a means of reducing concentrated local impacts that might cause local governments to overregulate oil and gas development and impede efficient bargaining for energy development.[113]

A key method of limiting local impacts is to require that operators clean up the damage they cause and post money that will be available for public clean-up efforts if operators do not adequately remediate sites. Many states and local governments require energy operators to submit bonds before obtaining a permit to drill an oil or gas well or construct a wind turbine.[114] A company pays a certain amount of money into a state fund or provides other financial assurance, and if the company fails to adequately plug and properly abandon a well or reclaim a site, or decommission a wind farm, the government can use the money to conduct these activities. Bonding amounts vary substantially, however, and often cover only well plugging, not environmental remediation.[115]

Beyond bonds that address the end of the life of an energy development, governments need ways to address impacts that occur during

---

[113] Spence, Local Vetoes, *supra*, n. 2, at 31–34.

[114] See Dana and Wiseman, *supra*, n. 28, at 1531, n. 19 (comparing bond amounts for oil and gas wells); Maryland Local Govt. Code § 13-706 (Westlaw 2014) (requiring bonds for wind energy conversion systems); 17 Okl. Stat. Ann. § 160.15 (Westlaw 2014) (requiring proof of financial security 'to cover the anticipated costs of decommissioning the wind energy facility').

[115] Dana and Wiseman, *supra*, n. 28, at 1531, n. 19 (showing a variety of different bond amounts).

energy development. They can make industry pay for road damage caused by heavy trucks, for example, as many communities do.[116] Further, as Pennsylvania has done, states can allow local governments to charge 'impact fees' for oil and gas wells, with the money going to the state and many of the funds being redistributed to local governments to address the short- to long-term impacts of energy development, including, for example, natural resource damage and housing scarcity.[117] These fees and similar taxes that are directly tied to impacts rather than, say, the amount of energy produced will help prevent communities from having to bear disproportionate costs of energy development.

CONCLUSION

Determining effective allocations of authority over energy development and identifying how these authority allocations need to shift over time is an enormous task that requires a detailed definition of 'good governance' and a far more comprehensive analysis of authority allocations that will lead to good governance. This chapter has, however, introduced the reader to some of the current allocations of government authority over two types of energy development that are increasingly common throughout the United States – unconventional oil and gas and renewable energy. It also has suggested that regardless of the metric that we use for measuring effective federalism approaches, we must ensure that all governments have some voice in the energy development process due to its complexity and the range of its impacts. Just as the nascent energy federalism literature has begun to do, it also has identified several strategies that will help to include all affected governments and people within the energy governance sphere, including more open permitting processes; the production of better information about impacts in order to inform those who participate in permitting processes; enlistment of local governments, industry and citizens in monitoring and enforcement; and enacting regulations designed to limit impacts – particularly through bonding in the event that energy infrastructure is not properly decommissioned – and providing compensation to communities that experience

---

[116] See Coon, Cheryl L., 'Environmental Law in the Barnett Shale,' in *64th Annual Institute on Oil and Gas Law* **255**, 271–72 (2008) (discussing road damage agreements).

[117] 58 Pa. Consolidated Stats. Annotated § 2302 (Westlaw 2014).

disproportionate harms. These are just several of a range of creative strategies that will be needed to ensure effective governance by the wide range of entities involved in energy development.

PART III

CLIMATE CHANGE AND FEDERALISM

7. Climate federalism, regulatory failure and reversal risks, and entrenching innovation incentives

William W. Buzbee

INTRODUCTION

To combat climate change successfully will require innovations in regulatory design, markets and technology. However, legal efforts to combat climate change encounter political economic dynamics and complexity arguably unmatched by any earlier social ill.[1] After all, the contributing sources are vast, investments in the status quo are great, matching regulatory structures mostly absent, distributional choices complex, many harms in the future and hard to discern or trace, costs of emissions reductions felt now, and the regulatory design menu large.[2] In addition, the low costs of energy and externalized harms do not now incentivize major behavioral changes absent legal mandates. This is a recipe for the stasis regarding climate change that has characterized much of the past few decades.

However, in recent years legal efforts to combat climate have emerged. Efforts during 2009 and 2010 to enact a comprehensive federal cap-and-trade-based climate change law met with failure. A new international agreement is also needed. Despite questions about the efficacy or logic of such efforts, states, local governments and even regions have stepped into

---

[1] Lazarus, Richard J., 'Super Wicked Problems and Climate Change: Restraining the Present to Liberate the Future' (2009) 94 Cornell L. Rev. **1153**, 1159 (calling climate change 'a super wicked problem that defies resolution because of the enormous interdependencies, uncertainties, circularities, and conflicting stakeholders').

[2] Buzbee, William W., 'Recognizing the Regulatory Commons: A Theory of Regulatory Gaps' (2003) 89 Iowa L. Rev. 1, 11–13, 22–36.

the breach.[3] In addition, federal regulations under the Clean Air Act have been promulgated or proposed to constrain GHG emissions. How a future comprehensive federal climate change law should be designed, however, remains a critical policy question.

This chapter analyzes climate regulation federalism choices, focusing on regional, state and local roles after enactment of federal climate legislation. (For ease of reading, I will generally refer to such subnational regulation simply as 'state' regulation, but states have sometimes addressed climate change through regional agreements and local governments have taken their own additional actions.) While scholars have analyzed, in the absence of federal legislation, the logic and efficacy of these state climate enactments, a separate question is whether such state climate regulatory authority should survive enactment of a federal climate law, especially one based primarily on a cap-and-trade strategy. (I return later to tax-based carbon regulation.) Prominent scholars, policymakers, and industry advocates contend that retaining state climate authority after enactment of a national climate law would undercut regulatory goals and be futile. They therefore contend that a future federal cap-and-trade regime should preempt state climate regulation.

This chapter takes issue with such claims, arguing that assessment of the efficacy of states' climate regulatory roles after enactment of federal climate legislation requires looking beyond an idealized or static view of regulation. Responses to regulation will inevitably be ongoing and dynamic; whatever regulatory instruments and design are chosen will shape and change the political and market terrain. Efforts to derail climate regulation and regulatory failure risks will remain persistent threats; all policy reforms are 'at risk,' facing post-enactment threats and a dynamic environment.[4] Climate scholarship has paid too little attention to these regulatory derailment risks and, especially, the implications of

---

[3] See Rabe, Barry G., *Statehouse and Greenhouse: The Emerging Politics of American Climate Change Policy* (Brookings Institution Press, Washington, DC 2004) (describing and analyzing state climate initiatives); Thomson, Vivian E., *Sophisticated Interdependence in Climate Policy: Federalism in the United States, Brazil, and Germany* (Anthem Press, London, New York, Delhi 2014), pp. xxvi–xxviii, 1–46 (describing and analyzing state climate initiatives in a comparative analysis of three nations' federalism regimes).

[4] Patashnik, Eric M., *Reforms at Risk: What Happens After Major Policy Changes Are Enacted* (Princeton University Press, Princeton NJ 2008). Patashnik's insights are applied to climate regulation in Biber, Eric, 'Cultivating a Green Political Landscape: Lessons for Climate Change Policy from the Defeat of California's Proposition 23' (2013) 66 Vand. L. Rev. **399**, 400–01, to explore why California's climate law survived a well-funded political attack.

such risks where a law-created market drives a substantial portion of related business investment and resulting technological innovation needed to mitigate climate risks. Retention of state climate authority can be part of an effective and durable regulatory design due to resulting incentives to commit to the federal regime, policy diffusion dynamics, and gradual entrenchment of supportive coalitions through a process of path dependent 'increasing returns' and 'costs of exit.'[5] While elements of these dynamics explain opposition to climate legislation, these dynamics also illuminate the importance of preserving state climate regulatory authority. One regulator, especially one creating and overseeing a unified carbon market, does intuitively seem the ideal answer for a quintessential global challenge requiring a response at the largest possible jurisdictional levels. Nevertheless, this policy intuition's flaws are apparent once one factors in innovation and investment incentives, persistent efforts to secure a policy reversal, overinclusion risks, policymakers' fallibility, and regulatory implementation failure risks.[6] Enactment is important, but legal durability is essential, especially where the law is the critical underpinning of linked investments and markets which in turn are critical to reduce GHG emissions.

After all, always underlying climate politics and linked markets is fear of all governments, citizens and market actors that their jurisdiction will

---

[5] For the most influential discussion of the path dependence and 'increasing returns' and 'costs of exit' concepts, see Pierson, Paul, 'Increasing Returns, Path Dependence, and the Study of Politics' (2000) 94 Am. Pol. Sci. Rev. 251. Others building on these concepts regarding climate change are few, but nuanced analysis, albeit in works with a different focus than this chapter, is provided in Biber, *supra*, n. 4 at 400–01 (comparing near simultaneous defeats of an anti-climate regulation initiative in California and federal climate bills and discussing Pierson and how policy initiatives change interest group incentives); Brewster, Rachel, 'Stepping Stone or Stumbling Block: Incrementalism and National Climate Change Legislation' (2010) 28 Yale L. & Pol'y Rev. **245**, 251, 311 (discussing such concepts in considering the dynamics of national and international climate regulation); and del Río, Pablo, and Xavier Labandeira, 'Barriers to the Introduction of Market-Based Instruments in Climate Policies: An Integrated Theoretical Framework' (2009) 10 Envtl Econ. & Pol'y Stud. **1**, 41 (mainly looking at how path dependence dynamics create resistance to climate regulation).

[6] For a review of the merits of a unitary or 'plural' regulatory answer, ultimately arguing for retention of latitude for state climate regulation alongside a future federal climate law, see Stewart, Richard B., 'States and Cities as Actors in Global Climate Regulation: Unitary versus Plural Architectures' (2008) 50 Ariz. L. Rev. **681**, 696–97.

act, but others will not, disadvantaging the climate-regulating jurisdiction, laying waste to investors in related businesses and markets and leaving GHG levels still on the rise.[7] For market actors supplying technological innovations and products to achieve climate and energy efficiency goals, a web of regulation resulting from multiple regulators, or at least potential regulators, will be far more resilient and resistant to wholesale derailment than would be complete dependence on a single federal regulatory scheme. A truly stable regulatory environment would not exist, but such a balanced regime could provide salutary play in the joints and, by changing incentives of both policymakers and businesses, reduce the risk of abrupt policy shifts or implementation failures. In short, even if state climate authority remained latent or little used after passage of a federal climate law, retaining that state authority would foster overall stability, create room for regulatory innovation, and thereby create conditions conducive to private investment in energy innovations and other climate-related markets and businesses.

I. THE CLIMATE REGULATION CHALLENGE AND BUSINESS NEED FOR REGULATION

This section provides a brief review of why climate regulation is difficult to enact, sure to trigger ongoing opposition, yet is needed to foster investment in needed technological innovation and more efficient modes of energy use (hereinafter 'clean energy' or 'energy efficiency').

This chapter assumes that the basic nature of climate change science and its causes are established.[8] Instead, the focus here is on how climate change's attributes make it a near perfect recipe for regulatory inaction, ineffective regulation and, especially, enduring opposition. The most prevalent GHG, carbon dioxide, is not a readily apparent pollutant. By itself, it causes no immediate harms, although it is often emitted with

---

[7] *Massachusetts v EPA*, 549 U.S. 497, 545–46 (2007) (Roberts CJ, dissenting) (stating concern with futile US regulation if China and India pollution increased). See also S. 15, 112th Cong. (2011) (proposing to prohibit carbon dioxide regulation until China, India, and Russia implemented climate change policies).

[8] For a succinct review of the science preceding analysis of climate federalism choices, see Carlson, Ann, 'Designing Effective Climate Policy' (2012) 49 Harv. J. on Legis. 207. For a more in-depth discussion, see Glicksman, Robert et al., *Environmental Protection: Law and Policy*, 7th edn (Wolters Kluwer, Austin TX, 2015), pp. 1172–90.

more risk-creating forms of pollution. Climate change's more severe impacts are generally anticipated to occur at least decades into the future and are difficult to predict with any precision; climate change's particularized manifestations remain the source of probabilistic predictions.[9] And although an array of horribles are part of the future due to climate change – rising temperatures, more severe storms, glacial melt and sea level rise being the most prevalent predictions – all are the result of numerous contributing causes. Climate skeptics can and do capitalize on the inability to trace particular harms to climate change.[10] Nevertheless, governments may see other reasons to regulate GHG emissions or energy efficiency, especially responsiveness to citizen calls for regulation, desires for greater energy independence, or other benefits of pollution reduction.[11]

Powerful interests, however, see climate regulation as a threat to their very existence. All carbon-intensive industries are threatened, but especially coal-burning utilities, coal-linked industries and other businesses linked to carbon-based forms of energy.[12] Unsurprisingly, threatened

---

[9] See e.g. Vandenbergh, Michael P., 'The China Problem' (2008) 81 S. Cal. L. Rev. **905**, 929–30 (listing different projections for growth in China's emissions) (citations omitted).

[10] Prominent federal politicians have seized on single events to claim evidence of lack of climate change. See e.g. Jim DeMint (Twitter) @JimDeMint (9 February 2010, 9.46 am), accessed 16 July 2015 at twitter.com/#!/JimDeMint/status/8863771523 (responding to Washington, DC blizzard: 'It's going to keep snowing in DC until Al Gore cries "uncle"'); Shogren, Elizabeth, 'Inhofe Offers Parting Shot at Global Warming,' NPR (7 December 2006, 6.00 am), accessed 16 July 2015 at www.npr.org/templates/story/story.php?storyId=6591614 (calling climate change a 'mass delusion').

[11] Dernbach, John C. et al., 'Making the States Full Partners in a National Climate Change Effort: A Necessary Element for Sustainable Economic Development' (2010) 40 Envtl. L. Rep. News and Analysis **10597**, 10602; see e.g. Symposium, 'Government's Role in Promoting Renewable Energy Solutions' (2008) 2 Env'tl & Energy L. & Pol'y J. **319**, 325 (statement of Congressman Nick Lampoon regarding desire for energy independence).

[12] See Biber, *supra*, n. 4, at 446–47 (noting that fossil fuel industries have fought an array of clean energy initiatives since their build up might lead to 'dynamic shifts in the economic and political landscape' and 'pose a threat' to their businesses); Brulle, Robert J., 'Institutionalizing Delay: Foundation Funding and the Creation of U.S. Climate Change Counter-Movement Organizations' in (2013) Climatic Change; Dunlap, Riley E. and Aaron M. McCright, 'Organized Climate Change Denial' in Dryzek, John S., Richard B. Norgaard, and David Schlosberg (eds), *The Oxford Handbook of Climate Change and Society* (Oxford University Press, Oxford, 2011), p. 148.

industries have financed climate regulatory opposition and efforts to question climate science.[13] Furthermore, state electric utility regulation often makes construction or modification of large carbon-burning power plants a source of guaranteed returns.[14] Because regulation that creates incentives for energy efficiency, reduced demand or a shift away from carbon-based energy might dramatically divert revenues from utilities, they are likely to remain opposed to climate regulation.[15] In addition, at least at this time, one political party seems heavily invested in denying the existence of climate change or opposing any climate regulation.

Structurally, the cross-border nature of GHG pollution adds a further complicating layer. A ton of carbon emitted or avoided has an equal impact everywhere: GHG levels and climate change are a global phenomenon. Any level of regulation smaller than the entire world will necessarily be partial and can be undercut by the actions or inaction of other jurisdictions. The pervasively shared atmosphere is also subject to 'regulatory commons' dynamics; because no jurisdiction owns or is legally responsible for climate change or on its own able to regulate it effectively, all jurisdictions face incentives not to act either due to free-rider dynamics, fears of regulatory futility, or lack of political benefit.[16]

However, the proliferation of states and regions now regulating GHGs undoubtedly shows that complete inaction is far from inevitable.[17] Indeed, the late Nobel Prize winner Eleanor Ostrom suggested that effective 'bottom-up' climate regulation was underway and theoretically understandable.[18] Nevertheless, the same attributes of climate change that

---

[13] See Biber, *supra*, n. 4, at 446–47; Brulle, *supra*, n. 12.
[14] 'Electricity Regulation in the US: A Guide,' Regulatory Assistance Project (March 2011), 42–46.
[15] Ibid. at 423–24 (observing that changed utility rate regulation law shifted California's utilities away from carbon-intensive modes of production).
[16] See Buzbee, *supra*, n. 2, 11–13, 22–36.
[17] See Thomson, Vivian E. and Vicki Arroyo, 'Upside-Down Cooperative Federalism: Climate Change Policymaking and the States' (2011) 29 Va. Envtl. L.J. 1; Thomson, *supra*, n. 3; Engel, Kirsten H. and Scott R. Saleska, 'Subglobal Regulation of the Global Commons: The Case of Climate Change' (2005) 32 Ecology L.Q. **183**, 223–26.
[18] Ostrom, Elinor, 'A Polycentric Approach for Coping with Climate Change,' WPS 5059 (October 2009) World Bank Policy Research. For a more succinct development of similar points, see Ostrom, Elinor, 'A Multi-Scale Approach to Coping with Climate Change and Other Collective Action Problems' (Feb 2010), 1 *Solutions* 27–36.

make regulation both difficult and an uphill battle create enduring incentives for opposition to GHG regulation.

This uncertain regulatory terrain has undercut investments in the green economy and means to combat climate change.[19] Law undoubtedly provides a crucial undergirding for all property rights and markets.[20] Nevertheless, opponents of retained state climate authority and much work on climate federalism have given little attention to how market stability links to the question of who should have authority to regulate climate ills. This linkage is important because some markets – especially markets linked to efforts to reduce GHG emissions and energy use – are substantially dependent on legally created incentives, scarcity and other legal strictures that punish or price those emissions.[21] Were it not for tax rewards and subsidies, mandates or market benefits unrelated to climate

---

[19] Cf. Porter, Michael E. and Claas van der Linde, 'Green and Competitive' (Sept–Oct. 1995) 73 Harv. Bus. Rev. **120**, 124, 129 (exploring neglected benefits of regulation, sometimes misguided reasons for business opposition, and how uncertainty and rigid regulation can trigger opposition and undercut regulatory benefits).

[20] Averich, Harvey and Leland L. Johnson, 'Behavior of the Firm Under Regulatory Constraint' (1962) 52 Am. Econ. Rev. **1052**, 1052, 1065–66, 1068; Brennan, Michael J. and Eduardo S. Schwartz, 'Consistent Regulatory Policy Under Uncertainty,' (1982) 13 Bell J. Econ. **506**, 506, 508–09, 518; Calabresi, Guido and A. Douglas Melamed, 'Property Rules, Liability Rules, and Inalienability: One View of the Cathedral' (1972) 85 Harv. L. Rev. **1089**, 1089–93; Coase, R.H., 'The Problem of Social Cost' (1960) 3 J.L & Econ. **1**, 15–16, 19, 23; Holmes, Oliver Wendell, 'The Path of the Law' (1897) 10 Harv. L. Rev. **457**, 460–61; Posner, Richard A., 'Creating a Legal Framework for Economic Development' 13 *World Bank Research Observer* **1**, 1, 3, 7–8 (1998).

[21] Aldy, Joseph E. and Robert N. Stavins, 'Using the Market to Address Climate Change: Insights from Theory and Experience' (2012) 141 *Daedalus* **45**, 48 (discussing how a carbon tax program incentivizes innovation and rewards producers who are able to cheaply reduce carbon emissions); Fabrizio, Kira R., 'The Effect of Regulatory Uncertainty on Investment: Evidence from Renewable Energy Generation' (2012) 29 J.L. Econ. & Org. **765**, 766, 768–69 (discussing how states 'designed (Renewable Portfolio Standard (RPS)) regulations to encourage investment in renewable electricity generation' and calling resulting business assets 'policy specific' because 'their value in their next-best use is substantially lower than their value under the governing policy'); Jaffe, Adam B. and Robert N. Stavins, 'The Energy Paradox and the Diffusion of Conservation Technology' (1994) 16 *Resource and Energy Economics* **91**, 97, 111–19 (stating that 'any policy that increased the profitability of a technology would speed its diffusion' and why there is need for 'those externalities to be internalized, such as through pollution taxes, tradable permit systems, or other economic instruments ... or through conventional command-and-control regulations').

concerns, market pressures today would provide little incentive for investment in companies and technologies that could prove crucial to combat climate change.[22] Especially since the 'fracking' natural gas revolution, cheap energy has undercut demand for low carbon forms of energy and linked technological innovation beyond possible switching from coal to natural gas. Moreover, prices for carbon-based forms of energy do not, without regulation, reflect and internalize resulting climate and other environmental harms. Although solar is becoming competitive over the long term with carbon-based energy sources, utilities may see little or no net benefit in such a switch given the norm of guaranteed returns to utilities in regulated markets for new power plant projects.

The climate challenge for law is, at its essence, figuring out effective means to respond to an innovation imperative. To combat climate change successfully will require successful innovations in regulatory design, new markets and major investments in technological innovation. Individual behavioral shifts may help, but regulatory mandates and inducements remain essential to strengthen incentives for both individual and business change.[23] Climate regulation durability and clean energy market viability are inextricably interrelated. Regulation will undergird clean energy markets, and growing proof of carbon and clean energy market viability and profitability is essential to help overcome citizen, market and political opposition to climate regulation and reduce incentives to derail such regulation.

II. THE CLIMATE FEDERALISM CHOICE POST-ENACTMENT OF A FEDERAL CLIMATE LAW

Several prominent scholars and policymakers have argued that effective and rational federal climate legislation should preempt state and local

---

[22] Sinden, Amy, 'The Tragedy of the Commons and the Myth of a Private Property Solution' 78 (2007) U. Colo. L. Rev. **533**, 571 ('Firms have neither "preferences" for permits nor any intrinsic desire to reduce pollution levels in the absence of any government-set limits on pollution.'); Merrill, Thomas W., 'Innovations in Environmental Policy: Explaining Market Mechanisms' (2000) U. Ill. L. Rev. **255**, 290 (stating that 'environmental resources are not, as a rule, under sufficient pressure to warrant the adoption of market mechanisms').

[23] Vandenbergh, *supra*, n. 9 at 929–30; Vandenbergh, Michael P. and Anne C. Steinemann, 'The Carbon-Neutral Individual' (2007) 82 N.Y.U. L. Rev. 1673.

climate regulation.[24] However, in the congressional arena the leading (but defeated) climate bills ultimately rejected such a framework, adopting language that would have retained substantial state climate regulatory authority.[25] After recapping the arguments for a preemptive federalized climate regime, this part turns to rationales for preserving state latitude to take regulatory steps to reduce GHG emissions.

The pragmatic political argument for displacing federal law is linked to political necessity; a preemptive bill may be the price of building enough industry support to enact federal climate regulation.[26] The main public-regarding argument for a preemptive federal climate bill is linked to its likely primary reliance on a cap-and-trade regime or other market-based regulation. Critics contend that disparate state and local actions could either hinder federal goals or merely be futile acts that would raise production costs, injure the regulating jurisdiction, but not actually lock in any climate-related benefits.[27] Analysis of these claims follows.

If climate regulation were to rely primarily on a cap-and-trade market, then ideally there would be one stable market at the largest scale possible, with one tradable currency, and ideally venues in which trades and prices would be transparent.[28] Market-based regulation would not depend on regulators who would need to learn vast amounts about each polluter.[29] And if the market and linked regulation rewarded the most

---

[24] Coglianese, Cary and Jocelyn D'Ambrosio, 'Policymaking Under Pressure: The Perils of Incremental Responses to Climate Change' (2008) 40 Conn. L. Rev. **1413**, 1423–25; Stavins, Robert N., 'Policy Instruments for Climate Change: How Can National Governments Address a Global Problem?' (1997) U. Chi. Legal F. **293**, 293–98; Wiener, Jonathan Baert, 'Global Environmental Regulation: Instrument Choice in Legal Context' (1999) 108 Yale L.J. **677**, 686; cf. Esty, Daniel C., 'What Is the Most Compelling Environmental Challenge Facing the World on the Brink of the Twenty-First Century? Stepping Up to the Global Environmental Challenge' (1996) 8 Fordham Envtl. L.J. **103**, 104–13 (exploring why anything less than a global agreement will be inadequate, but not discussing state–federal issues).

[25] See Glicksman et al., *supra*, n. 8 at 1190–211 (discussing regulatory design choices, climate federalism, the 2009–10 leading bills and federalism language).

[26] DeShazo, J.R. and Jody Freeman, 'Timing and Form of Federal Regulation: The Case of Climate Change' (2007) 155 U. Pa. L. Rev. **1499**, 1500–16.

[27] Wiener, Jonathan B., 'Think Globally, Act Globally: The Limits of Local Climate Policies' (2007) 1555 U. Pa. L. Rev. **1961**, 1966–73.

[28] See Esty, *supra*, n. 24.

[29] See Karkkainen, Bradley C., 'Bottlenecks and Baselines: Tackling Information Deficits in Environmental Regulation' (2008) 86 Tex. L. Rev. **1409**, 1413–20.

cost-effective producers of energy or methods to reduce GHG emissions, then over time market success and environmental benefits would go together. However, any partial regulation (whether state compared to national or national compared to international) could lead other jurisdictions to free-ride on the effective regulator's efforts.[30] If conflicting and uncertain climate regulation and carbon markets resulted from sub-national regulation, transaction costs and confusion would increase.[31] Furthermore, if federal or state regulation dictated pollution performance standards, or through subsidies and other monetary incentives chose winners and losers, then government choices would displace or distort market actors' search for cost-effective means to achieve goals.[32]

A second argument for preemptive federal legislation is rooted in claims of futility. Because GHGs are ubiquitous and climate change effects are rooted in worldwide GHG levels, more stringent or additional state actions could end up merely imposing costs locally and benefiting others.[33] A crackdown on GHG emitters by any governmental jurisdiction short of an all-encompassing international regime could cause a 'leakage' problem, leading production to shift to less regulated environments, creating little or no net climate benefit.[34] Those higher polluting, more lax jurisdictions might even develop a rigid anti-regulatory posture due to the influx of new regulation-avoiding emigrés.[35] Price effect leakage could also occur, where law-induced forbearance would reduce demand for carbon allowances, resulting in lowered prices and then a rebounding surge in demand and consumption by others. Under these perspectives, additional state and local climate actions could cause the regulating jurisdictions harm but with little or no net climate change benefit.

So why allow ongoing sub-national climate authority even if a federal climate bill were enacted? The answer hinges on regulatory derailment risks, the market impacts of such risks, and several regulatory rationales that can be distilled to the following: hedging; anticipating overinclusion

---

[30] Stavins, Robert N., 'A Meaningful U.S. Cap-and-Trade System to Address Climate Change' (2008) 32 Harv. Envtl L. Rev. **293**, 358.

[31] Ibid. at 298–99.

[32] See Carlson, *supra*, n. 8; Schoenbrod, David and Richard B. Stewart, 'The Cap-and-Trade Bait and Switch' (24 August 2009) *Wall Street Journal*, accessed 16 July 2015 at online.wsj.com/article/SB10001424052970203609204574314312524495276.html.

[33] Stavins, Robert N., 'State Eyes on the Climate Policy Prize' (2010) 27 *The Environmental Forum* No. 4, 16.

[34] Stavins, 'A Meaningful U.S. Cap-and-Trade System to Address Climate Change', *supra*, n. 30 at 370.

[35] See Brewster, *supra*, n. 5 at 287.

risks; and entrenching progress. In ways that may at first seem paradoxical, retaining state climate authority (and, for similar reasons, existing EPA regulatory power under the Clean Air Act) would create incentives and rewards for both climate-related regulatory and technological innovation. This part starts with a review of reasons that a federal scheme could fall short and the 'hedging' rationale, then develops at greater length arguments rooted in literature on policy diffusion and policy path dependence. Retention of state climate authority could help maintain a resilient web of climate regulation that would both incentivize business investment and build political, business, and citizen support for enduring climate regulation.

A. Hedging: Anticipating Failure and Opposition

If markets were perfect and regulatory implementation and enforcement also flawless and stable, the arguments would be quite strong for a unitary federal climate bill that preempted state climate regulatory authority. However, once one relaxes the assumption of perfection, and also realizes that a nation's laws send signals to other nations considering climate regulation (whether via an international agreement or national commitments), then the flaws of such unitary and preemptive federal legislation become apparent.

1. Federal laxity risks and state complementary actions and catalyst roles

Probably the biggest risk of federal climate legislation relying primarily on a cap-and-trade strategy is that it would prove too lax.[36] A national carbon cap-and-trade market would create substantial innovation incentives only if its cap were low enough to create economic rewards for innovations reducing emissions. Until a cap's stringency is on the immediate horizon, innovation incentives will be weak.[37] The leading 2009–10 cap-and-trade bills confirmed that this risk is substantial. They proposed to hand out a huge percentage of pollution allowances for free, to the largest polluters. The cap itself would not have kicked into effect for years, and the leading bills required little for many years. In addition, GHG allowances and offset credits could have been 'banked.' Thus, if

---

[36] McAllister, Lesley K., 'The Overallocation Problem in Cap-and-Trade: Moving Towards Stringency' (2009) 34 Colum. J. Envtl L. **395**, 400–03.

[37] Driesen, David M., 'Free Lunch or Cheap Fix?: The Emissions Trading Idea and the Climate Change Convention' (1998) 26 B.C. Envtl Affairs L. Rev. **1**, 41–46.

they had been enacted, the leading bills' minimal regulatory costs and rewards for innovation would not have been felt for years.

Preserving state and local latitude to address causes of climate change in the face of a lax federal law would provide several benefits. First, in the face of federal laxity, state and local action could, despite leakage concerns, complement federal efforts both directly and by supporting technological innovation. As would have been allowed under the leading climate bills, states could retire carbon allowances or charge more per unit of GHG emitted. Or state and local governments might reduce emissions from sources missed under a federal law or earlier than required under federal law. Allowing states or EPA to continue using old-fashioned 'Best Available Technology'-based performance standards could at a far earlier date lead polluters to ratchet back GHG emissions.[38] That regulatory pressure would create market rewards for creators and sellers of low-cost means to reduce GHG pollution. Similarly, state initiatives to diversify energy sources and reduce harms associated with energy production could continue to provide environmental benefits and educate both other policy-makers and constituencies about the implications of strategy choices.[39] As Professor Carlson and researchers at MIT have demonstrated, cap-and-trade plus complementary policies could lead overall costs of GHG reductions to increase but still provide other benefits and address predictable forms of market failure.[40] A broadened menu of tested cost-effective means to reduce GHGs and improve energy efficiency would also likely reduce resistance to a comprehensive national climate change law. Leakage risks, in the sense of movement of some production to more lax jurisdictions, would still exist. However, environmental compliance costs tend to be dwarfed by labor costs and other location-dependent advantages. In addition, some businesses, especially power plants, would find it difficult to move. (Of course, disparate regulatory burdens over the long term would influence choices about the movement of linked capital.) Thus, at the margins, climate and energy-directed state regulation might modestly influence locational choices, but an argument based on self-defeating regulatory futility seems an overly strong claim.[41]

---

[38] Glicksman, Robert L. 'Balancing Mandate and Discretion in the Institutional Design of Federal Climate Change Policy' (2008) 102 Nw U. L. Rev. Colloquy **196**, 204–06.

[39] DeShazo and Freeman, *supra*, n. 26 at 1522–23.

[40] Carlson, *supra*, n. 8 (citing studies from MIT and others predicting increased overall costs with cap-and-trade plus complementary policies, but also predicting lowered carbon allowance costs).

[41] See Wiener, *supra*, n. 24 (arguing the leakage and futility points).

Second, state environmental regulation has long been critical in catalyzing support for federal regulation, and whether due to implementation failures or policy reversals, no federal regulation is invulnerable to derailment.[42] As long as states could take climate-related actions to address laxity and implementation risks, some incentives for a revised federal law or improved federal implementation would remain. In contrast, if federal law were falling short, but state climate actions were preempted, then no one could turn to the states to press for action. No other venue for climate action would exist unless a new law re-empowered the states.

2. Risks of implementation failures and policy reversal

Risks of climate-related regulatory implementation failures and policy reversals are substantial and would undercut innovation incentives and climate progress. They are distinct from laxity risks, which focus on an undemanding environmental target. By regulatory implementation failure, I allude here to failures to implement a law after its enactment. Relatedly, policy reversals remain a risk.

First, both to secure favorable regulation or simply delay the effective date of regulatory burdens, industry will vigorously participate in climate-related regulatory venues. Even if industries benefited by climate regulation tried to keep implementation on track, agencies implementing a federal climate law might fall behind. Under the leading climate bills, hundreds of rulemakings and other complicated regulatory tasks were required, many of which would have led to regulatory challenges.[43] In addition, absent specific statutory mandates and deadlines, recent Supreme Court cases would make challenges to agency delay and inaction difficult.[44] Furthermore, even if the regulatory infrastructure were in place, GHG markets dependent on regulation would also need effective monitoring and enforcement. Especially if a federal climate law

---

[42] Engel and Saleska, *supra*, n. 17; Revesz, Richard L., 'Rehabilitating Interstate Competition: Rethinking the "Race-to-the-Bottom" Rationale for Federal Environmental Regulation' (1992) 67 N.Y.U. L. Rev. **1210**, 1244–47.

[43] Onken, Melissa et al., 'Litigating Global Warming: Likely Legal Challenges to Emerging Greenhouse Gas Cap-and-Trade Programs in the United States' (2009) 39 Envtl L. Rep. News & Analysis **10389**, 10390.

[44] See Blumm, Michael C. and Sherry L. Bosse, *Norton v SUWA and the Unraveling of Federal Public Land Planning*, (2007) 18 Duke Envtl. L. & Pol'y F. 105 (discussing *Norton v S. Utah Wilderness Alliance*, 542 U.S. 55 (2004)); Levin, Ronald M., 'Understanding Unreviewability in Administrative Law' (1990) 74 Minn. L. Rev. 689 (discussing *Heckler v Chaney*, 470 U.S. 821 (1985)).

credited offset-linked actions, risks of illusory beneficial activity would arise. If cheating were not caught or markets simply became muddled and lacking in transparency, the market could collapse. Authorizing additional state regulation, and ideally also state and citizen enforcement of federal law, might help preserve regulation-dependent markets.

A linked insight is also critical: if federal law provided the only significant climate regulation, polluters opposed to such regulation would work hard to cause such implementation delays, regulatory failures, or secure a policy reversal. They would undoubtedly engage in the sort of 'blood sport' regulatory attacks analyzed by Professor McGarity.[45] In fact, the regulatory payoff for regulatory obstruction at the federal level would be greater if that derailment promised a complete escape from regulation.[46] In contrast, if polluters were faced with a weak federal climate law and, instead of a regulatory vacuum, faced the possibility of more rigorous or diverse forms of state regulation, then they would have increased incentives to support more effective federal law over a wave of potentially disparate or stringent state regulation. Relatedly, a revival of climate-related actions under earlier laws like the Clean Air Act might lead industry to favor a more tailored, effective and likely less costly new climate bill. Hence, the mere retained possibility of state regulation would likely create greater commitment to the successful implementation of a federal law.

B. Anticipating Overinclusion Risks

Efforts to preempt state and local climate efforts would invariably create difficult line-drawing challenges that could themselves undercut climate markets and innovation incentives. With partial preemptive or displacing federal legislation, a major question concerns what would be preempted. GHGs are seldom regulated just for their climate effects. Either they cause other harms, are emitted with other co-pollutants, or might be regulated to achieve other state goals. For example, energy conservation might be motivated by desire to reduce rate hikes or to reduce power plants' use of vast amounts of water, rather than to address climate change. Broad preemptive language could lead to litigation challenging state regulation that, in effect, imposed burdens on emitters complying

---

[45] McGarity, Thomas O., 'Administrative Law as Blood Sport: Policy Erosion in a Highly Partisan Age' (2012) 61 Duke L. J. 1671.

[46] Blais, Lynn E. and Wendy E. Wagner, 'Emerging Science, Adaptive Regulation, and the Problem of Rulemaking Ruts' (2008) 86 Tex. L. Rev. **1701**, 1705–15.

with federal climate law. Industry would make conflict preemption claims, especially under 'obstacle' preemption case law since any state-imposed burdens might undercut federal cost-effectiveness goals.[47] Resulting uncertainty about the scope of preemption would create market uncertainty.

Although a familiar refrain in preemption battles, the anti-'patchwork' and 'fifty different states' arguments of industry favoring a unitary preemptive regime would both seek too much and disregard how the largest emitters of GHGs are actually regulated. First, the very ubiquity of GHG sources undercuts this argument. With a huge diversity of sources, and thousands of types of regulation directly or indirectly influencing GHG emission levels, a truly preemptive federal law could have a massive disabling effect on the states and agencies, even impinging on traditional state turf like utility rate regulation and state or local transportation, transit, and land use planning. It is hard to imagine that such massive preemption of state and federal power would be anyone's goal.

The anti-patchwork arguments also are misdirected due to how large stationary sources of GHG pollution are actually regulated. First, if the regulatory targets are energy utilities, most are subject to individualized state regulatory oversight for anti-monopoly and consumer protection reasons. Second, because federal emission standards set only a regulatory floor,[48] states and local governments have long been able to require greater pollution reductions and choose tradeoffs among pollutants and polluters, especially for existing pollution sources. Third, any large stationary source's regulatory compliance obligations are typically individualized and linked to its size, age, production techniques and many other variables.[49] Individualized source obligations also exist under the Clean Air Act's New Source Review program, where limitations are set

---

[47] Glicksman, Robert L., 'Federal Preemption by Inaction' in Buzbee, William W. (ed.) *Preemption Choice: The Theory, Law, and Reality of Federalism's Core Question* (Cambridge University Press, New York 2009), pp. 182–83; Buzbee, William W., 'Preemption Hard Look Review, Regulatory Interaction, and the Quest for Stewardship and Intergenerational Equity' (2009) 77 Geo. Wash. L. Rev. **1521**, 1545–46; Sharkey, Catherine M., 'Federalism Accountability: "Agency-Forcing" Measures' (2009) 58 Duke L.J. **2125**, 2190.

[48] Buzbee, William W., 'Asymmetrical Regulation: Risk, Preemption, and the Floor/Ceiling Distinction' (2007) 82 N.Y.U. L. Rev. **1547**, 1564–68.

[49] For example, even under New Source Performance Standards under Clean Air Act section 111(b)(2), promulgated regulations typically allow if not require obligations tailored to 'classes, types, and sizes' of regulated categories of polluters.

on a permit-by-permit basis based on referenced best performers or most stringent limitations imposed on other sources.[50] Such permit-by-permit review reduces the risk of stale and lax requirements and keeps progress moving.[51] Thus, large stationary sources are already subjected to individualized, negotiated pollution obligations; none expect simple 'off the rack' determinations about their regulatory obligations. Both within and among states, variety of obligations is hence already the rule.

C. Entrenching Climate Regulation Through a Web of Regulatory Authority

Somewhat counterintuitively, allowing for the possibility of federal, state and local climate regulation, and even different cap-and-trade regimes, could provide greater market stability and rewards for climate-linked investment than under an exclusively federal regime, even if such laws cause some increase in transaction costs and reduce economies of scale.[52] Of course, if a perfectly crafted, stable and enforced federal carbon cap-and-trade market existed, then the need for other regulatory actors would be greatly reduced. But such stability is far from a certainty, for reasons discussed above. Diffuse and diverse regulatory authority would provide substantial benefits in a real world where imperfection, opposition and instability are a near certainty. This section's discussion builds on several interrelated observations and theories about the political and economic dynamics of legislation and regulation leading to policy entrenchment.

The tendency of law and regulation to become entrenched and resistant to change is often noted as a problem since rigid and prescriptive regulation can create little inducement for ongoing improvement or updating.[53] However, where a regulatory challenge is pervaded by shared fears that regulatory commitments will prove unstable or unmatched by other jurisdictions, a central task is to balance the need for ongoing governmental and private sector learning and adjustment with regulatory

---

[50] Buzbee, William W., 'Clean Air Dynamism and Disappointments: Lessons for Climate Change Legislation to Prompt Innovation and Discourage Inertia' (2010) 32 Wash. U. J.L. & Pol'y **33**, 54–55.

[51] Ibid.

[52] Van de Ven, Andrew H., 'Central Problems in the Management of Innovation' (1986) 32 Mgmt. Science No. 5, **590**, 600 (noting that redundancy can sometimes increase innovation).

[53] See Coglianese and D'Ambrosio, *supra*, n. 24 at 1423–25 (opposing state-level climate regulation and noting 'lock-in' risks).

frameworks that are nonetheless stable and widely embraced. Professor Patashnik therefore suggests use of cap-and-trade regulation of GHG emissions because of how it will shape incentives and possibly 'create a business constituency' supportive of regulation.[54] Professor Lazarus has explored legislation 'pre-commitment' strategies that would discourage easy legislative reversals.[55] Professors Stewart, Biber and Brewster have each discussed how regulatory progress at the state level can over time create interest groups invested in that regulation.[56] Professors Engel and Adelman have analyzed how fostering technological innovation is an independent ground for retaining state climate regulatory authority.[57] This chapter's discussion builds on those analyses, in particular focusing on regulatory derailment risks and associated market instability, and showing how several conceptually related bodies of scholarship support the counterintuitive benefits of retained state and local climate power even after enacting national legislation.

First, a growing body of political science literature explores the dynamics of, and conditions conducive to, 'policy diffusion.'[58] Policy diffusion occurs when a jurisdiction's policy ideas or regulatory actions move to other jurisdictions, which either adopt similar measures or tailor them to the latter jurisdiction's context. Innovations inherently mean a degree of difference among jurisdictions, thus reducing economies of scale.

However, although political scientists analyze when and why jurisdictions follow and learn from each other, an important benefit of diffused policy innovations to market actors is perhaps neglected. Innovations will lead to some difference, but the critical point here is that the spread of *similarly targeted regulation* means that, overall, more and more jurisdictions would be invested in a regulatory field. From the perspective of private market actors, diffused but similarly targeted

---

[54] Patashnik, *supra*, n. 4 at 179.
[55] Lazarus, *supra*, n. 1.
[56] See (in order referenced in text) Stewart, *supra*, n. 6; Biber, *supra*, n. 4; Brewster, *supra*, n. 5.
[57] Adelman, David E. and Kirsten H. Engel, 'Adaptive Environmental Federalism' in *Preemption Choice, supra*, n. 47 pp. 277, 293, 296–98; Adelman, David E. and Kirsten H. Engel, 'Reorienting State Climate Change Policies to Induce Technological Change' (2008) 50 Ariz. L. Rev. 835.
[58] Shipan, Charles R. and Craig Volden, 'The Mechanisms of Policy Diffusion' (2008) 52 Am. J. of Pol. Sci. No. 4, **840**, 843. See also Karch, Andrew, 'Policy Diffusion and Climate-Change Policy' in Schlager, Edella C. et al. (eds) *Navigating Climate Change Policy: The Opportunities of Federalism* (University of Arizona Press, Tucson 2011), p. 104.

regulation can result in a web of regulation that in aggregate creates stable policy and resulting markets, even if some variety among jurisdictions remains. For the inventor of, for example, new battery technology, new high-efficiency solar energy technologies, an energy-efficient appliance or other means to reduce carbon emissions resulting from energy production, the existence of many jurisdictions driving markets for such products will maintain incentives for investment, even with regulatory variety.

Furthermore, every time a jurisdiction tailors its adoption of a diffused policy to its own distinctive needs, attributes and resources, it provides three benefits. First, that tailoring reduces the costs of adoption and, unless the jurisdiction is irrational, would also maximize local benefits and avoid misfitting regulation. Incremental regulatory innovations can teach other states and federal regulators, and the demonstration that regulation really is viable can also change federal regulatory and legislative dynamics.[59] States really can serve as 'laboratories' of democracy.[60] Second, every regulatory tweak and adjustment may open new market opportunities and reduce the costs borne by later following jurisdictions. Hence, regulatory costs would tend to drop, benefits increase, and sequential learning and regulatory and market innovations would follow.

The third benefit relates in a somewhat paradoxical way to the same dynamics that can drive race-to-the-bottom environmental concerns. States will inevitably compete against each other to attract businesses and their attendant employment and tax benefits.[61] They will also seek to grow and retain businesses linked to their particular economies, universities, research and development facilities and other endowments. And each state's different political environment will create different priorities and beneficial policy opportunities for politicians. That diversity is likely to generate a different mix of policy initiatives. That competitive state hunt for the next big industry or technological breakthrough is inherently a hunt for relative advantage. That many states would not want to be

---

[59] See DeShazo and Freeman, *supra*, n. 26 at 1533–38.

[60] See Sovacool, Benjamin K., 'The Best of Both Worlds: Environmental Federalism and the Need for Federal Action on Renewable Energy and Climate Change' (2008) 27 Stan. Envtl L.J. **397**, 430. But see Galle, Brian and Joseph Leahy, 'Laboratories of Democracy? Policy Innovation in Decentralized Governments' (2009) 58 Emory L.J. 1333 (critiquing the theory that states function as policy laboratories).

[61] See Engel, Kirsten H., 'State Environmental Standard-Setting: Is There a Race and Is It "to the Bottom"' (1997) 48 Hastings L.J. 271 (showing through survey how jurisdictions do compete for business investment).

regulatory innovators or do more than the federal government does not matter; all it takes is a state innovator to demonstrate new means to further regulatory ends. For example, states with businesses heavily invested in carbon offset activities would likely face interest group pressure to reward such climate change-fighting strategies even if the federal impetus weakened or disappeared.

The experience of state brownfield law innovations when the US federal Superfund law proved dysfunctional provides an important analogous lesson.[62] The federal Superfund law frustrated both private sector and state and local goals due to potentially vast and uncertain cleanup liabilities. States came up with improvements to reduce this uncertainty and encourage investment in former industrial sites known as brownfields. Other states learned and imitated. The federal government through regulatory measures then imitated the states and sought to reduce the harshness and liability uncertainty under the law. Ultimately, a federal legislative amendment encouraging brownfield reuse was enacted that modeled improvements on those state innovations.

Similarly, retaining latitude in the climate and energy areas for such state and local incremental improvement, experimentation and innovation would be of even greater value in devising regulatory responses to a federal climate law that would likely be under perpetual attack.[63] Such benefits were evident in the Obama Administration's 2015 Clean Power Plan, which promulgated Clean Air Act section 111(d) regulations for existing GHG-emitting power plants.[64] This regulation built substantially on diverse state and local initiatives already reducing GHG emissions.

As each state creates regulation that in turn fosters linked private investment, private and public constituencies will arise that are invested in that regulation and linked market. Those invested in the status quo

---

[62] Buzbee, William W., 'Contextual Environmental Federalism' (2005) 14 N.Y.U. Envtl. L.J. **108**, 119–21; Robertson, Heidi Gorovitz, 'Legislative Innovation in State Brownfields Redevelopment Programs' (2001) 16 J. Envtl L. & Litig. **1**, 11–15; Revesz, Richard L., 'Federalism and Environmental Regulation: A Public Choice Analysis' (2001) 115 Harv. L. Rev. **553**, 598–603.

[63] Kaswan, Alice, 'The Domestic Response to Global Climate Change: What Role for Federal, State, and Local Litigation Initiatives?' (2007) 42 U.S.F. L. Rev. **29**, 67, 69.

[64] See Carbon Pollution Emission Guidelines for Existing Stationary Sources: Electric Utility Generating Units, Proposed Rule (June 18, 2014) 79 Fed. Reg. 34,830. The regulations were released in final form on August 3, 2015, as this book went to press.

would oppose its wholesale abandonment.[65] A federal policy that precluded or hindered such state difference, however, could derail such a balance of beneficial innovation and a collectively large aggregate web of regulation supporting business investment.

When one starts to compare a single preemptive federal climate regime and a regime that embraces diffused authority with latitude for state difference and change, the benefits of non-preemptive regimes become especially apparent.[66] Federalism-facilitated policy diffusion ends up looking much like the 'learning by monitoring,' benchmarking and 'experimentalist' learning touted for many settings by Charles Sabel and other scholars working with his concepts, as well as the functioning of adaptive systems.[67]

Scholarship on 'path dependence' and 'increasing returns' or increasing 'costs of exit' similarly reveals how retaining state climate authority can over time increase investment in an ever-changing status quo.[68] As similarly directed policy initiatives are embraced in multiple jurisdictions, policymakers and dependent businesses and individuals will resist change that undercuts that investment. Time and changing increased investments create a path that is hard to abandon. This observation links closely to scholarship on legislative dynamics: any legislation, or even authoritative interpretation of legislation by an agency

---

[65] See Biber, *supra*, n. 4.

[66] See Richardson, Benjamin J., 'Enlisting Institutional Investors in Environmental Regulation: Some Comparative and Theoretical Perspectives' (2002) 28 N.C.J. Int'l L. & Com. Reg. **247**, 257 (discussing the need for greater communication between government and industry to reduce regulatory risk).

[67] See e.g. Dorf, Michael C. and Charles F. Sabel, 'A Constitution of Democratic Experimentalism' (1998) 98 Colum. L. Rev. **267**, 287–88 (arguing for benefits of continuous generation of new information and adjustment and improvement in an array of legal areas); Karkkainen, Bradley C., 'Environmental Lawyering in the Age of Collaboration' (2002) 2002 Wis. L. Rev. **555**, 567–71 (discussing 'collaborative ecosystem management' and the room it leaves for regionally tailored solutions with broad coordination and public accountability); Karkkainen, Bradley C., 'New Governance' in Legal Thought and in the World: Some Splitting as Antidote to Overzealous Lumping' (2004) 89 Minn. L. Rev. 471 (discussing similar legal innovations known by the 'new governance' label and related approaches to governance); Lobel, Orly, 'The Renew Deal: The Fall of Regulation and the Rise of Governance in Contemporary Legal Thought' (2004) 89 Minn. L. Rev. **342**, 396, 461 (discussing similar legal innovations and methods of governance); see also Ayres, Ian and John Braithwaite, *Responsive Regulation: Transcending the Deregulation Debate* (Oxford University Press, USA 1992) (exploring similar issues).

[68] See Pierson, *supra*, n. 5; Biber, *supra*, n. 4; Brewster, *supra*, n. 5.

or court, will lead to investment in that new status quo and create political opposition to change.[69] Again, each step down the legal path changes incentives. Even the growing body of behavioral economics observes a similar tendency at the individual level; people become attached to the status quo, especially circumstances that are familiar and recently available to them. Individuals hence may initially resist changes wrought by regulation, but once they start to adjust to a new normal, they may resist a return to the old ways or at least form new attachments.[70]

From the viewpoint of private market actors, an additional crucial insight is that universal change or deregulation is harder to achieve with diffused policy authority.[71] For example, if federal climate commitments waned or met with delay, that would not automatically lead states to abandon their own initiatives. States would invariably face different political dynamics, potentially including voters who care or businesses or interest groups invested in their own commitments to reduce GHGs or support clean energy innovations. Even if a new national majority, executive branch laxity or litigation challenges derailed a federal climate law, efforts to gut state climate and clean energy commitments would face different political opposition dynamics.

Furthermore, consideration of legislative inertia and status quo dynamics further reveals benefits of federal law retaining at least the possibility of multi-layered and institutionally diverse approaches to climate change. Legislative inertia would work in favor of retaining those state roles since interests seeking to derail climate efforts would not only have to derail federal implementation or repeal a federal climate law, but also gain supermajority support of federal legislators to disempower the states and unsettle bargains struck under other laws.[72] Or they would have to battle

---

[69] Eskridge, William N. Jr. and John Ferejohn, *A Republic of Statutes: The New American Constitution* (Yale University Press 2010), pp. 12–22; Eskridge, William N., '*Patterson v McLean*: Interpreting Legislative Inaction' (1988) 87 Mich. L. Rev. **67**, 99, 114. See also McCubbins, Mathew D. and Daniel B. Rodriguez, 'Superstatutory Entrenchment: A Positive and Normative Interrogatory' (2011) 120 Yale L.J. Online **387**, 395–401.

[70] Rachlinski, Jeffrey J., 'The Psychology of Climate Change' (2000) Ill. L. Rev. 299.

[71] See Freeman, Jody and Daniel A. Farber, 'Modular Environmental Regulation' (2005) 54 Duke L.J. **795**, 809–10, 813.

[72] See Ahdieh, Robert B., 'Dialectical Regulation' (2006) 38 Conn. L. Rev. **863**, 866 (noting that environmental law is prime example of 'intersystemic regulation'); Schapiro, Robert A. and William W. Buzbee, 'Unidimensional Federalism: Power and Perspective in Commerce Clause Adjudication' (2003) 88 Cornell L. Rev. **1199**, 1246–47.

in state after state to preclude state and local climate regulation. But because federalism politics are far more complicated and less predictable along party lines than are pro- or anti-environmental lines, or pro- or anti-climate legislation lines, federal level moves to disempower state and local governments would not automatically meet with success, even if national politics favored a weak or nonexistent climate law.[73]

Similarly, retaining or providing backstop EPA power to regulate GHGs under laws not initially meant to address climate change, such as the Clean Air Act, would make linked markets less vulnerable to collapse due to substantial interest group and political investment in those other laws. Due to its long existence, the Clean Air Act and similar laws might have more substantial supportive coalitions than would exist to defend a new climate bill.

To use a metaphor, a diffused regulatory environment is akin to a fabric with many different threads providing strength. To destroy that web of laws would require many successful political attacks. In contrast, if all climate regulatory authority rested on a single federal law, then intense federal lobbying, a sympathetic president or a slow or lax federal regulator could result in complete derailment of the only source of climate regulation supporting linked business investment.

1. A note regarding a carbon tax versus cap-and-trade regulation

This chapter has explored why retention of state climate regulatory authority can help create a more enduring and resilient web of regulation, thereby creating beneficial market stability for linked businesses. Cap-and-trade based regulation has generally been assumed. The other market-based regulatory strategy favored by economists and periodically revived by policymakers to deter harmful conduct is use of Pigouvian taxes.[74] If a price is affixed on each unit of carbon, incentives would exist

---

[73] Schapiro, Robert A., 'Progressive Federalism: Not Old or Borrowed: The Truly New Blue Federalism' (2009) 3 Harv. L. & Pol'y Rev. **33**, 33–42; Rabe, Barry G., 'State Competition as a Source Driving Climate Change Mitigation' (2005) 14 N.Y.U. Envtl. L.J. **1**, 2–8; Wiener, Jonathan Baert, 'On the Political Economy of Global Environmental Regulation' (1999) 87 Geo. L.J. **749**, 749–50 (noting that existing theory for environmental regulation lacks 'a convincing account' that is 'even more murky at the *global* level').

[74] Merrill, Thomas and David M. Schizer, 'Energy Policy for an Economic Downturn: A Proposed Petroleum Fuel Price Stabilization Plan' (2010) 27 Yale J. on Reg. **1**, 4.

to reduce pollution.[75] Large carbon emitters would be disfavored in the market and benefits would flow either to pollution reduction techniques or to other market actors able to provide the good (be it energy or a product) at a lower carbon cost. Tax-induced growth in tested viable means to reduce GHG emissions or energy use could help with regulatory stability.

However, when examined from a perspective focused on the stability of the regulatory regime and linked markets, tax-based strategies appear less likely than cap-and-trade schemes to create the invested constituencies that would fight against implementation failures and policy reversal. A carbon tax would create less path-dependent increasing returns or high costs of exit. After all, a tax involves little ongoing investment in and commitment to that regulatory regime. A tax can go away in a year or two with little disruption. Few if any entities would literally be invested in a carbon tax scheme, whereas a cap-and-trade regime, especially if it included offset credit rewards, would immediately create a host of businesses and perhaps governments here and abroad that would be substantially invested in the value of their carbon allowances or offset credits. Trading markets would create yet another source of wealth and regulatory entrenchment.[76] Thus, from the perspective of businesses and other jurisdictions looking for signals of dependable climate commitments, a tax-based strategy might provide little reassurance. If a carbon tax nonetheless became the preferred regulatory instrument, policymakers would need to create highly motivated supportive constituencies. For example, a guarantee that carbon tax revenues would go directly into taxpayers' pockets, much as a substantial portion of Alaska's oil revenue is allocated to its citizens, might over time entrench policy reducing GHG emissions.

CONCLUSION

Monopolies are always problematic. Recently floated proposals to preclude state climate efforts under a future federal climate change law would leave the United States almost completely dependent on a federal

---

[75] Pigou, A.C., *The Economics of Welfare* (Macmillan, London 1932), pp. 172–203. See also Baumol, William H. and Wallace E. Oates, *The Theory of Environmental Policy* (Cambridge University Press, Cambridge 1988), pp. 21–23, 29.

[76] Stavins, 'A Meaningful U.S. Cap-and-Trade System to Address Climate Change', *supra*, n. 30 at 298–99.

regulatory monopoly and a single law. Retaining state and local climate authority, and for similar reasons backstopping EPA climate power under the Clean Air Act, would create a more sturdy and resilient web of regulation, stabilize linked markets, and discourage efforts to derail a federal climate law. With more regulatory stability, market rewards for innovation would also be enhanced. Federal climate preemption and unitary regulatory scheme arguments may make sense in an idealized world of perfect, stable legal commitments, but in a real world pervaded by regulatory failure and reversal risks and political instability, such unitary preemptive regimes would undercut climate progress. The more a federal climate bill used preemptive and displacing strategies, the more all hopes for climate progress would rest on one imperfect and vulnerable federal vessel.

ACKNOWLEDGEMENT

This chapter benefitted from comments in connection with a related preliminary conference paper and presentation at the Yale Law School-Unitar Fall 2010 Conference on Climate Change Governance, *Strengthening Institutions to Address Climate Change and Advance a Green Economy*, and then in related papers presented at George Washington, Vanderbilt, UCLA, and University of Minnesota law schools, as well as linked conference and roundtable presentations at the American Association of Law Schools, Nova Law School, and the Center on Federalism and Intersystemic Governance (CFIG) at Emory University School of Law.

8. The enigma of state climate change policy innovation

Kirsten H. Engel

I. INTRODUCTION

For several years now, commentators, including the present author, have celebrated the innovation being demonstrated by states in the area of climate change policy.[1] Indeed, there is little question but that, starting in the 1990s, states began filling the gap left by the federal government's failure to enact climate change legislation. Policies adopted by states, such as regional greenhouse gas cap-and-trade regimes and renewable portfolio standards, have been lauded as demonstrations of the continuing ingenuity of the states as "laboratories of democracy,"[2] devising new and

---

[1] The literature on this point is now extensive. For just a snapshot of this literature, see Rossi, Jim, "Maladaptive Federalism: The Structural Barriers to Coordination of State Sustainability Initiatives" (2014) 64 Case W. Res. L. Rev. **1759**, 1965–67; Klass, Alexandra B., "State Standards for Nationwide Products Revisited: Federalism, Green Building Codes, and Appliance Efficiency Standards" (2010) 34 Harv. Envtl L. Rev. **335**, 341 (discussing state innovation in the areas of building codes and land use); Burger, Michael, "Empowering Local Autonomy and Encouraging Experimentation in Climate Change Governance: The Case for a Layered Regime" (2009) 39 Envtl L. Rep. **11161**, 11162–64 (discussing state, local and regional climate change initiatives); Carlson, Ann E., "Iterative Federalism and Climate Change" (2009) 10 Nw U.L. Rev. **1097**, 1099–1100 (discussing California and the federal government's iterative efforts developing vehicle emissions standards); Adelman, David and Kirsten Engel, "Adaptive Federalism: The Case Against Reallocating Environmental Regulatory Authority" (2008) 92 Minn. L. Rev. **1796**, 1846–49 (providing examples of states leading in the development of climate change policies).
[2] *New State Ice Co. v Liebmann*, 285 U.S. 262, 311 (1932) (Brandeis, dissenting). Justice Brandeis rebelled against the mandate for uniformity that he believed followed from the Court's decision to strike down an Oklahoma statute requiring the licensing of new ice business, stating "a single courageous State

innovative solutions to climate change, considered by many the most critical environmental problem facing the world.[3]

Although consonant with that of the famous jurist Louis Brandeis, this view of state and local government as the fount of innovation is in tension with the predictions of well-respected commentators applying an economic analysis to the drivers of regulatory innovation. These commentators, most prominently Susan Rose-Ackerman[4] but also including others,[5] cite dynamics that place a drag upon the ability of localities to innovate at levels desired by the electorate. Specifically, Rose-Ackerman predicts that politicians in one subnational jurisdiction will rather free-ride off the innovations developed by other subnational jurisdictions than generate new policies of their own. The upshot is that elected politicians will support innovation at levels below that preferred by their jurisdiction's voters. Rose-Ackerman's work is cited as a basis for supporting centralized policies by a national government.[6]

An examination of climate initiatives on the state and local levels tells a more nuanced story than that generally offered by either scholars of climate change policy or regulatory economists.[7] Despite appearances,

---

may, if its citizens choose, serve as a laboratory; and try novel social and economic experiments without risk to the rest of the country ... ."

[3] For commentators explicitly drawing this comparison, see Learner, Howard A., "Restraining Federal Preemption When There Is an 'Emerging Consensus' of State Environmental Laws and Policies" (2008) 102 Nw U.L. Rev. **649**, 649; Parenteau, Patrick Lead, "Follow or Get Out of the Way: The States Tackle Climate Change with Little Help from Washington" (2008) 40 Conn. L. Rev. **1453**, 1454.

[4] Rose-Ackerman, Susan, "Risk-Taking and Reelection: Does Federalism Promote Innovation?" (1980) 9 J. Legal Stud. **593**, 594.

[5] See e.g. Abramowicz, Michael, "Speeding Up the Crawl to the Top" (2003) 20 Yale J. on Reg. **139**, 157–59; Ribstein, Larry E., "Lawyers as Lawmakers: A Theory of Lawyer Licensing" (2004) 69 Mo. L. Rev. **299**, 327–62; Ribstein, Larry E. and Bruce H. Kobayashi, "State Regulation of Electronic Commerce" (2002) 51 Emory L.J. **1**, 60–62; Ayres, Ian, "Supply-Side Inefficiencies in Corporate Charter Competition: Lessons from Patents, Yachting and Bluebooks" (1995) 43 U. Kan. L. Rev. **541**, 545.

[6] See e.g. Hirsch, Jeffrey M. "Revolution in Pragmatist Clothing: Nationalizing Workplace Law" (2010) 61 Ala. L. Rev. **1025**, 1061 (the inability of states to achieve an optimal level of innovation due to the very dynamics discussed by Rose-Ackerman "may warrant a centralized, federal system of regulation that can correct the market failures of state governance").

[7] An important exception is a recent empirical study of climate change initiatives at the local level. Outka, Uma and Richard Feilock, "Local Promise for Climate Mitigation: An Empirical Assessment" (2012) 36 Wm. & Mary Envtl

state governments are the original source of only a few of the many climate policy initiatives. An analysis of the shortlist of the most touted state climate measures reveals that core aspects of the policies were first developed either by the federal government or by California, the latter being somewhat atypical of a state due to its size, population and history of environmental regulation. Instead of functioning as a consistent source of entirely new policy ideas, the local level climate policy picture highlights the role of state and local government in taking policy tools previously developed for the international or national levels, scaling them down to the state and local level, and adopting them in their revised form. As opposed to "policy innovators," state and local governments might more accurately be described as "scale innovators."

This chapter argues that, in contrast to what might be expected, the fact that state and local governments may be less original innovators may actually be good news, or at least not as bad an outcome as may first appear. What is occurring at the state level – scale innovation and policy adoption – is of unquestioned value to the ultimate goal of mitigating climate change.[8] Indeed, given the plethora of existing policy tools and the overarching necessity of cutting back on greenhouse gas emissions, scale innovation with respect to existing policy tools is of arguably greater social value than the development of additional new and original policy tools.[9]

L. & Pol'y Rev. 635. This study analyzed data from survey responses from Florida city planners to find that, outside early pioneers, local climate action has been newer and less pervasive than commonly presented in the legal literature.

[8] See Grant, Don, Kelly Bergstrand et al., "Effectiveness of US State Policies in Reducing CO_2 Emissions from Power Plants" (2014) 4 *Nature Climate Change* 977 (finding that several of the policies being implemented by states to reduce emissions from power plants are effective in lowering plants' carbon dioxide emissions).

[9] In its most recent report, the Intergovernmental Panel on Climate Change (IPCC) warns that increasing magnitudes of warming increase the likelihood of severe, pervasive and irreversible impacts, but that the overall risks of climate change impacts can be reduced by limiting the rate and magnitude of climate change. IPCC, "Summary for Policymakers" in: Climate Change 2014: Impacts, Adaptation, and Vulnerability. Part A: Global and Sectoral Aspects. Contribution of Working Group II to the Fifth Assessment Report of the Intergovernmental Panel on Climate Change 12 (2014), accessed 17 July 2015 at ipcc-wg2.gov/AR5/images/uploads/WG2AR5_SPM_FINAL.pdf.

II. STATE AND LOCAL CLIMATE CHANGE POLICY INITIATIVES

In an effort to gain an understanding of the innovation displayed by the states' adoption of climate change policies, the following discusses the origins of several initiatives that have served as the focus for discussions of state contributions to climate policymaking. These policies are greenhouse gas emission targets and registries, subnational greenhouse gas cap-and-trade regimes, emissions caps for electric utility plants, clean car standards, and low-carbon fuel standards and renewable portfolio standards. Although many more policies could legitimately be included in this survey,[10] this set has been the most frequently touted as state and local-level responses to climate change.

A. Greenhouse Gas Emission Targets and Registries

Greenhouse gas emission targets are among the foremost state innovations in response to climate change.[11] An emission target is a percentage reduction in greenhouse gas emissions that the state commits to achieve within a specified timeframe. A typical greenhouse gas reduction target might commit a state to reducing its emissions 20 percent below 2005 levels by 2020 and 80 percent below 2005 levels by 2050.[12] Twenty states plus the District of Columbia have adopted an emissions target.[13] The genius of a greenhouse gas emissions reduction target is that it provides a goal around which a jurisdiction can develop a detailed plan for reducing greenhouse gases. Indeed, this is the manner in which the targets function in the states that have adopted them.[14]

---

[10] For a more expansive list of state policies that bear on climate, including those targeted specifically at energy usage by the commercial, transportation and residential sectors, see Center for Climate and Energy Solutions, U.S. States and Regions, Climate Action, accessed 17 July 2015 at www.c2es.org/us-states.

[11] See "Green House Gas Emission Targets," Center for Climate and Energy Solutions, accessed 17 July 2015 at www.c2es.org/us-states-regions/policy-maps/emissions-targets.

[12] Ibid.

[13] Ibid.

[14] See Brawer, Judi and Matthew Vespa, "Thinking Globally, Acting Locally: The Role of Local Government in Minimizing Greenhouse Gas Emissions from New Development" (2008) 44 Idaho L. Rev. **589**, 606 (discussing efforts states are making to update their planning, zoning and building laws and regulations together with economic incentives and enforcement measures in order to achieve their emission reduction targets).

Greenhouse gas reporting and the maintenance of a greenhouse gas registry are companion policies to greenhouse gas emissions targets and plans. The registry is a mechanism to measure, track, verify and publicly report on greenhouse gas emissions.[15] Twenty-two states conduct their registry through the "Climate Registry," a nonprofit collaboration among states, provinces, territories and native nations to establish standards for measuring and reporting greenhouse gas emissions.[16]

The inspiration for greenhouse gas emission reduction targets and registries seem to have come, not from the state policymakers, but from the creators of the Kyoto Protocol, the international agreement to reduce greenhouse gases. Famously, the Kyoto Protocol imposes upon each member party a greenhouse gas emissions reduction target that, in the aggregate, amounts to reductions by all nations of 5 percent below 1990 levels by the first compliance period of 2008–2012. For instance, although not formally subject to a target because it never ratified Kyoto, the United States' target was 7 percent below 1990 levels.[17] Hence greenhouse gas emission reduction targets simply copy or elaborate upon the emissions targets of the Kyoto Protocol. Ditto greenhouse gas reporting and registries. The latter were originally developed to help countries ensure compliance with the Kyoto targets.[18] State greenhouse gas targets now reach much further into the future than the original Kyoto targets, routinely establishing a 2050 goal.[19]

---

[15] Greenhouse Gas Reporting and Registries, Center for Climate and Energy Solutions, accessed 17 July 2015 at www.c2es.org/us-states-regions/policy-maps/ghg-reporting-and-registries.

[16] The Climate Registry, accessed 17 July 2015 at www.theclimateregistry.org/.

[17] Kyoto Protocol to the United Nations Framework Convention on Climate Change, 11 December 1997, 2303 U.N.T.S. 148.

[18] "Registry Systems under the Kyoto Protocol," United Nations Framework Convention on Climate Change, unfccc.int/kyoto_protocol/registry_systems/items/2723.php.

[19] For example, Colorado established its emissions goal at 20 percent below 2005 levels by 2020 and 80 percent below 2005 levels by 2050. Illinois established emission reduction targets of 1990 levels by 2020 and 60 percent below 1990 levels by 2050. See Greenhouse Gas Emissions Targets, Center for Climate and Energy Solutions, accessed 9 Sept. 2015 at www.c2es.org/us-states-regions/policy-maps/emissions-targets.

B. Subnational Greenhouse Gas Cap-and-Trade Programs

One of the most touted climate change initiatives at the state and local level are greenhouse gas cap-and-trade programs. Under such initiatives, the aggregate amount of greenhouse gas emissions for a given category of sources is "capped" but, after an initial allocation of rights among individual emitting sources to emit up to the cap, such sources are free to trade among themselves which sources actually emit and by how much.[20] The adoption of greenhouse gas cap-and-trade programs at the subnational level can be traced to a 2005 Memorandum of Understanding between seven northeastern states. In this memo, the states gave birth to the Regional Greenhouse Gas Initiative by pledging to implement a cap on their respective fossil fuel fired electric generating facilities and allowing for the trading of emission allowances between regulated parties.[21] California first formally identified a state-wide greenhouse gas cap-and-trade program in its 2008 plan[22] for achieving the ambitious goals set forth in its landmark climate law, AB 32, calling for reducing greenhouse gases to 1990 levels by 2020.[23]

Cap-and-trade programs did not originate with the states. In the United States, cap-and-trade followed the more basic "offset" and "bubble" programs employed by EPA to enable states to allow new sources of emissions without further deteriorating air quality in areas where the air quality was already above health-based threshold levels.[24] Cap-and-trade gained prominence in 1990 when it served as the basis of Congress's approach to reducing acid rain under the Clean Air Act Amendments

---

[20] See Driesen, David, Robert Adler and Kirsten Engel, *Environmental Law: A Conceptual and Pragmatic Approach*, 2nd edn (Aspen, Wolters Kluwer, New York 2011), p. 305.

[21] Regional Greenhouse Gas Initiative, accessed 17 July 2015 at www.rggi.org.

[22] California Environmental Protection Agency, Air Resources Board, "Timeline of AB 32 Scoping Activities," accessed 17 July 2015 at www.arb.ca.gov/cc/scopingplan/timeline.htm.

[23] Assemb. 32, 2005–06 Leg., Reg. Sess. (Cal. 2006).

[24] Ellerman, A. Danny et al., *Emissions Trading in the U.S.: Experience, Lessons, and Considerations for Greenhouse Gasses* (Pew Center on Global Climate Change, 2003), p. 8, accessed 17 July 2015 at web.mit.edu/globalchange/www/PewCtr_MIT_Rpt_Ellerman.pdf; Hahn, Robert W., *A Primer on Environmental Policy Design* (Taylor & Francis, London 2013), pp. 35–37; Hahn, Robert W. and Gordon L. Hester, "Where Did All the Markets Go? An Analysis of EPA's Emissions Trading Program" (1989) 6 Yale J. on Reg. 109.

enacted that year.[25] Since that time cap-and-trade has been the prototype for allowance trading under the Kyoto Protocol and the favored policy framework in congressional bills to mitigate domestic sources of greenhouse gases. For instance, all ten of the climate legislative proposals pending before Congress in 2007 envisioned a cap-and-trade scheme for carbon dioxide emissions.[26]

C. Clean Car Standards

Alone among the 50 states, the federal Clean Air Act permits California to establish vehicle emission standards.[27] Other states may adopt the California standards, however, and, for those that do, these standards then replace federal vehicle emission standards within that state.[28] California has long used its unique authority to push ahead with standards to reduce conventional pollutants and, since 2002, to reduce the greenhouse gas emissions from motor vehicles.[29] In 2002, California enacted the Clean Cars Law to set vehicle emissions standards for greenhouse gases.[30]

Recently, California consolidated its program of controls upon vehicle pollutants contributing to both smog and climate change into the "Advanced Clean Cars Program" applicable to new vehicles in model years 2017 through 2025.[31] Currently, nine states have adopted the Zero Emission Vehicle (ZEV) part of this program, according to which major manufacturers of passenger cars and light trucks must procure a certain number of ZEV credits, depending upon the number of zero (fully electric vehicles) or low-emission vehicles produced and delivered for sale in the state.[32] An additional three states have adopted California's Low Emission Vehicle Program.[33]

---

[25] Clean Air Act tit. IV, §§ 401–16, 42 U.S.C. 7507 (2014).
[26] See Flatt, Victor, "Taking the Legislative Temperature: Which Federal Climate Change Legislative Proposal Is 'Best?'" (2007) 102 Nw. U.L. Rev. Colloq. **123**, 135.
[27] Clean Air Act § 209, 42 U.S.C. 7543 (2014).
[28] Clean Air Act § 177, 42 U.S.C. 7507 (2014).
[29] See Carlson, Ann E., "Iterative Federalism and Climate Change" (2009) 103 Nw U.L. Rev. **1097**, 1116–17.
[30] Assemb. 1493, 2001 Leg., Reg. Sess. (Cal. 2002).
[31] See "California's Advanced Clean Cars Program," Cal. Air Res. Bd., accessed 17 July 2015 www.arb.ca.gov/msprog/consumer_info/advanced_clean_cars/consumer_acc.htm.
[32] See "ZEV Program", Center for Climate and Energy Solutions, accessed 17 July 2015 at www.c2es.org/us-states-regions/policy-maps/zev-program.
[33] Ibid.

As Ann Carlson has demonstrated in detail, the California car program is not entirely the product of California's inventiveness, but instead reflects decades of back and forth between regulators at the state and the federal level as well as the automobile industry.[34] This history is rife with examples of California's adoption of federal standards and the federal government's adoption of a California emissions standard as federal law.[35]

D. Emission Caps for Electricity Generators

A small group of states has adopted carbon dioxide emission performance standards for electricity generation.[36] For instance, in 1997 Oregon enacted a law limiting new fossil fuel power plants to a net carbon dioxide emissions rate per kilowatt hour of electricity produced.[37] Washington state, in 2004, passed a law requiring new fossil fuel power plants to mitigate or offset 20 percent of their carbon dioxide emissions.[38]

Emission performance standards have a long history that does not necessarily originate with the states. Since its enactment in 1970, the federal Clean Air Act has imposed emissions standards upon electricity generators. These standards include the section 111 New Source Performance Standards, applicable to categories of new sources of air pollutants, as well as the section 111(d) guidelines for existing sources.[39]

E. Low Carbon Fuel Standards

While a late entrant to the climate change scene, low-carbon fuel standards are nevertheless a potent greenhouse gas mitigation measure. Low-carbon fuel standards restrict the sale or use of fuels based upon their carbon intensity. Life cycle analysis is one way of measuring a fuel's carbon intensity that takes into account the carbon emissions that

---

[34] Carlson, *supra*, n. 29.
[35] See e.g. ibid. at 1112.
[36] See "Standards and Caps for Electricity GHG Emission," Center for Climate and Energy Solutions, accessed 17 July 2015 at www.c2es.org/us-states-regions/policy-maps/electricity-emissions-caps.
[37] Title 36, O.R.S. § 469.503
[38] Wash. Rev Code § 80.70.
[39] Clean Air Act § 111(b), 42 U.S.C. 7411(b) (2014); Rubin, Edward S., *A Performance Standards Approach to Reducing CO_2 Emissions from Electric Power Plants* (Pew Center 2009), p. 13, accessed 17 July 2015 at www.c2es.org/docUploads/Coal-Initiative-Series-Rubin.pdf.

occur over the entire life cycle of the fuel, from extraction, to development, to transportation, to its ultimate combustion.[40]

California has been at the forefront of the development of a low-carbon fuel standard and indeed is responsible for enacting, in 2007, the first known low-carbon fuel standard mandate. The California Air Resources Board subsequently developed criteria for the standard that took effect in 2011. Nevertheless, the timing of similar proposals by other governments demonstrates that California was not alone in developing a low-carbon fuel standard at this time. Just three weeks after California passed the low-carbon fuel mandate in 2007, the European Commission proposed that a low-carbon fuel standard for the transportation sector requiring carbon intensity to be reduced by 10 percent between 2011 and 2020.[41] Similar legislation was approved by British Columbia in 2008.[42] It is impossible to attribute the entirety of the innovation to California alone.

F. Renewable Portfolio Standards

A key climate change initiative that *does* appear to originate with the states is the renewable portfolio standard (RPS). Under a renewable portfolio standard, a state requires that the energy portfolio of each retail electricity supplier serving its state include a minimum quantity of renewable energy or capacity, expressed in either units of energy or in a percentage of retail sales.[43] Retailers can satisfy this obligation either by owning a renewable energy facility and producing renewable energy or by purchasing power from a third party's renewable generating facility. Renewable portfolio mandates are perhaps the most widespread of any energy initiative. Currently, 32 states have adopted an RPS,[44] and for

---

[40] See ISO 14040.2, Envtl Mgmt Sys., Draft: Life Cycle Assessment – Principles and Guidelines (Int'l Org. for Standardization, Draft Int'l Standard).

[41] "EU Government Proposes Low Carbon Transport Fuel Standard," Env't News Serv. (31 Jan. 2007), www.ens-newswire.com/ens/jan2007/2007-01-31-05.html.

[42] Greenhouse Gas Reduction (Renewable and Low Carbon Fuel Requirements) Act, S.B.C. 2008, c. 16, accessed 17 July 2015 at www.bclaws.ca/EPLibraries/bclaws_new/document/ID/freeside/00 08016 01.

[43] Wiser, Ryan et al., *Renewable Portfolio Standards: A Factual Introduction to Experience from the United States* (LBNL, Berkeley 2007), p. 3; Rader, Nancy and Scott Hempling, *The Renewables Portfolio Standard: A Practical Guide* (National Association of Regulatory Utility Commissioners, 2001), p. ix.

[44] Center for Climate and Energy Solutions, *supra*, n. 10.

many, the standard has been through at least one or more iterations.[45] The more recent iterations require a higher percentage of renewable sources in a utility's portfolio.[46] The RPS is a type of subsidy justified by the market barriers that have historically prevented renewable energy from competing with fossil fuels on an even playing field.[47] The RPS sits astride the dividing line between a climate change initiative and an environmentally responsible energy initiative. RPSs are also about selling a particular product: renewable energy. Thus a strong motivation for adopting them is to build or support the renewable energy industry.[48] Part of their success may be attributed to being marketed, not only or even primarily as a greenhouse gas reduction tool, but instead as a way of creating jobs[49] and diversifying the sources of energy in a state's electricity portfolio.[50]

RPSs vary by state with respect to a few key characteristics. Important ones are the types of renewable energy sources covered, whether the scheme employs tradable renewable energy credits (TRECs or RECs) and whether the scheme requires a greater reliance upon a certain form of renewable energy or subtly or overtly favors the in-state generation of renewable power.[51]

The origins of the RPS can be traced back to the early 1990s as a means to protect the renewable power industry from the inroads of fossil fuel power resulting from the newly deregulated electricity industry. Iowa enacted the first RPS in 1991.[52] The RPS was integral to California's

---

[45] See Rabe, Barry, "Race to the Top: The Expanding Role of U.S. State Renewable Portfolio Standards" (Pew Center, 2006), 4, Table 1, 6, accessed 17 July 2015 at www.c2es.org/docUploads/RPSReportFinal.pdf.

[46] Ibid. at 4 (Table 1).

[47] Rader, Nancy A. and Richard B. Norgaard, "Efficiency and Sustainability in Restructured Energy Markets: The Renewables Portfolio Standard" (1996) *The Electricity Journal* **37**, 40–41.

[48] Lyon, Thomas P. and Haitao Yin, "Why Do States Adopt Renewable Portfolio Standards?: An Empirical Investigation" (2010) 31 *The Energy Journal* **131**, 132.

[49] See Lubber, Mind, "Protecting Renewable Portfolio Standards from Cynical Attacks," *Forbes*, 19 March 2013, accessed 17 July 2015 at www.forbes.com/sites/mindylubber/2013/03/19/protecting-renewable-portfolio-standards-from-cynical-attacks/.

[50] Ibid. See also Rabe, *supra*, n. 45 at 6.

[51] Lyon, Thomas P. and Haitao Yin, "Why Do States Adopt Renewable Portfolio Standards?: An Empirical Investigation" (2010) 31 *The Energy Journal* **131**, 132.

[52] Rabe, *supra*, n. 45 at 3.

electricity restructuring (California would enact an RPS in 2002), and several of the first state renewable energy mandates were incorporated into energy restructuring legislation.[53] The modern adoption of RPSs began in 1997 when Massachusetts, Nevada, Connecticut and four more states adopted RPSs between 1997 and 1999.[54]

III. STATE POLICY INNOVATION AND FEDERALISM THEORY

The question of state and local government policy inventiveness is pulled in opposite directions by two powerful narratives. Under the laboratory of democracy and related concepts, states and localities are the source of new policy ideas that are shaped by their diverse social, economic and natural environments.[55] Within this narrative, interstate competition fails to operate as a drag upon innovation. Why this may be so is subject to debate. It may be because of a continual pull toward a dominant policy that feeds federal legislation. Alternatively, it may be because the ideas that germinate at the local level are picked up by other local jurisdictions and eventually become the makings of national policy.[56] Finally, it may be that the population's continual search for the best fit between individual preferences and government choices fuels a continued demand for new and unique policies.[57] Regardless, this first narrative is in tension with a second in which interstate competition casts a dark shadow across the innovation potential of state and local governments, undermining confidence in the idea that they are a vibrant source of new policy ideas. Studying state and local adoption of climate change policies provides insights into the dynamics of innovation-generation at the state and local levels of government.

---

[53] Wiser et al., *supra*, n. 43, at 2.
[54] Bespalova, Olga, "Do Renewable Portfolio Standards (RPS) Promote Renewable Electricity Generation in the USA" (2011) 22 *U.S. Association for Energy Economics Dialogue* 1, accessed 17 July 2015 at dialogue.usaee.org/index.php/volume-22-number-1-2014/183-04-4-olga.
[55] This essential idea is manifest in a variety of forms. It is the foundation of the "democratic experimentalism" discussed by Michael Dorf and Charles Sabel, "A Constitution of Democratic Experimentalism" (1998) 98 Colum. L. Rev. **267**, 315.
[56] See Sager, Lawrence G., "Cool Federalism and the Life-Cycle of Moral Progress" (2005) 46 Wm. & Mary L. Rev. **1385**, 1387.
[57] Tiebout, Charles M., "A Pure Theory of Local Expenditures" (1956) 64 J. Pol. Econ. 416.

The theory set forth by Susan Rose-Ackerman, that state and local governments will innovate at suboptimal levels, rests on two assumptions: (1) that relatively secure incumbents will avoid backing innovative policy proposals owing to the risk of negative outcomes and the possibility that payoffs will occur, if ever, too late in the election cycle to benefit the sponsoring politician; and (2) that politicians will be tempted to free-ride on the innovations developed by other jurisdictions. With respect to the first, incumbents can be expected to support only low-risk proposals that promise payoffs in the short term.[58] Consequently, truly innovative proposals can be expected only from less secure politicians who have less to lose if a risky policy proposal flops or are willing to gamble that they will somehow be able to reap the benefits of innovative policies with long time horizons.

The potential for free-riding in the multi-jurisdictional context drastically increases the risk-averseness witnessed in the single-jurisdictional context. The attractiveness of free-riding is not hard to grasp. Developing solutions to society's current social, economic and environmental problems is costly and complex. State policymakers must invest large sums of money in hiring consultants, researching options, creating favorable political coalitions, and ultimately developing administrative structures capable of implementing new policies. Moreover, many policy innovations can be easily copied and adopted by these other jurisdictions. Policy ideas are not themselves "copyrightable"; there exist no intellectual property rights in new laws or regulations.[59] Hence politicians have an incentive to avoid the policy development costs where possible and free-ride on the investment made by others.[60] Knowing they can get identical results if their elected officials simply copy policies developed by other jurisdictions, Rose-Ackerman posits that voters will punish officials who spend scarce resources on developing innovative policies that they could get for free by copying the ideas of their neighbors.[61] Rose-Ackerman contends that politicians of multi-jurisdictional entities in a federal system will have only a slightly greater incentive to innovate. They may, for example, be expected to take larger risks in the hope that, even if unpopular with their own constituents, it might help distinguish them from their competitors and thereby raise their chances of being elected to a higher office.[62]

---

[58] Ibid. at 605.
[59] Rose-Ackerman, *supra*, n. 4, at 604.
[60] Ibid. at 594.
[61] Ibid. at 605.
[62] Ibid. at 614–16.

One can easily overstate Rose-Ackerman's thesis. Her argument is not that there exists *no* incentive to innovate, but that the incentive by politicians in the multi-jurisdictional context will be less than what the median voter would prefer. As a result, empirically verifying Rose-Ackerman's thesis is difficult. Simply pointing out examples of state innovation will not discredit her conclusions as she assumes a certain amount of such innovation will occur, but just not at socially optimal levels. Instead, testing the applicability of her theory must be done by comparing conditions in the real world to those that exist in her model.

Contemporary scholars of federalism have scrutinized Rose-Ackerman's claim that states will generate a sub-optimal amount of innovation. Although concluding that Rose-Ackerman's theory is generally borne out by subsequent studies, Brian Galle and Peter Leahy nevertheless decompose her thesis into subparts to demonstrate the critical assumptions upon which it stands.[63] For instance, they argue that whether a local government has incentives to free-ride depends upon a host of factors, such as the degree to which innovations are valuable to other jurisdictions, the costs involved in copying and adopting another's innovation, whether other governments have access to the relevant information and whether, regardless of the advantages of free-riding, there exist even greater advantages to innovating first.[64] Galle and Leahy conclude that localities are likely to "under-innovate" (innovate below the social optimum level) when it is relatively inexpensive for other jurisdictions to acquire information about and to adopt others' experiments.[65] Further, they conclude that because of the potential losses involved in innovation, only those jurisdictions most capable of bearing those losses will innovate. For the vast majority of jurisdictions, the potential gains from being a "first-mover" are considered too unlikely to overcome the benefits of free-riding.[66]

Galle and Leahy also critically examine Rose-Ackerman's assumption that local politicians are perfect reflections of voter preferences. They conclude that even relaxing this assumption and assuming instead that politicians act to further their own ends, as opposed to those of the voters, does little to undercut the conclusion that politicians will act in a risk-averse manner with respect to policy innovations. The exceptions to

---

[63] Galle, Brian and Joseph Leahy, "Laboratories of Democracy?: Policy Innovation in Decentralized Governments" (2009) 58 Emory L. J. **1333**, 1341–59.
[64] *Id.* at 1360.
[65] *Id.* at 1370.
[66] *Id.*

this are instances in which innovations are the responsibility of agency bureaucrats. Bureaucrats are mostly insulated from electoral pressures and hence have more freedom to pursue policies that carry risks of failure. As compared to elected politicians, bureaucrats reap greater benefits from innovating and they generally have greater access to the outside influences – organizations of agency officials and academic researchers, for example – associated with higher levels of innovation.[67] Nevertheless, the innovation potential of bureaucrats is tempered by their high propensity to collaborate and thus to develop similar innovations. Thus, according to Galle and Leahy, "their race to the top will be a race to the same summit."[68]

IV. STATE CLIMATE "INNOVATION": THEORY AND REALITY

This chapter does not pretend to perform a comprehensive empirical analysis of the innovation history of state and local climate change initiatives. Nevertheless, even the brief survey included here demonstrates the difficulty of matching a given innovation dynamic with any one particular theory. On the one hand and in contrast to the predictions of Rose-Ackerman, state and local government leaders are demonstrating a fair degree of risk by doing anything on climate change *at all* – a topic on which the federal government has been largely silent until the recent actions of the executive branch. On the other hand, the initiatives adopted tend to be "off the shelf" – pre-made, so to speak. The following examines the "riskiness" as well as the innovative originality reflected in state climate initiatives. I conclude that these initiatives reflect a policy innovative dimension not really explored by laboratory-of-democracy adherents or by the Rose-Ackerman thesis, that being "scale innovation," or the application to the state and local levels of policy tools previously limited to the nation or even international levels.

There is much in state and local climate initiatives that would appear to confirm the laboratory of democracy idea. When some states started to take action – in the late 1990s – states, at their own initiative, jumped in to fill the void left by the failure of Congress to address climate change. States were not required to do so; no federal law required or encouraged them to adopt a climate change-related law. Certainly the states' sheer

---

[67] *Id.* at 1386–87.
[68] *Id.* at 1389.

gumption in adopting measures to address climate change in the absence of any particular plan or guide demonstrates an experimental attitude.

It is when we get to the actual content of the climate change laws and regulations adopted that things get a bit more complicated. Several aspects of the actual content of the state laws adopted seem to verify Rose-Ackerman's predictions that states will not act as aggressive policy innovators but instead will adopt a risk-averse stance toward the adoption of new policy ideas. Most importantly, the critical features of the policies adopted by states are not really new, but have instead been fixtures of environmental regulation for decades. This characteristic especially mitigates the risk that would otherwise accompany adoption of a new policy.

A review of state climate initiatives is somewhat akin to a walk through the various approaches employed in environmental regulation. Perhaps the clearest example of this is the states' adoption of cap-and-trade regimes to mitigate greenhouse gas emissions. Cap-and-trade regimes are now ubiquitous throughout environmental law. The decades of experience with emissions trading under the Clean Air Act have sensitized regulators to their pitfalls. As a result, the adoption of the policy envelope represented by a cap-and-trade regime alone cannot be considered high risk. The same is true of electricity generation performance standards, which mirror the technology-based standards promulgated by EPA under the Clean Air Act to mitigate emissions of conventional pollutants from stationary sources. Not only are emissions targets, reporting and registries required of parties subject to the Kyoto Protocol, but the regulatory approach is similar to the information-based approaches seen in laws such as the Emergency Planning and Community Right-to-Know Act. Consequently, given this history of past adoption, the risk of failure by any of the policies adopted would appear to be low.

Adoption of the California clean car standards – by California itself and by the copycat states – might be considered to present greater risks than some of the other policies examined. Nonetheless, the iterative process between California and the EPA demonstrates the inaccuracy of labelling California's leadership in the development of vehicle emission standards as a pure product of state ingenuity.[69] Furthermore, to the extent that California is truly stepping out ahead in issuing these

---

[69] Carlson, *supra*, n. 29 at 1099 ("The most innovative state responses to climate change are neither the product of state regulation alone nor are they exclusively the result of federal action. Instead, such regulations are the results of repeated, sustained, and dynamic lawmaking efforts involving both levels of government – what I term 'iterative federalism'".).

standards, California is unique in having built a political culture that supports strong environmental regulation.[70] The constraints of the federal Clean Air Act reduce the risk that might otherwise be considered inherent in the adoption, by copycat states, of the California Clean Car standards. Such states are limited to adopting standards identical to those of California (thus ensuring that, if anyone catches blame for the new standards, it will be California, not them). Furthermore, if history is any guide, it is very likely that EPA will eventually adopt the California standards as the federal standards. This likelihood transforms any risk inherent in copying California's standards into a temporary state of affairs.

What is "new" and innovative in state climate policy initiatives is not so much the architecture of a given initiative as it is the adaptation of a pre-existing policy or regulatory framework to climate change mitigation and the adoption of the policy on the state level, as opposed to a higher level of governing authority. Here there are considerable risks. Looking just at the implementation risks, take for instance emissions performance standards for greenhouse gas emissions from electric utilities. In contrast to emission standards for conventional power plant emissions, the only end-of-the-pipe technology that exists for greenhouse gas emissions – carbon capture and sequestration – is not considered commercially feasible for new plants and is not technologically feasible for existing plants.[71] Thus states have had to adapt the standard in creative ways, allowing compliance through the purchase of offsets[72] or through the funding of energy conservation measures. Another example is that of implementing a cap-and-trade regime on the scale of a single state (California) or a region (the northeast, as in the Regional Greenhouse

---

[70] See Biber, Eric, "Cultivating a Green Political Landscape: Lessons from Climate Change Policy from the Defeat of California's Proposition 23" (2013) 66 Vand. L. Rev. **399**, 404–20.

[71] Sussman, Robert, "Power Plant Regulation Under the Clean Air Act: A Breakthrough Moment for U.S. Climate Policy?" (2014) 32 Va. Envtl. L.J. **97**, 100–02.

[72] See Wash. Rev. Code § 80.70.010 (2014) (allowing compliance with a performance standard requiring new fossil-fuel generating facilities to mitigate at least 20 percent of their carbon dioxide emissions by "1) payment to a third party to provide mitigation; 2) direct purchase of permanent carbon credits, or 3) investment in applicant-controlled carbon dioxide mitigation projects."); H.B. 3283, 77th Leg. Assemb., Reg. Sess. (Or. 1997). (Allowing existing plants to comply with a requirement that they reduce their emissions by 17 percent below the most efficient baseload plant by implementing carbon dioxide offset projects.)

Gas Initiative). While cap-and-trade may now have a track record on the national level, this is clearly not the case with respect to cap-and-trade on the state or regional level where there are a multitude of unknowns such as the extent of "leakage" of greenhouse gas emission reductions and the price of allowances.[73]

In addition to the implementation risks, the adoption of climate change innovations on the state and regional levels presents political risks. Such risks might be characterized as "taking a stand" against climate change. One would expect that climate innovations would tend to be limited to states for whom identification with climate change policy is considered a political advantage and thus for whom the political risk is at its lowest ebb. Indeed, the most "risky" of the state climate change initiatives – membership in a regional cap-and-trade program, zero-emission vehicle programs, for example – are limited to states with solid majorities of Democratic voters,[74] the party most supportive of climate change policies. Similarly, the political arena encompassed by climate change initiatives has been dominated by high-profile state-level politicians such as California Governor Arnold Schwarzenegger[75] who turned climate action into a signature issue that catapulted him into a subsequent career as a global climate activist.

The actual practice of state climate change innovation suggests that states have adopted numerous strategies to mitigate the implementation and even the political risks inherent in state-level climate initiatives. One of these is to adopt similar policies and another is to adopt policies as a group, often on a regional level. Adoption of similar policies protects politicians from being singled out for criticism should the policies prove politically unpopular down the road. Adoption of policies on a regional

---

[73] Ramseur, Jonathan L., "The Regional Greenhouse Gas Initiative: Lessons Learned and Issues for Congress" (Congress Research Service 2014) 13–14 accessed 17 July 2015 at www.fas.org/sgp/crs/misc/R41836.pdf (stating that "a critical design detail – electricity imports from non-RGGI states – remains unresolved, presenting an opportunity for 'emissions leakage'").

[74] See Climate Action, Center for Climate and Energy Solutions, Table "All State Initiatives," accessed 17 July 2015 at www.c2es.org/docUploads/all-state-initiatives-feb-2014.pdf.

[75] Goldenberg, Suzanne, "Arnold Schwarzenegger Demands Action at Final Climate Summit," *The Guardian* (15 Nov. 2010), accessed 17 July 2015 at www.theguardian.com/environment/2010/nov/16/arnold-schwarzenegger-climate-change-summit; Romm, Joe, "Showtime to Launch Landmark Climate TV Series 'Years of Living Dangerously' in April," *Climate Progress* (13 Jan. 2014, 5.23 pm) accessed 17 July 2015 at thinkprogress.org/climate/2014/01/13/3151271/showtime-years-living-dangerously/.

basis, such as is seen in the northeastern states' regional greenhouse gas cap-and-trade regime, ensures that the politicians in the participating states will either sink or swim together, depending upon the fate of the climate initiative.

A final insulating factor that bears mentioning is the dominant role in state climate innovation that is being played by state agency officials. Many of the initiatives have required no state legislative action, but have instead been carried out entirely by agency officials. For example, the renewable portfolio standards of all but two states are the product of executive branch officials. More insulated from electoral politics, bureaucrats have greater freedom to pursue more risky policies and are more likely to be influenced by policy think tanks and academic researchers. Their dominance in state climate innovation may account for the uniformity among many state-level climate policies.[76]

V. CONCLUSION

The experimentation demonstrated by states in adopting climate change initiatives is definitely present, but at the same time has been somewhat oversold. Many of the core aspects of the six state initiatives discussed in this chapter – greenhouse gas emission targets, reporting and registries, renewable portfolio standards, emissions caps for electric utility plants, clean car standards, regional greenhouse gas cap-and-trade regime and low-carbon fuel standards – are not really new, but instead have been fixtures of federal environmental policies for decades. Other than the federal government, the state initiatives display the handiwork of California, a state that not only has a long history of environmental regulatory leadership, but owing to its size and population has a greater capacity to absorb costs of policy failures.

Instead, what is new in state and local climate change policymaking is the adaptation of well-worn policies to the particular problem of climate change: greenhouse gas emissions, as well as the risks involved in adopting some of these policies on the subnational level. States and local governments have many strategies to counter these risks. For instance we see that states that are active on climate change policy are also active participants in regional groupings of states also active on climate change. States also appear to seek refuge in the adoption of policies identical to those of other states.

---

[76] See Galle and Leahy, *supra*, n. 63, at 1389.

While the analysis presented in this chapter might be considered disappointing from the vantage point of the high rhetoric of states as "laboratories of democracy," several of the risk-averse aspects of state climate innovation might be considered of overall social benefit. The uniformity among state policies and the tendency to act on a regional basis contribute to the effectiveness of state policy in mitigating climate change. Given that action at the international and national levels would be superior to action at the state level in terms of reducing a greater quantity of greenhouse gas emissions, this uniformity among state initiatives renders state action more effective in addressing the root problem of climate change. Thus the potential sub-optimality of state governments in terms of innovating policy to address climate change may be the makings of the most efficient response possible from state-level policy.

9. Cooperative federalism and adaptation

Alice Kaswan

Climate change adaptation will represent not just one, but many federalism issues. Climate change impacts will be felt throughout the physical world with pervasive environmental, economic and social consequences. Legal solutions to these impacts will transcend traditional legal boundaries, with implications for land use law, environmental law, disaster law, public health law, housing law, water law, immigration law, agricultural law and numerous other areas. Nonetheless, as our legal system struggles to build a response to climate change impacts, whether through piecemeal revisions to existing programs or through new overarching programs that attempt to rationalize our adaptation responses, similar federalism concerns will repeatedly arise and deserve explicit attention.[1]

One of the enduring features of climate change is that many of its impacts will be inherently multiscalar: they will be felt at the local, regional, state, federal and international levels. As a consequence, no single jurisdictional level can adequately respond.[2] In this chapter, I review the multiscalar nature of many climate impacts and then elaborate the federalism values that shape governance choices, including pragmatic

---

[1] Professors Dan Farber and Rob Glicksman have provided insightful accounts of the cross-cutting federalism issues raised by climate adaptation. Farber, Daniel A., "Climate Adaptation and Federalism: Mapping the Issues" (2009) 1 San Diego J. Climate & Energy L. 259; Glicksman, Robert, "Climate Change Adaptation: A Collective Action Perspective on Federalism Considerations" (2010) 40 Envtl. L. 1159.

[2] Erin Ryan characterizes these problems as falling in the "interjurisdictional gray area," and has promoted multilevel governance responses as essential to address many modern challenges, including climate change. Ryan, Erin, *Federalism and the Tug of War Within* (Oxford University Press 2012), pp. 145–80. Professors Robin Craig and J.B. Ruhl have also highlighted the multiscalar nature of climate change impacts. See Ruhl, J.B., "Climate Change Adaptation and the Structural Transformation of Environmental Law" (2010) 40 Envtl. L.

effectiveness, democratic legitimacy, and individual liberty and prevention of tyranny. Domestically, cooperative federalism regimes that structure and coordinate federal, state, and local roles can best bridge the multiscalar nature of adaptation challenges and satisfy key federalism values. Given the multiplicity of regimes implicated by adaptation, I do not pretend to advance a single adaptation federalism model. Instead, I identify generic types of federal requirements and federal support functions that could prove useful in particular contexts. I then turn to action in a few select substantive areas. I first identify areas, such as coastal planning, disaster management and recovery, and EPA programs, where existing cooperative federalism structures are already incorporating and could further incorporate adaptation. Lastly, I identify several substantive areas including water law, land use law, and housing law, in which existing reliance on state and local initiative might benefit from a greater federal role.

I. THE MULTISCALAR NATURE OF CLIMATE CHANGE IMPACTS

Climate change will lead to multiple physical environmental impacts that will have widespread ecological, social, economic and health impacts on multiple scales.[3] Climate scientists predict that sea levels will rise by three to four feet by 2100, leading to inundation of low-lying areas and infrastructure and to increased vulnerability from higher storm surges. In the northeast and Midwest, scientists predict increasing precipitation and more intense storms, with associated increases in flood risks. Other areas of the country, including the west, are facing decreasing precipitation, with increased risk of drought and wildfire. Global warming will bring increasing average temperatures as well as an increase in heat waves, with concomitant threats to public health.

363, 423–25; Craig, Robin Kundis, "'Stationarity Is Dead' – Long Live Transformation: Five Principles for Climate Change Adaptation Law" (2010) 34 Harv. Envtl L. Rev. **9**, 54–57.

[3] The United States Global Change Research Program has thoroughly documented US climate impacts in a series of comprehensive studies, the latest of which is its Third National Climate Assessment. US Global Change Research Program, "Climate Change Impacts in the United States: The Third National Climate Assessment" (2014), accessed 17 July 2015 at www.globalchange.gov/browse/reports/climate-change-impacts-united-states-third-national-climate-assessment-0.

These physical changes will have widespread and multiscalar impacts. Rising sea levels, increasing precipitation, more intense storms and, in other areas, wildfire risk created by heat and drought will increase the risk of disasters, with local, regional, statewide and national consequences. Damage caused by higher storm surges, flooding rivers and wildfires will have dramatic local impacts as local homes and businesses are damaged or demolished. The damage will have regional impacts as infrastructure such as roads, energy supply and communication lines, water treatment facilities and key businesses are impacted. And flooding or fire could have potentially national and international impacts when key ports are shut down, stopping trade, or when key resources are impacted, like oil and gas drilling and refining (as occurred when hurricane Katrina struck the Gulf Coast). Moreover, federal taxpayers experience the consequence of local disasters as they provide billions of dollars in disaster relief, such as the $51 billion in recovery funds Congress authorized in response to hurricane Sandy.[4] Disaster evacuees have local impacts as local governments provide shelters and hotels and rentals fill up, but can also impact multiple states as evacuees fan out in search of short- and long-term shelter, as 800,000 New Orleans residents did when they fled hurricane Katrina.

Rising sea levels, drought and changing precipitation levels will also impact water supplies for municipal and agricultural use. In some areas, sea level rise will cause saltwater to infiltrate freshwater supplies, with local, regional or statewide effects, depending upon the scale of reliance on the impacted water resources. In the western states, droughts and changing precipitation patterns that reduce the snowpack are significantly reducing available water supplies, posing questions about the long-term viability of habitation in some arid locations.

Droughts could have particularly severe consequences for agriculture. For example, in 2014, persistent drought led the federal Bureau of Reclamation to cut water supplies to California farmers to zero.[5] Climate change could cause additional challenges, as changing seasons, temperatures, precipitation patterns and weed and pest habitats shift. Many of

---

[4] Chen, David W., "U.S. to Release First Installment of $51 Billion in Hurricane Sandy Aid," *New York Times* (5 February 2013), accessed 17 July 2015 at www.nytimes.com/2013/02/06/nyregion/first-part-of-hurricane-sandy-aid-is-to-be-released.html?_r=0.

[5] Alexander, Kurtis, "Drought: Feds Cut Water to Central Valley Farmers to Zero," *SF Chronicle* (22 February 2014), accessed 17 July 2015 www.sfgate.com/news/article/Drought-Feds-cut-water-to-Central-Valley-farmers-5256131.php.

these challenges to agriculture have multiscalar impacts on local communities, on local economies, and on national and international food systems.

Several climate impacts will create public health threats with multiscalar implications. Rising temperatures and, in particular, heat waves are among the most significant threats to public welfare, causing more deaths than other forms of "natural" disasters. Because metropolitan design is critical to controlling the urban heat island effect, adapting to heat waves presents a regional, not just a local challenge. Increasing temperatures will also indirectly exacerbate air pollution, since ozone formation speeds up at higher temperatures, increasing the level of ozone pollution caused by a given level of precursor emissions. Increasing temperatures also exacerbate the impacts of existing water pollution. Such water quality challenges are almost always multiscalar, causing local impacts but stemming from and contributing to water quality issues throughout interconnected riparian systems. Increasing temperatures are also expected to affect the spread of disease, as disease vectors such as mosquitos or ticks spread their range, and are expected to affect the spread of allergens, as plants creating allergens thrive in a warmer climate. Disease vectors and allergens cause local impacts but do not respect jurisdictional boundaries; each jurisdiction's actions or inactions in addressing these concerns will impact its neighbors.

Climate change will affect not only the regions facing direct impacts, but the areas that appear relatively unscathed. As climate impacts make certain areas less habitable due to flood risks, insufficient water for urban and agricultural use, or unsustainable heat, internal migration is likely.[6] Moreover, globally, analysts predict that climate change will force millions – potentially hundreds of millions – to migrate.[7] Although these "climate refugees" do not have official refugee status, it is conceivable that the United States may, in the future, absorb some of those displaced by climate change. Thus, areas that do not experience direct climate impacts could indirectly experience in-migration. Greater demand for housing will likely increase housing prices. And, while the private market will likely respond to demand for higher-end housing, existing deficits in affordable housing could be exacerbated by internal migration. The Dust

---

[6] See Craig, *supra*, n. 2, at 55.

[7] The International Organization for Migration notes that estimates range from 25 million to 1 billion, with 200 million commonly cited. International Organization for Migration, "Migration and Climate Change" accessed 17 July 2015 at www.iom.int/cms/climateandmigration.

Bowl's homeless camps should provide a warning about potential future US housing challenges caused by national-scale population shifts.

Flooding, changing precipitation patterns, and increasing temperatures will not only impact human settlements, but have far-reaching impacts on the environment and other species. Scientists predict a significant increase in the rate of species endangerment. Human settlements themselves will create a significant barrier to natural adaptation. Coastal settlements will prevent the natural inland migration of coastal wetlands, and both urban and agricultural land uses will impede fluid species migration. Increasingly impaired water quality will impact aquatic species. Climate scientists also predict that climate change could increase the spread of invasive species, harming natural ecosystems.

The multiscalar nature of these impacts suggests that no single jurisdictional level can adequately respond. The critical question, then, is how to distribute governmental authority. As Professor Erin Ryan has made clear, federalism values provide a critical touchstone for determining what governance structure can best manage such multiscalar problems.[8]

II. FEDERALISM VALUES AND JURISDICTIONAL CHOICE

A first key federalism value is effectiveness: what governance structure will facilitate effective adaptation? A second key federalism value is democratic legitimacy: what governance structure best represents citizen interests and ensures accountability? A third key federalism value is the enhancement of individual liberty and prevention of tyranny: what governance structure would best protect the most vulnerable interests? Although adaptation will implicate many different kinds of impacts and legal regimes and the precise balance of governmental authority may vary for different impacts, there are numerous commonalities among adaptation challenges that warrant unified consideration.

---

[8] See Ryan, *supra*, n. 2. I provide a more detailed articulation of these three federalism values and their implications for adaptation in the land use context in Kaswan, "Climate Adaptation and Land Use Governance: The Vertical Axis" (2014) 39 Columbia J. Envtl. L. 390.

A. Effectiveness

From a practical standpoint, many adaptation challenges will require local action and control. For example, urban and building design initiatives to reduce disaster and heat risk, water conservation measures, and public health responses to cope with heat and disease are all driven largely by local institutions. Adaptation challenges will vary substantially from place to place, requiring locally tailored responses. Local officials will have detailed knowledge of local circumstances, challenges, and the implications of policy choices and tradeoffs. Maintaining strong local control also encourages local innovation, providing the nation with the benefit of their experimentation and containing the consequences of policies that might prove misguided. Moreover, in the adaptation context, the desire for uniformity does not provide a compelling rationale for federal or state control because so many relevant decisions concern matters that have traditionally been considered local, like land use, buildings, water use, public health and other matters for which we have long accepted local variation.

At the same time, local governments cannot go it alone. Although many local and state governments have begun to address adaptation,[9] in most cases their efforts are insufficient, and many at-risk jurisdictions are not adapting.[10] Even where local action might appear to be the best approach it does not always emerge, owing to a variety of collective action failures.[11] Local governments are the most knowledgeable about existing local conditions, but they do not have the resources to analyze climate science data and interpret their local implications. Moreover, collecting and analyzing such data at state and federal level would provide significant economies of scale. Most local governments also lack sufficient financial resources to engage in adaptation planning, much less implement expensive adaptation measures like buy-outs of vulnerable property or relocation of vulnerable transportation, energy, communications or wastewater infrastructure. Additional collective action failures emerge due to public choice pathologies, like the race to the bottom, free-riding and interest group distortions, failures that are discussed

---

[9] See "State and Local Adaptation Plans," Georgetown Climate Center, accessed 17 July 2015 at www.georgetownclimate.org/adaptation/state-and-local-plans.

[10] See Kaswan, *supra*, n. 8, at 414–15 (summarizing limitations of existing state and local adaptation efforts).

[11] See generally Glicksman, *supra*, n. 1 (describing likely collective action failures and the degree to which they justify a federal role in adaptation).

further below in connection with the democratic legitimacy dimensions of federalism analysis.

In many instances, the challenge is not simply that needed local action will fail to materialize, it is that local control is not the appropriate scale. The multiscalar nature of most climate impacts suggests that local governments cannot single-handedly, and in piecemeal fashion, address the larger scale problems they confront. For example, flooding, water quality impairments and water shortages will impact multiple jurisdictions all sharing the same resource; effective management requires coordinated action.

Moreover, and relatedly, the extra-jurisdictional impacts of local action and inaction justify a state or federal role.[12] Examples abound. If local governments build reservoirs that deplete downstream water supplies, or increase groundwater pumping to compensate for decreased surface water, these actions could jeopardize water availability for other jurisdictions. Beach armoring allowed in one jurisdiction could deplete beaches in a neighboring jurisdiction. If certain jurisdictions fail to control floodplain development, downstream communities will confront increased flooding. If communities do not adequately prepare for disasters, whether they arise from storm surges, river flooding or wildfires, then federal taxpayers are likely to pay the costs and neighboring communities and states will absorb the evacuees. If communities do not protect vital infrastructure, then neighboring areas, if not the nation, will experience disruptions in trade, energy and communications.

Policy makers do not have to choose among federal, state or local control. As is true in many areas of the law, structured multilevel governance can provide the best of all worlds by building upon the strengths of each jurisdictional level. Moreover, as writers espousing dynamic federalism have articulated, such multilevel governance structures provide their own inherent governance advantages.[13] When action is needed at multiple scales, a formal multilevel governance structure can

---

[12] See Farber, *supra*, n. 1, at 266–67 (describing numerous transboundary climate change impacts); Glicksman, *supra*, n. 1, at 1184–85 (describing numerous transboundary impacts that could emerge from state and local governments' failure to take needed adaptation measures).

[13] See e.g. Ryan, *supra*, n. 2; Adelman, David E. and Kirsten H. Engel, "Adaptive Federalism: The Case Against Reallocating Environmental Regulatory Authority" (2008) 92 Minn. L. Rev. 1796; Carlson, Ann E., "Iterative Federalism and Climate Change" (2009) 103 Nw. U.L. Rev. 1097; Osofsky, Hari M., "Diagonal Federalism and Climate Change: Implications for the Obama Administration" (2011) 62 Ala. L. Rev. 237.

coordinate otherwise fragmented and disjointed efforts. In addition, multilevel governance promotes dynamic engagement among differing jurisdictional levels, fostering dialogue, reflection and, ultimately, more innovation. Engaging multiple jurisdictions also increases accountability as different players pressure other players to fulfill their assigned roles. And, to the degree there is some overlap in roles (for example, simultaneous federal and state power to set standards), a multilevel governance structure provides a regulatory safety net that reduces the consequences if any one level were to fail to act.

Of course, having overlapping jurisdiction and complex systems of local planning reviewed by state or federal actors takes administrative resources. Nonetheless, whether structured into a formal multilevel governance process or not, the pressures of climate change will generate local, state and federal action, and that action could be more efficiently coordinated through formal attention to multigovernance structures rather than having such overlaps occur in a haphazard and fragmented manner. In addition, even where a multigovernance structure creates some duplication or overlap, the pragmatic benefits of coordination, enhanced dialogue and regulatory safety nets could outweigh a slight loss in administrative efficiency.

B. Democratic Legitimacy

Governance choices are informed not only by considering the effectiveness of alternative structures, but also by considering the democratic legitimacy and accountability values served by governance alternatives. Key parameters include a given jurisdictional level's capacity to represent citizen interests, its relative vulnerability to public choice pathologies, and its capacity to enhance accountability.

Theorists frequently laud the democratic virtues of local government decision-making. Citizens have easier and more direct access to local decision-making forums, and their voices appear more likely to be heard because they are less diluted by larger constituencies. Accountability is strong because, if local decision-makers fail to honor local preferences, they face the risk that citizens will vote out them out or exit the jurisdiction.

At the same time, however, local government decision-making has certain participatory deficits. Where larger-scale concerns are at stake, like the security of nationally significant infrastructure, then the relevant constituency is not just the local government where the infrastructure is located, but all those who depend upon it. And when local decision-making has extra-jurisdictional impacts, as is often the case in adaptation-related matters, then local decision-making fails to include all of those affected by the decisions. For example, downstream communities cannot participate in upstream communities' development decisions, and low-income migrants seeking safe housing cannot participate in community decisions that restrict affordable housing.

In addition, the ability to avoid potential public choice pathologies is relevant to determining the most democratically legitimate governance structure.[14] Where local or state governments retain primary decision-making authority, as is often the case in land use, infrastructure and water supply contexts, local governments could be tempted to free-ride on other jurisdictions' adaptation measures, like water conservation, wetland protection, or even disaster bail-outs if the worst comes to pass. Federal or state roles in adaptation could ensure widespread adaptation and lessen the risk of free-riding.

Moreover, the proverbial "race-to-the-bottom" could unduly constrain local action. Local governments may be reluctant to impose development restrictions or building code requirements because they fear that such restrictions could drive development to less restrictive jurisdictions. Federal or state minimum standards could create a more level playing field, dampening interjurisdictional competition. Rather than defeating local preferences, such federal minimum standards could enable local governments to provide desired protection without fearing adverse economic consequences.

Even without the threat of inter-jurisdictional competition, local governments could confront systemic political challenges in addressing climate change. For example, where climate change impacts suggest the need for restrictions on local development or retreat from existing settlements, local governments confront almost impossible political decisions.[15] Even areas subject to intense storm damage continue to rebuild, unwilling to believe that worse is yet to come. One cannot expect local governments to make collective decisions that require major and certain short-term sacrifices to community identity and to economic well-being, all in the name of preparing for long-term and seemingly speculative risks. Federal and state programs, based on up-to-date climate predictions

---

[14] See Glicksman, *supra*, n. 1, at 1186 (describing numerous political pressures that could prevent state and local governments from taking desired and needed adaptive measures).

[15] See Hudson, Blake, "Reconstituting Land-Use Federalism to Address Transitory and Perpetual Disasters: The Bimodal Federalism Framework" (2011) BYU L. Rev. **1991**, 1995.

and adequate resources, could work with local governments to ease the political and economic impediments that would otherwise stymie local action.

Multilevel governance structures could also help counter the risk of interest group capture. For example, at the local level, local development and real estate interests are often strong players in local politics, potentially impeding the adoption of land use measures that limit development in vulnerable areas. Similarly, agricultural interests could potentially impact water conservation measures. Creating multi-governance adaptation initiatives would reduce the risk of capture at any single level by multiplying the relevant political actors.

C. Individual Liberty and Prevention of Tyranny

Although ideal governance structures maximize meaningful democratic participation, they should also be designed to minimize potential abuses of government authority that could threaten individual rights. Multi-governance structures allow each governance level to check the other. For example, although some state or federal role may be necessary to facilitate retreat from vulnerable areas given local reluctance to make decisions that appear, in the short term, to be self-defeating, state and federal decision-makers might give too little attention to the property and community interests of those immediately impacted. The balance is tricky: a federal or state role in facilitating retreat is desirable to overcome unsurprising but nonetheless untenable local resistance. At the same time, local property rights and community interests cannot be ignored. A multilevel governance structure cannot eliminate these tensions, but it could provide a framework through which they could be resolved with greater respect for the competing values at stake than if power were lodged exclusively at one jurisdictional level.

Conversely, a state or federal role could address systemic local power imbalances that sometimes operate to the detriment of politically marginalized populations. Many adaptation decisions, particularly land use decisions, will require wrenching determinations about which areas to protect and which to abandon, about where and how to invest in measures to build resilience, and so on. Politically marginalized populations, often poor and minority, could be at risk in some local decision-making processes.[16] For example, as cities in Louisiana and Texas

---

[16] See Verchick, Robert R.M., *Facing Catastrophe: Environmental Action for a Post-Katrina World* (Harvard University Press, Cambridge MA 2010),

struggled to chart their post-hurricane path forward, questions of racial justice in rebuilding decisions were front and center.[17] Moreover, state and local policies could thwart climate-induced migration.[18] State or federal parameters could provide participatory and substantive guidelines that buttress the interests of potentially marginalized populations. The local role remains critical, but state or federal influence on local decision-making could better protect the rights of those whose interests might not be sufficiently considered at the local level.

Thus, in most contexts, partnerships between federal, state and local jurisdictional levels can provide more effective, legitimate and fair outcomes. The issue, then, is what form such partnerships should take.

III. ADAPTATION GOVERNANCE FUNCTIONS

There is no single "cooperative federalism" approach to addressing adaptation because of the multiplicity of impacted substantive domains. Nonetheless, it is possible to identify the kinds of governance functions that differing jurisdictional levels could serve, despite the variety of substantive contexts in which those functions would be realized.[19] Multiple forms of federal influence are possible, ranging from direct requirements, direct support, and mechanisms that harness market forces to induce safer behavior, such as taxes or flood insurance rates. For

---

pp. 105–70 (describing, in the disaster context, the greater vulnerability experienced by poor and of-color communities and the importance of designing policies to address their particular needs); Kaswan, Alice, "Domestic Climate Change Adaptation and Equity" (2012) 42 Envtl. L. Rep'r 1125; Ruhl, *supra*, n. 2, at 405 (observing that many adaptation policy decisions will have important equity implications).

[17] See Bullard, Robert D. and Beverly Wright, "Race, Place and the Environment in Post-Katrina New Orleans," in Bullard, Robert D. and Beverly Wright (eds) *Race, Place, and Environmental Justice After Hurricane Katrina: Struggles to Reclaim, Rebuild, and Revitalize New Orleans and the Gulf Coast* (American Sociological Association 2009), p. 19 (describing racial tensions in post-Katrina recovery decisions); Whelan, Robbie, "A Texas-Sized Housing Fight," *Wall Street Journal* 3 August 2012, at A3 (describing racial tensions in post-hurricane debates about rebuilding damaged public housing).

[18] See Glicksman, *supra*, n. 1, at 1190.

[19] See generally Camacho, Alejandro E. and Robert L. Glicksman, "Functional Government in 3-D: A Framework for Evaluating Allocations of Government Authority" (2014) 51 Harv. J. on Legis. 19 (analyzing how appropriate allocations of authority depend in part upon the governance function in question).

purposes of simplicity, this chapter focuses on direct regulatory mechanisms rather than market forces, including: (1) federal requirements that impose substantive or procedural requirements on subnational jurisdictions; and (2) federal support of subnational activity, including research, information sharing, financial support and coordination.

A. Federal Substantive and Procedural Requirements

1. Cross-cutting considerations

Some degree of substantive and procedural federal leadership on adaptation is appropriate, including clear statements of federal adaptation goals and, where appropriate, certain requirements or standards to guide state and local action.[20] State and local governments could fail to act because they lack resources or political will in light of the interest group pressures they face. Where state and local governments do act, some degree of substantive and procedural direction is also merited to overcome potential risks posed by state and local action, particularly risks of inter-jurisdictional impacts and risks to politically marginalized populations. Given local variation and the importance of community engagement, however, federal goals and requirements must at the same time provide substantial scope for local discretion and innovation.[21]

If the government imposes substantive standards or planning requirements, a key issue will be the relationship between such federally prompted initiatives and independent state and local action, or, in other words, the degree to which federal law should preempt state and local law.[22] As is the case in most cooperative federalism regimes, federal standards or requirements could provide a minimum floor that state and local governments can exceed.[23] Federal minimums can dampen the race to the bottom and avoid the public choice challenges that could arise at the local level. At the same time, there is no inherent justification for limiting state and local governments to the federal minimum. In the adaptation context, there is little need for nationwide uniformity, and

---

[20] See Glicksman, *supra*, n. 1, at 1183–86 (describing the need for minimum federally required adaptation measures to overcome transboundary externalities and race-to-the-bottom dynamics that would otherwise generate too little state and local action).

[21] See Craig, *supra*, n. 2, at 17, 29.

[22] See Glicksman, *supra*, n. 1, at 1186–92 (analyzing when federal law should and should not preempt state and local adaptation measures).

[23] See Buzbee, William, "Asymmetrical Regulation: Risk, Preemption, and the Floor/Ceiling Distinction" (2007) 82 N.Y.U. L. Rev. 1547.

some jurisdictions may justifiably choose to be more protective than required by the federal government.[24]

Although this chapter focuses primarily on the inherent federalism values guiding governance choices, it is important to recognize that the capacity of the federal government to impose substantive or procedural requirements on state and local government will be bounded by constitutional principles.[25] As a political matter, Congress – composed of state representatives – is unlikely to impose planning and implementation requirements on states without providing substantial federal funding. If Congress offers substantial resources in exchange for adaptation planning and implementation, then many states and local governments are likely to accept the funding, along with the associated conditions. Federal action would thus survive scrutiny under the Constitution's Spending Clause, which allows Congress to place conditions on the programs it funds.[26] Even without federal funding, some federal standards may be justified under the Commerce Clause.[27] For example, federal standards designed to protect infrastructure, such as energy and communications infrastructure, could be deemed to have a sufficiently strong relationship to interstate commerce and be considered critical components of a larger plan to avoid threats to national economic well-being.

2. Types of federal requirements

Given the complexity and diversity of adaptation settings and the complexity of the policy determinations, I outline the range of possible

---

[24] However, in a few instances, federal preemption could be warranted to prevent states from thwarting adaptation (e.g., to stop states from blocking climate-induced immigration), or to control state adaptation efforts that have adverse spillover or ecological impacts (e.g., to control water storage measures that deplete downstream supplies). See Glicksman, *supra*, n. 1, at 1189–91.

[25] See Farber, *supra*, n. 1, at 274–85 (discussing constitutional issues posed by adaptation).

[26] The Supreme Court's 2013 decision in *National Federation of Independent Businesses v Sebelius* imposed limits on Congress' authority under the Spending Clause; the conditions cannot be unduly coercive of state action. See Ryan, Erin, "Environmental Laws after Sebelius: Will the Court's New Spending Power Limits Affect Environmental State–Federal Partnerships?" (Am. Constitutional Soc'y 2013), accessed 17 July 2015 at www.acslaw.org/sites/default/files/Ryan-_After_Sebelius.pdf.

[27] See Farber, *supra*, n. 1, at 274–80 (discussing viability of federal adaptation measures under the Commerce Clause).

federal requirements without attempting to provide a monolithic determination about the appropriate form of federal action. Federal requirements could be realized through direct requirements on states or private actors or, alternatively, could be realized indirectly through federal conditions imposed on federal funding or licensing decisions.[28] They could also take a variety of forms, including specific requirements, more general goals and standards, and planning requirements.

At their most direct, the federal government could impose specific requirements that would control certain forms of state and local development. For example, the federal government could require that infrastructure, including roads, water treatment facilities and power plants, be built to withstand anticipated climate risks. The federal government could articulate specific rules, for example it could limit placement in flood zones or require the use of specified heat-resistant materials.

Alternatively, the federal government could set more general standards, like requiring that new infrastructure be able to withstand projected climate impacts and that existing infrastructure be retrofitted or moved as necessary. This approach would set a clear federal goal or standard, but give states or private entities more discretion in determining how to meet the standard or goal. Under this approach, state and local governments would be responsible for determining how to fulfill the federal standard.

Instead of or in addition to directly imposing federal rules or standards, the federal government could impose planning requirements. For example, the federal government could require state and local governments to engage in adaptation planning generally, or require adaptation planning in specific programs, for example highway or energy infrastructure, or land use planning to reduce climate risks. Planning requirements can vary in the degree to which they impose substantive requirements. At one extreme, they could simply indicate that state or local governments should engage in assessing risks and developing plans to address them, with little specification of what should be studied and little direction to the required planning. At the other extreme, planning requirements could identify specific types of risks to be addressed and establish specific standards or goals that such planning must meet.

---

[28] Professor Daniel Farber nicely outlines the forms federal adaptation requirements could take. Farber, *supra*, n. 1, at 265–66. See also Glicksman, *supra*, n. 1, at 1167, 1170–71 (describing model of adaptation federalism in which federal requirements displace state and local control by imposing direct federal requirements); ibid. at 1167, 1169 (describing model of adaptation federalism in which the federal government sets federal goals and then allows states to determine how to meet them).

In addition to establishing substantive planning parameters, federal requirements could create procedural standards or requirements. Federal law could require that state and local assessments and planning initiatives include minimum procedural mechanisms to enhance participatory processes. Potential parameters could include providing participatory opportunities for non-local stakeholders with an interest in the local decision, as well as requirements, like translation and outreach, to enhance participation by historically marginalized communities.

B. Federal Support Functions

In addition to imposing obligations on subnational actors, the federal government could provide essential support – either linked to or distinct from substantive and procedural obligations.[29] Given local and state governments' differing capacities to analyze climate data and their local implications, the federal government could perform essential information-sharing functions. In addition to data on climate impacts, the federal government could provide a clearinghouse for adaptation measures, and help local and state governments learn about and select adaptation strategies. The federal government could also monitor and assess local and state adaptation initiatives so that local and state governments can better evaluate the efficacy of alternative strategies.

The federal government could provide adaptation planning and implementation funds as well as information.[30] Many state and local governments are unlikely to have sufficient resources to engage in necessary adaptation planning and implementation. Given collective responsibility for the emissions causing climate harms, a collective role in responding to those harms is appropriate.[31] Federal funding on the necessary scale is unlikely at present. The need for adaptation funds, combined with the "polluter pays" principle, provides an important justification for market-based carbon mitigation schemes that generate revenue, whether a carbon tax or cap-and-trade.

In addition, the federal government could help coordinate the many local, state and federal initiatives that will be addressing climate-related

---

[29] See Glicksman, *supra*, n. 1, at 1181–83 (describing and justifying federal informational, financial, and planning assistance to state and local governments).

[30] For an in-depth discussion of the strengths and pitfalls of federal adaptation financing, see Farber, *supra*, n. 1, at 269–73.

[31] However, where communities knowingly make investments at risk from climate change, federal financial support to protect those risky investments is not appropriate. See Farber, *supra*, n. 1, at 273.

harms, irrespective of new federal programs. These initiatives cross not only scales but also scope, with numerous different programs within a single jurisdiction addressing parallel concerns, such as emergency management planning and land use planning. Independent of federal requirements, coordination of existing and new programs would provide a more efficient and better functioning government response to climate change.[32]

IV. IMPLICATIONS FOR LAW: MAINSTREAMING INTO EXISTING STRUCTURES AND NEW FEDERAL ADAPTATION INITIATIVES

Given the multiplicity of contexts in which adaptation must occur, the appropriate cooperative federalism structures are likely to vary considerably. In some contexts, adaptation measures could be "mainstreamed" into existing cooperative federalism programs in discrete substantive areas.[33] In others, new legislation to tweak existing authorities may be necessary. And in yet other contexts completely new legislation, with better integrated federal, state and local roles, may be necessary to enable an effective national response. I first highlight a range of existing federal programs, including both cross-cutting federal initiatives and particular agency initiatives. I then identify areas that have traditionally been left largely to state or local control but that could benefit from a more comprehensive multiscalar approach that includes a more robust federal role while preserving essential state and local autonomy.

A. Existing Federal Programs

The federal government has begun to assess its existing adaptation capacity, including its role in relation to the state and local government entities it funds and influences. In 2009 President Obama issued an executive order on sustainability that, among other things, created an Interagency Climate Change Adaptation Task Force. The Task Force, with over 20 members from a range of federal agencies, issued progress reports in 2010 and 2011 that identified a range of guiding principles for

---

[32] See Craig, *supra*, note 1, at 54–60 (describing need for increased coordination among sectors and governmental levels); Flatt, Victor B., "Focus and Fund: Executing Our Way to a Federal Climate Change Adaptation Plan" (2014) 32 VA. Envtl L.J. 157.
[33] See ibid.

federal agency adaptation planning, identified overarching goals, and set in motion agency-specific adaptation planning.[34]

Adaptation was a central theme in the President's 2013 Climate Action Plan, which reiterated the goal of federal support for strengthening and increasing the safety of communities and infrastructure, and which anticipates the need for extensive inter-jurisdictional cooperation.[35] Consistent with the Climate Action Plan, the President launched numerous cross-cutting projects in 2014. In March 2014 the President launched the Climate Data Initiative to facilitate information-sharing between the public and private sectors.[36] In June 2014 the President announced a $1 billion National Disaster Resilience Competition to provide funding to state, local governments and tribes for climate-resilient recovery in areas impacted by disasters in the last few years.[37] In November 2014 the State, Local, and Tribal Leaders Task Force on Climate Preparedness and Resilience, created pursuant to the Climate Action Plan, released a web-based *Climate Resilience Toolkit* to help public and private sector stakeholders across the nation better access existing federal information and planning tools.[38]

More comprehensively, in November 2014 the State, Local, and Tribal Leaders Task Force released recommendations on how the federal government could remove federal barriers to state and local adaptation

---

[34] See, "Progress Report of the Interagency Climate Change Adaptation Task Force: Recommended Actions in Support of a National Climate Change Adaptation Strategy" (White House Council on Envtl. Quality 2010), accessed 17 July 2015 at www.whitehouse.gov/sites/default/files/microsites/ceq/Interagency-Climate-Change-Adaptation-Progress-Report.pdf; Federal Actions for a Climate Resilient Nation: Progress Report of the Interagency Climate Change Adaptation Task Force (2011), accessed 17 July 2015 at www.whitehouse.gov/sites/default/files/microsites/ceq/2011_adaptation_progress_report.pdf.

[35] Executive Office of the President, The President's Climate Action Plan (The White House, Washington 2013), accessed 17 July 2015 at www.whitehouse.gov/sites/default/files/image/president27sclimateactionplan.pdf.

[36] Office of the Press Sec'y, The White House, Fact Sheet: The President's Climate Data Initiative: Empowering America's Communities to Prepare for the Effects of Climate Change (The White House, Washington 2014), accessed 17 July 2015 at www.whitehouse.gov/the-press-office/2014/03/19/fact-sheet-president-s-climate-data-initiative-empowering-america-s-comm.

[37] Fact Sheet: National Disaster Resilience Competition (The White House, 15 June 2014), available at www.whitehouse.gov/the-press-office/2014/06/14/fact-sheet-national-disaster-resilience-competition.

[38] "U.S. Climate Resilience Toolkit," accessed 17 July 2015 at toolkit.climate.gov/.

and better support subnational jurisdictions.[39] The recommendations identified overarching principles, including the importance of integrating climate risks into all federal programs and investments, as well as the importance of a federal role in strengthening inter-agency and inter-jurisdictional coordination, providing data and assistance to state and local decision-makers, and consulting with states, local governments and tribes on all features of climate resilience efforts. These principles are translated into more specific action recommendations in multiple domains, including community development, infrastructure, natural resources management, public health and safety, and disaster mitigation and recovery. While most of the recommendations address ways in which the federal government can support and coordinate action at multiple jurisdictional levels, the Task Force also called for a stronger federal role in shaping state and local adaptation actions through existing regulatory, planning and funding programs.

At the specific agency level, cooperative federalism structures relevant to adaptation already exist in many domains. Examples include coastal zone management, disaster law, stormwater management, water quality and transportation infrastructure, air quality, public health, housing, and endangered species protections. Without attempting to summarize the extensive adaptation-related efforts across all agencies, I provide a few illustrative examples below.

The Coastal Zone Management Act (CZMA) provides incentives for states (and where delegated, for local governments) to develop coastal zone management plans, and most coastal states have responded with coastal land use planning. However, the statute references a broad range of general goals and, although it explicitly encourages states to address sea level rise, the statute does not specifically direct states to account for it or to engage in adaptation planning.[40] And while the National Oceanic and Atmospheric Administration (NOAA) provides a wide array of informational and financial resources to support climate adaptation

---

[39] President's State, Local, and Tribal Leaders Task Force on Climate Preparedness and Resilience, Recommendations to the President (The White House, Washington 2014), accessed 17 July 2015 at www.whitehouse.gov/sites/default/files/docs/task_force_report_0.pdf.

[40] See Byrne, J. Peter and Jessica Grannis, "Coastal Retreat Measures" in Michael B. Gerrard and Katrina Fischer Kuh (eds), *The Law of Adaptation to Climate Change: U.S. and International Aspects* (American Bar Association, Chicago, IL 2012), pp. 267, 289–91.

planning and initiatives,[41] the agency does not have sufficient resources to comprehensively fund state and local adaptation efforts. More specific federal requirements that state and local coastal plans consider and plan for future sea level rise would improve the CZMA's capacity to ensure that this federal statute provides sufficient direction and incentives to state and local coastal planning.

Existing federal disaster law programs also have cooperative federalism dimensions relevant to adaptation. The National Flood Insurance Program creates incentives for local floodplain land use regulation and building codes[42] – although the existence of subsidized flood insurance rates may do more to encourage risky development than the floodplain and building codes do to mitigate the risk.[43] Federal statutes have also created a structure for funding and approving state and local disaster management plans. Although FEMA, the implementing agency, did not require consideration of climate risks in the past and many states failed to integrate such risks,[44] as of fall 2014 FEMA is proposing to require that states include climate risks in future mitigation plans.[45] More generally,

---

[41] See, e.g., "Climate Adaptation," NOAA, Digital Coast Office for Coastal Management, accessed 3 September 2015 at www.coast.noaa.gov/digitalcoast/topic/climate-adaptation.

[42] The federal government will guarantee federal bank mortgages for property in floodplains only if the local communities have adopted floodplain management measures, thus creating a federal incentive for local land use regulation. See Huber, Dan, "Fixing a Broken National Flood Insurance Program: Risks and Potential Reforms" (Center for Climate and Energy Solutions 2012), accessed 17 July 2015 at www.c2es.org/publications/fixing-broken-national-flood-insurance-program-risks-potential-reforms.

[43] Hecht, Sean B., "Insurance" in *The Law of Adaptation to Climate Change*, *supra*, n. 40, at 511, 518 (observing that offering subsidized insurance, even if conditioned on weather-proofing, could foster rather than inhibit development in risk-prone areas). 2012 federal legislation to adjust flood insurance premiums to better reflect risk was significantly rolled back in spring 2014.

[44] Babcock, Matthew, "State Hazard Mitigation Plans and Climate Change: Rating the States" (Columbia Law School 2013), accessed 17 July 2015 at web.law.columbia.edu/sites/default/files/microsites/climate-change/files/Publications/Students/SHMP%20Survey_Final.pdf; see generally Flatt, Victor B., "Domestic Disaster Preparedness and Response," in *The Law of Adaptation to Climate Change*, *supra*, n. 40, at 481.

[45] See "State Mitigation Plan Review Guide: Highlights of the Key Concepts" (FEMA 8 Sept. 2014), accessed 17 July 2015 at www.fema.gov/media-library-data/14103650924704dcaea71807b36f564f8e7841be4ff6b/State%20Mitigation%20Plan%20Review%20Guide_Key%20Concepts.pdf.

FEMA has expressed its intent to more fully incorporate climate risks and adaptation into its diverse programs.[46]

The Environmental Protection Agency is actively integrating climate change impacts into its programs. For example, in the water context, the agency has analyzed how it can help states and local governments address climate impacts on infrastructure for drinking water, wastewater and stormwater and how it can help states address climate impacts on water quality.[47]

Other federal programs will have significant influence over adaptation, and intersect with state and local efforts in important ways. The Army Corps of Engineers plays a key role in levee building and in wetland development, both areas that will be essential to adapting to higher flood risks. Mechanisms for integrating ACE decisions into longer-term adaptation planning at the federal, state and local level will be essential.[48] Transportation infrastructure decision-making at the federal, state and local levels will have important implications for resilience and require intergovernmental coordination. Many federal natural resource programs work in conjunction with parallel state agency programs, and will require integrated attention to climate impacts on forests, wildlands, and endangered species.[49]

B. New Multijurisdictional Initiatives

The substantial and wide-ranging challenges posed by climate change suggest that a greater federal role could be warranted in several contexts that have, historically, been left largely (though not exclusively) to state

---

[46] "Climate Change Adaptation Policy Statement" (FEMA 2011), accessed 17 July 2015 at www.fema.gov/media-library-data/20130726-1919-25045-3330/508_climate_change_policy_statement.pdf.

[47] National Water Program 2012 Strategy: Response to Climate Change (US Environmental Protection Agency 2012), accessed 17 July 2015 at www.water.epa.gov/scitech/climatechange/2012-National-Water-Program-Strategy.cfm.

[48] Flatt, Victor B. and Jeremy M. Tarr, "Adaptation, Legal Resiliency, and the U.S. Army Corps of Engineers: Managing Water Supply in a Climate-Altered World" (2011) 89 N. Car. L. Rev. 1499.

[49] See Council on Climate Preparedness and Resilience, "Priority Agenda: Enhancing the Climate Resilience of America's Natural Resources" (2014), accessed 17 July 2015 at www.whitehouse.gov/sites/default/files/docs/enhancing_climate_resilience_of_americas_natural_resources.pdf.

and local control.[50] For example, water law, land use planning, and housing (particularly affordable housing) are all areas where a cooperative federalism approach could lead to more effective and fairer adaptation.

Although clearly impacted by major federal water programs, states have nonetheless historically retained primary control over water supply and their own water rights jurisprudence. Climate change is expected to reduce water supplies in certain areas of the country, particularly in the southwest. State water policies are likely to have inter-jurisdictional impacts. For example, a failure to conserve, or even proactive water storage measures, could deplete flows to downstream states. Groundwater pumping could deplete aquifers that cross state boundaries. Tensions among states are already emerging. A federal role in promoting conservation, coordinating states and helping states adjust their water rights regimes could promote superior adaptation to changing water supplies than exclusive reliance on state institutions.[51]

Land use law presents another context where a stronger federal role is warranted. While many state and local governments are engaging in efforts to assess climate impacts and are recognizing the importance of land use planning and building codes in determining vulnerability and resilience, not all states or local governments have taken initiatives, and most have not moved to actively modify land use regulations to confront future climate risks. Revisions to existing programs, like the Coastal Zone Management Act, disaster planning, disaster recovery and flood insurance programs could improve local planning. But it is not clear that such piecemeal measures will be enough. A more direct requirement that states require local government adaptation planning, including appropriate land use planning, may be warranted.[52]

In the long term, housing law is another area deserving greater federal attention. Although federal housing programs have long provided support to local governments throughout the nation, federal housing programs are not set up to address the long-term shifts in population that could result from climate change impacts.[53] The federal government could help assess

---

[50] See Glicksman, *supra*, n. 1, at 1173–74 (observing that adaptation policy will require initiatives in areas that have traditionally been subject to state and local control).

[51] See Robert W. Adler, *Climate Change and the Hegemony of State Water Law*, 29 Stanford Envtl. L.J. 1 (2010).

[52] See Kaswan, *supra*, n. 8.

[53] See Craig, *supra*, n. 2, at 57 (observing that local land use law "operates at the wrong scale to deal with mass migrations").

long-term shifts, assess the degree to which the private market will provide adequate housing in areas experiencing in-migration, assist in the development of affordable housing and, as necessary, require state and local governments to reduce barriers to affordable housing.

V. CONCLUSION

Adaptation will be a messy affair. Given the multiplicity of fields impacted by climate change and the multiplicity of relevant actors already engaged in various degrees of climate change adaptation, there is no one-stop federal statutory fix that can generate a single coordinated federal–state–local structure for adaptation. Nonetheless, federalism issues will pervade the relevant areas, presenting common themes. Federalism values can guide how adaptation is mainstreamed into existing programs, can help shape new legislative initiatives to improve existing programs, and can inform the development of entirely new adaptation initiatives.

PART IV

THEORIES OF DIFFUSE REGULATORY POWER

10. Reverse preemption in federal water law

Ann E. Carlson[*]

INTRODUCTION

In this chapter, we explore an unusual form of federalism, what we call "reverse preemption."[1] Two reverse preemption provisions in federal law provide states with rather remarkable power to veto federal agency

---

[*] This chapter is excerpted from a larger article, "Reverse Preemption" (2014) 40 Ecology L.Q. 583, co-authored with Andrew Meyer, that explores not just the federalism implications of reverse preemption but also the relationship between the provisions and separation of powers between the legislative and executive branches.

[1] We recognize that the state veto provisions at issue in this chapter do not technically constitute preemption in that they do not prevent the federal government from legislating in the field or on the particular issue. Nevertheless, as we will show, the provisions can and do replace a federal agency decision with a state override, thus preempting the federal action in the dictionary sense of the word. And the provisions reverse the standard form of preemption in that they allow state policy to trump federal policy rather than the more traditional federal preemption of state law under the Supremacy Clause of the US Constitution. We thus adopt the label while recognizing its technical imprecision. To our knowledge, the term "reverse preemption" is regularly used in only one other circumstance and that is under the McCarran-Ferguson Act, which permits states to tax and regulate foreign insurance companies while exempting the insurance industry from antitrust laws. 15 U.S.C. §§ 1011–15 (2012). Section 1012(b) of the Act contains the reverse preemption provision and provides that "[n]o Act of Congress shall be construed to invalidate, impair, or supersede any law enacted by any State for the purpose of regulating the business of insurance, or which imposes a fee or tax upon such business, unless such Act specifically relates to the business of insurance." 15 U.S.C. § 1012(b). This provision was passed in response to the Supreme Court's ruling in *United States v South-Eastern Underwriters Ass'n*, 322 U.S. 533 (1944), in which the Court held that the business of insurance was "commerce," and therefore could be regulated by Congress under the Commerce Clause. *Humana, Inc. v Forsyth*, 522 U.S. 299,

213

decisions that conflict with state policy choices. These provisions, found in the Clean Water Act (CWA)[2] and the Coastal Zone Management Act (CZMA),[3] turn standard stories about federalism on their heads. Rather than preempting state power; setting up a scheme of cooperative federalism; or allowing the federal and state governments to operate in their own spheres (so-called "dual federalism"); by enacting two reverse preemption provisions, Congress has done something entirely different. It has granted power to the states – explicitly – to trump the policy decisions of federal agencies by imposing the states' own policy choices on federal actors even when those choices conflict with agency decisions.

Under the Coastal Zone Management Act, a state with a federally approved Coastal Zone Management Plan (CZMP) can veto any federal action inconsistent with the plan, subject to certain limits. For example, a state may challenge the approval of a federal oil and gas lease for exploration in coastal waters as inconsistent with its CZMP. Subject to certain limitations, the state determination will invalidate the lease.[4] The Clean Water Act contains a nearly identical provision. Under the CWA, if a state determines that a federal license or permit violates a state's water quality standards or other provisions of the Act, it may refuse to certify the activity unless it meets the state standards. This refusal to certify can be used to override the decision by a federal agency to allow the activity to proceed. These two veto provisions are not mere window dressing: states have used them to block oil leases, place conditions on the relicensing of hydroelectric dams, and veto proposed terminals for Liquefied Natural Gas (LNG) and other fuels.[5]

We argue in this chapter that providing states with veto power over federal agency decisions can promote important constitutional and policy values. Congress may, for example, trust states to implement its statutory commands more faithfully than the executive branch in some circumstances. Thus, reverse preemption provisions may bolster separation of powers values by deputizing states to execute federal statutory directives that an executive agency might otherwise fail to implement.[6] Congressional desire to limit executive power may be particularly strong in times

---

306 (1999). The McCarran-Ferguson "reverse preemption" provision sought to maintain a place for state regulation of the insurance industry. Ibid.

[2] 33 U.S.C. § 1342(a), (b) (2006) ("Section 401").
[3] 16 U.S.C. § 1456(c) (2006) ("consistency provision").
[4] See *infra* Part II.B.
[5] See *infra* Part II.A.
[6] Cf. Bulman-Pozen, Jessica, "Federalism as a Safeguard of the Separation of Powers" (2012) 112 Colum. L. Rev. **459**, 505 and discussion, *infra* Part II.A.

of divided government.[7] A Democratic Congress, for example, may empower states to check the regulatory biases of a Republican executive, reasoning that at least some states will share their policy preferences.[8]

Allowing states reverse preemption power may also allow Congress to bolster federalism values by granting those with knowledge about local political preferences and particular environmental resources a stronger say in the execution of federal law than federal agencies. This power is especially important for states with strong environmental preferences since the reverse preemption provisions work to implement statutes that provide for environmental protection. Thus, reverse preemption of federal agency actions can be thought of as a way to increase environmental protection, particularly when a federal agency's central mission includes promotion and protection of other non-environmental values.

We explore these reverse preemption provisions and their implications for federalism below.

I. REVERSE PREEMPTION PROVISIONS IN FEDERAL LAW: CLEAN WATER ACT SECTION 401 AND THE COASTAL ZONE MANAGEMENT PLAN

A. State Authority under Section 401 of the Clean Water Act

As with many of the major federal environmental laws, the CWA establishes detailed cooperative roles for both the federal and state governments.[9] Most federal environmental statutes, including the CWA, allocate specific powers to one level of government or another – for example, by providing the federal government with the authority to set standards and the states with the authority to implement a permitting program to enforce those standards.[10] By contrast, section 401 grants express veto power to states over certain federal decisions. Section 401 requires an applicant for a federal permit or license whose activity "may result in any discharge into the navigable waters" to obtain state certification. Specifically, the state must certify that the proposed activity complies with key provisions of the Act, including a state's water quality

---

[7] See Levinson, Daryl J. and Richard H. Pildes, "Separation of Parties, Not Powers" (2006) 119 Harv. L. Rev. 2311.

[8] Ibid. [10].

[9] Craig, Robin Kundis, *The Clean Water Act and the Constitution*, 2nd edn (Environmental Law Institute, Washington, DC 2009), p. 9.

[10] 33 U.S.C. § 1342(a), (b) (2006).

control standards and the Act's prohibition against discharges without a permit.[11] If the activity would violate the state's standards, the state can place conditions on federal approval of the license or permit in order to ensure that the standards are met. If the standards cannot be met through the imposition of conditions, the federal agency "shall not issue such license or permit."[12]

The state's water quality standards are part of a comprehensive set of requirements contained in the CWA that set limits on water pollution discharges, establish water quality standards to ensure that individual bodies of water are protected for their intended uses (for example swimming, fishing, drinking) and regulate the total amount of pollution specific water bodies can tolerate without violating the water quality standard (called the "total maximum daily load").[13] The CWA divides authority to implement these requirements between the federal and state governments. The CWA gives the EPA primary responsibility for setting technology-based limitations on discharges by individual "point sources" into the nation's navigable waters.[14] These limitations are implemented by approved states (or by the federal government for states without delegated authority) through the National Pollution Discharge Elimination System (NPDES).[15] States have the responsibility for setting the level of protection provided by a secondary layer of regulation: section 303 of the Act requires each state to institute comprehensive "water quality standards" (WQS) for all intrastate waters.[16] Water quality standards may be more stringent than the federal requirements[17] and contain two components: designated uses (for example swimming, fishing and recreation) and water quality criteria.[18] Water quality criteria may be expressed either as "numerical" limits on various pollutants, or as "narrative" requirements that set broad descriptive goals for various types

---

[11] 33 U.S.C. § 1341(a)(1).
[12] 33 U.S.C. § 1341(a)(2).
[13] See EPA, "Overview of Impaired Waters and Total Maximum Daily Loads Program" accessed 17 July 2015 at water.epa.gov/lawsregs/lawsguidance/cwa/tmdl/intro.cfm (last updated 6 March 2012) (explaining the relationship between individual effluent limitations on dischargers, water quality standards and the total maximum daily load program).
[14] 33 U.S.C. §§ 1252(a), § 1311(b).
[15] 33 U.S.C. § 1342(a)(b).
[16] 33 U.S.C. § 1313(a).
[17] 33 U.S.C. §§ 1311(b)(1)(C), 1370; see also 40 C.F.R. § 131.4(a) (2013) ("As recognized by section 510 of the Clean Water Act, States may develop water quality standards more stringent than required by this regulation.").
[18] 33 U.S.C. § 1313(c)(2)(A).

of water bodies (for example "[t]oxic, radioactive, or deleterious material concentrations shall be less than those which may affect public health, the natural aquatic environment, or the desirability of the water for any use"[19]), though criteria for toxic pollutants must, for the most part, be numerical.[20] Section 303 also contains an "anti-degradation" policy that requires states to ensure that bodies of water do not decline in quality even where the ultimate goal of the Act is to improve, not just maintain, overall quality.[21] The CWA also delegates to states the authority to implement a third type of regulation, the establishment of "Total Maximum Daily Loads," for bodies that fail to meet WQS.[22] These TMDLs are limits on the total amount of a pollutant that all sources can discharge into a particular body and are to be set at levels that bring the body of water into compliance with the WQS.[23]

Section 401 requires that federal permittees and licensees obtain state certification demonstrating that their activities comply with state WQS, TMDLs, and other limitations on discharges into waters covered by the Act.[24] State certifications must list any limitations and monitoring requirements necessary to assure that the applicant will be in compliance with various provisions of the CWA, as well as "any other appropriate requirement of State law."[25] Thus, under section 401, a state can withhold the necessary certification unless the applicant agrees to comply with federal *and* state water pollution requirements.

The most frequent use of Section 401 certification is for Federal Energy Regulatory Commission (FERC) licenses for hydroelectric power plants and Army Corps of Engineers permits to dredge and fill wetlands under section 404 of the Clean Water Act.[26]

---

[19] *PUD No. 1 of Jefferson Cnty. v Wash. Dep't of Ecology*, 511 U.S. 700, 716 (1994) (citing Washington State Water Quality Standards, WAC 173-201-045(c)(vii)h).

[20] 333 U.S.C. § 1313(c)(2)(B) (2006).

[21] EPA, Summary of Antidegradation Policy, accessed 17 July 2015 at water.epa.gov/scitech/swguidance/standards/handbook/chapter04.cfm#section2 (last updated 26 July 2013).

[22] 33 U.S.C. § 1313(d).

[23] EPA, "Impaired Waters and Total Maximum Daily Loads," accessed 17 July 2015 at water.epa.gov/lawsregs/lawsguidance/cwa/tmdl/index.cfm (last updated June 4, 2013).

[24] 33 U.S.C. § 1341(a)(1).

[25] 33 U.S.C. § 1341(d).

[26] 33 U.S.C. § 1344; EPA, "Section 401 Certification and Wetlands," accessed 17 July 2015 at water.epa.gov/type/wetlands/outreach/fact24.cfm (last

1. Section 401 certification and FERC

i. Legal authority over FERC permits The US Supreme Court has on several occasions addressed section 401 and FERC licensing of hydro-electric power plants. The Court has made clear that section 401 grants states significant power to condition or even veto FERC licenses.

Historically, the federal government had strong preemptive power over the states in the regulation of hydroelectric power plants.[27] In *California v FERC*,[28] the Court refused to allow the state to impose minimum stream flow requirements on an already existing federally authorized hydroelectric facility, following precedent set in 1940 in *First Iowa Hydro-Electric Cooperative v Federal Power Commission*.[29] But the question of state power to condition permits for *new* plants is made more complicated by section 401 of the Clean Water Act. The Court faced this question in *PUD No. 1 v Washington Dept. of Ecology*.[30]

In *PUD No. 1*,[31] a city-proposed, hydroelectric facility in Washington State would divert a large portion of the Dosewallips River's water to generate electricity before returning the water to the river downstream.[32] Pursuant to its authority to issue water quality standards under section 303 of the CWA, Washington had classified the Dosewallips River as "extraordinary," and designated it for uses including salmon spawning.[33] When the city applied for a CWA permit, the state refused to certify the project on the ground that the diversion would not leave enough water in the river's channel to allow for salmon spawning.[34] The city appealed, alleging that Washington lacked the authority under section 303 to impose minimum stream flow requirements as a permit condition.

After granting certioriari, the US Supreme Court upheld the state's refusal to certify the project.[35] Recall that section 401 applies to the

---

updated 28 March 2013); see Donahue, Deborah, "The Untapped Power of Clean Water Act Section 401" (1996) 32 Ecology L.Q. **201**, 277–95.

[27] *First Iowa Hydro-Electric Coop. v Fed. Power Comm'n*, 328 U.S. 152, 164 (1946).

[28] *California v Fed. Energy Regulatory Comm'n*, 495 U.S. 490, 498 (1990); Federal Power Act of 1920, 16 U.S.C. §§ 791–828(c) (2006).

[29] *First Iowa*, 328 U.S. at 152, 182.

[30] *PUD No. 1 of Jefferson Cnty. v Wash. Dep't of Ecology*, 511 U.S. 700, 723 (1994).

[31] Ibid. at 708 [36].
[32] Ibid. at 709 [37].
[33] Ibid. [38].
[34] Ibid. [39].
[35] Ibid. at 712–13 [41].

activity of any permit applicant "which may result in any discharge into the navigable waters."[36] The parties agreed that the construction of the power plant would result in discharges to the Dosewallips River, but petitioners argued that the condition the state imposed – compliance with minimum stream flows – did not pertain to the discharges.[37] The Court rejected the argument.[38] Under section 401(d), states may impose a variety of conditions as part of their certification: potential certification conditions are not constrained to discharge limits and may include compliance with state water quality. The state of Washington's water quality standards include its designated uses, including protecting salmon, as well as an antidegradation policy preventing the degradation of such uses.[39] Without minimum flow requirements, the dam could destroy the use of the river for salmon spawning.[40] By this reasoning, the Court held that the state was justified in conditioning permit approval on minimum stream flows.

In an important subsequent decision, *S.D. Warren Co. v ME Environmental Board of Protection,* the Court held that state authority under section 401 to issue conditions on federal permits and licenses extends to those seeking *relicensing* of privately held hydroelectric projects from FERC.[41] This is particularly consequential because FERC licenses are issued for periods not greater than 50 years.[42] Thus, states will have the opportunity to review nearly all of the nation's hydropower dams and either issue strict water quality requirements or deny certification altogether in the coming years.

ii. Evidence of section 401's influence in the FERC process   Whether the exercise of the section 401 power results in increased environmental protection is, of course, a more difficult question. Two studies at least suggest that the reverse preemption provisions result in the addition of a greater number of conditions in FERC licenses. The first, by Cornelius Kerwin, showed the number of environmental requirements in FERC

---

[36] 33 U.S.C. § 1341(a)(1) (2006).
[37] *PUD No. 1*, 511 U.S. at 711.
[38] Ibid. [44].
[39] Ibid. at 713–17 [45].
[40] Ibid. at 717 [46].
[41] *S.D. Warren Co. v Me. Envtl. Bd. of Prot.*, 547 U.S. 370 (2006).
[42] Ibid. at 373–74 [52]. For a complete list of issued licenses and their expiration dates, see Federal Energy Regulatory Commission, Applications for New Licenses, accessed 17 July 2015 at www.ferc.gov/industries/hydropower/gen-info/licensing/app-new.asp (last updated June 6, 2013).

licenses climbing from 1980 to 1986. The study does not provide an explanation for this increase and it occurred during a time when environmental pressures on FERC were increasing as a result of various court decisions.[43] However, part of the explanation could be that states were more systematically exercising their section 401 certification power. The second, a recent study of FERC decision-making over hydroelectric dams by Jody Freeman and J.R. DeShazo, found that when a greater number of public agencies participate in a FERC relicensing process, on average a greater number of environmental conditions are placed on the new license.[44] Their study counted the participation of federal and state agencies together, focusing not on the reverse preemption provision but on the effects of other federal environmental mandates.[45] Though the DeShazo–Freeman study does not disaggregate state from federal participation in determining the source of permit conditions, it shows that the involvement of public agencies, including state agencies, results in the inclusion of a larger number of environmental conditions.[46]

iii. Section 401 and wetlands protection The other substantive area in which states have potentially significant – though largely unrealized – power under section 401 is in the protection of wetlands. CWA section 404 requires any person seeking to dredge or fill wetlands to obtain a permit from the Army Corps of Engineers. Since any person seeking a federal permit or license for activity that may result in a discharge into navigable waters must obtain section 401 certification from the state in which the project is located, states must certify that a dredge and fill permit under section 404 is consistent with state water quality laws. Although virtually all of the states have section 401 certification programs for wetlands permits, to date, the limited evidence we have suggests that states do not appear to use their section 401 power very effectively to protect existing wetlands and connected water bodies.

Though section 404 does not require it, the policy of the United States since the George H.W. Bush Administration has been to administer the wetlands permitting program so that it results in no net loss of wetlands.[47]

---

[43] See Kerwin, Cornelius M., "Transforming Regulation: A Case Study of Hydropower Licensing" (1990) 50 Pub. Admin. Rev. **91**, 95.

[44] See DeShazo, J.R. and Jody Freeman, "Public Agencies as Lobbyists" (2006) 105 Colum. L. Rev. **2217**, 2265–67.

[45] Ibid. [57].

[46] Ibid. [58].

[47] For an excellent overview of the implementation of section 404, see Ruhl, J.B. and Jim Salzman, "No Net Loss – Instrument Choice in Wetlands Protection" in Freeman, Jody and Charles D. Kolstad (eds) *Moving to Markets in*

To achieve this goal, the Army Corps of Engineers prohibits wetland filling where possible. For those projects for which wetlands are filled, section 404 permittees must offset any wetlands loss with the replacement of an equal or greater amount of wetlands acreage, if possible.[48] The preferred mechanism for compensatory mitigation, by federal regulation, is participation in a wetlands mitigation bank.[49] Wetlands mitigation banks require federal approval and allow a permittee whose project will result in wetlands loss to replace the lost wetlands with wetland restoration performed by the mitigation bank.[50]

Many observers have criticized the performance of compensatory mitigation programs, arguing that the wetlands used to replace those to be dredged and filled are frequently of inferior quality.[51] After evaluating a number of mitigation sites, researchers concluded in one 2004 study that more than half of them did not adequately replace the wetlands lost.[52] Other studies have reached similar conclusions.[53]

Environmental Regulation: Lessons from Twenty Years of Experience (Oxford University Press, New York 2006), p. 323.

[48] For the regulatory guidance on wetlands mitigation, see EPA, Compensatory Mitigation, accessed 17 July 2015 at water.epa.gov/lawsregs/guidance/wetlands/wetlandsmitigation_index.cfm (last updated Feb. 22, 2013).

[49] The 1995 Federal Guidance for the Establishment, Use and Operation of Mitigation Banks establishes a preference for using mitigation banks for cumulative small impacts. The Transportation Equity Act for the 21st Century created a preference for the use of wetlands banks to replace wetlands destroyed as a result of transportation projects receiving federal highway funds. For an explanation, see EPA et al., Federal Guidance on the Use of the TEA-21 Preference for Mitigation Banking to Fulfill Mitigation Requirements Under Section 404 of the Clean Water Act (2003), accessed 17 July 2015 at water.epa.gov/lawsregs/guidance/wetlands/upload/2003_07_11_wetlands_TEA-21Guidance.pdf.

[50] Ibid. [64].

[51] See Kihslinger, Rebecca L., "Success of Wetland Mitigation Projects," *National Wetlands Newsletter*, Mar.–Apr. 2008, **14**, 14–15, accessed at www.tetonwyo.org/compplan/LDRUpdate/RuralAreas/Additional%20Resources/Kihslinger%202008.pdf.

[52] Ambrose, Richard F. et al., "An Evaluation of Compensatory Mitigation Projects Permitted Under the Clean Water Act Section 401 by the Los Angeles Regional Water Quality Control Board, 1991–2002" (2007), iii, accessed 17 July 2015 at www.waterboards.ca.gov/water_issues/programs/cwa401/docs/mitigation_finalreport_execsum081307.pdf ("Only 19 [percent] of the mitigation files were classified as optimal, with just over half sub-optimal and approximately one-quarter marginal to poor.").

[53] See Ambrose, Richard F., "Wetland Mitigation in the United States: Assessing the Success of Mitigation Policies" (2004), 9–11, accessed 17 July

The inadequacy of compulsory mitigation occurs despite the fact that states have the power to condition or even veto federal section 404 permits under section 401. Indeed, in an extensive review of wetlands permits under sections 401 and 404, researchers concluded that states appear to use this power largely to rubber stamp decisions already made by the Army Corps.[54]

Despite the states' apparent failure to exercise their power effectively under section 401 in the context of wetlands permits, every state in the country has a wetlands 401 certification program.[55] Through those certification programs, states could engage in more substantial oversight of wetlands permits. They could do so by either vetoing a permit altogether or conditioning a wetlands permit to ensure that permittees do not degrade or violate water quality standards, a condition that seems particularly well suited to permits authorizing the dredging and filling of wetlands. The power of the CWA reverse preemption provision to enhance the protection of wetlands subject to section 404 permitting, in short, seems significant but largely unrealized.

B. Reverse Preemption under the Coastal Zone Management Act

1. The consistency process under the CZMA

The Coastal Zone Management Act contains a reverse preemption provision nearly identical to section 303 of the CWA. Indeed, Congress explicitly modeled the CZMA provision after the CWA version.[56]

2015 at water.epa.gov/lawsregs/guidance/wetlands/upload/2004_10_28_wetlands _ambrose_wetlandmitigationinus.pdf; Kihslinger, *supra* note 51, at 14–15.

[54] See Ambrose et al., *supra*, n. 53, at i.

[55] Environmental Law Institute, State Wetland Protection: Status, Trends & Model Approaches (2008), 9, accessed 17 July 2015 at www.elistore.org/Data/ products/d18__06.pdf.

[56] Staff of S. Comm. on Commerce, 94th Cong., Legislative History of the Coastal Zone Management Act of 1972 (Comm. Print 1972), 254. In floor statements upon the passage of the CZMA, Senator William B. Spong made the following statement:

> I would be remiss if I failed to thank the committee and especially the distinguished Senator from South Carolina for accepting the suggestion I offered during the committee's consideration of the bill to require State certification of activities requiring a Federal license or permit. This provision parallels a requirement in the Federal Water Pollution Control Act that applicants needing a Federal license or permit must obtain a certificate from the State water pollution control agency that there is reasonable assurance that the activity in question will not violate applicable water quality standards. It

The CZMA sought to entice coastal states to use their traditional authority over land use to further the national interest in comprehensive coastal management. Unlike other environmental regulatory regimes, states are "encouraged," but not obligated, to participate in the program.[57] To participate, states must first create a Coastal Zone Management Plan (CZMP) that complies with several federal requirements. Each state's CZMP must define its "coastal zone"; provide a program for non point-source water pollution; identify land uses which may cause or contribute to the degradation of coastal waters; and provide for ongoing implementation and enforcement.[58,59] If the Secretary of Commerce and the Administrator of the EPA both agree that a CZMP meets the statutory requirements of the CZMA, the plan "shall" be approved.[60]

At its inception, the CZMA provided the states with two federal incentives: money and power. First, participating states were made eligible for federal funds for research, management and enforcement of the CZMP.[61] The second, more unusual incentive, referred to as the "consistency requirement," gave participating states a measure of authority over *federal* land use decisions that may affect the states' coastal zones.[62] The consistency requirement is what we refer to as a reverse preemption provision.

---

seems entirely reasonable to have a comparable provision in this legislation to guard against development that is inconsistent with the coastal zone management program. (Ibid. [71])

[57] See 16 U.S.C. § 1452(2). Congress sought to "encourage and assist the states to exercise effectively their responsibilities in the coastal zone through the development and implementation of management programs to achieve wise use of the land and water resources of the coastal zone ... ." Ibid. [75].

[58] 16 U.S.C. § 1455b(a), (b).

[59] 16 U.S.C. § 1455b(c)(1).

[60] 16 U.S.C. § 1456(b).

[61] 16 U.S.C. §§ 1454–55. These financial incentives are rather unremarkable: Congress frequently attaches conditions to the receipt of federal funds, and the Supreme Court long ago deemed such conditional grants constitutional, provided that the conditions bear some rational relationship to the purpose of the legislation. See *New York v United States*, 505 U.S. 144, 167 (1992).

[62] 16 U.S.C. § 1456(c). Over time, the amount of funding provided to states under the CZMP has waned, and the consistency requirement has become comparatively more important as an incentive. Kalo, Joseph J. et al., *Coastal and Ocean Law: Cases and Materials*, 2nd edn (West Publishing 2002), p. 192.

The consistency requirement provides that any federal agency activities or any private activities requiring a federal permit or federal funding that "affect ... any land or water use or natural resource of the coastal zone shall be carried out in a manner which is consistent to the maximum extent practicable with the enforceable policies of approved [CZMPs]."[63]

For federal agency activities, the acting federal agency must furnish the state agency charged with administration of the CZMP with a "consistency determination" explaining why the federal action is consistent with the CZMP "to the maximum extent practicable."[64] For private activities seeking federal approval, the applicant is required to request certification from the state that the project is consistent with the CZMP.[65] In the case of both federal activities in the coastal zone and permits and licenses, if the state finds that the action is consistent with the CZMP, the action may go forward.[66] If, by contrast, the state finds that the action is inconsistent, the action is effectively blocked unless the state's finding is overturned on administrative appeal by the Secretary or vetoed by the President.[67]

Federal agencies and permit applicants are entitled to administratively appeal a state's decision to the Secretary of Commerce. If the appeal fails, the President may veto the state's finding of inconsistency. This appeals process is, however, time-consuming and presidential vetoes are extremely rare. Thus, while the state's decision is not final, the appeals process gives the state significant leverage when bargaining for conditions or mitigation for a proposed project.

---

[63] 16 U.S.C. § 1456(c)(1), (3)(A). The CZMA regulations define "maximum extent practicable" as "fully consistent with such programs unless compliance is prohibited based upon the requirements of existing law applicable to the Federal agency's operations." 15 C.F.R. § 930.32 (2013).

[64] 16 U.S.C. § 1456(c)(1)(A), (C). If the federal and state agencies dispute whether a consistency determination is required, a state may resort to litigation under the Administrative Procedure Act. See *Sec'y of the Interior v California*, 464 U.S. 312 (1984); Administrative Procedure Act (APA), Pub. L. No. 79-404, 60 Stat. 237 (1946) (codified at 5 U.S.C. §§ 500–706 (2012)). See 5 U.S.C. § 706 (waiver of sovereign immunity).

[65] 16 U.S.C. § 1456(c)(3)(A).

[66] Ibid. [86]. If the state does not reply within three months to a "certification" submitted by a private applicant for a federal permit, then the states concurrence is conclusively presumed. Ibid. [87].

[67] 16 U.S.C. § 1456(c)(1)(B), (3)(A).

2. The scope of the reverse preemption provision: judicial interpretation and legislative amendment

The scope and application of the CZMA are exceptionally broad, extending not just to a state's own coastal zone but also to activities that could affect it. Congress clarified this broad scope after a Supreme Court decision construing state jurisdiction more narrowly, as we describe below.

Coastal states own the land in their "territorial sea," which includes "all lands permanently or periodically covered by tidal waters ... seaward to a line three geographical miles distant from the coast line of each such state."[68] The lands beyond the states' territorial seas – the outer continental shelf, or "OCS" – are owned by the federal government.[69] The Outer Continental Shelf Lands Act of 1953 granted the Secretary of the Interior the authority to lease the OCS for oil and gas exploration and drilling.[70] Absent the CZMA, states would not be able to affect federal management of OCS lands.[71] Given that the CZMA was inspired in part by the Santa Barbara oil spill of 1969, it is unsurprising that most of the major disputes over the consistency requirement have involved the federal leasing of tracts on the OCS – and thus outside a state's coastal zone – for oil and gas exploration or extraction.[72]

In *Secretary of the Interior v California*, the US Supreme Court construed the scope of the consistency requirement narrowly, confining its application to activities that took place directly within the geographical confines of the "coastal zone."[73] Congress quickly overturned the Supreme Court's narrow interpretation of the CZMA with the Coastal Zone Management Act Reauthorization Amendments of 1990.[74] The

---

[68] 43 U.S.C. § 1301(a)(2) (2006).

[69] 43 U.S.C. § 1302.

[70] Pub. L. No. 83-212, 67 Stat. 462 (codified as amended at 43 U.S.C. §§ 1331–56 (2006)).

[71] States would be relegated to lodging public comments in an environmental impact statement prepared pursuant to the National Environmental Policy Act for federal actions on the outer continental shelf, or exerting indirect political influence.

[72] See National Oceanic & Atmospheric Administration, Appeals Spreadsheet (2013), accessed 17 July 2015 at www.coastalmanagement.noaa.gov/consistency/media/appealslist.pdf.

[73] *Sec'y of the Interior*, 464 U.S. at 315.

[74] Coastal Zone Act Reauthorization Amendments of 1990, Pub. L. No. 101-508, 104 Stat. 1388-299–319 (codified at 16 U.S.C. §§ 1451–64 (2006)). The 1990 amendments were preceded by extensive congressional hearings. See e.g. *Coastal Zone Improvement Act of 1989: Hearing on S. 1189 Before the*

1990 amendments explicitly extended the Act to actions outside the coastal zone that affect the coastal zone itself.[75] The 1990 amendments also specifically provided that federal OCS leases for energy development under the Outer Continental Shelf Lands Act must comply with a state's CZMP.[76] These amendments extended state power under the CZMA markedly, beyond the Supreme Court's narrow interpretation in *Secretary of the Interior*. Not only did the amendments make clear that the reverse preemption provision extends to the OCS, but because states can require a consistency determination for any activity that *affects* the coastal zone, states can require consistency of federally approved activities that take place wholly within *another* state.[77] NOAA has established regulations that govern these interstate applications of the consistency requirement, and requires federal approval of any state request for an interstate consistency certification.[78]

3. The consistency requirement in practice

Many states appear to use their reverse preemption power under the CZMA robustly and successfully to challenge federal actions as inconsistent with their coastal plans. Although states find that proposed projects are consistent with the applicable CZMP about 95 percent of the

---

Subcomm. on National Ocean Policy Study of the S. Comm. on Commerce, Sci., & Transp., 101st Cong. (1990); *Coastal Environmental Monitoring: Hearings Before the Subcomm. on Natural Res., Agric. Research & Env't of the H. Comm. on Sci., Space, & Tech.*, 101st Cong. (1990); *Coastal Zone Management Act, Part II: Hearings on H.R. 4030 Before the Subcomm. on Oceanography & Great Lakes of the H. Comm. on Merch. Marine & Fisheries*, 101st Cong. (1990); *Coastal Zone Management: Hearings on Coastal Zone Management Before the Subcomm. on National Ocean Policy Study of the S. Comm. on Commerce, Sci., & Transp.*, 101st Cong. (1989); *Coastal Zone Management Act Reauthorization: Hearings on Discussion of Various Aspects of the Reauthorization of the Coastal Zone Management Act Before the Subcomm. on Oceanography & Great Lakes of the H. Comm. on Merch. Marine & Fisheries*, 101st Cong. (1989).

[75] Coastal Zone Act Reauthorization Amendments of 1990, Pub. L. No. 101-508, 104 Stat. 1388-29–319 (codified at 16 U.S.C. §§ 1451–64).

[76] 16 U.S.C. § 1456(c)(3)(B).

[77] See Office of Ocean & Coastal Resource Management, Interstate Consistency Fact Sheet (2011), accessed 17 July 2015 at coastalmanagement.noaa.gov/consistency/media/consistencyfact090111.pdf; see also 15 C.F.R § 930.1 (2013). NOAA notes that "[i]nterstate consistency does not affect the sovereignty of State B; it does not give State A authority to review the laws or policies of State B. It only allows State A to review the proposed *federal authorization* in the other state." Office of Ocean & Coastal Resource Management, *supra*.

[78] Office of Ocean & Coastal Resource Management, *supra*, n. 77.

time, findings of inconsistency have been used to block a significant number of large energy infrastructure projects. Even when a consistency finding is appealed,[79] many appeals are settled before final determination. Given the lengthy appeals process, these settlements are likely to be on terms favorable to the state. Thus, for large projects with significant effects on the coastal zone, the consistency requirement can be an effective tool for states to bargain for mitigation, or even to block the project altogether.

Those actions that states have contested are subject first to mediation – for which we have few data to evaluate the effects of state involvement.[80] It seems fair to assume, however, that successful mediation efforts result in states achieving at least some mitigation of the likely effects of an action subject to the consistency requirement. States would appear to have the upper hand in a mediation proceeding given their unilateral power to condition or veto a project (subject to appeal). It seems unlikely that if a state is willing to issue a determination of inconsistency in the first instance, the state would then simply back down during mediation and find a project to be consistent. Instead, our supposition is that mediation results in project applicants agreeing to mitigate the most deleterious effects of their projects on a state's coastal zone.

For those determinations of inconsistency that are not resolved via mediation, project applicants can choose the long path of appeal. As of March 2010, 144 determinations had been appealed.[81] Of those 144, 64 were settled or withdrawn, 32 were dismissed on procedural grounds, and 44 resulted in a formal decision by the Secretary.[82] Of the 44 appeals that yielded an administrative decision, 30 were resolved in favor of the state appellants.[83] States challenged oil and gas plans on the OCS, natural gas

---

[79] Nat'l Oceanic & Atmospheric Admin., *supra*, n. 72, at 1.

[80] As the Associate Deputy Assistant Administrator of NOAA noted in the Senate hearings on reauthorization of the CZMA in 2005:

Some will argue those statistics [indicating state findings of consistency in 95 percent of consistency reviews] leave out a number of cases where States have used consistency as leverage to bring people to the table to get some things done that the applicant or the Federal agency might not otherwise have wanted to do. Our response to that is that is the purpose of [the consistency provision] of the CZMA. (*Reauthorization of the Coastal Zone Management Act. Hearing Before the S. Comm. on Commerce, Sci., and Transp.*, 109th Cong. 7 (2005) (remarks of Dr Thomas Kitsos).)

[81] Ibid. [133].
[82] Ibid. [134].
[83] Ibid. [135].

pipelines and LNG terminals in 19 of the 44 appeals; ten of these energy-related appeals were resolved in favor of the states.[84] The lower success rate in energy-related appeals likely reflects the national interests in energy development, which weighs against the state in the balancing test Commerce applies in determining whether to approve the appeal.

It is difficult to extrapolate from these numbers to broad conclusions about the extent of state power under the consistency requirement. On the one hand, the relatively small number of appeals (only 5 percent of all actions reviewed by states) and the even smaller number of state victories may suggest that the actual significance of the consistency requirement is relatively minimal. However, states' success in blocking ten major energy projects, despite opposition from the Department of Interior and other federal agencies, is not insignificant. States may also have challenged many of the unfavorable appeals decisions in litigation, resulting in more favorable settlement agreements or judicial rulings.

Furthermore, the success rate of state appeals does not provide a complete picture of the influence wielded by states through consistency review. Just as states undoubtedly wield power through the mediation process described above, they also likely did so in the 64 appeals that were settled prior to resolution by the Secretary, as well as countless projects that were not formally appealed. The appeals process can take longer than four years to resolve – a fact that gives states substantial leverage in negotiating modifications or mitigation to undesired projects.[85]

It is also worth noting that not all states that participate in the CZMA process appear to use it uniformly. Thirty states and five US territories currently have CZMPs in place (including states such as Ohio whose coastline is not an ocean but a lake).[86] Of those 35 jurisdictions, ten states and one territory (Puerto Rico) have been involved in Commerce Department appeals.[87] California, unsurprisingly, has led the way with nine challenges, but South Carolina and North Carolina have also been active, with seven South Carolina projects appealed and six in North

---

[84] Ibid. [136]. Appeals not involving energy projects generally concern construction projects that involve the filling of wetlands, and so require a permit under section 404 of the CWA. The Army Corps of Engineers generally opposed the states in such appeals. Ibid. [137].

[85] Ibid. at 51 [137].

[86] National Oceanic & Atmospheric Administration, States and Territories Working on Coastal Management, accessed 17 July 2015 at coastalmanagement.noaa.gov/mystate/welcome.html (last updated July 20, 2012).

[87] National Oceanic & Atmospheric Administration, *supra*, note 86, at 3–5.

Carolina.[88] Though it is possible that a state may use its consistency power aggressively and not be subject to appeal, it seems logical to assume that the more aggressive users of the provision are those that are also subject to the appeals challenge.

The CZMA appears to grant states quite significant power to stop coastal activity that will negatively affect their coastal resources. The reverse preemption provisions in both the CWA and CZMA, then, provide a rather remarkable amount of power to states willing to assert it. They also tell a story about Congress and constitutional values that has to date gone unnoted. We turn next to that story.

II. REVERSE PREEMPTION AND CONSTITUTIONAL VALUES

Rather than abdicating responsibility to the executive branch, or preempting state power, or even allowing states and the federal government to exercise overlapping power as recent accounts of federalism suggest, Congress has used the reverse preemption mechanism to give states overt power over federal actions. This mechanism has multiple effects.

A. Preemption Trends

Many scholars have – appropriately – focused on congressional preemption of state power in a variety of substantive areas, including financial regulation, tort law, and the setting of national product standards.[89] Federal preemption of state power appears to be on the increase, continuing and perhaps accelerating a trend toward federal usurpation of state power that began in the 1960s.[90] The environmental field has seen congressional efforts to preempt state power (though states retain large swathes of authority in most environmental areas), and several court

---

[88] Ibid. [141].

[89] See e.g. William W. Buzbee, "Asymmetrical Regulation: Risk, Preemption and the Floor/Ceiling Distinction" (2007) 82 N.Y.U. L. Rev. **1547**, 1561–62, 1570–72; Roderick Hills et al., "Backdoor Federalization" (2006) 53 UCLA L. Rev. **1353**, 1389–98; Catherine M. Sharkey, "Preemption by Preamble: Federal Agencies and the Federalization of Tort Law" (2007) 56 DePaul L. Rev. **227**, 228–29.

[90] See "New Evidence on the Presumption Against Preemption: An Empirical Study of Congressional Responses to Supreme Court Preemption Decisions" (2007) 120 Harv. L. Rev. **1604**, 1611 (citing US Advisory Comm'n on Intergov't Relations, Federal Statutory Preemption of State and Local Authority (1992), 1).

decisions have held that Congress has either expressly or impliedly occupied areas of environmental law. The Clean Air Act, for example, preempts all states except California from regulating emissions from automobiles and from regulating fuels.[91] The Federal Fungicide, Insecticide and Rodenticide Act preempts state "breach of duty to warn" claims.[92] Several successive federal bills regulating appliance efficiency standards preempt states from issuing their own standards.[93] And one federal court has limited California's right to measure compliance with emissions standards using fuel economy under the Energy Policy and Conservation Act (EPCA) while another has preempted local building standards as inconsistent with federal appliance efficiency standards.[94]

Against this backdrop of increasing federal preemption, reverse preemption appears both to have gone largely unnoticed and to have defied congressional trends. What might explain why Congress would enact legislation – and subsequently strengthen it in the case of the CZMA – that weakens federal power at the expense of state preferences?

1. Reverse preemption as an enticement

The first explanation is a straightforward one. With respect to the CZMA, Congress appears to have enacted the reverse preemption provision in order to entice states to prepare CZMPs. Congress was reluctant to mandate land use planning given the long-standing respect for state and local control over land use decisions, making clear that the CZMA makes "no attempt to diminish state authority through federal preemption."[95] Instead, as the Senate Report accompanying the bill explained, "the intent of this legislation is to enhance state authority by encouraging and assisting the states to assume planning and regulatory powers over their coastal zones."[96] Despite its intent to respect local land use authority, the CZMA recognized that many states did not systematically protect coastal

---

[91] See 42 U.S.C. § 7542(a), (b) (2006) (emissions standards); 42 U.S.C. § 7545(c)(4)(A) (fuels).

[92] 7 U.S.C. § 136–36y (2012).

[93] For an explanation of the preemption provisions and background history, see Carlson, Ann E., "Energy Efficiency and Federalism" (2008) 107 Mich. L. Rev. First Impressions **63**, 65–66.

[94] See *Air Conditioning, Heating & Refrigeration Inst. v City of Albuquerque*, Civ. No. 08-633 MV/RLP, 2008 WL 5586316, at *1 (D.N.M. Oct. 3, 2008).

[95] S. Rep. No. 92-753, at 1 (1972), reprinted in 1972 U.S.C.C.A.N. 4776; but see Ashira Ostrow, "Land Law Federalism" (2012) 61 Emory L.J. **1398**, 1400–01 (outlining the involvement of the federal government in land use decision-making).

[96] S. Rep. No. 92-753, at 1 [150].

resources, a failure the Act sought to reverse through the enticement of the consistency determination (along with federal funding, since diminished).

2. Respect for environmental federalism

The initial impetus for inclusion of the reverse preemption provision in the CZMA does not, however, explain the inclusion of such a provision in the Clean Water Act or Congress's expansion of states' jurisdictional power under the CZMA in the 1990 amendments. A straightforward explanation for the reverse preemption provisions is that Congress may actually value federalism in particular substantive areas, especially when federalism aligns with the ideological preferences of Congress or serves practical ends.

There is a vigorous debate about which branch of the federal government should be entrusted to protect federalism values. These values are well known and include encouraging policy experimentation and diversity, respecting local preferences and taking advantage of local knowledge and information about the area of regulation.[97] The debate about the degree to which Congress actually respects federalism values is a vibrant one that often focuses on whether the judiciary should review – or review robustly – cases involving the division of powers between the federal government and the states.[98] Scholars divide on the question of

---

[97] See Carlson, Ann E., "Iterative Federalism" (2007) 103 Nw. U.L. Rev. **1097**, 1103 (discussing advantages).

[98] Herbert Weschler's article is a seminal one in the debate about federalism and political safeguards. See Wechsler, Herbert, "The Political Safeguards of Federalism: The Role of the States in the Composition and Selection of the National Government" (1954) 54 Colum. L. Rev. **543**, 547 (arguing that institutional design choices like the composition of the US Senate, with two representatives from each state regardless of population, protects the interests of states in the federal political system); see also Choper, Jesse H., *Judicial Review and the National Political Process* (University of Chicago Press, Chicago 1980), p. 175 (arguing that courts need not engage in robust judicial review of federalism cases because the political process protects federalism values); Kramer, Larry D. "Putting the Politics Back into the Political Safeguards of Federalism" (2000) 100 Colum. L. Rev. **215**, 219 (suggesting that political parties provide adequate political safeguards for federalism values); Baker, Lynn A. and Ernest A. Young, "Federalism and the Double Standard of Judicial Review" (2001) 51 Duke L.J. 75, 78 (arguing that Congress does not, in fact, systematically protect federalism values); Yoo, John and Sai Prakash, "The Puzzling Persistence of Process-Based Federalism Theories" (2001) 79 Tex. L. Rev. **1459**, 1462–63 (agreeing that political safeguards can protect federalism values but arguing that the judiciary should still play an important role in safeguarding federalism).

whether Congress has any institutional commitment to federalism values, with the divide very basically coming down to whether the structure of Congress and political parties that produce our congressional officials provide political safeguards for federalism. Those who believe that Congress has institutional features that are federalism-enhancing generally advocate a limited judicial role in the review of cases involving the appropriate division of power between states and the federal government, while those who doubt that Congress systematically respects federalism values are in favor of more robust judicial review.[99]

Setting aside the larger structural and institutional questions about the degree to which Congress's institutional design systematically protects states from federal aggrandizement, we argue here simply that reverse preemption provisions themselves promote the interests of state and local officials at the expense of federal agencies, and therefore promote federalism. Moreover, as we describe below, the fact that the reverse preemption provisions are federalism-promoting does not seem particularly surprising, given that they cover subject matters that the federal government did not traditionally regulate and that were long within state control.

The Clean Water Act represented a massive federal foray into an area traditionally regulated by the states. Indeed, President Eisenhower vetoed an early bill to consolidate power over water pollution on the ground that water pollution control was within the exclusive jurisdiction of the states.[100] In the Clean Water Act itself, Congress explicitly acknowledged the traditional role of states in water pollution control, stating in the Congressional Declaration of Goals and Policies section of the CWA that

> ... [i]t is the policy of the Congress to recognize, preserve, and protect the primary responsibilities and rights of States to prevent, reduce, and eliminate

---

[99] See citations in n. 98. For an argument that members of Congress are rarely motivated by a desire to strengthen the power of the federal government at the expense of states, see Levinson, *supra*, n. 7.

[100] Hines, N. William, "History of the 1972 Clean Water Act: The Story Behind How the 1972 Act Became the Capstone on a Decade of Extraordinary Environmental Reform", U. Iowa Legal Research Paper No. 12-12 (2012), p. 4. Hines wrote a series of important articles in the 1960s chronicling the role of states in water pollution control and describing the escalating federal role. See, e.g., Hines, "Nor Any Drop to Drink: Public Regulation of Water Quality, Part 1: State Pollution Control Programs" (1966) 52 Iowa L. Rev. 186; Hines, "Part II: Interstate Arrangements for Pollution Control" (1966) 52 Iowa L. Rev. 432; Hines, "Part III: The Federal Effort" (1967) 52 Iowa L. Rev. 799.

pollution, to plan the development and use (including restoration, preservation, and enhancement) of land and water resources, and to consult with the Administrator in the exercise of his authority under this chapter.[101]

Additionally, despite conventional wisdom that the states had not sufficiently protected their water resources, by the mid-1950s virtually every state in the country had a staff of water pollution professionals, and by the end of the 1960s most states required water pollution controls on sewage treatment plants and on industrial users, though enforcement was quite weak.[102] Moreover, Congress had already required states to develop water quality standards in the 1965 Water Quality Act and by 1970 all 50 had done so.[103] Thus, the states possessed significant regulatory expertise at the time the federal Clean Water Act was enacted in 1972. As William Hines concludes, "Congress' decision in the 1972 CWA to retain the traditional deference to the states to implement the new requirements was wise. It ... was ... based on the very practical recognition that, at that point in U.S. water pollution control history, nearly all the technical expertise and professional personnel needed to reach the ambitious new federal goals were located within the state programs."[104]

Nevertheless, despite the widespread involvement of states in regulating water pollution, their efforts were viewed widely as a failure.[105] Though the states had adopted water quality standards, only half had standards that were federally approved.[106] And by virtually all accounts the standards were poorly set, subject to manipulation by industry and woefully unsuccessful in actually cleaning up polluted water.[107]

Congress had already increased federal involvement by the time of the passage of the contemporary CWA; the 1972 Act dramatically escalated that involvement. The most significant change was to grant EPA the power to set effluent limitations on traditional point sources like paper mills, chemical plants and so forth and to require permits of polluters who discharged into the nation's water bodies.[108] This was a substantial

---

[101] 33 USC § 1251 (2006)
[102] Hines, *supra*, n. 100 at 4–5.
[103] Ibid. at 5.
[104] Ibid. at 5–6.
[105] Ibid. at 5.
[106] See Houck, Oliver, "The Regulation of Toxic Substances Under the Clean Water Act" (1991) 21 ELR **10528**, 10531.
[107] Ibid. at 10531–33 (describing failure of water quality approach)
[108] Ibid.

(and very intentional) move away from the traditional water quality/ambient approach as the dominant means of regulation.[109]

Nevertheless, given their long-standing role in regulating water pollution (albeit weakly) states retained significant authority both to implement the limitations through delegated authority and to continue to set ambient water quality standards.[110] Indeed states lobbied hard to retain their authority to set water quality standards.[111] This history of long-standing state authority over water quality combined with escalating federal involvement in setting technology based standards may help explain why Congress included the reverse preemption provision in the 1972 amendments.

The CZMA is even more explicitly designed to preserve state authority over land use decisions within a state's coastal zone, given that the statute includes no mandates or minimum standards. Instead, the entire statutory structure is about providing incentives to states to engage in good coastal planning rather than about exerting federal power over coastal resources. Again congressional intent to protect state power is clear:

> The key to more effective protection and use of the land and water resources of the coastal zone is to encourage the states to exercise their full authority over the lands and waters in the coastal zone by assisting the states, in cooperation with Federal and local governments and other vitally affected interests, in developing land and water use programs for the coastal zone, including unified policies, criteria, standards, methods, and processes for dealing with land and water use decisions of more than local significance.[112]

The idea that states and local governments have authority over land use issues has been noted by courts,[113] policy-makers[114] and scholars.[115]

---

[109] Ibid. Houck provides numerous examples of statements by members of Congress cataloguing the failure of water quality standards and the substitution of such standards with an effluent limitation/technology-based approach as the centerpiece of the 1972 amendments.

[110] 33 USC §1311 (2006).

[111] See Houck, *supra*, n. 106 at 10533.

[112] 16 U.S.C. § 1451(l) (2006).

[113] *Village of Euclid v Ambler*, 272 U.S. 365, 389 (1926) (endorsing the idea that zoning is a local issue).

[114] The text of the CZMA itself makes this clear. See *infra*, text accompanying n. 112.

[115] See e.g. Briffault, Richard, "Our Localism: Part I – The Structure of Local Government Law" (1990) 90 Colum. L. Rev. **1**, 3; Rose, Carol M., "Planning and Dealing: Piecemeal Land Controls as a Problem of Local Legitimacy" (1983) 71 Calif. L. Rev. **837**, 839; Tarlock, A. Dan, "Land Use Regulation: The Weak

Indeed, Congress considered "nationalizing" land use policy during the period of robust federal environmental expansionism in the early 1970s but rejected Senator Henry Jackson's National Land Use Policy Act. Part of the rationale for its defeat was the incursion of federal authority into an area of local control.[116] Thus, in both the CWA and the CZMA, Congress not only expressed policy sentiment in favor of federalism values, but did so in policy areas that had a long history of local domination.

The reverse preemption provisions, however, go beyond respecting state and local policy choices about how to implement coastal or water pollution control policy. As we explain below, the provisions privilege state and local decisions that protect the environment, bolstering them through federal law. Our conclusion, then, is that the provisions promote *environmental* federalism by granting authority to states willing to use it to advance environmental objectives.

3. Promotion of federalism with a twist

The reverse preemption provisions privilege federal statutory requirements that mandate state standards (in the case of the CWA) and encourage coastal planning (in the case of the CZMA). Once the states have established the required standards or plans, the reverse preemption provisions provide those states that have strong environmental preferences and effective bureaucracies an additional mechanism to ensure that their standards and plans are not overridden by federal agencies. Thus, the reverse preemption provisions enhance the power of only those states that are willing to exercise their authority to ensure the application of strong environmental standards against federal licensees or permittees.[117]

When both reverse preemption provisions were adopted in the 1970s, congressional concern for the environment was at its apex. Indeed, as the Senate Committee on Public Works explained in rebuffing an amendment to weaken section 401 of the CWA, "[a]ll we ask is that activities that threaten to pollute the environment be subjected to the examination of the environmental improvement agency of the State for an evaluation and a

---

Link in Environmental Protection" (2007) 82 Wash. L. Rev. **651**, 653. For an interesting exploration of the history of federal–state relationships over land use, see Ostrow, *supra*, n. 95, at 1401–12.

[116] See Ostrow, *supra*, n. 95, at 111 n. 43.

[117] See Buzbee, *supra*, n. 89, at 1586–87 (making the same point with respect to cooperative federalism schemes).

recommendation before the Federal license or permit be granted."[118] Thus the explanation that in adopting the reverse preemption provisions Congress sought to enhance federalism values seems too simple. Congress instead sought to enhance federalism values as long as state authority was used to enhance environmental protection.

Yet even the environmental federalism explanation seems insufficient to explain the strength of the reverse preemption provisions in allowing states to veto executive decisions. After all, the cooperative federalism arrangements in both the Clean Water and Clean Air Acts, for example, in requiring states to meet minimum standards while granting them authority to determine how to meet those standards, can also be explained on the grounds of environmental federalism. Like reverse preemption schemes, cooperative federalism also allows states to enforce environmental standards more rigorously, while providing a minimum floor of regulation. Something other than *just* the promotion of environmental values seems to be motivating the reverse preemption provisions. We explore the way in which reverse preemption provisions enhance and protect Congressional power below.

4. Protection of congressional power

i. Reverse preemption provisions as separation-of-powers enhancing One effect of the reverse preemption provisions is that they shift the balance of power between Congress and the executive branch. They do so by augmenting state power while reducing that of the executive in order to promote proper implementation of federal legislative requirements. In this respect, reverse preemption provisions bolster congressional power over executive power by deputizing state agents to carry out federal statutory provisions. These provisions, then, enhance the separation of powers between Congress and the executive branch, allowing Congress to check executive authority indirectly.[119]

Though states, not Congress, are the agents responsible for using the power granted to them by the reverse preemption provisions, they are doing so in a way that is consistent with federal statutory provisions enacted by Congress and in a way that limits federal agency discretion. The CZMA reverse preemption provision allows states to further coastal

---

[118] *A Legislative History of Amendments to the Federal Water Pollution Control Act of 1972* (Cong. Research Service 1972), 1388.

[119] We do not explore in detail here the values that separation of powers promote, but they include accountability and democratic responsiveness. See Bulman-Pozen, *supra*, n. 6, at 463.

protection according to congressional directives while constraining discretionary executive branch decisions. The Clean Water Act allows a state to condition a federal permit to require a permittee to comply with water quality standards required by a congressionally enacted statute. Thus the reverse preemption provisions allow Congress to ensure that its directives are not ignored by the executive branch.

The Madisonian idea of separating powers through competitive branches of government in order to check the concentration of power in one branch has long occupied constitutional thinking in both the courts and academic scholarship.[120] Reverse preemption could be viewed as a mechanism that does precisely what Madison envisioned: checking the exercise of executive power by making Congress more powerful. Many scholars have cast doubt on the accuracy of the Madisonian theory, noting that the legislative branch has both acquiesced in and explicitly granted large amounts of power to the executive.[121] The reverse preemption provisions appear to defy this trend.

Indeed, at the time of the passage of both reverse preemption provisions, executive agencies dominated the decision-making over the permitting of oil drilling and licensing of hydroelectric dams. The reverse preemption provisions afforded Congress an opportunity to exert some control over the executive branch's dam licensing and oil permitting. Both topics became increasingly controversial during this period as their environmentally damaging consequences became more evident.[122] The

---

[120] For a description of Madison's views of separation of powers as a way to cabin government aggrandizement of power, see Levinson, *supra*, n. 7, at 918–19. See also Merrill, Thomas W., "The Constitutional Principle of Separation of Powers" (1991) Sup. Ct. Rev. **225**, 259; Sargentich, Thomas O., "The Contemporary Debate About Legislative–Executive Separation of Powers" (1987) 72 Cornell L. Rev. **430**, 433. For a review of Supreme Court cases involving the separation of powers, see Manning, John, "Separation of Powers as Ordinary Interpretation" (2011) 124 Harv. L. Rev. 1939.

[121] As Levinson and Pildes put it, "There is some tension, to put it mildly, between the assumption that Congress is perpetually engaged in cutthroat competition for power with the Executive and the reality of massive congressional delegations of authority to the executive branch." Levinson and Pildes, *supra*, n. 7, at 2356–57; see also Bradley, Curtis A. and Trevor W. Morrison, "Historical Gloss and the Separation of Powers" (2012)126 Harv. L. Rev. **411**, 414–15; see generally *supra*, n. 7.

[122] The building of hydroelectric dams across the United States from the 1940s through the 1960s was extraordinary both in scale and in feats of engineering. Increasingly, however, as the Bureau of Reclamation proposed a number of federal dams on the Colorado River, environmentalists began to

heightened public attention provided Congress with incentives to exert more control over executive branch decisions.

Similarly, the deleterious consequences of oil drilling came to the fore with the 1969 oil spill off the coast of Santa Barbara, California.[123] The spill catalyzed public opinion and broadly influenced the direction of the environmental movement. Significantly for the CZMA's reverse preemption provision, the oil spill also highlighted the lax oversight exercised by the Department of Interior. Indeed the Secretary of the Interior at the time accepted some responsibility for the spill.[124] The CZMA reverse preemption provision, like its CWA counterpart, allowed Congress to exercise indirect control over Interior Department oil leasing decisions.

The timing of the 1990 amendments to the CZMA – overturning the Supreme Court decision holding that the consistency requirement did not apply to oil and gas leases on the Outer Continental Shelf – also supports the theory that the reverse preemption provisions were meant to bolster congressional power over executive branch decision making. The amendments followed a very contentious decade in which President Ronald Reagan's first Secretary of the Interior, James Watt, embarked on a massive program to lease almost a billion acres of offshore land for oil drilling over a five-year period.[125] Though he succeeded in dramatically expanding drilling, legal and political backlash allowed to him to achieve

---

protest. David Brower, the legendary Executive Director of the Sierra Club in the 1950s and '60s, led the charge to block dams proposed in Dinosaur National Monument. Though the Sierra Club acquiesced in the construction of Glen Canyon Dam in the late 1960s, the organization succeeded in killing two dams planned in the Grand Canyon. These very public battles over the environmental consequences of dam-building occurred just before the passage of the modern CWA. To be fair, the very public battles over the Grand Canyon dams were about federal dams built by the Bureau of Reclamation rather than about the nonfederal dams that must seek licenses from the Federal Energy Regulatory Commission. Nonetheless, the battles highlighted the environmental consequences of dams in the public's eye. The reverse preemption provision of the CWA allowed Congress to check FERC power to license or relicense dams without adequate environmental protection.

[123] See Clarke, Keith C. and Jeffrey J. Hemphill, "The Santa Barbara Oil Spill: A Retrospective" (2002) 64 Y.B. Ass'n Pac. Coast Geographers **157**, 158–59.

[124] Ibid. [169].

[125] See, National Commission on the BP Deep Water Horizon Oil Spill and Offshore Drilling, Final Report (Oil Spill Commission 2011), 63–65, accessed 18 July 2015 at www.oilspillcommission.gov/final-report.

only a quarter of his initial goal.[126] Congressional response was particularly strong. The Democratic House of Representatives imposed repeated moratoriums on the budget of the Republican Department of the Interior that had the effect of prohibiting new leases in areas other than the Gulf of Mexico and Alaska.[127] The Reagan expansion of offshore drilling was so politically controversial that in 1991 President George H.W. Bush cancelled numerous oil and gas sales authorized by the Reagan Department of the Interior in California, Oregon, Florida and other states.[128] Against this backdrop, the extension of the consistency requirement of the CZMA to OCS oil and gas leases again allowed Congress to check the expansive exercise of executive power over a controversial environmental issue.

ii. Reverse preemption to enhance congressional power during a period of divided government While we believe the reverse preemption provisions provide evidence that Congress sought to bolster its power vis-à-vis the executive branch, a more contemporary account of congressional behavior also provides a persuasive explanation of the reverse preemption provisions. Daryl Levinson and Richard Pildes question the degree to which Congress possesses either the institutional mechanisms or motivations to protect and enhance its own power at the expense of the executive, significantly undermining Madison's assertion that the separation of powers would check executive power.[129] They suggest instead that individual members of Congress work to improve their own electability and to advance the ideological goals of their political parties rather than to augment the institutional power of the branch in which they serve.[130] Put bluntly, members of Congress simply "lack any interest in the power of branches *qua* branches."[131] Instead, this account asserts that, particularly as party identity and ideological coherence among elected officials in Congress has intensified, members of Congress work to advance the interests of their parties, not their branch of government. Levinson and Pildes predict that if members of Congress are in fact driven by party loyalty, efforts to cabin executive power should be most apparent during times of divided government, when Congress is held by

---

[126] See ibid. at 66–67 [171].
[127] See ibid. [172].
[128] See ibid. at 67 [173].
[129] See Levinson and Pildes, *supra*, n.7, at 2347.
[130] Ibid. [175].
[131] Ibid. at 2316 [176].

one party and the Presidency by another.[132] In those circumstances, Democratic Congresses will pass legislation to constrain Republican presidents and vice versa.

The reverse preemption provisions are consistent with this view. Both provisions constraining executive power through reverse preemption were adopted by Democratic Congresses during a Republican presidency.[133] Section 401 of the CWA was adopted in the 1972 Clean Water Act, codifying and expanding upon a similar provision first adopted in 1970 in the Water Quality Improvement Act.[134] Richard Nixon was President in both years and Democrats held both houses of Congress.[135] Section 401 was amended in 1977 to clarify that its coverage included water quality standards, a slight expansion of state power.[136] The Democrats held both houses of Congress and the Presidency at the time of the 1977 amendments.[137]

The consistency provisions of the CZMA were enacted in 1972,[138] again a time when the Democrats held both houses of Congress and a Republican sat in the White House.[139] Congress's 1990 amendments expanded state power over federal actions to include actions that directly affect a state's coastal zone even if they occur outside it, including federal OCS energy leases. These amendments were passed by a Democratic Congress when Republican George H.W. Bush was President.[140]

With the exception of minor expansionary amendments to section 401 of the CWA in 1977, then, the enactment and subsequent expansion of reverse preemption provisions fits the Levinson–Pildes prediction that Congress will limit executive authority during times of divided government.[141]

---

[132] Ibid. at 2326.
[133] See Infoplease, "Composition of Congress, by Political Party, 1855–2015," accessed 18 July 2015 at www.infoplease.com/ipa/A0774721.html.
[134] See S. Rep. No. 92-414 (1971), reprinted in 1972 U.S.C.C.A.N. 3668, at 3669.
[135] See Composition of Congress, supra, n. 133.
[136] See Clean Water Act, 33 U.S.C. § 1341 (2006) (as amended in 1977).
[137] See Composition of Congress, supra, n. 133.
[138] See Composition of Congress, supra, n. 133.
[139] See Composition of Congress, supra, n. 133.
[140] See ibid.
[141] In the expanded version of this piece, we also explore the ways in which the reverse preemption provisions can mitigate the tendency of federal agencies to be dominated by the regulated parties they oversee. We concentrate in this chapter only on the relationship of the reverse preemption provisions to federalism.

III. CONCLUSION

As we have argued, reverse preemption provisions upend conventional accounts of federalism by codifying state supremacy into federal law through state vetoes of certain federal agency decisions. They also provide a novel and overlooked mechanism to Congress to enhance its oversight of executive branch decisions and promote environmental values that comport with local expertise and preferences.

One obvious and open question, then, is why these provisions appear to be confined to just two environmental policy areas, water quality and coastal protection. Relatedly, what policy areas might benefit from granting states veto power to check federal agency decision-making? Without fully answering these questions, we suggest very preliminarily that several factors may make certain policy areas well suited for reverse preemption provisions. First, reverse preemption provisions, at least to date, apply only when a federal agency is tasked with granting permission to engage in behavior through licensing or permitting. Other areas in which federal permitting or licensing occur include broadcasting,[142] banking,[143] grazing[144] and Medicare-approved facilities,[145] to name a few examples. Thus the federal government's involvement in granting permission to engage in a broad array of activity suggests that reverse preemption could expand beyond the narrow confines we have identified.

Second, reverse preemption seems well suited to policy areas in which states have overlapping jurisdiction with the federal government and where the values of federalism – for example local preferences, specialized knowledge and information about local conditions – are important. The delivery of health care through Medicaid and Medicare seems to be a good example.

---

[142] The Federal Communications Commission has jurisdiction over licensing and licensing of the electromagnetic spectrum. See Federal Communications Commission, "Business and Licensing," accessed 18 July 2015 at www.fcc.gov/business-licensing.

[143] The Office of the Comptroller of the Currency charters national banks. See Office of the Comptroller of the Currency, "About the OCC," accessed 18 July 2015 at www.occ.gov/about/what-we-do/mission/index-about.html.

[144] The Bureau of Land Management issues grazing permits. See US Department of the Interior, Bureau of Land Management, Fact Sheet on the BLM's Management of Livestock Management, accessed 18 July 2015 at www.blm.gov/wo/st/en/prog/grazing.html.

[145] See Centers for Medicare and Medicaid Services, Medicare Approved Facilites/Trials/Registries, accessed 18 July 2015 at www.cms.gov/Medicare/Medicare-General-Information/MedicareApprovedFacilitie/index.html.

Third, reverse preemption provisions may work especially well in checking agency behavior where there are real concerns about regulatory capture or industry dominance. Regulation of financial services is a paradigmatic example.

Fourth, Congress may seek to employ reverse preemption provisions in times of divided government where Congress believes the executive branch may run roughshod over statutory requirements. One can imagine reverse preemption provisions being employed by Democratic Congresses, as in the case of the environmental provisions we analyze, as well as Republican Congresses seeking to ensure that their legislative objectives are carried out. Medical cost containment could be an example of such an issue.

And finally, from the very few examples we have analyzed, states have played a more aggressive role in using their preemptive power where the number of licensing and permitting decisions to be reviewed is relatively small. Thus the provisions work better for FEC hydroelectric dam licensing and relicensing and for CZMP consistency than for providing a meaningful check on the thousands of wetland permits issued each year.

These are only preliminary suggestions and applying these factors to areas outside the environmental examples we have evaluated here is beyond our scope. Nevertheless reverse preemption appears to offer a twist on our standard conceptions of federalism, one that authorizes a role for states that can strengthen the implementation of federal law, enhance congressional power and oversight over the executive and counterbalance the influence of regulated parties. Its expansion to substantive areas outside water quality and coastal protection deserves further inquiry.

11. The cost of federalism: ecology, community, and the pragmatism of land use

Keith H. Hirokawa and Jonathan Rosenbloom

If there is a victim of federalism, it is undoubtedly the community. Self-governance demands that the persons affected by a governance decision have priority of control in decision-making over persons not so affected.[1] As indicated throughout this book, the notion of decentralized governance serves laudable and efficient purposes for democratic self-governance. In *Democracy in America*, Alexis de Tocqueville detailed several ways in which a decentralized authority encourages individuals to participate in enforcing the law to ameliorate lawlessness and injustice.[2] Other authors tend to prefer consequentialist justifications for decentralization as a mechanism to improve managerial and social economy.[3]

From a perspective that prioritizes community, citizens engage in the process of self-governance by utilizing the land and its associated ecosystems and resources to support the community's desired objectives. For example, some communities may seek to promote effective spaces for family and citizen engagement or spaces to interact with and learn

---

[1] Hills, Roderick M. Jr., "Is Federalism Good for Localism? The Localist Case for Federal Regimes" (2005) 21 J.L. & Pol. **187**, 190.

[2] Francis Bowen (ed.), (tr. Henry Reeve 1863) Alexis de Tocqueville, *Democracy in America*, vol. 1 (1835), pp 116–17, accessed 18 July 2015 at books.google.com/books?id=xZfiBEzcPTEC.

[3] Nussim, Jacob, "A Policymaker's Guide to Welfarism" (2007) 155 U. Pa. L. Rev. **227**, 234; Rubin, Edward and Malcolm L. Feeley, "Federalism: Some Notes on a National Neurosis" (1994) 41 UCLA L. Rev. **903**, 910. (One writer insists, "the main reason to decentralize is to achieve effective management.")

from ecology, while other communities may focus on spaces to improve mental and physical health or develop an economic advantage.[4]

Through the exercise of federal regulatory authority over local environmental conditions, citizens lose their ability to self-governance and thus to create communities. While we recognize that a uniform regulatory system may benefit the environment by, among other things, reducing collective action problems and may reduce costs associated with economic activities, a federal top-down regulatory scheme also imposes unwanted – and sometimes unwarranted – uniformity upon the diverse local prerogatives and priorities that are individually expressed among thousands of local jurisdictions. Of course, federalism is not intended to tear from communities the power to self-regulate and self-identify. Federalism is intended only to tear part of the power to self-regulate from communities by targeting the problems of parochialism and externalities. In the context of federal environmental regulations, however, the impact is the same – local communities are stripped of critical opportunities to self-identify and build a community around their natural environs.

From the principles that community is a worthwhile expression of values and that there are benefits in fostering local diversity, this chapter examines the exercise of federal control over environmental issues and its potential assault on the merits of community. This chapter explores whether imposed homogeneity or sameness at the federal level defeats the benefits of self-identifying communities through land use controls and, if so, whether that is a trade-off we are willing to accept given the benefits of federal environmental regulatory action. Our objective is to help clarify the impact of federal regulation on local land use control and to more completely articulate how federal regulation detaches a community from its local ecosystem.

The framework proposed herein is premised in the ecological economics of ecosystem services, which is defined as the "wide range of conditions and processes through which natural ecosystems, and the species that are part of them, help sustain and fulfill human life."[5] An ecosystem services analysis identifies the value of the otherwise invisible services that functioning ecosystems provide, such as mitigation of storm energy in wetlands, carbon sequestration and crop pollination. These

---

[4] For purposes of this chapter, we refer to "land use control" as broadly referencing the management and regulation of ecosystems within a geographic area. This definition is intended to include zoning, agricultural regulation, water, forest and wetland management, and many others.

[5] Daily, Gretchen et al., "Ecosystem Services: Benefits Supplied to Human Societies by Natural Ecosystems" (1997) 2 *Issues in Ecology* 1, 2.

services occur as natural processes in functioning ecosystems, and it is indisputable that they provide substantial benefits to humans and human well-being. The relevance of ecosystem services to the question of environmental federalism is how ecosystem services invoke the question of governance: once the local pond can no long sustain aquatic life, the neighborhood youngsters can no longer swim and fish; once riparian wetlands can no longer absorb storm surges, affected neighborhoods should fear flooding; once the local soils are depleted or have been washed away, communities will need to look elsewhere for employment and food. Localities, in contrast to the federal government, have a very real stake in the quality of ecosystem functionality, because localities rely on ecosystem services as the beneficiaries of those services. Hence, if there is a victim of federalism, it is undoubtedly the community.

I. THE LOSS OF COMMUNITY IN FEDERAL ENVIRONMENTAL LAW

American jurisprudence makes it clear that a local community is secondary to state and/or federal body politics and local laws are subordinate to state and/or federal laws. Establishing a community's authority to act in the US federalist system is predominantly decided by the actions of individuals and entities outside the community or local government. While a community may be empowered to take particular actions, it is rare that the community has exclusive control over a particular area. Rather, its authority is subject to federal and/or state government action that may preempt or withdraw the local power.[6]

While state and federal governments had the authority to regulate local environmental and land use issues, they did so only half-heartedly until the 1970s. Prior to the modern federal environmental regulatory scheme, environmental quality was largely dictated at the state and local levels. Historically, the litigation of claims concerning the environment was

---

[6] For a more complete discussion of preemption of local government actions see Rosenbloom, Jonathan, "Local Governments and Global Commons" (2015)__ B.Y.U. L. Rev. ___ (setting forth federal preemption of local actions); Rosenbloom, Jonathan, "New Day at the Pool: State Preemption, Common Pool Resources, and Non-Place Based Municipal Collaborations" (2012) 36 Harv. Envtl L. Rev. 445 (setting forth state preemption of local actions). But see *Robinson Twp. v Pennsylvania*, 83 A.3d 901 (Pa. 2014) (finding local governments to have an independent and distinct state constitutional obligation to sustainably manage resources).

considered, if at all, within the scope of state-based property protections or tort-based duties (such as nuisance, trespass and negligence) governing interactions among individuals and the public. Neither Congress nor common law supplied legal grounds to support a claim against environmental degradation, at least as that term is understood today. Litigation based in the environment often involved direct, physical, locally based impacts between and among neighbors, such as contamination of drinking water from pig farms[7] or the spread of disease through burning contaminated clothing.[8]

In contrast, state and local governments were active, albeit unsuccessful, in identifying regulatory roles in governing private actions affecting the environment.[9] Through zoning and other police power-based initiatives, local governments herded pollution sources to chosen locations (such as in industrial districts) to minimize exposure and protect the public, while still allowing activities to occur within local boundaries. Local governments used their planning powers to establish parks and natural settings, plant trees and protect waterfronts. Some municipalities adopted air pollution regulations.[10] Notwithstanding local efforts it became clear by the 1970s that many local communities simply lacked the resources necessary to protect the environment and the health of citizens.

As discussed in the next two subsections, the federal regulatory regime that sought to replace state and local regulation dramatically affected communities by discouraging them from exceeding federal standards in a "race-to-the-top" by failing to account for and maximize local communities' attachment to the environment. The attachment between local communities and their environment is critical in helping individuals create and define their communities. Environmental federalism strains that connection and treats broad categories of individual action, across diverse environments, in similar fashions, without regard for local environment and community values.[11]

---

[7] *Commonwealth* ex rel. *Woods v Soboleski*, 303 Pa. 53, 54–55 (1931).

[8] *Haag v Bd. of Comm'rs*, 60 Ind. 511, 512–15 (1878).

[9] Revesz, Richard L., "Federalism and Environmental Regulation: A Public Choice Analysis" (2001) 115 Harv. L. Rev. **553**, 578–79.

[10] Ibid. at 579.

[11] We recognize that there are clearly situations where a local community would prefer to overexploit a resource to the community's gain at great losses to individuals in other jurisdictions. This is obviously where federal environmental

A. Preeminence of Boundaries: How Federal Law Preempts Local Governance

When confronted with a question whether a local government has the legal authority to regulate in a particular area, judicial inquiry often hinges on whether local authority has been preempted by federal law. Two determining factors in a federal preemption analysis are: (i) what actions the federal government has taken, and (ii) whether the local government is regulating beyond its borders. These two factors focus the inquiry on individuals and impacts outside the local community's control, regardless of the local connection to, history with, and knowledge of the environment, ecosystems or relevant services.

The starting point to analyze a whether local community is subordinate to federal legal authority concerning a local environmental issue is the US Constitution. Although the US Constitution does not formally recognize local governments, the US federalist structure and US Supreme Court decisions concerning the Constitution help frame local communities' authority relative to federal law. The US Supreme Court has made it clear that local governments are subjects of their corresponding states.[12] As a matter of US constitutional law, local governments are "political subdivisions of the state, created as convenient agencies" by the state for undertaking state purposes.[13] As creatures of state law, local governments may have only that authority states did not transfer to the federal government. Thus, authority lies either with the federal government or with the state government – local governments do not have an independent source of authority.[14] If the federal government has the authority to act, states and local government are without the power to take action and vice versa.[15] While this form of dual sovereignty between the federal and state governments helps to define their respective

---

regulation excels. We are most concerned with the day-to-day decisions relevant to resources which communities are built around, such as potable water and forests.

[12] *Hunter v City of Pittsburgh*, 207 U.S. 161, 174–80 (1907). But see *Avery v Midland Cnty.*, 390 U.S. 474, 482–86 (1968) (finding that state law may not create a general purpose local government that apportions voting unequally in violation of the Constitution).

[13] *Hunter*, 207 U.S. at 178.

[14] But see *Robinson Twp.*, 83 A.3d at 901.

[15] *Printz v United States*, 521 U.S. 898, 900 (1997).

authority, it also makes it clear that local governments are not autonomous and local authority is not implicit.[16]

Determining whether local governments have been granted authority requires a review of the relevant provisions in the US Constitution, federal statutes, state constitutions and state statutes. In interpreting these legal sources, courts focus heavily on whether the federal or state governments have preempted local government actions. A reoccurring theme in the preemption analysis is that the scope of preemption is predominantly dictated by the federal and state governments and not by local governments. For example, assume a local government wanted to ensure that its citizens had the relevant health or environmental information pertaining to pesticides and/or the local government wanted to ban pesticide use on public or private lands. The federal government, however, regulates pesticide labeling and 43 states regulate the use, sale and transportation of pesticides.[17] The local community's desires here to protect its citizens from pesticide use would likely be prohibited as preempted by federal and state law. This determination is made predominantly based on actions of individuals outside the local community (that is, the state or federal legislative bodies), presumably not based on all of the information relevant to that particular local community, such as a desire for clean water and enhanced wildlife.

The Supremacy Clause makes it clear that the US Constitution and federal statutes regulating the environment "shall be the supreme law of the land" and may preempt state – and therefore, local – action.[18] By

---

[16] See Daily, *supra*, n. 5.

[17] See Federal Insecticide, Fungicide, and Rodenticide Act, 7 U.S.C. § 136 (2014) (stating that the federal government has exclusive authority over pesticide labeling); Cal. Food & Agric. § 11501.1 (West 2014) (stating local governments are prohibited from "attempt[ing] to regulate any matter relating to the registration, sale, transportation, or use of pesticides, and any of these [local] ordinances, laws, or regulations are void and of no force or effect."); see also Porter, Matthew, *Beyond Pesticides, State Preemption Law: The Battle for Local Control of Democracy*, accessed 18 July 2015 at www.beyondpesticides.org/lawn/activist/documents/StatePreemption.pdf ("Currently, 43 states have some form of state law that preempts local governments' ability to regulate the use of pesticides. In fact, state environmental preemption law often applies more broadly to local restrictions on genetically engineered crops and the use of synthetic fertilizers.").

[18] US Const. Art. VI; see also *Pac. Gas & Elec. Co. v State Energy Res. Conservation & Dev. Comm'n*, 461 U.S. 190, 203–04 (1983); *Rice v Santa Fe Elevator Corp.*, 331 U.S. 218, 230 (1947). But see *N.Y. State Conference of Blue Cross & Blue Shield Plans v Travelers Ins. Co.*, 514 U.S. 645, 655 (1995) (stating that "in cases ... where federal law is said to bar state action in fields of

doing so, when federal law conflicts with local community desires, it may limit local governments and communities by narrowing the issues they may address and the solutions they may propose. In *Metro. Taxicab Bd. of Trade v City of N.Y.*, the Second Circuit illustrated this point by striking down New York City's attempt to reduce its carbon footprint by, among other things, motivating taxi companies to consider fuel efficiency when purchasing vehicles.[19] The court ruled that New York City's effort was preempted by federal law. In this case, a local government sought to address a critical ecological challenge – clean air and climate change – but was not permitted to do so because it was preempted by federal law.[20] Pursuant to this case and others, communities are prohibited from addressing environmental challenges because of actions at other levels of government, *even though the local community's action would have a positive impact on the environment and would presumably be consistent with the prime objectives of the relevant federal law.*

In exercising its authority Congress has taken a number of steps to control environmental quality, including in the enactment of the 1969 National Environmental Policy Act (NEPA),[21] the 1970 Clean Air Amendments,[22] the 1972 Federal Water Pollution Control Act Amendments[23] (as amended by the 1977 Clean Water Act), 1973 Endangered Species Act,[24] and the Resource Conservation and Recovery Act (RCRA)[25] passed in 1976 and intended to create a system for the

---

traditional state regulation ... we have worked on the 'assumption that the historic police powers of the States were not to be superseded by the Federal Act unless that was the clear and manifest purpose of Congress.'").

[19] *Metro. Taxicab Bd. of Trade v City of N.Y.*, 615 F.3d 152, 155 (2d Cir. 2010).

[20] See generally *Cruz v United States*, 387 F. Supp. 2d 1057, 1073–75 (N.D. Cal. 2005) (striking down California law as it conflicts with US/Mexican agreements.). But see *Hillsborough Cnty. v Automated Med. Labs., Inc.*, 471 U.S. 707, 714 (1985) (holding that local law regulating blood plasma collection was not preempted by federal law because federal regulation was clear that it was not "usurp[ing] local power").

[21] National Environmental Policy Act of 1969, 42 U.S.C. § 4321 (1969).

[22] Clean Air Act of 1970, 42 U.S.C. § 7401 (1970).

[23] Federal Water Pollution Control Act of 1972, 33 U.S.C. § 1251 (1972) (amended 1997).

[24] Endangered Species Act of 1973, 16 U.S.C. § 1531 (1973) (amended 1978).

[25] Resource Conservation and Recovery Act of 1976, 42 U.S.C. § 6901 (1976).

disposal and reduction of solid waste. Unless specifically stated otherwise in the acts, these statutes have the potential to preempt a broad spectrum of local actions relevant to the environment and local land use control. For example, although Congress has not passed a comprehensive land use statute, it has passed a number of statutes directly affecting local land use decisions, including the 1996 Telecommunications Act (limiting local action over telecommunications facility siting). The US Constitution also has a number of provisions affecting local land use decisions, including the First Amendment, Equal Protection Clause and the Takings Clause of the Fifth Amendment. Because the federal constitution and statutes establish minimum standards for treatment of individuals, local governments and communities are prohibited from infringing upon those standards and must comply regardless of local sentiment, knowledge and history.

In addition to focusing on actions occurring outside the community (that is, federal and state actions), preemption jurisprudence restricts a community from acting extraterritorially – beyond its jurisdictional boundary.[26] This part of the preemption inquiry focuses intently on boundaries. It questions whether a local government is attempting to exercise authority, or will have an impact, outside its jurisdiction, regardless of whether the federal or state governments have acted or sought to expressly preempt local actions. Thus, where boundaries are drawn and who draws them becomes the focal point for identifying authority over environmental and land use issues.

At the federal level, it is clear that communities do not have the power to determine local government boundaries. The Supreme Court has held that individuals and communities have no protected constitutional right to localized self-government because states have almost complete authority to reshape local government boundaries as they see fit.[27] Individuals may not form a local government around communal beliefs without state authorization, and the US Constitution provides only limited protections from a state's intrusion into a community's attempt to draw a localized self-governance boundary.

Not only do states have almost complete authority over local boundaries, but federal and state law highlight the critical importance of those boundaries, further separating a community from its environment. The

---

[26] See e.g. *Seigles, Inc. v City of St. Charles*, 849 N.E.2d 456, 458 (Ill. App. Ct. 2006) (stating that it is "axiomatic" that a local government may not act outside its borders).

[27] *Hunter v City of Pittsburgh*, 207 U.S. 161, 178 (1907).

US Supreme Court highlighted the importance of being inside a boundary versus outside in *Holt Civic Club v City of Tuscaloosa*, holding that citizens who are serviced by a local government (including policing and sanitation services) have no US Constitution-protected right to representation in the administration of those services unless they are physically located in the local jurisdiction.[28] Thus, at its discretion, a state may place some people in and others out of a local government boundary, and those outside the boundary have no right to vote in how the local government is administered, even if they are receiving generalized services from the local government. Thus, not only do communities not have a right to be in one local government over the other, they do not have a right to vote in elections when drawn out of a local government. The *Holt* decision and others similar to it make it clear that the US Constitution does not recognize individuals' interest in a smaller form of government and their desire to be regulated one way or another based on a jurisdictional boundary that responds to their connection to their surroundings.

The Ohio Supreme Court's decision in *Bakies v City of Perrsburg* provides a typical example of state jurisprudence focusing on local boundaries, as opposed to the environment, communities, and the connection between them.[29] The plaintiffs in *Bakies*, landowners in unincorporated areas, challenged a local government's requirement that they execute an annexation agreement prior to receiving water and sewer services extraterritorially. The Court held that the local government may barter with extraterritorial customers desiring to use their services. While the local government may not barter with those inside the jurisdiction, it may with those outside. The Court ruled that "[m]unicipally owned public utilities have no duty to sell their products, including water, to extraterritorial purchasers absent contractual obligation."[30] Further, they can change the terms of existing services once the contract has expired. This decision, similar to the decision in *Holt*, hinged on where the local government boundary was drawn and whether the individuals were inside or outside the jurisdiction. If an individual or community is in the jurisdiction, then they are entitled to services.

An additional line of US Supreme Court cases further divides communities from their local services, the ecosystems in which they derive and democratic principles in the delivery of those services. In *Ball v*

---

[28] *Holt Civic Club v City of Tuscaloosa*, 439 U.S. 60 (1978).
[29] *Bakies v City of Perrsburg*, 108 Ohio St. 3d 361 (2006).
[30] Ibid. at 365.

James, the US Supreme Court ruled that individuals within a local government jurisdiction do not have a protected constitutional right to equal representation in the local government when those services are provided by a special purpose district.[31] For purposes of the constitutional analysis, a local government is considered a special purpose district when its actions are limited in nature (sufficiently specialized) and when the services have a disproportionately greater impact on a particular group. The majority in *Ball* held that if the local government is a special purpose district, the individual citizens serviced by the district do not have a constitutional right in stating how the service is to be run. The Court ruled that "districts remain essentially business enterprises, created by and chiefly benefiting a specific group of landowners."[32] The Court views the constitutional analysis as one analogous to a market transaction. It does not value the connection the community may have to the water and supporting ecosystems, and whether their form of government should be designed around it. Rather, it focuses its inquiry on legal constructs developed at the state or federal level.

The importance of boundaries often plays out in disputes between state and local laws as well. Because local governments derive their power from the state, it is not surprising that state law may preempt local actions. The predominant interpretation of state preemption laws weighs heavily in favor of state supremacy and restricting local governments from regulating beyond their borders. In analyzing whether a state has preempted local action, courts will look at state constitutional or statutory provisions to establish the boundaries of permissible local action.

There are four potential legal origins of local power: (i) Dillon's Rule, in which a local government may act only if the action was expressly authorized by the state, was incidental to an expressly stated authorization, or was "indispensable" to performing the local government's tasks;[33] (ii) legislative home rule;[34] (iii) imperio home rule;[35] and (iv) hybrid legislative/imperio home rule.[36] Whether a local government is authorized to take a particular action in a home rule state (ii–iv above) is a two-part inquiry: (1) has the local government been empowered to act? and (2) if empowered to act, has the local action nonetheless been

---

[31] *Ball v James*, 451 U.S. 355 (1981).
[32] Ibid. at 367.
[33] Dillon, John F., *Commentaries on the Law of Municipal Corporations*, vol. 1, 5th edn (Little Brown, Boston 1911), p. 449.
[34] See e.g. Ark. Const. Art. 10, § 11.
[35] See e.g. Cal. Const. Art. 11, § 5(a).
[36] See e.g. Iowa Const. Art. III, § 38A.

preempted? Zoning, for example, is an area in which states have traditionally empowered local governments to act, as opposed to international trade regulation, banking controls and immigration restrictions, which are not. If empowered to act, the court will then question whether the local action has been preempted by: (i) conflict preemption, where there is a direct conflict between the local ordinance and state law; (ii) express preemption, where the state specifically notes that it is preempting the subject matter; and (iii) implied preemption, where the state preempts a subject matter indirectly through prior actions, such as existing state legislation.[37]

Similar to federal preemption jurisprudence, judicial interpretation of state preemption[38] acknowledges the importance of jurisdictional boundaries, often at the expense of ecosystems and the ability of a community to connect to its environment. Preemption of a local action has often been decided based on whether the local action has an extraterritorial impact. While state courts differ on the precise meaning and terminology in describing local government extraterritorial impacts,[39] "many [courts] use a finding of extraterritoriality as the basis for the conclusion that the home rule ordinance ... has exceeded the [locality's] ... powers, or has been preempted by the state legislature."[40] If a local action encourages other local jurisdictions to adopt conflicting local legislation, results in

---

[37] See *Talbot Cnty. v Skipper*, 620 A.2d 880, 882–83 (Md. 1993); see generally Briffault, Richard and Laurie Reynolds *State and Local Government* 7th edn (West Academic Publishing, St Paul, MN 2009), pp. 422–49, 448.

[38] Similar to the theoretical justifications for federal preemption, state preemption is partially justified by the need to avoid a race to the bottom phenomenon stemming from local government competition. However, it is often state legal parameters that actually encourage local governments to unsustainably manage natural resources. "Local governments are often prohibited from having extraterritorial impacts and are limited to regulating solely within their borders. The combination of multi-jurisdictional natural capital resources and limited local government authority to regulate those resources creates inefficiencies that discourage local governments from seeking innovative solutions to commons challenges." Hudson, Blake and Jonathan Rosenbloom, "Uncommon Approaches to Commons Problems: Nested Governance Commons and Climate Change" (2013) 64 Hastings L.J. **1273**, 1307–08.

[39] Reynolds, Laurie, "Home Rule, Extraterritorial Impact, and the Region" (2009) 86 Denv. U. L. Rev. **1271**, 1274–78 (citing *Seigles, Inc. v City of St. Charles*, 849 N.E.2d 456, 458 (Ill. App. Ct. 2006) (stating that it is "axiomatic" that a local government may not act outside its borders) and comparing *Goodell v Humboldt County*, 575 N.W.2d 486, 492 (Iowa 1998) (treating the two legal questions separately), with *City of Northglenn v Ibarra*, 62 P.3d 151, 155 (Colo. 2003) (blending the two steps together)).

[40] Reynolds, *supra*, n. 39, at 1275.

"permeation, seepage, or cross border movement," or impacts "the marketplace generally," it may be preempted by state law.[41] Judicial interpretation of "extraterritorial impacts casts a wide net over the type of local actions that are preempted by state law ... It has been used to strike down local ordinances addressing noise pollution, wastewater, service contracts, telephone line installation, automated automobile photograph systems, sex offender controls, and others."[42]

The theoretical importance of addressing some environmental and land use issues at the federal or state level is clear. If it can overcome a number of internal obstacles including gridlock, Congress could be helpful in avoiding a tragedy of the commons among local governments. National legislation may reduce competition among local governments and may regulate their activity in a way that sustainably manages resources. This theory, of course, relies heavily on the assumption that local governments will set low environmental standards to incentivize local development. By unifying the law, Congress, it is assumed, may avoid this competition and more efficiently use resources at the local level. In doing so, however, Congress has consumed an area of environmental regulation, and left little space for local governments to flourish. The Supreme Court and state supreme courts have made it clear that local governments are vulnerable to federal and state preemption challenges. Among preemption jurisprudence there is very little acknowledgment that local governments could promote the goals of many federal acts and do so in a way that is more closely aligned with local conditions. Rather, preemption jurisprudence makes it clear that where federal or state governments have acted and, at times, when they have not acted local governments are prohibited from acting.

The combination of these two preemption themes – higher level action and boundaries – marginalizes local governments and their ability to address critical environmental challenges and build a community around the environment. The preemption analysis is deeply rooted in the federalist structure – a human-made, static institutional governance arrangement – to determine whether local governments have authority to regulate systems, such as the ecosystem, that do not respond to the government structures or their boundaries. The analysis does not consider the needs of the community trying to regulate and build a community identity. Further, it undermines and devalues the relationship between

---

[41] Ibid. at 1279–82.
[42] Rosenbloom, "New Day at the Pool," *supra*, n. 6, at 453.

ecology and community by focusing on institutional structures to determine the fate of communities and their connection to natural resources.

B. Specific Controversies over Local Decision-Making

In large part, land use decision-making has continued to occur at the local level. Yet the question of preemption in land use and local environmental decision-making is perpetually debated. It is noteworthy that in 1970 Congress considered adopting a federal policy "to encourage and assist the several States to more effectively exercise their constitutional responsibilities for the planning, management, and administration of the Nation's land resources."[43] The National Land Use Policy Act (NLUPA) was intended to coordinate land use governance under a federal agency that would facilitate an inventory of land use assets and plans across jurisdictional boundaries.[44] Although the bill was unsuccessful, the proposed NLUPA illustrates the importance of coordinating decision making over local environmental resources, as well as the political difficulties that the federal government faces in this arena.

Without a comprehensive federal statute on the subject, local governments typically confront federal restrictions on land use topics in a patchwork system of constitutional and statutory controls. Often the relevant laws are incidental to the concerns that dominate the land use process; for instance, the Religious Land Use and Institutionalized Persons Act of 2000 (RLUIPA)[45] protects religious freedoms from discrimination in the land use regulatory process and yet greatly influences local land use decisions. In other cases, federal preemption arises in statutory mandates that are limited to specific issues; for instance, the 1996 Telecommunications Act[46] imposes federal standards on the local regulation of telecommunications facility siting, with the purposes of facilitating development of a nationwide system of telecommunications access.

Air Conditioning, Heating and Refrigeration Institute v City of Albuquerque[47] provides a good example of the difficulties local governments face in trying to decipher a piecemeal federal preemption scheme.

---

[43] S. 3354, 91st Cong. § 402(a) (1970).
[44] Nolon, John R., "The National Land Use Policy Act" (1996) 13 Pace Envtl L. Rev. **519**, 522.
[45] Religious Land Use and Institutionalized Persons Act of 2000, 42 U.S.C. 2000cc (2000).
[46] Telecommunications Act of 1996, 47 U.S.C. §§ 1–1473 (1996).
[47] Civ. No. 08-633 MV/RLP, 2008 WL 5586316 (D.N.M. Oct. 3, 2008).

In this case, industry advocates successfully argued that the City of Albuquerque's attempt to require the construction of efficient buildings through a "green building code" was preempted by federal law that regulated the energy efficiency of appliances. Albuquerque adopted minimum energy efficiency standards that applied to the construction of new buildings and remodels. The Albuquerque code allowed applicants to consider several methods of building construction and design to meet the code's energy efficiency requirements. Most commercial construction was required to meet with one of two "performance" options, but the code also included a "prescriptive" option applicable to small commercial buildings. The code established minimum energy efficiency standards for building systems that were intended to exceed the EPCA "Energy Star" minimum ratings. Similarly, residential construction was subject to four "performance" options and a "prescriptive" option that considered installation of building components that exceeded minimum EPCA "Energy Star" product ratings.

Notably, appliance efficiency is a topic that has been preempted by a federal statutory scheme that governs the energy efficiency of appliances, but not of buildings. In *Air Conditioning, Heating and Refrigeration Inst.*, industry advocates insisted that Albuquerque's ordinances required builders to use particular appliances to meet the energy-efficiency demands. The court agreed that the City's building efficiency standards would require builders to choose particular appliances to meet the building performance levels. The court reasoned that even "if products at the federal efficiency standard are used, a building owner must make other modifications to the home to increase its energy efficiency in order to comply with the code,"[48] which the court found to serve as "a penalty imposed for selecting products that meet, but do not exceed, federal energy standards."[49] The court ruled that the code's effect of requiring the installation of certain appliances was clearly preempted by federal law.

---

[48] Ibid. at *9.
[49] Ibid. at *9.

In contrast, in *Building Industry Association of Washington v Washington State Building Code Council*,[50] a similar preemption challenge was rejected by the federal district court in Washington. Similar to the challenged provisions in the Albuquerque case,[51] the challenged provisions of the Washington State Energy Code applied to new residential construction and were based on the following findings:

> Energy efficiency is the cheapest, quickest, and cleanest way to meet rising energy needs, confront climate change, and boost [Washington's] economy. More than thirty percent of Washington's greenhouse gas emissions come from energy use in buildings. Making homes, businesses, and public institutions more energy efficient will save money, create good local jobs, enhance energy security, reduce pollution that causes global warming, and speed economic recovery while reducing the need to invest in costly new generation. Washington can spur its economy and assert its regional and national clean energy leadership by putting efficiency first. Washington can accomplish this by: Promoting super efficient, low-energy use building codes; requiring disclosure of buildings' energy use to prospective buyers; making public buildings models of energy efficiency; financing energy saving upgrades to existing buildings; and reducing utility bills for low-income households.[52]

As in the Albuquerque case, the plaintiff argued that the code's energy consumption mandates could be reached only by choosing particular appliances. However, the Washington Court recognized that the code did not mandate specific appliances, either directly or indirectly. Rather, the code allowed applicants to reach the energy efficiency levels through alternative "pathways." The Court found that the availability of options saved the energy code from impinging on the preempted subject matter.

Litigation has dulled the threat of federal preemption on some matters. However, it is clear that the federal government can unilaterally and completely obstruct local governments from governing matters of environmental importance. The question that remains unanswered is: at what cost do we achieve national uniformity among local governments in environmental matters?

---

[50] No. 3:10-cv-05373-RJB, 2011 WL 485895 (W.D. Wash. February 7, 2011), affirmed, 683 F.3d 1144 (9th Cir. 2012).

[51] In *Building Industry Association of Washington*, the building industry plaintiffs also relied on the preemption language of the Energy Policy and Conservation Act, Pub. Law No. 94-163, 89 Stat. 871 (1975) as amended by the National Appliance Energy Conservation Act of 1987, Public Law No. 100-12, and the Energy Policy Act of 1992, Public Law No. 102-486, 42 U.S.C. § 6297.

[52] Wash. Rev. Code §19.27A.130.

II. COMMUNITY IDENTITY AND LOCAL ENVIRONMENTS

This chapter now turns to what might be thought of as the *invisible costs* of federal control over natural resources. Specifically, we explore the effects of severing the legal authority to govern the environment from local communities. Our exploration suggests that *community* – an essential local concept – has no counterpart in the federalist vocabulary or the structure of federal environmental law. As noted above, the combination of federal and state preemption severely limits the ability of local governments to engage in the management of their local ecosystems as regulatory agencies. Because many ecosystems reach beyond the geographical borders of their local governmental entity, state and federal restrictions that limit local government's jurisdiction over natural resource management discourage and even prohibit local governments from considering externalities implicating ecosystems.[53] In light of these restrictions, local government regulations may be limited to goals and legal standards that do not reflect functionality or value in ecosystems, including forests, wetlands and agricultural resources. Yet, ecosystem functionality is an important concept to local governments because functioning ecosystems are relied upon and help define communities.

The point is an important one: the Millennium Ecosystem Assessment reports that 60 per cent of the ecosystems studied had been degraded beyond their capacity to regenerate or recover their previous level or type of functionality.[54] The observation about ecosystem functionality becomes more significant when it is framed in terms of natural capital: ecosystems that fail to function can provide neither the basis for formulating a community nor even the basic services on which human health and life rely, such as clear water and air, wildlife and biodiversity, climate and chemical regulation, nutrient cycling, and so on.[55] Of course, ecosystems are damaged in a number of different ways, and not all damage to the environment is due exclusively to lack of perception about ecosystem value or lack of access to information on the need for continuing ecosystem services. Nonetheless, efforts to value ecosystem functionality likely grow where ecosystem health coincides or converges

---

[53] Rosenbloom, "New Day at the Pool" *supra*, n. 6, at 453–61.

[54] Walter V. Reid et al., Ecosystems and Human Well-Being: Synthesis 1, 6 (2005).

[55] Daily, Gretchen C. et al., "Ecosystem Services in Decision Making: Time to Deliver" (2009) 7 Frontiers Ecology & Env't **21**, 23.

with some type of beneficiary interest, and in many ways recent ecology and economics make it clearer that communities are the primary beneficiaries of ecosystem processes. When framed in this way, the argument in favor of local power to regulate the environment becomes more persuasive.

A. What Federalism Is Not: Community as an Important Environmental Concept

As noted above, local governments have historically addressed environmental issues within the scope of home rule, police power regulation. That is, local governments have created communities,[56] and in the process have encountered, valued and managed local environmental resources in furtherance of baseline objectives for public health and the environment. To accomplish this task, local governments have identified and regulated the use of critical and locally important environments. As John Nolon describes:

> Communities have long used large-lot zoning as a crude way of protecting open space and its associated natural resources. Upzoning occurred in some suburban areas, aimed principally at lowering development densities to control population growth, maintain residential property values, and contain the cost of servicing development while, incidentally, limiting water use, preventing aquifer contamination, and containing nonpoint source pollution. As the environmental movement evolved and matured in the 1970s and 1980s, the sensitivity of local lawmakers was raised and early signs of the adoption of local environmental law became apparent. These signs emerged from a variety of sources, including the National Flood Insurance Program, which required local governments to adopt and enforce floodplain management programs as a prerequisite to local eligibility for national flood disaster assistance payments. Catastrophes influenced the movement towards increased regulation at the local level, leading to storm water management measures and stringent setback requirements along the coasts of barrier islands that are particularly vulnerable to hurricane damage. The 1990s saw the advent of local laws clearly designed to protect environmental functions and these, in the aggregate, now constitute a significant body of law.[57]

---

[56] In Ohio, for instance, municipal incorporation proceedings are driving by the necessity of findings that the area is compact and can be served by municipal services, and that "the general good of the community, including both the proposed municipal corporation and the surrounding area, will be served if the incorporation petition is granted." Ohio Rev. Code. § 707.07(D).

[57] Nolon, John, "In Praise of Parochialism" (2002) 26 Harv. Env. L. Rev. **365**, 374.

Nolon's historical detail illustrates the local concern for human welfare and its story as a powerful incentive for environmental regulation. Further, it highlights the ability of local governments to reflect community connectivity to environments and their ability to consider the value of local environmental resources.

When local governments interact with their local environments a very special type of governance happens. There is no counterpart in federal or state governance that could replicate local connectivity. Local governments, through their governed communities, interact as a means of expressing community identity. In the process of regulating use and abuse of the environment, local governments engage the democratic process as they envision and protect community assets. The traditional zoning and other police power tools enabled local governments to understand the relationship between the local environment and community goals.

In a report entitled *Community Culture and the Environment: A Guide to Understanding a Sense of Place*,[58] the EPA noted how important surroundings are to a determined policy of environmental protection:

> We live among, and are deeply connected to, the many streams, rivers, lakes, meadows, forests, wetlands, and mountains that compose our natural environment and make it the beautiful and livable place so many of us value. More and more often, human communities realize that the health and vibrancy of the natural environment affects the health and vibrancy of the community and vice versa. We value the land, air, and water available to us for material goods, beauty, solace, retreat, recreation, and habitat for all creatures. Throughout the nation, communities are engaging in efforts to protect these treasured natural resources and the quality of life they provide.[59]

The EPA's report builds on Nolon's observations and makes an important ecological point: what happens in local governments and the communities that they govern is very important to ecological identity and, conversely, what happens in ecosystems and the local environments they govern is very important to community identity.

The importance of this point is paramount: in contrast to federal environmental governance, local governments regulate the environment because communities are situated in the environment. Local governments

---

[58] Office of Water, U.S. EPA, Community Culture and the Environment: A Guide to Understanding a Sense of Place (2002).

[59] Ibid. at 2.

and communities need, and define themselves around, functioning ecosystems, whereas the same cannot (necessarily) be said for other governmental entities. The EPA's report also notes:

> Community-based environmental protection recognizes that values held both individually and as a group contribute to the quality of community life. Expression of values through social and cultural practices can create a "sense of community." Many of these values relate directly to the "place" in which people live, thus creating a strong "sense of place."[60]

One way of articulating this distinction is that "local environment" is synonymous with "governance" in very important ways. Many of the individual services that local governments provide to their residents – and the costs of providing those services – are substitutes for benefits that can be delivered (at least in part) by functioning ecosystems. Local governments are accountable in ways not felt at other levels of government. Recognizing such costs and the benefits of ecosystem investments is a local accountability issue. Dealing with ecosystem health is "governance" at the local level.

There's more. Because local governments are ecologically situated, the quality and character of the environment is essential to the identity and well-being of communities: the continuing receipt of ecosystem services (for example watershed services, such as water provision, water filtration, flood and climate control, wildlife habitat, and so on) is relied upon at the community level. However, we use land, and land use involves transformation of the landscape, and as such the types of changes that occur in land use development imply losses (in every instance) of some ecosystem attribute that affects expectations in social, economic and environmental ways. Local governments, with their experience in designing communities and protecting public health and safety, are constantly faced with accounting for ecosystem trade-offs and the losses that result. When local governments secure these ecological benefits through land use regulation, they are engaged in prioritization of local environmental functions and maximizing the interaction between community and nature.

B. Digging In: Examples of Local Governments Regulating within the Federal Scheme

The *Millennium Ecosystem Assessment* noted that, because of the special relationship that communities have with local ecosystems, community

---

[60] Ibid. at 4.

well-being in many cases drives priorities toward protecting ecosystem functionality. Evidence of this relationship is illustrated in the community priorities and preferences expressed in land use regulations and comprehensive land use planning. This makes sense: as beneficiaries of ecosystem processes, local governments have meaningful insights into the manner in which functioning ecosystems serve human needs.

When local governments regulate ecosystem characteristics, they confront a broad range of activities on the land that threaten to change how the ecosystem functions and how the community engages with the ecosystem. Local governments may regulate for the variety of lost values from land conversion, such as the wetlands ordinance in Branford, Connecticut that is triggered by activities that diminish inland wetland or watercourse capacities to support fisheries and wildlife, supply water, prevent flooding, process waste, facilitate drainage or provide open recreational space.[61] Local governments may protect open space, soil structure and function, critical habitats and other ecosystem features through the direct regulation of aquifer recharge,[62] subdivision regulations[63] and site design review processes,[64] and storm water and erosion

---

[61] See e.g. *Queach Corp. v Inland Wetlands Comm'n of the Town of Branford*, 779 A.2d 134, 140 and n. 12, 150 (Conn. 2001).

[62] Hernando County's groundwater protection ordinance is focused on the fact that the Floridan Aquifer underlying the county is unconfined and vulnerable to contamination. Hernando Cnty., Fla. Groundwater Protection and Siting Ordinance 94-8, § 2 (27 June 1994), accessed 18 July 2015 at www.co.hernando.fl.us/utils/PDF/ordinances/Ordinance%2094-08.pdf ("It is the intent and purpose of this Ordinance to protect and maintain the quality of groundwater in Hernando County by providing criteria for land uses and the siting of facilities which use, handle, produce, store or dispose of Regulated Substances; and by providing protection to vulnerable features which discharge directly to the Floridan aquifer. This Ordinance, through its provisions, shall protect the quality of water obtained from existing and future community public supply wells described in this ordinance, in addition to the County-wide groundwater resources.").

[63] *State Dep't of Ecology v Campbell & Gwinn, L.L.C.*, 43 P.3d 4, 10–13 (Wash. 2002) (finding that statutory exemptions from the groundwater permitting system for domestic wells were not applicable to applications to subdivide, recognizing that the exemption was not intended to exempt a water use of so many users).

[64] Dartmouth, Mass., Zoning Bylaws § 20.701(d) (2008) ("Site design shall incorporate natural drainage patterns and vegetation in order to maintain pre-development stormwater patterns and water quality to the greatest extent feasible.").

control programs.[65] Through their land use control programs[66] local governments are capable of committing to local ecosystem protection.

In an important respect, local governments engage politically with the environment because of the direct and often immediate impact on local economics. For instance, local governments are the primary economic beneficiaries of functional local forest resources. Of course, urban community forests are typically not valued as timber and other commodity resources. Instead, trees in urban areas contribute to community well-being by grounding an aesthetic and psychological identity, facilitating individual and community sense of place, mitigating the challenges of urban life.[67] Evidence of the value of urban forests is illustrated in increased property values, but also in the other non-commodity benefits. Hence, Roanoke, Virginia prepared an Urban Ecosystem Analysis to study the services provided to city residents by trees.[68] The Analysis measured property value and tourism, as well as ecosystem function features, such as storm water retention, shade, erosion control and pollution mitigation. The study identified a positive correlation between urban trees and property value, substantial value in storm water control services retention capacity at $128 million, and pollution sequestration potential at an annual value of $2.3 million. The urban forest in Roanoke saved the city from having to construct expensive water treatment facilities, saved residents in electricity bills from lower climate control needs, and provided a valuable sense of place. The conclusion of the report: increase the reach (and effectiveness) of the urban forest, because saving more trees means saving more dollars.

Local governments are also seriously concerned with actions that would impair the capacity of local aquifers to provide safe drinking water

---

[65] The New Jersey Administrative Code section 7:8-2.2 (2011), explicitly includes erosion control, as well as prevention of pollution and assurance of groundwater recharge as goals of the stormwater management regulation and permitting process.

[66] See Blackwell, Robert J., "Overlay Zoning, Performance Standards, and Environmental Protection After Nollan" (1989) 16 B.C. Envtl. Aff. L. Rev. **615**, 629, 632–34 and n. 152.

[67] In addition, urban forests provide ecosystem services as they "aid in stabilizing the environment's ecological balance by contributing to the processes of air purification, oxygen regeneration, groundwater recharge, and stormwater runoff retardation, as well as aiding in noise, glare, and heat abatement." Jackson Cnty., Fla., Code § 74-201(3) (1996).

[68] American Forests & City of Roanoke Town Council, Urban Ecosystem Analysis, Roanoke, Virginia: Calculating the Value of Nature (2002), accessed 18 July 2015 at www.systemecology.com/4_Past_Projects/AF_Roanoke2.pdf.

as well as sufficient flows for commercial and industrial purposes and for maintaining surface water flows.[69] Local governments regulate the manner in which land uses impact groundwater to ensure sufficient water supplies for domestic uses and economic development.[70] In addition, groundwater protections are designed to protect drinking water sources through regulation of contaminant discharges and prevention of pollution, such as the ordinance in Weston, Wisconsin which has as its purpose:

> The Village depends exclusively on ground water for a safe drinking water supply. Certain land use practices and activities can seriously threaten or degrade ground water quality. The purpose of this Section is to institute land use regulations and restrictions to protect the Village's municipal water supply and well fields, and to promote the public health, safety, and general welfare of the residents, employees, and visitors of the Village. The restrictions imposed in this Section are in addition to those of the underlying standard zoning district or any other provisions of this Chapter.[71]

What distinguishes local environmental regulation of ecosystem functionality is in the role and relevance of *local* priorities: local demands on the ecosystem goods, local advantages from geological conditions, local economies, local pressures on drinking water supplies, and the types of land use that are competing with the continued receipt of ecosystem benefits.

Notably, when local governments govern to capture the benefits of ecosystem services, they are not confined to thinking about only those

---

[69] About 35 percent of the US population – equating to more than 100 million people – get their drinking water from public groundwater systems that draw from aquifers. "Factors Affecting Public-Supply Well Vulnerability to Contamination: Understanding Observed Water Quality and Anticipating Future Water Quality," U.S. Geological Survey, accessed 18 July 2015 at oh.water.usgs.gov/tanc/NAWQATANC.htm; see also, "Science and Technology to Support Fresh Water Availability in the United States" (Subcomm. on Water Availability & Quality, Exec. Office of the President 2004), 5, accessed 18 July 2015 at water.usgs.gov/owq/swaq.pdf.

[70] Federal and state laws protecting specific resources have largely left local governments responsible for implementing land use regulation. Arnold, Craig Anthony (Tony), "Clean-Water Land Use: Connecting Scale and Function" (2006) 23 Pace Envtl. L. Rev. **291**, 302–03. Cities have a variety of land use controls that are capable of connecting conversion of ecosystems to public service needs, such as water supply. Tarlock, A. Dan, "How California Local Governments Became Both Water Suppliers and Planners" (2010) 4 Golden Gate U. Envtl. L.J. **7**, 20.

[71] Weston, Wis., Zoning Ordinances ch. 94, Art. 6, § 94.6.03(1) (2015), accessed at www.westonwi.gov/documentcenter/view/2330.

ecosystem processes that occur within jurisdictional boundaries. Hence, New York City and Santa Fe, New Mexico have acknowledged the direct relationship between ecosystem protection and securing reliable clean drinking water supplies, and have recognized that the relationship is defined by watershed boundaries rather than political ones. In Santa Fe, for example, the federally owned forested watershed supplies water for more than 30,000 homes and businesses.[72] Santa Fe's water supply is not risk-free: the basin is constantly monitored for the threats of forest degradation and fire catastrophe.[73] The solution was not obvious, but it illustrates the relevance of local involvement in environmental protection. Santa Fe balanced the cost of a substantial forest fire in the watershed (including the expenses of removing increased sedimentation, treating and filtering water supplies, and securing replacement water supplies[74]) against the costs of managing the watershed to reduce the likelihood of forest fire: "The cost to retain the restored forest condition is estimated at $4.3 million, an average of $200,000 per year. In contrast, the avoided cost that would result from a 7,000 acre fire in the watershed is estimated at $22 million."[75] To capitalize on the natural services provided to Santa Fe from the forested watershed, the city is pursuing its interests into federal lands with a plan to manage the federal forests to reduce the risk.[76]

CONCLUSION

At times, federalist jurisprudence seems to work reasonably well at accomplishing the stated goals of uniformity and standards setting among

---

[72] Margolis, Ellis et al., Santa Fe Municipal Watershed Plan, 2010–2029, (2009), 2, accessed 18 July 2015 at www.santafenm.gov/document_center/document/780.
[73] Ibid.
[74] Ibid. at 11.
[75] Ibid. at 1.
[76] The city is planning for ways to fund their proposal, including a payment for ecosystem services (PES) program. Under PES programs, some landowners are being paid to protect ecosystem services capacity, such as by enhancing flood storage, assisting in the management of critical habitats and aquifer recharge, and leaving wetlands intact. Majanen, Terhi et al., Ecoagriculture Partners, "Innovations in Market-Based Watershed Conservation in the United States: Payments for Watershed Services for Agricultural and Forest Landscapes" (2011), 6, 9, accessed 18 July 2015 at http://ecoagriculture.org/publication_details.php?publicationID=362.

potentially competitive states and local governments. However, through its design, the legal structure for a federal environmental program, including the resulting legal structure of local governments, may go too far in impinging upon individuals' collective desire to create community.[77] As Gerald Frug noted, "if we focus on cities as they are presently organized and managed, we will not see the argument for city power."[78] The argument in favor of local authority to regulate natural resources is not reflected in the federalist legal structure. The failure of many local governments to exceed federal regulations cannot be described simply as a failure of local governments to act or to care about their local environments. Rather, it is a failure of environmental federalism to account for local communities' connection to the environment and to incorporate that connection into the law, in particular land use controls.

Local governments face legal hurdles that are not only outside their ability to control, but also are crafted in a way that does not respond to a community's engagement with its surroundings. State and federal review of local authority essentially boil down to questions concerning external actions and boundary lines. Even assuming some divergence for the purposes and merits of decentralization as varied by discipline,[79] the inquiry into authority over the environment nonetheless marginalizes local governments' ability to know the importance of a given ecosystem, its historical and culture value, and the potential for it to impact local governments beyond their borders. It also fails to meet several classical notions of decentralization of power relative to community empowerment and involvement and give "better incentives, more opportunities to exercise their facilities, and fewer reasons to oppress each other."[80] Perhaps most importantly, the notion of centralized authority over natural resources avoids valuing the relationship between communities and

---

[77] We do note that many of the more pervasive threats to ecosystem health, such as land conversion, impervious surfaces, and other "nonpoint source" pollution problems, have been left to local governments in the federal scheme of environmental law. In some cases, the federal scheme appears to rely on the benign nature of such problems, while in others, Congress appears to cave to partisan politics and/or the object of regulation may simply be too miniscule or remote to justify uniform standards, such as small-scale soils displacement.

[78] Frug, Gerald E., "The City as a Legal Concept" (1980) 93 Harv. L. Rev. **1059**, 1067.

[79] Nussim, Jacob, "A Policymaker's Guide to Welfarism" (2007) 155 U. Pa. L. Rev. **227**, 234.

[80] Hills, Roderick M. Jr., "Is Federalism Good for Localism? The Localist Case for Federal Regimes" (2005) 21 J.L. & Pol. **187**, 191.

governance that only occurs in local governments and, in turn, in local self-governance.

Tocqueville believed that the individual, induced by the "spirit of ownership or any ideas of improvement," would act in his own self-interest and demand more gains or less waste from government.[81] The geographical proximity of the central authority to the individual ensures that it will be more accountable and hasten to repair inevitable mistakes.[82] Yet Tocqueville's argument also relies on observations of human nature. He believed that centralization of human affairs was a natural eventuality which helped form the first towns.[83] Tocqueville was not advocating sameness; some differences are essential yet expose the society to greater risk of external exploitation.[84]

Of course, the mere fact that local governments do engage in the protection of local ecosystem functionality is not a sufficient argument in favor of local control. Yet the inescapable observation in these local efforts is that they cannot be reproduced at the federal level: where local governments have regulated land uses to prevent degradation of local important ecosystems, they regulate from a purpose that non-local governments simply do not have.

---

[81] Tocqueville, *supra*, n. 2, at 116.
[82] Ibid. at 113, 119, 304.
[83] Ibid. at 74.
[84] Ibid. at 75.

PART V

COMPARING INTERNATIONAL REGIMES

12. The Australian experience with environmental federalism: constitutional and political perspectives

Robert Fowler

I. INTRODUCTION

The United States and Australia enjoy a common constitutional heritage through each having a vibrant federal system of government in which functions are distributed between, and often shared by, the federal and state levels. With respect to protection of the environment, they have also enjoyed a common experience of over 40 years of development of legislative and policy responses at both levels of government, with local and regional measures also employed in particular contexts.[1]

Within Australia, for most of this period, a cooperative federalism philosophy has strongly influenced the manner in which the Commonwealth[2] has pursued its particular role with respect to environmental matters. Pursuant to numerous intergovernmental agreements and national strategies and policies, the Commonwealth has acted collaboratively with state and territory governments[3] (hereinafter referred to collectively as the "state governments") in developing an extensive range

---

[1] For overviews of Australian environmental law, see Bates, G.M., *Environmental Law in Australia*, 8th edn (LexisNexis Butterworths, Chatswood NSW 2013); and Fisher, D.E., *Australian Environmental Law: Norms, Principles and Rules*, 2nd edn (Thomson Reuters, Pymont NSW 2010).

[2] Under s. 3 of the Australian Constitution (the Commonwealth of Australia Constitution Act 1901), the federal government is identified as the "Commonwealth".

[3] The two mainland territories (the Northern Territory and the Australian Capital Territory), which were surrendered to the Commonwealth in 1901, have each enjoyed powers of self-government since 1978 and 1988 respectively.

of environmental legislation. This legislation addresses matters such as environmental impact assessment of projects, national environmental standards, assessment of hazardous chemicals, nature conservation and natural resources management. But at times the Commonwealth has been prepared to take a more preemptive role, notably in relation to the implementation of international treaty obligations (for example, with respect to the protection of world heritage, wetlands of international significance and migratory species) or where pressing environmental challenges have demanded strong action. Examples in the latter context include the Water Act 2006, enacted in response to a drought-driven crisis in the Murray-Darling Basin and the carbon pricing scheme introduced in 2011 as Australia's principal mechanism for reducing carbon emissions.[4]

However, this blend of cooperative federalism qualified by occasionally coercive centralism is presently the subject of a substantial review by the Coalition[5] government (the "Abbott government") which was elected in late 2013. It has initiated a review of federal–state relationships through the proposed development of a White Paper on Reform of the Federation[6] and has also instituted a review of all environmental legislation and regulation with the aim of working with the states to "identify unworkable, contradictory or incompatible green-tape".[7] Even before the

---

[4] See the Clean Energy Act 2011 (Cth) 1, which was repealed by the Abbott government, and related legislation, including the Carbon Credits (Carbon Farming Initiative) Act 2011 (Cth).

[5] The Coalition government is a political partnership between two parties (the Liberal Party and the National Party) with the Liberal party being the dominant partner in terms of the number of seats held in the Commonwealth Parliament; its leader serves as the Prime Minister of Australia (at present, the Honourable Tony Abbott MP).

[6] A White Paper is a government report that sets out a formal policy position on a particular matter, often as a precursor to executive action or legislation. It is frequently preceded by a Green Paper in which various policy options are outlined for the purpose of obtaining feedback to be used in the preparation of a White Paper. For details of the White Paper Terms of Reference, see Prime Minister of Australia, White Paper on Reform of the Federation – Terms of Reference, 28 June 2014, accessed 19 July 2015 at www.pm.gov.au/media/2014-06-28/white-paper-reform-federation.

[7] See Liberal Party of Australia, Boosting Productivity and Reducing Regulation, para. 23, accessed 19 July 2015 at www.liberal.org.au/boosting-productivity-and-reducing-regulation.

completion of this review, the Abbott government has undertaken numerous actions to wind back existing Commonwealth environmental measures, most noticeably the abolition of the carbon price scheme introduced in 2011 by the Gillard government.[8]

The long-term impact of these recent initiatives on the Commonwealth's role in environmental matters and their implications for environmental federalism are difficult to predict given that any legislative reforms require the approval of the Senate, where the Coalition government lacks a majority. It must therefore deal with various minority parties and individual, independent senators in order to secure the passage of its amending or repealing legislation. To date, it has experienced both successes and failures in this regard and the situation therefore remains highly volatile.

This chapter will describe the general features of Australian federalism, in particular the tension that has been evident in recent years between cooperative and coercive approaches on the part of the Commonwealth. It will then examine the influence of the High Court on Australian federalism through its approach to interpretation of the Constitution and the resulting capacity of the Commonwealth to make laws with respect to the environment. This will be followed by a description of the various political mechanisms that have been employed over the past 40 years to promote a cooperative federalism approach to environmental management in Australia. Finally, there will be a summary of recent efforts by the Commonwealth to revive the notion of state sovereignty and to pursue reform of federalism in Australia through the White Paper process.

II. AUSTRALIAN FEDERALISM: GENERAL FEATURES

A. The Australian Constitution and the Federal System

The Commonwealth of Australian Constitution Act 1901, an Act of the United Kingdom Imperial Parliament, established a federal system that is comprised of six states, two territories and a central government (the Commonwealth). The framers of the Constitution deliberately chose to adopt the United States model, which they considered to be less centralist

---

[8] See *supra*, n. 4. The repealing legislation is the Clean Energy Legislation (Carbon Tax Repeal) Act 2014, assented to 17 July 2014.

than the Canadian federal system provided for by the Canadian British North America Act 1867 (UK).[9] Under the Australian Constitution, the principal matters on which the Commonwealth Parliament may legislate are set out in section 51.[10] The legislative authority provided by this section is concurrent with that of the states, but provision is made in section 109 for a Commonwealth law to prevail in the event of an inconsistency with state legislation on the same subject matter. This provision therefore enables Commonwealth preemption of state laws where it decides to cover a particular field or subject matter within its legislative competence under section 51.

The Constitution also provides in section 71 for the establishment of the High Court of Australia as the judicial body for determining disputes between the various governments within the federation. However, unlike the US Supreme Court, it has also been vested with the jurisdiction to serve as the ultimate court of appeal from the state Supreme Courts.[11]

Financial arrangements between the Commonwealth and the states are dealt with in Chapter IV of the Constitution and include a "free trade" clause (section 92) that declares that "trade, commerce and intercourse among the States ... shall be absolutely free".[12] At federation, the states agreed to surrender to the Commonwealth the power to impose customs duties, which at the time were their major source of revenue, on the assumption that they would be the beneficiaries of large surpluses expected to be generated by the Commonwealth after meeting its own needs. But the limited and time-bound measures included in the Constitution concerning distribution of Commonwealth revenues to the states[13] meant that the states became wholly dependent upon the discretion of the Commonwealth to distribute revenue to them from just ten years after

---

[9] See Selway, B. and J.M. Williams, "The High Court and Australian Federalism" (2005) 35 *Publius* **467**, 468–470.

[10] The Commonwealth also has exclusive legislative power with respect to a small number of matters; see in particular ss 52(i) (places acquired by the Commonwealth for public purposes) and 90 (customs and excise).

[11] Australian Constitution Act 1901, s. 73(ii). This function was frustrated to an extent by the continued availability of appeals from state Supreme Courts to the Privy Council on non-constitutional matters (see Australian Constitution Act, s. 74) until such appeals were finally abolished in 1975: see Privy Council (Appeals from the High Court) Act 1975 (Cth).

[12] For an application of this clause by the High Court to strike down a "protectionist" provision relating to bottle recycling, see *Castlemaine Tooheys Ltd. v South Australia* (1990) 169 CLR 553.

[13] See Australian Constitution Act 1901, ss 87, 89, 93 and 94.

federation.[14] Their financial vulnerability has been exacerbated by the subsequent assumption by the Commonwealth of the power to impose income tax, thereby depriving the states of the principal source of revenue available to governments within Australia. In addition, the ability of the Commonwealth, under section 96 of the Constitution, to provide financial assistance to any state on such terms and conditions as the Commonwealth Parliament thinks fit (often referred to as "specific purpose grants") has enabled the Commonwealth to determine the form of various financial programs that are delivered through the states. The end result has been a level of asymmetry between revenue raising and expenditure requirements (often referred to as "vertical fiscal imbalance") that has been described as "greater than in almost all established federations".[15]

Thus, despite the contrary intentions of the framers of the Australian Constitution, centralism has become the dominant characteristic of Australian federalism, with the trend having been reinforced over the period from 1995 to 2007 under the government of Prime Minister John Howard.[16] The combination of an expansive interpretation by the High Court of the legislative powers of the Commonwealth and a high degree of vertical fiscal imbalance have led to this outcome, but in practice it has been ameliorated over many years by political arrangements that have resulted in a high degree of shared functions and innovative approaches to cooperative federalism.[17]

There have been regular calls for federalism reform, in particular to reallocate roles and responsibilities and reduce vertical fiscal imbalance, but the means by which such reforms might be achieved remain difficult to pursue in practice.[18] Whilst there is some support, particularly among constitutional lawyers, for amendment of the Constitution to achieve a

---

[14] Selway and Williams, *supra*, n. 9, at 472.

[15] Ibid. at 486.

[16] Hollander, R. and H. Patapan, "Pragmatic Federalism: Australian Federalism from Hawke to Howard" (2007) 66 *Australian Journal of Public Administration* **280**.

[17] Twomey, A. and G. Withers, "Australia's Federal Future: Defining Growth and Prosperity", Federalist Paper 1, Report for the Council for the Australian Federation (April 2007), at 28, accessed 18 July 2015 at www.caf.gov.au/documents/australiasfederalfuture.pdf.

[18] Kildea, P., A. Lynch and G. Williams, "Introduction", in Kildea, P., A. Lynch and G. Williams (eds), *Tomorrow's Federation: Reforming Australian Government* (The Federation Press, Sydney 2012), pp. 1–4.

closer alignment between the political reality and its present form,[19] the experience of having just eight successful referenda for this purpose from a total of 44 attempts provides a significant deterrent. Instead, discourse on political rather than constitutional reform of federalism has been generated at regular intervals over the past 40 years, often at the initiative of the Prime Minister of the day. As noted above, with the election of the Abbott Coalition government in September 2013, a fresh initiative has been commenced recently which involves the preparation of a White Paper on the reform of Commonwealth–state relations. This initiative will be discussed further below.

B. Modes of Australian Federalism

Scholarship on the contested notions of federalism was limited at the time of the founding of Australia, with there being no equivalent to the Federalist Papers that were produced in the United States at federation.[20] In the absence of deeper theories regarding federalism, Australian scholars have focused generally on a practical analysis of the different modes of federalism that have been employed since federation. For example, Australian federalism has been described in recent years as having become "pragmatic", meaning that it is "characterised by a direct engagement or confrontation with pressing problems"[21] and remains "largely uninformed by imposing aspirations and grand political or legal theory, or shaped by party ideology or platform".[22] An alternative description that essentially reflects the same assessment is "opportunistic" federalism.[23]

The characterisation of Australian federalism as pragmatic or opportunistic focuses on the steady trend towards a centralised and coercive

---

[19] Ibid. at 4; see also Saunders, C., "Collaborative Federalism" (2002) 61 *Australian Journal of Public Administration* **69**, 75. For a contrary view, see Galligan, B., "Processes for Reforming Australian Federalism" (2008) 31 *University of New South Wales Law Journal* 616, arguing (at 630) that "most reforms can be done politically and through improving intergovernmental relations".

[20] Hollander and Patapan, *supra*, n. 16, at 281.

[21] Ibid.

[22] Ibid. at 285.

[23] See for example Twomey and Withers, *supra*, n. 17, at 33. This description was also used by Kirby, J. in his dissenting judgment in the High Court in *New South Wales v The Commonwealth (the Work Choices case)* (2006) 229 CLR 1, where he warned that the result of the majority decision could be for the states to be reduced, in effect, to service agencies of the Commonwealth (at 201).

version of federalism, but other commentators have described the existence of alternative "modes" of federalism that reflect varying levels of centralism on the part of the Commonwealth. Galligan, for example, identifies four such modes – cooperative, coercive, coordinate and competitive – each of which he suggests has been evident at some point since federation.[24] He dismisses coordinate federalism, which involves separate and distinct roles and responsibilities for the Commonwealth and the states respectively, as being inimical to "any sophisticated modern federal system",[25] particularly given that the Commonwealth and states today share roles and responsibilities within most major policy areas. But he suggests that it is possible to identify examples of all three other modes of federalism in operation today, with both competition and cooperation frequently operating together in dynamic combinations, and coercion replacing both on occasions.[26]

Competitive federalism, involving both vertical and horizontal contestation, is particularly favoured by economists as a description of the dominant mode of Australian federalism and the primary means of defining roles and responsibilities, whereas lawyers and political scientists have generally preferred to characterise Australian federalism as "cooperative" or "collaborative". In so doing, the latter point to a range of collaborative mechanisms, including legislative schemes that allow for harmonised or highly coordinated approaches; the use of the Council of Australian Governments (COAG) and Ministerial Councils to secure agreed policy outcomes; the entry into intergovernmental agreements; the referral of powers by the states to the Commonwealth pursuant to section 51(xxxvii) of the Constitution; and the provision of specific purpose grants under section 96 of the Constitution.[27] The use of various collaborative mechanisms of a political nature will be examined below.

---

[24] Galligan, *supra*, n. 19, at 639.
[25] Ibid. Whilst coordinate federalism was dealt a fatal legal blow in 1920 by the *Engineers case* (discussed below, Part II.C), it may still have some life politically in the assertion from time to time of the concept of state "sovereignty", as has occurred very recently: see further below, Part V.
[26] Ibid.
[27] Saunders, *supra*, n. 19, at 72–73.

C. The Influence of the High Court on Australian Federalism

During the first 20 years of federation, the High Court drew on United States jurisprudence[28] to develop doctrines of intergovernmental immunities and reserved powers that assumed the sovereignty of the states and Commonwealth respectively and thereby limited the legislative capacity of each level of government to impact upon the other in their respective fields of operation.[29] This version of the federal model reflects the concept of "coordinate" federalism referred to above.[30] It was decisively rejected in 1920 in the *Engineers* case,[31] where the High Court decided to pursue an approach (often described as a "textual" approach) to the interpretation of the Constitution that involves a search for its natural meaning and eschews any doctrine involving the implication of limits on legislative power.[32] With this decision, the legal concept of the sovereignty of the states was discarded, although it has been reasserted from time to time, including very recently, as a political doctrine or principle.[33]

The *Engineers* case has strongly informed the subsequent interpretation by the High Court of Commonwealth legislative powers, the end result of which has been described as "an evolutionary increase in federal power and influence and a corresponding decrease in the power and influence of state governments".[34] A number of landmark cases since the *Engineers* case have served collectively to support an expansive application by the Commonwealth Parliament of its concurrent legislative powers under section 51 of the Constitution. Early examples include the *First Uniform Tax Case*[35] and the *Second Uniform Tax*

---

[28] *McCulloch v Maryland* 4 Wheat 316 (1819); *Collector v Day* 11 Wall 113 (1871).

[29] *D'Emden v Pedder* (1904) 1 CLR 91; *Deakin v Webb* (1904) 1 CLR 585; see further, Selway and Williams, *supra*, n. 9, at 478–483.

[30] Galligan, *supra*, n. 19, at 639.

[31] *Amalgamated Society of Engineers v The Adelaide Steamship Co Ltd.* (1920) 28 CLR 129.

[32] Ibid., at 148–149. However, the High Court has recognised one implied limitation on Commonwealth power, this being for the purpose of protecting the existence or ability of a state to govern itself: see *Melbourne Corporation v Commonwealth* (1947) 74 CLR 31; and, more recently, *Austin v Commonwealth* (2003) 215 CLR 185, where the High Court reframed the *Melbourne Corporation* doctrine to focus its operation on the question whether the structural integrity of a state is threatened by a Commonwealth law.

[33] See further below, Part V.

[34] Selway and Williams, *supra* n. 9, at 483.

[35] *South Australia v Commonwealth* (1942) 65 CLR 373.

Case,[36] which together served to confirm that the states were precluded from imposing income taxes in light of the development of a uniform taxation scheme by the Commonwealth.

In the early 1980s, in the *Tasmanian Dam* case,[37] a narrow majority of the High Court ruled that the "external affairs" power under section 51(xxix) of the Constitution is not subject to any inherent limitation with respect to the subject matter of a Commonwealth law designed to implement a treaty to which Australia is a party. The High Court concluded that, provided a Commonwealth law made for this purpose is reasonably capable of being considered as appropriate and adapted to implementing the relevant treaty, it will be considered a valid exercise of the external affairs power.[38] This case was of critical significance in terms of confirming the capacity of the Commonwealth to legislate on environmental matters, given the extensive range of multilateral and bilateral agreements relating to the environment to which Australia has become a party.[39] Despite concerns expressed at the time of this decision by a number of parties (in particular some state Premiers) that it could result in the Commonwealth taking over the field of environmental regulation from the states, this has not proved to be the case in practice. As will be seen below, there has instead been a strong emphasis by the Commonwealth on securing collaborative political arrangements with the states in relation to a wide range of environmental matters,[40] with a more centralist or coercive legislative approach having been used only rarely.

More recently, the *Work Choices* case[41] confirmed the broad reach of the "corporations" power of the Commonwealth under section 51(xx) of

---

[36] *Victoria v Commonwealth* (1957) 99 CLR 575.

[37] *Commonwealth v Tasmania* (1983) 158 CLR 1.

[38] Ibid. at 25 (Mason J). See also, *Richardson v Forestry Commission* (1988) 164 CLR 261; *Polyukhovich v Commonwealth* (1991) 172 CLR 501; and *Leask v Commonwealth* (1996) 187 CLR 579.

[39] The Australian Department of Foreign Affairs and Trade (DFAT) provides on its website a list of some 272 treaties which are described as being in the field of "environment and resources" to which Australia is a party: accessed 18 July 2015 at www.info.dfat.gov.au/Info/Treaties/Treaties.nsf/WebView?OpenForm&Seq=2.

[40] Cf. Galligan, B., "Australian Federalism: A Prospective Assessment" (2002) 32 *Publius* **147**, 161: "The consequence has not been the demise of Australian federalism, but an enhanced role for the Commonwealth and greater reliance on political compromise and intergovernmental relations to work out the respective roles of Commonwealth and state governments."

[41] *New South Wales v Commonwealth* (2006) 229 CLR 1.

the Constitution,[42] in this instance to enable the Commonwealth to cover extensively the field of industrial relations. This decision has been widely regarded as the most significant in relation to Commonwealth legislative powers since the *Tasmanian Dam* case. Galligan notes that it "reinforces just how potent the High Court can be in shaping Australian federalism through sanctioning extensive centralisation of Commonwealth power".[43] The decision also lends weight to earlier predictions that section 51(xx) could provide a solid constitutional basis for an expanded legislative coverage by the Commonwealth of environmental matters,[44] although, as with the external affairs power, the Commonwealth has not sought to utilise this capacity to its fullest extent.

Despite the expansive interpretation of Commonwealth legislative powers by the High Court since the *Engineers* case in 1920, the general opinion amongst federalism scholars in Australia is that this has been less influential in relation to the dynamics of Australian federalism than has the political process[45] and the emergence of a national economy and welfare state.[46] Nevertheless, the High Court continues to provide a framework for further political developments concerning the federation through its essentially textual approach to the interpretation of the Commonwealth's legislative powers. In this regard it is interesting to note the observation by Perry in 2012 that the scope of the Commonwealth's executive power might be where "the battle between different conceptions of the federation may lie in the future".[47] This prophesy has since been borne out in the recent *School Chaplain* cases,[48] where the High Court has imposed limitations on the scope of the Commonwealth's

---

[42] Section 51(xx) refers to "foreign corporations, and trading or financial corporations formed within the limits of the Commonwealth".

[43] Galligan, *supra*, n. 19, at 631.

[44] Crawford, J.R., "The Constitution and the Environment" (1991) 13 *Sydney Law Review* **11**, 25.

[45] Sawer, G., *Australian Federalism in the Courts* (Melbourne University Press, Melbourne 1967), p. 8; Galligan, *supra*, n. 19, at 634.

[46] Selway and Williams, *supra*, n. 9, at 487.

[47] Perry, M., "The High Court and Dynamic Federalism", in *Tomorrow's Federation: Reforming Australian* Government, *supra*, n. 18, pp. 172, 190.

[48] *Williams v Commonwealth* (2012) 248 CLR 156; *Williams v Commonwealth (No. 2)* (2014) HCA 23 (judgment delivered 19 June 2014). Both cases involved challenges to a Commonwealth scheme to directly fund the provision of chaplains in schools independently of any state involvement. For an earlier decision on the extent of Commonwealth executive power that paved the way for these two decisions, see *Pape v Federal Commissioner of Taxation* (2009) 238 CLR 1.

executive power under section 61 of the Constitution, in particular by confining its spending power to matters within the heads of Commonwealth legislative power enumerated in the Constitution, in particular by section 51. This could have potentially significant implications in relation to both existing and future expenditure by the Commonwealth on environment-related matters.[49]

III. THE CONSTITUTIONAL POWERS OF THE COMMONWEALTH WITH RESPECT TO THE ENVIRONMENT

A. The Constitutional Extent of Commonwealth Legislative Power

Given the expansive interpretation afforded to section 51 of the Australian Constitution by the High Court, there is little room for debate today concerning the capacity of the Commonwealth to legislate on environmental matters. It is widely accepted among legal commentators that, through reliance on a number of the specific legislative powers set out in section 51, the Commonwealth has considerable, though not unlimited, power to legislate on environmental matters.[50] In addition to the external affairs and corporations powers, which have already been discussed, reliance may also be placed by the Commonwealth on powers in relation to international and interstate trade and commerce (section 51(i)); finance and taxation (section 51(ii)); defence (section 51(vi)); quarantine (section 51(ix)); fisheries in Australian waters (section 51(x)); and the "people of any race" (section 51(xxvi)). Also, the power to provide direct financial assistance to the states under section 96 may be used to achieve environmental objectives. Finally, reliance has also been placed by the

---

[49] For example, the question has been raised as to the constitutional validity of the Commonwealth legislation adopted during 2014 to establish an Emissions Reduction Fund for the purpose of implementing the Coalition government's Direct Action Plan on climate change (the Carbon Framing Initiative Amendment Act 2014): see Appleby, G., "Explainer: Is Direct Action Constitutionally Valid?" *The Conversation*, 3 November 2014, accessed 19 July 2015 at the conversation.com/explainer-is-direct-action-constitutionally-valid-33676.

[50] Crommelin, M., "Commonwealth Involvement in Environmental Policy: Past, Present and Future" (1987) 4 *Environmental and Planning Law Journal* 101; Crawford, *supra*, n. 44; Lindell, G., "Scope of Commonwealth Environmental Powers and Responsibilities", in Leadbeter, P., N. Gunningham and B. Boer (eds) *Environmental Outlook No. 3: Law and Policy* (The Federation Press, Sydney 1999), p. 107.

Commonwealth more recently on the referrals power (section 51(xxx–vii)), whereby the parliaments of the states may refer matters to the Commonwealth Parliament for the purpose of conferring legislative power on the latter.[51] This approach was used, for example, to bolster the constitutional validity of the Water Act 2007, which provided for new, centralised arrangements for the management of the Murray-Darling Basin in place of a highly consensual, collaborative model that dated back to 1914 but which had failed to produce effective outcomes.[52]

In 1999, the Senate Environment Committee conducted an enquiry into Commonwealth environment powers and received some 367 submissions, reflecting the substantial interest in this matter across the Australian community. The Committee concluded as follows:

> It is the view of the Committee that the Commonwealth Government has the constitutional power to regulate, including by legislation, most, if not all, matters of major environmental significance anywhere within the territory of Australia. The panoply of existing Constitutional heads of power confers on the Commonwealth extensive legislative competence with respect to environmental matters.[53]

The Australian Constitution shares with the American and Canadian Constitutions the absence of any specific reference to the environment, a situation that places these Constitutions in sharp contrast with the Constitutions of nearly three-quarters of the world's nations.[54] The inclusion of environmental clauses in many national constitutions that have been drafted in recent decades and the comparative ease with which

---

[51] See generally with respect to the use of this power since the early 1990s, Lynch, A., "The Reference Power: The Rise and Rise of a Placitum?" in *Tomorrow's Federation: Reforming Australian Government, supra*, note 18 p. 193.

[52] See Gardner, A., "Water Reform and the Federal System", in *Tomorrow's Federation: Reforming Australian Government, supra*, n. 18, p. 269, suggesting that the primary constitutional basis for the Water Act 2007 nevertheless was the external affairs power (p. 274).

[53] Parliament of the Commonwealth of Australia, Commonwealth Environment Powers, Report of the Senate Environment, Communications, Information Technology and the Arts Reference Committee, Parliamentary Paper No. 133 of 1999, ix.

[54] May, J.R., "Constitutional Directions in Procedural Environmental Rights" (2013) 28 *Journal of Environmental Law and Litigation* 27. See also, May, J.R., and E. Daley, *Global Environmental Constitutionalism* (Cambridge University Press, Cambridge 2014).

some older constitutions have been amended to insert such clauses,[55] gives pause for thought as to whether the Australian Constitution should also be amended to formalise the agreed legislative competency of the Commonwealth Parliament in relation to environmental matters. This possibility was canvassed, but rejected, in the late 1980s by a Constitutional Commission appointed by the Commonwealth to examine, among other things, the distribution of powers between the Commonwealth and state governments.[56] The Commission noted various submissions presented to it in support of such a power but concluded that it was not warranted as it would allow the Commonwealth to legislate on "matters which traditionally have been State concerns".[57] There has been little interest since this report in advancing the case for a constitutional amendment to insert an environment power in the Constitution. Instead, the Commonwealth has focused on the careful framing of its environmental legislation to ensure its constitutional validity and the pursuit of political accords with the states to produce collaborative approaches to various aspects of environmental management.

It should also be noted that Australia, unlike the United States, does not have a Bill of Rights and therefore does not have a framework within which to situate a declaration of environmental rights of the kind that, as noted above, has been common in many constitutions adopted in more recent years.[58] The absence of any specific rights of such a nature in the United States has been offset to some extent by the "environmental justice" movement,[59] a development that has been completely absent in Australia.

B. Legislative Drafting Techniques

One practical consequence of the so-called "panoply" of heads of power available to the Commonwealth to support its environmental legislation has been to induce its legislative drafters to identify relevant heads of

---

[55] May, *supra*, n. 54, notes that over the past two decades, nearly three dozen countries have embedded procedural rights in their constitutions (at 27).

[56] Commonwealth of Australia, Final Report of the Constitutional Commission, Volume Two 765 (Australian Government Publishing Service, 1988).

[57] Ibid. at 766.

[58] The case for adoption of an Australian Charter of Rights and Freedoms has been advanced in detail in Wilcox, M.R., *An Australian Charter of Rights?* (Law Book Co., Sydney 1992).

[59] See Cory, D.C. and T. Rahman, *Environmental Justice and Federalism* (Edward Elgar, Cheltenham, UK and Northampton, MA, USA 2012).

power explicitly in such legislation. Some Commonwealth environmental legislation relies solely on the external affairs power for its constitutional validity, particularly where its purpose is to implement obligations arising from a particular international treaty, and it is common in such circumstances to attach the relevant treaty as a schedule to the Act.[60] But in other cases, a legislative drafting technique is employed that utilises a combination of the heads of power previously mentioned to provide the required constitutional underpinning.[61] The most elaborate example of this approach is the Water Act 2007, which relies on a total of nine separate heads of power, at times citing several heads in support of a single provision. This approach is in stark contrast to federal environmental laws in the USA, which have been drafted largely on the assumption that their validity derives from the Commerce Clause.

The success of this approach is reflected in the fact that there has not yet been a successful challenge to the constitutional validity of any Commonwealth environment legislation since the Commonwealth first entered this field over 40 years ago. However, this situation is also a reflection of the highly collaborative approach taken by the Commonwealth when legislating on environmental matters, which has minimised the prospects of any constitutional challenge being brought.

C. Distinctions between Federal Legislative Authority in Australia and the USA

For the purposes of comparison, it should be noted that there are several significant differences between the constitutional authority of the federal governments in the USA and Australia in relation to environmental matters. These include the ambit of the Commerce Clause contained in each country's Constitution, the role of the respective federal governments as landowners and managers and the respective processes for treaty implementation.

Despite the similarity between section 51(i) of the Australian Constitution (the trade and commerce power) and the Commerce Clause in the US Constitution (Article 1, section 8(3)), the Australian High Court has construed the Australian provision in a more restrictive manner than has

---

[60] For a list of some 16 Commonwealth Acts that rely partly or in full on particular international treaties for their validity, see Bates, *supra*, n. 1, 137–138.

[61] See for example Therapeutic Goods Act 1989, s. 6; Industrial Chemicals (Notification and Assessment) Act 198, s. 4; Water Act 2007, ss 9–11; and Product Stewardship Act 2011, s. 40. See further, Lindell, *supra*, n. 50, 107; and Bates, *supra*, n. 1, 132–133.

the US Supreme Court in relation to the Commerce Clause, in particular by rejecting the argument that economic effects on interstate trade and commerce suffice to empower Commonwealth legislation under section 51(1).[62] This is a curious exception to its generally liberal approach to the interpretation of the heads of power contained in section 51. It is interesting to note, however, that since 1995 a narrow majority of the US Supreme Court has sought to restrict the reach of the Commerce Clause, although this does not appear as yet to have seriously threatened the constitutional validity of the wide range of federal environmental legislation that depends largely on this clause.[63]

The second significant difference relates to the respective roles of the Australian and US federal governments as landowners and managers. Whilst the Commonwealth has exclusive legislative power under section 52(i) of the Australian Constitution over "all places acquired by the Commonwealth for public purposes", it does not enjoy ownership of lands or "places" to anything like the same extent as does the US federal government. At federation in Australia, the former colonies retained title over the lands within their respective borders, together with the other natural resources situated therein (including water, minerals, oil and gas, uranium, forests and fisheries).[64] As a result, the Commonwealth has exercised a relatively limited role as a land manager, particularly compared with that performed by the Departments of Interior and Agriculture

---

[62] See for example *Attorney General (WA) v Australian National Airlines Commission* (1976) 138 CLR 492, at 508–510; see also Selway and Williams, *supra*, n. 9, 480–481. However, the High Court found in *Murphyores Inc. v Commonwealth* (1976) 136 CLR 1 that, in relation to international trade and commerce, the Commonwealth was entitled to consider environmental factors when determining whether to grant export approvals. This enabled the Commonwealth to apply its environmental assessment procedures under the Environment Protection (Impact of Proposals) Act 1974 (Cth) to export-related mining and forestry activities for a quarter of a century until this Act was repealed and replaced by the Environment Protection and Biodiversity Conservation Act 1999.

[63] Cory and Rahman, *supra*, n. 59, 88.

[64] The nature of this title, however, is open to debate following the decision of the High Court in *Mabo v Queensland (No. 2)* (19920 175 CLR 1, where the court rejected a long-standing proposition that Australia was *terra nullius* at the time of its settlement and held that a form of native title could survive colonisation until extinguished by the Crown. Thus, the Crown in right of the colonies acquired at settlement a "radical" title that is possibly distinct from full beneficial ownership: see further, Rogers, N., "The Emerging Concept of 'Radical Title' in Australia: Implications for Environmental Management" (1995) 12 *Environmental & Planning Law Journal* 183, noting similarities in this regard with the public trust doctrine in the United States (at 197).

in the United States. This has meant that it has been forced to rely primarily on mechanisms such as the provision of financial assistance to the states to exert its influence on natural resources management and biodiversity protection at the state level. However, it has also exercised a project assessment and approval role that has encompassed biodiversity considerations, particularly where natural areas have acquired international status as World Heritage Sites or Wetlands of International Importance.[65]

The Commonwealth's approach to biodiversity protection has focused particularly on supporting the National Reserves System (NRS), which was established in the early 1990s on the heels of the Rio Earth Summit, but which builds on a protected areas system at the state level that dates back to the nineteenth century.[66] The NRS is comprised primarily of protected areas, the vast majority of which are owned and managed by the states and some of which have been handed back to indigenous owners and placed under co-management arrangements with state national parks services. The Commonwealth has pursued a similar course with respect to two protected areas established by it in the 1970s within the Northern Territory.[67] Protected areas encompass almost 16 per cent of the Australian continent. Since the mid-1990s, lands owned and managed separately by indigenous people for conservation purposes have also been included within the NRS, and cover another 5 per cent of the continent. Finally, since 1999, several thousand protected areas on private land have been added, comprising another 1 per cent of the continent.[68] The Commonwealth has provided substantial funding to support the extension and management of the NRS. From 1997 until 2008 this was under the Natural Heritage Trust program. Since then, funds have been provided under its successor, the Caring for our Country Program, but a substantial

---

[65] Under the Environment Protection and Biodiversity Conservation Act 1999 (Cth).

[66] For details of the NRS, see www.environment.gov.au/land/nrs/about-nrs (accessed 19 July 2015).

[67] Kakadu National Park and Uluru National Park, both of which the Commonwealth retained responsibility for after the Northern Territory acquired self-government in 1978. These parks were established by the Commonwealth under its National Parks and Wildlife Conservation Act 1975 (Cth), which was repealed and replaced by the EPBC Act in 1999.

[68] NRS website, *supra*, n. 66.

reduction in funding for this program was announced by the Abbott government in late 2013, shortly after its election.[69]

The Commonwealth enjoys legislative authority in relation to two other types of "places": the oceans and its external territories. Although the High Court found in the *Seas and Submerged Lands* case[70] in 1975 that the Commonwealth enjoyed title to the sea and seabed up to the high-water mark, this verdict was overturned by a political accord reached between the Commonwealth and the states several years later, known as the "Offshore Constitutional Settlement" (OCS). Under this arrangement, which was implemented via uniform legislation of the Commonwealth and the states,[71] the Commonwealth returned to the states both title and legislative authority over the waters and seabed within the territorial sea, with the exception of the Great Barrier Reef region.[72] As a result, the states retain the capacity to regulate fishing, resource extraction and marine pollution within these coastal waters unless and until the Commonwealth introduces legislation of its own that overrides relevant state laws pursuant to section 109 of the Constitution. In practice, this has rarely happened.

With respect to marine conservation, the Commonwealth and the states agreed in 1998 to establish the National Representative System of Marine Protected Areas, whereby state and Commonwealth marine protected areas (MPAs) would be created on a coordinated basis across the respective jurisdictions.[73] In 2007 the Commonwealth established its first

---

[69] Hutchens, G. and P. Hannam, "Australian Government Cuts Billions of Dollars from Social Programs", *The Australian Sydney Morning Herald*, 18 December 2013, accessed 19 July 2015 at www.smh.com.au/federal-politics/political-news/australian-government-cuts-billions-of-dollars-from-social-programs-20131217-2zjbn.html.

[70] *New South Wales v Commonwealth* (1975) 135 CLR 337.

[71] The Commonwealth legislation comprises the Coastal Waters (State Title) Act 1980 and the Coastal Waters (State Powers) Act 1980.

[72] The Commonwealth had passed the Great Barrier Reef Marine Park Act 1975 in conjunction with the inclusion of the Great Barrier Reef on the World Heritage Register in order to confront threats by the Queensland government to allow oil drilling within the Reef. It decided to retain these special arrangements for what is arguably Australia's most iconic natural area outside the general scheme of the OSS. There is currently an intense debate concerning new threats to the Great Barrier Reef from coastal port development and shipping associated with extensive coal mine development in inland Queensland: see Bragg, J., "Queensland Litigation to Protect the Great Barrier Reef" (2014) 96 *Impact* 3.

[73] See further, www.environment.gov.au/topics/marine/marine-reserves/overview/background, accessed 19 July 2015.

MPA, covering the South East region, and a management plan for this area was adopted in July 2012. After extensive public consultation, five further Commonwealth marine reserves were proclaimed in November 2012, giving rise to one of the largest MPA systems in the world. However, in December 2013 the Abbott government re-proclaimed these MPAs, with the result that the management plans for these areas were set aside and now must be prepared again. The objective of this manoeuvre appears to be to lessen the level of restrictions on activities within MPAs through the development of substantially revised management plans.[74]

The Commonwealth's marine jurisdiction has been substantially extended by virtue of its possession of a number of territories that are comprised of islands (such as Christmas, Cocos (Keeling), Norfolk, Heard and Macdonald Islands) that are well distant from its continental shores, together with the Australian Antarctic Territory (AAT). This has enabled the Commonwealth to, for example, prohibit whaling activities within Australian waters comprised of its very large Exclusive Economic Zone.[75] In addition, the Commonwealth has legislated for environmental protection of the AAT, relying also in this regard on relevant international treaties.[76] Thus, although the Commonwealth is relatively limited in its role as a landowner and manager, it enjoys considerable authority to directly pursue conservation goals in its external territories and their associated marine waters.

A further difference between Australia and the United States is with respect to the manner in which treaties are ratified and implemented. In Australia, the negotiation, signing and ratification of treaties are executive functions that fall within the executive power defined in section 61 of the Constitution. There is no formal role for the Commonwealth Parliament with respect to these matters, unlike the requirement in Article II, section 2 of the US Constitution that the "advice and consent" of two-thirds of the Senate be obtained before the "making" (in practice,

---

[74] See Cox, L., "Fishing Interests Loom Large in Abbott Government Review of Marine Parks", *The Sydney Morning Herald*, 11 September 2014, accessed 19 July 2015 at www.smh.com.au/federal-politics/political-news/fishing-interests-loom-large-in-abbott-government-review-of-marine-parks-20140911-10fmsy.html.

[75] See Australian Whale Sanctuary Act 1999 (Cth). See also the Japanese whaling case, *Humane Society International Inc. v Kyodo Senpaku Kaisha Ltd* [2006] FCAFC 116.

[76] See Antarctic Treaty (Environment Protection) Act 1980; Antarctic Marine Living Resources Conservation Act 1981; and Antarctic Mining Prohibition Act 1991.

ratification) of a treaty by the President. As a result, there have generally been far fewer delays in Australia in proceeding from the signing of treaties to their ratification than have been experienced in the United States.

However, with the expansive interpretation of the external affairs power by the High Court, coupled with the burgeoning number of treaties being negotiated by the international community, the Commonwealth has felt it necessary to respond to state concerns about possible consequential impacts on state powers and functions by agreeing to consult regularly with them before taking action to implement a treaty. There has been established a Commonwealth–State–Territory Standing Committee on Treaties and state representatives are now regularly included in Australian treaty-negotiation delegations.[77] The Commonwealth has also adopted a practice of tabling treaties for at least 15 sitting days in the Commonwealth Parliament and referring treaties to a Joint Standing Committee on Treaties for advice.[78]

The other difference between the two countries in the context of treaty-making is that Australia does not have any legal concept of "self-executing" treaties such as operate in the United States with respect to those treaties that clearly create rights and obligations capable of enforcement in the courts. Under Australian domestic law, treaties cannot impose obligations or create rights in the absence of implementing legislation, so that in practice it is normal to pass appropriate legislation (where none already exists) before proceeding to ratify a treaty. The adoption by the Commonwealth of a cooperative approach to this matter was formalised in an Intergovernmental Agreement on the Environment adopted in 1992 which provides that the Commonwealth will:

> ... prior to ratifying or acceding to, approving or accepting any international agreement with environmental significance, consult the States in an effort to secure agreement on the manner in which the obligations incurred should be implemented in Australia, consistent with the roles and responsibilities established pursuant to this Agreement.[79]

---

[77] See Australian Government, Department of Foreign Affairs and Trade, Treaty-Making Process, accessed 19 July 2015 at www.dfat.gov.au/treaties/making/#constitution.

[78] Ibid.

[79] Australian Government, Department of the Environment, Intergovernmental Agreement on the Environment 1992, Clause 2.5.2.2.3, available at www.environment.gov.au/about-us/esd/publications/intergovernmental-agreement. This Agreement is discussed further below, Part IV.B.

This has meant that Commonwealth legislation that is designed to implement environment-related treaties has usually been drafted to reflect prior understandings reached with the states concerning its scope and effect.

IV. THE POLITICAL SETTING FOR ENVIRONMENT FEDERALISM

There are relatively few studies devoted specifically to the operation of Australian federalism in the context of environmental law and policy,[80] with the fullest treatment of this topic having been provided by Phillip Toyne in his book, *The Reluctant Nation*, some twenty years ago.[81] Also, despite a substantial interest by Australian legal scholars in US environmental law,[82] there are only a few studies of the respective systems

---

[80] See, for example, Davis, B.W., "Federalism and Environmental Politics: An Australian Overview" (1985) 5 *The Environmentalist* 269; Fowler, R.J., "New National Directions in Environmental Protection and Conservation", in Boer, B., R.J. Fowler and N. Gunningham (eds), *Environmental Outlook: Law and Policy* (Federation Press, Sydney 1994), 113; Fowler, R.J., "Environmental Impact Assessment: What Role for the Commonwealth" (1996) 13 *Environmental and Planning Law Journal* 246; Munchenberg, S., "Review of Commonwealth/State Roles and Responsibilities for the Environment" (1997) 14 *Environmental and Planning Law Journal* 148; Peel, J. and L. Godden, "Australian Environmental Management: A 'Dams' Story" (2005) 28 *University of New South Wales Law Journal* 668; Hollander, R., "Rethinking Overlap and Duplication: Federalism and Environmental Assessment in Australia" (2009) 40 *Publius* 136; and Holley, C., "Ageing Gracefully? Examining the Conditions for Sustaining Successful Collaboration in Environmental Law and Governance" (2009) 26 *Environmental and Planning Law Journal* 457.

[81] Toyne, P., *The Reluctant Nation: Environment, Law and Politics in Australia* (ABC Books, Sydney 1994). See also the Senate Committee Report in 1999, *supra*, n. 53, which recommended that the Commonwealth expand its role with respect to the environment and that its role be recognised in the Australian Constitution (at xiii–xviii).

[82] Some more recent coverage includes Baird, R., "Arresting Climate Change through Incremental Steps: *Massachusetts v Environmental Protection Agency*" (2007) 24 *Environmental and Planning Law Journal* 245; Fisher, D.E., "The Response of the United States Supreme Court to Global Warming: Injury in Fact or Conjecture" (2007) 24 *Environmental and Planning Law Journal* 241; Peel, J. and M. Power, "Climate Change Law: Lessons from the Californian Experience" (2010) 27 *Environmental and Planning Law Journal* 169; and Rackemann, M., "Environmental Dispute Resolution – Lessons from the States" (2013) 30 *Environmental and Planning Law Journal* 329.

from a comparative federalism perspective, and then mostly by US scholars.[83]

To examine how collaborative approaches have dominated environmental federalism in Australia, it is helpful to employ a distinction that has been drawn in this context between the "legal" Constitution, under which the Commonwealth enjoys extensive legislative power over environmental matters, and the "political" Constitution, under which the Commonwealth has relied upon a wide array of collaborative arrangements in developing both law and policy with respect to the environment.[84]

There are three distinct, but related, elements of the politically based cooperative approach to environmental matters that has evolved in Australia. First, there has been a reliance on intergovernmental forums in which cooperative approaches have been regularly negotiated. Second, intergovernmental agreements of a broader nature have been developed through these forums for the purpose of defining the roles and responsibilities of the Commonwealth and the states with respect to environmental matters generally or to address specific aspects of environmental management. Third, a wide range of national strategies and policies have been developed, again through intergovernmental forums, often leading to Commonwealth legislation to give effect to undertakings entered into by the Commonwealth therein. The combined effect of these intergovernmental agreements, strategies and policies has been to define through political processes a more limited role for the Commonwealth regarding environmental matters than is legally available to it, given its substantial constitutional capacity in this context.

---

[83] See Battle, J., "Environmental Law and Co-operative Federalism in the United States" (1985) 2 *Environmental and Planning Law Journal* 302; Murchison, K.M., "Environmental Law in Australia and the United States: A Comparative Overview (Parts 1 and 2)" (1994) 11 *Environmental and Planning Law Journal* 179 and 254. For a comparative study involving Australia and Canada, see Gardner, A., "Federal Intergovernmental Cooperation on Environmental Management: A Comparison of Developments in Australia and Canada" (1995) 11 *Environmental and Planning Law Journal* 104. A detailed comparative study of environmental federalism involving Australia, USA, Canada and the European Union was undertaken by the author in an unpublished report prepared for the Australian Conservation Foundation and Greenpeace Australia (Fowler, R.J., "Proposal for a Federal Environment Protection Agency" (1991) (unpublished manuscript on file with the author).

[84] Crawford, *supra*, n. 44, 11–13.

A. The Council of Australian Governments (COAG) and Ministerial Councils

Extensive use has been made of intergovernmental Councils to negotiate collaborative responses by the Commonwealth and the states to many environmental issues. Since its establishment in 1992, the over-arching body for this "Council system" has been the Council of Australian Governments (COAG), comprised of the Prime Minister, the State Premiers and Territory Chief Ministers, and the President of the Local Government Association of Australia (ALGA).[85] COAG has addressed a wide range of environmental matters, including salinity and water quality, the Murray-Darling Basin, a renewable energy target and national energy efficiency standards, in almost every instance arriving at outcomes that have been reflected in an intergovernmental agreement or a national strategy or policy.

Under the Council system administered by COAG, other specific purpose Ministerial Councils also have operated, including the Standing Committee on Environment and Water (SCEW)) with respect to environmental matters. This Council was established in 2010 and succeeded a line of predecessors[86] dating back well before COAG to the Australian Environment Council, which came into existence in 1972. This long history of using specialist Ministerial Councils to address environmental matters collaboratively across jurisdictions has recently been the subject of a serious reverse. In December 2013, at the first meeting of COAG following the election of the Abbott government, the Commonwealth insisted upon a reorganisation of COAG Ministerial Councils to reduce their number. This resulted in the abolition of SCEW,[87] meaning that, for the first time in 40 years, there is no longer an intergovernmental forum specifically dedicated to the discussion of collaborative national approaches to environmental matters. An informal meeting of Commonwealth and state Environment Ministers was subsequently convened in April 2014, the principle outcome being to give priority to a National Review of Environmental Regulation for the purpose of "identifying

---

[85] The COAG website is located at www.coag.gov.au/ (accessed 19 July 2015).

[86] These were the Australian and New Zealand Environment and Conservation Council (ANZECC), from 1990 to 2001, and the Environment Protection and Heritage Council (EPHC), from 2001 to 2010.

[87] The announcement of the abolition of SCEW may be found on its website, which currently is being maintained for historical purposes: accessed 19 July 2015 at www.scew.gov.au/.

unworkable, contradictory or incompatible regulations and seeking opportunities to harmonize and simplify regulations".[88]

These developments appear to signal a significant departure from the long-standing cooperative federalism approach to environmental matters in favour of a decentralised approach that leaves environmental responsibilities largely in the hands of the states. This impression is reinforced by the statement in the COAG Communiqué of December 2013 that: "The Commonwealth respects the States and Territories (the States) are sovereign in their own sphere. They should be able to get on with delivering on their responsibilities, with appropriate accountability and without unnecessary interference from the Commonwealth".[89]

As was noted above, this resurgence of the notion of state "sovereignty" appears to reflect the coordinate mode of federalism that has been considered redundant since the *Engineers* case in 1920. What this will mean in practice is still difficult to discern, but it bodes ominously for the future of much existing Commonwealth environmental legislation.[90]

B. Intergovernmental Agreements Defining Roles and Responsibilities

The cooperative federalism model has found its fullest expression, at least until recently, through the development of intergovernmental agreements which have defined the respective roles and responsibilities of the Commonwealth and the states concerning environmental matters – both in the general sense, and in relation to particular areas such as environmental impact assessment (EIA). The occasional contemplation from time to time of a more expansive role for the Commonwealth in environmental management has been essentially quashed by these political accords.

Concerns have been raised by commentators about the so-called "democracy deficit" associated with the development of such intergovernmental agreements through COAG and its associated Ministerial Councils, in particular that the process for the development of such agreements has been exclusively managed by senior government officials

---

[88] Agreed Statement – Environment Ministers' Meeting, 29 April 2014, accessed 19 July 2015 at www.environment.gov.au/minister/hunt/2014/mr 20140429.html.
[89] See COAG, Meeting 13 December 2013, accessed 19 July 2015 at www.coag.gov.au/node/516.
[90] This matter is discussed further below, Part V.

and has not allowed for regular involvement in outcomes by either parliaments or the community.[91] It has also been noted that the substantial number of intergovernmental agreements emanating from this mode of federalism are not systematically recorded.[92] These criticisms have strong relevance in the context of environmental policy, where key intergovernmental agreements have been developed without any form of public consultation and not subjected to any discussion or scrutiny within either the Commonwealth or state parliaments. The result has been a substantial reframing of the constitutional capacity of the Commonwealth on environmental matters through political accords reached behind closed doors.

The most comprehensive of these political accords is the Intergovernmental Agreement on the Environment (IGAE),[93] entered into in May 1992, which was supplemented by the Heads of Agreement on Commonwealth and State Roles and Responsibilities for the Environment 1997 (HoA).[94] Both agreements were adopted at meetings of COAG.

The IGAE is particularly significant in that it provided, for the first time, a politically agreed definition of the role and responsibilities of the Commonwealth concerning environmental matters. It was developed primarily by state government officials, who negotiated its terms in private, and was signed on behalf of the Commonwealth by Prime Minister Keating shortly after he had taken up this office and without having had any involvement in its development. It was never the subject of any public consultation.

In defining the role and responsibilities of the Commonwealth, the IGAE referred to the "responsibilities and interests of the Commonwealth in safeguarding and accommodating national environmental matters", which of itself is a reasonably broad test, but then cited as examples of this definition a very limited range of circumstances, as follows: the negotiation of international agreements relating to the environment and ensuring that consequential international obligations are met by Australia; ensuring that states do not allow significant environmental impacts to

---

[91] Saunders, C., "The Constitutional, Legal and Institutional Foundations of Australian Federalism", in Carling, R. (ed.), *Where to for Australian Federalism?* (Centre for Independent Studies, Sydney 2008), p. 1; Kildea, P., "Making room for Democracy in Intergovernmental Relations" in *Tomorrow's Federation: Reforming Australian Government, supra*, n. 18, p. 73.

[92] Saunders, *supra*, n. 91, at 5.

[93] *Supra*, n. 79.

[94] Accessed 19 July 2015 at www.environment.gov.au/resource/heads-agreement-commonwealth-and-state-roles-and-responsibilities-environment.

result in other states or Commonwealth territories or marine waters; and facilitating the cooperative development of national standards and guidelines.[95] Elsewhere, the agreement states that the states have responsibility for "resource assessment, land use decisions and approval processes",[96] thereby reinforcing the restrictive definition of the role of the Commonwealth just referred to.

The IGAE also provided for the creation by uniform legislation of a National Environment Protection Authority (which the states subsequently insisted should be called a "Council", given it was to be comprised of Commonwealth and state environment Ministers) for the purpose of "establishing measures for the protection of the environment".[97] The National Environment Protection Council (NEPC) was established in 1995 through uniform legislation of the Commonwealth and the states[98] and since then has developed a number of national environment protection measures (NEPMs).[99] This has proved to be a relatively limited mechanism for the setting of national environmental standards, particularly when compared with the broad approach adopted in the United States by the federal Environment Protection Agency. A significant difference between Australia and the United States is that Australia has elected to employ a statutory Ministerial Council for this purpose rather than develop a specific federal authority or agency, as occurred in the USA in the early 1970s. Inevitably, this has required extended negotiations across all the jurisdictions involved and resulted in slow progress in the development and amendment from time to time of NEPMs. With the termination of the COAG Standing Committee on Environment and Water (SCEW) in late 2013, it remains to be seen what will be the future of the NEPC.

The 1997 HoA was executed at a time when the Commonwealth was engaged in a rewrite of its EIA legislation that resulted ultimately in the adoption of the Environment Protection and Biodiversity Conservation

---

[95] *Supra*, n. 79, Cl. 2.2.1.
[96] Ibid. at Sch. 2.
[97] Ibid. at Sch. 4.
[98] The relevant Commonwealth legislation is the National Environment Protection Council Act 1994.
[99] See NEPC website for details: www.environment.gov.au/protection/nepc (accessed 19 July 2015). Matters addressed by NEPMs include air toxics; ambient air quality; assessment of site contamination; diesel vehicle emissions; movement of controlled wastes; a National Pollutant Inventory and used packaging. For a critique, see Fowler, R.J., "Law and Policy Aspects of National Standardisation" in Boer, B., R.J. Fowler and N. Gunningham (eds), *Environmental Outlook No. 2: Law and Policy* (Federation Press, Sydney, 1996), p. 318.

Act (the "EPBC Act") in 1999. The HoA was drafted with this development in mind. It provided that Commonwealth involvement in environmental matters should focus on various "matters of national environmental significance" (MNES) identified in Appendix 1, thus reframing and elaborating the concept of "national environmental matters" adopted in the IGAE some years earlier. The MNES list presented in Appendix 1 of the HoA comprised seven items that eventually were provided for in the EPBC Act as the triggers for the operation of its EIA procedures. These were World Heritage Sites; RAMSAR Wetlands of International Importance; places of national significance (as identified on the national heritage list); nationally endangered and vulnerable species and ecological communities; migratory species and cetaceans; nuclear activities; and management and protection of the marine and coastal environment. An additional 23 matters were identified in the second part of Appendix 1 in which it was agreed the Commonwealth has an "interest" but which would not serve as triggers for its EIA process. It was noted that the Commonwealth would not vary or add to this MNES list without consulting the states. Thus was established the foundation for the environmental assessment and approvals provisions in the future EPBC Act.

The HoA also indicated that the Commonwealth and the states would seek to establish bilateral agreements that would provide for Commonwealth accreditation of state EIA processes and, in appropriate cases, state decisions.[100] The EPBC Act subsequently adopted this proposal by including specific provisions concerning the making of both "procedures" and "approvals" bilateral agreements.[101] Whilst procedures bilateral agreements were subsequently entered into by the Commonwealth and the states for the purpose of harmonising their respective EIA processes, the Abbott government recently has taken the extra step of pursuing approvals bilateral agreements with the states through its "One Stop Shop" initiative.[102] This is intended to secure the accreditation of state environmental approval processes, thereby removing the Commonwealth from active involvement in the approval of projects under the EPBC Act, but it is being sternly opposed by a wide range of environmental

---

[100] *Supra*, n. 94, Attachment 2.
[101] EPBC Act, Part 5.
[102] For further details of this initiative, see www.environment.gov.au/topics/about-us/legislation/environment-protection-and-biodiversity-conservation-act-1999/one-stop (accessed 19 July 2015).

organisations that are concerned it will lessen environmental protections under the Act.[103]

There has been no attempt since 1997 to further address the subject of roles and responsibilities with respect to the environment through either the amendment or replacement of these two agreements. However, the election of the Abbott government in late 2013 has given rise to a fresh discussion of this matter at the behest of the Commonwealth. A revision of these established political understandings now appears possible, particularly through the proposed White Paper on federal–state relations. This matters is re-canvassed further below (Section V).

C. Other Types of Intergovernmental Agreements on Environmental Matters

Other intergovernmental agreements have addressed specific aspects of environmental management, rather than broader jurisdictional matters, and often are reflected in, or even appended to, related Commonwealth environmental legislation. The need for transboundary approaches has been met, for example, by agreements concerning the Murray-Darling Basin that date back to 1914, but which in their most recent form have provided the framework for the Commonwealth's Water Act 2007.[104] Another example is provided by the Lake Eyre Basin Intergovernmental Agreement, signed in 2000, which provides for the adoption of policy and strategies concerning water and related natural resources management issues in the Lake Eyre Basin.[105] This Basin, an area of 1.17 million square kilometres in the interior of Australia, comprises 17 per cent of the Australian continent. The Agreement has been ratified by legislation of the Commonwealth and participating states,[106] but it has been observed by the Commonwealth that the Agreement "does not override the statutory responsibilities of the states for natural resources

---

[103] See for example "Places You Love Alliance, Media Backgrounder, Removal of Federal Environmental Approvals", accessed 19 July 2015 at www.placesyoulove.org/wp-content/uploads/2014/06/Media-Backgrounder-EPBC-legislation.pdf. For a critique of the One Stop Shop initiative, see McGrath, C., "One Stop Shop for Environmental Approvals a Messy Backward Step for Australia" (2014) 31 *Environmental and Planning Law Journal* 164 (2014).

[104] For a review of this Act, see Gardner, *supra*, n. 52.

[105] Accessed 19 July at www.environment.gov.au/resource/lake-eyre-basin-intergovernmental-agreement. See also www.lakeeyrebasin.gov.au/collaborative-management (accessed 19 July 2015)

[106] The Commonwealth legislation is the Lake Eyre Basin Intergovernmental Agreement Act 2001.

management and relies to a large degree on the goodwill and commitment of State governments".[107] In this respect, it very much reflects the statement of roles and responsibilities presented in the 1992 IGAE. Given, as noted previously, that there is no official record of the many intergovernmental agreements that have been made, including with respect to environmental matters, it is not possible to provide a complete account of their content and reach here. This is a task that still awaits the attention of environmental federalism scholars in Australia.

D. National Strategies and Policies

Finally, it should be noted that the Commonwealth and the states also have developed an extensive array of national strategies or policies on a wide range of topics, including ecologically sustainable development, Australia's Natural Reserves System, climate change, oceans, forests and the conservation of biological diversity.[108] These instruments are entirely political in nature and have no legal force or effect. It is intended that their implementation will be achieved collaboratively through the operation of state and Commonwealth legislation and/or executive action.

One particular strategy that deserves special mention is the National Strategy for Ecologically Sustainable Development (NSESD), which was adopted by COAG in June 1992.[109] Work on this strategy commenced in 1990 at the direction of the Commonwealth, very much as a response to the 1987 Report of the World Commission on Environment and Development (the "Bruntland Commission").[110] An extensive public consultation process was followed over almost two years, culminating in almost 500 recommendations being proposed. The basic purpose of the Strategy is stated as follows: "... to set out the broad strategic and policy framework under which governments will cooperatively make decisions and take actions to pursue ESD in Australia".[111] The strategy was

---

[107] Australian Government, Department of the Environment, Integrated Water Resource Management in Australia: Case Studies – Lake Eyre Basin Agreement, accessed 19 July 2015 at www.environment.gov.au/node/24405 (viewed 12.1.2015).

[108] For a fuller list, see Bates, *supra*, n. 1, 166.

[109] www.environment.gov.au/about-us/esd/publications/national-esd-strategy-part1 (accessed 19 July 2015).

[110] World Commission on Environment and Development, *Our Common Future* (Oxford University Press, Oxford and New York 1987).

[111] See Australian Government, Department for the Environment, What Does the National Strategy for ESD Contain?, accessed 19 July 2015 at www.environment.gov.au/about-us/esd/publications/national-esd-strategy-part1.

intended to be used to guide policy- and decision-making, particularly in relation to natural resources use and management. In practice, its main impact has been to provide inspiration for the drafting of objects clauses in Commonwealth and state environmental legislation that require consideration of the principles of ESD, including the integration of economic and environmental considerations in decision-making and the precautionary principle.[112] The IGAE, which was adopted by COAG just months prior to the NSESD, has also been influential in this regard by setting out four principles that were designed to guide "the development and implementation of environmental policy and programs by all levels of government", these being the precautionary principle, the principle of intergenerational equity, the conservation of biological diversity and ecological integrity and improved valuation, pricing and incentive mechanisms.[113] Through the combined influence of the NSESD and the IGAE, both the precautionary principle and the principle of intergenerational equity have been embedded to a significant extent in Australian environmental law and are applied from time to time by the courts when reviewing government administrative action.[114] It is altogether another matter whether the NSEDS has met its fundamental goal of achieving "development which aims to meet the needs of Australians today, while conserving our ecosystems for the benefit of future generations".[115] The rate at which biodiversity in Australia continues to decline suggests a substantial failure on this score.[116]

V. THE REVIVAL OF THE CONCEPT OF STATE SOVEREIGNTY

Following its election in September 2013, the Abbott Coalition government moved quickly to pursue its pre-election commitment to boost

---

[112] For a list of over a hundred statutes across the Commonwealth and states that expressly incorporate ESD principles in their objects clauses (i.e. clauses setting out the objects of each statute), see Stein, P., "Are Decision-Makers Too Cautious with the Precautionary Principle?" (2000) 17 *Environmental and Planning Law Journal* **3**, 22–23.

[113] IGAE, *supra*, n. 79, Section 3.

[114] See Peel, J., *The Precautionary Principle in Practice* (The Federation Press, Sydney 2005) for a detailed account of the operation of the precautionary principle in Australian environmental law; also Stein, *supra*, n. 112.

[115] NESDS, *supra*, n. 109, Part 1.

[116] See Ritchie, E.G. et al., "Continental-Scale Governance Failure Will Hasten Loss of Australia's Biodiversity" (2013) 27 *Conservation Biology* 1133.

productivity and reduce regulation, including through reform of the taxation system and Commonwealth–state relations. At its first COAG meeting in December 2013, it secured agreement from the states to work together closely on the preparation of Commonwealth White Papers on Taxation and Reform of the Federation.[117] As noted above, the Communiqué from this meeting included an acknowledgement that: "The Commonwealth respects the States and Territories … are sovereign in their own sphere."[118] It therefore seems possible that the Commonwealth has in contemplation a form of coordinate federalism based on the recognition of state sovereignty in relation to particular matters within the state "sphere".

This impression is reinforced by the Terms of Reference that were issued for the White Paper on Reform of the Federation in June 2014, which state that the objective of the White Paper is to "clarify roles and responsibilities to ensure, as far as possible, that States and Territories are sovereign in their own sphere".[119] The Terms of Reference also provide that the White Paper will explore how to achieve "agreement between State and Commonwealth governments about their distinct and mutually exclusive responsibilities and subsequent funding sources for associated programs".[120] They also indicate that the principal areas of interest in this context will be health, education, housing and homelessness, but proceed to include a list of additional areas to be addressed "to a lesser degree", including the environment.[121]

In 2009, while serving in the Opposition, Tony Abbott described himself as a "pragmatic nationalist" committed to securing greater Commonwealth authority over the states.[122] However, now that he is in office as Prime Minister, it appears that this commitment is matched by a desire to limit Commonwealth activities to a narrower range of matters and to hand over responsibility to the states for certain areas in which the Commonwealth has previously engaged. There are strong indications that the Commonwealth government considers that the so-called "sphere" of state sovereignty extends to the environment, for example in the avid pursuit of its "one stop shop" initiative noted above, which involves the

---

[117] www.coag.gov.au/node/516 (accessed 19 July 2015).
[118] Ibid.
[119] www.pm.gov.au/media/2014-06-28/white-paper-reform-federation (accessed 19 July 2015).
[120] Ibid.
[121] Ibid.
[122] See for example Abbott, T., *Battlelines* (Melbourne University Press, Melbourne 2009).

handing over to the states of its environmental assessment and approval functions under the EPBC Act.

In reality, it is most unlikely that such a radical reform of Australian federalism will be achievable, particularly insofar as it involves the revival of a coordinate mode of federalism that was rendered obsolete almost a century ago by the *Engineers* case. In a speech delivered on 24 October 2014, the Prime Minister offered a substantially revised version of his reform agenda that appears to reflect recognition of these realities.[123] Whilst declaring that he remains a "pragmatic nationalist", he indicated that "rather than pursue giving the Commonwealth more authority over the states, as I proposed in my 2009 book, *Battlelines* – [I think] better harmonising revenue and spending responsibilities is well worth another try".[124] In terms of making each government "sovereign in its own sphere", he indicated that this is meant to refer to "resolving the mismatch between what the states are supposed to deliver and what they can actually afford to pay for".[125] Finally, he indicated that the Commonwealth will pursue only changes that the states are willing to consider, on the basis that "reform of the federation has to be owned by the states as well as by the Commonwealth".[126] These statements suggest a less radical reform agenda, but the nature and extent of any federalism reforms, and their impact upon environmental federalism, will not become apparent until the publication by the Commonwealth of its White Paper, due at the end of 2015.

VI. CONCLUSIONS

Overwhelmingly, the mode of federalism that has been adopted in relation to environmental management in Australia over the past forty-plus years has been, until most recently, cooperative or collaborative in nature. This has been so to such an extent that this approach has been criticised for its failure to deliver adequate and effective protection of the environment due to its tendency to generate lowest common denominator outcomes.[127] The agenda of the current Commonwealth government to reduce its involvement in environmental matters, in deference to state

---

[123] For the full text of this speech, see australianpolitics.com/2014/10/25/abbott-henry-parkes-tenterfield-speech.html (accessed 19 July 2015).
[124] Ibid.
[125] Ibid.
[126] Ibid.
[127] See generally Toyne, *supra*, n. 81; also, Fowler, *supra*, nn 83 and 99.

"sovereignty", appears to mark a significant departure from the general attitude of previous Commonwealth governments over the past four decades, even allowing for the ebbs and flows in philosophy that have been evident from time to time concerning the appropriate level of engagement by the Commonwealth. This latest development appears to signal a substantial disengagement by the current Commonwealth government from environmental matters, rather than merely an adjustment to its level of engagement.

There is a pressing need to pursue in Australia a more mature and sophisticated conversation about the case for strong and clear leadership by the Commonwealth on environmental matters, particularly one which moves beyond the current political rhetoric concerning state sovereignty and excessive "green tape". As has been noted recently by a group of prominent Australian scientists, the serious threats to biodiversity in Australia are essentially a consequence of the "failure of government".[128]

In summary, the current situation in Australia is that the desire of the current Commonwealth government to disengage with the environment is being exacerbated by state indifference to environmental concerns and a preoccupation with income generation from resources development. Given the environmental challenges that are facing Australia, this situation calls for different political leadership and radically revised approaches. In this regard, it is pertinent that the most recent Constitutional Values Survey, published in October 2014, has indicated that there is a very strong public expectation of, and preference for, Commonwealth leadership on environmental matters.[129] This reinforces the suggestion that it is time for a serious reappraisal of the respective roles and responsibilities of the Commonwealth and the states with respect to environmental matters, with the aim of defining a stronger leadership role for the Commonwealth.

However, the means by which such a reappraisal might be triggered are difficult to envisage in the current political climate. It is most unlikely that an amendment of the Constitution to vest legislative power with respect to the environment in the Commonwealth would be pursued or be likely to succeed at any time in the near future, given the contention it would generate and past referendum failures. But the decision by the Abbott government to produce a White Paper on federal–state relationships by the end of 2015 provides a convenient opportunity for the

---

[128] Ritchie, *supra*, n. 114.
[129] Griffith University/Newspoll, Australian Constitutional Values Survey 2014, accessed 19 July 2015 at www.griffith.edu.au/__data/assets/pdf_file/0015/653100/Constitutional-Values-Survey-Oct-2014Results-2.pdf.

suggested conversation to be held and, in particular, for an alternative view to that held by the current Commonwealth government to be advanced.

The assumption of a stronger leadership role by the Commonwealth on environmental matters would not require the abandonment of the cooperative federalism model, but would involve a greater effort by the Commonwealth to establish processes, plans and standards (with appropriate levels of associated resources) that would complement and enhance the performance of regulatory functions at the state level. It should also involve an examination of new types of collaborative mechanisms that might replace or supplement those that have been examined in this chapter. In this regard, there is a compelling case for undertaking comparative studies of how environmental federalism operates in other countries with federal constitutional systems similar to that which exists in Australia.

POSTSCRIPT

On 14 September 2015, the Liberal Party replaced the Honourable Tony Abbott PM as its leader, appointing the Honourable Malcolm Turnbull in his place. Mr Turnbull was duly sworn in as the new Prime Minister of Australia on 15 September 2015. It is not yet clear whether he will pursue all of the policies of his predecessor outlined in this chapter but there is some expectation that he will adopt a less strident approach in a number of contexts. This would likely involve a return to the longstanding forms of cooperative environmental federalism described in this chapter.

13. German environmental federalism in the multilevel system of the European Union

Nathalie Behnke and Annegret Eppler

I. INTRODUCTION

Germany is a typical case of intrastate federalism:[1] policy-making is marked by intense interdependencies, usually described as joint decision-making,[2] aimed at securing comparable living conditions throughout the territory.[3] Competences are divided vertically between the federal and the Länder levels. While legislation involves a high number of veto players and often several stages of ratification in parliaments at different levels of government, implementation typically involves cooperation and negotiation with non-state actors (industries, pressure groups). This general description is true all the more for the field of environmental politics. Here, not only different levels of government, but also different policy sectors and environmental media as well as groups of actors need to be coordinated. The Europeanization of environmental policy-making adds a further layer of complexity, as actors have to coordinate across four levels of government. It is thus a major task for national actors to manage the interdependency resulting from the joint use of instruments of governance of different levels of government.[4] On the one hand, under those conditions it seems almost impossible to enact and implement a

---

[1] Broschek, Jörg, 'Federalism and Political Change. Canada and Germany in Historical-Institutionalist Perspective' (2010) 43 *Canadian Journal of Political Science* 4.
[2] Scharpf, Fritz W. 'The Joint-Decision Trap: Lessons from German Federalism and European Integration' (1988) 66 *Public Administration* 239–278.
[3] Abromeit, Heidrun, *Der verkappte Einheitsstaat* (Leske+Budrich, Opladen 1992).
[4] Pehle, Heinrich and Roland Sturm, 'Die Europäisierung der Regierungssysteme' in *Die EU-Staaten im Vergleich* (Springer, 2008), 156.

coherent policy. This impression is mirrored by the fact that the aim of drafting and legislating an encompassing environmental protection statute has still not been accomplished in Germany. On the other hand, given that environmental policy is 'the' paradigmatic case of a policy field involving externalities, it is a sheer necessity to involve a great number of actors as early as possible in order to become aware of and to adequately address external effects, to balance benefits and burdens and to secure compliance of addressees of regulations. Indeed, empirical analyses of the German policy process show that substantial policy output is produced in spite of the institutional checks and balances.[5] In this contribution, we thus argue that, on the one hand, the multilevel distribution of competences and the number of actors involved in environmental policy-making create considerable obstacles to smooth implementation of environmental policies; on the other hand, the complexity of the institutional structure creates multiple access points for interested actors, thus securing a high level of input legitimacy,[6] and the high autonomy of the Länder in execution and implementation secures a high level of output legitimacy.

The chapter is structured as follows: we first outline the structure of German intrastate federalism with its distribution of competences between the levels of government and its embedding in the bigger EU system in general (section II). We then describe the legislative and executive competences (and their recent developments) for environmental policy specifically (section III). The actual process of environmental policy-making along the policy cycle is explained in section IV, analysing in greater detail the role of different actors involved and the way in which they interact, thus enabling policy coordination. Based on this analysis, we conclude with a brief and balanced account on the merits and pitfalls of the organization of environmental policy in the federal system of Germany (section V).

---

[5] Behnke, Nathalie and Arthur Benz, 'The Politics of Constitutional Change between Reform and Evolution' (2009) 39 *Publius* 213; Hegele, Yvonne and Nathalie Behnke, 'Die Landesministerkonferenzen und der Bund – Kooperativer Föderalismus im Schatten der Politikverflechtung' (2013) 54 *Politische Vierteljahresscharift* 21.

[6] Scharpf, Fritz W., 'Legitimationskonzepte jenseits des Nationalstaats', MPIfG Working Paper.

II. THE STRUCTURE OF EXECUTIVE FEDERALISM IN GERMANY

In German federalism, we distinguish four levels of government: the federal and the subnational (Länder) levels are endowed with full sovereign powers and divide competences in a classic federal manner. The communal level holds extensive rights of self-government, but is constitutionally part of the Länder, fulfilling executive tasks in direct relation to the citizens. The EU level has increasingly gained influence on German policy-making. In a series of constitutional treaties, the member state governments transferred legislative competencies to the EU level in a number of policy areas. Environmental policy-making thus involves all levels of government in different roles.

The distribution of competences between levels of government follows primarily a functional, not a sectoral logic. That is, legislation is primarily a federal function with strong rights of co-decision of Länder governments, while the executive function is the Länder's stronghold. Step by step, a supranational political system developed at the European level. It gained influence on legislation, causing the emergence of new coordination patterns of all levels and actors involved. As an overall picture, we thus see that environmental policies in the 16 Länder are based on the same legal requirements, with several differences in implementation.

According to the letter of the constitution, the Länder hold the residual (primary) legislative competence,[7] while the competences of the federal level are secondary and derived from the Länder. Consequently, matters of federal legislative competences are listed specifically in the constitution. Transfer of legislative competences to the federal level requires a change to the German constitution (Basic Law) for which the approval of a two-thirds majority in the first chamber (Bundestag) as well as in the second chamber (Bundesrat, composed of the executives of the Länder) is necessary. The Basic Law distinguishes exclusive[8] and concurrent legislative powers of the federal level.[9] Any matter not listed in Articles 73 and 74 of the Basic Law falls automatically in the jurisdiction of the Länder. In matters of concurrent legislation, the Länder have the right to

---

[7] Grundgesetz für die Bundesrepublik Deutschland [Grundgesetz] [GG] [Basic Law], 23 May 1949, I, Arts 30 and 70ff (Ger.).

[8] Grundgesetz für die Bundesrepublik Deutschland [Grundgesetz] [GG] [Basic Law], 23 May 1949, I, Arts 71 and 73 (Ger.).

[9] Grundgesetz für die Bundesrepublik Deutschland [Grundgesetz] [GG] [Basic Law], 23 May 1949, I, Arts 72 and 74 (Ger.).

legislate as long as the federal level does not claim this right for reasons of uniform regulation and standards across the territory. Concurrent legislation is thus a typical instance of the German tradition of 'unitary' federalism, where uniform living standards and implementation regulations formed the normative core of federalism policies. The same logic of competence distribution applies to the relationship between Germany and the EU. The residual competence lies with Germany, while the EU level has the right to attract matters only if they are listed in the body of the European treaties. To establish new EU competences, in most cases the unanimous vote of all Member States to change the treaties is necessary. Once the legislative competences in a policy field are allocated at the higher level, decisions of the latter are binding: federal law overrides the law of the Länder, and European primary as well as secondary law is binding on every national law (that is federal and Länder law). In practice, however, the federal level holds the overwhelming part of legislative competences (with a steadily increasing proportion moving further 'upwards' to the EU level), leaving only a restricted number of issues to the Länder, whose primary competence is not legislation but the execution of laws.[10] In executing European, federal and Länder laws, the Länder governments have leeway of interpretation and implementation. In environmental legislation, most legislative competences have been transferred to the EU level. The other levels need to coordinate their actions in development, ratification and implementation of environmental policy.

The more or less voluntary relinquishment of autonomous legislative competences to the federal level via concurrent legislation and further to the European level is compensated by extensive 'shared rule': the Länder executives send representatives to the second chamber, the Bundesrat, where they have rights of co-decision in all federal legislative matters. The Basic Law distinguishes between bills requiring the consent of the Bundesrat and those not requiring it.[11] Bills require the consent of the Bundesrat if they change the constitution, if they have an impact on Länder's finances or if they interfere with executive competencies of the

---

[10] Grundgesetz für die Bundesrepublik Deutschland [Grundgesetz] [GG] [Basic Law], 23 May 1949, I, Arts 30 and 83 (Ger.).

[11] Matters requiring the consent of the second chamber according to Art. 77 Basic Law are about 25–30 per cent of all legislative matters: Burkhart, Simone and Philip Manow, 'Was bringt die Föderalismusreform?' (MPIfG Working Paper 6 June 2006); Harald, Georgii and Sarab Borhanian, 'Zustimmungsgesetze nach der Föderalismusreform' (Wissenschaftliche Dienste des Deutschen Bundestages 2006).

Länder. Consent of the Bundesrat is reached with an absolute majority (50 per cent) of votes or more. If bills do not require Bundesrat consent, they can nonetheless be vetoed by a Bundesrat majority which must be overridden by a Bundestag majority. This structural principle of shared rule is again mirrored at the EU level: the governments of EU Member States constitute the Council; the Council is, so to say, the first legislative chamber of the EU: it has more legislative competences than the European Parliament. On the one hand, the *parliaments* of the lower levels (Länder, federal level) lose legislative competences to the higher levels (federal, EU). On the other hand, the *executives* of the lower levels are compensated for the loss of parliamentary self-rule by increased shared rule, that is by the possibility to influence legislative decision-making at the higher levels (Bundesrat, Council). While a certain balance of power is retained between levels of government even after vertical transfers of competences, in the horizontal dimension within one level the parliaments lose and the executives win. This is why parliaments are seen as the losers not only of executive federalism but also of European integration.

Formal competences of legislation and execution are, however, only one part of the story. Actors from both levels of government meet not only in parliament, but in manifold committees and bodies of horizontal and vertical coordination.[12] Those bodies are in part obligatory; in part they are voluntary, such as the conferences of the ministers of the Länder with their various working groups and subcommittees. The dense network of joint decision-making provides continued coordination and thus secures a smooth working of executives in everyday tasks between the levels of government, even if it is often said to block major reforms and to hinder effective governance.

III. CHARACTERISTICS OF GERMAN ENVIRONMENTAL POLICY-MAKING UNDER EU INFLUENCE

Environmental policies and politics expose four specific features in the multilevel power distribution of German federalism which impact strongly on the policy process. These are, first, the fragmentation of the policy field among environmental media which led to the creation of a

---

[12] Kropp, Sabine, *Kooperativer Föderalismus und Politikverflechtung* (VS-Verlag, Wiesbaden 2009).

deeply fragmented body of laws and regulations (which stands contrary to the cross-media approach of the EU); second, and tightly intertwined with the first, a shift over time in legislative competences for specific media from the Länder to the federal level and later to the EU; third, a traditional focus on standards and detailed regulatory instruments which is at odds with the focus on quality standards and impact assessment the EU has been following since the 1990s; and fourth, a complicated structure of legislative competences split between the EU, the federal and the Länder level which provides a major obstacle to fast ratification and uniform implementation of environmental legislation. All those features are rooted in German history, depend strongly upon one another, and developed in a path-dependent manner over the years, so that even today the stickiness of inherited institutions and patterns of behaviour hinders the establishment of more effective procedures.

1. Fragmentation of the Policy Field and Shift of Competences

The policy field of environmental protection evolved comparatively early in Germany. First environmental laws date back to the late 1960s, and in 1970 Bavaria was the first Land to establish an environmental ministry with all other Länder following suit in the next few years. The conference of environmental ministers of the Länder was established in 1973, the federal agency for the environment (Umweltbundesamt – UBA) in 1974, and the federal ministry of the environment in 1986.[13] Traditionally, jurisdiction for environmental legislation was at the Länder level. Indeed, the Länder took the lead and gave the issue a high priority. In those early years institutions as well as policy solutions emerged at the Länder level in response to specific problems, leading to a fragmented structure among the 'objects' of regulation which persists until today. Different laws and regulations exist, for example for nature protection, soil protection, prevention of air pollution, water protection, emission policy and so on, involving overlapping yet distinct communities of actors. The fragmented approach among policy objects went hand in hand with a preference for regulatory instruments such as obligations and prohibitions, licensing procedures and setting limit values. Those detailed regulations were fitted neatly to single objects of regulation.

Those Länder, however, which implemented environmental legislation feared that a successful environmental protection within their own

---

[13] Eppler, Annegret, 'Deutsche Umweltpolitik im europäischen Mehrebenensystem' in Wolfgang Renzsch, et al. (eds), *Föderalismus in Deutschland* (Oldenbourg, München 2009), 323ff.

borders would jeopardize their economic competitiveness compared to other Länder. Hence they pushed for the adoption of their progressive policies at the federal level and for uniform regulation.[14] Step by step, competences for environmental legislation were transferred to the federal level alongside environmental media, thus perpetuating the sectorial division of their environmental law to the federal level as well. This shift of competences from the Länder to the federal level, on the other hand, enlarged Länder influence on federal legislation in the Bundesrat.

Also, the EU increasingly gained competences to rule environmental policy.[15] Beginning in the 1970s, the EU began to legislate in all areas of environmental policy in order to create favourable conditions for the evolution of the internal market on the basis of the blanket clause for law harmonization. The cross-border nature of many environmental problems, as well as the prevalent perception in the 1970s and 80s that national economies might suffer from a strict environmental policy at national level, prepared the ground for Member States' willingness to transfer more legislative competences to the EU. In 1987, with the Single European Act,[16] a particular environmental chapter was added to the European treaties, thus acknowledging explicitly the necessity of establishing uniform high levels of environmental protection throughout the EU.[17] Nevertheless, beside specific environmental EU programmes, most environmental law is still based on the harmonization clause. The German federal government has a voice concerning EU environmental policy in the Council. Nevertheless, with the introduction of qualified majority voting in environmental policy[18] since the Treaty of Maastricht,[19] the introduction of Co-Decision with the European Parliament,[20] and the enlargement of the EU to 28 Member States, this voice became

---

[14] Müller Brandeck-Bouquet, Gisela, *Die institutionelle Dimension der Umweltpolitik. Eine vergleichende Untersuchung zu Frankreich, Deutschland und der Europäischen Union* (Nomos, Baden-Baden 1996).

[15] Treaty on European Union (TEU) consolidated version, 26 October 2012, Art. 194ff., see also Knill, Christoph, *Europäische Umweltpolitik. Steuerungsprobleme und Regulierungsmuster im Mehrebenensystem* (VS Verlag für Sozialwissenschaften Zweite Auflage 2008).

[16] Single European Act, 29 June 1987.

[17] Treaty on European Union (TEU), consolidated version, 26 October 2012, Art. 194ff.

[18] Treaty on European Union (TEU), consolidated version, 26 October 2012, Art. 16 Abs. 4.

[19] Treaty on European Union, Maastricht Treaty, 1 November 1993.

[20] Treaty on European Union (TEU), consolidated version, 26 October 2012, Art. 224.

less and less powerful. The Länder can advise and influence the position of the federal government in European negotiations in the Council by formulating opinions.[21]

The sectorally fragmented structure of German environmental regulation caused problems not only in advocating German style environmental policy-making at EU level, but also in the implementation of European environmental policy in Germany, as the EU gradually developed a more coherent approach of regulation.[22] Thus, in terms of policy drafting, German policy interests at EU level became increasingly outdated and it became increasingly difficult to broker majorities to enforce those interests. And in terms of implementation, one single law or directive issued by the EU needs to be transposed into a multiplicity of objective-related laws at the federal and Länder levels, thus causing implementation delays which more than once have led to reprimands from Brussels.

2. Policy Instruments

Since the 1990s, the types of policy instruments used in environmental policy have multiplied. While initially hard instruments prevailed (for example regulatory policies, laws, regulations, fixed term limits), governance of new environmental topics such as an ecology tax or regenerative energies has relied increasingly on soft cooperative instruments such as financial and structural incentives, dialogue strategies, networking and active participation of environmental and trade associations in policy-making as well as on economic control instruments.[23] As the effect of individual instruments and measures is limited, integrated strategic approaches such as context management, goal orientation and complex governance tools are used for improved performance.

---

[21] Grundgesetz für die Bundesrepublik Deutschland [Grundgesetz] [GG] [Basic Law], 23 May 1949, I, Arts 23 and 72ff. (Ger.), Treaty on European Union (TEU), consolidated version, 26 October 2012, Art. 254ff.

[22] Holzinger, Katharina, 'Environmental Policy in the Joint-Decision Traps: The Critical Balance between "Market Making" and "Market Correcting"', in Falkner, Gerda (Ed.) *The EU's Decision Traps: Comparing Policies* (Oxford University Press, Oxford 2011), 112.

[23] Böcher, Michael and Annette Elisabeth Töller, *Umweltpolitik in Deutschland. Eine politikfeldanalytische Einführung* (VS Verlag für Sozialwissenschaften 2012).

The European Union's environmental policy is focused on fixed goals and procedures. Quantitative objectives regarding the effects of environmental policies, coupled with temporal deadlines, leave the actors free to choose their means of action. With stakeholders' consensus concerning the aim, the importance of the instruments decreases. Moreover, in setting targets the EU is not concentrating on one specific environmental medium or single instrument; rather, EU environmental policy is following a cross-media and instruments approach, because both instruments and media are seen as interrelated in many ways. Typically, multiple policy areas and actors need to be involved in environmental problem-solving. Thus in Germany the traditional 'environmental management approach', with its legislation segmented among policy media, is fundamentally incompatible with European environmental governance.

3. Legislative Competences

Today, the EU issues most environmental legislation. European directives need to be transposed into national law to come into effect.[24] The Member States can be reprimanded by the European Court of Justice (CJEU) for implementation delays, as EU law is superior to national law. Within the German multilevel system, the responsibility of one level to implement EU law in a timely manner depends on its legislative competences for specific policies. Most environmental laws have federal jurisdiction under concurrent legislative competence, while the Länder issue implementation laws ('Ausführungsgesetze') or administrative instructions ('Verwaltungsvorschriften') to specify federal legislation. Indeed, this distribution of environmental legislative competences (fragmented among objects) tended to collide with European requirements, because decentralized ratification often caused implementation delays, thus causing reprimands from the CJEU. As a consequence of this misfit, a major institutional reform of legislative competences in 2006 was enacted to secure a faster and more straightforward ratification and implementation of European directives and to avoid further reprimands.[25]

Before 2006 national legislative competences for many environmental media had been listed as matters of framework legislation. On matters of

---

[24] Treaty on European Union (TEU), consolidated version, 26 October 2012, Arts 288, 294.

[25] Eppler, Annegret, 'Föderalismusreform I im Politikfeld Umweltpolitik als Europäisierungsschritt' in von Blumenthal, Julia and Stephan Bröchler (eds) *Föderalismusreform in Deutschland. Bilanz und Perspektiven im internationalen Vergleich* (Springer VS, Wiesbaden 2010).

framework legislation, the federal level was entitled to pass legislation on general guidelines which provided a framework for legislation at Länder level. If EU directives were issued in matters falling under those areas of framework legislation, then all 16 Länder and their parliaments had to individually implement the EU directives after the federal level had implemented a framework law. Obviously, the necessity to get through 17 legislative processes caused great delays in implementation. This was all the more so when EU directives concerned more than one environmental medium, since it then had to be split into different laws with some parts of the directive (those concerning concurrent legislation) being implemented through federal law and some (concerning framework legislation) through federal and Länder legislation.

In the course of a major federalism reform in 2006, legislative competences were reorganized and the framework legislation abolished with the aim of making the process of legislation in Germany more efficient. While before the reform, some environmental matters had been in the concurrent and some in the framework legislation, after the reform all environmental matters falling formerly under framework legislation were then allocated to concurrent legislation. As a compensation for this empowerment of the federal level, the Länder were given the right to deviate from federal legislation under certain circumstances and to varying degrees,[26] thus enabling asymmetric arrangements. The effect is a simplification of the implementation process of EU law: now, the federal level can transpose all environmental European law into binding national legislation, thus avoiding the violation of European deadlines caused by ratification in 16 Länder parliaments. The Länder can later modify the regulations in their own legislation, while obviously they cannot depart from the content of the original European regulation. It is not yet clear how extensively deviation rights are being used in practice. But the insertion of the clause into the constitution is an absolute novelty in the normative backbone of German federalism and marks a clear break with the German tradition of 'unitary' federalism towards a specific model of a more asymmetric ruling.

After the abolition of framework legislation, the next step – in order to minimize misfits between EU and national environmental policy – should be the abolition of the traditional fragmentation of environmental legislation among environmental media. A major project of several successive governments was the drafting and passage of a new and encompassing

---

[26] Grundgesetz für die Bundesrepublik Deutschland [Grundgesetz] [GG] [Basic Law], 23 May 1949, I, Art. 72, s. 3 (Ger.).

environmental statute updating and unifying the diverse sectoral laws, for example to issue uniform guidelines for different environmental media. In terms of policy instruments, the recent change of focus as described above aims at enabling an integrated management approach in Germany which, however, collides with the still persistent fragmented regulatory structure among policy objects. In the 1990s, a draft federal environmental Act had been prepared by the federal government without ever reaching parliamentary debate. After 1998, the newly elected red–green coalition abandoned this draft, presumably because they were aiming at more far-reaching legislation.[27] To date, political constellations in the Bundestag and the Bundesrat have never allowed the passage of a unified environmental law. Instead, the German tradition of slicing environmental protection according to its 'objects' persists, and different aspects of what was meant to be the new environmental statute were inserted in other laws. The most encompassing new statute was the Nature Protection and Landscape Conservation Act of 2010. The new law was subject to concurrent legislation with deviation rights for the Länder.[28] As it superseded existing Länder legislation, it needed to be complemented by new Länder laws implementing and substantiating several provisions of the federal law and – where they wished to – deviating from them. Three years after the federal statute entered into force, 11 of the 16 German Länder have passed new laws, all of them deviating from the federal law in varying degrees. This complicates the practical application of the law, because the federal law first needs to be consulted and then the respective Länder law needs to be checked for specifications or deviations. While the deviation rights may be useful in adapting general regulations to regional needs, it becomes obvious that a uniform application of environmental regulations will not be attained in Germany in the near future.

To catch the whole picture, and not only formal competences of legislation and implementation, it must be borne in mind that – just because the field of environmental policy is so diversified among its objects – the actor constellation varies according to the object at stake. Typically, environmental policy-making is achieved through negotiations in networks. Networks are generally conceived as a governance mode contrasting hierarchic decision-making. In practice, negotiations are

---

[27] Eppler, Föderalismusreform I im Politikfeld Umweltpolitik als Europäisierungsschritt, *supra*, n. 25, at 207–209.

[28] Grundgesetz für die Bundesrepublik Deutschland [Grundgesetz] [GG] [Basic Law], 23 May 1949, I, Art. 72 s. 2 cl. 3 (Ger.).

conducted under the 'shadow of hierarchy',[29] in other words, although state actors negotiate with business companies, both negotiating partners are aware of the possibility that the state might always take hierarchical and regulatory action. In several sub-areas, networks of actors are dense, as for example in energy policy, where state and non-state actors had been stuck together for years in series of negotiation rounds, struggling to find solutions to the exit from nuclear energy. In sub-areas strongly influenced by the EU, in contrast, more open networks prevail, because the EU promotes a process-oriented environmental policy and involvement of the public as an external control.

IV. ACTORS AND PROCESSES IN ENVIRONMENTAL POLICY-MAKING

Since the late 1960s or early 1970s, the number of political institutions concerned with environmental policy has expanded at all levels of government, but also non-state actors have become increasingly involved (environmental organizations, business associations and companies, also pro-environmental companies and 'green economy', media, academia, civil society, etc.). In the course of Europeanization, the complexity of actors, processes, and interdependencies increased further. In the following we outline the formal position and effective role of the most important actors, exemplifying the process of environmental policy-making in an ideal type policy cycle.

1. Agenda-Setting

The EU is the main legislator in environmental policy. Therefore, the policy cycle for German environmental policy starts in Brussels. It is highly important for German policy-makers to influence EU environmental policy early on, before a law comes into force, because any law issuing from the European level – not just the primary contract work, but also secondary legislation such as directives and regulations – is in the hierarchy of norms prior to the national legal systems and must necessarily be implemented in the German multilevel system.

---

[29] Benz, Arthur et al., *Horizontale Politikverflechtung* (Campus, Frankfurt 1992).

Almost all legislation at EU level is initiated by the European Commission. Environmental legislation is initiated by the Directorate-General for the Environment[30] ('DG Environment'), which was founded in 1981, even before the competence for environmental legislation was laid down formally in the Single European Act in 1987.[31] The DG Environment has mainly shaped the style and mix of instruments in EU environmental policy over the last decades. Today, as outlined above, the model of process orientation prevails, setting broader target agreements or procedural rules (for example of admission or impact assessment), which are however not specific to individual environmental media but are to be applied generally. The early stage of legislation drafting in the DG Environment is thus a crucial time for inserting national interests in the process. The German federal government uses different access points to make its voice heard in the DG and to state its position: the permanent representation of Germany at the EU in Brussels keeps close contact with the administrative staff of the DG. Experts of the German federal government are working both in Berlin and Brussels to shape future EU environmental laws and give information and political opinions to the permanent representation as well as directly to the experts in the DG.[32]

German Länder governments are active, too, in influencing the European environmental policy agenda. All German Länder governments maintain offices in Brussels independently of the federal permanent representation. The offices of the bigger Länder, like Baden-Wuerttemberg, Bavaria or Saxonia, host experts of each Land ministry, thus mirroring the departmental and organizational structure of the Länder governments directly in Brussels. Like the federal permanent representation, the Länder offices and their environmental experts keep contact with DG bureaucrats and do individual lobbying.[33] Furthermore, they act collectively, coordinating their positions in bodies of horizontal coordination, for example via the Länder Conference of Environment

---

[30] ec.europa.eu/dgs/environment/index_en.htm (accessed 19 July 2015). In the new Commission (2014–2019), Karmenu Vella from Malta is Commissioner for Environment, Maritime Affairs and Fisheries.

[31] Single European Act, 29 June 1987.

[32] Grünhage, Jan, *Entscheidungsprozesse in der Europapolitik Deutschlands. Von Konrad Adenauer bis Gerhard Schröder* (Nomos, Baden-Baden 2007); Laffan, Brigid, 'Core Executives', in Graziano, Paolo and Maarten P. Vink (eds), *Europeanization. Research Agendas* (Palgrave Macmillan, Basingstoke 2007).

[33] Große Hüttmann, Martin and Annegret Eppler, 'Die Europapolitik Baden-Württembergs im Dreieck Stuttgart-Berlin-Brüssel', in Frech, Siegfried et al. (eds) *Handbuch Europapolitik* (Kohlhammer, Stuttgart 2009).

Ministers ('UMK'), as well as in horizontal working groups in Brussels. The UMK gives advice to the federal and Länder governments as well as at the European level. It serves as an interface between technical and administrative issues and political discourse, laying programmatic groundwork with a specific view to Länder interests and concerns for later implementation. Decisions of the UMK are taken unanimously. In the case of no agreement, discussions served at least to clarify the positions of individual Länder. At this early stage, the Länder and the federal level thus act as separate players, sometimes pursuing different interests, having their own networks with other Member States and subnational regions, as well as with non-state actors who pursuit their own agenda.

To counter executive dominance of both the federal and the Länder governments, the parliaments became increasingly active at the EU level. Since 2007 the German Bundestag as well as the Bundesrat and three German Länder parliaments (Baden-Wuerttemberg, Bavaria and Hesse) have opened their own offices in Brussels, not only to influence policy-making from the earliest stage, but also to observe what 'their' governments are doing in Brussels. Thus they fulfil the parliamentary control function towards both the EU level (via subsidiarity control) and their 'own' government.

When the Commission has concluded its decision-making process, it sends a legislative draft to the Council, the European Parliament and to all chambers of national parliaments. According to the Lisbon Treaty, all chambers of national parliaments have the right to give a reasoned opinion on subsidiarity and proportionality issues of all legislative initiatives of the European Commission within eight weeks.[34] The decision-making process of the EU organs continues only after this eight-week period. The German Bundestag as well as the Bundesrat therefore check all environmental initiatives at this early stage between the setting of the agenda and the decision-making at European level. In order to manage this task within the limited time frame, the Bundestag established not only a Committee for European Affairs, but also a specific administrative unit, staffed it with experts, extended the budget for EU affairs, and changed its internal rules of procedure.[35] The EU

---

[34] Raunio, Tapio, 'The Gatekeepers of European Integration? The Functions of National Parliaments in the EU Political System' (2011) 33 *Journal of European Integration* 303.

[35] Vollrath, Sven, 'Herausforderungen bei der Umsetzung der neuen Rechte nach dem Vertrag von Lissabon durch den Deutschen Bundestag und die Begleitgesetzgebung', in Abels, Gabi and Annegret Eppler (eds), *Auf dem Weg*

policy experts work closely with the expert committee for the environment that is responsible for subsidiarity control in the environmental field.

The Bundesrat, as the second parliamentary chamber, gives the executives of the Länder a say in all legal decisions at the federal level, in the negotiations of the federal government in EU affairs as well as in European subsidiarity control. At the agenda-setting stage, the Bundesrat Committee of European Affairs, as well as the Committee for the Environment, are involved in the control of European initiatives. In Bundesrat decisions, party political and Länder interests typically intersect, leaving room for flexible coalition-building. With regard to EU subsidiarity control, a kind of 'gentlemen's agreement' has evolved, implying that the concern of one Land in a case of an EU initiative leads to a reasoned opinion of the Bundesrat as a whole. The Länder parliaments are involved in subsidiarity control, too, according to the procedures laid down in their respective Land constitutions.

If a specific quorum of chambers of national parliaments within the EU has subsidiarity concerns on an initiative, the European Commission has to answer and give reasons for its initiative or even to change the initiative. After the involvement of the national (and subnational) parliaments and eventual correction by the Commission, the legislative initiative at European level is sent to the Council and the European Parliament.

2. Decision-Making

Legislative decisions at EU level are taken by the Council and the European Parliament. The Council is composed of the executives of the Member States and has traditionally been more powerful in legislation than the European Parliament. In European environmental policy-making, with the Treaty of Amsterdam,[36] the co-decision procedure was introduced specifically for environmental law. The co-decision procedure has been in force since as early as 1993[37] for the sweeping clause on legal harmonization that is the basis for most environmental law. Since then the European Parliament has been on a par with the Council, and thus with national governments, in environmental decision-making. It was the

---

zum Mehrebenenparlamentarismus? Zukünftige Funktionen von Parlamenten im Integrationsprozess (Nomos, Baden-Baden 2011).

[36] Treaty of Amsterdam amending the Treaty on European Union, the Treaties establishing the European Communities and certain related acts, 10 November 1997.

[37] Treaty on European Union, Maastricht Treaty, 1 November 1993.

Maastricht Treaty,[38] as well, which provided that decisions in the Council be taken with qualified majority voting (before that decisions were taken unanimously), and the enlargement rounds between 1995 and 2013, bringing the EU from 12 to 28 Member States, continuously restricted the influence of a single national government on EU environmental policy.

The European Parliament traditionally plays an active role in environmental policy, advocating severe and far-reaching measures. As the European Parliament is a so-called 'working parliament', most of the work is done in the committees. The ENVI Committee (Environment, Public Health and Food Safety) consists of about 70 members and is currently the biggest legislative committee of the EP. About ten of the Committee members are German MEPs. Since the European elections in May 2014, the German group has consisted of 96 MEPs who also form Länder groups and are closely connected to other political levels and actors in Germany who are trying to influence 'their' MEPs in important questions.[39]

In the Council, Germany is represented by its federal government. In the process of shifting legislative competences step by step from the Länder to the federal level, as described above, the federal level became the most important German actor in environmental policy. The German position, as it is defended at the European level, is however the result of an intense coordination between a number of national executive and legislative actors.[40] The lead in executive coordination is taken by the Federal Ministry for the Environment, Nature Conservation and Nuclear Safety (established in 1986 in consequence of the leaking nuclear power plant in Chernobyl in the Ukraine). The cross-cutting nature of environmental policy calls for cross-sectoral coordination with other federal departments (for example economy, traffic and agriculture) and with EU policy experts in those departments. At cabinet level, environmental policies are coordinated by the Cabinet Committee on the Environment (Kabinettsausschuss für Umweltfragen), and there are other permanent committees of State Secretaries and heads of divisions of different ministries concerned with environmental policy. The environmental ministry receives expert advice from the Expert Advisory Board for Environmental Issues (Sachverständigenrat für Umweltfragen) as well as from a

---

[38] Treaty on European Union, Maastricht Treaty, 1 November 1993.
[39] Große Hüttmann and Eppler, 'Die Europapolitik Baden-Württembergs im Dreieck Stuttgart-Berlin-Brüssel', *supra*, n. 33.
[40] Grünhage, *Entscheidungsprozesse in der Europapolitik Deutschlands. Von Konrad Adenauer bis Gerhard Schröder*, *supra*, n. 32.

number of federal agencies, specialists on, for example, nature conservation and radiation protection.

Before the representative of the German government is able to negotiate and take a vote in the Council, the government's position has to be adjusted at national level with the two legislative bodies.[41] This is the second formal opportunity for the Bundestag and the Bundesrat – after the EU subsidiarity control – to influence EU legislation. Compared to the Bundestag, the Bundesrat is vested with privileged competences, thus acknowledging its role as representative of the interests of Länder governments (rather than as a typical parliamentary chamber). In line with the rationale of federal distribution of legislative competences (see section III above), the Bundesrat has a graded veto position in EU affairs, depending on its degree of impact on German legislation in the respective policy area. In very specific cases of very high Länder concerns, Germany is to be represented in the Council of Ministers by a representative designated by the Bundesrat. There have been only a few cases in which the Bundesrat has insisted on its veto position. But typically, the shadow of this veto position contributes to a cooperative opinion formulation between the federal government and the Länder governments.[42]

In terms of self-rule, however, the upwards shift of legislative competences, as well as the network character and technical nature of environmental regulation, has relegated parliaments at federal and Länder levels to ratifying higher-level legislation or to passing secondary legislation rather than passing their own legislation. Still, parliaments retain an important function of articulating and representing the public interest and promoting public discussion in environmental issues, which are traditionally of high profile in Germany, not least due to the relative strength of the Green Party.[43]

After the Bundestag and the Bundesrat have given their opinions to the national government, representatives of Germany negotiate in the Council

---

[41] Grundgesetz für die Bundesrepublik Deutschland [Grundgesetz] [GG] [Basic Law], 23 May 1949, I, Art. 23 (Ger.).

[42] Eppler, Annegret, 'Weiterentwicklung der Zusammenarbeit von Bund und Ländern in der deut-schen Europapolitik durch die erste Stufe der Föderalismusreform', in Baus, Ralf et al. (eds), *Competition versus Cooperation. German Federalism in Need of Reform – A Comparative Perspective* (Nomos, Baden-Baden 2007).

[43] Eppler, Annegret, 'Die Umweltpolitik von Bund und Ländern zwischen Kooperation und Ent-flechtung angesichts europäischer Vorgaben und heterogener sachpolitischer Herausforderungen', in Scheller, Henrik and Josef Schmid (eds), *Föderale Politikgestaltung im deutschen Bundesstaat. Variable Verflechtungsmuster in Politikfeldern* (Nomos, Baden-Baden 2008).

at European level. As in Bundestag and Bundesrat decisions, different lines of conflict (party political conflicts, specific Länder or issue-specific interests) intersect, and it often happens that no common agreement can be arrived at. In those situations, the German representative in the Council will abstain from voting, a strategy which coined the expression of a 'German vote' for abstention in Council voting.

The European Parliament and the Council discuss the legislative draft in three readings. The formal procedure allows the application of a conciliation committee and also the failure of an act if the positions of Council and Parliament remain incompatible. In environmental policy, the European Parliament and the Council are equally involved in the legislative process and the Council decides with qualified majority.[44] That means that the German representative in the Council alone cannot veto environmental legislation. If the European Parliament and Council agree on a legislative act, it is not automatically in force: as most of the European environmental legislative acts are directives, they enter into force only after the Member States have transposed them into their national law.

3. Ratification and Implementation

While regulations enter into force automatically after having been issued by the EU, directives must be implemented by the Member States to come into operation. As explained above, Germany has been and still is slow in implementing European law. The delays result from the shared responsibilities for implementing European law: the simple rule is that the level and institution that would have the legal competence to legislate on the same issue in Germany is responsible for making a law that implements the European directive. The need to pass legislation through two chambers if not through 16 Länder parliaments on the one hand, and to split European directives among the different environmental media and policy instruments in German lawmaking on the other, has often caused delays in ratification and implementation and cases of reprimand before the European Court of Justice. While the first problem was abolished with the federalism reform in 2006 (see section III.3 above), the problem

---

[44] In qualified majority voting the votes of Member States are weighted. According to the Treaty of Lisbon, three conditions have to be met to reach a qualified majority, at least 55 per cent of the members of the Council, at least 15 countries and at least 65 per cent of the EU population represented. Four States may form a blocking minority.

that European legislation must be split among environmental media for transposition into German law is still unresolved.

The Länder's primary role is to secure implementation of any environmental ruling. At the stage of administrative implementation, the UMK again plays an important role. The technical character of an environmental ruling and its high relevance in terms of external and long-term effects gives a high priority to the efficient coordination of implementation among the Länder and between levels. In the UMK, the environmental ministers of the Länder and of the federal government meet twice a year, supported by a permanent secretariat.[45] The meetings take place behind closed doors, and the results of the negotiation are made available to the public, but only in a highly condensed form. On the one hand, this encourages debate beyond party political lines of conflict; on the other hand, the lack of transparency to the public and the merely executive composition of the conference raises questions as to its democratic and parliamentary legitimacy.

The environmental outcome is highly dependent on the work of the Länder and their administrative sub-structure, especially of the local level as the lowest administrative authority. At the local level, again, the network character of environmental policy-making is strongly emphasized, as there, administrators, citizens, industry, environmental organizations and pressure groups typically cooperate to make environmental policy work.

4. Policy Review: The Judicature in Environmental Policy

Despite the fact that the Federal Constitutional Court (Bundesverfassungsgericht) has been involved in defining the relationship between the levels of government in other policy areas, it has not yet taken a major role in environmental federalism.[46] Judicial treatment of environmental policy is embedded in the general adjudication of federal jurisdictional litigation.[47] Jurisdiction on those issues has contributed to shifting power towards the federal level and to strengthening the veto position of the Bundesrat at federal level.

---

[45] Kropp, *Kooperativer Föderalismus und Politikverflechtung*, *supra*, n. 12

[46] Eppler, 'Die Umweltpolitik von Bund und Ländern zwischen Kooperation und Ent-flechtung angesichts europäischer Vorgaben und heterogener sachpolitischer Herausforderungen', *supra*, n. 43

[47] Grundgesetz für die Bundesrepublik Deutschland [Grundgesetz] [GG] [Basic Law], 23 May 1949, I, Art. 84 s. 1 and Art. 72, s. 2 (Ger.).

But the European level has also gained importance in policy review. The European Court of Justice plays a crucial role in German environmental policy, in establishing the guidelines for proper implementation of European law. The Court does not decide on national law unless a national court appeals it and asks for an interpretation of the 'fit' of national and European law. Nevertheless, the CJEU plays an important role when the European environmental law is not correctly implemented in time or substance. In those cases, the Court is allowed to sentence the Member State to a penalty payment. As Germany has had considerable problems in the implementation of goal-orientated European policy across different environmental media, it has been convicted of incomplete implementation of EU directives on several occasions.[48]

V. CONCLUSION: STRENGTHS AND WEAKNESSES OF MULTILEVEL ENVIRONMENTAL POLICY-MAKING

Since the beginning of environmental policy-making by the German Länder in the 1970s, the number of governmental levels and actors involved, and the complexity of the process, have increased continuously. In this process, the EU integration has taken effect, multiplying actors and interdependencies. Today, the European Union is the most powerful actor, setting the agenda and issuing most environmental laws. There is no such thing as 'German environmental policy-making'; rather, the German levels of government are closely intertwined with European policy-making. The German federal level and the Länder have to adapt to the European policy cycle by establishing specialized units serving as channels for influence, information and communication as well as developing mechanisms to coordinate EU policy between the involved actors and institutions within Germany. The Europeanization of environmental policy-making even led to a reform of legislative competences between the federal level and the Länder and to the adaptation of implementation processes and policy styles – from segmented and media-specific environmental management to environmental governance setting targets and overall aims.

---

[48] Knill, *Europäische Umweltpolitik. Steuerungsprobleme und Regulierungsmuster im Mehrebenensystem, supra*, n. 15.

The high number of actors involved in a long and complex policy process inevitably calls for intense coordination across levels of government, policy sectors and groups of stakeholders. On the one hand, in terms of output legitimacy, that is, effective policy-making, it is questionable whether the system is able to produce an efficient outcome. Decision-making takes time, and the final decisions incorporate compromises at the smallest common denominator. EU Member States with relatively high environmental standards, such as Germany, cannot act independently but are constrained by 27 other Member States. While decision-making is a complex process involving all levels of government, actual implementation is exclusively vested with the Länder governments, thus securing the necessary closeness to regional needs and citizen interests.

On the other hand, in terms of input legitimacy, the multiplicity of actors involved, of access points for interests in the agenda-setting process and of veto points in the decision process possibly enhances acceptance of the decisions agreed upon, thus promoting their implementation and application in the long run. From this point of view, a higher input legitimacy might counterbalance the questionable output legitimacy. Critics argue, however, that the lack of transparency in the decision-making process systematically gives priority to executives and highly organized economic interests while disadvantaging parliaments and smaller, less powerful, interest representations of civil society.

As environmental politics crosscuts policy sectors and does not stop at state boundaries, a joint approach to regulation is undoubtedly appropriate for Europe. It is widely acknowledged that international regimes of environmental protection are fundamentally flawed due to the dilemma structure of the decision situation, the high number of veto players, the non-existence of a norm-enforcing instance and the low incentives for adherence. Compared to this situation, environmental policy-making in the German and European multilevel systems can be accorded reasonable levels of input- and output-legitimacy despite the shortcomings outlined above.

REFERENCES

Jörg Broschek, 'Federalism and Political Change. Canada and Germany in Historical-Institutionalist Perspective' (2010) 43 *Canadian Journal of Political Science*.
Fritz W. Scharpf, 'The Joint-Decision Trap: Lessons from German Federalism and European Integration' (1988) 66 *Public Administration*.
Heidrun Abromeit, *Der verkappte Einheitsstaat* (Leske+Budrich, 1992).

Heinrich Pehle and Roland Sturm, 'Die Europäisierung der Regierungssysteme', in *Die EU-Staaten im Vergleich* (2008).
Nathalie Behnke and Arthur Benz, 'The Politics of Constitutional Change between Reform and Evolution' (2009) 39 *Publius*.
Yvonne Hegele and Nathalie Behnke, 'Die Landesministerkonferenzen und der Bund – Kooperativer Föderalismus im Schatten der Politikverflechtung' (2013) 54 *Politische Vierteljahresscharift*.
Fritz W. Scharpf, 'Legitimationskonzepte jenseits des Nationalstaats' (MPIfG Working Paper).
Simone Burkhart and Philip Manow, 'Was bringt die Föderalismusreform?' (MPIfG Working Paper 6 June 2006).
Harald Georgii and Sarab Borhanian, *Zustimmungsgesetze nach der Föderalismusreform* (Wissenschaftliche Dienste des Deutschen Bundestages, 2006).
Sabine Kropp, *Kooperativer Föderalismus und Politikverflechtung* (VS-Verlag, 2009).
Annegret Eppler, 'Deutsche Umweltpolitik im europäischen Mehrebenensystem', in Wolfgang Renzsch et al. (eds), *Föderalismus in Deutschland* (2009).
Gisela Müller Brandeck-Bouquet, *Die institutionelle Dimension der Umweltpolitik. Eine vergleichende Untersuchung zu Frankreich, Deutschland und der Europäischen Union* (Nomos, 1996).
Christoph Knill, *Europäische Umweltpolitik. Steuerungsprobleme und Regulierungsmuster im Mehrebenensystem* (VS Verlag für Sozialwissenschaften Zweite Auflage edn, 2008).
Katharina Holzinger, 'Environmental Policy in the Joint-Decision Trap? The Critical Balance between "Market Making" and "Market Correcting"', in Gerda Falkner (ed.) *The EU's Decision Traps: Comparing Policies* (2011).
Michael Böcher and Annette Elisabeth Töller, *Umweltpolitik in Deutschland. Eine politikfeldanalytische Einführung* (VS Verlag für Sozialwissenschaften, 2012).
Annegret Eppler, 'Föderalismusreform I im Politikfeld Umweltpolitik als Europäisierungsschritt', in Julia von Blumenthal and Stephan Bröchler (eds), *Föderalismusreform in Deutschland. Bilanz und Perspektiven im internationalen Vergleich* (2010).
Arthur Benz, et al., *Horizontale Politikverflechtung* (Campus, 1992).
Jan Grünhage, *Entscheidungsprozesse in der Europapolitik Deutschlands. Von Konrad Adenauer bis Gerhard Schröder* (Nomos, 2007).
Brigid Laffan, 'Core Executives', in Paolo Graziano and Maarten P. Vink (eds), *Europeanization. Research Agendas* (2007).
Martin Große Hüttmann and Annegret Eppler, 'Die Europapolitik Baden-Württembergs im Dreieck Stuttgart-Berlin-Brüssel', in Siegfried Frech, et al. (eds), *Handbuch Europapolitik* (2009).
Tapio Raunio, 'The Gatekeepers of European Integration? The Functions of National Parliaments in the EU Political System' (2011) 33 *Journal of European Integration*.
Sven Vollrath, 'Herausforderungen bei der Umsetzung der neuen Rechte nach dem Vertrag von Lissabon durch den Deutschen Bundestag und die Begleitgesetzgebung', in Gabi Abels and Annegret Eppler (eds), *Auf dem Weg zum Mehrebenenparlamentarismus? Zukünftige Funktionen von Parlamenten im Integrationsprozess* (2011).
Annegret Eppler, 'Weiterentwicklung der Zusammenarbeit von Bund und Ländern in der deutschen Europapolitik durch die erste Stufe der Föderalismusreform', in Ralf Baus, et al. (eds), *Competition versus Cooperation. German Federalism in Need of Reform – A Comparative Perspective* (2007).

Annegret Eppler, 'Die Umweltpolitik von Bund und Ländern zwischen Kooperation und Ent-flechtung angesichts europäischer Vorgaben und heterogener sachpolitischer Herausforderungen', in Henrik Scheller and Josef Schmid (eds), *Föderale Politikgestaltung im deutschen Bundesstaat. Variable Verflechtungsmuster in Politikfeldern* (2008).

14. The paradox of environmental federalism in India

Sairam Bhat

AN INTRODUCTION TO FEDERALISM

The Constitution of India is one of the longest-written constitutions of any sovereign country in the world, containing 448 Articles in 22 parts, 12 schedules and more than 100 amendments. The Constitution of India is of the federal type.[1] It establishes a dual polity, a three-tier governmental system, with the central government at one level and the state and local governments at the other. Some schools of thought believe that India is not a true federation: it combines features of a federal government and features of a unitary government[2] which can also be called the non-federal features.[3] Federalism is an expression of plurality, heterogeneity and diversity and India poses unique challenges in all these three areas.

Federalism is essentially about sharing of powers between a central government and two or more local governments, including state governments, that are subordinately useful entities but with some 'real' powers. In this sense, India is a federal state. Federalism in India is a matter of administrative convenience, but also one of principle,[4] because India was

---

[1] Part XI of the Constitution of India defines the power distribution between the federal government (the centre) and the states in India: India Constitution, Arts 245–63. This part is divided between legislative, administrative and executive powers. Ibid.

[2] 6 Constituent Assemb. of India (1948).

[3] Among the bones of contention are powers such as those that central government has under Art. 356 wherein the executive powers of the state governments are subject to the powers of the central government. Under this provision the central government may dismiss a state government and impose 'President's rule'.

[4] Jain, Mahabir Prashad et al., *M.P. Jain Indian Constitutional Law*, 6th edn (LexisNexis India 2010), 791.

a unitary state by political action prior to the Constitution being adopted in 1949. Hence, we see a federal state as one of transition to a larger unity. Further, the federal scheme in the Constitution is one of administrative and legislative federalism. Part IV of the Constitution of India contains the Directive Principles of State Policy (DPSP) formulating the fundamental principles of state policy casting a duty on state governments to follow the same in both legislative and administrative policies.[5] Further, Article 245 of the Constitution of India strengthens this duty by making the legislative power 'subject' to the provision of the Constitution.[6]

The current approach with a strong federal structure of governance shows an approach which is more hierarchal and less consensus-driven. In green matters, this view is strengthened by the fact that all the major enactments governing the conservation and protection of natural resources are enacted and governed through federal legislation.[7] India is regarded by some as a semi-federal state. Professor K.C. Wheare describes it as 'a quasi-federal state'.[8] The Supreme Court of India also describes it as 'a federal structure with a strong bias towards the Centre'.[9]

The fundamental organization of government between federal and state bodies significantly affects allocation of authority over environmental and pollution matters.

The division of environmental policy-making and allocation of environmental functions between the central, state and local governments is

---

[5] India Const. Art. 37. Legislative entries in Seventh Schedule may be given wide interpretation for effecting Directive Principles. Constitutional provisions may be constructed in the light of Directive Principles. See *Laxmi Kant v Union of India*, AIR 1987 SC 232; *Mukesh v Madhya Pradesh*, AIR 1985 S.C. 537; *A.B.K. Singh v Union of India*, AIR 1981 SC 298.

[6] Art. 245 states that Parliament may make laws for the whole or any part of the territory of India, and the legislature of a state may make laws for the whole or any part of the state. Further, Parliament can make laws with extraterritorial application: India Const. Art. 245(2).

[7] See Indian Forest Act, No. 16 of 1927, India Code (2014); The Forest (Conservation) Act, No. 69 of 1980, India Code (2014); The Water (Prevention and Control of Pollution) Act, No. 6 of 1974, India Code (2014); The Air (Prevention and Control of Pollution) Act, No. 14 of 1981, India Code (2014); The Wild Life Protection Act, No. 53 of 1972, India Code (2014); The Environment (Protection) Act, No. 29 of 1986, India Code (2014); Biological Diversity Act, No. 18 of 2003, India Code (2014).

[8] See generally Wheare, K.C., *Federal Government*, 4th edn (Oxford University Press, London 1963).

[9] *S.R. Bommai v Union of India*, AIR 1994 SC 1918.

regulated by the Constitution of India.[10] The Constitution marks off the sphere of action of each level of government through an elaborate scheme of distribution of legislative, administrative and financial powers between the centre and the states. Environmental protection is clearly provided for in the Constitution of India as a DPSP[11] and judicial activism over the years has further strengthened the 'right to Environment'.[12] The Constitution also mandates a fundamental duty on citizens to protect and improve the natural environment.[13]

The Constitution, in the Seventh Schedule, clarifies the scheme of division of powers between federal and state government.[14] The environmental subjects over which state legislatures can legislate are public health and sanitation; agriculture; communication; preservation, protection and improvement of stock and prevention of animal diseases; water; land, and so on. Parliament and state legislatures have overlapping, concurrent and shared jurisdiction over 52 subjects ranging from forests, protection of wild animals, and mines and mineral development to population control and family planning, minor ports, factories and electricity.[15]

This chapter will examine in its first part environmental federalism in India by tracing its growth under the Constitutional framework. In its second part the chapter will critically analyse the centre–state relationship in green matters. The third part will consider the implementation of federal legislation through cooperative federalism, with a special emphasis on institutional structures, and lastly the chapter questions whether decentralization can be effected in green matters. The scheme of the

---

[10] The division of legislative functions can be seen in the Seventh Schedule of the Constitution of India. Union Powers are defined in List I, State in List II and Concurrent Powers in List III.

[11] Art. 48A of the Constitution of India states that the state shall endeavour to protect and improve the environment and to safeguard the forests and wild life of the country: India Const. Art. 48A.

[12] Under Art. 21 of the Constitution of India, the Indian judiciary has held that 'right to life include right to clean and healthy environment [sic]'. See *Subhash Kumar v Bihar*, AIR 1991 SC 420; *M.C. Mehta v Union of India*, AIR 1988 S.C. 1037; Vellore Citizen's Welfare Forum (1996) 5 SCC 647; *Indian Council of Enviro-Legal Action v Union of India* (1996) 3 SCC 212.

[13] India Const. Art. 51A(g).

[14] List I is the Union List, List II is the State List and List III is the Concurrent List. For the use of the powers in the Seventh Schedule *see* Indian Constitution Art. 246.

[15] See the Indian Constitution Sch. 7 (Concurrent List).

chapter revolves around constitutional, institutional, legislative and judicial perspectives of the environment and then goes on to scrutinize various elements of the international order to establish the degree, if any, of the link between federalism, decentralization and the environment.

Genesis of Green Federalism in India

Indian federalism has a long history going back to the way in which the British unified the country under their rule and later the way in which the territories under the direct control of the British and various principalities were integrated in the Indian union.[16] The founding fathers of the Constitution decided to have a federation with a strong central government to hold together the diverse economic, linguistic and cultural entities and to avoid fissiparous tendencies. Centralization was also found desirable to unify the country, comprising regions directly ruled by the British and 216 princely states and territories.[17] A federation is not founded on the principle of equality between the union and states; states are only subordinately useful entities. The degree of subordination can vary but states must have some 'real' powers.[18] The central government in India has the powers, and it actually does invade the legislative and executive domains of the states.

Twenty-first century federalism has come to be understood as a dynamic process of cooperation and shared action between the two levels of government, with increasing interdependence and centrist trends. The concept of 'cooperative federalism' held the federal system, with its divided jurisdiction, to act in union. It minimizes friction and promotes cooperation among the various constituent governments of the federal union so that they can pool their resources to achieve certain desired

---

[16] The sole exception, of course, was the state of Jammu and Kashmir, which under Art. 370 of the Constitution of India had special status. For more see Arora, Balvir, 'Adapting Federalism to India: Multilevel and Asymmetric Innovations', in Arora, Balvir and Douglas Verney (eds), *Multiple Identities in a Single State* (Konark, New Delhi 1995).

[17] Chanda, Asok K., *Federalism in India: A Study of Union–State Relations* (Hillary House, New York 1965).

[18] Art. 3 of the Constitution of India vests the Parliament with powers to constitute new states by separating territories from the existing ones, alter their boundaries, and change their names: India Const. Art. 3. The only requirement for this is that the 'Bill' for the purpose will have to be placed in the Parliament on the recommendation of the President and after it has been referred to the relevant state legislature for ascertaining their views (their approval is not necessary).

national goals.[19] Where the goals are specified in the Constitution itself as fundamental to the governance of the country, cooperation becomes inevitable.

The role of people and communities is absolutely essential for federalism to be effective. It was emphasized that while factoring in environment, development goals cannot be overlooked. Therefore, the greatest challenge is in responding to development and aspirational pressures from different stakeholder groups, yet ensuring environmental quality. For this purpose, a holistic understanding of 'green' is required at all levels.[20]

There is also a long Concurrent List[21] containing subjects of common interest and Parliament gets superior legislative as well as administrative powers to govern in these areas. To strengthen this idea over green matters, in 1980 the Tiwari Committee[22] recommended that a new entry

---

[19] Examples of Cooperative Green Federalism can be seen in the protection of biosphere reserves. In 1973, 'Project Tiger' was launched with the help of the World Wide Fund and International Union for Conservation of Nature and Natural Resources. It earmarked reserves with a core area free from human interference and cattle grazing. There are now 21 tiger projects. In 1991–92 'Project Elephant' was launched, with an aim of ensuring long-term survival of the population of elephants, relocating populations outside national parks and sanctuaries, restoring migration corridors, strengthening anti-poaching infrastructure, etc.

[20] For further information, see the report on the Conference organized by the Energy and Resources Institute (TERI), in collaboration with the Forum of Federations, Ottawa; Ministry of Environment and Forests, Government of India; Inter-state Council Secretariat, Government of India; and the World Bank. Strengthening Green Federalism: Sharing International Practices (2012), accessed 19 July 2015 at interstatecouncil.nic.in/downloads/gfc-summary-proc.pdf. These entities organized a two-day event, the 'International Conference on Strengthening Green Federalism: Sharing International Practices'. Ibid.

[21] India Const. list 3 (17) ('Prevention of cruelty to animals') (Parliament has enacted the Prevention of Cruelty to Animals Act 1960); India Const. list 3 (17A) ('Forests') (Parliament has enacted the Forest Conservation Act 1980); India Const. list 3 (17B) ('Protection of wild animals and birds') (Parliament has enacted the Wildlife Protection Act 1972).

[22] Empowered committee (Tiwari Committee) set up in February 1980 for reviewing and recommending legislative measures and a suitable administrative machinery to ensure environmental protection, recommended the setting up of a separate Department of Environment. Thus, in November 1980, a separate Department of Environment was set up to act as the focal agency in the administrative structure of central government for planning, promotion and coordination of environmental programmes. During 1985 the Departments of Forest and Wildlife were annexed and the Ministry of Environment and Forests

on 'Environmental Protection' be introduced in the Concurrent List to enable the central government to legislate on environmental subjects.[23] The Recommendations of the Tiwari Committee, however, did not consider Parliament's power under Article 253, which empowers Parliament to make any law for implementing any treaty, agreement or convention, which in green matters are plenty and India is a signatory to them.

The 42nd Amendment to the Constitution in 1976 and the enactment of the Environmental Protection Act in 1986 can be considered as the phase in which green federalism became structured in India. The 42nd amendment introduced a new entry, 'Population Control and Family Planning', while subjects like 'Forest' and 'Protection of Wild Animals and Birds' were moved from the State List to the Concurrent List, with a purpose of having uniform conservation and protection strategies for the whole nation.[24] The 42nd amendment also introduced several notable changes in the area of the centre–state relationship, the inevitable thrust of which was to strengthen the centre vis-à-vis the states in several respects, and thus to make Indian federalism more centralized.[25] The central government has a large sphere of action and thus is required to play a more dominant role than the states in green matters.[26]

The Bhopal Disaster of 1984[27] prompted the federal government to bring about strong policy, legislative as well as institutional measures in

---

was thus created. See Committee for Recommending Legislative Measures and Administrative Machinery for Ensuring Environmental Protection, Report, para. 3.15 (1980).

[23] The Committee's recommendation was based on a note from the Indian Academy of Environmental Law which observed that there was no direct entry in the Seventh Schedule enabling Parliament to enact comprehensive environmental laws.

[24] India Const., amended by the Constitution (Forty-Second Amendment) Act 1976.

[25] The following entries were eliminated from the State List: Education, Forest, Wild Animals, Weight and Measures. See Jain, *supra*, n. 4, at 1823.

[26] Art. 256 of the Constitution states that the executive power of every state shall be so exercised as to ensure compliance with laws made by Parliament, further the executive power of the union shall extend to giving directions to a state as may appear necessary to the Government of India: India Const. Art. 256.

[27] Union Carbide Corporation India Limited was charged with the death of nearly 20,000 people due to the leak of a gas in the city of Bhopal in Madhya Pradesh. In 1991 a court settlement was reached for US$470 million compensation. In June 2010 a Bhopal District Session Court sentenced six persons, who were at the helm of affairs at the factory, to two years' imprisonment for causing death by negligence. The matter is still not fully resolved. See Rosencranz,

green matters. The government in India established a fully fledged Ministry of Environment and Forest (prior to this, it was a Department of Environment under the Ministry of Science and Technology). After the Bhopal disaster, environmental issues and problems were given importance in its legislative formulations and administrative set-up. Central government embarked on various policy initiatives for conservation of resources, such as the Water Policy 1987, New Water Policy of 2002 and 2012, the National Forest Policy 1988, the National Policy Statement for Abatement of Pollution 1992, the National Conservation Strategy and Policy Statement on Environment and Development 1992, and the National Environmental Policy of 2006.[28]

Moving to legislative responses following the Bhopal disaster, what became increasingly evident was the central government legislation, like the Water Act 1974 and the Air Act 1981, which were merely sectoral, as they focused on only one specific type of pollution. Though they were consistent with the limited objectives of their times, they failed to regard the 'environment' as a whole. The need for a general legislation for environmental protection, and the aftermath of the Bhopal disaster, therefore, led to the enactment of the Environment (Protection) Act 1986. While this Act provides the central government with greater powers to set environmental as well as effluent and emission standards, the enforcement powers have been delegated entirely to the states. The Act established a basic structure of centralized legislation on green matters through section 3 read along with section 5 of the Environment Protection Rules 1986, empowering the central government to legislate on all matters concerning the protection and conservation of the 'environment'.[29] Rule 3(2) of the Environment (Protection) Rules tilts the balance firmly towards the centre. It clearly specifies that the states can have

---

Armin and Sairam Bhat, 'Requirement of Justice', *Econ. & Political Weekly*, 13 November 2010.

[28] The policy was a response to clean environment, mandated in the Constitution in Arts 48A and 51A(g), strengthened by judicial interpretation of Art. 21. See Ministry of Env't & Forests, Gov't of India, National Environmental Policy (2006), accessed 19 July 2015 at envfor.nic.in/sites/default/files/introduction-nep2006e.pdf.

[29] As defined under s. 2(a) of the Environment Protection Act 1986. The Environment (Protection) Act, No. 29 of 1986, India Code (2014).

more but not less stringent standards than the centre.[30] Thus, in terms of environmental standards, this law always states the minimum morality that must be respected.

The Bhopal industrial tragedy triggered the need to safeguard and protect the environment and also bring in an effective system of laws, rules and regulations, their enforcement and implementation, along with a speedier adjudicatory mechanism to combat exploitation, depletion and degradation of the environment.[31] Judicial activism in green matters gained momentum and federalism, with a strong centralization, was apparently catalysed.[32]

I. FEDERALISM AND THE CONSTITUTION OF INDIA

Environmental federalism relates to the proper assignment of various roles in green matters to the different tiers of government.[33] The Constitution of India divides powers between the union, state government and local governments. The Seventh Schedule of the Constitution includes three lists of subjects – the Union List, the State List and the Concurrent List. The central or union government has exclusive power to make laws on the subjects which are mentioned in the Union List. With regard to the Concurrent List, both the central and state governments can make laws on the subjects mentioned in the Concurrent List, but a federal law will override the state law.[34] Finally, the subjects which are not mentioned in the above three lists are called residuary powers and the union government can make laws on them.[35] 'Environment' does not feature in the Constitution of India as a separate entry under the schedule demarcating legislative rights. Thus 'land'[36] and 'water'[37] are state

---

[30] Chandiramni, Nilima, 'Environmental Federalism: An Indian View Point' (2004) 3(2) ICFAI J. Envtl. L. 29–48.

[31] See Divan, Shyam and Armin Rosencranz, *Environmental Law and Policy in India*, 2nd edn (Oxford University Press India, New Delhi 2001), 66.

[32] See Oluem gas leak case where J.P.N. Bhagwati propounded the 'Absolute liability' principle as a deviation from 'strict liability' – which has a loophole for its application in environmental matters: *M.C. Mehta v Union of India*, AIR 1987 SC 1086, writ petition (civil) No. 12739 of 1985.

[33] Oates, Wallace E., 'On Environmental Federalism' (1997) 83 Va. L. Rev. 1321.

[34] India Const. Art. 254.

[35] India Const. Art. 258.

[36] India Const. list 2 (18).

[37] India Const. list 2 (17).

subjects, 'forests'[38] and 'wildlife'[39] are concurrent,[40] and 'environment' in general is a residuary subject.

Law-making in green matters can be traced to the use of parliamentary powers under Article 252. Under that Article, two or more states can delegate their powers to the central government to enact legislation on any subject in the State List. The states of Bihar (now Jharkhand) and Bengal authorized Parliament to legislate for setting up the Damodar Valley Corporation.[41] Similarly, under Article 252 Parliament enacted India's first specialized legislation relating to environmental protection, the Water (Prevention and Control of Pollution) Act 1974.[42]

The next provision in the Constitution which central government has often used is Article 253,[43] which empowers Parliament to make laws implementing India's international obligations as well as any decision made at an international conference, association or other body. Article 253 read with Entry 13 of the Union List, Seventh Schedule, apparently gives Parliament the power to enact laws on virtually any entry contained in the State List. Based on this power, Parliament has enacted the Air (Prevention and Control of Pollution) Act 1981 and the Environment (Protection) Act 1986.[44] The broad language of Article 253 suggests that in the wake of India's being a signatory to various international Conventions, such as the Stockholm Declaration 1972, the Rio Declaration 1992, World Summit on Sustainable Development 1992, United Nations

---

[38] India Const. list 2 (17A).

[39] India Const. list 3 (17B).

[40] Introduced by the 42nd Amendment to the Constitution in 1976, 'forest' and 'wildlife' were moved from the State List to the Concurrent List of the Seventh Schedule of the Constitution.

[41] Damodar Valley Corporation (DVC) is a thermal and hydro power generating unit. DVC has a network of four dams: Tilaiya and Maithon on River Barakar, Panchet on River Damodar and Konar on River Konar.

[42] States of Assam, Bihar, Gujarat, Haryana, Himachal Pradesh, Jammu and Kashmir, Karnataka, Kerala, Madhya Pradesh, Rajasthan, Tripura and West Bengal authorized Parliament to enact legislation on 'Water' which is a state subject.

[43] India Const. Art. 253 ('Legislation for giving effect to international agreements: Notwithstanding anything in the foregoing provisions of this Chapter, Parliament has power to make any law for the whole or any part of the territory of India for implementing any treaty, agreement or convention with any other country or countries or any decision made at any international conference, association or other body').

[44] The Preambles of both these laws state that these Acts were passed to implement the decisions reached at the United Nations Conference on the Human Environment held at Stockholm in 1972.

Conference on Climate Change 1992, and others, the Indian Parliament has the power to legislate on all matters linked to the outcomes of such international meetings, treaty obligations and Conventions.[45] Validating the use of Article 253, the Supreme Court in India, in *S. Jagannath v Union of India*,[46] upheld the power of the union government under Article 253 read with Entry 13, List I of the Seventh Schedule to frame the Coastal Regulation Zone Notification 1991,[47] which was passed under sections 3(1) and 3(2)(v) of the Environment (Protection) Act 1986.[48] This notification attempted to regulate 'developmental' activities on the ecologically fragile coastline in India. Interestingly, the Court went further and recognized that the coastal regulations 'shall have overriding effect and shall prevail over the law made by the legislatures of the States'.

Another green matter of national importance in India is the allocation of water resources in inter-state rivers. Most rivers in India are inter-state rivers and hence the role of central government is significant, not only in the matter of equitable distribution of river waters but also in settling disputes on distribution of water resources equitably and amicably among the state governments. Inter-state river water is within the jurisdiction of the central government and powers in Article 262 help in maintaining balance between the different interests of state government with respect to the national interest. Article 262 of the Constitution confers exclusive power on the federal Parliament to enact a law providing for the adjudication of any dispute or complaint with respect to the use, distribution or control of waters of or in any inter-state river or river valley. Further, according to item 56 of List I, the union/federal government is responsible for regulation and development of inter-state rivers and river valleys to the extent that it is declared by Parliament by law to be expedient in the public interest.

In exercise of the power conferred by Article 262, the Indian Parliament enacted the Inter-State Water Dispute Act 1956, and the jurisdiction of all courts, including the Supreme Court, is barred with respect to such disputes, which are to be settled by the tribunal set up under that Act.

---

[45] *Supra*, n. 31, at 47.
[46] AIR 1997 SC 811, 846. It is popularly called the *Shrimp Culture* case.
[47] Currently, this law is replaced by the Coastal Zone Notification of 2011.
[48] Under the Environmental (Protection)Act 1986, the union government under s. 3, read with s. 6, is empowered to take measures to protect and improve the environment. Thus, using s. 3 of this Act, the central government has issued Notifications (Law) regarding Noise Regulations, Waste Managements and Handling, Environmental Impact Assessment, Public Hearing and others.

Sharing of water resources asks for resolution of competing claims by integrating development with justice and the human right to life claims in water and food. The normative ordering within the Constitution compels the participants of federalism to cooperate towards this objective.[49] Hence, the rights of the state over water are subject to their duty not to affect the rights of those states that are lower in riparian use of the river water.

II. COOPERATIVE FEDERALISM: CENTRE–STATE RELATIONSHIP IN GREEN MATTERS

The centre–state relationship in India's federalism has always been on tenterhooks. Harmonious relationship and construction of federal powers in light of state aspirations should be the way forward.

On several occasions, the division of power under India's federal structure has led to tension between the centre and the states in matters concerning regional development and the preservation of natural resources. The areas of stress include coastal development[50] and the commercial exploitation of mineral resources around federally protected areas.[51] Central statutes designed to protect forests and prevent the destruction of wildlife habitat are viewed as a needless fetter on industrial activity and mining by some states anxious to encourage the commercial exploitation of minerals.[52]

---

[49] Bhat, P. Ishwara, 'Constitutionalism's Challenges and Responses in the Domain of Inter-State Water Dispute Law: An Analysis Towards Enhancement of Social Acceptability' in Bhat, P. Ishwara (ed.) *Inter-State and International Disputes* (Eastern Book Company, Lucknow, 2013), 31.

[50] Goa and Kerala have disregarded the Federal Coastal Zone Management Regulations 2011, which state that the ecologically fragile regions on the coastline including mangroves must be a strictly 'no-development' zone. The CRZ area in Kerala is reduced to 50 metres (earlier under the 1991 notification it was 500 metres) from High Tide Line (HTL) on the landward side. This area is a 'No Development Zone' where no new construction can be carried out. One of the stated objectives of the Notification is 'to ensure livelihood security to the fishermen's communities and other local communities, living in the coastal areas ... and to promote development through sustainable manner [*sic*] based on scientific principles taking into account the dangers of natural hazards in the coastal areas, [and] sea level rise due to global warming'.

[51] *Supra*, note 31, at 46–48.

[52] See *Tarun Bharat Sangh, Alwar v Union of India*, (1993) 3 SCC 115, 128; *Consumer Educ. & Research Soc'y v Union of India*, AIR 1995 Guj. 133.

In 1983 the Sarkaria Commission was established by the central government to study the question of the centre–state relations and to suggest reforms if necessary. This commission emphasized cooperative federalism in India. It is a fact that India has a strong central government but it should not always try to interfere in the matters of the states. Both governments should respect one another's power or authority and work harmoniously.

A kind of centre–state partnership to promote the welfare of the people has thus come into existence, which has slowly transformed the whole concept and character of Indian federalism. In the beginning, the centre–state relationship was one of competition, each trying to claim more powers for itself, but this has now given place to cooperative federalism.[53] In India, cooperative federalism can be seen more evidently in the environmental sphere.

In environmental matters cooperative federalism is significant on three counts. First, the environment concerns all citizens, irrespective of territorial boundaries. Resources and political capacity to manage the environment cannot be compromised by a disintegrated approach to the protection and conservation of the environment. In that sense, environmental issues and challenges are national concerns.

Secondly, federal legislation does not tend to usurp the command and control of environmental matters with a view to over-centralization. States are mandated with responsibilities and administrative roles. Giving consent for establishment of industrial units, permission for access to resources, ensuring environmental quality and so on are all state-centred approaches in environmental legislation.

Thirdly, under Article 256 state governments have the primary share in the enforcement and implementation of environmental laws. State Pollution Control Boards, state government, and the Ministry of Environment are involved in the decision-making process of granting 'environmental clearance' for projects and can enforce conditions and compliance in such licences and grants. State governments have the final word in all 'developmental' activities within their jurisdiction, while inter-state issues are handled by the central government.

---

[53] Jain, Mahabir Prashad, 'Some Aspects of Indian Federalism' (1968) 28(2) Zeitschrift für Ausländisches öffentliches Recht und Völkerrecht: ZaöRV 305.

III. COOPERATIVE GREEN FEDERALISM: AN INSTITUTIONAL PERSPECTIVE

In this part we cover cooperative federalism from those institutions that govern green matters in India. Water for example is a state subject.[54] The Water Act 1974, being federal legislation, establishes Central and State Pollution Control Boards.[55] The real implementation of the Act is with the State Boards,[56] who are assigned functions[57] of controlling and regulating the activities that pollute resources like water and air. The State Boards not only lay down effluent discharge standards but are also responsible for complete monitoring of compliance of such standards. In exercise of their functions, the State Boards are subject to directions from the central government from time to time.[58]

Another instance is Entry 56 in the Union List, which states: 'Regulation and development of inter-state rivers and river valleys to the extent to which such regulation and development under the control of the Union is declared by parliament by law to be expedient in the public interest.' Article 262 explicitly grants Parliament the right to legislate over the matters in Entry 56, and also gives it primacy over the Supreme Court.[59] The Inter-State Water Disputes Act of 1956 was legislated to deal with conflicts, and included provisions for the establishment of tribunals to adjudicate where direct negotiations have failed. If the central government feels that the water dispute referred to it cannot be settled by negotiation, then it can refer the dispute to adjudication by a tribunal

---

[54] India Const. list 2 (17).

[55] As per s. 4 of the Water Act and s. 4 of the Air Act, the State Boards are 'Pollution Control Boards'.

[56] See the Air (Prevention and Control of Pollution) Act, No. 14 of 1981, ch. 4 India Code (2014); The Water (Prevention and Control of Pollution) Act, No. 6 of 1974, ch. 4 India Code (2014).

[57] See the Air (Prevention and Control of Pollution) Act, No. 14 of 1981, § 17 India Code (2014); The Water (Prevention and Control of Pollution) Act, No. 6 of 1974, § 16 India Code (2014).

[58] In a recent National Green Tribunal direction in *International Marwari Association v West Bengal Pollution Control Board*, Appeal No. 53(THC)/2013, order dt. 21-08-2013, the NGT stated that state governments, through the State Pollution Control Boards, cannot dilute or enhance the standards of noise levels in contravention of those that are laid down by the central government (MoEF).

[59] Richards, Alan and Nirvikar Singh, Dep't of Econ., Univ. of Cal., Water and Federalism: 'India's Institutions Governing Inter-State River Waters', accessed 19 July 2015 at people.ucsc.edu/~boxjenk/waterdom.pdf.

constituted under the Act. The tribunal shall then investigate the complaint and forward a report to the central government known as an 'order' or 'award' of the tribunal. Within three months of the report, the central government or any of the state governments concerned can approach the tribunal for clarification. The central government shall publish the tribunal's decision in the Official Gazette, when the decision will be final and binding on the parties to the dispute. Neither the Supreme Court nor any other court shall exercise jurisdiction in respect of any water dispute referred to a tribunal. India's water laws give the appearance of clarity. Actual practice, however, is far more opaque.[60]

Interestingly, major water resources projects need clearance from the Central Water Commission, an arm of Central Water Resources Ministry and Central Electricity Authority, a wing of the Energy Ministry. Nevertheless, permission for construction of dams on inter-state rivers[61] has also been an issue within the domain of the inter-state river tribunals.

In India, the fresh controversy of the unsafe Mullaperiyar dam between Kerala and Tamil Nadu has erupted over a dam built on an inter-state river.[62] The Supreme Court in *State of Tamil Nadu v State of Kerala and Union of India*[63] has clarified the issue and seems to have resolved the matter for the time being.[64]

Yet another example of cooperative federalism can be seen in the governance of 'forest'. 'Forest', being in the Concurrent List, has two

---

[60] The Act permits considerable discretion, and different disputes have followed quite different paths to settlement, or in a few cases, continued disagreement. See the Cauvery and Krishan river disputes.

[61] On the face of it, inter-state water disputes involve issues of: (i) allocation of waters between divergent states; (ii) apportionment of construction costs and benefits if a project is developed jointly by more than one state; (iii) compensation to the states prejudicially affected by the implementation of a project by another state; (iv) dispute settlement relating to interpretation of agreements and; (v) excess withdrawals by a state. Jain, Srimandir Nath et al., *Inter-State Water Disputes in India: Suggestions for Reform in Law* (Indian Law Inst., New Delhi 1971).

[62] The dam is now 116 years old and has developed leaks and cracks during the earthquake in 1979. The dam, in existence since October 1895, lies on the soil of Kerala, and it is the people of Kerala that would be at risk if the dam were to collapse. The reason for the Tamil Nadu government's stand against decommissioning of the Mullaperiyar dam is that the dam provides irrigation water to at least five districts in that state.

[63] Writ No. 3 of 2006 SC.

[64] Bhat, Sairam, 'Interlinking Dam Safety Within Inter-State Water Dispute', in Bhat, Ishwara, *Inter-State and International Water Disputes* (Eastern Book Company 2013), 217–32.

major laws. The Forest Act 1927 and the Forest Conservation Act 1980 have significant roles for state governments in the management of 'forest' as a resource. Management of forests is distributed between the centre, state and to some extent local bodies, depending upon the nature of the forests and subject area. The combined effect of the forest laws is that state governments are empowered to notify reserve forests and protected areas.[65] Under the Forest Act 1927, state governments may make rules to regulate the cutting, sawing, conversion and removal of trees and timber; the granting of licences to the inhabitants of towns and villages in the vicinity of protected forests to take trees, timber or other forest produce; the cutting of grass and pasturing of cattle in such forests; hunting, shooting, fishing, poisoning water and setting traps or snares in such forests and similar activities.[66]

However, the Forest Conservation Act of 1980 provides that states must seek prior permission from the centre before diversion of forest land.[67] Further, state government must also seek permission from the central government for use of forest land for 'non-forest activities'.[68]

Likewise, 'wildlife' is also a Concurrent List subject. The Wildlife Protection Act 1972 was enacted under Article 252 of the Constitution of India. This federal law provides under section 6 for the constitution of a State Board for Wildlife. This Board, to be constituted by the state government, advises the state government in the selection and management of 'protected areas',[69] in the formulation of policies for protection

---

[65] The Indian Forest Act, No. 16 of 1927, § 4 India Code (2014). Under s. 27 of this Act, state government through a notification has power to declare forest no longer reserved. The Indian Forest Act, No. 16 of 1927, § 27 India Code (2014). This power under s. 27 has been overridden by s. 2 of the Forest Conservation Act 1980. The Forest (Conservation) Act, No. 69 of 1980, § 2 India Code (2014).

[66] See the Indian Forest Act, No. 16 of 1927, § 32 India Code (2014).

[67] The Forest (Conservation) Act, No. 69 of 1980, § 2 India Code (2014).

[68] Ibid. Non-forest activities do not include any work relating or ancillary to conservation, development and management of forests and wildlife, namely, the establishment of check-posts, fire lines, wireless communications and construction of fencing, bridges and culverts, dams, waterholes, trench marks, boundary marks, pipelines or other like purposes. In *T N Godavarman v Union of India 1*, writ petition of 1995, decided by J. Verma and J. Kirpal B, the court held that states have to receive prior permission from the centre before diversion of any forest land for non-forest activity.

[69] See the Wild Life Protection Act, No. 53 of 1972, §§ 35, 36A India Code (2014).

and conservation of wildlife and specified plants, and also in harmonizing the needs of tribals and forest dwellers.[70]

Similarly, the Biodiversity Act 2002, being federal legislation,[71] creates a three-tier system comprising a National Biodiversity Authority, State Biodiversity Boards and Biodiversity Management Committees for the protection of biological diversity. It is the legal duty of the central government to devise and execute national strategies, actions and programmes for conservation, but also to issue directives to state governments to take immediate steps where biodiversity and habitats are threatened by overuse, abuse or neglect. This could very well apply to forest in India.[72] The National Biodiversity Authority (NBA)[73] grants approval to use genetic resources and the associated knowledge for commercial utilization by foreign nationals and entities. The State Biodiversity Boards grant similar approvals to domestic entities.[74] Applications for intellectual property rights in biodiversity areas are received and approved only by the NBA.[75] The Act does not mandate a role for the states in granting the approval for applying a patent, or even imposing a benefit-sharing fee or royalty for commercial utilization. Nevertheless, the NBA is increasingly referring applications to the relevant State Biodiversity Boards for response or consultation/consent for access of bio-resources.[76]

Other issues under cooperative federalism stem from the Environmental Protection Act 1986 and numerous notifications vested under this umbrella law. These notifications enacted by the federal government dominate areas and roles that traditionally would have been governed by the state government. This domination is with the single purpose of setting a national agenda and goals for the conservation and protection of the environment.

---

[70] Ibid. at § 8.

[71] The Act was enacted by Parliament by its powers under Art. 253, which gives powers to Parliament to make any law for implementation of any treaty, agreement or convention or any decision made at any international conference. India Const. Art. 253.

[72] Biological Diversity Act, No. 18 of 2003, § 36 India Code (2014).

[73] As per s. 8 of Biological Diversity Act 2002.

[74] See ibid. at ch. 6.

[75] Ibid. at s. 6.

[76] Kohli, Kanchi and Shalini Bhutani, *The Balancing Act: Campaign for Conservation and Community Control Over Biodiversity* (ABS 2013), 31.

In 2000, under the Environmental Protection Act, the central government notified the Noise Regulation Rules 2000.[77] Under section 3(3), this notification mandates that the state government shall take measures for abatement of noise pollution from vehicles, loudspeakers and firecrackers so as to ensure that noise levels do not exceed the ambient air quality standards for noise. State governments are also responsible for categorizing areas into industrial, commercial, residential and silent zones for the purposes of implementation of noise standards. The responsibility of enforcement is left to the respective State Pollution Control Boards.[78]

Another instance of federal intervention can be seen in the coastal environment. The federal government has enacted the Coastal Regulation Zone Notification 2011.[79] With a view to ensuring livelihood security to the fisher and other local communities living in the coastal areas, to conserve and protect coastal stretches, their unique environment and marine area and to account for the dangers of natural hazards in the coastal areas and sea level rise due to global warming, the federal government enacted this law asking state governments to draw up comprehensive plans[80] for sustainable growth and development in these areas. The notification prohibits activities such as setting up new industries, handling hazardous waste, discharge of trade effluents, dumping, and mining of sand, which may have adverse effects on the coastal environment. The implementation of this notification is left to the respective state governments.[81] Articles 256 and 355 impose duties on the union government to ensure compliance with the laws.

Similarly, other notifications under the Environmental Protection Act, such as the Bio-Medical Waste (Management and Handling) Rules 1998,[82] also make provision for state governments to manage and monitor the state of the environment.

---

[77] Enacted under s. 3 of the Environmental Protection Act read with rule 5 of the Environmental Protection Rules 1986.

[78] Noise Regulation Rules, § 4 (2000) (as amended in 2006).

[79] Enacted under ss 3 and 5 of the Environmental Protection Act 1986. The Environment (Protection) Act, No. 29 of 1986, § 3, 5 India Code (2014).

[80] Under s. 5(vi) the state government has to draw Coastal Zone Management Plans in line with this law. Coastal Regulation Zone Notification, s. 5(vi) (2011).

[81] Ibid. at s. 6(c).

[82] Section 7 mandates state government/s to establish a prescribed authority for implementation of the Rules. Ibid. at s. 7.

Another bone of contention from a 'development' perspective that the states seek to achieve is the Environmental Impact Assessment (EIA)[83] and environmental clearances that are required for industrial activities. The EIA Notification of 2006, enacted under the Environmental Protection Act 1986, mandates that environmental clearance is necessary from the central and state governments. This makes environmental clearance for developmental activities a cumbersome process. The centre gives environmental clearance; the enforcement of conditional clearance is left to the state agencies. The notification classifies projects: category A is for clearance by the centre and category B for clearance at state level. All inter-state and most high-impact projects come within category A, thus raising vital questions whether in green matters the government is committed to constitutional and legal imperatives of meaningful devolution and local governance.[84]

Many state governments raised their objections to the EIA law stating clearly that it is against the principle of federalism.[85] In fact the EIA process weighs heavily in favour of centralization before environmental clearances can be granted, and further, the 2006 law added newer developmental activities such as construction projects, industrial estates and power projects under the EIA process, hence the resulting reluctance from the state governments.

Another recent development in green federalism has been the establishment of the National Green Tribunal (NGT) in 2010 by parliamentary legislation.[86] The purpose of the NGT has been for effective and expeditious disposal of cases relating to environmental protection and conservation of forests and other natural resources including enforcement

---

[83] EIA is a tool for sustainable development through evaluation of the potential impact of a project or activity. EIA notification should contain some key elements including screening, scoping, comprehensive study, public participation, progress reports, review, decision and follow-up.

[84] Saldanha, Leo et al., *Green Tapism: A Review of the Environmental Impact Assessment Notification 2006* (Env't Support Group 2007).

[85] See Kohli, Kanchi, 'States Unhappy with Centralized Clearances', *India Together* (14 June 2006), accessed 19 July 2015 at indiatogether.org/eiastates-environment.

[86] National Green Tribunal or the concept of an Environmental Court is not new. Different courts in India had recommended the establishment of an Environmental Court to take up the cases relating to environmental degradation. See *M.C. Mehta v Union of India* 1986 SCC (2) 176; *Indian Council for Enviro-Legal Action v Union of India* AIR 1996 SC 2715; *A.P. Pollution Control Bd. v M.V. Nayudu* AIR 1999 SC 812; see also Law Commission of India, 186th Report on Proposal to Constitute Environment Courts (2003).

of any legal right relating to the environment and giving relief and compensation for damage to persons and property.

The tribunal's dedicated jurisdiction in environmental matters will provide speedy environmental justice and help reduce the burden of litigation in the higher courts. The tribunal has original jurisdiction on matters of 'substantial questions relating to environment' (in other words, where a community at large is affected, or damage to public health at a broader level) and 'damage to environment due to specific activity' (such as pollution). The tribunal is also competent to hear appeals or any person aggrieved by an order or decision of state governments, under several Acts such as the Forest (Conservation) Act,[87] the Biological Diversity Act,[88] the Environment (Protection) Act,[89] the Water and Air (Prevention and Control of Pollution) Act,[90] and also has appellate jurisdiction related to the above Acts within a period of 30 days of award or order. Any person aggrieved by order or decision made under any environmental legislation can approach the NGT for relief. There have also been cases in which the NGT has initiated *suo moto* enquiry into some matters. Articles 256 and 355 came to the rescue.

The establishment of this tribunal has raised certain issues on federalism. This tribunal is established under the federal law and has taken over all matters of dispute resolution relating to 'environment' which are dealt with by federal legislation such as the Environmental Protection Act 1986.[91] The definition of 'environment' includes water, air and land and the interrelationship which exists among and between water, air and land, and human beings, other living creatures, plants, micro-organisms and property.[92] Hence, although subjects such as 'water' and 'land' fall under the State List,[93] it is inevitable that under the NGT Act the matters will be adjudicated by this tribunal created for the purpose. Supporting this federal adjudication in environmental matters is Article 323B of the Constitution of India, which states that 'the appropriate legislature may, by law, provide for the adjudication or trial by tribunals of any dispute,

---

[87] The National Green Tribunal Act, No. 19 of 2010, § 2A India Code (2014).
[88] Ibid. at § 52.
[89] Ibid. at § 5A.
[90] Ibid. at § 33B.
[91] This Act was enacted to give effect to India's commitment to the United Nations Conference on the Human Environment held at Stockholm in June 1972.
[92] The Environment (Protection) Act, No. 29 of 1986, § 2(a) India Code (2014).
[93] See India Const. list 2 (17), (18).

complaints or offences with respect to all or any of the matters with respect to which such Legislature has power to make laws'. Thus, 'environment' being a residuary subject,[94] Parliament by virtue of its powers under Article 248 of the Constitution of India has exclusive powers to make any law with respect to any matter not enumerated in the Concurrent List or State List.

In *Goa Foundation and Peaceful Society v Union of India*,[95] the state government of Goa raised a contention that the NGT cannot issues orders and directions to state governments, and the state governments are not bound by such orders.

J. Swatanter Kumar, Chairperson of NGT,[96] entertained an application from Goa Foundation[97] that sought protection of the ecology in Western Ghats and for suitable directions to state governments not to issue any consent/environmental clearance or permission under different laws within Western Ghat areas. Overruling the contention raised by state governments, the NGT held that 'all civil cases', 'substantial questions relating to environment' and 'disputes' were expressions of wide connotation and had to be liberally construed to achieve the objective of the NGT Act 2010. Once the legislature had used such expressions of wide connotation intentionally and intended to enlarge the scope of the Act to consider all civil cases raising questions of environment, then by process of interpretation it would not be permissible to restrict that jurisdiction that springs from such legislative intent. In civil cases which raise questions relating to the environment, the NGT should have jurisdiction to decide disputes arising out of such questions. Therefore there was no need to carve out any exception for exclusion which was not spelt out by the legislature itself. There is a statutory obligation upon state governments to protect environment and ecology and to ensure that they are not degraded so as to harm the public and environment at large. The tribunal held that the NGT would have jurisdiction to provide appropriate directions to state governments under section 5 of the Environmental Protection Act 1986 for achieving the objects of any legislation in order to protect and conserve the environment.

---

[94] Residuary subjects are those that do not fall under any of the three lists of the Seventh Schedule.

[95] M.A. No. 49 (2013).

[96] The National Green Tribunal is headed by a former Supreme Court judge and all adjudication before it is heard by one judicial and one expert member.

[97] A non-governmental organization in the state of Goa, working for the cause of environmental protection in general and coastal protection in particular.

Federal environmental laws often require states to constitute state environmental management boards/authorities, meet minimum national standards, monitor conditions laid down for compliance, supervise the implementation of environmental legislation and aid and advise the central government on effective legislative and administrative set-up for environmental conservation. They generally do not preempt state law except in narrowly defined circumstances.[98]

IV. DECENTRALIZATION: WHETHER EFFECTUATED?

As a part of the democratic order, federalism decentralizes power into diverse regional centres and allows regionalism to respond to these values.[99] In India, it is generally believed that planning has failed to maintain environmental sustainability and fulfil local subsistence demands. A recent realization[100] has been that decentralization policies can contribute towards sustainable livelihoods and conservation of natural resources, where the optimism is in community collective action and protection of indigenous knowledge along with participatory resource management.[101] The emergence of arguments for decentralization can be linked to the disillusionment felt in different quarters, in the ability of centralized governments to oversee the development process.[102] There is a long theoretical literature on the advantages of decentralized service delivery. The benefits include better information revelation, as citizen preferences are more easily perceived at local level, as well as improved

---

[98] Percival, Robert V. et al., *Environmental Regulation: Law Science and Policy*, 6th edn (Aspen, New York 2009), 115.
[99] *Supra*, n. 48, at 32.
[100] Bhat, Sairam, *Natural Resources Conservation Law* (2011), 441.
[101] The enactment of the Forest Dwellers Act, 2006 is a clear example of this realization. The Scheduled Tribes and Other Traditional Forest Dwellers (Recognition of Forest Rights) Act, No. 2 of 2007, India Code (2014). The Forest Dwellers Act is a central law which provides for land tenure rights to tribal (indigenous) people living in forest areas. The balance between tenure rights to these forest dwellers along with their duty to conserve and protect natural resources shows Green Federalism flourish. 'Land' is in the State List of the Seventh Schedule, whereas 'Forest' is under the domain of the central government, cooperation between state and union has ensured protection of rights of indigenous persons in India.
[102] Torri, Maria Costanza, 'Decentralising Governance of Natural Resources in India: Lessons from the Case Study of Thanagazi Block, Alwar, Rajasthan, India' (2010) 6/2 Law, Envn't & Dev. J. 228.

accountability since it is easier to link the performance of local services to local political representatives.[103]

Local government and village administration is a subject in the State List.[104] Hence, it is the states which have to set up local governments. Consequently, local governments are completely under the jurisdiction and control of their respective state governments. They derive their powers, functions and jurisdiction from their 73rd and 74th Amendment Acts of 1992 to the Constitution of India, inserting Parts IX and IXA into the Constitution. Part IX (Articles 243–243(0)) deals with panchayats and Part IXA (Articles 243(P)–243(Za)) relates to municipalities.[105]

'Decentralization' of governance in this sense refers to the process of transferring decision-making powers in all these areas to lower, more localized levels.[106] Decentralized governance by no means precludes a role for higher levels of the state. Rather, it refers to a 'more appropriate' allocation of rights and responsibilities across levels.[107]

The states are not obliged to devolve all or even some of these listed functions on the panchayats and municipalities. However, local governments do perform some environmental functions such as public health and sanitation, garbage collection and sewerage. But there is considerable variation across Indian states in the range and nature of environmental functions discharged by the panchayats and municipalities.[108]

Under federal environmental legislation, decentralization of governance can be prominently seen in forest management. Under section 28 of the Forest Act 1927, state government may assign to any village

---

[103] Corbridge, Stuart and John Harriss, *Reinventing India: Liberalization, Hindu Nationalism and Popular Democracy*, vol. 1 (Polity, Cambridge 2001).

[104] India Const. list 2 (5).

[105] The 73rd and 74th Constitutional Amendments added XI and XII Schedules to the Constitution. While XI Schedule distributes powers between the state legislature and the panchayat, XII Schedule distributes powers between the state legislature and the municipality. Both Schedules contain environmental subjects.

[106] See the Karnataka Panchayat Raj Act, §§ 66.69, 77, 82–87, 100–06 (1993). The Act empowers Gram Panchayats in matters of water supply, maintaining tanks, wells, and water sources, prohibiting pollution, abatement of nuisance, etc. The Guidelines for Watershed development of the Ministry of Rural Development, Government of India 1994 contemplates a key role for panchayats in watershed development projects.

[107] Lélé, Sharachchandra, 'Decentralising Governance of Natural Resources in India: A Review' (Centre for Interdisciplinary Studies in Environment and Development, Bangalore 2004).

[108] *Supra*, n. 31.

community the rights of government to or over any land which has been constituted a reserved forest, and may cancel such assignment. All forests so assigned shall be called 'village-forests'. Administrative decentralization in India operates under various labels such as 'joint management', 'co-management' or 'participatory development'.[109] The Joint Forest Management programme (JFM)[110] initiated in the 1980s was one such effort.[111] JFM has always been seen as an 'instrument' for addressing the problem of continued forest degradation, as a cost-effective mechanism for reforesting degraded lands and sustaining regenerated forests. A state-initiated decentralization system carried out through the local administrative unit, the Gram Panchayat[112] is the most suited in the Indian context.

The role of the Gram Panchayats in environmental governance can also be seen through legislation such as the Biodiversity Act 2002[113] (central legislation), which seeks Gram Sabha to maintain a 'biodiversity register' or the Panchayat (Extension to the Scheduled Areas) Act 1996, which under section 4 states that 'every Gram Sabha shall be competent to safeguard and preserve the traditions and the customs of the people, their cultural identity, community resources and the customary mode of dispute resolution'.

The debate over decentralization is still strong, its pros and cons still being analysed. Nevertheless, India's National Environment Policy 2006 insists that natural endowments can be better managed and effectively

---

[109] This was attempted through the Panchayati Raj system (a three-tier system of self-governance) that was introduced after the 73rd Amendment to the Constitution of India was passed in 1992.

[110] See Exec. Order No. 6-21/89-P.P. (1990). Such initiatives are generally state-initiated partnership programmes which transfer some rights to forests and its resources to user groups with a promise of resource conservation from them. JFM is a strategy under which the Forest Department and the village community enter into an agreement to jointly protect and manage forest lands adjoining villages and to share responsibilities and benefits. For more, see Jeffery, Roger and Nandini Sundar, *A New Moral Economy for India's Forests?: Discourses of Community and Participation* (Sage, New Delhi 1990).

[111] Participatory (canal) irrigation management, participatory tank irrigation management, and participatory watershed development were other initiatives.

[112] The Gram Panchayat is an elected body with a local administrative role at the village unit level.

[113] See Biological Diversity Act, No. 18 of 2003, ch. 9 India Code (2014) (seeking coordination between centre and state government in achieving and promotion of in situ, and ex situ, conservation of biological resources).

regulated at the local level.[114] Environmental activists insist that natural endowments can be better managed and effectively regulated at the local level. But they also apprehend a dilution of regulatory enforcement at the local level.[115] Decentralization is ceding or transfer of power from a central authority to state or local authorities, in order to empower public authorities with jurisdiction at the spatial level at which particular environmental issues are salient, to address these issues. Need for a decentralized approach has been recognized and developed since the Constitution of India came into being. Over the years, the centralization and decentralization have been a dynamic feature of Indian federalism.

V. CONCLUSION

Green federalism is strongly centralized in India. Apart from the federal consolidation that has happened in terms of taxing powers, it is powers such as in Article 249, which enable Parliament to legislate with respect to a matter in the State List in the 'national interest', that prove that the parliamentary supremacy is firmly rooted in the Constitution of India. In green matters, the same is being established with more and more federal legislation being enacted. Article 39(b) of the Constitution[116] alone would suffice to take the 'environment' as a material resource of the community and allow Parliament to regulate so as to serve the interests of the community and the people of India as a whole. This chapter, though, has not covered the taxation and revenue matters that govern the centre–state relationship, which also have an impact on green federalism.[117]

---

[114] Approved by the Union Cabinet on 18 May, 2006. For more, visit Ministry of Environment, Forests and Climate Change, accessed 20 July 2015 at envfor.nic.in.

[115] See generally Bhatt, S. and Akhtar Majeed, *Environmental Management and Federalism: The Indian Experience* (Uppal, New Delhi 2002).

[116] India Const. Art. 39(b) states that the ownership and control of the material resources of the community are so distributed as best to serve the common good.

[117] For instance, the Compensatory Afforestation Fund Management and Planning Authority (CAMPA) collects funds that are released among the state governments to be utilized for conservation efforts. The CAMPA fund was created in 2004 on the direction of the Supreme Court to ensure project proponents deposit the net value of diverted forest land with state governments for taking up afforestation and management of forests. Also the emerging literature on environmental federalism deals with the fiscal decentralization which may determine environmental quality and balance inter-jurisdictional

The states, though by no means unimportant in the country's constitutional and administrative processes, have however come to occupy a position somewhat inferior to the central government whose primacy is now an established fact.[118]

In the Indian federation, centre and state governments share their responsibilities towards environmental governance. In certain environmental spheres, the power and control of the centre is high even though the states are responsible for taking action for protecting the environment at the state level, and therefore more accountable. Cooperative federalism is the right and suitable approach.

The environment and its effect are not territorially bound. The impact of environmental harm is mostly transboundary and hence uniformity of rules, regulations and compliance structures may be necessitated. Further, challenges such as those posed by climate change[119] call for federal coordination and compliance, especially to fulfil India's obligations under international conventions and treaties. Climate mitigation and adaptation policies will have very different effects in different regions, and importantly these policies may contain significant comparative economic advantages for different states. These call for shared responsibilities between the centre and state. These shared responsibilities across different government levels, including the panchayats, are based on the understanding that some levels are better positioned to respond to the governance challenges. This approach of 'race-to-the-bottom' has not been implemented due to lack of devolution of powers by the state governments to the panchayats. This assumes greater importance in the context of the

---

competitiveness to attract industrial activity by lax environmental standards, which will result in sub-optimal outputs of local public good including the environmental quality. See Chakraborty, Lekha S., 'Determining Environmental Quality in a Federal Setting: An Empirical Analysis of Sub-National Governments in India' (Nat'l Inst. of Pub. Fin. & Policy, Working Paper), https://mpra.ub.uni-muenchen.de/7605/1/MPRA_paper_7605.pdf; see also Shankar, U., 'Ecology, Environment and Sustainable Development in Indian Fiscal Federalism' (Madras Sch. Econ., Working Paper No. 47, 2009), accessed 20 July 2015 at www.mse.ac.in/pub/working%20paper%2047.pdf.; Thirteenth Finance Commission, 'Report on Integrating Environment, Ecology and Climate Change Concerns in Indian Federalism Framework; Government of India' (The Energy and Resources Institute, New Delhi 2009).

[118] *Supra*, n. 49, at 305.

[119] The National Action Plan on Climate Change was finalized in 2008. This federal plan asks states to prepare action plans for mitigation and adaptation strategies to address climate change for their respective jurisdictions.

environment and natural resources, owing to different conditions, capacities and priorities as well as localized impacts of many environmental challenges, which cut across state boundaries. The unique feature should achieve state level implementation of rules, policies and schemes which are designed with central supervision and monitoring.

In times of global concerns about environmental issues, a system of cooperative federalism can offer a framework where responsibilities are shared. One can assume that such a structure of cooperative federalism in India has resulted in a 'race-to-the-top' approach, in which both the central legislation and the supervision of the top court, the Supreme Court of India, have resulted in a centralized approach to environmental protection. The author partially disagrees with this approach. Instead of just imposing national or international mandates on the lower tiers of governance, environmental protection would be better managed if the latter were given a greater share in regulation and enforcement. Environment is an area where federal devolution can provide the solution for welfare governance.[120]

ACKNOWLEDGEMENT

I thank Professor Devidas, Adjunct Professor of Law, National Law School of India University and Professor Smita Shrivastava, Reader, Sarawat Vidyalaya's Sridora Caculo College of Commerce and Management Studies, Mapusa, Goa for improving this chapter.

---

[120] *Supra*, n. 107.

PART VI

CONCLUDING THOUGHTS

15. Environmental federalism's tug of war within

Erin Ryan

I. INTRODUCTION

Anyone paying attention will have noticed that, of late, many of the most controversial issues in American governance involve questions of federalism. Lawmakers, judges, pundits and average citizens are regularly embroiled in arguments over the federalism implications of pollution law,[1] health care reform,[2] energy policy,[3] marriage rights,[4] farm and

---

[1] E.g. *EPA v. EME Homer City Generation, L.P.*, 134 S. Ct. 1584 (2014) (upholding EPA's Clean Air Act interstate pollution regulations); *Rapanos v. United States*, 547 U.S. 715 (limiting federal authority to regulate certain wetlands under the Clean Water Act); *CTS Corp. v. Waldburger*, 134 S. Ct. 2175 (2014) (holding that the federal Superfund statute does not preempt state statutes of repose).

[2] E.g. *National Federation of Independent Businesses v. Sebelius*, 132 S. Ct. 2566 (2012) (upholding certain mandates of the Affordable Care Act under the federal taxing power but invalidating other mandates relating to the state–federal Medicaid partnership for exceeding the spending power).

[3] E.g. Vann, Adam et al., "Proposed Keystone XL Pipeline: Legal Issues," U.S. Congressional Research Service (R42124, 20 January 2012) (discussing state–federal conflicts over the proposed pipeline, including siting issues pitting state land use law against federal authority under the Commerce Clause and dormant Commerce Clause); Osofsky, Hari M. and Hannah Wiseman, "Dynamic Energy Federalism" (2013) 72 Md. L. Rev. 773 (discussing federalism issues in energy policy); Williamson, Jeremiah I. and Matthias L. Sayer, "Federalism in Renewable Energy Policy" (2012) 27 Nat. Resources and Environ. 1 (listing different state programs).

[4] E.g. *Hollingsworth v. Perry*, 133 S. Ct. 2652 (2013) (enforcing the District Court's ruling that California's gay marriage ban was unconstitutional after concluding that the initiative sponsors lacked standing to appeal), *U.S. v. Windsor*, 133 S. Ct. 2675 (2013) (invalidating important parts of the federal Defense of Marriage Act).

forest regulation,[5] immigration,[6] species protection,[7] national security,[8] climate change,[9] and other hot-button political controversies.[10] Each one elicits diverging views about the appropriate policy content of the regulatory response, and federalism is sometimes invoked for purposes that are more strategic than principled.[11] Nevertheless, each one also forces us to confront the ultimate federalism dilemma of who, exactly, should have the final say over policy content.[12] Should ultimate control rest with the local community? The state? The national government? Some collaborative alliance among them? The dilemma is heightened in

---

[5] E.g. *Decker v. Northwest Environmental Defense Coalition*, 133 S. Ct. 1326 (2013) (examining the Clean Water Act Silviculture Rule and holding that certain discharges from logging roads are exempt from Clean Water Act permitting requirements); *Alt v. EPA*, No. 2:12-CV-42, at 17–18 (N.D.W. Va. Oct. 23, 2013) (holding a concentrated animal feeding operation exempted from Clean Water Act permitting requirements as agricultural exemption).

[6] E.g. *Arizona v. U.S.*, 132 S. Ct. 2492 (2012) (affirming broad federal authority over immigration and naturalization while allowing some state regulation relating to immigration).

[7] E.g. *In re Polar Bear Endangered Species Act Listing and Section 4(d) Rule Litigation*, 709 F. 3d 1 (DC Cir. 2013) (upholding federal action listing the polar bear under the Endangered Species Act and rejecting, inter alia, Alaska's claim that the agency failed to properly account for state management recommendations).

[8] E.g. Dickey, Christopher, "The Spymaster of New York" *Newsweek*, 9 February 2009, 40–41, accessed 20 July 2015 at www.newsweek.com/2009/01/30/the-spymaster-of-new-york.html (reporting on overlapping counter-terrorism intelligence gathering by the CIA and NYPD).

[9] E.g. *Massachusetts v. E.P.A.*, 549 U.S. 497 (2007) (upholding a state's challenge to the federal agency's decision not to regulate greenhouse gases under the Clean Air Act). Several states have also initiated cap-and-trade programs in the absence of comprehensive federal climate regulation. See Western Climate Initiative, accessed 20 July 2015 at www.westernclimateinitiative.org/milestones (detailing California's program); Midwestern Greenhouse Gas Reduction Accord, accessed 20 July 2015 at www.c2es.org/us-states-regions/regional-climate-initiatives/mggra (reporting on the Midwestern states' program and noting that although it has not been suspended, participating states have ceased moving forward with it).

[10] See Ryan, Erin, *Federalism and the Tug of War Within* (Oxford University Press, Oxford 2012), pp. xviii-xx (cataloging high-profile federalism controversies in all fields of law, including gun control, violence against women, minimum wage requirements, marijuana policy, radioactive waste disposal, and others) (hereinafter, "*Tug of War*").

[11] Ibid. pp. 35–37 (discussing the strategic use of federalism rhetoric).

[12] Ibid. pp. xii–xvii.

contexts of jurisdictional overlap, where different local, state and national regulatory interests or obligations are simultaneously implicated.[13] The intensity of federalism disputes reflects the inexorable pressure on all levels of government to meet the increasingly complicated challenges of governance in an ever more interconnected world, where the answers to jurisdictional questions are less and less obvious.[14]

Yet even as federalism dilemmas continue to erupt all from all corners of the regulatory map, the foregoing chapters show that environmental law remains at the forefront of federalism controversy, and that it is likely to do so for some time. From mining[15] to nuclear waste[16] to water pollution[17] to climate change,[18] the Supreme Court's environmental federalism cases have always been among the most contentious of its jurisprudence,[19] a phenomenon matched in the lower courts.[20] Environmental cases have also produced some of the most fractured judicial opinions on record (including some that have produced famously unworkable precedent going forward).[21] Federalism dilemmas are usually

---

[13] Ibid. pp. 146–50.

[14] Ryan, Erin, "The Once and Future Challenges of American Federalism" in Basaguren, Alberto López and Leire Escajedo San-Epifanio (eds), *The Ways of Federalism in Western Countries and the Horizons of Territorial Autonomy in Spain*, vol. 1 (Springer, Berlin, Heidelberg 2013).

[15] *Hodel v. Virginia Surface Mining & Reclamation Assn.*, 452 U.S. 264 (1981).

[16] *New York v. United States*, 505 U.S. 144 (1992).

[17] *Solid Waste Agency of Northern Cook County v. United States Army Corps of Engineers* (SWANCC), 531 U.S. 159, 173–74 (2001); *Rapanos v. United States*, 547 U.S. 715, 739 (2006).

[18] Cf. *Massachusetts v. Environmental Protection Agency*, 549 U.S. 497 (2007). As discussed further, *infra*, while this case is not usually viewed as a federalism decision, it raises the core environmental federalism problem of which aspects of environmental regulation are the primary prerogative of the federal and state governments.

[19] See Ryan, *Tug of War, supra*, n. 10, pp. 145–46, 147–80 (discussing the intensity of environmental federalism disputes).

[20] E.g. *Gibbs v. Babbit*, 214 F.3d 483 (4th Cir. 2000) (upholding under the Commerce Clause the Endangered Species Act's regulation of the hunting of endangered red wolves); *Connecticut v. Am. Elec. Power Co., Inc.*, 582 F.3d 309, 314 (2d Cir. 2009) rev'd, 131 S. Ct. 2527, 180 L. Ed. 2d 435 (U.S. 2011) (allowing municipal plaintiffs to bring a public nuisance suit against defendant power plants over alleged harms from greenhouse gas emissions).

[21] See e.g. *Rapanos v. United States*, 547 U.S. 715, 739 (2006) (limiting federal authority over certain wetlands but failing to set forth an articulable

hard, and often divisive. But why is this so accentuated when the subject at hand is the environment?

In fact, environmental law is uniquely prone to federalism discord because it inevitably confronts the core question with which federalism grapples – *who gets to decide?*[22] – in contexts where state and federal claims to power are simultaneously at their strongest. Environmental problems tend to match the need to regulate the harmful use of specific lands (among the most sacred of local prerogatives) with the need to regulate border-crossing harms caused by these uses (among the strongest of national prerogatives). As a result, it is often impossible to solve the problem without engaging authority on both ends of the spectrum – and disputes erupt when local and national ideas on how best to proceed diverge.[23]

Famous environmental decisions like *New York v. United States* (invalidating parts of a state–federal plan to manage radioactive waste),[24] *Rapanos v. United States* (limiting federal authority over intrastate wetlands under the Clean Water Act),[25] and even *Massachussets v. EPA* (allowing a state to sue the federal government for failing to regulate greenhouse gases under the Clean Air Act)[26] all feature variations on the theme of jurisdictional conflict over competing regulatory concerns. Together with ongoing jurisdictional controversies in energy policy, pollution law and natural resource management, they reveal environmental law as the canary in federalism's coal mine, showcasing the underlying reasons for jurisdictional conflict in all areas of law. And they indicate the critical need to better cope with the problems of jurisdictional overlap at the level of federalism theory.[27]

Concluding the book, this chapter explores why environmental law regularly raises such thorny questions of federalism, and how environmental law has specifically adapted to manage federalism conflicts. Drawing from the theoretical framework I introduced in *Federalism and*

---

principle for state or federal agency interpretation going forward). *Rapanos* is discussed further *infra* in Part III.

[22] Ryan, *Tug of War*, *supra*, n. 10, pp. xii–xvii (defining federalism as the constitutional means for allocating decision-making authority among the federal and state governments).

[23] See ibid., pp. 105–80 (discussing the challenges of jurisdictional overlap for the traditional "dual federalism" model of state–federal relations).

[24] 505 U.S. 144 (1992).

[25] 126 S. Ct. 2208, 2224 (2006).

[26] *Massachusetts v. E.P.A.*, 549 U.S. 497 (2007). All three cases are discussed further *infra* at Part IV.

[27] Ryan, *Tug of War*, *supra* n. 10, pp. 7–17, 30–33.

the Tug of War Within,[28] Part II reviews the central objectives of federalism, examining the conflicting values they imply and the resulting tension that suffuses all federalism-sensitive governance. Against this theoretical backdrop, Part III evaluates why federalism conflicts are especially heightened in the context of environmental law. The characteristic divisiveness of environmental federalism reflects the intense competition among federalism values in environmental governance, while also providing key insights into the core theoretical dilemmas of jurisdictional overlap more generally.

After analyzing why environmental federalism is so fraught, the second half of the chapter assesses how environmental law has responded to the challenges of jurisdictional overlap at the structural level. Part IV probes how different environmental statutes asymmetrically allocate local, state, and federal authority within various models of collaborative governance or cooperative federalism, including programs of coordinated capacity, federally supported state implementation, conditional preemption, and shared and general permitting programs. Part V concludes with consideration of what the larger discourse can learn from the dynamic federalism innovations emerging from the study and practice of multi-scalar environmental governance.

This analysis, supported by others in the book, reveals that the most successful environmental governance is conducted through processes of consultation, compromise and coordination that engage stakeholders at all levels of jurisdictional scale. Indeed, the broader federalism discourse is increasingly recognizing environmental federalism[29] for lighting a path away from the entrenched "zero-sum" model, which treats every assertion of authority at one jurisdictional level as a loss of authority for the others.[30] Many areas of environmental law doubtlessly remain imperfect in their implementation of these ideals, and emergency circumstances will occasionally require less deliberative government action. Still, the most successful examples of environmental governance suggest that, at the end of the day, good multiscalar governance is essentially a project of negotiation.

---

[28] Ibid.
[29] See Gerken, Heather K., "Federalism as the New Nationalism: An Overview" (2014) 123 Yale L.J. 1889, 1902, 1909 (noting that environmental federalism has been "ground zero for much of the new thinking on federalism").
[30] Ibid. at 267–68; see also Erin Ryan, "Negotiating Federalism" (2011) 52 B.C. L. Rev. 1, 4–5.

II. FEDERALISM AS A TOOL OF GOOD GOVERNANCE

To understand why environmental federalism is especially fraught, we must first understand why federalism itself is so fraught. This Part prepares the analysis of environmental federalism specifically by exploring the purposes and challenges of federalism more generally, beginning with the principles of good governance that federalism and other multi-scalar forms of government are designed to promote. It then examines the governance challenges that arise when federalism interpreters are forced to grapple with the inevitable tension among these principles, at the level of both theory and practice.[31]

A. The Objectives of Federalism

Federalism is a system of government that divides sovereign power between a central authority and regional political subunits – American states, Canadian provinces, German Länder, the nation states of the European Union, etc. – each with the authority to directly regulate citizens within its own jurisdiction.[32] The American system of "dual sovereignty" recognizes separate sources of sovereign authority in the federal and state governments but, as demonstrated by the chapters in Part V of this book,[33] the range of federal systems worldwide demonstrates many different ways of allocating regulatory authority within the overall model.[34] Federalism issues usually present as questions about which level of government is entitled to decide the unfolding course of a

---

[31] Some of this analysis draws on previous scholarship. To avoid unduly reiterating that work, it provides supporting citations to the deeper analysis in earlier publications, usually without further reference in the main text.

[32] Ryan, *Tug of War*, *supra*, n. 10, pp. 7–8.

[33] See Fowler, Robert, "The Australian Experience with Environmental Federalism," *supra*, Chapter 12; Behnke, Nathalie and Annegret Eppler, "German Environmental Federalism in the Multi-Level System of the European Union," *supra*, Chapter 13; Bhat, Sairam, "The Paradox of Environmental Federalism in India," *supra*, Chapter 14.

[34] Ibid. The Forum on Federations, which researches federalism and devolved governance, reports that the countries of the world include 25 federal systems at present, governing 40 percent of the world's population, with an additional two countries in transition to federalism. See "Federalism by Country," The Forum on Federations, accessed 20 July 2015 at www.forumfed.org/en/federalism/federalismbycountry.

given regulatory policy.³⁵ Each demands that we resolve whether the given regulatory matter is within the jurisdiction of local, state, regional, national or international authorities – or some combination thereof.

In the United States and other formal federal systems, federalism questions are embedded within larger issues of constitutional structure, implicating additional questions about the separation of powers between state and federal sovereigns and interpretive authority among the three branches of government.³⁶ But even in non-federal national and international contexts, similar issues arise concerning regulatory scale, competition and collaboration. And even within the American system, issues of regulatory scale and dynamic interaction extend beyond constitutionally cognizable state–federal relations to the various ways that towns, cities, counties, metropolitan partnerships and regional associations manage interjurisdictional governance (not to mention the growing phenomenon of international partnerships between subnational actors).³⁷

Nevertheless, for every system of multiscalar governance, the fundamental issue is the same: how to manage regulatory challenges in a way that best balances the good governance ideals that its framers seek to accomplish. In opening *Federalism and the Tug of War Within*, I argue that "federalism is best understood not just in terms of the conflict between states' rights and federal power, or the debate over judicial constraints and political process, or even the dueling claims over original intent – but instead through the inevitable conflicts that play out among

---

[35] See Ryan, *Tug of War*, *supra*, n. 10, at pp. xii–xvii (defining federalism as the constitutional means for allocating decision-making authority among the federal and state governments).

[36] See ibid. (addressing constitutional interpretive questions associated with American federalism in detail).

[37] See e.g. Gerken, Heather K., "Federalism All the Way Down" (2010) 124 Harv. L. Rev. 4; Osofsky, Hari M., "Diagonal Federalism and Climate Change: Implications for the Obama Administration" (2011) 62 Ala. L. Rev. 237 (discussing the significance of government levels beyond the state–federal dichotomy); Resnik, Judith, "Lessons in Federalism from the 1960s Class Action Rule and the 2005 Class Action Fairness Act: 'The Political Safeguards' of Aggregate Translocal Actions" (2008) 156 U. Penn. L. Rev. 1929 (discussing the role of local actors in federalism dilemmas); Davidson, Nestor M., "Cooperative Localism: Federal–Local Collaboration in an Era of State Sovereignty" (2007) 93 Va. L. Rev. 959 (discussing how local and federal actors can align against state actors); Barron, David J., "A Localist Critique of the New Federalism" (2001) 51 Duke L.J. 377, 378–79 (discussing the distinct spheres of local, state, and national power).

federalism's core principles."[38] This chapter's exploration of that conflict is based on the American model, because it was within the American constitutional experiment that the innovation of federalism was first born.[39] However, the principles of good multiscalar governance that undergird the American federal system have taken root within international norms, influencing governance in many other parts of the world as well.

B. Federalism Values and the Tug of War Within[40]

Analysis of the legislative history of the American Constitutional Convention, later Supreme Court interpretations, congressional and executive pronouncements and the academic literature yields five foundational good governance values that American federalism is designed to advance.[41] These emphasize the maintenance of (1) checks and balances between opposing centers of power that protect individuals; (2) governmental accountability and transparency that enhance democratic participation; (3) local autonomy that enables interjurisdictional innovation and competition; (4) centralized authority to manage collective action problems and vindicate core constitutional promises; and finally (5) the regulatory problem-solving synergy that federalism enables between the

---

[38] See Ryan, *Tug of War*, *supra*, n. 10, p. xi.

[39] See generally Lacroix, Alison L., *The Ideological Origins of American Federalism* (Harvard University Press, Cambridge MA 2010); Purcell, Edward A. Jr., *Originalism, Federalism, and the American Constitutional Enterprise: A Historical Inquiry* (Yale University Press, New Haven CT 2007).

[40] This section summarizes key insights from my book by the related title, *Federalism and the Tug of War Within*, Ryan, supra, n. 10.

[41] Ibid. pp. 34–67. In the book, I discuss the four federalism values most directly voiced in American federalism jurisprudence: checks and balances, transparency and accountability, localism values, and the problem-solving value implied by subsidiarity. Here, I add overt discussion of the values of centralized power that counterbalance the localism values within federalism. Because they are implicit in the creation of an overall nation-state, these values are debated less directly in the many cases that presume the value of centralized national authority but debate its appropriate relationship with subnational authority. These values are also implied by the value of intergovernmental problem-solving synergy. That said, so many environmental laws especially tap these values of central authority that I believe it is worth explicitly highlighting here as the fifth in the series.

unique governance capacities of local and national actors for coping with problems that neither can resolve alone.[42]

Governance in pursuit of these values advances individual dignity within healthy communities. It enhances democratic governance principles of self-determination while recognizing the responsibilities that group members hold toward one another. It creates a laboratory for innovations in governance from multiple possible sources[43] and facilitates multiple planes of negotiation among competing interests and interest groups.[44] It appropriately honors both sides of the subsidiarity principle – the directive to solve problems at the most local level possible[45] – which notably couples its preference for local autonomy in governance with the expectation of effective regulatory problem-solving (and by implication, at whatever level will achieve it).[46]

However, identifying what federalism is designed to accomplish is only the first part of the puzzle. The harder task is figuring out how these goals fit together. The core federalism values are doubtlessly all good things in and of themselves, and American governance has long aspired to realize each of them independently. Yet our success has been complicated by the fact that each individual good governance value is suspended in a web of tensions with the others. No matter how we may try, the hard truth is that they all cannot always be satisfied simultaneously in any

---

[42] See ibid. pp. xiv, 34–67 (specifically detailing the values of checks, transparency, localism, and synergy and dealing more holistically with the nationalism values necessarily implied by a federal system).

[43] For the most famous statement of this principle, see *New State Ice Co. v. Liebmann*, 285 U.S. 262, 311 (1932) (Brandeis J. dissenting) (comparing the states to laboratories in which to "try novel social and economic experiments").

[44] See Ryan, *Tug of War*, supra, n. 10, pp. 265–367 (discussing negotiated federalism among the various levels and branches of government). See also Ryan, "Negotiating Federalism," supra, n. 30 (introducing the analysis that evolved into this final part of the book).

[45] See e.g. Vischer, Robert K., "Subsidiarity as a Principle of Governance: Beyond Devolution" (2001) 35 Ind. L. Rev. 103, 103. For various accounts of the subsidiary principle, see Currie, David P., "Subsidiarity" (1998) 1 Green Bag 2D 359; Huffman, James L., "Making Environmental Regulation More Adaptive Through Decentralization: The Case for Subsidiarity" (2004) 52 U. Kan. L. Rev. 1377; Stinneford, John F., "Subsidiarity, Federalism, and Federal Prosecution of Street Crime" (2005) 2 J. Cath. Soc. Thought 495; Vause, W. Gary, "The Subsidiarity Principle in European Union Law – American Federalism Compared" (1995) 27 Case W. Res. J. Int'l L. 61; Bayer, Jared, Comment, "Re-Balancing State and Federal Power: Toward a Political Principle of Subsidiarity in the United States" (2004) 53 Am. U. L. Rev. 1421.

[46] See Ryan, *Tug of War*, supra, n. 10, pp. 59–66.

given context. The regulatory choices we make inevitably involve trade-offs, in which one value may partially eclipse another.[47] Conflicts between localism and nationalism are obvious, but the network of tension runs much deeper and among all the various values.

To take another example, consider the tension between the values of (1) checks on sovereign authority and (2) transparent and accountable government. Federalism promotes a balanced system of checks on sovereign authority at both the state and federal level, enabling the useful tool of governance that I have previously called "regulatory backstop," which protects individuals against government excess or abdication by either side.[48] When sovereign authority at one level fails to protect the vulnerable, regulatory backstop ensures that it remains available to do so at a different level. The history of civil rights law reveals especially famous examples, matching periods in which the federal government protected the rights of African-Americans forsaken by state law[49] with more modern examples in which states have acted to protect rights unrecognized by federal law, including those of LGBT citizens[50] and the owners of property subject to eminent domain.[51] Environmental law showcases equally compelling examples of dual sovereignty at its best,[52] including the 1970s era in which the federal government acted to prevent

---

[47] Ibid. pp. 38–39 (and more generally pp. 34–67).

[48] Ibid. pp. 39–44 (discussing checks and balances); 42–43 (discussing regulatory backstop).

[49] E.g. Howard, Marilyn K., "Discrimination," in Brown, Nikki L.M. and Barry M. Stentiford (eds), *The Jim Crow Encyclopedia*, vol. 1 (Greenwood, Westport, CT 2008), pp. 222, 226-27

[50] See e.g, Vt. Stat. Ann. tit. 15, § 8 (2009) (amending marriage definition from union between a man and woman to a union between two people); Colo. Rev. Stat. §§ 24-34-401 and 24-34-402 (2007) (barring discrimination in hiring based on sexual orientation); *Goodridge v. Dep't of Pub. Health*, 798 N.E.2d 941 (Mass. 2003) (asserting that the Massachusetts constitution is more protective of civil rights than the federal Constitution in invalidating a state statutory ban on same-sex marriages). Cf. Gerken, Heather K. "Dissenting by Deciding" (2005) 57 Stan. L. Rev. 1745 (discussing San Francisco's decision to issue gay marriage licenses despite contrary state law). More recently, the Supreme Court removed an important federal obstacle to state efforts to legalize gay marriage. *U.S. v. Windsor*, 133 S. Ct. 2675 (2013) (invalidating parts of the federal Defense of Marriage Act).

[51] See e.g. Tim Hoover, "Eminent Domain Reform Signed" *Kan. City Star*, 14 July 2006, at B2 (reporting on new state law property rights).

[52] See Ryan, *Tug of War*, *supra*, n. 10, pp. xxvii–xxix.

excessive air and water pollution when most states had failed to do so,[53] and the current era in which many states are moving to address the causes and effects of climate change at a time when the national government has not succeeded.[54]

Yet the availability of a regulatory backstop exacts a price. The very maintenance of checks and balances between state and national actors itself frustrates the independent value of transparency, making it harder for the average citizen to navigate the lines of governmental accountability (and know whom to blame for bad policy choices).[55] This is especially problematic in realms of extreme jurisdictional overlap, such as environmental or criminal law, where legitimate state and federal governance takes place simultaneously.[56] As I describe in *Federalism and the Tug of War Within*, if all we cared about were the good governance values of transparency and accountability, the best alternative would be a unitary system of government, such as that in use by France or China.[57] Alternatively, if checks and balances were the primary governance ideal, then we should do away with the Constitution's Supremacy Clause,[58] which gives the national government a powerful edge in many state–federal conflicts.[59] If localism values were primary, then our best course of action would be a confederal system among powerful states and a weak center, lacking federal constitutional supremacy (not unlike the nation's first experiment with the Articles of Confederation).[60]

Instead, we tolerate the open tension between checks and transparency, and the obvious conflicts between localism values and strong national power, and all the other trade-offs that palpably manifest among the five – precisely to reap the federalism-facilitated benefits of local autonomy when desirable, national uniformity when preferable, regulatory backstop

---

[53] Clean Air Act, 42 U.S.C. § 7401 *et seq.* (2006); Clean Water Act, 33 U.S.C. § 1251 *et seq.* (2006).

[54] See e.g. Engel, Kirsten H., "Whither Subnational Climate Change Initiatives in the Wake of Federal Climate Legislation?" (2009) 39 Publius 432; Engel, Kirsten, "State and Local Climate Change Initiatives: What Is Motivating State and Local Governments to Address a Global Problem and What Does This Say About Federalism and Environmental Law?" (2006) 38 Urb. Law. 1015. See also Engel, Chapter 8; Buzbee, Chapter 7; Kaswan, Chapter 9.

[55] See Ryan, *Tug of War*, *supra*, n. 10, pp. 43–50.

[56] Ibid. pp. 145–80.

[57] Ibid. pp. 48.

[58] U.S. Const. Art. VI.

[59] See Ryan, *Tug of War*, *supra*, n. 10, pp. 43–44.

[60] Notably, this unsuccessful experiment was rejected in favor of true federalism. Ibid.

when necessary, and interjurisdictional problem-solving when inevitable.[61] Strong local authority expands opportunities for democratic participation, encourages well-tailored governance, facilitates diversity, inspires innovation and encourages interjurisdictional competition.[62] Strong national power resolves collective action problems, facilitates markets, manages border-crossing harms and large-scale public commons, speaks to the world with a unitary voice and vindicates non-negotiable constitutional promises.[63] Ideally, coupling healthy local authority with strong national power facilitates the kind of dynamic interjurisdictional synergy in governance that makes for the most effective regulatory response – drawing on the distinctive forms of governance capacity that develop respectively at the local and national levels to solve pressing interjurisdictional problems that require both.[64]

C. The Once and Future Challenges of Federalism Theory[65]

With values-based competition implicit in all federalism quandaries, each dilemma demands that decision-makers choose, consciously or otherwise, how to prioritize among conflicting federalism values. Navigating the tension to a conclusion usually provides good direction on the related issue of where to assign regulatory responsibility within zones of jurisdictional overlap, or realms of governance that legitimately implicate both state and federal authority (discussed further in Part IV). Reconciling competing values and allocating authority are daunting tasks. Yet federalism theory – the conceptual roadmap that jurists have created over the centuries to help interpreters meet the challenge – has not always been helpful.

To be sure, there are some easy cases, in which federal supremacy cleanly resolves a given conflict in favor of nationalism, or a clear constitutional command resolves it in favor of localism values.[66] But

---

[61] Ibid. pp. 34–67.
[62] Ibid. pp. 50–59.
[63] See e.g. Millican, Edward, *One United People: The Federalist Papers and the National Idea* (University of Kentucky Press, Lexington, KY 1990).
[64] Ibid. pp. 59–66, 145–80, 265–367. See also Ryan, "Negotiating Federalism" *supra*, n. 30 (exploring intergovernmental bargaining as a means of harnessing interjurisdictional synergy).
[65] See generally Ryan, "The Once and Future Challenges of American Federalism," *supra*, n. 14 (inspiring the title of this section).
[66] Compare U.S. Const. Art. VI (federal supremacy) with U.S. Const. amend. X (reserving non-enumerated powers to the states); compare U.S. Const. amend. XV (conferring clear federal authority to ensure that voting rights are not

even when the federal government *can* legally trump local initiative, does that necessarily mean that it *should*? Consider the current debates over the respective state and federal roles in regulating marijuana and immigration. In recent cases addressing these subjects, the Supreme Court affirmed that the federal government holds trumping regulatory authority.[67] But what are the competing considerations in each context that guide your own opinion about the relative strength of state claims for input into final regulatory policies? What theoretical tools are available to help answer these questions?

Indeed, the federalism discourse is only just beginning to appreciate how this unresolved "tug of war" for privilege among these competing values has led to the Supreme Court's notoriously fluctuating federalism jurisprudence.[68] Over the nation's history, the Court, Congress and others

---

abridged on the basis of race) with U.S. Const. Art. I, § 2, amend. XVII, Art. II § 1, amend. XII (conferring clear state responsibility for conducting congressional and presidential elections).

[67] See *Gonzales v. Raich*, 545 U.S. 1 (2005) (upholding the criminalization of intrastate marijuana growers under the Commerce Clause); *Arizona v. U.S.*, 132 S. Ct. 2492 (2012) (affirming federal primacy in immigration law).

[68] The federalism literature has exploded in recent years with interesting new perspectives on dynamic and innovative federalism theory. While all sources are too numerous to list, a worthy tour would include Ryan, *Tug of War*, supra, n. 10; Schapiro, Robert A., *Polyphonic Federalism* (University of Chicago Press, Chicago 2009); Nugent, John, *Safeguarding Federalism: How States Protect Their Interests in National Policymaking* (University of Oklahoma Press, Norman 2009); Chemerinsky, Erwin, *Enhancing Government: Federalism for the 21st Century* (Stanford University Press, Stanford CA 2008); Feeley, Malcolm M. and Edward Rubin, *Federalism: Political Identity and Tragic Compromise* (University of Michigan Press, Ann Arbor MI 2008); Bulman-Pozen, Jessica, "Partisan Federalism" (2014) 127 Harvard L. Rev. 1077; Gluck, Abbe, "Federalism's Domain" (2014) 123 Yale L.J. (forthcoming); Gerken, "Federalism All the Way Down," *supra*, n. 37; Bulman-Pozen, Jessica and Heather Gerken, "Uncooperative Federalism" (2009) 118 Yale L.J. 1256; Buzbee, William W., "Interaction's Promise: Preemption Policy Shifts, Risk Regulation, and Experimentalism Lessons" (2007) 57 Emory L.J. 145; Engel, Kirsten H. "Harnessing the Benefits of Dynamic Federalism in Environmental Law" (2006) 56 Emory L.J. 159. More traditional and historical perspectives are also an important part of the recent federalism discourse. See e.g. Greve, Michael S., *The Upside-Down Constitution* (Harvard University Press, Cambridge MA 2012); Lacroix, Alison L., *The Ideological Origins of American Federalism* (Harvard University Press, Cambridge MA 2010); Bednar, Jenna, *The Robust Federation* (Cambridge University Press, New York 2009); Purcell, Edward A. Jr., *Originalism, Federalism, and the American Constitutional Enterprise: A Historical Inquiry* (Yale University Press, New Haven CT 2007).

have experimented with various theoretical models of federalism in which one value has been uncritically elevated above the others in importance, with corresponding costs for good governance.[69] At various points, most recently during the Rehnquist Court's New Federalism revival, the Court has grounded its federalism adjudication in an idealized model of "dual federalism."[70] Dual federalism privileges the check-and-balance value in idealizing a system of mutually exclusive state and federal jurisdictional spheres – notwithstanding the marked departure of this ideal from the reality of an American system suffused with jurisdictional overlap.[71] By contrast, the preferred model of federalism during the New Deal era privileged nationalism in service to the problem-solving value – elevating the need for strong federal power to solve critical societal problems after the Great Depression – but with less regard for the values of checks, localism or accountability (and arguably fomenting the social frustration that would later lead to the modern New Federalism and Tea Party Movements).[72]

Notwithstanding the ghost of dual federalism that continues to haunt the Supreme Court's federalism jurisprudence, the model of cooperative federalism predominates in the actual practice of federalism-sensitive governance.[73] Cooperative federalism acknowledges the reality of jurisdictional overlap between legitimate state and federal interests, and it allows for regulatory partnerships in which state and federal actors take responsibility for interlocking parts of a larger regulatory whole.[74] This model seeks a middle ground between the excessive jurisdictional separation of pure dual federalism and the fear that New Deal federalism would obliterate dual sovereignty. Nevertheless, the critics of cooperative

---

[69] See Ryan, *Tug of War*, *supra*, n. 10, pp. 68–104 (analyzing the different theoretical models of federalism in use over the history of American governance and jurisprudence).

[70] See ibid. pp. 98–104 (reviewing dual federalism), 109–44 (analyzing the Rehnquist Court's New Federalism revival).

[71] In fact, jurisdictional overlap is so prevalent in American governance that it has been famously compared to "marble cake," with entangled swirls of interlocking local and national law. Grodzins, Morton (Daniel J. Elazar, ed.), *The American System, A New view of Government in the United States* 2nd edn (Transaction Books, New Brunswick 1984), pp. 8, 60–153. See also Ryan, *Tug of War*, *supra*, n. 10, pp. 145–80 (reviewing the interjurisdictional challenge to dual federalism).

[72] See Ryan, *Tug of War*, *supra*, n. 10, at pp. 84–88 (reviewing New Deal Federalism), 98–104 (reviewing the rise of New Federalism and the Tea Party).

[73] See ibid. pp. 89–98 (reviewing cooperative federalism).

[74] Ibid.

federalism variously assail the model as overly ad hoc, undertheorized, and coercive.[75]

In response to shortcomings in these paradigmatic models, a host of new scholarship is developing newer theoretical conceptions of federalism,[76] including the Balanced Federalism model that I proposed in *Federalism and the Tug of War Within*.[77] Balanced Federalism emphasizes dynamic interaction among the various levels of government and shared interpretive responsibility among the three branches of government, with the overall goal of achieving a balance among the competing federalism values that is both dynamic and adaptive over time.[78] As I describe it there, the Balanced Federalism model involves:

> a series of innovations to bring judicial, legislative, and executive efforts to manage the tug of war into more fully theorized focus. [Balanced Federalism] mediates the tensions within federalism on three separate planes: (1) fostering balance among the competing federalism values, (2) leveraging the functional capacities of the three branches of government in interpreting federalism, and (3) maximizing the wisdom of both state and federal actors in so doing. [This initial foray] imagines three successive means of coping with federalism's values tug of war, each experimenting with different degrees of judicial and political leadership at different levels of government. Along the way, the analysis provides clearer theoretical justification for the ways in which the tug of war is already legitimately mediated through various forms of balancing, compromise, and negotiation.[79]

The full elaboration of Balanced Federalism in the book helps provide the missing theoretical justification for the tools of cooperative federalism that predominate modern environmental law, as well as support for future moves by environmental governance toward even greater dynamic

---

[75] See ibid. pp. 96–98 (discussing frustration with cooperative federalism), 273–76 (discussing the federalism safeguards debate). See also Greve, *supra*, n. 68 (assailing cooperative federalism as coercive and collusive).
[76] See e.g. Chemerinsky, *supra*, n. 68, Schapiro, *supra*, n. 68, Greve, *supra*, n. 68.
[77] See generally Ryan, *Tug of War*, *supra*, n. 10.
[78] See ibid. pp. 181–214, 265–70, 339–67.
[79] Ibid. pp. xi–xii.

engagement.[80] It emphasizes the skillful deployment of legislative, executive and judicial capacity at each level of federalism-sensitive governance, allocating authority based on the specific forms of decision-making in which they excel.[81]

In so doing, Balanced Federalism demonstrates how well-crafted multiscalar governance deflates the pervasive presumption of "zero-sum federalism," a misunderstanding of state–federal relations with roots in dual federalism that continues to haunt the American discourse.[82] Zero-sum conceptualizations of federalism assume that the state and federal governments are locked in an antagonistic, winner-takes-all competition for power, in which every victory by one side constitutes a loss for the other.[83] While this is sometimes true,[84] closer examination of federalism-sensitive governance reveals that the line between state and federal power is just as often a project of negotiation, through ongoing processes of consultation and coordination that can accrue to the advantage of both sides.[85] Several authors in this book have highlighted the theory of negotiated federalism that is central to the Balanced Federalism model as an essential step toward more rational environmental governance.[86]

While this chapter does not further explore Balanced Federalism, it is no coincidence that the Balanced Federalism proposal was inspired by my own experience and research of environmental governance. Environmental law, land use planning and public health and safety regulation address problems in which the tensions among federalism values and the questions of who should arbitrate among them are heightened, sometimes viscerally so.[87] The pressures of jurisdictional overlap in environmental law have driven the Supreme Court's federalism decisions to its

---

[80] See generally Ryan, *Tug of War*, *supra*, n. 10.

[81] See ibid.; Ryan, "Negotiating Federalism and the Structural Constitution: Navigating the Separation of Powers both Vertically and Horizontally (A Response to Aziz Huq)" (forthcoming, 2015) Colum. L. Rev. Sidebar.

[82] Ryan, *Tug of War*, *supra* n. 10, at pp. 267–68; see also Ryan, "Negotiating Federalism" (2011) 52 B.C. L. Rev. 1, 4–5.

[83] Ibid.

[84] See e.g. *Arizona v. United States*, 132 S. Ct. 2492 (2012) (holding most of a state immigration statute preempted by federal law).

[85] Ryan, *Tug of War*, *supra* n. 10, at pp. 267–68; see also Ryan, "Negotiating Federalism" (2011) 52 B.C. L. Rev. 1, 4–5.

[86] See Wiseman, "Evolving Energy Federalism: Current Allocations of Authority and the Need for Inclusive Governance," *supra*, Chapter 6; Kaswan, "Cooperative Federalism and Adaptation," *supra*, Chapter 9.

[87] Cf. Doremus, Holly, "Shaping the Future: The Dialectic of Law and Environmental Values," (2003) 37 U.C. Davis L. Rev. 233.

extremes, exposing the fault lines between competing values that exist, if less ostentatiously, in all fields of federalism-sensitive governance.[88] But for the same reasons, environmental law can lead the way for all fields in developing innovative forms of collaborative multiscalar governance, in which policymaking is appropriately informed by consultation, negotiation and compromise among all participants.

III. ENVIRONMENTAL FEDERALISM AND THE TUG OF WAR WITHIN

Tension among the core federalism values is especially heightened in the context of environmental law, where compelling claims for the importance of local autonomy and tailoring are coupled with equally compelling claims about the need for national capacity and uniformity. Concerns over accountability, checks and problem-solving point decision-makers in different directions. Climate governance, other air and water pollution, coastal and forest management, wildlife protection, hazardous waste, energy law and related environmental fields all demonstrate the difficulties of managing these tensions in regulatory territory where both local and national actors hold unique authority, interests, obligations and expertise. Intertwined with both land use law and public health and safety regulation, environmental law implicates federalism's tug of war within perhaps more dramatically than any other single area of law.

Casting environmental law as the canary in the coal mine of wider federalism controversy, this Part explores why environmental federalism disputes so often become so intense. With analysis of current environmental challenges and examples from the Supreme Court's environmental docket, it examines how environmental dilemmas uniquely expose the underlying competition among good governance values. Clashes often arise because of the way the regulatory target matches the need for state authority to manage the local harms and benefits of particular land uses with the need for national authority to cope with the externalities and collective action implications of those uses. The first section illustrates these points in the context of several ongoing controversies in energy law, and the second section explores them through the competing opinions in three noteworthy Supreme Court decisions.

---

[88] See Ryan, *Tug of War, supra,* n. 10, p. xi.

A. The Canary in Federalism's Coal Mine

Environmental law is prone to extreme federalism controversy because it effectively allocates power in regulatory contexts where state and federal claims to authority are simultaneously at their strongest. Environmental problems very often match a need to regulate the harmful use of a specific parcel of land with the need to police border-crossing harms associated with that use.[89] The state claim for regulatory priority is supported by the hallowed understanding that governing land use is among the most sacred of local prerogatives,[90] while the federal claim is buttressed by the fact that regulating externalities is among the original predicates of national authority.[91] Criminal law and public health federalism might be fraught for similar reasons, because they also implicate the state's police power to regulate for health and safety, and they also portend spillover harms to other states if poorly managed. And indeed, these realms of law are also marked by federalism controversy, as the recent Obamacare upheaval attests.[92] Yet most of the time, environmental federalism controversies are even more heightened, for reasons that appear to hinge on the special relationship between land use regulation and environmental law.

Conventional environmental laws regulate pollution or natural resources, but both are intertwined with regulation of the local lands on which resources are regulated or pollution produced. Harmful land uses must be regulated to prevent spillovers, and the failure of state environmental laws to accomplish this before the enactment of the major federal pollution statutes in the 1970s suggests that central authority may be necessary.[93] However, the regulation of land poses questions to which the answers are intensely more idiosyncratic – and more locally variegated – than most regulatory issues involving crime or public health. There is

---

[89] See Ryan, "The Once and Future Challenges of American Federalism," *supra*, note 14, at Part 3.1.

[90] See e.g. *Young v. American Mini Theaters*, 427 U.S. 50, 80 (1976) (Powell J. concurring) (identifying local land use regulation as among the essential functions of local government).

[91] See e.g. *Missouri v. Illinois*, 200 U.S. 496 (1906) (strongly affirming federal jurisdiction to resolve an interstate nuisance claim over discharges by Chicago of raw sewage into the Mississippi River).

[92] See e.g. *National Federation of Independent Businesses v. Sebelius*, 132 S. Ct. 2566 (2012).

[93] See e.g. Percival, Robert V., "Environmental Federalism: Historical Roots and Contemporary Models" (1995) 54 Md. L. Rev. 1141, 1160 (describing the failure of state law efforts as the precursor to federal environmental law).

widespread consensus on what constitutes health, theft or murder; state public health and criminal laws do differ, but mostly at the margins. By contrast, the answers to questions about how best to regulate land use can differ radically between states, or even between neighborhoods, because the nature of the land in question is so locally unique.

As Hirokawa and Rosenblum argue in Chapter 11, the contours of the land, soil quality, climate, precipitation levels, elevation, prevailing winds, habitat, population density, zoning laws and the local economies dependent on that land will all differ dramatically from one community to the next. Managing water pollution in Oregon, Arizona, Iowa, New York and Florida requires wholly different sets of local expertise – you have to know what the watershed looks like, what the major stressors are, where the local industry is operating, the seasonal weather patterns – and these will likely result in diverging, locally tailored strategies. Moreover, bad land use decisions made without the benefit of local expertise can portend serious environmental, cultural and economic harm if things go wrong. Applying an inappropriate regulatory strategy for given conditions could damage soil, water and other local resources, with enormous collateral consequences for entire communities. Nevertheless, if one community fails to prevent spillover harms to another, then the stakes are equally high.

For these reasons, jurisdictional conflicts have long been part of the legal and political controversies that erupt within the vast gray area of environmental governance. Should EPA be able to regulate manmade irrigation ditches as wetlands?[94] Can California impose costs on "dirtier" energy imported from out-of-state?[95] Should municipalities have the right to ban fracking operations?[96] On the surface, these conflicts play out as

---

[94] See "Definition of Waters of the United States Under the Clean Water Act," EPA, 80 Fed. Reg. 37,054 (June 29, 2015 (to be codified at, e.g.) 40 C.F.R. 230.3), accessed Sep. 30, 2015 at www2.epa.gov/cleanwaterrule/definition-waters-united-states-under-clean-water-act (proposed rule extending Clean Water Act authority to, inter alia, agricultural ditches); Missouri Farm Bureau, "That's Enough" ("Let it Go" Parody), *You Tube*, 23 May 2014, accessed 20 July 2015 at www.youtube.com/watch?v=9U0OqJqNbbs&feature=youtu.be (video parody of Disney Film, *Frozen*, criticizing the proposed rule's application to agricultural ditches).

[95] See *Rocky Mountain Farmers Union v. Corey*, 730 F.3d 1070 (9th Cir. 2013) cert denied 134 S. Ct. 2875 (2014) (overturning the lower court's conclusion that California's "lifecycle analysis" of imported fuel's carbon intensity unconstitutionally burdens interstate commerce in energy).

[96] Compare *Robinson Township v. Pennsylvania*, ___ A.3d ___, 2013 WL 6687290 (Pa. 2013) (upholding municipal rights to regulate fracking under the

contests between state and federal jurisdiction, where each has a legitimate claim to regulate. But environmental conflicts are especially charged because of the values contest that extends beneath the surface task of assigning primary responsibility. Regardless of who gets the final say, making that call requires the decision-maker to forge a path forward through the tension among federalism's core values – checks and balances, accountability and transparency, local autonomy, central authority, and problem-solving synergy – each pointing regulatory response in a different direction.

Should the primary consideration be the facilitation of interjurisdictional innovation, given uncertainty about the best regulatory approach (an interpretation favoring values of local autonomy)? Should the primary consideration be the need for preemptive central regulation to fully police collective action problems that may unravel other regulatory solutions (favoring values of central authority)? Is it the need for simultaneous local and national regulation to provide a regulatory backstop and prevent regulatory capture (favoring checks and balances)? Or is this a situation in which state and federal regulation is needed to simultaneously manage different elements of an interjurisdictional regulatory problem that requires both local and national capacity (favoring problem-solving synergy)? If so, how do concerns about governmental transparency and accountability factor in?

Regulatory decision-makers navigate these conflicting values to establish a rough order of priority, and this enables them to determine which level of governance has the best capacity to act on the primary concerns. But in environmental law clear answers are especially elusive. In some regulatory contexts the value that cries out for primacy may seem clear to most observers – for example, the need for preemptive central authority in managing the war power. For generally accepted reasons, the armed forces ultimately respond to only one commander in chief. But in environmental contexts the answer is often less clear. Sometimes the need for regulatory innovation really does clash with the need to resolve collective action problems – as powerfully demonstrated by the challenges of climate governance. In others, the majority of observers may firmly believe that one value clearly cries out for primacy – but they lack consensus on exactly which one it is.

---

state constitution) with *Colorado Oil & Gas Assn. v. City of Fort Collins*, ___P.3d ___, 2014 (case number 13CV31385, Larimer County District Court, Aug. 7, 2014) (holding a local fracking ban preempted by contrary state law).

Examples abound in environmental law, especially in realms where land use factors heavily, including the examples of nuclear waste disposal, water pollution law, coastal management and climate governance, discussed further below. But for an initial example, consider how the tension among federalism values manifests in several ongoing challenges for energy law.

(1) Federalism tension in energy policy

Federalism-sensitive energy law dilemmas include how to allocate authority over different aspects of energy harvest and infrastructure; how to share state and federal oversight of energy pricing and transmission; and how to appropriately structure energy markets to respect different realms of local, state and federal prerogative. Energy law pits federalism's underlying values against one another as intensively as any other realm of environmental law, and in many respects more interestingly – because intergovernmental conflicts here are as likely to arise between local and state government as they are between state and federal government.

As Hannah Wiseman explains in Chapter 6, most energy governance takes place at the state and local levels, which maintain primary authority over the siting and operation of in-state energy facilities and markets. States remain the primary regulators of oil and gas drilling operations and electric utilities, a jurisdictional realm explicitly preserved by the Federal Power Act.[97] In general, states regulate the intrastate elements of the energy industry (including production and retail sales), while the federal government regulates the interstate elements (including interstate transmission and wholesale pricing), mostly through the Federal Energy Regulatory Commission.[98] Drawing on federal authority over interstate commerce, the Commission oversees interstate energy markets and wholesale rate-making, interstate oil and gas pipelines and other fuels transportation, liquefied natural gas terminals, hydropower projects, and reviews certain mergers, acquisitions and corporate transactions by electric companies.[99] State agencies regulate virtually all else (except

---

[97] 16 U.S.C. §§ 824, 824a–824w (2012) (distinguishing state and federal roles in regulating electric utilities).

[98] See e.g. Hoecker, James J. and Douglas W. Smith, "Regulatory Federalism and Development of Electric Transmission: A Brewing Storm?" (2014) 35 Energy L.J. 71 (arguing that the distinctions are blurring).

[99] Federal Energy Regulatory Commission, "What FERC Does," accessed 20 July at www.ferc.gov/about/ferc-does.asp (last updated 24 June 2014) (listing

nuclear power plants, under the separate jurisdiction of the federal Nuclear Regulatory Commission).[100]

Recently, federalism litigation has arisen over the extent to which state Renewable Portfolio Standards, carbon-intensity preferences and other creative means of promoting sustainable energy use within state markets are preempted by federal authority under the dormant Commerce Clause. These policies capitalize on the regulatory innovation and interjurisdictional competition that local autonomy enables within federalism's laboratory of ideas, all in the service of solving critical problems associated with climate change, energy independence and environmental sustainability. Nevertheless, they come into heated conflict with claims for the preeminent value of central authority to promote free markets and national uniformity in interstate commerce.

For example, in *Rocky Mountain Farmers Union v. Corey*, the Ninth Circuit recently upheld California regulations favoring low carbon-intensity fuels against a claim that they unconstitutionally regulated extraterritorial production, finding that they did not facially discriminate against out-of-state production.[101] Overturning a contrary conclusion by the lower court, the panel was persuaded by the localism values of innovation and competition, essentially holding that California was entitled to experiment with regulatory means of avoiding serious harms from climate change to its citizens, and that any interstate burden was justified by the fact that the formula accurately measured carbon intensity.[102] Highlighting the clash of values, however, a strongly stated dissent defended the importance of national uniformity and unfettered interstate commerce notwithstanding respect for California's "long history of innovative solutions to complicated environmental problems."[103] Advocates for California's rule praised the decision's reasoning,

---

agency responsibilities and distinguishing the related responsibilities of state and other federal agencies).

[100] Ibid.

[101] 730 F.3d 1070 (9th Cir. 2013), cert. denied 134 S. Ct. 2875 (2014) (overturning the lower court's conclusion that California's "lifecycle analysis" of imported fuel's carbon intensity unconstitutionally burdens interstate commerce in energy).

[102] Ibid.

[103] Ibid. at 1108, 1110 (Murguia, Circuit Judge, dissenting).

while critics called it "a thin veil attempting to mask a result-based conclusion."[104] The Supreme Court denied review.[105]

Nevertheless, perhaps the most interesting dilemmas of energy law include intrastate controversies over where, how and whether to harvest different sources of energy when state and local preferences conflict. As Professor Wiseman describes, both traditional and renewable energy harvest are land-use intensive in ways that can disproportionately disperse the costs and benefits of extraction, leading to community protest.[106] For example, sprawling solar and wind power operations lay claim to large surface areas that can interfere with wildlife and community aesthetics. Citing harm to scenic resources and migratory birds, Massachusetts residents have unsuccessfully sought to block the establishment of a large offshore wind farm off the coast of Cape Cod.[107] Controversy over the siting of transmission facilities, including the proposed XL Pipeline, further embroils all levels of government in conflicts in which state and local interests are not always aligned.[108]

More poignantly, the drilling and hydraulic fracturing (fracking) of oil and gas wells has led to divisive regulatory conflicts between state and local interests. Local opposition to fracking, which can cause troubling air and water pollution,[109] has spawned a series of clashes between municipalities seeking to ban it and state efforts to preempt the local bans. In 2013 the Pennsylvania Supreme Court invalidated state efforts to preempt a local fracking ban under the state's Environmental Rights Amendment, an expanded and constitutionalized version of the public

---

[104] Jonathan Marsh, "Ninth Circuit Holds that 'California's Regulatory Experiment' Does Not Discriminate Against Out-of-State Ethanol and Crude Oil Producers," *King & Spaulding Energy Newsletter*, October 2013, accessed 20 July at www.kslaw.com/library/newsletters/EnergyNewsletter/2013/October/article5.html.

[105] See 134 S. Ct. 2875 (2014).

[106] See Wiseman, "Evolving Energy Federalism," *supra*, Chapter 6.

[107] See e.g. Fox, Jeremy, "Federal Judge Dismisses Cape Wind Lawsuit," *Boston Globe*, 4 May 2014, accessed 20 July 2015 at www.bostonglobe.com/metro/2014/05/03/district-court-judge-dismisses-suit-block-cape-wind-project/hiMjvDh22jsc10fqRPNV3N/story.html (reporting on local opposition to a large offshore wind project).

[108] See Vann, *supra*, n. 3 (discussing XL Pipeline controversy).

[109] See e.g. Morris, Jason, "Texas Family Plagued with Ailments gets $3M in 1st-of-Its-Kind Fracking Judgment," CNN, 26 April 2014, accessed 20 July 2015 at www.cnn.com/2014/04/25/justice/texas-family-wins-fracking-lawsuit/ (reporting on a successful private nuisance suit).

trust doctrine.[110] By contrast, two district courts in Colorado have concluded that local bans by the cities of Fort Collins and Longmont are preempted by the Colorado Oil and Gas Conservation Act.[111] The Colorado controversy prompted a widely reported dispute between state and local interests leading up to the 2014 election, involving multiple competing ballot initiatives about local authority over fracking operations, culminating in a state task force to reconsider the extent of state and local authority over fracking and other locally sensitive energy extraction.[112]

The recent fracking controversies demonstrate an important disjuncture that the federalism debates often mask: the occasionally stark gap between state and local interests. Pure constitutional federalism presumes a false identity between state and municipal interests in vindicating localism values. The Constitution treats the state as the "local" branch of government, a historical conceit that is barely defensible in application to Wyoming (population: 576,412) or Delaware (land area: 2,489 square miles, 6,446 square kilometers) and laughable in application to California (population: 37,253,956; land area: 163,695 square miles, 423,698 square kilometers).[113] Effectively balancing localism values with other good governance values ultimately requires multiscalar governance with greater sensitivity to the distinction between state and local interests than is enabled by the more simplistic models of dual federalism and even cooperative federalism.[114]

---

[110] *Robinson Township v. Pennsylvania*, ___ A.3d ___, 2013 WL 6687290 (Pa. 2013).

[111] *Colorado Oil & Gas Assn. v. City of Fort Collins*, ___P.3d ___, 2014 (case number 13CV31385, Larimer County District Court, Aug. 7, 2014). Two weeks earlier, on 24 July 2014, the Boulder County District Court held the City of Longmont's hydraulic fracturing ban was similarly preempted.

[112] Olson, Bradley and Jennifer Oldham, "Colorado Fracking Opponents Losing Local Control Fight," *Bloomberg*, 4 Aug. 2014, accessed 20 July 2015 at www.bloomberg.com/news/2014-08-04/colorado-governor-strikes-deal-seen-avoiding-fracking-curbs.html (reporting on ballot initiatives and a new state task force in Colorado).

[113] US Census Bureau, "Annual Estimates of the Population for the United States, Regions, States, and Puerto Rico: April 1, 2010–July 1, 2012," accessed at www.census.gov/popest/data/national/totals/2012/ (providing state population statistics); US Census Bureau, "State Area Measurements and Internal Point Coordinates," accessed 20 July 2015 at www.census.gov/geo/reference/state-area.html (providing state area measurements).

[114] See e.g. Gerken, Osofsky, Resnik and Davidson sources cited *supra*, n. 37.

More specifically, federalism tension arises in the fracking disputes between values of localism, centralized authority at both the state and federal level, and checks on sovereign authority. Fracking, wind farm and pipeline controversies implicate core localism values regarding a community's right to self-determine local land uses and economic opportunities, with different municipalities reaching different conclusions about the kinds of communities they want to live in. Yet they also implicate competing values of centralized state and/or federal authority to protect larger-scale public interests in stable access to affordable supply, environmentally sustainable production or transmission safety. In addition, the virtually unlimited ability of most states to preempt or control conflicting municipal choices – vastly more powerful than the ability of the federal government to control the states – raises troubling questions about the protection of checks and balances between local and centralized power within states, a problem that is constitutionally invisible in the general federalism discourse.

B. Environmental Federalism and the Supreme Court

With such embedded tension at play, environmental cases are often among the most contentious on the docket. Judicial federalism analyses in environmental conflicts often fracture into multiple opinions, revealing greater theoretical instability than other areas of the Supreme Court's federalism jurisprudence. However, they are valuable to the overall study of American federalism for exactly this reason – and especially so because they leave such a clear paper trail, providing unparalleled windows into individual justices' efforts to grapple with the underlying tensions. Contrasting judicial analyses prioritize competing values differently, revealing federalism's fault lines in ways that mainstream economic regulation rarely does.[115] Famous environmental decisions invalidating state-led efforts to cope with radioactive waste,[116] limiting federal authority over intrastate wetlands,[117] and even allowing a state to force more thoughtful federal climate governance[118] all highlight environmental federalism's tug of war within. They also suggest weaknesses in the Court's preferred theoretical tools for managing jurisdictional overlap within a fuller conception of federalism.[119]

---

[115] See Ryan, *Tug of War*, *supra*, n. 10, pp. 145–46.
[116] *New York v. United States*, 505 U.S. 144 (1992).
[117] *Rapanos v. United States*, 547 U.S. 715, 739 (2006).
[118] *Massachusetts v. E.P.A.*, 549 U.S. 497 (2007).
[119] See Ryan, *Tug of War*, *supra*, n. 10, pp. 7–17, 30–33.

(1) New York v. United States and radioactive waste management

New York v. United States, the controversial environmental case that inaugurated the Rehnquist Court's New Federalism revival of dual federalism ideals, offers a vivid example of federalism values in conflict.[120] In New York, the Court invalidated key parts of the Low Level Radioactive Waste Policy Act, the statutory product of state-led efforts to more safely and equitably manage mounting streams of nuclear waste.[121] With few proper disposal facilities, hazardous waste was being stored without adequate safety precautions or shipped thousands of miles to the few states with open disposal sites.[122] Proposed to Congress by the National Governors Association, the Act required all states to share equitably in the burden of waste management by rotating responsibility within regional interstate compacts.[123] New York initially advocated for the Act, but later challenged it when it failed to identify a local disposal site.[124] When the majority agreed that the Act's enforcement provisions coerced state action in violation of the Tenth Amendment, it dismantled decades of negotiations between state and federal actors to resolve a critical public safety issue that, as a result, remains largely unresolved today.[125]

New York remains among the most famous federalism decisions of the twentieth century, setting forth the anti-commandeering doctrine that became a regular basis on which to challenge other programs of cooperative federalism (though usually unsuccessfully).[126] It also showcases many of the features that position environmental law as such a powerful federalism exemplar. Safe and equitable waste disposal draws on simultaneously strong local and national regulatory interests, requiring state land use authority to site local disposal facilities and national authority over interstate commerce and spillover harm. Siting a toxic waste dump implicates core aspects of local governance, including land

---

[120] 505 U.S. 144 (1992).
[121] Ibid. at 187–88.
[122] See also Ryan, *Tug of War*, *supra*, n. 10, pp. 215–30.
[123] Ibid.
[124] Ibid.
[125] Ibid. at 215–41 (discussing the evolution of the Low Level Radioactive Waste Policy Act partially invalidated in *New York* and the chaos that ensued after the decision). See also Ryan, Erin, "Federalism at the Cathedral: Property Rules, Liability Rules, and Inalienability Rules in Tenth Amendment Infrastructure" (2010) 81 Colorado L. Rev. 1 (same).
[126] 505 U.S. at 187–88. See also Ryan, *Tug of War*, *supra*, n. 10, p. 199 n. 35 (reporting more than 70 such challenges filed in the first 14 years after *New York* was decided.)

use planning that protects public safety and empowers citizens to create the kinds of communities they want to live in. (Indeed, New York State challenged the law it had once supported precisely because it could not find a municipality willing to host a disposal site.) Yet the problem also implicates critical aspects of national governance, including centralized authority to impose uniform obligations when needed to resolve collective action problems among the states. In this case, the states voluntarily sacrificed some local autonomy when they partnered with Congress to create the intergovernmental synergy that they believed was necessary to solve an ominous environmental problem they had failed to manage on their own.

The opposing arguments of the justices themselves provide the best evidence of the intense competition among underlying federalism values. Justice O'Connor's majority opinion was driven by explicit concerns over accountability and checks on sovereign authority. She argued that the intergovernmental partnership impermissibly compromised accountability, openly worrying that voters might not understand whether to hold state or federal representatives accountable for the results.[127] She also appealed to the importance of checks and balances in maintaining that state consent to the initial partnership was immaterial, because a state's sovereign authority against federal incursion was an inalienable right of its citizens that the state cannot waive.[128] Justice White vociferously opposed the majority's analysis, focusing on values of local autonomy, central authority and problem-solving synergy. He would have upheld the law in affirmation of local autonomy, respecting the state's ability to bind itself to a regulatory promise, and of the central authority needed to give the interstate agreement binding legal force.[129] His opinion further

---

[127] 505 U.S. at 168.

[128] 505 U.S. at 180–82 ("How can a federal statute be found an unconstitutional infringement of state sovereignty when state officials consented to the statute's enactment? The answer follows from an understanding of the fundamental purpose served by our Government's federal structure. The Constitution does not protect the sovereignty of States for the benefit of the States or state governments as abstract political entities, or even for the benefit of the public officials governing the States. To the contrary, the Constitution divides authority between federal and state governments for the protection of individuals. State sovereignty is not just an end in itself; 'Rather, federalism secures to citizens the liberties that derive from the diffusion of sovereign power.'"). See also Ryan, *Tug of War*, supra, n. 10, pp. 231–41, and Ryan, supra, n. 125, 39–64 (critiquing this analysis).

[129] Ibid. at 196–97 (White J. concurring and dissenting) (arguing that "these statutes are best understood as the products of collective state action, rather than

stressed the importance of regulatory synergy between local capacity (to site waste disposal facilities) and national capacity (to prevent free-riders) in resolving the hazardous waste crisis.[130]

(2) *Rapanos v. United States* and water pollution

Since then, the Court has continued to issue divisive environmental decisions, several suggesting that federal regulation may be approaching the limits of federal authority under the Commerce Clause.[131] In the most recent, *Rapanos v. United States*, a private landowner successfully challenged the reach of federal Clean Water Act authority over certain intrastate wetlands, including those connected to navigable waters by manmade channels or separated by artificial berms.[132] The Court's rationale for limiting federal jurisdiction was splintered among four opinions, none of which commanded a solid enough majority to issue a clear principle for state and federal regulators to follow. Justice Scalia's plurality opinion explicitly invoked dual federalism theory to limit federal assertions of jurisdiction over remote and altered wetlands,[133] while Justice Kennedy's concurring opinion focused on the need to scientifically establish a hydrological connection to navigable waters in each individual enforcement action.[134]

With its multiplicity of conflicting opinions and unclear mandate for future regulation, *Rapanos* may rank among the least helpful Supreme Court decisions of all time. The jurisdictional uncertainty left in its wake

---

as impositions placed on States by the Federal Government. [New York clearly signified] assent to the agreement achieved among the States as codified in these laws ... As it was undertaking these initial steps to honor the interstate compromise embodied in the 1985 Act, New York continued to take full advantage of the import concession made by the sited States, by exporting its low-level radioactive waste for the full 7-year extension period provided in the 1985 Act. By gaining these benefits and complying with certain of the Act's 1985 deadlines, therefore, New York fairly evidenced its acceptance of the federal–state arrangements").

[130] Ibid. at 196–97.

[131] *Solid Waste Agency of Northern Cook County v. United States Army Corps of Engineers* (SWANCC), 531 U.S. 159, 173–74 (2001); *Rapanos v. United States*, 547 U.S. 715, 739 (2006).

[132] 547 U.S. 715, 739 (2006) (rejecting the federal agency's interpretation of the CWA for infringing on traditional state control over land and water use and pushing the limits of congressional commerce power).

[133] Ibid. at 737–38 (noting that "the Government's expansive interpretation would 'result in a significant impingement of the States' traditional and primary power over land and water use'").

[134] Ibid. at 780–82 (Kennedy J. concurring).

has substantially altered enforcement of the statute and arguably led to declining water quality nationwide.[135] A major investigation several years after *Rapanos* found that regulators had abandoned nearly 1500 water pollution investigations because establishing jurisdiction was too difficult, time-consuming or expensive.[136] Eight years later, as this book goes to press, federal agencies have promulgated new rules to replace those *Rapanos* invalidated,[137] but the process has been politically strained and fraught by uncertainty about what the Court will approve in the inevitable next round of litigation.[138] This uncertainty reflects the multiplicity of views on the Court to this point, which itself reflects the underlying turmoil among competing good governance values.

---

[135] See e.g. Berman, Mark, "Toledo's Water Ban and the Sensitivity of Our Water Systems," *Wash. Post*, 4 Aug. 2014, accessed 20 July 2015 at www.washingtonpost.com/news/post-nation/wp/2014/08/04/toledos-water-ban-and-the-sensitivity-of-our-drinking-systems/ (reporting on recent drinking water bans in major metropolitan areas across the nation as a result of harmful water pollution); Duhigg, Charles, "Clean Water Laws Are Neglected, at a Cost in Suffering," *N.Y. Times*, 12 Sept. 2009, accessed 20 July 2015 at www.nytimes.com/2009/09/13/us/13water.html?pagewanted=all&_r=0 (reporting on the results of an extensive review of water pollution records showing that "in recent years, violations of the Clean Water Act have risen steadily across the nation"); "Toxic Waters Project: A Series About the Worsening Pollution in American Waters, and Regulators' Response," *N.Y. Times*, August 2009–March 2010, accessed 20 July 2015 at projects.nytimes.com/toxic-waters (a collection of reports on the subject).

[136] See Duhigg, Charles and Janet Roberts, "Rulings Restrict Clean Water Act, Foiling EPA," *N.Y. Times*, 28 Feb. 2010, at A1, accessed 20 July 2015 at www.nytimes.com/2010/03/01/us/01water.html?emc=eta (also noting indications by EPA officials that they may be "unable to prosecute as many as half of the nation's largest known polluters because officials lack jurisdiction or because proving jurisdiction would be overwhelmingly difficult or time consuming"); Kinney, Jeff, "Internal EPA Memo Finds Enforcement Decreased Following Rapanos Decision," (2008) 39 Env't Rep. (BNA) 1392.

[137] EPA, "Definition of Waters of the United States Under the Clean Water Act," see *supra* n. 94.

[138] Cf. Liebesman, Lawrence, Elizabeth Lake and Joanna Meldrum, "Obama Administration Releases Proposed Rule on 'Waters of the United States,'" *Holland & Knight*, 4 April 2014, accessed 20 July 2015 at www.hklaw.com/publications/obama-administration-releases-proposed-rule-on-waters-of-the-united-states-04-04-2014/ (extensive analysis of the proposed rule by an industry-side law firm warning that the rule "is unprecedented in its reach and scope," "has received broad praise from environmentalists," and that clients

Like the regulation of radioactive waste disposal, the environmental dilemma in *Rapanos* pits local interests in land use sovereignty against federal interests in protecting the nation's waterways and preventing the boundary-crossing harm of water pollution. Its various opinions are also marked by consideration of competing values, though because it is primarily a statutory interpretation case, they are featured less forthrightly than in the explicit federalism dialogues of *New York*. Still, Justice Scalia focused on localism and check-and-balance values in limiting the expansion of federal authority beyond the traditional boundary of navigability, while Justice Kennedy was willing to privilege central authority and problem-solving values when extended federal jurisdiction is proved necessary to achieve the statutory goal of preventing water pollution. Justice Kennedy acknowledges the tension explicitly, noting that "[t]he possibility of legitimate Commerce Clause and federalism concerns in some circumstances does not require the adoption of an interpretation that departs in all cases from the Act's [commitment to resolving water pollution]."[139] Dissenting arguments by Justices Stevens and Breyer pull in still different directions, favoring deference to federal interpretive authority on the need for a centralized response to resolve a clearly interjurisdictional problem.[140]

(3) *Massachusetts v. EPA* and climate change

While not overtly a federalism decision, even the famous *Massachussets v. EPA* climate change decision speaks to the fractious relationship between state and federal authority in the realm of environmental law.[141] There, a sharply divided Court allowed the state standing to force EPA's reconsideration of regulating greenhouse gases under the Clean Air Act, on grounds that EPA's failure to adequately justify its inaction harmed state sovereign authority over threatened coastal lands.[142] Quoting Justice Oliver Wendell Holmes in an environmental federalism case of the previous century, Justice Stevens wrote for the majority that "the State has an interest independent of and behind the titles of its citizens, in all

---

should engage policymakers to "lessen ... the impact on the regulated community."). See also Missouri Farm Bureau ("Let it Go" Parody), *supra*, n. 94 (urging members to fight the proposed rule).

[139] 547 U.S. 715, at 783 (2006) (Kennedy J. concurring).

[140] Ibid. at 788 (Stevens J. dissenting); ibid. at 811 (Breyer J. dissenting) (noting that his "view of the statute rests in part upon the nature of the problem").

[141] 549 U.S. 497 (2007).

[142] Ibid.

the earth and air within its domain. It has the last word as to whether its mountains shall be stripped of their forests and its inhabitants shall breathe pure air."[143]

More than any other area of environmental law, climate governance intersects local, state, federal, and even international claims to regulatory authority and obligation where they are strongest. With greenhouse gases from all parts of the world mixing evenly in the upper atmosphere, it is the quintessential collective action problem in which centralized authority is necessary to police free-riders and prevent boundary-crossing harms. Yet human contributions to climate change span virtually the entire range of human activity – from personal decisions about diet and transportation, to municipal building codes, to state energy policy, to federal tax incentives, to international treaty-making. Some contributions to climate change are more easily regulated than others, and some modifications more easily encouraged, but as William Buzbee, Kirsten Engel and Alice Kaswan argue in Part III of this book, effective climate governance requires coordinated efforts at all levels.

Indeed, Justice Holmes' famous passage points to the grand dilemma for environmental federalism more generally. In a nutshell, it is that both the federal and state governments have regulatory interests and obligations regarding their citizens' ability to enjoy a clean, safe and productive environment for generations to come. Environmental problems like radioactive waste, water pollution and climate change pair local land use problems with border-crossing public health and safety problems. Like the problems with which energy law grapples, they cannot be resolved without partnering elements of state-specific expertise and authority with corresponding elements of national capacity. And while constitutional federalism sees the issue only in terms of state and national governance, the challenges of multiscalar governance go far deeper, extending into the productive possibilities for regulation at the local, regional and international level as well, in various permutations and combinations.[144]

The grand project for federalism and multiscalar regulation more generally is to figure out how these different levels of government can best work together in realms of jurisdictional overlap. The following Part explores how environmental law has responded to the challenge.

---

[143] Ibid. at 518–20 (quoting *Georgia v. Tennessee Copper Co.*, 206 U.S. 230, 237 (1907)).
[144] See sources cited *supra*, n. 30.

IV. THE RESPONSE OF ENVIRONMENTAL GOVERNANCE

Having analyzed the rip tides of federalism that so complicate environmental law, the chapter now turns to the question of how environmental governance has risen to meet the challenge, reviewing specific adaptations within programs of environmental federalism to cope with jurisdictional overlap.

While the dilemmas of environmental federalism are divisive for reasons that run deep among the underlying values of good governance, they surface in the jurisdictional disputes that erupt regularly in environmental law. As discussed in Part II of this book, zones of overlapping state and federal regulatory jurisdiction complicate the administration of federalism-sensitive governance in ways that earlier theories of federalism did not always comprehend.[145] As a theoretical matter, jurisdictional overlap is the formal result of the underlying conflicts within federalism-sensitive governance, where implicated values are sometimes best served by state and local regulation just as others are best served by national action. As a practical matter, jurisdictional overlap provides the framework within which different levels of government advocate for their distinct concerns and a platform for their coordinated response.

Nevertheless, contests for regulatory dominance within realms of jurisdictional overlap often lead to divisive federalism controversies, requiring sensitive response from environmental governance. Sometimes dilemmas arise because of the way environmental law wrestles with newly identified problems, such as climate change, where there is no historically settled answer to the question of where primary regulatory authority should be seated (contrasted with, say, land use planning, historically regarded as a local matter). Other times, the evidence increasingly reveals that even problems once presumed to be essentially "local" in nature – such as water allocation, waste disposal, and even land use planning – have important regional, national or even international dimensions. At the same time, such seemingly "national" problems as energy policy, telecommunications and even international relations are increasingly bound up with the exercise of state authority over local land use and natural resource management. The ideal seat of regulatory authority over these matters is often hotly contested.

---

[145] See *supra*, text accompanying nn. 65–75.

Environmental law has contended with jurisdictional controversy by experimenting with the available tools of cooperative federalism, exploring variations that might enable the right balance of flexibility, durability and responsiveness to address each particular constellation of concerns. This Part explores how environmental law deals with the challenges of jurisdictional overlap that are present in all federalism dilemmas but endemic in environmental governance. After reviewing the classic challenges of jurisdictional separation and unstructured overlap, it reveals how environmental federalism has adapted contrasting structures of intergovernmental coordination, including models of coordinated capacity, federally supported state implementation, conditional preemption, and shared and general permitting programs.

A. The Problem of Jurisdictional Overlap

Environmental law is hardly unique among realms of governance that include a zone of concurrent state and federal regulatory jurisdiction, but it does so in an especially palpable way. Jurisdictional overlap arises in regulatory contexts where both the federal and state governments have legitimate regulatory interests or obligations simultaneously.[146] Federal interests are created by constitutional delegations of federal responsibility, while state interests arise from the reservoir of police power that is constitutionally reserved to the states.[147] However, distinct state and federal regulatory mandates are often triggered by related or interdependent areas of law, creating an "interjurisdictional gray area" between clearer areas of primarily state or federal prerogative.[148]

There are, to be sure, areas of relative jurisdictional clarity within American dual sovereignty. The Constitution plainly enumerates some powers specifically to the federal government, such as the powers to declare war and manage foreign relations, while explicitly reserving

---

[146] See Ryan, *Tug of War*, *supra*, n. 10, pp. 145–80.
[147] U.S. CONST. amend. X.; see also Ryan, *Tug of War*, *supra*, n. 10, pp. 1–33 (discussing indeterminacy among the details of constitutional delegations).
[148] See Ryan, *Tug of War*, *supra*, n. 10, pp. 145–80; see also Ryan, Erin, "Federalism and the Tug of War Within: Seeking Checks and Balance in the Interjurisdictional Gray Area" (2007) 66 Md. L. Rev. 503 (providing the initial impetus for the fuller theoretical exposition in the book, *Tug of War*, *supra*, n. 10).

others to the states, such as the authority to manage federal elections.[149] But even the states' exclusive constitutional obligation to manage elections collides with exclusive federal obligations to interpret the voting rights of citizens casting ballots in those elections.[150] And increasingly, states are engaging in regulatory activities with ramifications for the nation's conduct of international relations,[151] some of which the federal government has tolerated (including several international subnational climate governance partnerships)[152] and some of which it has not.[153]

Even seemingly simple delegations of exclusive authority can reveal jurisdictional overlap in application. For example, bankruptcy law is

---

[149] U.S. Const. Art. I, § 8 (empowering Congress to declare war); Art. I, § 4 (delegating responsibility for the mechanics of congressional elections to state legislatures).

[150] U.S. Const. amend. XIV (promising the equal protection of the laws); amend. XV (promising that voting rights will not be abridged on account of race); amend. XIX (promising that voting rights will not be abridged on account of sex). See also *Bush v. Gore*, 531 U.S. 98 (2000) (overturning state electoral decisions in a presidential election on federal equal protection grounds, though in a decision famously confining its reasoning to its facts).

[151] See e.g. Gerken, Osofsky, Resnik, and Davidson sources cited *supra*, n. 37.

[152] In the West, California has joined four Canadian provinces to form the Western Climate Initiative, a carbon trading partnership. See e.g., "Western Climate Initiative," accessed 20 July 2015 at www.westernclimateinitiative.org/milestones. In the Midwest, six states and one Canadian province formed the Midwest Greenhouse Gas Reduction Accord, pledging to establish a multi-sector cap-and-trade system to meet regional greenhouse gas reduction targets. "Midwestern Greenhouse Gas Reduction Accord," accessed 20 July 2015 at www.c2es.org/us-states-regions/regional-climate-initiatives/mggra. However, although a Model Rule was produced in 2010 and the accord formally remains in effect, "the participating states are no longer pursuing it." Ibid.

[153] For example, in *Crosby v. National Foreign Trade Council*, 530 U.S. 363, 388 (2000), the Supreme Court invalidated a Massachusetts law that prohibited state and local actors from purchasing goods or services from companies doing business with the nation of Burma, also known as Myanmar, on grounds that the state law undermined the President's ability to conduct diplomacy. Similarly, the Court invoked the dormant foreign affairs power to invalidate a California law mandating public disclosure of in-state insurance companies' holocaust policies, which had been enacted so that consumers could patronize companies that had rectified Nazi-era practices (when many had failed to honor the policies of Jewish holders). *Am. Ins. Ass'n v. Garamendi*, 539 U.S. 396, 417–20 (2003).

explicitly delegated to the federal government, but its actual administration relies on legal definitions of property provided by state law.[154] Although the federal commerce power implies a navigational servitude across all navigable waters in the United States,[155] the submerged lands beneath many of them are considered property of the states, held in trust for their citizens, under the public trust and equal footing doctrines.[156] With so many avenues for regulatory overlap, the interjurisdictional gray area runs deep in American law, from environmental law to criminal law to national security to financial services regulation and beyond.[157]

Still, the gray area is especially visceral in the environmental context. As noted in Part III of this book, jurisdictional overlap is common here because so many environmental problems partner the need for (1) local land use regulation, to control the actual source of the harm at issue, with (2) federal authority, often under the Commerce Clause, to prevent locally uncontrolled harm from spilling over into neighboring jurisdictions that lack direct regulatory authority over the source of the harm.[158] Consider the prevention of water pollution. The best way of preventing harmful stream sedimentation by a local construction project is probably through the municipal construction permitting process (as EPA itself recognizes in its Clean Water Act regulations for preventing stormwater pollution by constructing sites).[159] But if the state or its local subdivisions fail to regulate that pollution, it can cause problems for

---

[154] U.S. Const. Art. I, § 8 (delegating bankruptcy administration to the federal government); Nadborny, Felicia Anne, Note, "'Leap of Faith' into Bankruptcy: An Examination of the Issues Surrounding the Valuation of a Catholic Diocese's Bankruptcy Estate," (2005) 13 Am. Bankr. Inst. L. Rev. 839, 889 (discussing the role of state law).

[155] See *Fed. Power Comm'n v. Niagara Mohawk Power Corp.*, 347 U.S. 239, 249 (1954) (describing how the Commerce Clause creates a dominant servitude to regulate navigation).

[156] See e.g. *Illinois Cent. R. Co. v. State of Illinois*, 146 U.S. 387 (1892) (affirming application of the common-law public trust doctrine to state ownership of the submerged lands beneath the navigable waters of the Great Lakes); *PPL Montana, LLC v. Montana*, 132 S. Ct. 1215 (2012) (recognizing the general rule of state ownership of submerged lands under the public trust doctrine).

[157] See Ryan, *Tug of War*, supra, n. 10, pp. 145–80.

[158] See *supra*, text accompanying nn. 89–94.

[159] Office of Water, EPA, Stormwater Phase II Final Rule: Fact Sheet 2.1, at 2 (2005), accessed 20 July 2015 at www.epa.gov.npdes/pubs/fact2-1.pdf (discussing the Phase II Rule); Office of Water, EPA, Stormwater Phase II Final Rule: Fact Sheet 2.9, at 3 (2005), accessed 20 July 2015 at www.epa/gov/npdes/pubs/fact2-9.pdf (discussing the conferral of municipal discretion under the general permit system); *Environmental Defense Center v. EPA*, 344 F.3d 832,

downstream communities in other states that lack the means to control out-of-state activity. Federal authority is needed to effectuate the ability of these other states to perform their traditional police power obligations to protect the health and safety of their own citizens.

With so many independent but overlapping sovereign interests, uncertainty can arise over which sovereign should be able to make which regulatory choices – the "who decides?" jurisdictional question at the heart of federalism dilemmas.[160] This uncertainty breeds additional controversy within federalism-sensitive governance that is already implicitly struggling with the tension among conflicting federalism values. Notably, jurisdictional uncertainty can arise both when we manage the problem by attempting to separate regulatory authority along bright jurisdictional lines, and also when we explicitly recognize overlapping local and national jurisdiction. Federalism dilemmas are thus marked by two different kinds of uncertainty: what happens after we draw a jurisdictional line, and what happens when we don't.[161]

In contexts of true overlap, the uncertainty resulting from efforts at jurisdictional line-drawing creates the more obvious problem. For example, as Blake Hudson describes in Chapter 4, managing forest resources at the local level provided short-term order but long-term difficulties as spillover issues eventually transcend local jurisdictional boundaries. The uncertainty that results from a decision not to draw jurisdictional lines is perhaps more the interesting problem, creating different challenges and opportunities for interjurisdictional governance. For example, the authors in Part III of this book provide sophisticated analyses of the different challenges and opportunities of multiscalar climate governance. Meanwhile, the classical model of cooperative federalism splits some of these differences, eschewing both strict jurisdictional lines and unstructured regulatory overlap. The following discussion visits these three separate approaches to managing jurisdictional overlap.

845–46 & n. 20 (9th Cir. 2003) (discussing the Phase II Rule's regulation of construction site sedimentation).

[160] See e.g. Buzbee, William (ed.), *Preemption Choice: The Theory, Law, and Reality of Federalism's Core Question* (Cambridge University Press, New York 2011).

[161] See Ryan, "The Once and Future Challenges of American Federalism," *supra*, n. 14, Part 2 (discussing the two kinds of uncertainty).

(1) Untangling jurisdictional separation

Federalism uncertainty often arises about the actual boundary line between state and federal authority, in contexts where a bright line of separation seems important. For example, in *Arizona v. United States*, the Supreme Court recently reviewed state immigration legislation that, among other provisions, required immigrants to carry documentation of their immigration status at all times and punished those who hire or shelter the undocumented.[162] Distinguishing legitimate local regulation from exclusively federal authority, the Court invalidated all provisions except one (allowing state police to investigate immigration status under specified conditions).[163]

Environmental law has struggled with issues of jurisdictional separation since its inception. For example, as *Rapanos* demonstrates, line-drawing uncertainty has plagued decades of rulemaking about the boundary between state and federal reach over wetlands regulation relating to water pollution control.[164] The location of that boundary will determine when a landowner must seek permission to fill wetlands that are not directly subject to the Clean Water Act, but which may bear a relationship to pollution in other waterways that are subject. After the Solid Waste Agency of Cook County, IL, successfully sued to invalidate

---

[162] 132 S. Ct. at 2497–98. Arizona argued that the law was a necessary assertion of its police power to protect local communities, while the Department of Justice argued that the law exceeded the state's legitimate role, usurped federal authority to regulate immigration, and critically undermined US foreign policy objectives. Ibid.; Press Release, Dep't of Justice Office of Pub. Affairs, Citing Conflict with Federal Law, Department of Justice Challenges Arizona Immigration Law (6 July 2010), accessed 20 July 2015 at www.justice.gov/opa/pr/2010/July/10-opa-776.html.

[163] *Arizona v. United States*, 132 S. Ct. at 2510 (invalidating provisions allowing state police to arrest individuals on suspicion of undocumented status and criminalizing the presence and work of undocumented immigrants in the state, while upholding a provision enabling state police to investigate immigration status under certain circumstances). See also *United States v. Alabama*, 691 F.3d 1269, 1301 (11th Cir. 2012) (granting in part and denying in part a preliminary injunction enjoining enforcement of the state's new immigration law); *Georgia Latino Alliance for Human Rights v. Governor of Georgia*, 691 F.3d 1250, 1267 (2012) (holding that sections of the Georgia immigration law were preempted by federal law); Elias, Stella B , "The New Immigration Federalism," (2013) 74 Ohio St. L.J. 703 (discussing federalism issues in immigration law).

[164] See Ryan, *Tug of War, supra*, n. 10, pp. 151–53, 160–62 (discussing the interjurisdictional problem of water pollution and recent controversy in wetlands regulation).

federal authority over hydrologically isolated wetlands,[165] the issue of what would constitute a jurisdictional connection embroiled the Supreme Court in the *Rapanos* decision that failed to produce clear regulatory direction despite four separate opinions.[166] As noted above, years of regulatory turmoil have followed, in which enforcement efforts have plummeted and water quality has degraded.[167] Federal agencies have recently promulgated a new rule to clarify jurisdiction after the two wetlands cases, but the new rule has already been drawn into further legal challenges.[168]

(2) Untangling jurisdictional collaboration

Other federalism-sensitive contexts are more tolerant of concurrent jurisdiction and less committed to jurisdictional line-drawing, demonstrated by broadly overlapping state and federal roles in criminal law,[169] or even cooperative state–federal management of the national highway system.[170] But environmental law provides the most interesting examples, from realms in which state and federal actors regulate separately in related legal territory (such as energy law, discussed above in Part III), to complex programs of cooperative federalism that require deference to both state and federal concerns in different circumstances (discussed further below in Part IV). In areas where concurrent jurisdiction is the norm, less energy is spent resolving the proper spheres of state and federal authority on either side of a bright-line boundary, because no such

---

[165] *Solid Waste Agency of Northern Cook County v. U.S. Army Corp of Engineers*, 531 U.S. 159, 173–74 (2001) (limiting federal authority over "hydrologically isolated" wetlands).

[166] *Rapanos v. United States*, 547 U.S. 715, 739 (2006) (casting further doubt on the reach of federal regulatory authority over wetlands without direct surface connections to navigable waters). Strictly speaking, *Solid Waste Agency* and *Rapanos* were both statutory decisions interpreting the Clean Water Act. However, the justices and their observers clearly understood their task of statutory interpretation as taking place in the looming shadow of ongoing debate over the reach of federal Commerce Clause authority.

[167] See *supra*, nn. 136–38 and accompanying text.

[168] See *supra* n. 94 (new rule); Cf. Liebesman, et al., *supra*, n. 138 (critiquing points of the new rule).

[169] See Logan, Wayne A., "Creating a 'Hydra in Government': Federal Recourse to State Law in Crime Fighting" (2006) 86 B.U. L. Rev. 65, 104–06; Klein, Susan R., "Independent-Norm Federalism in Criminal Law" (2002) 90 Cal. L. Rev. 1541, 1553.

[170] Federal-Aid Highway Act of 1956, Pub. L. 84-627, 70 Stat. 374 (29 June 1956) (creating a National Highway System jointly administered by the states and federal government).

boundary exists. However, uncertainty here arises over whose judgment should prevail when simultaneously operating state and federal choices conflict. When both have a role to play, the federalism question shifts from the relatively simpler "who gets to decide?" to the vexing permutation "whose decision trumps?" Should national objectives preempt, or should local priorities prevail?[171]

The Constitution's Supremacy Clause affirms that the legitimate exercise of federal authority can always trump conflicting state law,[172] but federal law often leaves purposeful space for local participation even when Congress could theoretically preempt an entire regulatory field – especially in environmental law.[173] Notwithstanding enumerated federal authority over commerce and the channels of interstate commerce, international treaties and foreign relations, federal property, military readiness, national security and others,[174] Congress usually leaves space for local participation to engage regulatory expertise or capacity that local governments have, but the federal government does not.[175] For that reason, the more difficult preemption question in these contexts is not whether the federal government *could* preempt, but whether (and to what degree) it *should*.[176]

---

[171] E.g. Adler, Jonathan H., "Jurisdictional Mismatch in Environmental Federalism" (2005) 14 N.Y.U. Envtl L.J. 130, 172–73 (questioning increasing federalization of environmental regulation formerly within state prerogative); Logan, *supra*, n. 169, at 104–06 (questioning the increasing federalization of criminal law).

[172] U.S. Const. Art. VI, cl. 2.

[173] See Ryan, *Tug of War, supra*, n. 10, pp. 145–80, 271–314 (reviewing regulatory realms in which the federal government invites state involvement even though it could legitimately preempt the field, including many fields of environmental law).

[174] U.S. Const. Art. I, cl. 8 (enumerating most of Congress's constitutionally delegated authority).

[175] See Ryan, *Tug of War, supra*, n. 10, pp. 326–38 (discussing reasons federal actors cede authority to local actors); Ryan, "Negotiating Federalism," *supra*, n. 30 (providing additional source information for these conclusions).

[176] See Ryan, *Tug of War, supra*, n. 10, pp. 339–67; cf. Buzbee, William, "Asymmetrical Regulation: Risk, Preemption, and the Floor/Ceiling Distinction" (2007) 82 NYU L. Rev. 1547 (discussing the advantages of narrowly tailored "floor preemption," which enables state discretion to exceed a federal standard, over the alternative "unitary federal choice" or "ceiling preemption," which does not); Carlson, Ann, "Iterative Federalism and Climate Change" (2009) 103 Nw. U. L. Rev. 1097 (discussing the advantages of declining to fully preempt state discretion within a national program of air pollution prevention).

Ongoing dilemmas about federal scope and restraint in environmental law – from wetlands to forests to air pollution regulation – demonstrate the force with which federalism and preemption controversies preoccupy American governance.[177] In some realms of open jurisdictional overlap, such as education[178] and health care law,[179] a significant federal presence is matched by trumping local authority, usually because the federal presence has been purchased with the federal spending power and is untethered to independently enumerated federal power.[180] In others, federal priorities routinely trump local concerns, as demonstrated by federal finance law under the Commerce Clause,[181] and a spate of

---

[177] See Ryan, *Tug of War*, supra, n. 10, pp. 132–41.

[178] See e.g. Martin, Benton, "An Increased Role for the Department of Education in Addressing Federalism Concerns" (2012) 2012 BYU Educ. & L.J. 79, 81–84 (discussing the role of state and federal actors over the history of American education law). Education federalism issues have recently erupted over the Common Core, a set of curricular goals created by a partnership of states that were initially embraced by nearly every state. However, some states are now withdrawing from the initiative amid criticism that federal support for the standards represent federal overreach into a realm of state sovereignty. See e.g. Jackson, Nancy M., "Core Withdrawal? Some States Seem to Be Reconsidering their Common Core Commitments," Scholastic Administrator, Summer 2013, accessed 20 July at www.scholastic.com/browse/article.jsp?id=3757959 (listing states that have recently withdrawn from the common core standards); Layton, Lyndsey, "How Bill Gates Pulled Off the Swift Common Core Revolution," *Wash. Post*, 7 June 2014, accessed 20 July 2015 at www.washingtonpost.com/politics/how-bill-gates-pulled-off-the-swift-common-core-revolution/2014/06/07/a830e32e-ec34-11e3-9f5c-9075d5508f0a_story.html (noting emerging federalism controversy over the Common Core standards).

[179] See e.g. Clark, Brietta, "Safeguarding Federalism by Saving Health Reform: Implications of *National Federation of Independent Business v. Sebelius*" (2013) 46 Loy. L.A. L. Rev. 541, 571 (describing federalism conflicts in health care law and the Affordable Care Act); Leonard, Elizabeth W., "The Rhetoric Hits the Road: State Challenges to the Affordable Care Act Implementation" (2012) 46 U. Rich. L. Rev. 781 (discussing the strategies some states have taken to combat implementation of the Affordable Care Act, including drafting state legislation).

[180] See Ryan, Erin, "The Spending Power and Environmental Law After *Sebelius*" (2014) 85 Colorado L. Rev. 1003 (discussing the difficulties of Medicaid regulation because health law is beyond Congress's enumerated powers, reachable in federal law only through the spending power).

[181] See e.g. Markham, Jerry W., "Banking Regulation: Its History and Future" (2000) 4 N.C. Banking Inst. 221 (discussing federal banking and finance

Supreme Court cases aggressively preempting state health and safety laws under competing federal regulations.[182]

Yet environmental law represents a substantial realm of overlap where the scales of state and federal influence go back and forth. Sometimes federal environmental law trumps all competing considerations, perhaps demonstrated by the force with which the Endangered Species Act is usually enforced against state actors as strictly as it is against everyone else.[183] Often, environmental law resolves conflicts among independently operating state and federal regulators by allowing state judgment to trump federal judgment when state law is more protective, but federal judgment to trump state judgment when state law is less protective.[184] This "floor preemption" regime, adopted by most federal environmental laws, creates a federal "floor" of environmental protection that states may exceed but not undermine.[185]

In other legal regimes, states hold a privileged position in environmental decision-making that goes beyond mere cooperation, and despite available federal supremacy. From the perspective of environmental federalism, these are among the most interesting. For example, as Bill Andreen notes in Chapter 2, states play an important role in allocating water from interstate rivers,[186] notwithstanding clear Supreme Court

---

law). See also Ryan, *Tug of War, supra*, n. 10, pp. 284–85 (discussing jurisdictional overlap despite federal supremacy in the field of financial services regulation).

[182] See e.g. *Lorillard Tobacco Co. v. Reilly*, 533 U.S. 525, 530, 550–51 (2001) (holding that state tobacco advertising regulations were preempted by the Federal Cigarette Labeling and Advertising Act); *Geier v. American Honda Motor Co.*, 529 U.S. 861, 863–64 (2000) (holding that a common law defective design claim for failure to equip an automobile with a driver-side airbag was preempted by a Federal Motor Vehicle Safety Standard); but see *Wyeth v. Levine*, 129 S. Ct. 1187, 1194–98 (2009) (declining to overrule *Geier* but creating confusing precedent going forward by upholding a common law failure-to-warn claim based on a dangerous method of injecting a pharmaceutical that had satisfied FDA labeling regulations). See also Buzbee, *supra*, n. 160 (engaging the preemption issue from multiple angles); Chemerinsky, *supra*, n. 68, at 225–37 (discussing conflicts between the Supreme Court's preemption jurisprudence and the principles of federalism).

[183] Endangered Species Act of 1973, Pub. L. No. 93-205, 87 Stat. 884 (1973) (codified as amended at 16 U.S.C. §§ 1531–1544, § 1538 (2012)).

[184] See Buzbee, William W., "Asymmetrical Regulation: Risk, Preemption, and the Floor/Ceiling Distinction" (2007) 82 N.Y.U. L. Rev. 1547 (comparing floor-preemption and ceiling-preemption alternatives).

[185] Ibid.

[186] Dan Tarlock, *Law of Water Rights and Resources* (Westlaw 2009), § 10.

precedent affirming federal supremacy in the allocation of interstate water[187] and requiring congressional approval for state compacts that empower state decision-making at the expense of federal prerogative.[188] In 2005, eight states negotiated the Great Lakes-St Lawrence River Basin Compact to prevent the diversion of Great Lakes waters out of the watershed.[189] Congress approved the agreement, as it has for many similar state-led water compacts, even though it weakens federal prerogative in limiting the federal government's ability to move water from the Great Lakes basin to the high plains or arid west.[190] In interpreting terms of the Yellowstone River Compact that require consent by Montana, North Dakota and Wyoming for any water diversions outside the water basin,[191] the Ninth Circuit has held that congressional consent immunizes water compacts that encroach on the federal commerce power this way.[192] In allowing these compacts, federal courts and legislators have ceded federal supremacy to the states on the theory that state and local actors possess superior regulatory capacity for administering this scarce natural resource.

As Ann Carlson describes in Chapter 10, states hold a similarly privileged position in managing coastal resources under the Coastal Zone Management Act (CZMA), which enables states to veto federal permitting decisions that conflict with state priorities in an approved Coastal Zone Management Plan.[193] Under a limited waiver of federal supremacy known as the "consistency provision," federal actors must seek state permission for any actions that could impact coastal resources protected under a state's coastal management plan, a regulatory program previously negotiated between state and federal actors.[194] States may review not only those activities conducted by or on behalf of a federal agency, but also activities that require a federal license or permit, including activities conducted pursuant to an Outer Continental Shelf Lands Act exploration

---

[187] *Sporhase v. Nebraska ex rel. Douglas*, 458 U.S. 941, 953–54, 959–60 (1982).

[188] Tarlock (2009), *supra*, n. 186, at § 10–24.

[189] Ibid. at § 10–32.

[190] Ibid. at § 10–32.

[191] Yellowstone River Compact Comm'n, accessed 20 July 2015 at yrcc.usgs.gov/ (last visited Nov. 25, 2010).

[192] *Intake Water Co. v. Yellowstone River Compact Comm'n*, 769 F. 2d 568, 570 (9th Cir. 1985).

[193] Coastal Zone Management Act of 1972, Pub. L. 92-583, 86 Stat. 1280 (1972) (codified as amended at 16 U.S.C. §§ 1451–1466 (2012)).

[194] 16 U.S.C. § 1456(c); NOAA, Basic Statutory Tenets of Federal Consistency, 71 Fed. Reg. 789–90.

plan, and any federally funded activities that may impact the coastal zone.[195] The Act also provides a mechanism for resolving potential conflicts between state and federal priorities, fostering early consultation and negotiated coordination.[196]

Indeed, as I have described in previous work, the Consistency Provision represents the final stage in the Act's larger project of intergovernmentally negotiated coastal management policy.[197] Congress initiates the first stage of bargaining under its spending power, offering financial and technical assistance for voluntary state participation. In the second stage of bargaining, state and federal agencies haggle over the terms of a state's proposed coastal management plan, negotiating the provisions that each side most prefers to see in the final plan. Federal leverage climaxes here, because the federal agency maintains final approval authority and holds the ultimate carrot of federal funding. However, federal leverage is tempered by the fact that only the state possesses the local land use planning authority and governance capacity needed to implement effective management. In the final stage, the consistency principle shifts the negotiating leverage further toward the states. Once the federal government approves the state plan, it effectively agrees *itself* to be bound by the state plan going forward, ensuring that all federal activities directly or indirectly affecting the coastal zone will be consistent with the approved state plan.

These various platforms for state–federal negotiation set the stage for ongoing state–federal dialogue, exchange and innovation in regulatory decision-making, openly defying the assumptions of zero-sum federalism. The three stages of bargaining "effectively engage state and federal actors in an ongoing, *ad infinitum* dialogue about coastal management,

---

[195] Ibid. States may disapprove activities that "affect any land or water use or natural resource of the coastal zone" unless they are "consistent to the maximum extent practicable" with accepted state management programs. 16 U.S.C. § 1456(c)(1)(A). A federal agency may override objection only if it demonstrates that its activity is consistent with the approved plan to the maximum extent practicable. CZMA §307(c)(1)–(2).

[196] CZMA s. 307 (16 U.S.C. §1456(h)(2)). See also Florida Department of Environmental Protection, Coastal Zone Management Act, accessed 20 July 2015 at www.dep.state.fl.us/secretary/oip/czma.htm.

[197] For more detail on intergovernmental power-sharing and negotiation under the Coastal Zone Management Act and other areas of law, see Ryan, "The Once and Future Challenges of American Federalism," *supra*, n. 14, at Part 3.1; Ryan, "Negotiating Federalism," *supra*, n. 30, at 59–62; Ryan, *Tug of War, supra*, n. 10, pp. 302–05.

informed by both local and national insight in exactly the way that federalism intends":[198]

> The CZMA enables broadly negotiated local initiative within a framework of federal law that ensures fidelity to both local and national concerns. It provides a useful model for interjurisdictional governance matching broad national goals with policies best implemented at the local level, especially where local land use authority or "place" is a necessarily salient feature of the regulatory problem.[199]

Hydroelectric licensing decisions by the Federal Energy Regulatory Commission similarly include negotiations between state and federal actors over permission to violate the otherwise applicable federal navigational servitude,[200] because the Clean Water Act's section 401 certification process gives states a regulatory hook over an otherwise federal process.[201] These programs of environmental federalism represent unusual cases in which the states can hold legally trumping authority, creating rare instances in which the federal government must negotiate for state approval when regulatory policies diverge.

(3) Classical cooperative federalism

As the previous sections have shown, the challenges of jurisdictional overlap can alternatively inspire jurisdictional separation and less structured, simultaneous regulation. However, most environmental governance

---

[198] Ryan, "The Once and Future Challenges of American Federalism," *supra*, n. 14, at Part 3.1.
[199] Ibid.
[200] See *Fed. Power Comm'n v. Niagara Mohawk Power Corp.*, 347 U.S. 239, 249 (1954) (describing how the Commerce Clause creates a dominant servitude to regulate navigation).
[201] 33 U.S.C. § 1330 (2006); see also Coggins, George and Robert Glicksman, *Public Natural Resources Law*, 2nd edn (Thomson/West, St Paul MN 2009), § 37:41 (noting that the state certification process "represents the states' best opportunity to significantly affect the licensing process for hydroelectric facilities on waters within federal jurisdictions"). The major federal licenses and permits subject to § 401 are (1) FERC hydropower licenses, 16 U.S.C. § 797(e) (2006) (authorizing FERC to license hydroelectric facilities); (2) Rivers and Harbors Act section 9 and 10 permits, 33 U.S.C. §§ 401, 403 (2006) (regulating construction in navigable waters); and (3) CWA §§ 402 and 404 permits in the few states that have not assumed NPDES permitting authority, 33 U.S.C. § 1342 (outlining the "National Pollutant Discharge Elimination System" permitting regime); see also Donahue, Debra L., "The Untapped Power of Clean Water Act Section 401" (1996) 23 Ecology L.Q. 201, 219–20.

falls between the extremes of strict separation and unstructured overlap. Instead, it generally leans toward state–federal regulatory collaboration, often through programs of cooperative federalism in which the roles of state and federal actors are formally prescribed as asymmetrical complements.

Evolving climate and energy governance offers great opportunity to craft new models of dynamic intergovernmental regulation, but even the most established environmental laws – including the Clean Air[202] and Water Acts,[203] the Safe Drinking Water Act,[204] the Resource Conservation and Recovery Act,[205] the Surface Mining Control and Reclamation Act,[206] the Superfund Act,[207] the Emergency Planning and Community Right-to-Know Act,[208] and even the Endangered Species Act[209] – all incorporate programs of cooperative federalism in which state and federal actors simultaneously operate within a single regulatory organism.[210] Rather than merely colliding over separate efforts that occasionally overlap, these traditional programs of cooperative federalism all purposely engage state and federal actors in an ongoing series of consultation, negotiation, and compromise.[211] The following section explores in

---

[202] Clean Air Act, Pub. L. 88-206, 77 Stat. 392 (1963), codified as amended at 42 U.S.C. §§ 7401 et seq. (2011).
[203] Clean Water Act, Pub. L. 92-500, 86 Stat. 816 (1972), 33 U.S.C. §§ 1251 et seq. (2011).
[204] Safe Drinking Water Act, Pub. L. 93-523, 88 Stat. 1660 (1974), 42 U.S.C. § 300f et seq. (1996)
[205] Resource Conservation and Recovery Act, Pub. L. No. 94-580, 90 Stat. 2795, codified as part of the Solid Waste Disposal Act, 42 U.S.C. §§ 6901 et seq. (2006).
[206] Surface Mining Control and Reclamation Act, Pub. L. 95-87, 91 Stat. 445 (1977), codified as amended at 30 U.S.C. §§ 1201 et seq. (2006).
[207] Comprehensive Environmental Response, Compensation, and Liability Act (Superfund), Pub. L. No. 96-510, 94 Stat. 2767 (1980), amended by Superfund Amendments and Reauthorization Act of 1986, Pub. L. No. 99-499, 100 Stat. 1613, codified as amended throughout 42 U.S.C. §§ 9601 et seq. (2011).
[208] Emergency Planning and Community Right-to-Know Act, Pub. L. No. 99-499, 100 Stat. 1728 (1986), 42 U.S.C. § 11001 et seq. (2011).
[209] Endangered Species Act, Pub. L. No. 93-205, 87 Stat. 884 (1973), codified as amended at 16 U.S.C. §§ 1531 et seq. (2012).
[210] See Ryan, "The Spending Power and Environmental Law," *supra*, n. 180 (separately describing each of these programs of environmental cooperative federalism with special attention to their spending power-related elements).
[211] My own research focuses heavily on the phenomenon of how much federalism-sensitive governance is, in fact, the product of intergovernmental

more detail how the more traditional models of environmental federalism allocate state and federal authority in realms of jurisdictional overlap.

B. The Tools of Cooperative Environmental Federalism

Interjurisdictional environmental problems cannot be managed exclusively at the local or national level, because they require governance capacity from the full spectrum of governance scale.[212] For that reason, cooperative environmental federalism models strive to partner the needed elements that tend to be superior at the federal level with elements that are usually superior at the state and local level, ideally through processes that empower each level to perform to their strengths.

Federally superior governance capacity often includes, inter alia: scientific, technical and financial resources; the legal authority to enforce nationally uniform standards; the ability to appropriately scale regulation for large-scale public commons; and the ability to police spillover effects from one autonomously acting state to another. Elements of governance capacity that tend to be superior at the state and local level often include: detailed expertise about local environmental, geographic, economic, demographic, political and cultural factors that bear on the needs and workability of regulatory proposals; locally situated enforcement personnel; the legal authority to regulate local land use and engage in comprehensive land use planning; and other police power-based legal authority to regulate beyond the more limited set of federally enumerated powers. (Of course, these generalizations bear exceptions.) Governance that skillfully partners complementary capacity across levels enhances the regulatory voice of each, harnessing synergy in a way that belies the old zero-sum federalism game.

Intergovernmental partnerships may involve direct state–federal coordination, but they are often mediated by statutory structures that asymmetrically allocate decision-making authority within programs of coordinated capacity, federally supported state implementation, conditional preemption, and shared and general permitting programs. Each of these methods strives to maximize local and national authority where

---

bargaining. Negotiated federalism includes examples of conventional political haggling, formalized methods of collaborative policymaking, and even more remote signaling processes by which state and federal actors share responsibility for public decision making over time. Ibid. First explored in "Negotiating Federalism," *supra*, n. 30, the negotiation of federalism-sensitive governance became a core insight of *Federalism and the Tug of War Within*, *supra*, n. 10.

[212] See Ryan, *Tug of War*, *supra*, n. 10, pp. 145–80.

each can best contribute, and many have been pioneered by environmental law.

(1) Coordinated capacity

Environmental federalism programs that coordinate capacity partner the distinct regulatory skill sets of state and federal actors relatively straightforwardly. For example, the Emergency Planning and Community Right-to-Know Act, codified as a later addition to the larger Superfund statute, engages state and local experts in coordinated planning for chemical and other emergencies.[213] It harnesses local capacity by requiring each state to establish an Emergency Response Commission drawing on technical expertise from all relevant state agencies.[214] It partners local expertise with federal capacity by authorizing the US EPA to require compliance by all relevant facilities with the emergency planning provisions created by each state's commission.[215] This structure drew praise as an early cooperative federalism model, enhancing interjurisdictional synergy by trading a fully federalized response for one enabling more expert state implementation.[216] However, it was also criticized for not allowing states to opt out of participation in favor of direct federal regulation.[217]

(2) Federally supported state implementation

More often, however, environmental federalism partnerships are crafted around complex regulatory regimes that offer states greater regulatory choices. One model that is common in environmental law and elsewhere

---

[213] 42 U.S.C. § 11001–11050 (2011).

[214] See ibid. §§ 11001(a), 11045; see also www.epa.gov/region4/air/epcra/sercs.htm (listing commissioners) (accessed 20 July 2015). For an example of the wide range of state capacity included in a state commission, see the membership of North Carolina's State Emergency Response Commission. North Carolina Department of Public Safety, "Commission Members," accessed 20 July 2015 at www.ncdps.gov/Index2.cfm?a=000003,000011,003240 (listing participants from state agencies addressing law enforcement, transportation, medical services, environment, agriculture, fire, and others).

[215] 42 U.S.C. §§ 11001(a), 11045 (2011).

[216] See Humphrey, Hubert H. III and LeRoy C. Paddock, "The Federal and State Roles in Environmental Enforcement: A Proposal for a More Effective and More Efficient Relationship" (1990) 14 Harv. Envtl. L. Rev. 7, 27 (noting that EPCRA "for the first time gave states extensive direct authority to enforce a federal environmental law in federal court").

[217] See Johnson, Nicholas J., "EPCRA's Collision with Federalism" (1994) 27 Ind. L. Rev. 549, 550 (arguing that EPCRA "[e]schew[s] traditional incentives for eliciting state regulation," instead "issu[ing] a flat command").

is the model of federally supported state implementation, in which the federal government offers state governments financial and technical resources to help implement federal goals. Relying on Congress's power under the Spending Clause,[218] the federal government offers grants to states in exchange for their participation and to facilitate state accomplishment of related regulatory goals.[219] In this way, the federal government negotiates for state participation in spending power-based partnerships, with federal support for state implementation. (And while the Supreme Court recently constrained spending power bargaining that would tie very large federal grants to indirectly related conditions,[220] few if any environmental programs are likely to be impacted.[221])

Spending power partnerships are attractive to states because they come with fiscal incentives and because they offer states the choice of participation, enhancing the potential for synergy with respect for local autonomy. In some cases, such as the Coastal Zone Management Act, a state maintains total discretion over whether the regulatory program will exist within its boundaries, because the law provides for no federal intervention if the state declines the deal.[222] Spending power partnerships are attractive to the federal government because they enable Congress to negotiate with states for policymaking influence in regulatory realms that lie beyond its more directly enumerated powers[223] – and is thus an important device in federal education,[224] social services,[225] and health

---

[218] US Const. Art I, § 8.

[219] See e.g. Ryan, "The Spending Power and Environmental Law," *supra*, n. 180, at 1009–17 (discussing spending power bargaining and its legal history).

[220] *National Federation of Independent Businesses v. Sebelius*, 132 S. Ct. 2566 (2012).

[221] See generally Ryan, "The Spending Power and Environmental Law," *supra*, n. 180 (evaluating all environmental spending power programs under the new precedent and concluding that all of them, even potentially vulnerable Clean Air Act highway fund sanctions, should survive scrutiny).

[222] See Ryan, *Tug of War*, *supra*, n. 10, p. 303.

[223] See Ryan, "The Spending Power and Environmental Law," *supra*, n. 180, at 1011–13 (explaining spending power bargaining), 1027–28 (listing spending power partnerships in various areas of law), 1033–34 (discussing the limited constitutional footing of certain spending power partnerships beyond the federal spending power).

[224] See e.g. No Child Left Behind Act of 2001, 20 U.S.C. §§ 6301–7941 (reauthorizing the Elementary and Secondary Education Act of 1965, 20 U.S.C. § 6301).

[225] See e.g. Temporary Assistance for Needy Families, 42 U.S.C. §§ 601–79, 603 (authorizing federal grants to states to offer assistance to qualifying poor families).

care law.[226] By contrast, however, environmental law is usually grounded in such federally enumerated powers as the Commerce Clause,[227] the Property Clause,[228] and occasionally other grants of federal authority, such as the Treaty Clause.[229] In programs of cooperative environmental federalism, spending power partnerships are mostly used to invite state participation in regulatory efforts that the federal government could theoretically administer exclusively, but which will be far more effective when incorporating the local expertise and enforcement capacity of state and local partners.

For example, in the larger Superfund program – the Comprehensive Environmental Response, Compensation, and Liability Act – Congress incentivized state participation in the management of toxic waste through a series of spending power partnerships.[230] As Klass and Fazio describe in Chapter 3, the Act imposes liability for involvement with hazardous substances that endanger human health or the environment, and it is mostly federally administered. However, the statute authorizes discretionary grants to encourage state participation and leadership in cleanup efforts,[231] and it makes states and tribes eligible for Brownfield Grants to lead management efforts at less contaminated sites.[232] The Endangered Species Act is also primarily administered by federal actors, but it also invites collaborative state enforcement through several small federal grant

---

[226] See e.g. Medicaid, 42 U.S.C. § 1396, §1396a (authorizing state–federal partnerships in the administration of health insurance).

[227] U.S. Const. Art. I, § 8, cl. 3 (empowering Congress to regulate the channels, persons, and things of interstate commerce, as well as activities having a substantial relationship to interstate commerce).

[228] U.S. Const. Art. IV, § 3, cl. 2 (conferring federal authority over all federal lands and other resources that constitute the property of the United States).

[229] U.S. Const. Art. II, § 2, cl. 2 (together with the Supremacy Clause, Art. VI, cl. 2, conferring federal authority to make and enforce international treaties with environmental implications).

[230] Pub. L. No. 96-510, 94 Stat. 2767 (1980), amended by Superfund Amendments and Reauthorization Act of 1986, Pub. L. No. 99-499, 100 Stat. 1613 (codified as amended throughout 42 U.S.C. §§ 9601–9675 (2011)).

[231] See ibid. § 9604.

[232] Ibid. §§ 9604(k) (discussing brownfields revitalization funding), 9628(a)(1)(B)(ii) (providing that states and tribes may use grants to capitalize a revolving loan fund for brownfield remediation). Section 128(a) was added to CERCLA in 2002 by the Small Business Liability Relief and Brownfields Revitalization Act. Pub. L. No. 107-118, § 128(a), 115 Stat. 2356, 2376–2377 (2002) (codified as amended at 42 U.S.C. § 9628 (2011)).

programs.[233] As Kalyani Robbins explains in Chapter 5, the Act provides various protections for threatened and endangered species of animals and plants through federal consultation and enforcement,[234] but the statute also authorizes small-scale spending-power partnerships capitalizing on local capacity through the Cooperative Endangered Species Conservation Fund, Habitat Conservation Planning Assistance grants and Habitat Conservation Plan Land Acquisition grants.[235]

(3) Conditional preemption

Still, the classic model of cooperative environmental federalism that has been pioneered, if not invented, in environmental law is the model of conditional preemption, by which the federal government sets goals or standards that may be implemented by the states.[236] In this model, the states are invited to participate in accomplishing the overall regulatory goal by tailoring the implementation of federal standards in a way that best suits local political, geographic, economic and demographic circumstances. However, if the states decline to participate, the federal government will regulate in-state activity directly, preempting any conflicting state law. These programs safeguard a centralized response while opening possibilities for local autonomy and interjurisdictional synergy. Of note, many environmental laws deploy federally supported state implementation and conditional preemption simultaneously.

For example, under the Clean Water Act, state and federal actors share supervision of the National Pollution Discharge Elimination System, which prohibits the discharge of federally designated pollutants into protected water bodies without a permit.[237] The law is designed around a program of conditional preemption that allows EPA to act as the permitting authority or to delegate authority to willing states.[238] However,

---

[233] Endangered Species Act, Pub. L. No. 93-205, 87 Stat. 884 (1973), codified as amended at 16 U.S.C. §§ 1531–1543 (2012).
[234] Ibid.
[235] "Section 6 of the Endangered Species Act," U.S. Fish & Wildlife Serv. (16 July 2014), accessed 20 July 2015 at www.fws.gov/midwest/endangered/grants/S6_grants.html.
[236] See e.g. Tushnet, Mark, *The New Constitutional Order* (Princeton University Press, Princeton NJ 2009), p. 87, (discussing conditional preemption); see generally Rotunda, Ronald D., "The Doctrine of Conditional Preemption and Other Limitations on Tenth Amendment Restrictions" (1984) 132 U. Penn. L. Rev. 289.
[237] Clean Water Act, 33 U.S.C. §§ 1251–1387, 1342(b) (2012).
[238] Ibid. at § 1342(a). See also Andreen, Chapter X.

nearly all states have chosen to administer their own permitting programs, in order to maximize regulatory autonomy in managing in-state water resources and economic development.[239] The Clean Water Act also uses the federal spending power to support state implementation directly, authorizing various federal grants to states to improve water quality,[240] including those made under the State Revolving Fund (SRF).[241] The Safe Drinking Water Act further authorizes federal standards implemented by state and local agencies,[242] coupled with the Drinking Water State Revolving Loan Fund that helps public water agencies finance the infrastructure projects needed to comply with federal drinking water regulations.[243]

The Surface Mining Control and Reclamation Act, which regulates the environmental, social and economic harms of surface mining,[244] uses a similar combination of conditional preemption and federally supported state implementation. The law enables states to implement their own regulatory programs or opt for direct federal regulation,[245] and it authorizes federal grants to assist states in developing their own permitting programs.[246] This Act takes the possibilities for state initiative one step further, authorizing cooperative agreements by which states may act as the primary regulators of coal mining operations on federal lands within

---

[239] E.g. N.M. Env't Dep't, NPDES State Program Authorization Briefing Paper (2004), accessed 20 July 2015 at www.nmenv.state.nm.us/swqb/PSRS/NPDES-DelegationBriefingPaper_June-04.pdf (discussing the benefits of self-administration).

[240] The CWA includes 14 categorical grant programs to states, including those to provide water pollution control program support, public water system supervision, underground water source protection, beach monitoring and non-point source pollution control. EPA, National Water Program Guidance Fiscal Year 2011, at 49–50 (April 2010), accessed 20 July 2015 at nepis.epa.gov/Exe/ZyPDF.cgi?Dockey=P100E5WU.pdf.

[241] 33 U.S.C. § 1381 (2006).

[242] Safe Drinking Water Act §1443, 42 U.S.C. § 300f.

[243] Pub. L. 104-182, 110 Stat. 1613 (1996) (codified as 42 U.S.C.A. § 300f–j (1996)).

[244] Surface Mining Control and Reclamation Act of 1977, Pub. L. 95-87, 91 Stat. 445 (1977) (codified as amended at 30 U.S.C. §§ 1201–1328 (2006)).

[245] See ibid. §§ 1253, 1254 (describing the state and federal programs for regulating surface coal mining and reclamation operations).

[246] Ibid. § 1295; Office of Surface Mining Reclamation & Enforcement, "Regulatory Programs Overview," in *Federal Assistance Manual* (2010), accessed 20 July 2015 at www.osmre.gov/lrg/fam/5-100.pdf; "Basics of SMCRA Title IV," W. Pa. Coal. for Abandoned Mine Reclamation (May, 2007), accessed 20 July 2015 at www.wpcamr.org/projects/smcra_reauth/TitleIV%20Basics.pdf.

the state.[247] Under these agreements, federal supremacy and federal sovereignty over nationally owned lands are exchanged for the efficiencies of scale and regulatory continuity offered by unified state management. The Resource Conservation and Recovery Act,[248] which regulates hazardous substances through life-cycle oversight, similarly enables states to choose whether to submit to federal regulation or implement the program within state boundaries.[249]

The Clean Air Act also merges a version of conditional preemption with spending power bargaining, though – perhaps uniquely among environmental law – as less of a carrot and more of a stick.[250] The Act anticipates that EPA will set ambient air quality standards and that states will design and administer State Implementation Plans for attaining these standards.[251] States that fail or decline to do so will eventually be regulated directly by EPA under a Federal Implementation Plan, a variation on the conditional preemption model discussed above.[252] In the meanwhile, however, noncompliant states may be threatened with the loss of federal highway funds offered under a separate spending partnership with the federal Department of Transportation.[253] The threatened

---

[247] 30 U.S.C. § 1273 (2006).

[248] Resource Conservation and Recovery Act of 1976, Pub. L. No. 94-580, 90 Stat. 2795 (codified as part of the Solid Waste Disposal Act, 42 U.S.C. §§ 6901–6992 (2006)).

[249] EPA, Authorizing States to Implement RCRA, in *RCRA Orientation Manual 2011*, at III-133, III-134 (2011), accessed 20 July 2015 at www.epa.gov/osw/inforesources/pubs/orientat/rom311.pdf ("As of August 2008, all states, with the exception of Alaska and Iowa, are authorized to implement the RCRA hazardous waste program.").

[250] 42 U.S.C. §§ 7401–7671(q) (2012).

[251] Ibid. at § 7509(b)(1) (mandating state implementation plans).

[252] If a state declines to create a State Implementation Plan (SIP), or if the EPA concludes that a submitted SIP fails to meet statutory criteria, the EPA is required to create a Federal Implementation Plan (FIP) for that state within two years. 42 U.S.C.A. § 7410(c)(1).

[253] Clean Air Act §179 requires that federal highway funds be withheld from a state that has failed to prepare an adequate SIP or failed to implement requirements under an approved plan when that state includes "non-attainment areas," or areas that have not achieved the federally established National Ambient Air Quality Standards. 42 U.S.C. §§ 7401–7671q, 7509(b)(1) (2012). The EPA has considerable discretion about how and when to apply sanctions (and indeed, has done so on only one occasion), but the Act mandates withholding of certain federal highway funds if noncompliance extends beyond 18–24 months. 42 U.S.C.A. §7509(a). For a fuller discussion of the mechanics of the Clean Air Act highway fund sanctions, see Ryan, *supra*, n. 180, at 1049–59.

loss of federal funds for noncompliance sets the Clean Air Act apart from other environmental laws, most of which use federal funds as an enticement for action rather than as a sanction for inaction.[254] Nevertheless, the conditional preemption elements of the partnership limit the impact of the highway fund sanctions, because when EPA assumes regulatory responsibility within a noncompliant state, the threat of highway fund sanctions is lifted.[255]

As Glicksman and Wentz explain in Chapter 1, the design of the Clean Air Act reflects its architects' intentions that the federal government remain the senior partner in this state–federal partnership, reserving dominant centralized authority to resolve the collective action elements of the interstate air pollution problem. After all, this is a problem that results not only from polluting activities solidly rooted in place but also from countless mobile pollution sources (both domestically and internationally) that are less meaningfully related to local expertise and land use authority.[256] Nevertheless, the Clean Air Act remains an intergovernmental partnership that enables states to more efficiently manage the benefits and burdens of regulation on in-state communities and economies than a fully preemptive model – explaining why nearly all states have chosen to assume responsibility for State Implementation Plans rather than submit to a Federal Implementation Plan.[257]

(4) Shared and general permitting programs

The Clean Air Act especially showcases the asymmetry of state and federal roles within environmental federalism, but most state–federal

---

[254] See Ryan, "The Spending Power and Environmental Law," *supra*, n. 180, at 1034–49.

[255] Section 179 itself is ambiguous on this point, but EPA has formalized this interpretation in the implementing regulations, 40 C.F.R. § 93.120 (2013), to which a reviewing court must defer. See *Chevron v. NRDC*, 467 U.S. 837 (1984). For a discussion of how this regulatory design likely immunizes the Clean Air Act highway fund sanctions against challenge under new spending power limits set forth in *National Federation of Independent Businesses v. Sebelius*, 132 S. Ct. 2566 (2012), see Ryan, *supra*, n. 180, at 1034–49.

[256] For this reason, federal authority can intrude on state discretion even within state implementation plans, through federal regulations of tailpipe emissions and new source review and performance standards associated with large stationary sources. 42. U.S.C. § 7411 (2012).

[257] See United States Environmental Protection Agency, "Status of SIP Requirements for Designated Areas" (last updated 21 Sept. 2014) accessed 20 July 2015 at www.epa.gov/oar/urbanair/sipstatus/reports/map_s.html (providing details on all individual state SIPs).

partnerships follow a similar model, in which federal judgment usually trumps regulatory goals and standards, while local judgment usually gets federal deference on matters of design and implementation that account for diverse local circumstances. In fact, environmental law has pioneered different ways of formalizing this asymmetrical allocation of state and federal authority through its different approaches to shared and general permitting programs.

The conditional preemption model of shared permitting responsibility emerged in various formats over the 1970s in the Clean Air and Water Acts, the Surface Mining Control and Reclamation Act, and the Resource Conservation and Recovery Act, and also in the Occupational Safety and Health Act (OSHA), which enables states to assume permitting responsibility over safe working conditions or opt for direct federal regulation.[258] Interestingly, however, while nearly all states elect to assume permitting responsibility in the environmental context, fewer than half the states have opted to participate as co-regulators under OSHA.[259] While it is impossible to know the reason for this with confidence, it may suggest that environmental law sits at the equipoise of state and federal regulatory interests in a way that more conventional commercial regulation does not. If a state believes that federal decision-makers will be just as capable at regulating worker safety, then allowing the feds to absorb the political and financial costs of regulation is a rational choice. The fact that states usually make the opposite call in environmental contexts – choosing the burdens of regulating over the risk that federal regulators will cause damage – affirms that environmental governance includes factors that are intensely more local in valence, including regulation of land use.

Nevertheless, the environmental model is being viewed with increasing interest in other realms of cooperative federalism, for example, health law. After the Supreme Court invalidated portions of the Affordable Care Act for exceeding the federal spending power,[260] the architects of national health policy are taking great interest in the Clean Air Act's model of partnering mandatory state implementation plans with a federal

---

[258] Occupational Safety and Health Act of 1970, 29 U.S.C. §§ 651–78. (2012).

[259] See Occupational Safety and Health Administration, "All About OSHA," accessed 20 July 2015 at www.osha.gov/Publications/3302-06N-2006-English.html.

[260] *National Federation of Independent Business v. Sebelius*, 132 S. Ct. 2566, 2606–07 (2012).

fallback option.[261] Especially where federal authority is grounded primarily by the Spending Clause,[262] the conditional preemption model is likely to become a fixture in state–federal partnerships far beyond environmental law.[263]

Yet another regulatory device pioneered by environmental law for coordinating state and federal authority in realms of jurisdictional overlap is the use of general permitting programs. The general permit is a tool of regulatory governance that maximizes discretion and minimizes the regulatory burden for applicants, allowing permit applicants to obtain permission to engage in regulatory activity by following a general set of instructions that provide guidance about acceptable and unacceptable activity.[264] For example, the Army Corps of Engineers uses a general permit to govern the filling of wetlands protected by section 404 of the Clean Water Act, allowing countless public and private actors nationwide to obtain permission to fill wetlands with minimal regulatory oversight according to a specified set of federal guidance, with state input.[265]

---

[261] See Ryan, "The Spending Power and Environmental Law," *supra*, n. 180, at 1061 (noting that "one scholar intimate with the development of the ACA suggests that if the drafters could do it again, they would likely have structured some sort of federal fallback provision [like the Clean Air Act's] into the Medicaid expansion"). See also Rosenbaum, Sara and Patricia Gabow, "Open Exchanges to the Poor in States that Opt Out of Medicaid," Roll Call (26 July 2013), accessed 20 July 2015 at www.rollcall.com/news/open_exchanges_to_the_poor_in_states_that_opt_out_of_medicaid_commentary-226677-1.html.).

[262] U.S. Const. Art I, § 8.

[263] See Ryan, "The Spending Power and Environmental Law," *supra*, n. 180, at 1061. While spending power partnerships face new scrutiny after the Affordable Care Act case, very few will involve federal grants large enough to trigger scrutiny under the doctrine, especially those that are also grounded in independent sources of constitutional authority. See Ryan, *supra*, n. 180, at 1027–30.

[264] See e.g. Biber, Eric and J.B. Ruhl, "The Role of Permits in the Regulatory State," RegBlog, 1 July 2014, accessed 20 July 2015 at www.regblog.org/2014/07/01-biber-ruhl-permits-in-the-regulatory-state.html. See also Biber, Eric and J.B. Ruhl, "The Permit Power Revisited: The Theory and Practice of Regulatory Permits in the Administrative State" (forthcoming, 2014) 64 Duke L. J.

[265] United States Environmental Protection Agency, "Section 404 Permitting" (2013) accessed 20 July 2015 at water.epa.gov/lawsregs/guidance/cwa/dredgdis/ (explaining the section 404 general permit program); US Army Corps of Engineers, ORM Permit Decisions, accessed 20 July 2015 at geo.usace.army.mil/egis/f?p=340:1:0) (providing direction on how to apply for a § 404 general permit. See also Biber and Ruhl, *supra*, n. 264 (discussing the § 404 general permit option).

Section 404 also allows states to assume responsibility for general permitting programs within their boundaries, combining the devices of general permitting and conditional preemption.[266]

More interestingly, though, general permitting can also be used to asymmetrically allocate state and federal authority within particularly federalism-sensitive governance, especially when state actors must seek federal approval for their own regulated activity or for state regulation of private activity that is also subject to federal regulation. For example, section 404 of the Clean Water Act also enables states themselves to seek coverage under a State Program General Permit to discharge dredged and fill material to wetlands.[267] Like other methods of allocating asymmetrical authority within environmental federalism programs, the general permit allows federal actors to establish the boundaries of permissible activity while enabling state and local actors to move creatively but responsibly within those parameters (at least in comparison to more intensive preemptive regulation).

When used in these federalism-sensitive contexts, general permits balance central authority with local autonomy by enabling state actors to satisfy broadly framed federal standards by whatever means they choose. Ideally, the general permit alternative encourages synergy and innovation while streamlining the regulatory process. For example, the Clean Water Act's Phase II Stormwater rule administers municipal stormwater discharges under a general permit that enables localities to develop their own unique programs for meeting overarching federal goals.[268] The regulation of stormwater pollution sits "vexingly at the crossroad

---

[266] United States Environmental Protection Agency, "State, Tribal, Local, and Regional Roles in Wetlands Protection" (2012), accessed 20 July 2015 at water.epa.gov/type/wetlands/outreach/fact21.cfm. EPA notes that states and tribes may also strengthen their roles in wetlands protection by: "undertaking comprehensive State Wetland Conservation Plans ... developing wetland water quality standards; applying the Clean Water Act Section 401 Water Quality Certification program more specifically to wetlands; incorporating wetlands protection into other State and Tribal water programs"; and comprehensive resource planning, including the protection of specified river corridors and watersheds. Ibid.

[267] Ibid. (noting that states "may strengthen their roles in wetlands protection by ... obtaining State Program General Permits from the Corps for discharges of dredged and fill material in wetlands").

[268] 33 U.S.C. §1342(p)(4) (2000) (authorizing the "Phase I" and "Phase II" Stormwater Rules); EPA, Permits for Municipal Separate Storm Sewer Systems (MS4s) (14 July 2014), accessed 20 July 2015 at water.epa.gov/polwaste/npdes/stormwater/Municipal-Separate-Storm-Sewer-System-MS4-Main-Page.cfm; see also Ryan, *Tug of War*, supra, n. 10 at pp. 153–56, 300–01.

between land uses regulated locally and water pollution regulated federally,"[269] because most regulated stormwater discharges are by municipal storm drains.[270] Through a decade of intense negotiated rulemaking, federal, state, municipal, environmental and industrial stakeholders designed a general permitting program to empower local discretion as much as possible while still accomplishing federal Clean Water Act goals.[271] The resulting rule allows municipal dischargers to be covered under the general permit by tailoring local management plans to best address local circumstances while meeting five basic federal criteria.[272] Such general permitting programs mirror the classical environmental federalism balance of state and federal power, in which federal judgment prevails on matters of standards and state judgment prevails on matters of design.

General permitting represents another important tool of regulation that is not widely understood beyond the realm of environmental law. In fact, the legal community's failure to grasp the significance of general permits in environmental law may have led the Supreme Court astray in another environmental decision with important federalism implications,[273] *Utility Air Regulatory Group v. EPA*, limiting EPA's ability to regulate stationary sources of greenhouse gases.[274] The Court upheld Clean Air Act regulation of stationary greenhouse gas sources if they also emit other regulated pollutants, but not stationary sources that only emit greenhouse

---

[269] Ryan, *Tug of War*, supra, n. 10 pp. 300–01; Ryan, "Negotiating Federalism," *supra*, n. 30, at 55–56.

[270] See *Envtl. Def. Ctr. v. EPA*, 344 F.3d 832, 840–41 (9th Cir. 2003).

[271] Ibid. at 864. The Phase II Final Rule was published in the Federal Register on 8 December 1999. See Regulations for Revision of the Water Pollution Control Program Addressing Storm Water Discharges, 64 Fed. Reg. 68722 (Dec. 8, 1999) (codified at 40 C.F.R. pts. 9, 122, 123, 124).

[272] See *Envtl. Def. Ctr. v. EPA*, 344 F.3d at 847–48. Specifically, dischargers may develop any program that: (1) educates the public about stormwater hygiene, (2) incorporates public participation, (3) prevents illicit discharges, (4) controls construction debris, and (5) manages pollutant runoff from municipal operations. 40 C.F.R. § 122.34(b) (2010).

[273] Biber, Eric and J.B. Ruhl, "General Permits and the Regulation of Greenhouse Gases," RegBlog (23 July 2014), accessed 20 July 2015 at www.regblog.org/2014/07/23/23-biber-ruhl-general-permits-and-the-regulation-of-greenhouse-gases/.

[274] 134 S. Ct. 2427 (2014) (upholding portions of the Clean Air Act's Prevention of Significant Deterioration Program and Title V permitting program that regulated greenhouse gases from stationary sources under regulation for other pollutants, but invalidating them as applied to stationary sources only subject to regulation for greenhouse gases).

gases.275 The majority concluded that allowing greenhouse gas emissions to be regulated independently would produce "calamitous consequences," because "extravagant" federal authority and resources would be required to administer so many sources.276

But as Professors Eric Biber and J.B. Ruhl have argued, general permitting represents an "alternative between complete exclusion of a range of activities from regulation and burdensome, complex permitting structures," alleviating the Court's seemingly unresolvable concerns about expansive federal reach.277 Indeed, these scholars predict that general permitting structures will prove critical in the future regulation of climate change precisely because they enable streamlined regulation "of widespread and common activities in ways that are politically, legally, and administratively feasible."278 Emerging climate federalism partnerships should take note of the potential of these tools for effective multiscalar governance.

V. CONCLUSION: WHO SHOULD DECIDE?

Wrestling with the incendiary tensions at the intersection of local land use and spillover harm, environmental federalism has helpfully exposed the fault lines underlying our federal system to analysis. Some of the structural tools that environmental law has developed for managing these tensions may be instructive for health reform, education law, marijuana policy and other areas of law contending with similar federalism controversies. To be sure, not every aspect of federalism can be generalized from the environmental experience, and environmental law has yet to perfect its task. Nevertheless, the challenges of environmental governance provide critical insight into the core conflicts of federalism-sensitive governance more broadly, and the successes of environmental governance indicate the potential for exporting effective regulatory strategies. This

---

[275] Ibid. at 2449.
[276] Ibid. at 2442–44.
[277] Biber and Ruhl, *supra*, n. 273 (arguing that "the Court dismissed general permits out of hand as a way of addressing the challenges that greenhouse gases present to the Clean Air Act when, in fact, general permits have already been widely adopted by states and the EPA as a tool to manage permitting problems under both the Clean Air Act and the Clean Water Act. General permits are not novel, untested tools, as Scalia's footnote seems to imply. They are workhorses of the regulatory state").
[278] Ibid.

conclusion suggests a few potential lessons from the environmental experience for related areas of law.

Environmental governance has experimented with different means of allocating regulatory authority across multiscalar lines, often asymmetrically. Different statutory programs engage multiple regulatory stakeholders while allocating roles according to the distinctive strengths of local and national capacity. The conventional tools of cooperative environmental federalism – including coordinated capacity, federally supported state implementation, conditional preemption, and shared and general permit programs – may prove useful in other realms of jurisdictional overlap, especially where the need for a centralized response is matched by strong local capacity rooted in core expressions of the states' police power. Education law, social services delivery and public health laws may be good candidates, as might national security partnerships, criminal law enforcement and even financial services regulation.

For example, the Affordable Care Act might have fared better on judicial review had the Medicaid Expansion been coupled with a federal fallback provision, borrowing from the environmental federalism model of conditional preemption.[279] Perhaps the skilled use of a general permitting partnership could help harmonize state and federal regulation of the complex financial services industry,[280] as Bieber and Ruhl argue it could for the complex project of greenhouse gas regulation, by streamlining points of contact around clear and critical standards. Programs of coordinated capacity and federally supported state implementation already exist in other areas of law, but the results in environmental law and elsewhere clearly show that programs enabling two-way exchange are more successful than federal efforts at unidirectional policymaking.[281] Famous failures in cooperative federalism, such as the No Child Left Behind Act or the REAL ID Act,[282] could learn from the channels of exchange cultivated in the most successful examples of environmental law, such as the Coastal Zone Management and Clean Water Acts.

Indeed, environmental scholars – especially among the emerging dynamic federalism literature – are increasingly emphasizing the values of overlap, fluidity, exchange and negotiation among separately regulating local, state and federal actors. Innovations in federalism theory, such

---

[279] See *supra*, text accompanying nn. 260–61.
[280] Cf. Ryan, "Negotiating Federalism," *supra*, n. 30, at 30–31.
[281] Compare ibid. at 62–63 (discussing state-based innovations under the Social Security Act) with ibid. at 88–90 (discussing state resistance to the No Child Left Behind Act).
[282] See ibid. at 88–90 (No Child Left Behind), 56–58 (REAL ID).

as the Balanced Federalism model in Part II, should help the architects of governance further tailor the tools of conventional cooperative federalism in service of federalism's underlying values.[283] Architects could capitalize on the existing asymmetrical allocation of authority to more effectively engage insight and capacity at the local level, and to more strategically allocate roles among executive, legislative and judicial decision-makers where each is most able. For example, a Balanced Federalism evaluation of New York's challenge to the Low Level Radioactive Waste Management Act[284] might have led the Supreme Court to defer to a federal legislative plan forged by nearly universal consent among state executives (one negotiated behind the veil of regulatory ignorance, before more parochial interests took hold), heading off the current crisis of regulatory abdication.[285]

Relatedly, federalism theory should push regulators to recognize that many of the difficult dynamics of jurisdictional overlap that are formally recognized within state–federal relations are equally meaningful in municipal–state relations. While the US Constitution falsely presumes that municipal interests are synonymous with that of their state, federalism controversies over fracking and other energy harvesting especially reveal intrastate conflicts. Local–state conflicts may be cognizable under state constitutions, which occasionally empower local prerogative over other state interests.[286] At any rate, these conflicts should be duly considered in the elaboration of good federalism-sensitive governance.

One important lesson of environmental governance is that there is no one size to fit all regulatory needs, and different federalism values may take priority in different circumstances. For example, the CZMA, a federal statutory framework that enables multiple iterations of open bargaining between state executive actors toward the creation of corresponding state legislation, provides a good example of how to integrate state/federal and legislative/executive capacity where place-based local diversity is the most critical factor.[287] A very different model is taken by the Clean Air Act's mechanism for regulating motor vehicle emissions, which enables states to follow either the federal or California standard – limiting the variability of regulation within the national market of

---

[283] See *supra*, text accompanying nn. 76–86.
[284] *New York v. United States*, 505 U.S. 144 (1992).
[285] See Ryan, *Tug of War*, *supra*, n. 10, pp. 215–64.
[286] See e.g. *Robinson Township v. Pennsylvania*, ___ A.3d ___, 2013 WL 6687290 (Pa. 2013) (upholding municipal rights to prevent fracking, notwithstanding contrary state law, under the state constitution).
[287] See Ryan, *Tug of War*, *supra*, n. 10, pp. 305 (analyzing the CZMA).

automobile manufacturing while still enabling the benefits of regulatory competition.[288] This model enables effective dynamic interaction within a more centralized regime, in which the constraints of a national market are the most critical factor.[289]

In general, governance architects designing new regulatory structures of cooperative federalism must consider all of the implicated federalism values, weighing carefully whether any one takes priority over another. While most federalism-sensitive governance should incorporate some means of multiscalar coordination, the balance may shift as needed toward a more centralized approach, such as conditional preemption under the Clean Air Act, or a more locally empowering approach, such as the CZMA's reverse preemption within a program of federally supported state implementation. The more all values are in equipoise, the more the regulatory framework should allow for adaptive management through ongoing deliberation among regulatory stakeholders.

To that end, the preceding chapters demonstrate that ongoing environmental dilemmas require continued innovation and ongoing adaption. Improving the coordination of local, state and federal capacity in realms of jurisdictional overlap remains the central challenge of environmental law. Several earlier chapters identify statutory systems in which more federal authority may be needed to resolve collective action problems, including Blake Hudson's discussion of forest resources (Chapter 4), Kalyani Robbins' discussion of species protection (Chapter 5), and Bill Andreen's discussion of water law (Chapter 2). Glicksman and Wentz defend the importance of federal authority in the Clean Air Act regulatory partnership (Chapter 1), prompted by competing claims for greater local devolution. These authors persuasively describe environmental regulatory contexts in which the values of central authority may outweigh countervailing values of local autonomy.

In their discussions of climate and energy law, Bill Buzbee (Chapter 7), Kirsten Engel (Chapter 8), Alice Kaswan (Chapter 9), and Hannah Wiseman (Chapter 6) tout the benefits of jurisdictional overlap between strong local and national regulators, in the hopes that regulatory dynamism will promote well-informed decisions, focus different regulatory capacity at different elements of the overall problem, and overcome agency capture through regulatory backstop. Here, the values of local autonomy and central authority each make strong claims for primacy, but

---

[288] See ibid. at 310 (analyzing the Clean Air Act).
[289] See ibid. See also Ryan, "The Once and Future Challenges of American Federalism," *supra*, n. 14, at Part 3.

the overall goals of regulatory problem-solving are most furthered by dynamic interaction. Robert Fowler (Chapter 12), Behnke and Eppler (Chapter 13), and Sairam Bhat (Chapter 14) describe how similar tensions are respectively navigated within the Australian, German and Indian federal systems.

In still other areas of environmental law, localism values may appropriately take priority. Hirokawa and Rosenbloom argue that preserving the primacy of local land use authority is necessary to protect ecosystems and communities (Chapter 11). Ann Carlson shows how environmental regulation of coastal and water resources appropriately privileges local concerns over central oversight through mechanisms of "reverse preemption" (Chapter 10). However, Klass and Fazio warn that new Supreme Court precedent privileging state laws of repose over federal Superfund mandates can effectively "reverse preempt" hazardous waste cleanup, in ways that compromise the overall statutory mission (Chapter 3).

With so many considerations at play, it is hard to imagine environmental law – or any federalism-sensitive governance – reaching a definitive answer to the question of who should decide. Strictly segregating state and federal efforts in interjurisdictional contexts is unlikely to work well, as demonstrated by failed environmental governance over radioactive waste management and nonpoint source water pollution.[290] Yet leaving jurisdictional matters fully unresolved can also have serious consequences. Doctrinal uncertainty may deter effective regulatory problem-solving where it is needed if regulators fear becoming embroiled in legal challenges to their assertion of contested authority.[291] The sharp decline in Clean Water Act enforcement after *Rapanos* demonstrates this peril, leading to worsening water quality across the country. Alternatively, doctrinal uncertainty can encourage self-serving regulatory abdication, if all levels of government cast the regulatory dilemma as someone else's responsibility.[292] And the two are sometimes related. As noted, there has been precious little movement in managing the problem of radioactive waste after *New York* eviscerated the enforcement provisions of the Low Level Radioactive Waste Policy Act.[293]

---

[290] See Ryan, *Tug of War*, supra, n. 10, pp. 109–45 (discussing the pitfalls of jurisdictional separation).
[291] See ibid. pp. 162–65.
[292] See ibid. pp. 165–67.
[293] See ibid. pp. 226–41 (discussing the chaos that ensued after the Court's decision).

From the Balanced Federalism perspective, the lessons from these failures in environmental federalism suggest that the allocation of federalism interpretive responsibilities should not only better track national and local capacity, but the unique capacities of the different branches of government.[294] Judicial federalism constraints should be reserved for clear legal questions that courts are equipped to answer, and political constraints should operate in contested contexts of overlap where multiscalar interests are well represented.[295] If the purpose of federalism is to ensure that governance affecting distinctively local and national interests appropriately accounts for both, then governance that is the product of informed, accountable, multiscalar collaborative process warrants deference because it accomplishes that goal.[296] At a minimum, courts reviewing federalism claims should carefully consider the larger ramifications for good governance when evaluating difficult jurisdictional questions.

Heeding these lessons, well-crafted multiscalar governance belies the perverse presumption of zero-sum federalism, which assumes that the allocation of decision-making authority among levels and agents of government is always a zero-sum game.[297] Defying the presumption that authority exercised by one is categorically removed from others, environmental governance has experimented with different ways of enhancing authority among multiple agents simultaneously, through structured programs of consultation and exchange. This empirical assault on the mythos of zero-sum federalism warrants emphasis, drawing attention to what most American federalism actually looks like in practice, and how federalism in practice increasingly departs from the rhetoric of conventional federalism theory.[298]

In the end, perhaps the problem that stymies all federalism-sensitive governance is the assumption underlying the question with which we began. "*Who should decide?*" presumes a simple answer, and in contexts of profound jurisdictional overlap, there is rarely a simple answer. Environmental federalism has shown that the best response is often to inform interjurisdictional governance with multiple perspectives as feasibly as possible, through ongoing processes of exchange, adaptation and

---

[294] See generally ibid.; ibid. pp. xi–xii; Ryan, "Negotiating Federalism and the Structural Constitution," *supra*, n. 81.

[295] See ibid. pp. 339–67; see also Ryan, "Negotiating Federalism," *supra*, n. 30.

[296] Ibid.

[297] See *supra*, nn. 82–86.

[298] See Ryan, "The Once and Future Challenges of American Federalism," *supra*, n. 14, at Part 2; Ryan, *Tug of War*, *supra*, n. 10, p. 268.

negotiation among stakeholders at all levels of jurisdictional scale. Balanced federalism suggests that similar principles apply to the allocation of decision-making authority along the horizontal separation of powers. Good interjurisdictional governance engages not only the distinctive capacity at different levels of government vertically but from the different branches of government within each level. Legislative, executive and judicial coordination at all levels of scale are needed to manage the difficult trade-offs that federalism-sensitive governance always has required, and always will require, of us.

ACKNOWLEDGEMENTS

This chapter draws on material previously published in Erin Ryan, *Federalism and the Tug of War Within* (Oxford, 2012), and several related articles: Erin Ryan, "The Once and Future Challenges of American Federalism" in Alberto López Basaguren and Leire Escajedo San-Epifanio, eds., *The Ways of Federalism in Western Countries and the Horizons of Territorial Autonomy in Spain*, Vol. 1 (Springer, 2013); Erin Ryan, "Negotiating Federalism" (2011) 52 B.C. L. Rev. 1; Erin Ryan, "Federalism at the Cathedral: Property Rules, Liability Rules, and Inalienability Rules in Tenth Amendment Infrastructure" (2010) 81 Colorado L. Rev. 1; and Erin Ryan, "Federalism and the Tug of War Within: Seeking Checks and Balance in the Interjurisdictional Gray Area" (2007) 66 Md. L. Rev. 503.

I am most grateful to Ann Carlson, David Adelman, Craig Johnston, and Kalyani Robbins for their comments, and to Ashley Garcia and Gabe Hinman for their research assistance.

Finally, I am very thankful for the excellent suggestions I received on a draft version of this piece from participants in Professor Ann Carlson's Climate and Energy Law Workshop at UCLA Law School.

Index

adaptive federalism 109–13
Adelman, David 109–10
Adler, Jonathan 105
Affordable Care Act 2010 413
Air Conditioning, Heating and Refrigeration Institute v. City of Albuquerque (2008) 255–7
air pollution
  shift from state to federal controls 13
  CAA Amendments 1977 16–18
  CAA Amendments 1990 18–19
  CAA 1970 13–16
Alaska Department of Environmental Conservation v. EPA (2004) 4–5
Amalgamated Society of Engineers v. Adelaide Steamship Co Ltd (1920) 278, 280
Arizona v. United States (2010) 391
Australia
  constitutional law
    background 271, 273–4
    Commonwealth power, scope of 279–81
    state and Commonwealth relationship 274–5, 279–81
    treaties, ratification and implementation processes 288–90
  cooperative federalism
    coercive centralism, and 271–2
    Council of Australian Governments (COAG) 292–3
    democracy deficit 293–4
    intergovernmental agreements 293–8
    Ministerial Councils 292–3
    reform proposals 272–3, 297–301
    trends 271–2, 277, 291, 301–2

environmental federalism
  challenges 273, 295, 302–3
  Commonwealth powers 281–3, 287–8
  compared with US authority 284–90
  cooperative approach 291
  external territories, Commonwealth authority over 288–9
  generally 271–2, 290–91
  initiative impacts 273
  Intergovernmental Agreement on the Environment (IGAE) 294–5
  intergovernmental initiatives 291–8
  National Environment Protection Council (NEPC) 295
  national strategies 291, 298–9
  oceans, Commonwealth authority over 287–8
  preemption 272
  Standing Committee on Environment and Water (SCEW) 292
  trends 301–2
environmental protection policy
  biodiversity 286–7
  carbon price scheme 273
  Commonwealth initiatives 286–7
  Commonwealth legislative power 281–3, 287–8
  cooperative approaches 291
  Environment Protection and Biodiversity Conservation Act 1999 295–7
  Lake Eyre Basin 297–8
  legislative drafting 283–4

matters of national environmental
significance (MNES) 296
Murray-Darling Basin 272, 282,
297
National Strategy for Ecologically
Sustainable Development
298–9
Natural Reserves System 286–7,
298
federalism
centralism, and 271–2, 274–5
coercive approach 271–2, 277
competitive approach 277
federal land ownership and
management role 285–6
general features 273–7
judicial influences on 278–81
opportunistic focus 276–7
pragmatism 276–7
reform proposals 275–6
state sovereignty, revival proposals
298–303

Bakies v. City of Perrsburg (2006) 251
balanced federalism 369–70, 414,
417–18
Ball v. James (1981) 251–2
Bankhead, John 88
Bedford Affiliates v. Sills (1998) 59–60
Bentsen, Lloyd 19
Bieber, Eric 412–13
biodiversity *see also* endangered
species
Australian protection mechanisms
286–7
climate change impacts on 111–12,
258–9
cooperative federalism
adaptive management approach,
need for 110–13
climate change impacts, and
110–13
geographic range changes 111–12
*Board of County Com'rs v. Brown
Group Retail (2009)* 61
*Building Industry Association of
Washington v. Washington State
Building Code Council (2012)* 257

Burger, Michael 134
*Burlington N. and Santa Fe Ry. Co. v.
United States* (2009) 54
Buzbee, William 109, 126

Clean Air Act 1970
amendments
compliance deadlines 19
criticism of 19
generally 6, 10
1977 16–18
1990 18–19
cooperative federalism
conditional preemption 406–7, 409
emphasis shifts 13–19
enforcement powers and penalties
8–9
initial approach 3–6
limitations of 21–5, 183–4
need for 7, 26–7
performance of 20–23
shared and general permit
programs 407–8
EPA role and powers
development of 13–19, 25–7
dominance of 5–10
emissions guidelines 25–6
enforcement 8–10
purpose 25–6
state program supervision 9–10
generally
amendments 6, 10, 16–19
background 3–4
California's emissions standards 9,
14, 24–5
environmental law, influences on
development 4–5
non-compliance penalties 406–7
purpose 7–8, 13–16, 407
successes and limitations of 20–23,
27
suitability for addressing climate
change 23–5
state role and powers
changing emphasis 13–19
distrust of 14–15, 17–18
higher standards adoption 9, 14, 16
limitations 8–9, 24–5

non-attainment penalties 8–9, 17
preemption of state laws 229–30
rights *vs.* responsibilities 7–10, 17–18
state implementation plans (SIPs) 8, 406
uniformity, and 24–5
California v. FERC (2008) 218
cap-and-trade programs 145, 153–6, 166–7, 174–5, 183–5
CERCLA (Comprehensive Environmental Response, Compensation and Liability Act 1980)
  cooperative federalism
    Congressional intention 49, 54–5
    discovery rule 63
    federal claims preemption 53–5, 57–67
    limitations 163
    personal injury or property damage 62–6
    remediation costs recovery 63–4
    spending power partnerships 403–4
    statutes of limitations or repose 62–6
    successes 401
  generally
    background 49–50
    cost recovery and contribution claim 51–2
    hazardous substances, definition 52
    limitations 52–3
    National Contingency Plan (NCP) 51, 57–8
    purpose 49–54, 63–4
  state role and powers
    common law, reliance on 56–7
    contribution claims 59–62
    cost recovery claims 57–62
    double recovery claims 60–61
    NCP non-reliance implications 57–8
    personal injury or property damage claims 62–6

    preemption of state law claims 53–5, 57–67
    presumption against preemption 66
    scope of claims function 53–5
    state Superfund statute variations 55–6
    statutes of limitations or repose 62–6
    unjust enrichment claims 61–2
clean car standards 175–6, 183–4
Clean Power Plan (2015) 163–4
climate change, generally
  adaptation challenges 209
    democratic legitimacy 195–7
    effectiveness 193–5
    free-riding 196
    liberty rights protection 197–8
    prevention of tyranny 197–8
  federal adaptation initiatives
    Climate Action Plan 204
    Climate Data Initiative 204
    Climate Resilience Toolkit 204
    disaster law programs 206–7
    federal agency role 205–7
    Interagency Climate Change Adaptation Task Force 203–4
    multi-jurisdictional programs 207–9
    National Flood Insurance Program 206–7
    program development and interaction 203–7
    support recommendations 204–5
  impacts
    economic 190–92
    ecosystem degradation 258–9
    human settlements 191–2
    infrastructure 190–91
    natural adaptation 192
    physical 190–91
    public health 191
    scale of 188–91
    significance of 23
  predictions 189
    challenges 148–9
climate change policies
  bottom-up approaches 150–51

cap-and-trade methods 145, 153–6,
    166–7, 174–5, 183–5
carbon taxes 166–7
cooperative federalism
  adaptation governance functions
    198–203
  anti-patchwork arguments 159–60
  biodiversity and wildlife protection
    challenges 110–13
  clean car standards 183–4
  Coastal Zone Management Act 205
  collective response role 202–3
  democratic legitimacy 195–7
  dynamic federalism, and 194–5
  effectiveness 193–5
  extra-jurisdictional impacts 194–5
  federal standards or requirements
    199–202
  federal support functions 202–3
  federalism values 192–8
  first mover advantage 181
  funding 200, 202
  housing programs 208–9
  incremental improvements 163–4
  individualized source obligations
    159–60
  initiative support
    recommendations 204–5
  innovation incentives 160–61, 179
  inter-jurisdictional challenges
    196–7
  interest group capture, and 197
  judicial challenges 384–5
  justifications for 194–5
  liberty rights protection 197–8
  multi-jurisdictional program
    development 207–9
  multilevel structure, advantages of
    194–5
  path dependence 164–5
  policy diffusion 161–6
  political incentives 180–82, 185–6
  potential benefits 152–3
  prevention of tyranny 197–8
  program development and
    interaction 203–7
  regulatory webs 161–3
  similarly targeted regulation 161–3

  suboptimal innovation theory
    180–82
  substantive and procedural
    requirements 199–202
  suitability for addressing 23–5
  systemic political challenges
    196–7
  water programs 207–8
federal role and powers
  implementation failure risks 157–8
  laxity risks 155–7
  limitations 167–8
  preemption of state law 146,
    152–4, 158–64
  regulatory limitations and
    challenges 154–5
international approach, need for
  145–6
legal durability, need for 147, 165–6
legal influences 145–7, 151–2,
  165–6, 188
market influences 147–8, 151–4,
  165–7
regulatory challenges
  authority, establishing 151–2
  conservation motivations 158–9
  cross-border nature of problem
    150, 154
  derailment risks 146–8, 154–8
  free-riding 154, 170, 180–81, 196
  hedging 155–7
  implementation failure 157–8
  innovation incentives 155–7,
    169–71, 180–82
  inter-jurisdictional competition
    196–7
  interest group capture 197
  leakage 154–6
  legislative inertia 165–6
  liberty rights protection 197–8
  market forces 147–8, 151–4
  overinclusion risks 158–60
  policy reversal 157–8
  prediction variations 148–9
  private and corporate interest
    149–50, 167–8
  regulation avoidance 154
  regulatory commons dynamics 150

regulatory entrenchment 160–66
skepticism 149
state, local and federal conflicts 153–4
under-innovation 181–2
state role and powers
adaptation effectiveness, and 193–4
advantages 147, 151–2, 169–70
catalyst roles 155–7
clean car standards 175–6, 183–4
electricity generation emission caps 176
extra-jurisdictional impacts 194
federal preemption of 146, 152–4, 158–64
free-riding, and 170
GHG emission targets and registries 172–3, 183
individualized oversight 159–60
innovation incentives 156–7, 169–71, 179
inter-jurisictional policy impacts 207–9
'laboratories of democracy' theory 162, 169–70, 179, 182–3, 187
limitations 147, 193–4
low carbon fuel standards 176–7
path dependence risks 164–5
policy diffusion, and 161–3, 165–6
policy reversal 157–8
political risks, and 185–6
regional agreements 146
renewable portfolio standards 177–9
risk aversity, and 180–82
scale innovation, and 171, 182–7
standard adoption creativity 184–5
state agencies 186
subnational cap-and-trade programs 174–5
Coastal Zone Management Act 2006 205, 208
amendments 238–9
reverse preemption 214
judicial interpretation and legislative amendment 225–6
practical application 226–9, 397–8

state veto of inconsistent federal actions 214, 222–4, 238–9, 396–7
collective action theory 10–13, 16
cooperative federalism, justifications for 10–13, 16–17, 23–5, 105
'not in my back yard' (NIMBY) syndrome 12–13, 25, 115–16
'race to the bottom' 4–5, 12, 16–18
resource pooling 11–12, 16
transboundary externalities 11, 18, 24
uniform standards 12, 16, 24–5
Commonwealth v. Tasmania (1983) 279–80
Comprehensive Environmental Response, Compensation and Liability Act 1980 *see* CERCLA
constitutional federalism, in US
forestry management policies 76–81, 87
wetland management policies 78–9
constitutional law
Australia, in
background 271, 273–4
Commonwealth power, scope of 279–81
state and Commonwealth relationship 274–5, 279–81
treaties, ratification and implementation processes 288–90
federalism, relationship with 361–2
US, in
definitions of state 247–8
local governance rights and controls 250–52
Supremacy Clause 248–9, 365, 393
treaties, ratification and implementation 288–90
cooperative federalism, generally
adaptive management approach, need for 109–13
advantages 368–9
climate change mitigation, suitability for 23–5
collective action theory, and 10–13
criticism of 368–9
enhanced approach 107–10

environmental policy applications
    398–400
  capacity coordination 401, 413
  conditional preemption 404–7, 409
  federally supported state
      implementation 401–4, 413
  intergovernmental partnerships
      400–401
  shared and general permit
      programs 407–12
  spending power partnerships
      402–3
  flexibility, and 414–15
  functions 3–4, 368–9
  health policy 408–9
  judicial interpretation role 417
  jurisdictional overlaps, and 398–400,
      415–16
  justifications for 10–13, 16–17, 23–5,
      105
  matching principle 105–6, 134
  merits and criticism of 4–5
  'not in my back yard' (NIMBY)
      syndrome 12–13, 25, 115–16
  'race to the bottom' 4–5, 12, 16–18
  regulatory opportunities 399–400
  resource pooling 11–12, 16
  standard approach 106–7
  successes and failures 413
  transboundary externalities 11, 18, 24
  uniform standards 12, 16, 24–5
CTS Corp. v. Waldburger (2014) 64–7
Clean Water Act 1972
  amendments 35–6, 39, 43–7
    best management practices 45
    coastal zones regulation 44–5
    state authority 45–7
  cooperative federalism
    best management practices 45
    Coastal Zone Management Act
        (CZMA) 44–5
    Coastal Zone Reauthorization
        Amendments (CZARA) 44–5
    conditional preemption 404–5
    dynamic federalism, development
        of 43–8
    hydromodifications 30–31, 47–8

  judicial restrictions on reach of
      382–4
  non-point source program 30–31,
      35–7, 43–7, 77
  point source program 33–5, 43
  quality standards 34
  rights *vs.* responsibilities 7–8
  State Revolving Fund 405
  stormwater permits 410–11
  successes and failures 30–32
  water quantity/ flow management
      38–40, 47–8
EPA role and powers 29
  best management practices 45
  enforcement 34
  non-point source program 36–7,
      43–7, 77
  oversight authority 33–4, 37
  point source program 33–5
  successes and limitations 45–6
  total maximum daily load (TMDL)
      36–7, 45–7
  water quantity/ flow management
      36–7, 40, 45–8
generally
  amendments 35–6, 39, 43–4
  background 28–9, 32
  importance 28–9
  judicial challenges 382–4
  pollution, definition 39
  successes and limitations 28–32,
      40–46, 48
state role and powers
  authority restrictions 41, 45–7
  coastal zone management 44–5
  enforcement 34, 41–2
  higher standards adoption 42–3
  legislative amendments regarding
      45–7
  non-point source program 35–6,
      41, 44–7
  point source program 33
  preemption 34–5, 39
  regulatory and quality standards
      33–4
  restrictive legislation 40–41
  reverse preemption provisions
      214–17

savings clauses 35
successes and limitations 40–43
total maximum daily load (TMDL)
    41, 45–6
veto of FERC permits 218–22
veto of inconsistent federal actions
    214–17
veto of wetlands permissions
    220–22
water quality certification 42–3,
    216–17
water quantity/flow management
    39–40, 47–8

*Decker v. Northwest Environmental
    Defense Center (2013)* 77–8
DeShazo, J.R. 220
Dillon, John F. 252–3
Dole, Bob 19
Duane, Timothy 107–8
Dwyer, John 106–7

ecosystems
    ecological economics of 244–5
    exosystem services analysis 244–5,
        261–3
    functionality degradation predictions
        258–9
    local governance and protection role
        261–5, 267
Emergency Planning and Community
    Right-to-Know Act (2011) 401
Endangered Species Act 1973 99–104
    critical habitat designation 100
    Joint Task Force on Endangered
        Species Act Policy (ESA JTF)
        103–4
    listed species recovery plans 100–101
    state conservation programs 100–102
    state–federal cooperation
        benefits 94, 102, 104–6
        enhanced model 107–10
        jurisdiction conflicts 108–9
        limitations 103
        in practice 102–4
        requirements 100–102
        spending power partnerships
            403–4

    standard model 106–7
endangered species policies, in US
    game laws 96–7
    migratory birds 97
endangered species protection policies,
    in US
    common law development 95–6
    cooperative federalism
        adaptive management approach,
            need for 110–13
        climate change impacts, and
            110–13
        cooperation in practice 102–4
        cooperation requirements 100–102
        critical habitat designation 100
        dual system, benefits of 94, 102,
            104–5
        enhanced approach 107–10
        Joint Task Force on Endangered
            Species Act Policy (ESA JTF)
            103–4
        jurisdiction conflicts 108–9
        limitations 103
        listed species recovery plans
            100–101
        standard approach 106–7
        state conservation programs
            100–102
    Endangered Species Act 1973
        99–104
    federal role and powers 96–100
        advantages of 104
        federal aid for wildlife restoration
            97
        game laws 96–7
        maritime mammals 98–9
        migratory birds 97
        preemption of state powers 97–9
        wild horses 98
    fragmentation 71
    geographic range changes 111–12
    Montana gray wolf 107–8
    state role and powers 95–6, 104
        federal preemption 97–9
energy policy, in US
    cooperative federalism
        environmental regulation
            interaction 125

governance impacts 134–6
implementation 138–9
information sharing 137–8
initiative overlaps 125–6
justifications for 115–16, 135–6
local–federal conflicts 378–9
matching principle 134
negotiated federalism 135–6
participation maximisation 136–7
preemption, avoiding 136
federal role and powers
  potential advantages of 134–5
  regulatory overlaps 125–6, 375–6
generally
  controversies in 375–9
  costs 119–23
  damage mitigation and compensation 139–40
  development benefits 123–4
  development duration 120
  electricity generation emission caps 176
  endangered species regulation impact 125
  environmental impacts 120–22
  location impacts 119–20, 122
  standardized approach, need for 140–41
  transportation impacts 120–21
industry trends 117–18
  development costs 119–23
  development impacts 119–23
  development times 120
  economic impacts 123–4
  industry governance role 131–2
  private sector governance role 131–2
  renewable energy 117–21, 129–30, 377–9
  shale gas fracking 117, 131–2, 377–9
  wind energy 117–20, 129–30
state role and powers 375–9
  damage mitigation and compensation 139–40
  development burdens 123
  economic benefits 124
  federalised approaches 138–9

hybrid regulatory controls 130–31
interstate jurisdiction conflicts 376–9
judicial interpretation 132–4, 376–7, 379–85
local governance and state joint regulation 129–30, 375–6
local governance preemption 127–9, 133–4
local governance role 126–7
local impact minimisation 139–40
participation maximisation 136–7
preemption, avoiding 136
production and transportation change influences 114–15, 377
regulatory challenges 133–4, 376
regulatory floors and ceilings 129–30
regulatory overlaps 125–6, 376
regulatory standards 127–9, 131
regulatory variations 126–7
Engel, Kirsten 109–10
environmental federalism, generally
  controversies in 357–8, 371–5
  causes 371
  crime or public health impacts 372–3
  decision-making goals and priorities 374
  energy policy, and 375–9
  greenhouse gas regulation 384–5
  judicial interpretation 132–4, 376–7, 379–85
  jurisdictional overlaps 370–74
  radioactive waste management 380–82, 416
  regulatory overlaps 372–4
  state regulatory claims 372–5
  ultimate control dilemma 358, 371, 374, 384–5, 392–8, 416–18
  water pollution 382–4
governance responses 386–7
  cooperative federalism 398–400
  jurisdiction overlaps 389–400
  jurisdictional collaboration 392–8
  jurisdictional separation 391–2

environmental federalism, in Australia
    see Australia
environmental federalism, in Germany
    see Germany
environmental federalism, in India see
    India
environmental federalism, in US
    Australian authority, compared with
        284–90
    challenges 246, 250–51
        decision-making controversies
            255–7
        greenhouse gas regulation 384–5
        invisible and social costs 258–65
        judicial rulings 379–85
        National Land Use Policy Act 1996
            (proposed) 255
        radioactive waste management
            380–82, 416
        Religious Land Use and
            Institutionalized Persons Act
            2000 255
        water pollution 382–4
    cooperative federalism 398–400
        capacity coordination 401, 413
        conditional preemption 404–7, 409
        federally supported state
            implementation 401–4, 413
        intergovernmental partnerships
            400–401
        shared and general permit
            programs 407–12
        spending power partnerships
            402–3
    historical development 248–9, 255
    local governance
        boundaries, importance of 252
        community role, importance of
            258–67
        ecological identity, and 260–61
        ecosystem regulation and
            protection 261–5, 267
        local priorities, role of 264–5
        political engagement, and 263
    preemption
        conditional 404–7, 409
        examples 255–7
        extraterritorial impacts 253–4

    floor preemption 395
    judicial influences 249–50, 253–4,
        265–7, 394–6
environmental policy, in US see also
    environmental federalism
    federal role and powers
        Australian approach, compared
            with 284–90
        Commerce Clause 76, 78–9, 87,
            98, 284–5, 394–5
        constitutional supremacy 248–9,
            393
        historical development 245–6,
            249–50
        implications 245–6
    governance challenges
        generally 412–13
        multiscalar approach 413–14
    Resource Conservation and Recovery
        Act 1976 406, 408
    state and local role and powers 245–6
        community role, importance of
            258–67
        historical development 245–6
    Surface Mining Control and
        Reclamation Act 1977 405–6,
        408
equal footing doctrine 389

Federal Aid in Wildlife Restoration Act
    1937 97
federalism, generally see also
    cooperative federalism;
    environmental federalism;
    federalism theory; reverse
    federalism
    constitutional structure, relationship
        with 361–2
    definition 247–8
    democracy, and 363
    disadvantages 243–4
    federal-sensitive governance 370
    functions 244, 362–6
    good governance, and 361–3
    judicial interpretation 247–57
    jurisdictional overlaps 387–9, 414,
        415–16
    local governance, and

authority of 247–8
boundaries, role of 252–4
challenges of 266–7
community role, importance of 259–67
constitutional rights and controls 250–52
controversies 255–7
decision making controversies 255–7
extraterritorial impacts of local actions 253–4
limitations of 249–50
marginalization 254–5
origins of power 252–3
preemption of 247–55, 253–7
self-governance implications 243–4, 250–51
objectives 360–63
preemption, judicial interpretation 249–50, 253–4
regulatory backstop, as 364–5
sovereignty, and 247–8, 360
Supremacy Clause of US Constitution 248–9, 365, 393
trends 108
ultimate control dilemma 355–7, 366–7, 392–8, 416–18
uncertainty, and 390–400, 416
values 362–3
   flexibility, and 414–15
   tensions and conflicts between 363–6
federalism theory *see also* cooperative federalism
   adaptive federalism 109–13
   balanced federalism 369–70, 414, 417–18
   benefits of 414
   challenges of 366–71
   dual federalism 368–9
   negotiated federalism 370
   New Deal federalism 368
   zero-sum federalism 370, 417
First Iowa Hydro-Electric Cooperative v. Federal Power Commission (1946) 218
forestry policies, in US

federalism, fragmentation of
   Capper Report (1919) 88
   Commerce Clause authority 76, 78–9, 87
   constitutional federalism 76–81, 87
   federal prescription policies 86–8
   historical influences 86–92
   institutional influences 81–4
   legal influences 80–81
   overcoming, need for 91–2
   political culture influences 84–6
   public/private forest ownership influences 81–4, 92
   Roosevelt administration influences 86–9
   spillover effects 81–3
   state preemption influences 79–81
   vertical and horizontal controls 71–5, 79
   voluntary assistance and incentive programs 92
generally
   federal role 71–2
   flexibility advantages 73–4
   forest fire, influences on policy development 86–7, 90
   forestry land loss forecasts 72–3
   forestry parcelization 82–3
   fragmentation 71–5
   interconnected nature of forestry, implications 80–81
   National Industrial Recovery Act 1933 87
   policy focus patterns 86, 90–91
   political and legal impacts 73
   public/private ownership patterns 81–3, 92
   regional management trends 86–92
   REIT ownership 83, 92
   social and economic impacts 72–3
   state and local government role 72
resource management approaches
   forest preservation 75
   timber operations 74–5
state role and powers
   attitudes to land use management 76–9

federal controls, resistance to 78–9
forest preservation 75
management success trends 91–2
policy preemption 79–81
timber management 74–5
Freeman, Jody 220
Frug, Gerald 266

Galle, Brian 181–2
Galligan, B. 277
Gavin, Steven 135
Geer v. Connecticut (1896) 95
Germany
  environmental federalism
    challenges 305, 309, 311, 323–4
    concurrent legislation 312–14
    deviation rights 313–14
    EU legislative role 312–16
    European Court of Justice
      oversight 312
    executive dominance, and 317
    framework legislation 313–14
    national and local government
      interaction 316–17
    strengths and weaknesses 323–4
  environmental protection policy
    agenda-setting process 315–18
    Bundestag and Bundesrat role
      306–8, 314, 317, 320–21
    challenges 305, 309
    co-decision procedure 318–19
    Conference of Ministers (UMK)
      role 316–17, 322
    decision-making process 318–21
    development 313–14
    EU influences 310–21, 323–4
    fragmentation 311
    judicial review 322–3
    legislative competences 312–15
    multi-level governance conflicts
      312
    national interests, promotion of
      316–17
    Nature Protection and Landscape
      Conservation Act 2010 314
    networks, role of 314–15
    policy instrument trends 311–12
    ratification and implementation
      321–2
    regulatory conflicts 312–15
    shift of competences 309–11
  federalism
    Basic Law/ constitutional
      influences on 306–7
    concurrent legislation 307–8,
      312–14
    deviation rights 313–14
    EU influences on 304–8, 317–21
    general principles 304–8
    Länder role and powers 306–8, 313
    legislative powers 306–8
    reform 313, 321–4
    shared rule principle 307–8
    sovereignty and self-government
      powers 306
    structure 306–8
    subsidiarity, and 317–18, 320
    unitary federalism 307, 313
*Goa Foundation and Peaceful Society v.
  Union of India (2013)* 346
greenhouse gas emissions
  cap-and-trade programs 145, 153–6,
    166–7, 174–5
  carbon taxes 166–7
  clean car standards 175–6
  emissions targets 172, 183
  energy generation emission caps 176
  low carbon fuel standards 176–7
  regulation, judicial challenges 384–5
  renewable portfolio standards 177–9
  reporting and registries 173
Guercio, Lara 107–8

Hart, Gary 46
*Holt Civic Club v. City of Tuscaloosa
  (1978)* 250–51
Hughes v. Oklahoma (1979) 95, 98

*Illinois Central Railroad v. Illinois
  (1892)* 95
India
  Bhopal Disaster
    policy, influences on 332–4
  constitution
    amendments 332

division of powers 328–9, 334–5
general principles 327–8
international obligations 335–6
semi-federal status 327–8
environmental federalism
  background 330–34
  biodiversity protection regulation 342, 349–50
  centre–state relationships 332–5, 337–338
  challenges 331, 337–8, 351–2
  coastal zone regulation 343
  Concurrent List policies 331–2, 334, 340–42
  cooperative federalism 337–47, 351–2
  decentralization, and 347–50
  dispute resolution 336–7, 339–40, 344–6
  division of powers 328–9, 334–5
  Environmental Impact Assessments 344
  forestry regulation 340–41, 348–9
  implementation 338
  international obligations 335–6
  judicial role 336–7, 339–40
  legislative powers 333–4
  local administrative units *(Gram Panchayat)* 349–50
  National Green Tribunal (NGT) 344–6
  public interest impacts 339–40
  reforms 338
  residuary powers 334–5, 345–6
  state law preemption 347
  State List policies 332, 334–5, 345–6, 348, 350
  structural influences on 328
  water regulation 339–40
  wildlife protection 341–2
environmental protection policy
  Bhopal Disaster influences on 332–4
  biodiversity 342
  coastal environment 336–7, 343
  commercial conflicts 337
  Concurrent List policies 331–2, 334, 340–42
  Environmental Protection Act 1986 342–4
  forestry 340–41
  fundamental duties 329
  implementation and enforcement 338
  inter-state rivers 336–7
  National Biodiversity Authority (NBA) 342
  noise pollution control 343
  population control 332
  state controls 343
  water resource allocation 336–7
  wildlife 341–2
federalism
  centre–state relationships 337–8
  cooperative federalism 330–31, 337–8
  general features 327–8
  government organization 328–9
  structure 328, 348
  subordination, role of 330

Jefferson County v. Washington Department of Ecology [PUD No.1] (1994) 42, 46, 218
Joint Task Force on Endangered Species Act Policy (ESA JTF) 103–4

Kerwin, Cornelius 219–20
Kleppe v New Mexico (1976) 98
Kyoto Protocol 173, 183

'laboratories of democracy' theory 162, 169–70, 179, 182–3, 187
Lacey Act 1900 96–7
Leahy, Peter 181–2
Levinson, Daryl 239
local governance
  energy policy
    governance preemption 127–9, 133–4
    local and state joint regulation 129–30
    local governance role 126–7
  environmental governance
    boundaries, role of 252–4

community role, importance of
    259–67
  ecological identity, and 260–61
  ecosystem regulation and
    protection 261–5, 267
  local priorities, role of 264–5
  political engagement, and 263
federalism, and
  authority of 247–8
  challenges of 266–7
  constitutional rights and controls
    250–52
  controversies 255–7
  decision making controversies
    255–7
  extraterritorial impacts of local
    actions 253–4
  limitations of 249–50
  marginalization 254–5
  origins of power 252–3
  preemption of 247–55, 253–7
  self-governance implications
    243–4, 250–51
  origins of power 252–3
low carbon fuel standards 176–7

McDonald v. Sun Oil Co. (2008) 65
Madisonian theory 236–9
Maritime Mammal Protection Act 1972
    98–9
Massachussets v. EPA (2007) 358,
    384–5
matching principle 105–6, 134
*Metro. Taxicab Bd. of Trade v. City of
    N.Y. (2010)* 249
Migratory Bird Treaty 1918 97
Minnesota Environmental Rights and
    Liability Act 2014 (MERLA) 56
Missouri v. Holland (1920) 97
Montana gray wolf 107–8
*MPM Silicones v. Union Carbide Corp.
    (2013)* 60–61

*National Audubon Society v. Superior
    Court (1983)* 96
National Contingency Plan (NCP) 51
National Land Use Policy Act 1996
    (proposed) 255

natural resources *see also* endangered
    species policies; forestry policies
  US policies, generally
    federal role 71–2
    fragmentation 71–2
    wetland management 78–9
negotiated federalism 370
*New South Wales v. Commonwealth
    (2006)* 279–80
*New South Wales v. Commonwealth
    (1975)* 287
New York v. United States (1992) 358,
    380–82, 416
New York v. West Side Corp. (2011) 60
*Niagara Mohawk Power Corp. v.
    Chevron USA (2010)* 59
Nolon, John 135, 259
'not in my back yard' (NIMBY)
    syndrome 12–13, 25, 115–16

Outka, Uma 135

Percival, Robert 106–7
Perry, M. 280
Pharmacia v. Union Elec. Co. (2013) 62
Pildes, Richard 239
PMC. v. Sherwin-Williams Co. (1998)
    61
pollution
  air pollution
    Clean Air Act amendments 16–19
    shift from state to federal controls
      13
  definitions 39
  noise pollution policy in India 343
  water pollution
    judicial rulings 382–4
preemption, generally *see also* reverse
    preemption
  conditional preemption 404–7, 409,
    413
  conflict preemption 253
  express preemption 253
  extraterritorial impacts 253–4
  implied preemption 253
  judicial interpretation 249–50, 253–4
public trust doctrine 95–6, 389

'race to the bottom' 4–5, 12, 16–18
radioactive waste management 380–82, 416
Rapanos v. United States (2006) 358, 382–4, 391–2, 416
Religious Land Use and Institutionalized Persons Act 2000 255
renewable energy 117–21, 129–30, 377–9
renewable portfolio standards 177–9
Resource Conservation and Recovery Act (1976) 406, 408
resource pooling 11–12, 16
reverse preemption
  Clean Water Act permissions
    veto of FERC permits 218–22
    veto of inconsistent federal actions 214–17
    veto of wetlands permissions 220–22
  Coastal Zone Management Act permissions
    judicial interpretation and legislative amendment 225–6
    practical application 226–9
    veto of inconsistent federal actions 214, 222–4, 238–9, 396–7
  generally 213–14, 241
    background 237–9
    congressional power, and 236–40, 242
    environmental federalism, and 231–5
    federalism promotion, and 235–6
    incentive function 230–31
    motivations for 230–40
    potential benefits 214–15, 241–2
    separation of powers, and 236–9
    trends 229–30
Robinson Township v. Commonwealth of Pennsylvania (2013) 80
Rocky Mountain Farmers Union v. Corey (2013) 376
Rose-Ackerman, Susan 170, 180–81
Ruhl, J.B. 412–13

S.D. Warren Co. v. ME Environmental Board of Protection (2006) 219
self-governance
  constitutional protections 250–51
  federalism implications for 243–4, 250–51
  state powers of 250–51
  US judicial interpretation 245–6, 250
separation of powers
  reverse preemption, and 236–9
shale gas fracking 117, 131–2, 377–9
Solid Waste Agency of Northern Cook County v. US Army Corp of Engineers 391–2
South Australia v. Commonwealth (1942) 278–9
Spence, David 134, 139
standards
  clean car standards 175–6, 183–4
  energy policy regulation 127–9, 131
  justification for federal action 12, 16, 24–5
  low carbon fuel standards 176–7
  renewable portfolio standards 177–9
  state higher standards adoption 9, 14, 16, 42–3
State of Tamil Nadu v. State of Kerala and Union of India (2014) 340
Superfund *see* CERCLA
Surface Mining Control and Reclamation Act (1977) 405–6, 408

Tennessee Valley Authority v. Hill (1978) 99
Tocqueville, Alexis de 243, 267
Toyne, Philip 290–91
transboundary externalities 11, 18, 24

Utility Air Regulatory Group v. EPA (2014) 411–12

Victoria v. Commonwealth (1957) 278–9

Wallop, Malcolm 46–7
Washington Department of Fisheries v. Gillette (1980) 96

water law *see* Clean Water Act; Coastal Zone Management Act
water pollution
  judicial rulings 382–4
wetlands
  regulation, judicial interpretation 391–2
  reverse preemption of federal permissions 220–22
  US management policies 78–9
Wild Free-Roaming Horses and Burros Act 1971 98
wildlife regulation, in US *see also* Endangered Species Act
  common law development 95–6
  cooperative federalism 94, 104–5
    adaptive management approach, need for 110–13
    climate change impacts, and 110–13
    enhanced approach 107–10
    jurisdiction conflicts 108–9
    standard approach 106–7
  federal role and powers 96–9
    advantages of 104
    Commerce Clause power 98
    federal aid for wildlife restoration 97
    game laws 96–7
    maritime mammals 98–9
    migratory birds 97
    preemption of state laws 97–9
    scientific role development 98–9
    wild horses 98
  police powers 95
  property-based protection 95–6
  public trust doctrine 95–6
  state role and powers 95–6, 104
    federal preemption of 97–9
Williams v. Commonwealth (2012) 280–81
wind energy 117–20, 129–30

Zero Emission Vehicle programs 175–6
zero-sum federalism 370, 417